HITLER'S THIRD REICH

A
Documentary
History

Edited by

Louis L. Snyder

**The City University
of New York**

Nelson-Hall nh Chicago

This book is for
Faye Lieberman
With love and admiration

Library of Congress Cataloging in Publication Data

Main entry under title:

Hitler's Third Reich.

Includes index.
1. Germany — History — 1933-1945 — Sources.
2. Germany — Politics and government — 1918-1933 —
Sources.   3. Hitler, Adolf, 1889-1945.   I.   Snyder,
Louis Leo, 1907-
DD256.5.H536   943.086   81-9512
                                   AACR2

ISBN 0-88229- 705-8 (cloth)
ISBN 0-88229-793-7 (paper)

Contents

Preface   xvii

Introduction   1

Part One: Background: War, the Weimar Republic, and the Experiment in Democracy   13

1.   The Victorious Allies Impose the Treaty of Versailles upon a Humiliated Germany   **15**

2.   Article 48: The Achilles Heel of the Weimar Constitution   **20**

3.   A Small Group of Dissidents, Calling Themselves the German Workers' Party, Issues a Manifesto of Twenty-Five Points Designed to Invigorate the Fatherland   **22**

4.   Hitler Begins His Personal War Against the Jews: An Early Speech in His Anti-Semitic Campaign   **26**

Part Two: The Crucial Decade: 1923 to 1933   31

5.   The Beer-Hall *Putsch*: Hitler Makes His First Attempt to Seize Power, November 8, 1923   **33**

6.   Tried with Hitler for Treason, General Erich Ludendorff, World War I Hero, Exalts Himself, March 27, 1924   **37**

7.   Hitler Delivers His Final Speech at His Trial for Treason, March 27, 1924   **40**

8.   *Mein Kampf*: In Prison at Landsberg, Hitler Writes the Story of His Life and Presents the Blueprint for His Future Career   **42**

9.   The Nazi Leader Issues a Warning Against the Red Dragon in a Speech at Munich, May 23, 1926   50

10.   Dr. Paul Joseph Goebbels, Later to Become Propaganda Minister of the Third Reich, Writes a Pamphlet Excoriating the Jews   53

11.   Hitler Repeats His Basic Political Demand — Revision of the Treaty of Versailles, September 28, 1930   56

12.   In an Interview with the *Times* (London) Hitler Warns About the Possibility of a Bolshevist Germany, October 14, 1930   58

13.   Hitler's Düsseldorf Speech to Rhineland Industrialists Sets the Groundwork for Financial Backing, January 27, 1932   60

14.   Re-election of von Hindenburg to the Presidency: Hitler Fails in a Bid for Power, April 10, 1932   70

15.   Von Hindenburg and Hitler Fail to Come to Terms, August 13, 1932   75

16.   A Confident Hitler Turns Down von Hindenburg's Offer of a Conference, November 24–30, 1932   77

17.   Resignation of the von Schleicher Cabinet, January 28, 1933   80

18.   Von Hindenburg Names Hitler to the Office of Reich Chancellor, January 30, 1933   81

Part Three: Coordination: "Ein Volk, Ein Reich, Ein Fuehrer"   83

19.   Chancellor Hitler Issues a Proclamation to the German People, February 1, 1933   85

20.   The *Fuehrer* Speaks to the NSDAP, the Nazi Party, February 1, 1933   90

21.   The New German Chancellor Makes a Radio Appeal for Support, February 4, 1933   92

22.   Hermann Goering Orders the Prussian Police to Combat All "Subversive Organizations," February 17, 1933   93

23.   The *Reichstag* Fire — I: The *Manchester Guardian* Suspects
      That an Act of Arson Was Committed by the Nazis   **95**

24.   The *Reichstag* Fire — II: The Oberfohren Memorandum
      Presents the Communist Case Against the Nazis   **102**

25.   The Enabling Act: The Law to Remove the Distress of
      People and State Legalizes the Nazi Revolution, March 24,
      1933   **106**

26.   The Chancellor Explains to President von Hindenburg His
      Attitude Toward the Jews and Their Role in Germany, April
      5, 1933   **108**

27.   Law for the Restoration of the Civil Service: The Opening
      Stage in the Persecution of the Jews, April 7, 1933   **111**

28.   The Burning of the Books — I: "Un-German Literature" Is
      Consigned to the Flames in a Nazi Ceremony, May 10,
      1933   **113**

29.   The Burning of the Books — II: Dr. Goebbels, Minister for
      Public Enlightenment and Propaganda, Delivers His Speech
      of Justification, May 10, 1933   **120**

30.   Romain Rolland Denounces the Nazi Regime and Receives
      a Strained Rebuke, May 14, 1933   **123**

31.   Hitler's Decree for the *Gleichschaltung* (Coordination) of
      All Activities in the Third Reich, June 30, 1933   **129**

32.   Law Concerning the Formation of New Parties: The
      Fuehrer Abolishes All Opposition, July 14, 1933   **131**

33.   Law for the Protection of Heredity Health: The Attempt to
      Improve the German Aryan Breed, July 14, 1933   **132**

34.   Propaganda Minister Goebbels Sums Up Six Months of
      Accomplishments of the Nazi Regime, July 17, 1933   **134**

35.   Concordat Between the Holy See and Nazi Germany: An
      Agreement to Regulate Tensions, July 30, 1933   **139**

36.   Hereditary Farm Law: The Nazi Government Seeks to
      Preserve the German Peasantry as the Blood Source of
      German Society, September 29, 1933   **143**

37.   Law to Promote National Labor: The German Worker Is Brought Under State Control, January 20, 1934   **145**

38.   Law for the Reorganization of the Reich: Hitler Decrees Legality for His Dictatorship, January 30, 1934   **152**

39.   Propaganda Minister Goebbels Addresses the Film Industry at Kroll Opera House, February 9, 1934   **153**

40.   The *Horst Wessel Lied*: The Nazis Find Their Poet of the Barricades   **158**

41.   Nazi Ideology – I: Alfred Rosenberg, Official Nazi Philosopher, Discourses on the Myth of the Blood   **160**

42.   Nazi Ideology – II: Professor Hermann Gauch Compares Nordics with Non-Nordics   **162**

43.   Nazi Ideology – III: Ewald Banse, Professor of Military Science, Publishes a Book Approving German Militarism   **164**

44.   Twenty-Five Points of the German Religion: Professor Ernst Bergmann's Catechism for "Positive Christianity"   **167**

45.   From London, Author and Refugee Lion Feuchtwanger Denounces the Nazi Regime   **170**

46.   Vice-Chancellor Franz von Papen's Marburg Speech: A Call for More Freedom, June 17, 1934   **173**

47.   Blood Purge, June 30, 1934: The SA Advocates of a "Second Revolution" Are Eliminated   **178**

48.   Official Communiqué on the Crushing of the Radical Nazi Revolt, June 30, 1934   **185**

49.   Hitler Appoints Viktor Lutze New SA Chief of Staff and Issues an Order for Its Reform, June 30, 1934   **187**

50.   Proclamation by Viktor Lutze, June 30, 1934   **190**

51.   The *Stahlhelm*, Organization of War Veterans, Is Ordered to Support Hitler, June 30, 1934   **191**

52.   President von Hindenburg Sends Telegram of Congratulations to Hitler and Goering, July 2, 1934   **192**

53. Hitler Issues a Decree Designed to Prevent Further Revolts Against His Authority, July 3, 1934 **193**

54. Death of von Hindenburg: Hitler Becomes President of the Third Reich, August 2, 1934 **194**

55. Personal Oath of Loyalty to the *Fuehrer* Is Required of All Soldiers of the Armed Forces, August 2, 1934 **195**

56. Von Hindenburg's Political Testament Is Published, August 16, 1934 **196**

57. Franco-German Agreement: The Saar Is Returned to Germany, February 18, 1935 **201**

58. Law Regarding Labor Service: The Coordination of Labor Is Completed, June 26, 1935 **206**

59. The Nuremberg Laws on Citizenship and Race: Legal Sanction Is Given to Nazi Anti-Semitism, September 15, 1935 **211**

60. Hitler's Decree to the Army on the Introduction of the Reich War Flag, November 7, 1935 **215**

61. Dissolution of the *Stahlhelm*: The Veterans Organization Is Subjected to Coordination, November 7, 1935 **216**

62. Heinrich Himmler Praises His *Schutzstaffel* as an Anti-Bolshevist Fighting Organization, November 12, 1935 **219**

63. Occupation of the Rhineland: Hitler Breaks Versailles Curb, Citing the Franco-Soviet Treaty as a Reason, March 7, 1936 **224**

64. The *Fuehrer* Inaugurates a Four-Year Plan Designed to Improve the Economy of the Third Reich, August 1936 **229**

65. The German Evangelical Church Issues a Manifesto Defending Its Faith and Attacking Hitler's Conception of "Positive Christianity," August 23, 1936 **233**

66. Decree on the Strength of the Reich Labor Service: Attention Is Given to Labor Service for Female Youth, September 6, 1935 **238**

67.   The Third Reich and the Japanese Government Sign an
       Agreement to Oppose the Spread of Communism, November
       25, 1936   **239**

68.   The Hitler Youth Is Formally Declared to Be a State
       Agency, December 1, 1936   **241**

69.   The University of Bonn Cancels Thomas Mann's Honorary
       Degree, and the Famous Author Replies in a Scathing
       Denunciation, December 19, 1936   **242**

70.   Racial Purity: Hitler Reverts to the Dominant Theme of
       the National Socialist Program, January 30, 1937   **247**

71.   *"Mit Brennender Sorge"*: Papal Encyclical Expresses Deep
       Anxiety for the Future, March 14, 1937   **249**

       Part Four: The Road to War   261

72.   The Hossbach Memorandum: Hitler Expresses His
       Intention of Obtaining *Lebensraum* for the German People,
       November 5, 1937   **263**

73.   Hitler Dismisses His Two Top Generals and Appoints
       Himself Commander-in-Chief of All the Armed Forces,
       February 4, 1938   **274**

74.   Hitler Again Expresses His Contempt and Loathing for
       Communism and Bolshevism, February 20, 1938   **276**

75.   Report on the Accomplishments of the *Kraft Durch Freude*
       Organization, 1938   **278**

76.   *Anschluss:* Hitler Completes the Union Between Germany
       and Austria, March 12, 1938   **279**

77.   Decree on Jewish-Owned Property: The Campaign
       Against the Jews Is Intensified, April 26, 1938   **284**

78.   The People of Czechoslovakia Learn That Their Nation
       Has Been Wrecked, September 21, 1938   **286**

79.   The Munich Agreement: The Western Allies Abandon
       Czechoslovakia in a Classic Case of Appeasement,
       September 29, 1938   **291**

80. Night of Broken Glass: Nazis Smash, Loot, and Burn
     Jewish Shops and Synagogues, November 10, 1938   **295**

81. Goering Issues Three Decrees Holding the Jews
     Responsible for the Excesses of *Kristallnacht*, November 12,
     1938   **302**

82. Reich Propaganda Minister Goebbels Comments on the
     Grynszpan Case in the *Völkischer Beobachter*, November 12,
     1938   **305**

83. Questionnaire for the Euthanasia Program, Spring
     1939   **309**

84. In a Blistering Speech to the *Reichstag*, Hitler Responds to
     President Roosevelt's Peace Message, April 28, 1939   **311**

85. To the Commanders-in-Chief of the *Wehrmacht* Hitler
     Reveals His Decision for War, August 21, 1939   **327**

86. The Hitler-Stalin Pact: The Third Reich and the USSR Join
     in a Pact to Carve Up Poland, August 23, 1939   **330**

87. The British Guarantee the Integrity of the Polish State,
     August 25, 1939   **332**

88. The *Fuehrer*'s Reply to the British Government Is Handed
     to the British Ambassador, August 29, 1939   **333**

89. German Ultimatum to Poland: Hitler Gives Poland
     Twenty-four Hours to Accept a Sixteen-Point Proposal,
     August 30–31, 1939   **337**

90. Failure of a Mission: Sir Nevile Henderson Reports on His
     Unsuccessful Negotiations with Hitler to Prevent War,
     1939   **341**

Part Five: The Third Reich in World War II
349

91. Nazi Germany Goes to War: The German Assault on
     Poland Is Reported by the London *Times*, September 1,
     1939   **351**

92.   Hitler Speaks to the *Reichstag* Justifying His Decision to
       Go to War and Asking for Support by the German People,
       September 1, 1939   **353**

93.   War Lord to the Front: The German Press Reports How
       the *Fuehrer* Goes to His Troops, September 4, 1939   **358**

94.   The German Foreign Office Publishes an Official Reply to
       the British War Blue Book and Claims that England Started
       the War, September 15, 1939   **359**

95.   German-Soviet Treaty: Hitler and Stalin Complete the
       Partition of Poland, September 28, 1939   **367**

96.   Hitler as Military Leader: The *Fuehrer's* War Directives,
       1939–1945   **371**

97.   Order of Battle of the Thirty-Nine *Waffen-SS* Divisions in
       World War II 1939–1945   **377**

98.   Defeat at Sea: The *Graf Spee* Is Scuttled in Montevideo
       Harbor, December 17, 1939   **382**

99.   The Nazi War Machine Crushes Norway: Correspondent
       Leland Stowe Tells the Story of a Paralyzing Conquest, April
       9, 1940   **386**

100.   Bombing of Rotterdam: Hitler Sets a Standard of Air
       Attack for Which German Cities Would Pay Heavily, May
       14, 1940   **395**

101.   Fall of France: Hitler's Hour of Triumph at Compiègne,
       June 21, 1940   **399**

102.   A Triumphant Hitler Makes a Peace Offer to England,
       June 19, 1940   **405**

103.   Berlin-Rome-Tokyo Axis: The Three Have-Not Powers
       Sign a Ten-year "Tripartite Pact," September 27, 1940   **406**

104.   Coventry: Massive *Luftwaffe* Attack on British Midlands
       Manufacturing Center, November 15, 1940   **408**

105.   *Dolchstoss*: In His Berlin Speech Hitler Supports the
       Stab-in-the-Back Theory, February 1, 1941   **412**

106.   In the Midst of War Hitler Denounces Churchill as the
       Victim of a Paralytic Disease or Drunken Delusions, May 4,
       1941   **414**

107.   The Hess Flight: The No. 3 Nazi Parachutes to Scotland
       After an Eight-Hundred-and-Fifty-Mile Flight to Warn the
       British, May 10, 1941   **417**

108.   Nazi Authorities Claim That Hess Was Mentally Deranged
       and a Victim of Hallucinations, May 12, 1941   **420**

109.   The German Conquest of Crete: First Airborne Invasion in
       History, May 20, 1941   **422**

110.   The Third Reich Declares War on the USSR: The German
       Ambassador at Moscow Presents the Declaration, June 22,
       1941   **426**

111.   In an Emotional Speech Hitler Justifies His Invasion of the
       Soviet Union, June 22, 1941   **430**

112.   German Declaration of War on the United States,
       December 11, 1941   **439**

113.   The Battle for Moscow: Soviet Reporter Konstantin
       Simonov Records the German Defeat on Soviet Soil, January
       29, 1942   **441**

114.   El Alamein: The Third Reich Sustains a Major Defeat in
       One of the Decisive Battles of World War II, October 23,
       1942   **445**

115.   Stalingrad: Nazi Germany Is Defeated in a Major Turning
       Point of the War, February 2, 1943   **450**

116.   Opposition: Students of the *Weisse Rose* Distribute a
       Leaflet Denouncing Nazism and Pay for It with Their Lives,
       February 22, 1943   **453**

117.   On the Fall of Italy, Hitler Calls on Almighty God to
       Bestow the Laurel Wreath of Victory on Germany,
       September 10, 1943   **456**

118.   The Schweinfurt Raid: Allied Air Power Helps Turn the
       Tide of War Against the Third Reich, October 14,
       1943   **460**

119.   D-Day: Beginning of the End for Nazi Germany, June 6,
       1944   **466**

120.   Dr. Theodor Morell, Hitler's Personal Physician and
       Injection Specialist, Prescribes an Extraordinary Variety of
       Drugs for His Patient, 1936–1945   **473**

121.   Conspiracy: Hitler Survives Bomb Attempt on His Life at
       His Secret War Headquarters, July 20, 1944   **477**

122.   Escape from Assassination: Texts of Talks by Hitler,
       Goering, and Doenitz, July 20, 1944   **482**

123.   The Allies Prepare a Protocol on the Occupation and
       Administration of the Greater Berlin Area, September 12,
       1944   **487**

124.   In a Last Gamble to Change the Tide of War Hitler
       Unleashes His Vengeance Weapons Against Britain,
       November 10, 1944   **491**

125.   The Allies Agree on Control Machinery for Germany,
       November 14, 1944   **493**

**Part Six: Götterdämmerung and
Residue   499**

126.   Nero Decree: Hitler Orders the Destruction of All
       Industrial Installations, March 30, 1945   **501**

127.   Buchenwald: Weimar Germans Are Forced to View the
       Horrors of a Nazi Death Factory, April 16, 1945   **503**

128.   Berlin Bunker: The Last Days of Hitler in His
       "Cloud-Cuckoo Land," April 20–30, 1945   **507**

129.   Belsen: A British Reporter Gives an Eyewitness Account of
       a Nazi Concentration Camp, April 24, 1945   **511**

130.   Hitler's Last Will: The Trapped *Fuehrer* Dictates His Final
       Bequests, April 29, 1945   **516**

131.   Hitler's Political Testament: Apologia and Last Warning
       Against "International Jewry," April 29, 1945   **518**

132. JCS/1067: The U.S. Military Government Issues a Directive for the Occupation of the American Military Zone in Defeated Germany, April 1945 **522**

133. Admiral Karl Doenitz, Hitler's Successor, Broadcasts a Proclamation to the German People, May 1, 1945 **528**

134. Admiral Doenitz Issues His First Order of the Day to the German Armed Forces and Calls for Further Resistance, May 1, 1945 **529**

135. Final Capitulation at Reims: Collapse of the Third Reich, May 7, 1945 **531**

136. The Formal Act of German Military Surrender, Berlin, May 8, 1945 **535**

137. Devastated Berlin: Newsman Describes the Capital of the Third Reich as a Modern Carthage, May 9, 1945 **537**

138. Allied Declaration on the Defeat of Germany and the Assumption of Supreme Authority by the Victor Powers, June 5, 1945 **540**

139. The Potsdam Conference: The Allies Decide the Future of Germany, July 17–August 2, 1945 **545**

140. Nuremberg Trial: Hermann Goering Takes the Stand and Begins His Defense, March 13, 1946 **551**

141. Justice Robert H. Jackson, Chief American Prosecutor, Makes His Summation at the Conclusion of the Nuremberg Trial, July 20, 1946 **560**

142. Judgment at Nuremberg: The International Military Tribunal Brings in Verdicts on Twenty-Two Individuals and Seven Organizations, October 1, 1946 **571**

143. Finale: Kingsbury Smith of International News Service Witnesses the Executions at Nuremberg, October 16, 1946 **607**

Index **615**

Preface

The documentary – in books as well as in television – retains its popularity because it gives the reader or viewer access to the facts. What an individual author has to say about Hitler and the Third Reich may well be of interest, but documentary material has an even greater import.

As an addition to the growing literature on Hitler and Nazism, this book aims to tell the story of the Third Reich exclusively in documents. New material has been added only to bring each entry into focus. The value of such a treatment, of course, lies in its selectivity. There are literally tens of thousands of documents available, but space is given here only to the most important.

The present approach is chronological. Major sections are devoted to the immediate post-World War I years and the Weimar Republic, the early stages of Hitler's career, his drive for political power, the consolidation of the Nazi dictatorship, the background of World War II, the Third Reich during World War II, the suicide in the *Götterdämmerung* – the twilight of the gods – and Germany immediately after the end of the Third Reich. All the documents here fit into this framework.

The term *document* is used here in its broadest sense. No attempt has been made to reproduce at length archival documents with page after page of clauses and subclauses. That approach may be useful for advanced students of diplomacy and adjunct disciplines. Here, however, the aim has been to provide a running account of the history of the Third Reich in a variety of documents, including official publications, reportage, speeches, excerpts from diaries, letters, radio talks, court records – in short, written and oral documents that dramatically convey the flavor and events of the period.

There are introductions to each selection that place each in its historical context and provide guidelines to its relevance to the total story. The documentary material then delivers the impact of immediacy. Above all, an effort has been made to avoid a presentation of many snippets of documentary material introduced by long explanations. Enough of each document is given — on most occasions the entire document — to give continuity to the history.

For the student of the Nazi phenomenon, for the armchair historian, and for the general reader, this documentary approach may well serve to bring alive the history of that unique experience in human affairs.

This book was made possible by the staffs of two superb libraries: the Firestone Library of Princeton University and the Wiener Library in London. Without them, this special combination of documents would have lain dormant. Again, as on many past occasions, I express my appreciation for the special assistance of my wife, Ida Mae Brown Snyder, whose patience and understanding have been far beyond the call. In doubtful cases, consultation with her has been decisive in solving many problems in a project of this kind.

March 1981
Princeton, New Jersey   Louis L. Snyder

Introduction

There has been little in historiography to compare with the extent and depth of the examination of the Third Reich. Books, television programs, and films, all dealing with special elements in Hitler's life or in Nazism, are appearing in a cascading proliferation of attention to this historical era. The 1979 television program *Holocaust* won a huge worldwide audience. Scholars everywhere continue to examine every phase of this extraordinary development in human affairs.

Since the suicide of Hitler on April 30, 1945, in his Berlin bunker, people everywhere have asked how it was possible for the people of Bach, Beethoven, and Brahms to turn to the leadership of Hitler, Himmler, and Hess. There has been nothing in recorded history like those twelve tragic years of the Third Reich, that empire which Hitler confidently expected to last for a thousand years. There is an enduring fascination with the personality and character of Germany's Napoleon, with the trappings of Nazism, and the moral and political issues raised by Germany's era of horror.

Fascination with the Third Reich exists at many levels. Psychoanalysts and psychohistorians busily explore the mind of Hitler, seeking to throw psychological light on his thought and actions. Doctoral candidates devote dissertations to the minutiae of the National Socialist movement. History buffs find the dramatic tale unendingly absorbing.

The Hitler craze has extended to the collector's world. Young people, without any regard or understanding for the morality of Nazism, prize memorabilia of the Hitler era — medals, flags, banners, songs, books, pamphlets, anything adorned with the swastika. This kind of collecting has become big business.

The revival of interest is worldwide. But in Germany, scene of Nazi triumphs, the same intensive interest is lacking. There have been occasional revivals of neo-Nazism in the Federal Republic, but they have never gained much headway and are discouraged by the government. The older generation of Germans, who lived through the trauma of Nazism, prefer to dismiss it from their minds in the way an individual tends to forget the painful moments of his life. Younger Germans are appalled by their parents' sins of omission and commission during the years from 1933 to 1945. They reject any ideological or self-exculpatory attempts to distort the truth. Significantly, many thousands of the people who trek to the shrine of Anne Frank in Amsterdam are teenage Germans who are deeply affected by the tragedy of the young Jewish girl's experience.

When the film *The Final Solution* was shown in Germany, one young German left the theater shaking his head and muttering, "How in the world could my parents have been taken in by that clown?" It was an attitude in sharp contrast to that of the Hitler youth who saw in the *Fuehrer* the messianic leader who would revive Germany's greatness.

To understand the rise of Hitler and the emergence of the national socialist dictatorship, one could go far back to the roots of German history. For this story in documents, a convenient point of origin is the Weimar Republic — that illegitimate child of defeat which Hitler replaced with the Third Reich.

As late as 1918, despite their hunger, privation, and misery, with defeat on World War I battlefields very near, the German people hoped for victory until the very last moment. They believed that somehow, some way, everything would be straightened out and the day would come when bells would peal and people would cry with the joy of victory. In October 1918, official communiqués from the fighting fronts still spoke of German triumphs. German soil had been almost untouched by the scourge of war.

Then, seemingly overnight, came the news of disaster. William II, the Hohenzollern who had pronounced himself "William the Great," retreated in disgrace to Holland and a new government was proclaimed.

They called it the Weimar Republic in the belief that the cultural milieu of Goethe and Schiller would replace the Potsdam of Clausewitz and von Treitschke. A new political system was pieced together from American, British, French, and Swiss models. Germany was to be a democratic republic, with universal suffrage, a president, a ministry headed by a chancellor, and a *Reichstag* (legislature) to represent the people. Democrats everywhere were delighted by the news that a German bill of rights insured the legal equality of the sexes, established free and compulsory education until the age of eighteen, and projected an excellent system of social legislation. The Weimar Constitution was truly one of the most advanced documents of its kind in the history of government.

Such was the promise, but great was the disappointment. Germany's experiment in democracy – her first – was burdened from the beginning with problems that she was never able to overcome. The new republic was not the willing creation of the German people. It was imposed upon them from the outside by powers that had demonstrated their superiority on the battlefields. The victorious Allies were not at all helpful to the struggling democracy. They occupied German territory; they maintained the blockade; they refused to release prisoners of war. Hohenzollern Germany was to be punished for its sins. All this was fiercely resented, and all of it came to be associated in the German mind with the nascent Weimar Republic.

In fact, the Weimar Republic had been born with little or no preparation – almost as an afterthought. The men who created it wanted above all the approval of Allied leadership as a prerequisite for a soft peace. Those who had to live under it came to regard it as a temporary measure, a pause awaiting the restoration of the Hohenzollerns and the good old days. The Weimar Republic was unwanted, misunderstood, unloved from its very inception.

The men of Weimar never quite understood the feebleness of German liberalism. The old fragility had led to the failure of the Revolution of 1848, when the first attempt has been made to introduce a semblance of democracy into Germany. A new opportunity came in 1919. But again the will was lacking. The Weimar Republic turned out to be a republic without republicans. Its leaders meant well, but they were operating in a vacuum without a broad base of support among their constituents.

It was a tragic situation. The Weimar regime, unsupported by public opinion, lacking help from the indifferent Alllies, was doomed from its start. The statesmen of Weimar would have to try desperately to defend it from attacks from both the right and the left. It struggled to survive in an era of political chaos, economic dislocation, social distress, and psychological anxiety. Buffeted by energetic Communists on the left and by Nazi extremists on the right, the bold experiment in democracy which was Weimar soon degenerated into the nightmare of Hitlerism.

Economic Roots of National Socialism

Why? This is the ultimate question of recent German history. Why this turn to the monstrosity of national socialism?

The answer is deeply rooted in the history of the German people for the last several centuries. The issue of causality cannot be treated simply. The late great German historian Friedrich Meinecke attempted to find the answer: Nazism was a disastrous stroke of lightning which hit the unsuspecting German people from the heavens. Never has so great a historian been so self-deceptive in assigning the causes of a historical movement.

On the contrary, the causes for the rise of Hitler and Nazism are complex and pluralistic. They were rooted in economic, political, social, military, and psychological motivations, none of which separately can tell the entire story. Marxist materialists place overwhelming emphasis on the economic factors of any historical movement and regard all others as only ideological veils hiding the true reality. Holding this view, they assiduously seek for economic causes alone to explain the rise of the Hitler regime. The result is an incomplete picture of exactly what happened.

This does not mean that there were no economic motives behind Hitlerism. They were, indeed, of major importance. For four years the Germans had taken part in a debilitating war, and the cost to their economic structure was enormous. The German currency collapsed in 1923. Money speculators and big industrialists made huge profits. The Weimar Republic was held responsible for the rapidly deteriorating economic situation. There were many political and social repercussions. The old idea of personal property was suddenly thrust aside. The middle class saw its pensions, bank accounts, and insurance protection vanish. It was a bitter experience – and Hitler was to profit from it.

When the great depression struck in 1929, major states abandoned the gold standard but the German administration refused to follow. Instead, the government turned to currency manipulations, which were politically desirable but economically dangerous. The country was hit by a heavy wave of unemployment.

To meet the crisis Weimar extended state control over economic life to a point where the coming transfer to totalitarianism could be made easily. It was an unconscious drive to suicide. By this time the economy was in chaos. More than fifty thousand PhDs had poured out from the universities only to find themselves jobless. The establishment dreaded the increasing possibility of social change and gradually came to the conclusion that the fanatically rightist Hitler might be of some use in preventing the progress of communism. Conservatives, nationalists, aristocrats, *Junker* landowners, army officers, Rhineland steel magnates – all saw salvation in the curious man with his hypnotic eyes and oratorical power. His anticapitalist propaganda, they were sure, was mere claptrap. They gave him the funds he needed – an elemental mistake.

The Milieu and the Man

Added to these economic causes for the rise of national socialism was a mixture of political, social, cultural, and psychological factors. Let us limit ourselves here to two motivating causes: (1) the milieu in which Nazism emerged; and (2) the personality of Hitler.

The eighteenth-century Enlightenment, the Age of Reason, called the *Lumière* by the French and the *Aufklärung* by the Germans, was centered in England, France, and the United States. Unfortunately, it bypassed Germany. This is not to say that the Germans did not know about the Enlightenment and its implications. German intellectuals understood all its ideas – constitutionalism, parliamentarianism, liberty, equality, fraternity, freedom of speech, press, and assembly, toleration of dissent. These were the ideals of a free society, though not necessarily completely achieved ideals, and Germans were well aware of them.

The course of German history, on the other hand, took an opposite turn following the regime of Frederick the Great. Prussian ideals took over once the Prusso-German symbiosis began to operate. The beliefs of the *philosophes* did not win the German mind. Instead, the Germans rejected the rationalist's belief in the supreme importance of the individual in favor of the *exaltation of the state*.

This was the crux of German intellectual development in the nineteenth and early twentieth centuries. The German mind was trained in the tradition of regarding the state as the be-all and end-all of human existence. The champion of the process was the philosopher Hegel. Civilization, in Hegel's view, was a process of upward movement from primitive times to its highest level – Prussian society. Hegel deemed it necessary that the individual be subordinated to the state. This became the theme of German home life, education, and activities from social life to the military. Before 1919 most German teachers could not hold jobs in the educational system unless they were Hegelian trained.

The Prussian way of life was superimposed upon all of Germany during the octopus-like expansion of Prussia. Prussian characteristics became German characteristics. By the early twentieth century Prussia ran Germany. Political control was extended into social and cultural life.

Clamped in the rigid Prussian formula, the Germans took on characteristics decidedly hostile to the Enlightenment. The changing German national character adopted many Prussian traits and they were more than mere stereotypes. These included discipline, obedience, an exaggerated attitude toward law and order, a passion for legality, worship of authority (*die Obrigkeit*), and an inordinate respect for the military.

So what? asks the skeptic. Other peoples, too, have such characteristics in small or large part. Granted. But the *combination* of characteristics, something uniquely German, was responsible in part for the tragic descent into Hitlerism.

The most dangerous element in this combination of traits was the deep sense of obedience to what was regarded as the proper authority. This was an offshoot of the German attitude toward dissent. Where other peoples, stimulated by the spirit of the Enlightenment, developed a strong tradition of dissent and disagreement with authority, the Germans were trained from childhood to remain rigidly loyal to the legal head of government, no matter who he might be. This attitude persisted through the Bismarckian Second Reich and the era of William II. What was *legal* was right.

This explains in part German acceptance of a regime foreign to their concept of good and evil. The central fact of Hitler's political ideology was to obtain power *legally*. After the Munich beer-hall fiasco, he was determined to drop his policy of power-by-revolution and to win his way to the chancellorship by legal means. He did just that. Voted into power, he became the lawful authority in

Germany. For the Germans this solved all kinds of immediate problems. They had a legal master and they remained obedient to him.

By the time the Germans realized the real nature of the man and the regime that they had catapulted into power, it was far too late. They were caught in a straightjacket, which they had unconsciously prepared for themselves.

Hitler: Psychopath or Neurotic?

Added to the milieu and peculiarly fitted to take advantage of it was the person of Adolf Hitler. There has been much speculation about the mind of this unique human being, certainly one of the most puzzling individuals of the twentieth century. No psychoanalyst has ever been able to bring him to a couch. There is no record of any Hitler conversations with psychiatrists. There is much evidence available, however, to allow a limited glimpse into the personality and character of the man. This material includes his autobiography, *Mein Kampf,* recorded secret conversations, speeches, and documented actions. All this material has been examined with painstaking care by scholars and psychiatrists to find clues to the mind of Hitler.

Some psychiatrists suggest that Hitler was the victim of several kinds of insanity, ranging from paranoia (systematic delusions), schizophrenia (disintegration of personality), dementia praecox (incoherence of thought and action); or monomania (paralyzing hatred of Jews). There is no general agreement.

Some stress Hitler's psychotic suspicions: "I have never met an Englishman who didn't say that Churchill was off his brain." "There is no doubt about it – Roosevelt is a sick brain." Others emphasize the *Fuehrer's* delusions of grandeur. "When one enters the Reich Chancellery, one should have the feeling that he is visiting the master of the world." Still others point to his *idée fixe:* "Jews are destroyers of civilization, parasites on the bodies of other peoples."

It takes but a little imagination to realize what kind of leadership would be projected by a man with these bizarre ideas. There is general agreement among students of human behavior that Hitler was a political genius, an evil genius to be sure, but there is disagreement on whether or not he stepped over the line between genius and insanity.

Erich Fromm, the psychoanalyst, believed that Hitler was not insane in the clinical sense, but that he was a victim of crippling neurosis. There is much to be said in favor of this thesis. Hitler had the half-educated mind of a backwoods Austrian. Similar characters are often seen in barrooms and cafes, where they discourse on every subject as if they knew the last word on it. Hitler's knowledge was severely limited, but he believed himself to be a man of tremendous intelligence. He was shrewd. He had an extraordinary understanding of mass psychology. In the long run, however, his was an inferior mind, governed by passion and emotions.

Hugh R. Trevor-Roper, the Oxford historian, described Hitler's mind in a remarkable sentence: "A terrible phenomenon, imposing in its granite harshness and yet infinitely squalid in its miscellaneous cumber — like some huge barbarian monolith, the expression of giant strength and savage genius, surrounded by a festering heap of refuse — old tins and dead vermin, ashes and eggshells and ordure — intellectual detritus of centuries."

It is an accurate and knowing appraisal. The pity of it was that such a depraved mind could come to a position of political power and control the destiny — the life and death — of millions of his compatriots and other peoples all over the world. His capacity for evil was enormous. The history of the Third Reich was colored from its beginning by the half-baked ideology of a midget who was propelled by fate into the seat of the mighty. He was responsible for the ultimate degradation of a great and gifted people.

Anatomy of the Third Reich

The Third Reich set up by Hitler has been variously described as "a cloud-cuckoo land," "a lunatic structure," and "the house of a megalomaniac." The Germans accepted Hitler as the expected political messiah and took as legitimate the compound of *Nibelungen* nonsense presented to them by their flawed high priest.

Once installed in office, Hitler deliberately set about the task of obliterating the Weimar democracy and fashioning a totalitarian state in its place. He smashed all other political parties, dissolved the trade unions and confiscated their property and funds. He abrogated all individual rights guaranteed by the Weimar constitution. He coordinated every phase of national life — church, press, education, industry, and the military.

The world was shocked by the extent of Hitler's campaign "to protect German honor" against the Jews — who numbered about one percent of the population. It had been said that Hitler's anti-Semitism was merely a political ploy to win power, but now it was seen that he was earnest in his desire to rid Germany of its Jews. The Nuremberg Laws officially delegated the Jews for the time being to the role of secondary citizens. Later there were to be more terrible consequences.

Hitler assumed for himself executive as well as judicial powers. There would be only one political party, the National Socialist. In a sweeping program of centralization, he placed federal, state, and local governments under his absolute authority. He smashed all internal opposition, even within his own party. On June 30, 1934, in a barbaric blood purge, he liquidated several hundred of his own followers who had dared to advocate a Second Revolution led by the socialist wing of his National Socialist party.

Hitler had no patience with any religion that opposed his theory of racialism. He insisted on the subordination of all religion to the state. He threw pastors and priests alike into concentration camps. He tried to split Protestantism by organizing a new German Christian church, which as a new form of "Positive Christianity" was to bow to state control. In July 1933 he made a concordat with the Catholic church, by which Catholics would not be molested as long as they remained aloof from politics. He promptly violated the agreement. Meanwhile, he sought to win public approval by presenting a neopagan movement which denied Christianity and recreated old Teutonic mythology. Zealous advocates placed Hitler's photograph on altars alongside candlelight and reverted to the mystic rites of ancient days.

The churches did not submit as quietly as did most German citizens. There were spirited, if unsuccessful, protests from all corners of the Third Reich against religious intolerance.

An economically illiterate Hitler relied on Gottfied Feder for his bizarre economic theories but later had to settle for more conventional procedures. His goal was to bring the national economy in line with self-sufficiency. He solved the unemployment problem by the simple expedient of placing the jobless in the army, providing for extensive public works, and organizing labor camps. He obtained funds for remilitarization by a system of forced loans from banks, industries, and insurance companies, using the lever of patriotism as the reason. He also suspended payment on foreign debts. In 1936 he launched a four-year plan to make the nation economically independent. Lacking an adequate gold supply, he adopted a barter system to compete with other countries for world markets.

Radical cultural innovations were designed to bring the entire nation in line with the special mystical intuitions of its *Fuehrer*. A country that had long been in the forefront of artistic endeavor sank to the level of the ideologies professed by an Austrian "hick" who announced himself as the greatest German of all time. It was an extraordinary spectacle to a disbelieving world to witness this dizzying slide into mediocrity.

All cultural activities in the Third Reich were subordinated to Nazi ideology. Schools were transformed into propaganda agencies, and women were relegated to the kitchen — *Kirche, Küche, Kinder* (kirk, kitchen, kids). All cultural activities were required to imbue citizens with glorification of the Leader, fanatical worship for the *Fuehrer*, racial prejudice, and hatred for the enemies of the Third Reich. Dr. Paul Joseph Goebbels, as Reich minister for public enlightenment and propaganda, was assigned the task of implementing Hitler's special views of what German culture was to be.

Hitler's foreign policy was simple and direct — to regain Germany's prestige as a world power, to bring about the restoration of German colonies, to promote Pan-Germanism ("One Reich, One People, One *Fuehrer*"), and to revive the *Drang nach Osten* (Drive to the East). To free Germany from what he called the chains of Versailles, Hitler in March 1935 announced the rearmament of Germany, introduced conscription, enlarged the army and navy, and launched a formidable air force.

In 1936, in violation of the Locarno treaties, Hitler sent his troops — unopposed — into the Rhineland. Emboldened, he repudiated Article 231, the war-guilt clause of the Treaty of Versailles. On March 15, 1938, in order "to preserve Austria," he formally incorporated her into the Third Reich. After signing the Munich Pact in September 1938, which sold Czechoslovakia down the river, Hitler piously announced that his territorial aims in Europe were satisfied. Then his invasion of Poland on September 1, 1939, brought on World War II.

The Vulgarization of Power

The Nazi regime in power represented a descent into bestiality such as the world had seldom witnessed. Hitler, the self-professed omniscient and omnipotent *Fuehrer*, promised the German people a way out of their misery and a mission of global power.

Originally skeptical about this strange Austrian, the Germans became more and more convinced of his infallibility as he delivered one crippling blow after another to the system of Versailles. They were impressed by his promise of a Thousand-Year Reich. Politically illiterate Germans had little understanding of what was happening to them before the bar of humanity. The slaughter of Jews and others deemed unfit in a barbaric attempt to cleanse biologically the "Aryan" race had no parallel in the history of civilization. The massacre of other millions, the devitalization of nations, the inhuman behavior of Nazis, the condoning of horrors, all this shocked and embittered people all over the world. There has been little to compare with it in the entire history of civilization. It took a worldwide coalition to bring down the Third Reich and to destroy its fanatical *Fuehrer.*

Part One:

Background: War, the Weimar Republic, and the Experiment in Democracy

1. The Victorious Allies Impose the Treaty of Versailles upon a Humiliated Germany

"The Allied and Associated Governments affirm and Germany accepts. . . ."

As the hands of the clock finally reached eleven on November 11, 1918, there was at first a dead silence and then the sound of men cheering from the Alps to the sea. At long last an end had come to World War I. After four years of misery and suffering and bloodshed, the fires of hell had been watered down. In the Allied world there was unrestrained joy as the people of Paris, Rome, London, and New York gave way to hysterical celebration. Little wonder. Sixty-five million men had been mobilized in the Great War, of whom eight-and-a-half million were killed or died of illness, and more than twenty-one million men were wounded. In addition there were an estimated nine million civilian deaths from causes related to the war.

It was a different story in Berlin and in all the cities and towns of Germany. No celebrations here – instead bewilderment, gloom, pain, anger. Not a square inch of German soil was in enemy hands. The great legions of the Kaiser had come marching home, defeated on the battlefields. But there was disbelief that so magnificent an army could have been defeated by the enemy. The real reason must have been far from the battlefields. Perhaps there were traitors at home who had stabbed Germany in the back – the *Dolchstoss* theory – which, indeed, would appear soon to explain the catastrophe.

U.S., Congress, Senate, *Treaty of Peace with Germany*, 66th Cong., 1st sess., 1919, Senate doc. 49.

The Germans laid down their arms in the belief that they would receive a just and lasting peace based upon the Fourteen Points of President Woodrow Wilson. But when the peacemakers came to Versailles, the truculent French Tiger, Georges Clemenceau, angrily faced Wilson and bellowed: "God Almighty had only ten points – Wilson has to have Fourteen!" It was not a pleasant or a desirable atmosphere for an effective peace. The men of Versailles were determined to punish Germany to the hilt – and they succeeded. When they were finished and demanded that the Germans sign upon pain of invasion, they set the stage for the arrival of a human monster who would lead them to the disaster of another massive blood bath. To understand Hitler, one must be familiar with the treaty that paved his way to power.

The Treaty of Versailles between the Allies and Germany was signed in the Hall of Mirrors at Versailles on June 28, 1919. Both the time and place were selected in a deliberate attempt to humiliate the beaten Germans. The time was the fifth anniversary of the assassination of the Austrian heir apparent, Archduke Franz Ferdinand, at Sarajevo, the event that had triggered the outbreak of the First World War. The place was the same hall where in 1871 Otto von Bismarck had proclaimed the Second German Reich.

The Treaty of Versailles was to become the object of vilification of virtually every political leader in the Weimar Republic, the democratic state that succeeded the empire of William II. Hitler was to take advantage of that treaty in his drive for political power.

Following are the most important articles of the Versailles Treaty affecting Germany. Attention is directed to Article 231, the war-guilt clause, which held Germany and her allies responsible for causing the loss and damage "imposed by the aggression of Germany and her allies."

PART III
Political Clauses for Europe

ARTICLE 31. Germany, recognizing that the Treaties of April 19, 1839, which established the status of Belgium before the war, no longer conform to the requirements of the situation, consents to the abrogation of the said treaties and undertakes immediately to recognize and to observe whatever conventions may be entered into by the Principal Allied and Associated Powers, or by any of them, in concert with the Governments of Belgium and of the Netherlands, to replace the said Treaties of 1839. If her formal adhesion should be required to such conventions or to any of their stipulations, Germany undertakes immediately to give it. . . .

ARTICLE 42. Germany is forbidden to maintain or construct any fortifications either on the left bank of the Rhine or on the right bank to the west of a line drawn 50 kilometers to the East of the Rhine. . . .

ARTICLE 45. As compensation for the destruction of the coal-mines in the north of France and as part payment toward the total reparation due from Germany for the damage resulting from the war, Germany cedes to France in full and absolute possession, with exclusive rights of exploitation, unencumbered and free from all debts and charges of any kind, the coal-mines situated in the Saar Basin. . . .

ARTICLE 51. The territories which were ceded to Germany in accordance with the Preliminaries of Peace signed at Versailles on February 26, 1871, and the Treaty of Frankfurt of May 10, 1871, are restored to French sovereignty as from the date of the Armistice of November 11, 1918.

The provisions of the Treaties establishing the delimitation of the frontiers before 1871 shall be restored. . . .

ARTICLE 80. Germany acknowledges and will respect strictly the independence of Austria. . . .

ARTICLE 81. Germany, in conformity with the action already taken by the Allied and Associated Powers, recognizes the complete independence of the Czecho-Slovak State. . . .

ARTICLE 87. Germany, in conformity with the action already taken by the Allied and Associated Powers, recognizes the complete independence of Poland, and renounces in her favor all rights and title over the territory [of Poland].

The boundaries of Poland not laid down in the present Treaty will be subsequently determined by the Principal Allied and Associated Powers. . . .

PART IV
German Rights and Interests Outside Germany

ARTICLE 119. Germany renounces in favor of the Principal Allied and Associated Powers all her rights and titles over her oversea possessions. . . .

PART V
Military, Naval, and Air Claims

ARTICLE 160. By a date which must not be later than March 31, 1920, the German Army must not comprise more than seven divisions of infantry and three divisions of cavalry.

After that date the total number of effectives in the Army of the States constituting Germany must not exceed one hundred thousand men, including officers and establishments of depots. The Army shall be devoted exclusively to the maintenance of order within the territory and to the control of the frontiers.

The total effective strength of officers, including the personnel of staffs, whatever their composition, must not exceed four thousand.

. . . The Great German General Staff and all similar organizations shall be dissolved and may not be reconstituted in any form.

ARTICLE 180. All fortified works, fortresses and field works situated in German territory to the west of a line drawn fifty kilometres to the east of the Rhine shall be disarmed and dismantled.

ARTICLE 181. After the expiration of a period of two months from the coming into force of the present Treaty the German naval forces in commission must not exceed:

6 battleships of the *Deutschland* or *Lothringen* type,

6 light cruisers,

12 destroyers,

12 torpedo boats,

or an equal number of ships constructed to replace them. . . .

No submarines are to be included.

All other warships, except where there is provision to the contrary in the present Treaty, must be placed in reserve or devoted to commercial purposes. . . .

ARTICLE 198. The armed forces of Germany must not include any military or naval air forces. . . .

PART VI
Reparation

ARTICLE 231. The Allied and Associated Governments affirm and Germany accepts the responsibility of Germany and her allies for causing all the loss and damage to which the Allied and Associated Governments and their nationals have been subjected as a consequence of the war imposed upon them by the aggression of Germany and her allies. . . .

PART X
Special Provisions

ARTICLE 245. Within six months after the coming into force of the present Treaty the German Government must restore to the French Government the trophies, archives, historical souvenirs or works of art carried away from France by the German authorities in the course of the war of 1870–1871 and during this last war. . . .

ARTICLE 246. Within six months from the coming into force of the present Treaty, Germany will restore to His Majesty the King of the Hedjaz the original Koran of the Caliph Othman, which was removed from Medina by the Turkish authorities and is stated to have been presented to the ex-Emperor William II.

Within the same period Germany will hand over to His Britannic Majesty's Government the skull of the Sultan Mkwawa which was removed from the Protectorate of German East Africa and taken to Germany. . . .

PART XIV
Guarantees

ARTICLE 428. As a guarantee for the execution of the present Treaty by Germany, the German territory situated to the west of the Rhine, together with the bridgeheads, will be occupied by Allied and Associated troops for a period of fifteen years from the coming into force of the present Treaty. . . .

ARTICLE 431. If before the expiration of the period of fifteen years Germany complies with all the undertakings resulting from the present Treaty, the occupying forces will be withdrawn immediately.

2. Article 48: The Achilles Heel of the Weimar Constitution

"The Reich President may . . . take such measures
as are necessary to restore public safety and order."

It is a strange phenomenon of history that great constitutions, the products of brilliant minds, can be negated by one clause that cancels the spirit and even legality of the broader document. That is what happened to postwar Germans and led them straight into the trap of Hitlerism.

The Weimar Republic, the first democratic regime in German history, was not the willing product of German citizens. It was imposed upon them from the outside. It was burdened from its very beginning by an overwhelming combination of problems: the bitter humiliation of defeat, a currency debacle, reparations, and acute economic distress. Not only were the Germans ill prepared for it, but the victorious powers showed little sympathy or understanding for the fledgling republic. The new government had to fight for its existence against determined opposition from both left and right. It smashed the Communist onslaught only to fall victim to fascism on the right.

The draft of the constitution of the Weimar Republic, written by Dr. Hugo Preuss, a political science teacher, and adopted on August 11, 1919, was – on paper – one of the most advanced constitutions in history. It was carefully based on the American, British, French and Swiss forms of government. Germany was to be a democratic republic, with universal suffrage for all citizens over twenty years of age. The constitution provided for a president elected for

Die Verfassung des deutschen Reichs von 11 August 1919 (Reklams Universal Bibliothek, no. 6051: Leipzig, 1930). Translated by the editor.

seven years by direct vote of the people, after which term he was eligible for re-election. Actual executive authority was vested in a ministry headed by a chancellor, appointed by the president but responsible to the *Reichstag*. The *Reichstag*, elected for a period of four years, had the power of initiating bills. The old *Reichsrat*, the upper body, was retained, but it had only secondary importance. A comprehensive bill of rights insured the legal equality of the sexes, established free and compulsory education up to the age of eighteen, and provided for a system of social legislation.

The most controversial part of the constitution was Article 48, which provided that, if any state (*Land*) did not live up to its constitutional obligations, the president could force it to do so by use of the armed forces. He could abrogate – temporarily, wholly, or in part – the fundamental freedoms guaranteed by the constitution. These included Article 114 (freedom of the individual); Article 115 (freedom of residence); Article 117 (secrecy of postal, telegraph, and telephone communications); Article 118 (freedom of expression); Article 123 (freedom of assembly); Article 124 (freedom of organization); and Article 153 (personal property guarantee).

Article 48 played a critical role in the history of the Weimar Republic. It provided a perfect wedge for weapons to destroy the Republic. It was abused in such a way that it eventually led to the Nazi dictatorship and in effect gave this dictatorship legal sanction. The men who made the constitution, operating in times of political instability, were anxious to provide for effective control of both right and left. What they did, perhaps unwittingly, was to provide the enemies of the constitution with a deadly loophole that they could use to squeeze the life out of the Republic. Article 48 in reality was the suicide clause of the Weimar Constitution, and as such played an important part in the emergence of Nazi totalitarianism.

ARTICLE 48. If a Land fails to fulfill the duties incumbent upon it according to the Constitution or the laws of the Reich, the Reich President can force it to do so with the help of the armed forces.

The Reich President may, if the public safety and order of the German Reich are considerably disturbed or endangered, take such measures as are necessary to restore public safety and order. If necessary, he may intervene with the help of the armed forces. For this purpose he may temporarily suspend, either partially or wholly, the Fundamental Rights established in Articles 114, 115, 117, 118, 123, 124, and 153.

The Reich President shall inform the Reichstag without delay of all measures taken under Paragraph 1 or Paragraph 2 of this Article. On demand by the Reichstag the measures shall be repealed. . . .

3. A Small Group of Dissidents, Calling Themselves the German Workers' Party, Issues a Manifesto of Twenty-Five Points Designed to Invigorate the Fatherland

"The party . . . combats the Jewish-materialist spirit. . . ."

The old saying has it that giant oaks from little acorns grow. Equally apt is the aphorism that overwhelming political movements grow from modest beginnings. While the Weimar Republic struggled for its very existence from assault on both right and left, a tiny group of dissidents — the German Workers' party (which eventually became the National Socialist German Workers' party) — emerged to win Germany for Hitler and lead her straight to the defeat of 1945. The beer-guzzling politicos were to bring tragedy not only to all Germans but to the entire world.

It all started at the close of World War I, when an angered veteran, Adolf Hitler, an Austrian who had fought in the German army, returned from war. He was angered by the revolution in Germany and the rise of the Weimar Republic, which he considered to be a product of "crazy democratic brains." He turned to politics as a means of working against both the Treaty of Versailles and the new German democracy. At first, remaining on the roster of his old regiment, he was assigned to spy on political parties of the left. In September 1919 he was ordered to investigate a small group of nationalistic veterans who called themselves the German Workers' party. With only a few marks in its treasury, the party was insignificant, but Hitler was impressed with its ideas, which coincided with his own. He joined the party as member No. 55 and later was made No. 7 on its executive committee.

U.S., *Department of State, National Socialism*, Publication no. 1864, pp. 222–25.

The official program of the German Workers' party, which consisted of twenty-five points, was officially proclaimed on February 25, 1920. The manifesto was primarily the work of Anton Drexler, a toolmaker who called for the founding of a national movement, and Gottfied Feder, a journalist and an early editor of the *Völkischer Beobachter*. Hitler, too, contributed to the program. After its presentation he said: "A wolf has been born which is destined to break into the herd of swindlers and misleaders of the people."

THE PROGRAM of the German Workers' party is limited as to period. The leaders have no intention, once the aims announced in it have been achieved, of setting up fresh ones, merely in order to increase the discontent of the masses artificially and so ensure the continued existence of the party.

1. We demand the union of all Germans to form a Great Germany on the basis of the right of self-determination enjoyed by nations.

2. We demand equality of rights for the German people in its dealings with other nations, and abolition of the peace treaties of Versailles and Saint-Germain.

3. We demand land and territory [colonies] for the nourishment of our people and for settling our excess population.

4. None but members of the nation may be citizens of the state. None but those of German blood, whatever their creed, may be members of the nation. No Jew, therefore, may be a member of the nation.

5. Anyone who is not a citizen of the state may live in Germany only as a guest and must be regarded as being subject to foreign laws.

6. The right of voting on the leadership and legislation is to be enjoyed by the state alone. We demand therefore that all official appointments, of whatever kind, whether in the Reich, in the country, or in the smaller localities, shall be granted to citizens of the state alone. We oppose the corrupting custom of Parliament of filling posts merely with a view to party considerations, and without reference to character or capacity.

7. We demand that the state shall make it its first duty to promote the industry and livelihood of citizens of the state. If it is not possible to nourish the entire population of the state, foreign nationals (non-citizens of the state) must be excluded from the Reich.

8. All non-German immigration must be prevented. . . .

9. All citizens of the state shall be equal as regards rights and duties.

10. It must be the first duty of each citizen of the state to work with his mind or with his body. The activities of the individual may not clash with the interests of the whole, but must proceed within the frame of the community and be for the general good.

We demand therefore:

11. Abolition of incomes unearned by work.

12. In view of the enormous sacrifice of life and property demanded of a nation by every war, personal enrichment due to a war must be regarded as a crime against the nation. We demand therefore ruthless confiscation of all war gains.

13. We demand nationalization of all businesses (trusts). . . .

14. We demand that the profits from wholesale trade shall be shared.

15. We demand extensive development of provision for old age.

16. We demand creation and maintenance of a healthy middle class, immediate communalization of wholesale business premises, and their lease at a cheap rate to small traders, and that extreme consideration shall be shown to all small purveyors to the state, district authorities, and smaller localities.

17. We demand land reform suitable to our national requirements.

18. We demand ruthless prosecution of those whose activities are injurious to the common interest. Sordid criminals against the nation, usurers, profiteers, etc., must be punished with death, whatever their creed or race.

19. We demand that the Roman Law, which serves the materialistic world order, shall be replaced by a legal system for all Germany.

20. With the aim of opening to every capable and industrious German the possibility of higher education and of thus obtaining advancement, the state must consider a thorough reconstruction of our national system of education. . . .

21. The state must see to raising the standard of health in the nation by protecting mothers and infants, prohibiting child labor, increasing bodily efficiency by obligatory gymnastics and sports laid down by law, and by extensive support of clubs engaged in the bodily development of the young.

22. We demand abolition of a paid army and formation of a national army.

23. We demand legal warfare against conscious political lying and its dissemination in the press. In order to facilitate creation of a German national press we demand:

a) that all editors of newspapers and their assistants, employing the German language, must be members of the nation;

b) that special permission from the state shall be necessary before non-German newspapers may appear. These are not necessarily printed in the German language;

c) that non-Germans shall be prohibited by law from participation financially in or influencing German newspapers. . . .

It must be forbidden to publish papers which do not conduce to the national welfare. We demand legal prosecution of all tendencies in art and literature of a kind likely to disintegrate our life as a nation, and the suppression of institutions which militate against the requirements above-mentioned.

24. We demand liberty for all religious denominations in the state, so far as they are not a danger to it and do not militate against the moral feelings of the German race.

The party, as such, stands for positive Christianity, but does not bind itself in the matter of creed to any particular confession. It combats the Jewish-materialist spirit within us and without [around] us. . . .

25. That all the foregoing may be realized we demand the creation of a strong central power of the state. Unquestioned authority of the politically centralized Parliament over the entire Reich and its organizations; and formation of chambers for classes and occupations for the purpose of carrying out the general laws promulgated by the Reich in the various states of the confederation.

The leaders of the party swear to go straight forward — if necessary to sacrifice their lives — in securing fulfillment of the foregoing points.

4. Hitler Begins His Personal War Against the Jews: An Early Speech in His Anti-Semitic Campaign

"My feeling as a Christian leads me to be a fighter for my Lord and Saviour."

Hitler's obsessive hatred of the Jews amounted to a monomania. This deep-rooted private hatred lasted throughout his life. He blamed the Jews for all of Germany's ills. They were the traitors, he thought, who had stabbed unwitting Germans in the back during World War I. With inconsistency, he accused the Jews of being Communists as well as capitalists. He was certain that they wanted to run the entire world.

Hitler's capacity for hatred was almost limitless, but his fear of and contempt for Jews were so deep-rooted that they never left him. He was convinced that the Jews were intent upon domination, not only of Germany but of the entire world. In the days when he was striving for political power, he reprinted millions of copies of a pamphlet called *The Protocols of the Elders of Zion,* an absurd forgery, which contended that Jewish leaders from all over the world came to Switzerland once a year to meet in a cemetery to report how they were getting on in the campaign to run their own countries. To the budding politician this phony document was the epitome of truth.

Hitler imbibed his anti-Semitism in the cafés of Vienna, which for years had been hotbeds of anti-Semitic hysteria. Here he heard stories about Jewish rabbis drinking Christian blood in rituals, about Jewish doctors giving dope to German girls, about Jews causing all suffering in Germany. When he became a politician, he made anti-

---

Völkischer Beobachter, April 22, 1922. Translated by the editor.

Semitism the major platform of his political appeal. "The wretched Jew," he said, "is the enemy of the human race. The Jew is the devil in human form."

Where others used anti-Semitism merely for its political appeal, Hitler was convinced to the marrow of his bones of the truth of his allegations. He expressed his hatred in speech after speech. By 1922, as absolute and undisputed master of the National Socialist German Workers' party, he was in a position in which he could carry on his self-appointed campaign against "this alien and despised race."

In the following speech, delivered in Munich on April 12, 1922, and published ten days later in the *Völkischer Beobachter* (later the official Nazi newspaper), Hitler presented himself as a warrior for Christ in an unending struggle against the Jews. He referred to Jews as "Orientals." By "100,000 Jews from the East," he meant Polish Jews who emigrated to the Weimar Republic and took advantage, he charged, of the German inflation. He accused Jews of having played a central role in the Russian Revolution and insisted that they had profited by it.

I ASK YOU: Did the Jews have an interest in the collapse of 1918? It is possible for us to discuss that objectively today. You are undoubtedly aware that on a comparative basis very few Jews have suffered at all. Let no one tell me: Oh, the poor Eastern Jew! Of course, they did not possess anything to begin with, for the simple reason that they lived in a country which they had robbed and stripped to the bone for centuries. They never have been nor will they ever be productively active.

They were poor when they came here. But look at any Oriental after he has been here for five or six years. Look at those millions of workers in Berlin in 1914 and look at them today. Now they are thinner; their clothes ragged and torn; they are poverty-stricken.

And now take a look at the 100,000 Jews from the East who came here during the first years of the war. Most of them have gotten rich and even own automobiles. That is so not because the Jews are more clever, because I challenge you to say that millions of decent and hard-working citizens are only stupid people.

The only reason is that these 100,000 Jews were never really ready to work in an honorable manner in a national organism for the common good of all. From the beginning they regarded the whole national organism as nothing more than a hothouse in which they could thrive.

The Jew has not become poorer. Slowly he is puffing himself up. If you do not believe me, take a look at our health resorts. There you find two kinds of people: the German who tries to catch a breath of fresh air for the first time in a long while and who wants to recuperate; and the Jew, who goes to the resorts as a means of getting rid of his excess fat. When you go to the mountain resorts, whom do you find in new yellow shoes, with large knapsacks, in which you do not find much of anything? And why should they? The Jews travel to the hotel, usually as far as the train goes, and where the train stops, they also stop. They just sit within a kilometer of the hotel, like flies on a corpse.

Certainly this is not our own "working class," neither of our intellectual or laboring workers. You will usually find the "working classes" wearing old clothing, climbing about somewhere along the sides of the hotel, because they are ashamed to enter this perfumed atmosphere in their old clothes dating from 1913 and 1914.

Watch the Oberammergau Passion Plays this summer and see who have the time and leisure and the money to enjoy nature and the spectacle of Christ's sufferings.

That same Jew, who was a Majority Socialist or an Independent in those days of November 1918, led you then and he leads you now. He can be either an Independent or a Communist, but he remains the same.

And just as he did not look after your interests at that time but after the interests of his own capital and his own race, so today he will certainly not lead you in the struggle against his race and against his capital. To the contrary, he will try to stop you from fighting against your real exploiters. He will never give you any help in liberating you, because he is just not the one who is enslaved.

Today in Soviet Russia millions are starving and dying. Some 30 million so-called "proletarians" lie prostrate, digging roots and grass from the soil in order to prolong their lives even for a few days, or for a few weeks. Chicherin and his delegation of some two hundred Soviet Jews travel through Europe on special trains, visit night clubs, attend strip-tease joints, and live in the best hotels. Really, they are better off than the millions of so-called "bourgeois" you thought at one time you had to fight. The four hundred Soviet commissars of Jewish nationality are not suffering, nor are the thousands of deputy commissars. Quite the opposite. All the wealth which the "proletarians" in their madness took from the so-called "bourgeois" in order to fight against so-called capitalism, is now concentrated in the hands of the Soviet commissars.

It is quite true that some workers in those days appropriated the pocketbooks of the landlords or employers. It is true that the proletariat annexed rings and diamonds and was happy in possession of the treasures owned at one time by the "bourgeoisie." But in his hands these possessions are dead, really dead gold. They just do not help. He is lost in the woods and he just cannot feed himself on diamonds. He gives millions in value just for a crust of bread. But the bread is controlled by the central state organization and that organization is controlled by the Jews. In that way everything, absolutely everything, which the ordinary man once thought he had won for himself, goes right back to the hands of those who have seduced him.

It was done by the Jew. There was, indeed, a redistribution of wealth, but not the way the masses wanted it to be. It was nothing more than a mere shifting of wealth from one hand to another. Millions of men lost their last ruble, which they had saved honestly, honorably, and with great care. These millions of rubles now became the property of those who as leaders had not done anything at all and who are not doing anything now except to starve and bleed the people.

And now, my dear fellow countrymen, do you really believe that those people who are doing the same thing here will end the revolution of 1918? They do not want to end the Revolution because there is no need for them to do so.

The Aryan looks upon work as the foundation of the national community. The Jew looks upon work as a means of exploiting others. The Jew never works as a productive creator but rather always with the idea of becoming a master. He works unproductively, utilizing and profiting from the work of others.

We, therefore, quite understand those iron words of [Professor] Mommsen: The Jew is the ferment of the decomposition of people. This means that it is in the nature of the Jew to destroy, and he must destroy, because he lacks altogether any idea of working for the common good. It is of no matter whether or not the individual Jew is decent or not. He possesses certain characteristics given to him by nature and he never can rid himself of those characteristics. The Jew is harmful to us. . . .

We were the ones who warned the people about the danger which has come into our midst, a danger which millions did not realize, but a danger — the Jewish peril — which will lead all of us to ruin. People today say that we are agitators. In this respect I refer to someone greater than I. In the last session of the *Reichstag*, Count Lerchenfeld said that his feeling "as a man and as a Christian" keeps him from being an anti-Semite.

I say this: My feeling as a Christian leads me to be a fighter for my Lord and Saviour. It leads me to the man who, at one time lonely and with only a few followers, recognized the Jews for what they were, and called on men to fight against them, and Who, believe me, was greatest not as a sufferer but as a fighter.

As a Christian and as a man with boundless love, I read that passage which told how the Lord finally gathered His strength and used the whip in order to drive the money-changers, the vipers, and the cheats from the temple.

Today, some two thousand years later, I understand with deep emotion Christ's tremendous struggle on behalf of the world against the Jewish

poison. I understand it all the more by the fact that He has given His blood
on the cross in this struggle. It is not just my duty as a Christian to allow
myself to be cheated, but it is my duty to be a champion of truth and of
right.

As a human being it is my duty to see to it that humanity will not suffer
the same catastrophic collapse as did that old civilization two thousand
years ago, a civilization which was driven to its ruin by the Jews. However, in the days when Rome fell, new and endless masses of Germanic
peoples came in from the North to take the place of the old metropolis. But
if our Germany were to fall today, who will come after us? . . .

As a Christian, I owe something to my own people. I see how our people
are working and working, laboring and exerting themselves, and still at
the end of the week they have nothing but misery and poverty to show for
it. That just is not understood in the homes of the nobility.

But when I go out in the mornings and see those people in the bread lines
and look into their drawn faces, then I am convinced that I am really a
devil and not a Christian if I do not feel compassion and do not wage war,
as Christ did two thousand years ago, against those who are stealing from
and exploiting these poverty-stricken people.

People today, of course, are aroused by this misery. Outwardly, the
people may seem to be indifferent, but inwardly they are boiling mad.
Some people say that it is an accursed crime to arouse passions in these
circumstances. However, I tell myself passion will be aroused by increasing misery and this passion will reveal itself in one way or another. I ask
this question of those who today call us agitators: "What do you have to
offer the common people in the way of a belief they might hold to?"
Nothing at all. For you yourself do not believe in your own prescriptions.

Such is the mightiest mission of our movement — to give the searching
and bewildered masses a new, strong belief, a belief which will not leave
them in these days of chaos, to which they will swear and abide by. . . .

Two thousand years ago a man was similarly denounced by this particular race which today denounces and blasphemes all over the place, by a
race which agitates everywhere and which regards any opposition to it as
an accursed crime. That man was dragged before a court and they said: He
is arousing the people! So He, too, was an agitator! And against whom?
Against "God," they cried. Indeed, He is agitating against the "god" of the
Jews, because that "god" is nothing more than money.

Part Two:

The Crucial Decade: 1923 to 1933

5. The Beer-Hall *Putsch*: Hitler Makes His First Attempt to Seize Power, November 8, 1923

"Herr Hitler, who seemed to be extraordinarily excited, fired a pistol into the roof. . . ."

As his movement gained momentum, Hitler began to think in terms of political power. Under a democratic regime he had to be voted into office, but he was unwilling to wait. In the confused milieu of the early 1920s, one way to win control was through a *coup d'état*, what the Germans called a *Putsch*, a forcible takeover of political control. With wild abandon, Hitler decided that his fledgling movement was strong enough to take a chance.

Convinced that the Weimar Republic was on the verge of collapse, Hitler decided to act. He worked in conjunction with World War I hero General Erich Ludendorff, Hermann Goering, and Ernst Röhm, leader of the Storm Troopers. Hitler decided to gain control of the Bavarian government and force it at gun point to acknowledge Nazi leadership. Several plots went astray, but on November 8, 1923, when it was announced that Gustav von Kahr, state commissioner for Bavaria, Colonel Hans von Seisser, chief of the Bavarian State Police, and General Otto von Lossow, commander of the German armed forces in Bavaria, would address a gathering at a beer hall in Munich, Hitler made his move. The intention was to make Ludendorff dictator.

The scene was the *Bürgerbräu Keller,* one of the largest beer halls in Munich, where thousands of thirsty Germans gathered to drink beer out of stone mugs and sing rousing drinking songs. On the evening of November 8, 1923, some three thousand people were gathered in the beer cellar to hear political speeches by Bavarian

---

Times (London), November 10, 1923.

officials. The crowd was unaware that Hitler, leader of the National Socialist German Workers' party, had decided to take over control of the Bavarian government at one stroke in a popular uprising.

What happened in the Munich beer hall was an immediate overnight sensation, not only in Germany but throughout the world. There were conflicting reports. The following dispatch from the *Times* (London) gave tentative reports from "Our Own Correspondent." The exact details were to be published later, but there was enough here to note what was happening in Munich.

Ludendorff Captured.
Munich Revolt Checked.
Von Kahr Changes Sides.

THE ATTEMPT OF General Ludendorff and Herr Hitler, with the support of their extreme Nationalist followers, to seize power in Bavaria and challenge the Berlin Government has failed. The two leaders have been arrested, though it has been reported that Hitler has since escaped.

Details of the events in Munich on Thursday night and yesterday morning are lacking, but it is understood that Herr von Kahr and General von Lossow, the Reichswehr commander, were surprised into giving their assent at first to the drastic programme of the Ludendorff-Hitler party, but as soon as they had time to make the necessary arrangements they set about suppressing the movement.

From Our Own Correspondent

BERLIN, Nov. 9

I learn that General Ludendorff and Herr Hitler, who led the Nationalist coup d'état in Munich yesterday, were taken prisoner this afternoon after a fight in which the Reichswehr troops rushed the Bavarian military administration offices, in which the rebels had taken refuge. There were losses on both sides.

At noon news was received in Berlin that the Ludendorff *Putsch* could be considered at an end. It was stated that the authorities had the situation well in hand, and that all official buildings were again in the hands of the Government, with the exception of the Ministry of War, where Ludendorff and Hitler had barricaded themselves in. Herr Pohner has been arrested. Herr von Kahr had issued orders to all local authorities to exercise strict passport control. Adherents of the National Socialists and the Oberland Bund were to be arrested.

The Central Government has issued a proclamation appointing General von Seeckt to the Dictatorship in place of the Minister of Defense, Dr. Gessler. It has also cut off all communications with Bavaria and given instructions that no payments on behalf of the Reich are to be made until normal conditions have been restored in accordance with the Constitution. Orders have also been issued to Reichswehr officers informing them that if they enter Bavaria they are to obey the orders of Herr von Kahr and General von Lossow.

Manifesto to Troops.

General von Seeckt has issued a manifesto to the Reichswehr informing them that he has been appointed to sole control, and calling upon them loyally to support him. In his manifesto he states that his first duty will be to ensure the food supply and to preserve order.

News received from Bavaria states that the Bavarian Government (not the Provisional Government) has issued a manifesto to all officials, both of the Reich and of Bavaria, members of the police, and the Reichswehr, to refuse to obey any commands given by the rebels. It instructed the officials that all persons not conforming with this order would be considered as guilty of treason.

The comment of the Berlin Press in general is one of satisfaction that Ludendorff has thrown off his mask and has been so easily dealt with. Some surprise is expressed at the sudden change in attitude of Herr von Kahr and General von Lossow. Their conversion to support of the Constitution they had so recently violated is considered very sudden. Everything is quiet in Berlin.

Owing to the censorship of Bavarian news and the occupation of the telegraph and telephone offices by the military, it is still not possible to get an exact view of events of the *Putsch.* It seems clear, however, that there was a combination of Herr von Kahr and General von Lossow on the one side, and General Ludendorff and Herr Hitler on the other. By a surprise action the Ludendorff-Hitler combination succeeded in running the Kahr-Lossow combination off its feet and intimidated it into taking part in the revolution.

As usual, the *Putsch* seems to have been extraordinarily ill-prepared. Neither General Ludendorff nor Herr Hitler seems to have taken the trouble to find out what would be the attitude of the Reichswehr under General von Lossow, or of the Bavarian National police. As might have been expected, these followed their officers, who followed their chief.

It has now become known that Herr von Kahr and General von Lossow soon began suppressing the movement of General Ludendorff and Herr Hitler, and in a very little while it was clear that they had gained the upper hand. The *Putsch,* in fact, did not really last more than 12 hours. During all this period news was being received by wireless in Berlin.

Well Kept Secret.

The secret had been well kept, the speech of Herr von Kahr to the professional classes having been arranged some time previously. The meeting at which it was delivered was held in the hall of a Munich brewery, and was well attended. Besides Dr. von Knilling (Premier), three Ministers of the Bavarian Government were present, Dr. Schweyer (Minister of the Interior), Herr Wutzelhofer (Agriculture) and Dr. Krausneek (Finance). Herr von Kahr's speech was of a distinctly reactionary character, and in general formed his apologia for his dictatorship. It was, he said, on that day five years ago that Germany had collapsed, and today the foundations for a new national army were to arise in Germany. As he said this there was a commotion in the hall, and Herr Hitler, with some men at his back, forced his way to the platform. He had brought in all some 600 men, with whom he had surrounded the building.

From the platform he delivered a speech, in which he said that the revolution which had begun five years ago was now done with, the von Knilling Government overthrown, and a national dictatorship was set up. He caused Dr. Schweyer and Dr. von Knilling to be arrested, and declared that the new Bavarian Government had been formed, with Herr von Kahr as President of the Bavarian State, Herr Pohner (the former Chief of Munich Police) as Prime Minister, General Ludendorff as Commander-in-Chief of the whole German Army, General von Lossow as Minister of the Reichswehr, and Colonel von Seisser as Reich Minister of Police. Thereupon the various personages who were present, are stated to have declared amid enthusiasm that they accepted their office, and then to have withdrawn for a discussion. The hall remained in occupation of Hitler's troops.

Subsequently, it is stated, Herr von Kahr, Herr Pohner, and other members of the Bavarian Government returned to the hall. Herr von Kahr said that he took over the direction of Bavarian affairs in trust for the Monarchy, and Herr Pohner declared his readiness to act with Herr von Kahr. According to some reports, General Ludendorff also made a speech, in which he said that he would lead the armies to victories.

Several accounts said that Herr von Kahr seemed a little astonished at the way at which the thing was carried off. One account of the proceedings said that Herr Hitler, who seemed to be extraordinarily excited, fired a pistol into the roof when he found that he could not obtain a hearing.

At this point the direct news from Munich ceased, but I learned subsequently that news had been received from Bamberg that Herr von Kahr, General von Lossow, and Colonel von Seisser had declared that their sanction to the Ludendorff-Hitler *Putsch* had been forced from them. At a very early stage General von Lossow gave orders for the arrest of General Ludendorff and Herr Hitler. A further message from Bamberg stated that the National Socialists (Herr Hitler's followers) were being disarmed.

6. Tried with Hitler for Treason, General Erich Ludendorff, World War I Hero, Exalts Himself, March 27, 1924

*"The world's history sends me, who has fought for
the Fatherland, not to prison but to Valhalla."*

Hitler was crushed by the immediate failure of his Beer-Hall *Putsch* on the evening of November 8, 1923. He suggested to General Erich Ludendorff, hero of World War I who took part in the attempted seizure, that the three thousand Storm Troopers be disbanded, but the hard-bitten old general would not hear of it. He would lead a march to take the city.

At 11:00 A.M. the next day, the Storm Troopers, bearing huge swastika banners and war flags, marched to the center of Munich with Ludendorff, Hitler, Hermann Goering, and Julius Streicher at their head. At the Odeonplatz, a detachment of police barred the way. On Hitler's cry of "Surrender!" the police replied with a hail of bullets. Within minutes, sixteen Nazis, later to become martyrs of the National Socialist movement, and three policemen lay dead or dying on the pavement.

Hitler, dispatch bearer of World War I, instinctively hit the ground, saving his life but injuring his shoulder. Old General Ludendorff, scowling, his eyes straight ahead, marched through the ranks of the policemen, who respectfully turned their guns aside.

Both Ludendorff and Hitler were arrested on a charge of treason. Brought to trial, each defended himself in his own way. The old general's behavior was described in this dispatch to *The New York Times* by Thomas B. Ybarra. Ludendorff was found innocent.

The New York Times, March 28, 1924.

BERLIN, March 27. — General Ludendorff stood up before his judges today to speak for the last time in his own defense at the Munich treason trial
wherein he is one of the two principal defendants. His defense had a ring of
dignity and eloquence lacking in his previous laborious attempts to whitewash himself and blacken everybody else concerned in the abortive uprising last November against the German Government.

For once Ludendorff, the man of deeds, outshone as a speaker Hitler,
the man of words, and the other principal defendant. Hitler poured out a
torrent of eloquence, as usual, but somehow his harangue, uttered at the
top of his lungs, only served to bring Ludendorff's quiet, halting and
shorter speech into sharper relief.

After declaring that he had done his utmost duty in the World War,
Ludendorff said that after Germany's defeat every German should have
continued making all possible efforts to save the Fatherland, but only the
Nationalists had done so.

"These men now stand before your seat of judgment, gentlemen," he
continued, "but they also stand before the seat of judgment of the world's
history. The world's history sends me, who has fought for the Fatherland,
not to prison but to Valhalla. Again I raise my voice and tell you in this
most fateful hour that if the German nationalistic movement is unsuccessful, we Germans are lost forever, because before us will lie a Versailles and
the menace of enslavement to France. If the nationalistic movement does
not succeed, Germany's name will be struck from the roll of nations.

"Listen, gentlemen, to the cry of the German soul for freedom. Remember that the verdict in this trial will be announced on the birthday of the
old Emperor and Chancellor who knew how to lean upon the German
nation and army. Give these men who sit before you back to the German
nation, since it is their duty to school the German people. Not words but
only deeds make world history."

Ludendorff's speech brought him a tremendous ovation from his
hearers.

After him came Hitler who jeered at attempts to brand men like him
traitors because they had sought Germany's welfare by armed revolt
against the Republican government. He pointed out that Bismarck had
dissolved the Reichstag and ruled by force without parliamentary sanction, wherefore he had been called a traitor by his foes, yet his course was
justified by the extreme benefit which it brought Germany.

Hitler found further justification for the revolt of last November in the
example of the coronation in 1871 of William I, which upset the government then existing in the German States and substituted the Empire.

"On that day when the German Emperor was crowned outside Paris,
high treason was legalized," he thundered.

Ludendorff and Hitler were wildly acclaimed by the Munich crowds after today's final session of the treason trial, in fact, it was some time before Ludendorff's automobile could take him homeward, so dense was the wildly cheering crowd pressing around him.

All is over now at the trial except the announcement of the verdict, which has been set for next Tuesday.

7. Hitler Delivers His Final Speech at His Trial for Treason, March 27, 1924

". . . the goddess of the eternal court of history
. . . finds us not guilty."

At the trial for treason, which began on February 26, 1924, in the *Kriegsschule,* an old red brick building in the officers' training school in Munich, Hitler acted as his own lawyer. For the first time he had an audience outside of Bavaria and he was determined to take full advantage of the opportunity. In court were representatives of newspapers from all over the world, fully a hundred reporters from both the German and world press.

The up-and-coming politician turned the proceedings into a personal triumph. Putting on a dazzling display of oratory, Hitler admitted that he was the only one who planned the *Putsch.* He confessed that he deliberately intended to overthrow the Weimar Republic. He had done only what the dictators of Bavaria had wanted to do themselves. With his final words, Hitler built up his failure at the Beer Hall into a great propaganda legend.

The verdict was mild. Hitler was sentenced to five years in prison. Together with Rudolf Hess, he was sent to the prison at Landsberg-am-Lech, more of a sanitarium than a prison.

It was a political debacle, but from it Hitler learned a precious lesson: Why go to all the trouble of fighting for political power through a *Putsch* when obviously his movement was attracting such support that he might well obtain power by legal means? From

---

Quoted in Ernst Forsthoff, ed., *Deutsche Geschichte seit 1918 in Dokumenten* (Leipzig; n.p., 1935), pp. 213-14. Courtesy of Alfred Kroner Verlag. Translated by Forsthoff.

that moment on, he cast aside all thoughts of revolutionary activity and relied on the polls to bring his movement to power. So intent was he on this procedure that he was given the nickname of *"Adolf Légalité"* – Adolf the Legal One. (Another nickname, *Adolf der Schöne* – Adolf the Handsome One – indicated his immense appeal to German womanhood.)

I AIMED FROM THE FIRST at something a thousand times higher than being a minister. I wanted to become the destroyer of Marxism. I am going to achieve this task, and, if I do, the title of minister will be an absurdity as far as I am concerned. . . .

At one time I believed that perhaps this battle against Marxism could be carried on with the help of the government. In January 1923 I learned that that was just not possible. The hypothesis for the victory of Marxism is not that Germany must be free, but rather Germany will only be free when Marxism is broken. At that time I did not dream that our movement would become great and cover Germany like a flood.

The army that we are building grows from day to day, from hour to hour. Right at this moment I have the proud hope that once the hour strikes these wild troops will merge into battalions, battalions into regiments, regiments into divisions. I have hopes that the old cockade will be lifted from the dirt, that the old colors will be unfurled to flutter again, that expiation will come before the tribunal of God. Then from our bones and from our graves will speak the voice of the only tribunal which has the right to sit in justice over us.

Then, gentlemen, not you will be the ones to deliver the verdict over us, but that verdict will be given by the eternal judgment of history, which will speak out against the accusation that has been made against us. I know what your judgment will be. But that other court will not ask us: Have you committed high treason or not? That court will judge us, the quartermaster-general of the old army, its officers and soldiers, who as Germans wanted only the best for their people and Fatherland, who fought and who were willing to die. You might just as well find us guilty a thousand times, but the goddess of the eternal court of history will smile and tear up the motions of the state's attorney and the judgment of this court: for she finds us not guilty.

8. *Mein Kampf*: In Prison at Landsberg, Hitler Writes the Story of His Life and Presents the Blueprint for His Future Career

"I, however, decided to become a politician."

Sentenced to five years in prison at Landsberg-am-Lech for his part in the Beer-Hall *Putsch,* Hitler served only eight and one-half months under highly favorable circumstances. To while away the time he began to dictate, first to several other prisoners and then to Rudolf Hess, a book about his life and struggles. The manuscript soon ran to a printed version of eight hundred pages. At first it was entitled *Four and a Half Years of Struggle Against Lies, Stupidity, and Cowardice,* which Max Amann, an enterprising Nazi publisher, changed to *Mein Kampf* (My Struggle).

The book was a combination of nationalism, racialism, and gross historical errors. One critic at the time called it "a queer *mélange* of half-truths and nonsense, combined with an almost uncanny insight into the mind of the mob." But this wordy, repetitious, and badly written book was destined to become the bible of the Nazi movement. It was a best seller inside Germany: by 1939 more than five million copies had been sold, and by 1943 there were 9,740,000 in print. Couples were expected to buy a copy when they were joined in matrimony, and it became a favorite birthday gift. Hitler became independently wealthy from its sales.

Following is a *précis* of the leading ideas expressed by Hitler in *Mein Kampf.* The first part was concerned with his early life and struggle for power, the later chapters with his personal philosophy.

Adolf Hitler, *Mein Kampf* (Munich: Zentralverlag der NSDAP, 1943), two volumes in one. All quotations in this section are from this 809th printing. Translated by the editor.

In the opening pages of *Mein Kampf*, Hitler tells of his life in the house of his parents and about his education and years of suffering in Vienna. He was born on April 2, 1889, in the Bavarian-Austrian town of Braunau, the son of a pensioned customs official. He attended the *Realschule* in the Austrian city of Linz. At eleven years of age he informed his father that he did not wish to follow in his footsteps; instead he wanted to become a painter or an architect. "When I look back now after so many years, I see two things of importance in my childhood. First, I became a nationalist. Second, I learned to understand and grasp the real meaning of history. . . . When I was but fifteen years old, I understood the difference between dynastic 'patriotism' and racial 'nationalism,' and at the time I knew only the latter." Even though he was an Austrian, as a child he sang *"Deutschland über Alles!"* with fervor. He preferred it to the *"Kaiserlied"* in spite of all the warnings and punishments of his teachers at school. "In a short time I developed into a fanatical German nationalist."

After his father died, he left for Vienna, where he was advised, after failure to pass the entrance examination for the Painting Academy, to follow the career of architect. He described long hours of work, incompatibility with fellow workers, and a physical hunger which seemed to be his only "true friend." He found his only joy in books. In a few years he laid the foundation for all his knowledge.

What impressed Hitler most in Vienna was the lack of national pride (*Nationalstolz*). He learned something here he had never dreamed of before, that "only he through education learns to know the cultural, industrial, and above all, the political greatness of his Fatherland, only he is able to win and will win that inner pride which ought to go with the honor of belonging to a nation. And I can only fight for something I love; I can love only that which I esteem; I can esteem only that which I at least know."

In 1912 Hitler went to Munich, the capital of Bavaria. "A German city! What a difference from Vienna!" First, he made a bare living by doing drawings and sketches for magazines and newspapers. These were the happiest days of his life. Here his first interest in politics was awakened, and he got his first taste of Social Democracy, which he found "nationally unreliable." It seemed to him to breathe the very spirit of Judaism; therefore, he became a pronounced enemy of the Jews. "I developed from a weakling, from a citizen of the world [*Weltbürger*], to a fanatical anti-Semite."

The young Hitler studied Karl Marx, but found that "the Jewish teachings of Marxism rejected the aristocratic principles of nature." It denied the value of the individual in mankind and disputed the importance of nationalism and race. He observed the parliamentary system and found it wanting: "A feeling of national self-preservation convinced me even then that I ought to care little for national representation." He came to the conclusion that such terms as "authority of the state," "democracy," "pacifism," and "international solidarity" were doctrinaire conceptions: "There is only one thing of importance in a nation — the general national necessity of existence [*allgemeine nationale Lebensnotwendigkeiten*]."

When World War I began, Hitler preferred to fight for Germany. He disliked Austria, with its conglomeration of races and its Hapsburg ruler: that country aroused no sense of patriotism in his bones. He penned a note to the king of Bavaria and asked that he be allowed to serve in the ranks of the German army. His application was accepted almost immediately, and he was sent to the front. For four years he was in the thick of battle, performing the difficult duties of a dispatch bearer. He was wounded and gassed severely, was awarded the Iron Cross, first class, but was not promoted beyond the rank of lance-corporal.

The news of the fall of the monarchy in November 1918, and the formation of the German Republic left him bitter. His hatred of the men who had brought about the crime grew and grew. "I, however, decided to become a politician," he wrote.

Hitler soon came under the influence of Gottfried Feder, who awakened his interest by a new idea — "the breaking of interest-servitude [*Zinsknechtschaft*]." In a flash he saw the national idea that could save Germany. Germany must be awakened and must become truly national; there must be no Communists, no Jews, no financial enslavement to the rest of the world.

Hitler then became a member of the German Workers' party (*Deutsche Arbeiterpartei*). The organization expanded quickly, and in 1923 Hitler led it in an abortive beer-hall *Putsch* in Munich. (See document 5.)

Hitler attributed his sense of nationalism to his early training. Though he did not do especially well in his classes, he was always at the top in history: "We sat at the feet of our old professor, often enthused to the bursting point, sometimes even breaking into tears. Our little version of national fanaticism was a means by which he could educate us: he only had to appeal to our national honor in order to bring us around to his viewpoint more quickly than he could in any other way."

To Hitler the composer Richard Wagner, who immortalized the spirit of Teutonic gods in crashing martial music, was the ideal representative of the "Nordic race." Wagner's dictum that "the Jew is the plastic demon of the decline of mankind" appealed to young Hitler. The young Austrian first heard *Lohengrin* when he was but twelve years old. "At one stroke I was captivated. My youthful enthusiasm for the Bayreuther master knew no bounds. Again and again this enthusiasm drew me to his works, and even today I am especially happy to say that I can attribute my later rise to these modest provincial performances."

As a youth, Hitler had never heard the word "Jew." There were few Jews in Linz, and his father avoided any mention of them. When he came to Vienna, he was asked by friends to read an anti-Semitic newspaper, but he refused, and described such publications as "unworthy of the cultural mission of a great people." Then came the great moment of decision. He saw a black-haired Jew on the street and asked himself: "Could this be a German?" Then followed a soul-searing battle in his mind. He decided that the Jew was a spiritual pestilence in art, literature, and the theater. "The fact that nine-tenths of all obscene literature, of artistic claptrap, and theatrical foolishness is traceable to these people, who number scarcely one percent of the people in this country, cannot be denied very easily."

Hitler began to study the ideas of Adolf Stoecker, William II's court-chaplain, whose views about the Jewish menace appealed to him. "I gradually began to hate them. I became a fanatical anti-Semite."

Hitler then turned his interest to his conception of the State and the political situation. He denounced the German Republic as "the greatest miscarriage of the twentieth century" and "a monstrosity of the human mechanism." Three conceptions of the State were prevalent among the people. First were those who saw in the State simply a more or less voluntary collection of people under a government. This was by far the most numerous group, the "crazy brains" of which had created a state authority (*Staatsautorität*) and which forced people to serve the State instead of the State serving the people.

The second group, a smaller one, recognized a state authority under certain conditions, such as liberty, freedom, and other rights of man. It expected that the State be run in such a manner that the individual's pocketbook would be filled comfortably. This group was recruited mainly from the German bourgeoisie, from liberal democracy.

The third and weakest group looked for the unity of all peoples speaking the same language. It sought to win nationalization through language. This group was dominated by the Nationalist party and was handicapped by fundamentally false conceptions. The various peoples of Austria could never be Germanized. A Negro or a Chinese could never become German simply because he spoke the German language fluently.

According to Hitler, nationality and race lay in blood, not in language. It would be possible to better the racial situation in Germany if lower elements were gradually weeded out. Especially bad was the mixture in eastern Germany, where foreign Polish elements had crept into German blood. Germany had gotten a bad reputation by the belief prevalent in America that all German immigrants were Germans. On the contrary, they were, in Hitler's view, Jewish "imitation Germans."

All three concepts of the State — the voluntary, the liberal-democratic, and the nationalistic — were, in Hitler's view, fundamentally false. They did not recognize that the cultural powers of the State rested essentially upon racial elements. It was the prime duty of the State to preserve and encourage its racial elements. The State was no end, but a means to an end. It was, indeed, the prerequisite to a higher *Kultur*,* but not the cause of it. The cause lay exclusively in the existence of a race capable of improving the *Kultur*: "The highest aim of the national state should be the care and maintenance of these primeval racial elements (*Urelemente*), which create the beauty and dignity of a higher civilization. We, as Aryans, understand by the word *State*, then, only the living organism of a nation, which not only ensures the preservation of this nation, but leads to the higher freedom through the development of its spiritual and idealistic power."

Hitler contended that what the rest of the world thought about Germany, or what Germany thought about the world, was of absolutely no moment when such interests conflicted with German values. "The German Reich must, as a state, include all Germans. Its task is to collect and maintain the most valuable primeval racial elements of the nation, which it must lead upward to a dominating position."

At this point, Hitler summarized seven points as the business of the state:

1. It must place race at the center of attention.
2. It must keep the race clean.
3. It has the duty to maintain the practice of modern birth control. No diseased or weak persons should be allowed to have children.
4. It must promote sport among the youth to an unheard-of efficiency.
5. It must make the army the final and highest school.
6. It must emphasize the teaching of racial knowledge in schools.
7. It must awaken patriotism and national pride in all its citizens.

Hitler was certain that the Aryan or Indo-European stock, especially the Germanic or Teutonic, was actually what the Jews claimed to be — a chosen people. The survival of mankind depended on this race. "Everything we admire on this earth, whether in science, art, technology, or invention, is the creation of only a few nations and, perhaps, orginally, of one race. The whole success of our *Kultur* depends on these nations." For Hitler there was only one race of consequence — the Aryan. "History shows in striking clarity that every mixture of blood between the Aryan race with lower races had resulted in the downfall of the bearer of *Kultur*. North America, whose greater proportion of population consist of Germanic elements, mixed but little with lower colored races, shows a civilization and a *Kultur* different from that of Central or South America, where the

---

*The German word *Kultur* cannot be translated accurately by the words "culture" or "civilization." It is a peculiar German expression denoting the whole range of a nation's philosophy and progress.

Romanic immigrants become assimilated to a greater extent with the native inhabitants." Race mixture, Hitler said, did not affect Germanic North America in this way. North America was "racially clean."

Hitler warned his countrymen that he who failed to understand the laws of race would bring misfortune upon himself. He beseeched them to join the parade of victory (*Siegeszug*) of the best races. He repeated again and again that the one race which held the fate of civilization was the Aryan. Cut the Aryan race from the face of the earth and deep blackness, comparable to the Dark Ages, would descend upon mankind.

Hitler divided all humanity into three classes: (1) founders of civilization (*Kulturbegründer*); (2) bearers of civilization (*Kulturträger*); and (3) destroyers of civilization (*Kulturzerstörer*).

By founders of civilization Hitler meant the Aryan race residing in Germany and North America. The gradual global spread of Aryan *Kultur* to such countries as Japan and other "morally subjugated races" led to the creation of the second class, the bearers of civilization. Hitler included the Orient generally in this category. Only in outward forms would Japan and other bearers of civilization remain Asiatic; inwardly, they would become Aryanized. In the third class, the destroyers of civilization, Hitler placed first of all the Jews.

Hitler went on to proclaim the superiority of the Aryan race. Just as mankind produces the individual genius, so did the various races have a sort of genius race among them — the Aryan. It was an inborn characteristic, just as genius was born in the brain of the child. When the Aryan race came into contact with lower races, it conquered them and imposed its will upon them. Instead of maintaining the purity of his blood, however, the Aryan mixed it with that of the natives, until he began to take on the spiritual and bodily characteristics of the lower races. Continuation of this blood mixture meant to Hitler the destruction of old civilizations and the loss of a power of resistance (*Widerstandskraft*), which was alone the possession of those of pure blood. The Aryan race had maintained its high place in civilization precisely because it understood the meaning of duty, i.e., the Aryan individual always was eager to offer his life for the benefit of the majority. In Hitler's eyes, this willingness to endure sacrifice revealed the crowning feature of mankind — the essence of sacrifice.

Hitler saw the Jew in strong contrast to the Aryan. "Scarcely any people on earth has its instinct of self-preservation so well developed as the so-called 'chosen people.' " Hitler insisted that the Jew never had a culture of his own, that he always borrowed from others, and that he developed his mind from contact with other peoples. Unlike the Aryan, the Jew's desire for self-preservation did not go beyond the individual. The Jewish feeling of belonging together (*Zusammengehörigkeitsgefühl*) was based on a primitive herd instinct. The Jewish race was nakedly egotistic, and it had only an imaginary *Kultur*. It had no idealism. The Jews were not even a race of nomads, because the nomads had at least an idea of what work meant. Jews were parasites on the bodies of other peoples. They formed a state within the state, and they refused to leave.

Hitler never considered Judaism a religion. Religion, in his view, represented a people with positive racial characteristics. The Talmud was not a religious book dedicated to preparation for immortality, but rather was devoted to the practical life of the present world. The religious teachings of Judaism were concerned primarily with the task of keeping Jewish blood pure, not to religion itself.

Hitler saw the Jewish spirit as working for the ruin of Germany. "The black-haired youth waits for hours with satanic joy in his eyes for the unsuspecting [Aryan] whom he shames with his blood and thereby robs the nation. He seeks to destroy the racial characteristics of the German with every means at his command. It was the Jews who brought the Negro to the Rhine, always with the same thought and clear aim in the back of their heads — to destroy the hated white races through 'bastardizing,' to tumble them from their cultural and political heights, and to raise themselves to the vacant place."

Hitler believed that organized Marxism and its dictatorship of the proletariat ideology was responsible for corruption of the national blood and German national ideals. Hitler predicted that Marxism would overcome German nationalism until Hitler himself appeared to act the role of savior. This was attributable to the Jews, who wanted to root out the "national bearers of intelligence and make slaves in the land." A terrible example was Russia, "where 30 million were allowed to die of hunger in a truly savage manner and undergo inhuman torments while literary Jews and stock-exchange bandits obtained control over a great people."

Hitler insisted that a racially clean people could never be subjugated by the Jews. Everything on earth could be bettered. Every defeat could become the victory of a later epoch. There could be a "renaissance of the German soul" as long as the blood of the German people was kept pure. Germany's defeat in 1918 could well be explained on racial grounds: 1914 saw the final attempt of forces making for national preservation against steadily advancing pacifistic-Marxist crippling of the German national body. "What Germany needs today is a Teutonic State of the German Nation."

Hitler then turned to economic nationalism. Under the influence of Gottfried Feder's economic teaching and his own nationalistic feeling, Hitler came to the conclusion that national self-sufficiency and economic independence had to replace international trade. This principle — *Autarkie* — was based on the assumption that economic interests and economic leaders had to be subordinated ruthlessly to racial and national considerations. Hitler pointed out that the nations of the world were erecting higher and higher barriers against commercial intercourse and cutting imports to a minimum.

Hitler revealed that he would go to even greater extremes. Germany would cut herself off from the rest of Europe altogether and be self-sufficient. Enough food could be raised in Germany and in eastern Europe to assure the existence of the Reich. Hitler admitted that this would undoubtedly mean a severe economic revolution, but Germany, he argued, had already undergone enough strain to be inured to such a situation.

In Hitler's view, the struggle against international finance and loan capitalism had become the most important point in the program of the battle of the German nation for independence and freedom. The steel axe of national socialism was breaking interest-servitude (*Brechtung der Zinsknechtschaft*). Farmers, workingmen, bourgeoisie, industrialists — the entire nation — all of whom had to borrow foreign capital, were under the influence of this interest-servitude. State and people must be freed from their interest debts to loan-capitalism. There must be a new national state capitalism. The *Reichsbank* must be under governmental control. Money for all public works (water power, roads) must be obtained through issue of governmental coupons (*Staatskassengutscheine*) with no interest. Building associations and industrial banks had to be formed to grant loans without interest. Hitler had no trust in international capital.

Hitler made it clear that any wealth obtained during World War I should be regarded as criminally acquired. War profits had to be confiscated. All trusts had to be placed under governmental ownership. All large industries had to adopt a profit-sharing system. The importance of personality in business had to be recognized. There had to be a comprehensive development of the old-age pension system. Large department stores, such as Tietz, Karstadt, and Wertheim, had to be placed on a cooperative basis and leased to small tradesmen at small profit.*

In summary, from the pages of *Mein Kampf* there emerged the views of a man who was strongly nationalistic, violently anti-Semitic, "truly" socialist, anti-democratic, anti-Catholic, anti-Marxian, anti-French. It was a predominantly negative philosophy. It was also an accurate blueprint in light of later events. Statesmen in the democratic world paid little attention to it — a tragic mistake.

---

*Hitler's views on economics later underwent considerable modification. He saw his best road to political power in cooperation with Rhineland industrialists and quickly abandoned these bizarre economic views for more orthodox ones. He conveniently sidetracked Gottfied Feder, his economic mentor, in favor of Dr. Hjalmar Schacht.

9. The Nazi Leader Issues a Warning Against the Red Dragon in a Speech at Munich, May 23, 1926

"We are convinced that there will be a final show-down in the struggle against Marxism."

From the beginning of his political career Hitler exhibited an extraordinary ability as an orator. He discovered his talent to hold audiences in the cafés of Vienna, and he improved his techniques in his long drive for political power. There is no doubt that he was one of the most effective speakers of modern times. He understood the magic of the spoken word. A spellbinder without humor, his jokes were feeble and stale, but he knew how to hold an audience.

He would start his speeches in a slow, tenor voice. Then, as he gathered momentum, he would speed up his delivery until, finally, he was shouting and barking in near hysterical fashion. His speeches were often chaotic, full of contradictions, and at times meaningless. Many who heard him were entranced for several hours but later could not remember what he had said. He had held them in a kind of hypnotic trance. All they knew was that he had started with troubled, gloomy phrases and had ended with triumphant shouts.

"His words," said one listener, "were like a scourge. When he spoke of the disgrace of Germany, I was ready to spring on my enemy. I looked around to see that his magnetism was holding these thousands as one. The intense will of the man, the passion of his sincerity, seemed to flow from him into me. I was exalted. It was just like a religion. I gave him my soul."

In the later stages of Hitler's drive for political power, Nazi

---

Völkischer Beobachter, May 26, 1926. Translated by the editor.

officials planned Hitler's speeches with all the care devoted to a stage production. After a long wait, the hall would suddenly darken. In utter silence a spotlight fingered its way to the entrance. Then, in a blare of trumpets, the slight figure of Hitler appeared. The spotlight followed him to the platform. Bowing and smiling to the audience, Hitler stood quietly acknowledging the loud, monotonous chant of "*Sieg Heil! Sieg Heil!*" "Hail to Victory!"

He would raise his hand and the thunderous chant would stop as if by magic. His podium was specially rigged: with a row of electrical buttons he could regulate the volume of sound and the lighting. Pressing one button, he gave the audience a go-ahead signal to applaud. When he pressed another, there was an immediate halt to the applause and shouting.

Among Hitler's favorite subjects throughout his career were Marxism and its concomitants – communism and the bolshevik threat. In speech after speech he denounced bolshevism as a reversion to Asiatic barbarism. He regarded Marxism as the deadly enemy of his own movement. The following excerpt from a speech at Munich given on May 23, 1926, reveals this favorite theme.

THE WIDESPREAD FEELING that Marxism is finished is madness and insanity, and it requires great stupidity to believe in this madness. I have said in the past that there is going to be a final confrontation, and that will not come in the *Reichstag* but in an overall showdown which will result in the destruction of either Marxism or ourselves. Since I said that, a year has passed. Now from 90,000 to 120,000 Red Front fighters are ready to parade in Berlin.

Communism is not being put down, but rather it is being radicalized. Marxism is not becoming weaker; it is getting stronger. For that the bourgeois parties are responsible today. After seven years of this we are standing, not beside the corpse of communism but alongside our own coffin. That is the result of the measures taken by the know-it-alls of the Bavarian Government and also the result of their ban on public speaking.

These gentlemen will never be able to justify themselves before German history for what they have done by issuing this ban on public speaking. They attempted to throttle the one party which would have been able to counteract this Red pestilence.

What do they expect further in Germany? In 1919 there were not even 20,000 Communists in Berlin, in 1923 there were 140,000, in the first election of 1924 there were more than 200,000, and at the second election in that same year there were 357,000. Today you may be sure there are from 600,000 to 700,000 Communists in Berlin. In other cities of Germany it is much the same as in the German capital. What can be expected of a German future if this increase is not halted?

In Bavaria we have the wonderful solution of bringing out the Royalists to oppose the Red dragon as it lifts its head and blows steam from its nostrils. Just as long ago Pope Leo went forth to meet the hordes of Attila and calmed them by his majestic appearance, so some day Professor Bauer will go out to meet the Asiatic hordes, royal crown and umbrella in his hands, and will make this movement, which extends from Vladivostok to Königsberg, halt at the sight of war veterans, those who march and cry: "Hail to our King, stop!"

In Berlin the Red mob is threatening while here we talk about Monarchy!

My dear friends! If something should happen today, how in the world can the war veterans, armed with umbrellas, take up the struggle? How can those who were finished so quickly in 1918 be able suddenly to out-yell the international *Marseillaise*? These gentlemen are nodding themselves into beautiful dreams. They say that we are a danger to the state. No, they themselves are destroying the state by seeking to destroy that force which alone, through its knowledge of the past, can make moves against the Red mob.

The war veterans will not be the ones to decide the issue. Only a fanatical will is enough to meet the attack, and these gentlemen do not possess that will. Their claim that we are a danger to the state is an unbelievable lie. During all these years we have been the ones who are fighting for the German Reich and the German state.

It is our own mission to forge a strong weapon — will and energy — so that when the hour strikes, and the Red dragon raises itself to strike, at least some of our people will not surrender to despair. I myself represent the same principles that I stood for a year ago.

We are convinced that there will be a final showdown in this struggle against Marxism. We are convinced that it will come, for two ideologies are fighting one another and there can be only one outcome. One will be destroyed and the other will be victorious.

It is the great mission of the National Socialist movement to give our times a new faith and to see to it that millions will stand by this faith. Then, when the hour comes for the showdown, the German people will not be completely unarmed when they meet the international murderers.

10. Dr. Paul Joseph Goebbels, Later to Become Propaganda Minister of the Third Reich, Writes a Pamphlet Excoriating the Jews

"The Jew is . . . the conscious destroyer of our race."

The conglomeration of misfits, ambitious demagogues, adventurers, and ruffians who formed Hitler's immediate entourage learned quickly that the surest way to his attention was to imitate his fanatical anti-Semitism. His comrades, from Rudolf Hess to Julius Streicher, from Hermann Goering to Heinrich Himmler, outdid one another in expressions of hatred to win the goodwill of their *Fuehrer.* In newspapers and pamphlets, in speeches and radio talks, they repeated Richard Wagner's dictum about the Jews as the plastic demon of the fall of mankind, as a blood-sucking race which had to be eliminated from German life.

Among those who vied for the *Fuehrer's* attention was Paul Joseph Goebbels, a short, club-footed, hatchet-faced man with a loud, booming voice. Joining Hitler in the early stages of the National Socialist movement, he was at first disposed to support the radical (socialist) side of the party that called for a Second Revolution, but he was careful to mount the Hitler bandwagon when it became certain that the latter was headed for the top post in the fledgling Nazi party. An unsuccessful playwright, he found his niche at the side of Hitler as his propaganda expert. He enjoyed Hitler's confidence until the day when they both committed suicide. To envious members of the Nazi hierarchy, he was contemptuously known as "The Little Mouse Doctor."

Goebbels, from the beginning, concentrated heavily on Hitler's

From Goebbels-Mjoinir, *Die verflüchten Hakenkreuzler,* published in the late 1920s. Translated by the editor.

monomania on Jews. He never let slip an opportunity to denounce the Jewish peril, because he was certain that Hitler would approve. The following extracts from a Goebbels pamphlet of the early days shows the tenor of Nazi ideology.

WHY are we enemies of the Jews?

We are enemies of the Jews because we are warriors for the freedom of the German people. THE JEW IS THE CAUSE AND THE BENEFICIARY OF OUR SLAVERY. He has used the social troubles of our broad masses in order to widen the split between right and left among our people, he has made TWO HALVES OF GERMANY. Here is the real reason for the loss of the World War on one side and for the betrayal of the revolution on the other side. . . .

The Jew has no interest in the solution of the question of German fate. He CAN'T have it, since he lives because it remains unsolved. . . . He has a better trump in his hand, when a nation lives in slavery than when it is free, busy, self-conscious and self-contained. THE JEW HAS CAUSED OUR MISERY, AND TO-DAY HE LIVES ON OUR TROUBLES.

That is the reason why as NATIONALISTS AND AS SOCIALISTS WE ARE ENEMIES OF THE JEW. HE HAS RUINED OUR RACE, ROTTED OUR MORALS, CORRUPTED OUT TRADITIONS AND BROKEN OUR POWER. We can thank him for being the goats of the world to-day. As long as we were Germans, he was a leper among us. Since we have forgotten our Germanic character, he has triumphed over us and our future.

The Jew is the plastic demon of the decline of mankind. Where he scents rubbish and putrefaction, there he appears and begins a criminal game of chess with the people. He takes on the mask of those whom he wants to deceive, pretends to be the friend of his victim, and before the unfortunate one knows it, he has his neck broken.

The Jew is uncreative. He does not produce anything, HE DEALS ONLY WITH PRODUCTS. With junk, clothes, pictures, precious stones, grain, stocks and bonds, shares, people and states. And he has STOLEN somewhere everything he uses in his trading. As long as there is a storm raging in a state he is a REVOLUTIONARY, as soon as he is in possession of POWER, he preaches peace and quiet, in order to chew his booty in comfort.

What has ANTI-SEMITISM to do with SOCIALISM? I ask it the other way round: what has the Jew to do with SOCIALISM? SOCIALISM is the gospel of WORK. Who ever saw a Jew work and not plunder, steal, sponge (*schmarotzen*) and live from the sweat of the other man's brow? As SOCIALISTS we are all JEW-HATERS, because we see in the Hebrew the incarnation of capitalism. . . .

What has ANTI-SEMITISM to do with NATIONALISM? I ask it the other way around: what has the JEW to do with NATIONALISM? NATIONALISM is the gospel of BLOOD, of RACE. The Jew is the enemy and the destroyer of unity of blood, the conscious destroyer of our race. We are AS NATIONALISTS JEW-HATERS, because in the HEBREW we see the eternal enemy of our national honor and our national freedom.

The Jew is indeed ALSO A HUMAN BEING. Certainly, and none of us has ever doubted it. We only doubt that he is a DECENT person. He doesn't belong to us. He lives according to other inner and outer laws. Because he is a human being is no reason why we should allow him to oppress us in the most inhuman manner. He is indeed a human being — BUT WHAT KIND? If someone beat your mother in the face with a whip, would you then say: "Thank you, sir! HE IS ALSO A HUMAN BEING!?" That is no human (*Mensch*), that is a savage (*Unmensch*)! How much worse has the Jew done to OUR MOTHER GERMANY and how much worse does he still do to-day?

. . . ANTI-SEMITISM is unChristian. That is to say then that the Christian means to look on as the Jew cuts our skin into strips. . . . In order to be Christian: YOU MUST LOVE YOUR NEIGHBOR AS YOURSELF! MY NEIGHBOR IS MY COMRADE IN BLOOD AND NATIONALITY. IF I LOVE HIM, THEN I MUST HATE HIS ENEMIES. HE WHO THINKS AS A GERMAN, MUST DESPISE THE JEW. One statement depends on the other.

Even Christ saw once that one doesn't find love sufficient in all situations. When he came across the thieves in the temple, he didn't say: "Children, love each other!"; instead HE TOOK a whip and drove the pack away.

WE ARE JEW-HATERS BECAUSE WE ADMIT THAT WE ARE GERMANS. THE JEW IS OUR GREATEST CALAMITY.

It isn't true that we eat a Jew with every breakfast.

But it is true the HE IS EATING US UP SLOWLY BUT SURELY, TOGETHER WITH ALL OUR POSSESSIONS.

THAT IS GOING TO CHANGE, AS SURE AS WE ARE GERMANS.

11. Hitler Repeats His Basic Political Demand — Revision of the Treaty of Versailles, September 28, 1930

"Even a camel will lie down and refuse to move. . . ."

On September 28, 1930, the London *Sunday Express* published an article contributed by Hitler, in which the German political leader claimed that the economic proletarianization of a people would be followed by their political proletarianization. He warned of the implications of the German election of September 14, just two weeks earlier, in which his party had received nearly 6.3 million votes and returned 107 deputies to the *Reichstag.* "It tore away the veil and partly revealed the soul of Germany," he wrote. The world was shocked, he said, to discover Germany in a high fever, which was bound to continue – to rise against existing conditions and unbearable burdens.

The concluding part of Hitler's article follows.

GERMANY MAY STILL be saved by reopening the Versailles Treaty and the Young Plan. When delirium sets in it will be too late. . . .

No people, I do not care who they are, can endure such conditions, carry such burdens, be conscious that they, their children and their children's children are foreign tribute slaves and yet retain their self-respect. It is impossible.

Even a camel will lie down and refuse to move, even a horse will baulk when cruelly overloaded. Why should not a people revolt against burdens

---

Sunday Express (London), September 28, 1930.

they know they cannot carry, after having given the world the sincerest proof of their loyal efforts to do so? . . .

We demand the revision of the Young Plan.

We demand the return to us of the Polish Corridor, which is like a strip of flesh cut from our body. It cuts Germany into two. It is a national wound that bleeds continuously, and will continue to bleed till the land is returned to us.

All this is founded on the hypocritical basis that Germany was guilty of causing the World War. The National Socialists reject that accusation. It is untrue. It has been thoroughly exploded, but all Germany is suffering from the Versailles Treaty and the Young Plan, which are based on that accusation.

The National Socialist Movement proposes to rouse all Germans against this injustice, to rouse them to say unitedly that there shall be "No more."

President Wilson solemnly promised the German people that if they laid down their arms and overthrew the Imperial regime they would not be held responsible for the War, and no indemnities would be laid on them. That promise and others were broken in the most contemptuous manner.

"Indemnities" were renamed "reparations."

If the German people must suffer as they are suffering to-day and will be suffering to-morrow, then let us have suffering that may come from saying "No" rather than that laid on us by our "Yes."

12. In an Interview with the *Times* (London) Hitler Warns About the Possibility of a Bolshevist Germany, October 14, 1930

". . . Germany would be like a powder barrel that a single spark could set off."

By 1930, Hitler was strong enough politically to begin lecturing the world about the possibility of a bolshevist Germany and his own mission to prevent that catastrophe. In an interview with a correspondent of the *Times* (London), he told how effective a national socialist Germany would be in combating communism and in honoring all obligations to repay private foreign loans and investments. He warned that Western civilization might not survive the bolshevization of Germany.

IF ECONOMIC DEVELOPMENTS continued as at present, before the winter was out Germany would be like a powder barrel that a single spark could set off. The Middle parties in the Reichstag would be hopelessly split, and the world would have the choice between a Bolshevist Germany and a National Socialist Germany. A Bolshevist Germany would repudiate everything – reparation debts and private obligations too. Those who, with a helpless shrug of the shoulders, had signed the Treaty of Versailles and the Dawes Plan and the Young Plan had been giving bad cheques. A National Socialist Germany would never sign cheques it could not honour. It would not make the political payments, because it would not honestly be able to; but, like any honest merchant, it would honour all obligations to repay private foreign loans and investments. If the world insisted on the political payments being made, then Germany would go under.

Times (London), October 15, 1930.

The Bolshevization of Russia had already given the whole civilized world a jolt; if Germany became an annex of Bolshevist Russia, Western civilization would get a much worse and probably fatal jolt. Even Oswald Spengler, who had at least given the decline of Western civilization three hundred years to complete itself, would then prove to have been an optimist.

13. Hitler's Düsseldorf Speech to Rhineland Industrialists Sets the Groundwork for Financial Backing, January 27, 1932

"The movement . . . does not retire from the scene in cowardly fashion, but rather it brutally enforces its will."

From the beginning of his movement, Hitler was forced to face the contradictory motivations of nationalism and socialism. Fascism in the form of national socialism meant the combination of two essentially opposite historical phenomena. From the beginning, a radical wing called for the extension of the movement into a Second Revolution and emphasized socialist goals. The second major element — nationalism — turned to the right instead of to the left. Hitler, a pragmatist, saw his best chance for power by discouraging the leftist elements of the Storm Troopers and seeking support on the right.

On the right were the industrialists of the Rhineland, who had the money and the political clout that Hitler needed if he was to be successful in his drive for political power. In the early stage of his political career, money was the primary need. When the opportunity arose, he was quick to meet it.

On January 27, 1932, Hitler went to Düsseldorf, in the heart of Germany's industrial complex, as a guest of the Industry Club, an important body of Rhineland-Westphalian industrialists. It was the first time that German financial lords had an opportunity to meet the politician about whom everyone was talking.

At first the reception was cool and reserved. Who was this loud-

---

Condensed from the official German version, January 27, 1932. Translated by the editor.

speaking Austrian who dared to seek assistance? The industrialists thought they would hear him and then turn him down as a crackpot agitator. They had invited him because they were attracted by his fanatical anticommunism.

Hitler made good use of his opportunity. For two and a half hours he harangued the assembled coal and steel barons. In perhaps the shrewdest speech of his life, he presented, one after another, the stock ideas that had already impressed the German public. He wanted big business to know that it could trust him and his National Socialists. All that Nazi propaganda about interest-slavery (*Zinsknechtschaft*) was so much electioneering rubbish, and the industrialists need not take it seriously, he told them. The only hope of salvation from the Bolshevik bugaboo lay in cooperation with his Nazi movement. He denounced democracy and praised national socialism as the only key to a great German future.

It was a virtuoso performance. The skeptical audience gradually warmed up to this hypnotic speaker. When Hitler finally finished his oration, he saw the assembled industrialists rise to their feet and give him tremendous round of applause. True, this loud little man was lacking in tone, tact, and taste, but he had the right ideas. It was an extraordinary day; the industrialists now had their champion to protect them against the rise of communism and the trade unions. For Hitler, too, it was a triumph. Now he had access to the purse strings of the country, and he would take good advantage of the situation.

Hitler's speech to the Düsseldorf industrialists was a long one. Following is a condensed version of this historic address.

TODAY THE NATIONAL SOCIALIST movement is widely regarded in Germany as being opposed to our business life. It seems to me that the reason for this viewpoint is that we have looked at the events that have shaped our development to the present, in a different way from all other organizations in our public life.

I believe it is most important that once and for all we break with the concept that our destiny is determined by world events. It is just not true that our present misery was caused by a world crisis, a world catastrophe. What really happened was that we have reached a state of general crisis. From the beginning many mistakes were made.

I need not say: "According to the general view the Peace Treaty of Versailles is the cause of our misfortune." The Peace Treaty of Versailles is only the work of men. It is not a burden that has been placed upon us by destiny. It is the work of men. Both the Peace Treaty of Versailles and

effects of that treaty have been the result of a policy which, fifteen, fourteen, or thirteen years ago, was looked upon as the right policy, at least in
the enemy states. From our point of view it has been fatal — when ten or
fewer years ago its true character was revealed to millions of Germans.

It is, furthermore, my own view that it is false to say that life in Germany today is solely determined by considerations of foreign policy.
Certainly a people can reach the point where foreign relations influence
and completely determine political life. But that is neither natural nor
desirable.

Politics is nothing else and can be nothing else than the safeguarding of a
people's vital interests and the waging of the life-battle by every means. All
functions of the body politic must in the final analysis fulfill only one
purpose — to secure in the future the maintenance of that body which is the
people.

Neither foreign policy nor economic policy is of primary importance.
Of course, a people needs the business world in order to live. But business
is only one function of the body politic. The essential thing, then, is the
starting point — and that is the people themselves.

The greatness of a people is to be found in the final analysis in the sum of
its outstanding achievements. The whole edifice of civilization is in its
foundations and in all its stones nothing else than the result of the creative
capacity, the achievement, the intelligence, and the industry of individuals. In its greatest triumphs it represents the crowning achievements of
individual God-favored geniuses.

It is only natural that when the capable intelligences of a nation, always
in a minority, are regarded only as the same in value as all the rest, then
genius and personality are subjected to the majority and this process is
falsely named the "rule of the people." This is not really the rule of the
people, but in reality it is the rule of stupidity, of mediocrity, of half-
heartedness, of cowardice, of weakness, and of inadequacy.

In the long run democracy leads to the destruction of a people's real and
enduring values. That is why it is that peoples with a great past lose their
dominant position as soon as they surrender themselves to the unlimited,
democratic rule of the masses.

Added to this is another factor — namely, the view, that life in this world
is not to be maintained through conflict. That will have appalling consequences because it slowly poisons an entire people.

It is wholly absurd to build up economic life on the idea of achievement,
on the value of personality, and therefore in practice on the authority of
personality, and then in the *political* sphere to deny the authority of
personality and to put in its place the law of the greater number —
democracy.

What will happen is that there will be a gap between the economic and
the political points of view, and to bridge that gap an attempt will be made

to assimilate the former into the latter. This gap is not merely bare theory. Life in its practical form is grounded on the importance of personality. Now it is gradually being threatened by the supremacy of mere numbers. In the state there is an organization, the army, which cannot in any way be democratized without surrendering its very existence.

In Germany today we witness an internal conflict between the representatives of the democratic principle and the representatives of the principle of authority.

The conception of pacifism is logical if I once admit a general equality among peoples and human beings. But in that case what sense is there in conflict? Pacifism translated into practice must gradually lead to the destruction of the competitive instinct, and to the destruction of the ambition for outstanding achievement.

To sum up the argument: I see two diametrically opposed principles: the principle of democracy, which, no matter how you look at it, is the principle of destruction; and the principle of the authority of personality, which I call the principle of achievement.

The worth of a people, the character of their internal organization, and the character of their education — these are the starting points for political action.

The world today is quite different from that of fifty, eighty, or a hundred years ago. The position which faces you today is not the result of a revelation of God's will, but the result of human weaknesses, of human mistakes, of false judgments by men. It is but natural that there must be a change in this situation, and that men must be transformed inwardly.

Look at the world today. We have nations which, through their innate outstanding worth, do not have the life-space (*Lebensraum*) which is rightfully theirs. We have the so-called white race which, since the fall of ancient civilizations, in the course of some thousand years has created for itself a privileged place in the world. This privileged position, this economic supremacy, has been due to a *political* conception of supremacy.

Take any single area you like. England did not conquer India by way of justice and law; she conquered India without any regard for the wishes or views of the natives, and when necessary upheld her supremacy with the most brutal ruthlessness. Just as in the same way Cortez or Pizarro annexed Central America. The white race was convinced that it had the right to organize the rest of the world. Superficial disguises make no difference: in practice it was the exercise of an extraordinarily brutal right to dominate others (*Herrenrecht*).

Today we are faced with a world condition which is for the white race understandable only if it brings about a marriage of the spirit of domination in political will and the spirit of domination in economic activity. The white race can maintain its position only as long as the difference in standard of living in different parts of the world continues to exist. If today you give our export markets the same standard of living as we ourselves possess, it will be impossible for the white race to maintain its position of superiority.

The world condition today can be stated briefly. Germany, England, France, and the United States, together with a whole series of lesser states, are industrial nations depending upon exports. At the close of the Great War, all these people were faced with markets emptied of commodities. With new improved methods, new entrepreneurs rushed into the void. The process continued successfully for two, three, four, or five years.

But there has been no further extension of export markets. On the contrary, now we see those export markets contracting, the number of exporting nations increased, and a great many former export markets themselves industrialized. And the new wholesale exporter, the United States, while not yet all-powerful in all spheres, can reckon on advantages in production which we in Europe just do not possess.

Alongside the gradual growth of confusion in thought of the white race in Europe, a world view (*Weltanschauung*) has grown in one part of Europe and in a great part of Asia which threatens to tear this continent out of its base of international economic relations altogether. German statesmen today seem to neglect this portent with an astonishing lightheadedness.

Why is it that people just do not see how a cleavage has opened up, a cleavage which is not merely a fancy born in the heads of a few people but whose spiritual idea forms the foundation of one of our great world powers? Why do they not see that Bolshevism today is not just a mob storming about in some of our streets in Germany, but rather an idea of the world which is taking over the whole Asiatic continent?

This is emphatically not merely a theory which is held by a few visionaries or evil-minded individuals. No! This is a *Weltanschauung* that has won for itself a state, and from that base it can gradually take over the entire world and bring it down in ruins. If the advance of Bolshevism is not interrupted, it will transform the entire world completely just as Christianity in the past changed the world.

In three hundred years people will speak about a new religion, though its basis will not be Christianity. If this movement develops further, in three hundred years people will regard Lenin not merely as a revolutionary of the year 1917 but as the founder of a new world doctrine.

This gigantic phenomenon cannot be wished away in the modern world. It is a reality, and of necessity it must destroy the existence of our white race. We can see the stages of the process: first the lowering of civilization; then the construction of an independent system of production; and then the final stage — its own production to the complete exclusion of other countries.

I know well that the gentlemen of the Reich Ministry and gentlemen representing German industry will object: we just do not believe that the Soviets will ever build up an industry which can really be able to compete with us. Gentlemen: They could really never build up such an industry if they were confined to the natural resources of Bolshevist Russia. But this industry will be built up by valuable elements drawn from the white peoples themselves. And furthermore, let it be known that a lower standard of living will fully compensate for any advantage which we possess in our own methods of production.

If European and American modes of thought remain the same as today, we shall find Bolshevism gradually spreading over Asia. Thirty or forty years, when it is a question of *Weltanschauung*, count for nothing. If this process continues and our outlook remains unchanged, it will not then, gentlemen, be possible to say: "How does that affect our economic life?"

Gentlemen, the development is there for all to see. The crisis is serious, very serious.

It is natural for us to try to save labor power. Increase in achievement means reduction in the number of workmen employed. Unemployment — that has become the characteristic feature of our European nations — means that gradually a certain percentage of the population is proved statistically to be superfluous. To this must be added the fact that the struggle of all European nations for the world export market results naturally in a rise of prices which forces us to practice further economies. The final result will be the downfall of the white race, especially of those peoples who live in a narrow living-space. For her protection England will then raise her tariff barriers today and tomorrow still higher, and all other peoples will be forced to follow suit.

Germany's position today is melancholy, and it is right to call attention to that. But it is wrong to seek the cause of our distress in externals.

Germany lost the war. Do you believe for a minute that seven to eight million men, who have for ten or twenty years been excluded from the national process of production, will regard Bolshevism as anything else than the logical theoretical complement of their actual economic situation?

The essential thing to remember is that at the present time we find ourselves in a condition which has existed several times before in the history of the world. There have been occasions when the volume of certain products in the world exceeded the demand. Today we experience the same thing on the largest possible scale.

It is not the spirit which formerly opened up the world to the white race. Germans, too, took part in opening the way into the economic life of the world. But it was not German business which conquered the world and then came the development of German power.

In our case, too, it was the power-state (*Machtstaat*) which created for the world the general condition for its subsequent prosperity. In my view it is to put the cart before the horse if people today believe that by business methods they can recover Germany's power position. One must realize that the power position is also the condition for the improvement of the economic condition.

There can be no economic life unless behind that economic life there stands the determined political will of the nation absolutely ready to strike and strike hard. And here I would enter a protest against those who believe that the Treaty of Versailles is, according to the almost universal view, the cause of our misfortune. No, that treaty is in itself only the consequence of our own slow inner confusion.

We find ourselves, no one can doubt it, in a period in which the world is faced with extraordinarily difficult mental conflicts. One cannot escape these conflicts by simply regretting them. These struggles are not merely caused by the ill will of a few men. They have their deepest roots in the facts of race.

If Bolshevism is spreading today in Russia, this Bolshevism is for Russia just as logical as Czardom was in the past. It is a brutal regime which cannot be held together as a state except through a brutal government. We must watch out — we must not forget that our people, too, are racially a mixture of varied elements.

We must see in that watchword: "Proletarians of all countries, unite!" much more than a political battle cry. It is in reality the expression of men who have a certain kinship with like-minded people at a low level of civilization.

I beg you to think about it — when one comes under the conflicts of *Weltanschauungen*, one just cannot overcome them by simple emergency decrees. Gentlemen, these conflicts strike at the very power and strength of the nation as a whole.

It is quite conceivable that Germany could become a Bolshevist state — it would be a catastrophe, but it is conceivable. But it is quite inconceivable that one can create a strong and sound Germany with 50 percent of its citizens German and 50 percent nationally minded.

Germany once had its basis in Christianity. When this basis was shattered, we see how the strength of the nation turned from external affairs to internal conflicts.

There were great periods of civil wars, wars of religion, etc., struggles and confusions during which a nation either finds a new basis for its existence or splits into two and falls into chaos. The religious struggles meant that Germany withdrew inward, exhausted internally, and failed to react to great events of worldwide significance. It is an error to say that world politics alone determined Germany's fate in the sixteenth century.

No, our own internal condition at that time contributed to form that attitude toward the world which later caused us so much suffering — the position of the world without Germany.

Once again the same historical experience is repeated. Germany lost her religious unity, and the two Confessions [Catholics and Protestants] are now icebound and neither one can overcome the other. A new platform appears: the new conception of the state. First a legitimist one, and then the age of nationality. Bit by bit Germany united her forces and consolidated the Reich, which had fallen into decline. That increase in strength led to the August days of 1914, an experience which we ourselves were proud to share.

At this point I must say this: No matter what the *Reichstag* undertakes, especially in the way of emergency decrees, unless Germany can manage to master its internal divisions in *Weltanschauungen*, no measures taken by the legislature can halt the decline of the German nation.

Too much time has been lost in useless work. If the process of reconstruction had begun in 1918, then Germany's external developments would have taken a different course during the last eleven years. The Versailles Peace Treaty was imposed on us because at that time Germany had no influence at all. And Germany had no definite will of her own to change the treaty. We are not really the victims of the treaties, but rather they are the result of our own errors.

If I want to better the situation in any way, then I must first of all change the values of the country. I must first of all recognize the fact that it is not the primacy of foreign policy which can determine our actions but rather the character of our nation in the domestic sphere.

As an example, Bismarck's idea of a new Reich with the exclusion of Austria could not have been achieved without creating the instrument — the Army — to realize his political purpose. He carried that idea through in the teeth of the madness of Parliament. That rendered possible the end of Königgrätz and at Versailles, when the Reich was founded.

The same thing today — I cannot formulate an aim without obtaining the political means which are absolutely necessary for such a plan. And the political means is reorganization of an army. It makes no difference if that army is composed of 100,000 men, or 200,000, or 300,000. The essential thing is that Germany needs eight million reservists whom she can transfer into her army without falling into the catastrophic *Weltanschauung* of 1918.

If anyone wants to accuse me as a National Socialist of the greatest possible crime, he says: "You want to force a decision by violence. You want one day to destroy your political opposition. We stand on the Constitution and the right of all political parties to exist." To that I reply: It is no good appealing for national unity when 50 percent of the people are pacifist and do not want to fight for the national colors. Any state which declares treason to the country to be ethical and moral does not deserve to live.

Gentlemen: Germany in the long run cannot exist unless we find our way back to a quite extraordinary, newly created political force which can exercise effective influence abroad.

It matters not which problem we want to solve. If we want to support our export trade, the political will is all-important. If we want to construct a new internal market, if we want to solve the problem of *Lebensraum*, once again we shall need the collective political strength of our nation.

We need more than a few heavy batteries, eight or ten tanks, twelve aircraft, or a few air squadrons. The technique of arms has changed. But what remains unchanged is the formation of the will. If that fails, weapons are not of any use. With the body politic as it is today, we can no longer conduct any practical political policy.

When I returned from the front in 1918, I found a situation which I, like all the others, might simply have accepted as a *fait accompli*. I said to myself: "It is just not enough to realize that we are ruined. It is also necessary to know why."

In 1918 I looked at the situation coolly and with considered judgment. I realized that coming before the people with a new organization was a difficult course to follow. It would have been easier to join one of the existing organizations. I was naturally forced to say to myself that it would be an appalling struggle, because I was not fortunate enough to possess an outstanding name.

I was only a nameless German soldier, with a very small zinc identification dog tag on my breast. But I came to realize that if a new body politic were not formed to halt the existing fermentation, then the nation would never rise again.

Today that movement cannot be destroyed. It is there. People must reckon with it whether they like it or not. They see before them an organization which does not preach as mere theory the views which today I have presented to you as essential, but puts them into practice. That organization is inspired to the highest degree by national sentiment, based on the idea of an absolute authority in leadership in all spheres. It has overcome not only internationalism but also democracy. It acknowledges only responsibility, command, and obedience. It has an indomitable aggressive spirit. It does not retire from the scene in cowardly fashion, but rather it brutally enforces its will and hurls to its enemies the retort: "We fight again! We fight tomorrow." It is no provocation when *German* Germany expresses itself.

We have formed an inexorable decision to destroy Marxism in Germany down to its last root. That decision does not come from love of brawling. I could easily have imagined a better life than one which means to be hunted throughout Germany, persecuted by countless government regulations, and with one foot in jail.

I could imagine for myself a better destiny than what was regarded by all as an insane chimera. I have been guided by nothing but my own faith, my indestructible confidence in the natural forces of our people, and by the necessity for good leadership.

Behind us lie twelve years of struggle. We are ready to fight on a larger scale. I recall the time when with six other unknown men I formed this association, when I spoke before eleven, twelve, fourteen, twenty, thirty, and fifty people. I recall how after a year I had won sixty-four members for the movement, how our small scale kept growing. Today a stream of millions of our German fellow-countrymen is flowing to our movement. That is unique in German history.

Today we stand at a turning point in Germany's destiny. Either we shall succeed in working out a body politic as hard as iron from this conglomeration of parties, or Germany will fall into final ruin. Today no one can escape the obligation to complete the regeneration of the German body-politic. Everyone must show his personal sympathy, and everyone must take his place in the common effort. I speak to you today not to ask for your votes or to induce you to do this or that for the party. No, I am here to present a point of view. I am convinced that victory for this point of view is the only starting point for German recovery.

Remember that it means sacrifice when today hundreds of thousands of S.A. and S.S. men mount their trucks, protect meetings, undertake marches, sacrifice themselves day and night, and then return in the grey dawn to workshop and factory, or, as jobless, take the pittance of a dole. It means sacrifice when these little men spend all their money to buy uniforms, shirts, badges, and even pay their own fares.

But there is in all this the strength of an ideal — a great ideal. If the entire German nation today had this idealism, Germany would look far different in the eyes of the world than she does now!

The first necessity is to restore a sound national German body politic armed to strike. To realize this I founded the National Socialist movement thirteen years ago.

I have led that movement during the last twelve years. I hope that one day it will accomplish this task and that, as a result of its struggle, it will leave behind a German body politic completely renewed internally, intolerant of anyone who sins against the nation and its interests, intolerant of anyone who will not acknowledge its vital interests or who opposes them, intolerant and pitiless against anyone who would attempt once again to destroy or ruin that body politic.

And yet it is at all times ready for friendship and peace with all those who have a desire for peace and friendship.

14. Re-election of von Hindenburg to the Presidency: Hitler Fails in a Bid for Power, April 10, 1932

"Elaborate police preparations proved unnecessary."

The presidency of Paul von Hindenburg came to an end in early 1932 in the midst of severe political and economic crises. The old war-horse was now eighty-four and declining in health. He grew ever more dependent upon his son Oskar, who acted as his secretary. He was highly susceptible to the influence of the camarilla surrounding him, especially by General Kurt von Schleicher, known as "His Gray Eminence." Although reluctant to run for another term, von Hindenburg allowed himself to be persuaded by von Schleicher to stand for election again. In 1925 the old man had been the candidate of the conservatives, but now he was supported by defenders of the republic against attacks from the right.

On the first ballot, in March, von Hindenburg polled 18,650,000 votes (49.6 percent); Hitler received 11,339,285 (30.1 percent); Thälmann, the Communist party candidate, 4,983,197 (13 percent); and Düsterberg, the Nationalist party candidate, 2,558,000 (6.8 percent). Again, as in 1925, because no candidate had won a majority, a second ballot was required. In the run-off election held a month later, von Hindenburg received 19,359,635 votes (53 percent); Hitler 13,418,451 (26.8 percent); and Thälmann 3,796,655 (10.2 percent). This time the nationalist *Stahlhelm,* the veterans organization, threw its votes to Hitler, but the gesture was not enough to elect him. There was a lack of interest in the election — a million fewer voters came to the polls than in 1925.

The New York Times, April 11, 1932; Associated Press, April 11-12, 1932.

Coverage of the election by both *The New York Times* and the Associated Press was excellent. The following reports appeared the next day, before the final corrected figures were known.

HINDENBURG WINS ELECTION; HITLER IS 6,000,000 BEHIND; COMMUNISTS LOSE HEAVILY

13,417,460 VOTES FOR NAZI

Fails to Poll 15,000,000 He Claimed in Run-Off, but Gains 2,078,175.

THAELMANN A POOR THIRD

Red Vote Cut to 3,706,388, a Loss of 1,276,809 From the First Presidential Test.

BRUENING IS STRENGTHENED

Hitler Launches Fight for Diet Elections — One Killing in the Polling Throughout Reich.

By GUIDO ENDERIS
Special Cable to THE NEW YORK TIMES

BERLIN, April 10. — President Paul von Hindenburg won the run-off election for the Presidency of Germany with an absolute majority today, defeating Adolf Hitler, his National Socialist rival, by almost 6,000,000 votes.

With an estimated total of 36,491,694 votes cast, provisional official returns gave the 84-year-old President 19,359,642, an increase of 708,912 over his showing in the first balloting March 13; Herr Hitler, 13,417,460, an increase of 2,078,175, and Ernst Thaelmann, Communist and the only other candidate, 3,706,388. . . .

Eighty-three percent of the electorate voted, compared with 86 percent March 13, when 37,647,115 ballots were cast.

The fact that President von Hindenburg bettered his vote in the first election by more than 700,000 was regarded by the backers of the veteran Field Marshal as an excellent showing in view of the fact that the total poll today was more than 1,000,000 less than in the first contest.

Hitler's Gain Surprises

With the President's victory a foregone conclusion and speculation turning only on the size of his vote, today's surprise came from Herr Hitler's running more than 2,000,000 ahead of his total on the first ballot-

ing, indicating that he had obtained the lion's share of the Nationalist and
Steel Helmet vote for Colonel Theodor Duesterberg in the initial test,
which totaled 2,500,000.

President von Hindenburg obtained a majority in twenty-two of the
thirty-five federal election districts today, while Herr Hitler succeeded in
obtaining a majority in only one—Pomerania, one of the Nazi strong-
holds—and gained a plurality in only a few other districts.

A conspicuous feature of the day's voting was the fact that Herr Hitler
gained consistently wherever Herr Thaelmann lost, tending to confirm
intimations from Communist quarters that the Reds' leaders would not
discourage their following from voting for Herr Hitler since their own
candidate had no prospect of bettering his first showing.

Herr Hitler's gain is therefore being attributed to a voluntary contribution from the Communists and liberal support from Dr. Alfred
Hugenberg's Nationalists and the Steel Helmet League.

Bruening Strengthened

President von Hindenburg's decisive victory not only stabilizes the
present Bruening Government but disposes of the possibility that the so-
called National Opposition, represented by the Nazis and Dr. Hugenberg's
Nationalists, will be able to brow-beat the government, both as far as its
domestic and foreign policies are concerned.

Dr. Bruening will now have a freer hand, especially as he is assured of
the continued support and powerful moral backing of President von Hindenburg.

The outcome of today's voting, by converting hope into certainty,
should greatly stiffen the forces of liberalism that have been the mainstay
in the fight for Herr von Hindenburg and on which Dr. Bruening must lean
in the prosecution of his foreign policies, as he stressed in his campaign
speeches.

It is especially with regard to the impending negotiations at Geneva and
Lausanne that today's re-election of President von Hindenburg by a decisive majority amounts to vindication of Dr. Bruening's stand on reparations and disarmament as well as his internal economic policies, and to this
extent it constitutes a mandate from the majority of the German people to
continue the present course.

Throughout the Reich election day passed with a tranquility exceeding
that on the day of the first balloting. Yesterday the election fever was at its
height, but no collision of consequence was reported anywhere today and
there was little in the way of public demonstrations and few cases of
violence and rows.

Elaborate police preparations proved unnecessary. In Berlin police afoot, mounted, on bicycles and in motor lorries kept patrolling the streets but had little to do except suppress sporadic attempts at forbidden electioneering and scatter gathering crowds in the workers' districts, notably the Buelowplatz, a Communist storm centre.

In the early hours it seemed that the vote would be considerably lighter than last time. By noon a little more than a quarter of the electors had voted, whereas on March 13, 40 to 50 percent of the vote was then already in.

In the afternoon, however, the voting picked up, and in contrast with the first election, when the polls were virtually deserted after 5 P.M., something like a rush developed in many places in the last hour before closing time at 6.

The Iron Front and the Nazis followed up last week's intensive campaigning by running a "drag service" to the polls all day to counteract the "what's-the-use" feeling, a feeling strengthened by the Spring weather.

Among the earliest voters in the capital was Dr. Bruening, who returned from Koenigsberg, where he wound up his campaign tour last night, and deposited his ballot at 9 A.M. As in the first balloting, President von Hindenburg did not vote, and spent the day at home. Herr Hitler, forbidden to hold his final meeting in Munich last night, stayed over in Stuttgart, where he had talked in the afternoon, and voted there, later flying to Munich, where he watched the returns at the Brown House, Nazi headquarters.

Hitler Falls Short of Claim

BERLIN, April 10 (AP). — Adolf Hitler fell short of reaching the 15,000,000 votes he had claimed in the run-off election for the German Presidency today.

The Nazi leader again carried Pomerania, however, receiving 511,000 votes to President von Hindenburg's 396,000 and Ernst Thaelmann's 64,000, and apparently obtained most of Colonel Theodor Duesterberg's following of last month. He also carried Chemnitz-Zwickau again with 557,000 votes, as against 445,000 for the President and 177,000 for Herr Thaelmann.

East Prussia, perhaps the most hotly-contested district of all, where both Chancellor Bruening, in behalf of President von Hindenburg, and Herr Hitler had made their supreme efforts, again endorsed Herr von Hindenburg, who obtained 546,000 votes to Herr Hitler's 493,000 and Herr Thaelmann's 85,000.

Herr Hitler, while gaining 90,000 over his East Prussian vote of March 13, nevertheless failed to draw to himself all the 133,879 Nationalist votes for Colonel Duesterberg in the first poll.

Hindenburg Carries Brunswick

Brunswick, Nazi "paradise," where the police are in the hands of Dietrich Klagges, National Socialist Minister of the Interior, gave President von Hindenburg a majority with 53,000 out of the 105,000 votes cast. Herr Hitler gained from both the Communists and Nationalists there, however, polling 44,700, or 42.5 percent of the vote, compared with 36.4 percent March 13. President von Hindenburg's vote was 47.7 percent four weeks ago.

Rainstorms and dismal weather over a greater part of the nation held down the vote.

A National Socialist was shot and killed in a clash between the Nazis and Communists in Hamburg and several persons were wounded there, with a few others injured elsewhere in minor clashes, but the alert police kept down the disturbances.   The police of Berlin kept extremists of the Right and Left running, arresting 200 last night and twenty more this morning. Most were released, however. Homes of National Socialists were searched throughout the day for weapons.

Communists in some of the central thoroughfares pasted over the nameplates of streets with signs, renaming them "Thaelmannstrasse," "Leninstrasse" and after other Communist leaders.

With the Presidential election out of the way, political interest centered upon the Diet elections in Prussia and other States April 24, which it is felt will give a true measure of the political strength of the Fascist movement. On that date elections will be held for the Diets of Prussia, Bavaria, Württemberg, Hamburg and Anhalt.

Hitler Grateful for "Victory."

MUNICH, Monday, April 11 (AP). — Adolf Hitler issued a call today for his adherents to gird for the Prussian Diet elections April 24 in an effort to march a step further toward the goal he calls "German liberation." He expressed pleasure with the number of votes given him in yesterday's runoff Presidential election.

Before retiring early this morning he sent to leaders and party workers the following message:

"Victory obliges me to thank all who worked to create the basis of the victory. The confidence of 13,500,000 Germans is the highest reward of our work, but it carries a heavy obligation to continue.

"The National Socialists know not what rest is and must not tarry until the goal of German liberation has been reached. Our work begins tomorrow."

15. Von Hindenburg and Hitler Fail to Come to Terms, August 13, 1932

"We are ready and willing to take over full responsibility."

So strong was Hitler's showing at the polls that President Paul von Hindenburg decided to receive him at the president's palace to discuss the possibility of Nazi participation in the new government. The chilly interview lasted only fifteen minutes. Offered a post in the cabinet, Hitler curtly turned it down. Instead, he demanded the chancellorship. Von Hindenburg coldly refused. The old man admonished his arrogant visitor to conduct himself properly.

Following is a report of the interview as published in the *Völkischer Beobachter,* later to become the official Nazi newspaper.

ON SATURDAY [August 13], the *Fuehrer* was received by Reich Chancellor von Papen, who invited him to be interviewed by Reich President von Hindenburg. To the question as to whether he and the Party were ready to enter the von Papen cabinet, the *Fuehrer* declared: "We are ready and willing to take over full responsibility for German political policies in every form, provided that that means unequivocal leadership of the government. If that is not the case, then the National Socialist Movement can accept neither power nor responsibility. Specifically, it declines entrance into a cabinet headed by von Papen."

Since the Reich President, however, declined to entrust the National Socialist movement even though it is the strongest party in the country,

---

Völkischer Beobachter, August 14, 1932. Translated by the editor.

with control of the government, the negotiations were broken off as fruit-less.

Appropriate measures for the continuation of the struggle of the National Socialist movement will take place in conferences led by the *Fuehrer* in the next several weeks.

The *Fuehrer* left Berlin on Saturday.

16. A Confident Hitler Turns Down von Hindenburg's Offer of a Conference, November 24–30, 1932

". . . I therefore beg the esteemed Reich President most respectfully to be kind enough not to press his invitation at this moment."

By late November 1932, Hitler was convinced that nothing on earth could halt his march to the chancellorship. By now Reich President Paul von Hindenburg on several occasions had made it a point to invite Hitler to come to see him "on political matters," undoubtedly to discuss the possibility of a coalition government. Hitler was not inclined to dilute his power by subjugating himself to the whims of *Junker* politicians interested in their own survival. The invitations were extended through Dr. Otto Meissner, the state secretary. Following are two replies sent to President von Hindenburg through his state secretary. Before sending the second letter, Hitler carefully edited out several highly offensive passages.

as from Berlin, 24 November, 1932

Dear Herr Staatssekretär,
   In acknowledging your letter rejecting my proposals for the solution of the present crisis, allow me to make the following final comments.
   1) I did not describe the attempt to form a parliamentary majority government as hopeless but called it impossible in view of the conditions attached.

National Archives, Washington, D.C.

2) I have pointed out that if conditions are to be laid down these must be based on the Constitution.

3) I have not asked for leadership of a presidential cabinet, but have merely submitted a proposal for the solution of the German government crisis.

4) Unlike others, I have constantly stressed the need for collaboration with the people's representatives based on the Constitution and have given express assurances that I would only serve under such legal conditions.

5) Not only have I not asked for a party dictatorship but I was prepared, just as I was in August of this year, to open negotiations with all other suitable parties in order to form a government. These negotiations were doomed to failure so long as there was a firm intention to preserve the von Papen Cabinet as a presidential cabinet at all costs. There is thus no need to convince me of the need for collaboration with other constructive, national forces because, despite the grossest vilifications during the summer, I have done everything in my power to achieve just that. However, I simply refuse to look upon the presidential cabinet as a constructive force. Moreover, all my judgments of the activities and failures of this cabinet have thus far been proved right.

6) This knowledge has caused me to warn against an experiment that is bound to lead to the use of naked force and hence to end in failure.

7) Above all, I was not, and shall never be, prepared to place the Movement I have built up at the service of interests other than those of the German people. In all this I feel responsible to my own conscience, to the honour of the Movement I lead and to the lives of millions of Germans whom recent political experiments have thrown into ever-deeper misery.

For the rest, I beg you now as before to convey to His Excellency the Herr Reichs President the expression of my deepest respect.

Yours very truly,
Adolf Hitler

as from Weimar, 30 November, 1932

Dear Herr Staatssekretär,

Herr Göring, President of the Reichstag, has just handed me your summons to present myself once again to the Herr Reichs President for a discussion of the political situation and the appropriate measures. Since I have explained my view on these matters in great detail both by word of mouth and in writing first to the Reichs President and also the public, and since, moreover, I stayed on one whole week in Berlin for any further explanations, I cannot, with the best will in the world, think of anything that I could usefully add to my previous arguments, the less so as there has been no essential change in the political situation.

Moreover, I have respectfully submitted to the Herr Reichs President what positive suggestions I sincerely believe can alone produce a lasting solution of the crisis. You, Herr Staatssekretär, now inform me that these suggestions are not to be the basis of our discussion. In that case, I do not think that I can defend my entering in further discussions that are bound to awake false hopes and hence cause grave disappointments. Since, furthermore, I am engaged in an election battle in Thuringia, I find it most difficult to take time off for a purely informative talk, and I therefore beg the esteemed Herr Reichs President most respectfully to be kind enough not to press his invitation to me at this moment.

May I furthermore ask you, Herr Staatssekretär, once again to convey to the Herr Reichs President the expression of my deepest esteem.

Yours very truly,

Adolf Hitler

17. Resignation of the von Schleicher Cabinet, January 28, 1933

". . . lost the confidence of the Reich President. . . ."

Toward the end of January 1933, Chancellor Kurt von Schleicher, desperately holding on to political power in the face of Hitler's increasing popularity, asked President Paul von Hindenburg to dissolve the *Reichstag*, which was due to reconvene on January 31, 1933. Von Schleicher preferred, as a solution, a military dictatorship. To his dismay, however, the old president refused to grant him the requested authority. Von Schleicher then resigned on January 28, 1933.

Berlin 28 January [Telegram]
Reich Chancellor von Schleicher today informed the Reich President about the situation. He declared that the present Reich government would be unable to defend itself *vis-a-vis* the *Reichstag* if it did not obtain in advance the power to dissolve parliament. Reich President von Hindenburg stated that he could not grant this proposal because of current conditions. Reich Chancellor von Schleicher then announced the resignation of the government since it had lost the confidence of the Reich President and therefore could not continue in office. The Reich President thanked the Reich Chancellor and his colleagues in the cabinet for their services in difficult times.

Reich President von Hindenburg summoned former Reich Chancellor von Papen and requested him to clarify the political situation and to suggest possible procedures.

Kölnische Zeitung, January 28, 1933. Translated by the editor.

18. Von Hindenburg Names Hitler to the Office of Reich Chancellor, January 30, 1933

"At noon today the Reich President received the Fuehrer. . . ."

At noon on January 30, 1933, President Paul von Hindenburg received Hitler and Franz von Papen in his office. Von Papen informed the president that Hitler had succeeded in forming a government of national concentration. The oath of office was then administered to the Nazi leader. Hitler promised to uphold the constitution and rule by legal means. That night, von Hindenburg and Hitler, at a window of the Reich Chancellery, reviewed a great torchlight procession of Hitler's followers.

AT NOON TODAY the Reich President received the *Fuehrer* of the National Socialist Party, Hitler, as well as former Reich Chancellor von Papen in an extended interview. The Reich President named Herr Hitler to the office of Reich Chancellor. At Hitler's nomination the following cabinet was named:

Former Reich Chancellor von Papen, Reich Vice Chancellor and Reich Commissioner for Prussia

Baron von Neurath, Reich Minister for Foreign Affairs

State Minister Dr. Frick, Reich Minister of the Interior

General Lieutenant von Blomberg, Reich Minister of War

Count Schwerin von Krosigk, Reich Minister of Finance

Privy Finance Councillor Hugenberg, Reich Minister of Economics and Agriculture

---

Kölnische Zeitung, January 30, 1933, evening edition. Translated by the editor.

Franz Seldte, Reich Minister of Labor

Baron von Eltz-Rubenbach, Reich Postal and Communications Minister,

and

Reichstag President Goering, Reich Minister without Portfolio and at the same time Reich Commissioner for the *Luftwaffe*. Reich Minister Goering was entrusted with the task of supervising the business of the Prussian Ministry of the Interior.

Reich Commissioner for Employment Opportunities Gereke was retained in his post.

Nominations for the Reich Ministry of Justice are postponed for the moment. The Reich Chancellor will begin discussions today with the Center Party and the Bavarian People's Party. The first cabinet session will take place today at 5:00 P.M.

Part Three:

Coordination: *Ein Volk, Ein Reich, Ein Fuehrer*

19. Chancellor Hitler Issues a Proclamation to the German People, February 1, 1933

"May Almighty God bless us in our work. . . ."

At long last, after a fanatical struggle lasting more than a decade, Hitler was on his way to top power in Germany. In the battle of the streets, his Storm Troopers had defeated the cadres of communist fighters who stood in his way. In a shrewdly devised campaign he had won mass support by opposing all the elements the German people feared in their national life. He took good advantage of a combination of negative feelings: his party was anti-Semitic, anti-Marxist, anti-bolshevik, anti-Catholic, antiliberal, antidemocratic, anti-Masonic, and, most of all, anti-Treaty of Versailles. The German public was impressed by the obvious sincerity of this man.

Within twenty-four hours after becoming chancellor, Hitler issued a glowing proclamation to the German people. It was a euphorious compendium of political arguments, a summary of all the tried formulas he had used in the years of struggle for political power. Again and again he called upon the German people to support him in his task of reconstruction and help raise Germany like a phoenix out of the ruins caused by fourteen years of the ineffectual Weimar Republic. Hitler invoked the assistance of Almighty God, a call which became progressively weaker as the dictatorship was consolidated.

OVER FOURTEEN YEARS have passed since that unholy day when, deluded by

---

Völkischer Beobachter, February 2, 1933. Translated by the editor.

domestic and foreign promises, the German people forgot and thereby lost the highest values of its past, of the Reich.

Since that day of treason the Almighty has withheld His blessing from our people.

Discord and hatred made their entrance. In deep distress millions of the best German men and women from all stations of life saw the unity of the nation break apart and dissolve in a chaos of political and personal opinions, economic interests, and ideological differences.

As so often in our history, we have faced since that day of revolution a picture of heartbreaking disunity. We never received the promised equality and fraternity, and we also lost our liberty. For the dissolution of the spiritual and moderately intended unity of our people in domestic affairs, there followed the dissolution of our political position in the world.

Hotly convinced that the German people went to war in 1914 without any feeling that they were guilty of starting the war, and filled with the desire to defend the freedom of the Reich and the very existence of the German people, we can see in the disastrous fate which has burdened us since November 1918 the result of our own domestic disunity. Since that time the rest of the world, too, has been no less shaken by overwhelming crises.

The historical balance of power, which at one time contributed to the understanding for the internal unity of a nation, with all the resultant advantages for trade and commerce, has been shattered. The insane idea of winner and loser destroyed the trust between nations and with it the industry of the whole world.

The misery of our people has been terrible to behold. The unemployed millions of industrial proletariat are starving. The entire middle class and the small artisans have been impoverished. When this situation reaches the farmers, then we shall see a catastrophe of incalculable consequences.

The Reich will not only fall apart but with it our two-thousand-year inheritance of the loftiest values of human culture and civilization.

There have been threatening signs of this collapse. With extraordinary will power the Communists have used their insane methods to poison a shattered and uprooted people. . . .

Fourteen years of Marxism have just about ruined Germany. One year of Bolshevism will destroy us. What is today the most beautiful and richest cultural area of the world would be smashed into chaos and ruin. Even the troubles of the last decade and a half could not be compared with the misery of a Europe in whose heart the red banner of destruction has been raised.

The thousands of wounded, the uncounted dead, which this domestic war has already cost Germany, should be the warning before the storm.

In these hours of overpowering troubles of the German nation, we men of the national party once again call on our venerable leader of the World War, just as we did at one time at the front, to fight with us again on the domestic front in unity and loyalty for the salvation of the Reich. Because the honorable Herr Reich President in this great-hearted sense has extended his hand to us and beseeched us to work together, we as national socialists make this solemn vow, before our conscience and before the German people, to fulfill the mission of a National Government with steadfast and firm persistence.

The heritage we have assumed is of the utmost gravity.

The task which we must solve is the most difficult one that has ever faced German statesmen. Faith in us, however, is unlimited, for we believe in our people and in their imperishable honor. Peasants, workers, and townsmen, all must work together to lay the foundation stones of our new Reich.

The national government sees as its first and foremost task to reestablish the spiritual unity of our people. It will preserve and protect the fundamentals on which our nation rests. It regards Christianity as the basis of our system of morality, the family as the germ cell of the body of the people and the state. It will look beyond ranks and classes in order to bring our people to the consciousness of a national and political unity and the duties which go along with it. To educate German youth it will use as a basis the glory of our great past and pride in our old traditions. In that way it will counter the spiritual, political, and cultural annihilation of a cruel war. Germany should not and will not sink into anarchism and communism.

That government will install a national discipline to replace turbulent instinct as the guiding principle of our lives. Thinking carefully in terms of such adjustments, it will thereby guarantee the energy and vitality of our nation.

The national government will see to the reorganization of the economy of our people through two great Four Year Plans: rescue of the German peasantry as a means of assuring the nourishment and thereby the life of the nation; and salvation of the German worker through a powerful and wide-ranging attack against unemployment.

In fourteen years the November parties* have ruined the German agricultural class. In fourteen years they created an army of millions of unemployed.

The national government will, with iron will and tenacious perseverance, accomplish the following plan: Within four years the German farmer must be relieved of his misery. Within four years unemployment

---

*Hitler here refers to the politicians who formed the Weimar Republic in 1919.

will be conquered. At the same time this hypothesis holds for the rest of industry.

The national government will combine the gigantic task of cleansing our economy with the task of accomplishing the cleansing of the Reich, the states, and the local communes in administrative and fiscal matters.

In that way only will the idea of a federated existence of the Reich be implemented.

To the foundation stones of this program belong the ideas of workers' responsibility and the politics of land settlement.

Care to guarantee daily bread will be combined with care for illness and old age.

In the economy of the administration, in the extension of work, in the attitude of the farmer, as well as in the use of initiative by the individual, lie the best guarantees for avoiding those experiments which would endanger our standards.

In its foreign policy, the national government regards it as its highest mission to preserve the right to life and with it the re-establishment of freedom for our people. Because it is dedicated to the task of bringing an end to the chaotic conditions inside Germany, it will work along in common with other nations in the task of fashioning a state of equal value and along with it of equal rights. For that purpose it bears the great responsibility of representing this free and equal people in the goal of winning and maintaining the peace, which all the world needs even more than in the past. Let us hope that all others will cooperate and understand the nature of this deep-felt wish for the benefit of Europe, indeed of all the world.

As great as is our love for our army as bearer of our weapons and as symbol of our great past, we would be happy if the world through its limitation of armaments would make it no longer necessary for us to increase our own weapons.

As Germany experiences this political and economic awakening and scrupulously fulfills its obligations to other nations, one overriding fact emerges: the overcoming of the communist disintegration of Germany.

We men of this government feel ourselves responsible before German history for the reconstruction of an ordered folk community and with it for the definite elimination of that crazy class warfare. We do not represent one class, but all the German people, the millions of farmers, city folk, and workers, who will either together overcome the troubles of these times or succumb to them.

We are determined, true to our oath, and despite the incompetence of the present *Reichstag*, to accomplish this goal, and to place its implementation where it belongs, on the German people, whom we represent.

Reich President General Field Marshal von Hindenburg has called on us to use our courage to bring about the reconstruction of the nation.

We appeal, therefore, once more to the German people to give its support to this act of conciliation.

The government of the national uprising will work, and you will work. It was not responsible for the fourteen years during which the nation fell apart, but it will lead the nation upward. It is determined to make good within four years all the damage done in fourteen.

All alone it just cannot effect the reconstruction necessitated by the collapse.

The parties of Marxism and their collaborators have had fourteen years to show what they can do. The result has been desolation. Now, German people, give us four years and then judge and try us!

True to the command of the General Field Marshal shall we begin: May Almighty God bless us in our work, maintain our will, bless our judgment, and favor us with the trust of our people. For we desire not to struggle for ourselves alone, but for Germany!

20. The *Fuehrer* Speaks to the NSDAP, the Nazi Party, February 1, 1933

"Give me your trust and your support. . . ."

The night of January 30, 1933, was a great moment for the man who had been a miserable tramp on the streets of Vienna. Far into the night, exuberant Nazis with flaming torches marched by the window of the Chancellery to cheer Germany's new leader. Hitler had kept his promise – there had been no *Putsch,* no revolution. All was constitutional and legal!

Hitler was especially proud of the performance of the political party he had built up. The next day he delivered a call (*Aufruf*) to the members of the party that had propelled him to power.

NATIONAL SOCIALISTS! National Socialists! My party comrades, men and women!

Fourteen years of what in German history has been an unparalleled political arena has now led to a great political success.

Reich President von Hindenburg has named me, the *Fuehrer* of the National Socialist movement, Chancellor of the German Reich.

National organizations and parties now join together in a common struggle for Germany's resurrection.

For the honor before German history of taking a leading role in this task I am indebted in addition to the great-hearted decision of the General Field Marshal to your loyalty and support, my party comrades.

For this success we can be thankful to those of you who have followed

---

Völkischer Beobachter, February 1, 1933. Translated by the editor.

me with unbreakable loyalty in the darkest days as well as in days of happiness and have remained true to me even during severe setbacks.

The tasks that lie before us are staggering. We must solve them, and we shall solve them.

To you, my party comrades, I address only one request: Give me your trust and your support in this new huge and great arena exactly as you have done in the past — then also will the Almighty not deny us His blessing for the reconstruction of a German Reich noted for its honor, freedom, and social peace.

21. The New German Chancellor Makes a Radio Appeal for Support, February 4, 1933

"May the good-will of others aid us. . . ."

Several days after being named chancellor, Hitler made a radio address in which he appealed for support of the German people. In the following excerpt from his speech, Hitler promised that within four years unemployment would be definitely overcome. In foreign policy he repeated his demand for German rights and for "the restoration of the liberty of our people."

THE NATIONAL GOVERNMENT, with firm will and tenacious perseverance, will realize the following plan: Within four years the German farmer must be relieved from impoverishment; within four years unemployment must be definitely overcome. Concurrently, conditions will be established for prosperity in the other branches of industry.

As regards foreign policy, the national government sees its highest mission in maintenance of the vital rights and therewith restoration of the liberty of our people. While it is determined to put an end to the chaotic conditions in Germany, it will help to add a state of equal worth and, of course, equal rights to the community of nations. It is thereby filled with a sense of the greatness of its duty to stand up with this free and equal people for the preservation and strengthening of peace, which the world needs today more than ever before.

May the good-will of others aid us, in order that our most sincere wish for the welfare of Europe, and, indeed, the world, be brought to fulfillment.

The New York Times, February 5, 1933.

22. Hermann Goering Orders the Prussian Police to Combat All "Subversive Organizations," February 17, 1933

". . . weapons must be used relentlessly when necessary."

As soon as he held the reins of power, Hitler made it plain that he intended to have nothing to do with democratic institutions and thinking. His ideology always took into account the necessity for a strong hand at the helm of state, a euphemism for dictatorship. He was convinced that it was his mission to lead the Aryan-Nordic-Teutonic "superrace," a culture-bearing people, to its proper role in the leadership of world society.

From the beginning of his regime, Hitler turned to *Gleichschaltung,* or coordination. There was to be no political opposition to the National Socialist German Workers' party. Every phase of national life – from schools to labor to army – was to be coordinated as a limb of Nazi ideology. The Third Reich would be a monolithic structure governed from above – with no nonsense about liberty, equality, and fraternity.

Only several weeks elapsed before Hitler inaugurated his plan to rid the country of all political dissent. He named his number-two Nazi, Hermann Goering, air hero of World War I and close colleague since the Munich beer-hall *Putsch,* to take the initiative in Prussia and thereby set an example for the rest of the country. Goering did as he was told. He dismissed all police chiefs in Prussia who belonged to the Social Democratic, Center, or any other party. On February 17, 1933, he sent the following order to all police chiefs in Prussia. It was a harbinger of orders to come.

Times (London), February 21, 1933.

I ASSUME THAT IT IS unnecessary to point out especially that the police must in all circumstances avoid giving even the appearance of a hostile attitude, still less the impression of persecuting the patriotic associations [the Nazi Storm Detachments and the Stahlhelm]. I expect all police authorities to maintain the best relations with these organizations which comprise the most important constructive forces of the State. Patriotic activities and propaganda are to be supported by every means. Police restrictions and impositions must be used only in the most urgent cases.

The activities of subversive organizations are on the contrary to be combated with the most drastic methods. Communist terrorist acts and attacks are to be proceeded against with all severity, and weapons must be used ruthlessly when necessary. Police officers who in the execution of this duty use their firearms will be supported by me without regard to the effect of their shots; on the other hand, officers who fail from a false sense of consideration may expect disciplinary measures.

The protection of the patriotic population, which has been continually hampered in its activities, demands the most drastic application of the legal regulations against banned demonstrations, illegal assemblies, looting, instigation to treason and sedition, mass strikes, risings, press offences, and the other punishable acts of the disturbers of order. Every official must constantly bear in mind that failure to act is more serious than errors committed in acting. I expect and hope that all officers feel themselves at one with me in the aim of saving our fatherland from the ruin which threatens it by strengthening and unifying the patriotic forces.

23. The *Reichstag* Fire – I: The *Manchester Guardian* Suspects That an Act of Arson Was Committed by the Nazis

"Before the tribunal of history, it is not the Communists, not the wretched van der Lubbe . . . but the German Government that is arraigned."

Hitler had been in power nearly a month when it happened. He needed a big propaganda victory, for the next month there would be elections and attention had to be paid to democratic ways for the time being. The propaganda coup came with the burning of the *Reichstag* on the night of February 27, 1933, a major event in the history of the Third Reich.

The blaze served Hitler well. It achieved exactly what he had hoped for – the end of the Weimar Republic. It not only made a hollow shell of the imposing *Reichstag* building, it also gave Hitler what he believed to be a legitimate reason to crush his opponents. The day after the fire he proclaimed a "national emergency." He suspended such civil rights as freedom of speech, of the press, and of assembly. Along with a million marks worth of glass and masonry, the pacifists, liberals, democrats, and socialists were ruined by the catastrophe.

Most Germans were convinced by Nazi propaganda that the *Reichstag* fire was to be the signal for a communist revolt. That conviction played an important role in the elections that came on March 5, 1933. The NSDAP increased its number of deputies in the *Reichstag* from 196 to 288, its popular vote from 11,737,000 to 17,277,200. This was 44 percent of the total vote. This together with

---

Manchester Guardian, April 26, 27, 1933.

the Nationalist party vote gave Hitler control of 52 percent of all votes.

That was the power Hitler wanted. The first act of the new *Reichstag* was to bury itself and the constitution. By the Enabling Act (q.v.) they turned legislative power over to Hitler.

Soon after the *Reichstag* fire emerged reports that the burning had been committed not by the Communists but by the Nazis themselves. Among the first to make this accusation was the *Manchester Guardian,* which in its issues of April 26 and 27, 1933, published a two-part feature presenting the case against the Nazis. Much of this report was based on the Oberfohren Memorandum (see document 24).

26 April 1933

THE REICHSTAG FIRE
I. Who was Guilty?
THE CASE AGAINST THE NAZIS
Germany, April.

WHEN Hitler became Chancellor — with von Papen as Vice-Chancellor — at the end of January, the Nazis and their partners in office, the Nationalists, had antagonistic ambitions. The Nazis, above all Captain Goering and Dr. Goebbels, wanted absolute and undivided power. Von Papen, as well as the Nationalist leader, Dr. Hugenberg, and the President, von Hindenburg, wanted the Nazis, with their enormous following, to provide a 'National' Government with the popular support which was denied to the Nationalists themselves. The Nazis, in other words, were to share power with the Nationalists while being denied that preponderance which, by virtue of being by far the biggest party in the Reich, they considered their due.

The Nationalists, though a very small party, had certain sources of strength. They represent all that is left of Imperial Germany; they, and not the Nazis, incarnate old Prussian traditions. They were supported by a large part of the higher bureaucracy, by the higher ranks of the Reichswehr, by the Stahlhelm, a powerful conservative league of ex-servicemen, and by President von Hindenburg, whose personal authority was still considerable. Nor were they, in case of need, disinclined to negotiate for the support of the trade unions and even of the Reichsbanner, a strong militant force (made up chiefly of workmen) whose leaders had developed certain militarist and nationalist tendencies.

The Nazis were showing signs of disintegration. The Brown Shirts were growing mutinous in different parts of the Reich; several units had to be disbanded, and in the electorate there were symptoms of waning enthusiasm. Another election might (if sufficient time were allowed to lapse) mean a heavy loss of votes. And would not a movement that had arisen so rapidly and so high suffer a correspondingly precipitous decline?

NAZIS AND NATIONALISTS

Thus the Nazis were under a strong compulsion to take a share of power, lest the time might come when even a share would be denied to them. Hitler had become Chancellor of the 'Government of National Concentration' only on condition that there would be no changes in the Cabinet without the sanction of President Hindenburg. Thus the Nazis, although in a position of great influence, achieved nothing comparable with that complete transformation of the whole economic and social order to which they and the millions of their enthusiastic followers had aspired. Had they respected the terms imposed on Hitler, the disappearance of those millions would only have been a matter of time. They were indeed in a trap.

The Nationalists had no particular faith in Hitler's word, which had been broken more than once before. But they were vigilant, and on the slightest sign of bad faith they were ready, with the sanction of the President and the army, to proclaim a military dictatorship (in which case they could have counted on the support not only of the Stahlhelm but also of the police, amongst whom Socialist influences were still strong). How were the Nazis to get out of the trap? If there were a general election without loss of time they might still increase their vote, for Hitler's Chancellorship had the appearance of almost absolute power without the substance, and new hope had revived the ardour of his followers, though, with the inevitable emergence of the reality, it was bound to cool in a very short time. He therefore demanded a general election at the earliest possible date. His promise to the President was, it is true, binding, irrespective of the result of that election. At the same time, an increase of his already heavy vote could only be welcome. Indeed, if he obtained an absolute majority, could his promise be considered binding against the manifest 'will of the people'? Or would not Hindenburg give way before that 'will'?

But the chances that he would get such a majority were small, and as the election campaign developed it seemed probable that revived enthusiasm was ebbing once again and that the elections would show a loss in the Hitlerite vote. This would have bound Hitler to his promise and the Nazis permanently to the Nationalists. It was clear to their more adventurous and ambitious leaders, Captain Goering and Dr. Goebbels, that 'something' must be done to keep Nazi enthusiasm at its height, indeed to drive it still higher, and to precipitate a new situation in which Hitler could either be freed from his promise or that promise would lose its meaning. The election campaign promised to be violent, there was a tense atmosphere, extravagant rumours were abroad. The moment was favourable to men of imaginative daring and unscrupulous ambition.

NOT A SURPRISE

Everyone — including the correspondents of British, French, and American newspapers in Berlin — expected 'something' — a staged Communist uprising, a fictitious attempt to murder Hitler, or a fire. The Reichswehr warned the Communists, through an intermediary, that they must not allow themselves to be provoked into any rash action. On no account must they provide an excuse for raising an anti-Bolshevik scare.

When on 27 February the Reichstag burst into flames no serious observer of German affairs was at all surprised. Nevertheless, there was widespread horror and panic. Many understood the signal well and fled the country forthwith, fearing to wait until they should be arrested or until the frontiers should be closed. There were workmen who, with shrewd foresight, at once buried their 'Marxist' literature. It was the Reichstag fire, not the Chancellorship of Hitler nor his electoral victory on 5 March, that began the Brown Terror.

The fire was instantaneously attributed to the Communists by the Government, which at once began to manufacture false evidence, thereby not inculpating but rather exculpating the Communists and deepening the suspicion felt by all objective observers that the real incendiaries were to be found within the Cabinet itself. Before the tribunal of history it is not the Communists, not the wretched van der Lubbe, (their alleged instrument, whose public execution Hitler has threatened before his guilt has been proved, before he has even been tried), but the German Government that is arraigned.

A confidential memorandum on the events leading up to the fire is circulating in Germany. It is in manuscript, and the Terror makes any open mention or discussion of it impossible. But it is a serious attempt by one in touch with the Nationalist members of the Cabinet to give a balanced account of these events. In spite of one or two minor inaccuracies it shows considerable inside knowledge. While not authoritative in an absolute and final manner, it is at least a first and a weighty contribution towards solving the riddle of that fire. The memorandum contains certain allegations of high interest that will be discussed in the next article.

27 April 1933

THE REICHSTAG FIRE
II. Nazis Guilty?
A NATIONALIST VERSION
Storm Troopers Accused

Germany, April.

THE 'Karl Liebknecht Haus', the headquarters of the Communist Party, and editorial office of the 'Rote Fahne', had been searched again and again by the police, but no incriminating matter had been found. The Nationalists were opposed to the suppression of the Communists, for without the Communist members the Nazis would have had an absolute majority in the Reichstag. This the Nationalists wished to avoid at any cost.

But the chief of the Berlin Police, Melcher, a Nationalist, resigned under Nazi pressure. He was replaced by Admiral von Levetzow, a Nazi. On 24 February the Karl Liebknecht Haus was again searched. On the 26th the 'Conti', a Government news agency, issued a report on the sinister and momentous finds that were supposed to have been made 'in subterranean vaults' and 'catacombs' that had long been cleared of everything by the forewarned Communists. The report also hinted darkly at plans for a Bolshevik revolution. The confidential Nationalist memorandum mentioned in the first article describes the annoyance of the Nationalist members of the Cabinet over the clumsiness and transparent untruthfulness of this report. They refused to allow the suppression of the Communist Party.

On 25 February a fire started in the old Imperial Palace. It was quickly extinguished. The incendiary escaped, leaving a box of matches and some inflammable matter behind. From various parts of the country came news — all of it untrue — of arson and outrage perpetrated by Communists. On the 27th, according to the memorandum, the chief Nazi agitators, Hitler, Goering, and Goebbels, all three of whom are members of the present German Government, were, 'strangely enough', not touring the country to address election meetings, although the campaign was at its height, but were assembled in Berlin 'waiting for their fire'.

THE ACCUSATION

The Reichstag is connected with the Speaker's residence by a subterranean passage. Through this passage, according to the memorandum, 'the emissaries of Herr Goering (the Speaker) entered the Reichstag'. Each of these emissaries — they wore civilian clothes — 'went to his assigned place, and in a few minutes sufficient inflammable matter was distributed throughout the building' (after the fire had been quenched several heaps of rags and shavings soaked in petrol were found unburnt or half-burnt).

The Storm Troopers then, so the memorandum continues, withdrew through the passage to the Speaker's residence, put on their brown uniforms, and made off. They left behind them in the Reichstag building Van der Lubbe, who, so as to make sure that the Communists could be incriminated, had taken the precaution to have on his person his Dutch passport, a Communist leaflet, several photographs of himself, and what seems to have been the membership card of some Dutch Communist group.

THE OFFICIAL STORY

On the following day, the 28th, the fire was announced by the official 'Preussische Pressedienst' as intended to begin the Bolshevik revolution in Germany, the plans for this revolution having been discovered amongst 'the hundreds of hundredweights of seditious matter' found in the 'vaults and catacombs' of the Karl Liebknecht Haus. According to these plans 'Government buildings, museums, palaces, and essential plants were to be fired', disorders were to be provoked, terrorist groups were to advance behind screens of women and children, if possible the women and children of police officers', there were to be terrorist attacks on private property, and a 'general civil war' was to commence.

It is peculiar that no preparations for this civil war had been made by the German Government – there had been time enough, for the alleged plans had been discovered on the 24th. Whenever there has been the slightest reason to suspect violent action against the State, carbines are served out to the police, Government buildings are specially guarded, and the Wilhelmstrasse is patrolled night and day. No precautions of this kind were taken against the 'general civil war', not even after the fire in the Imperial Palace.

The 'Angriff', of which Dr. Goebbels is editor, announced that the documents found in the Karl Liebknecht Haus would be 'placed before the public with all speed'. Eight weeks have passed and this has not been done.

FALSE REPORTS

The full political effects of the Reichstag fire could not be achieved merely by the presence of a Communist (with leaflet and membership card) in the Reichstag building. The Nazis have all along been bent on the destruction of 'Marxism' as a whole – that is to say, of Social Democracy as well as Communism. The communiqué of the 'Preussische Pressedienst' therefore added that 'the Reichstag incendiary has in his confession admitted that he is connected with the Socialist Party. Through this confession the united Communist-Socialist front has become a palpable fact.' Since then the Nazi press has repeatedly published false reports that arms and ammunition have been found hidden in rooms owned by the Socialist trade unions.

So as to incriminate the Communists still further, it was announced (in the *Deutsche Allgemeine Zeitung*) that their leaders Torgler and Koenen had spent several hours in the Reichstag on the evening of the 27th, and had been seen not only with van der Lubbe but also with several other persons who were carrying torches, these persons having eluded arrest by escaping through the passage to the Speaker's residence. Why did no one telephone to the Speaker's residence to have them arrested there? The question remains unanswered.

Two persons happened to get into the Reichstag almost immediately after the fire broke out. One of them rang up the 'Vorwärts' with the news. He was promptly cut off at the exchange, and was, together with his companion, arrested. Neither has been heard of since – the memorandum describes the one as a member of the staff (*Redakteur*) of the 'Vorwärts', but this is an error. The arrest of Stampfer, the editor, was at once ordered, and the editorial office was occupied by police within an hour (Stampfer eluded arrest by flight). The entire Socialist press throughout Prussia was suppressed on the night of the fire. The first edition of the 'Vorwärts' was already out, but all copies were confiscated by the police. On the morning of the 28th, Torgler gave himself up to the police of his own free will, accompanied by his solicitor, Dr. Rosenfeld, and prepared to face and answer any charges that might be brought against him. This was most inconvenient — 'his flight', according to the memorandum, 'would have been much more desirable'.

A SCARE CREATED

But the fire made a deep impression on the electorate. The elimination of the Socialist press in Prussia and the rigorous censorship on all other papers allowed hardly a suspicion to get into print. The Nationalists could not speak up, for even if they did not want the Nazis to have the mastery they could not afford to see them collapse — and the truth about the fire if publicly known, would have meant the collapse of the Nazi movement. The scaremongering story of the impending Bolshevik revolution was supplemented by others — an alleged plot to assassinate Hitler, the alleged discovery of Communist arsenals and munition dumps, and so on. Such stories are still being invented and appear in the Nazi papers almost every day.

A Bolshevik scare was created, especially in the country districts (stories of burning villages were calculated to impress the imagination of the peasantry). Hitler seemed the one saviour from anarchy and red revolution. That scare not only gave the Nazis and Nationalists a joint majority, it also unleashed that inhuman persecution of Communists, Socialists, Liberals, pacifists, and Jews which is still going on. It made the complete suppression of the Communist Party possible, thus eliminating its members from the Reichstag and giving the Nazis the absolute and overwhelming majority which the elections alone had not given them.

Despite the clumsiness with which it was staged, and despite the grossness of the falsehoods with which facts and motives were concealed, the fire turned out to be a big success. The legend that it was the work of Communists and Social Democrats is the main foundation of the Hitlerite Dictatorship and of the Brown Terror.

24. The *Reichstag* Fire — II: The Oberfohren Memorandum Presents the Communist Case Against the Nazis

> *"The incendiaries, Goebbels and Goering, had thought out everything very cleverly."*

In the bitter struggle between Nazis and Communists before and after Hitler's accession to power, both sides used every means possible, including forgeries, to denigrate the other. Each accused the other of responsibility for the *Reichstag* fire. Nazis claimed that Marinus van der Lubbe, a half-crazed Dutch Communist, set the fire by himself, while the Communists attributed the deed to Nazis.

In the April 27, 1933, issue of the *Manchester Guardian* there appeared what has since become known as the Oberfohren Memorandum. It was supposedly written by Dr. Ernst Oberfohren, parliamentary leader of the German Nationalist People's party, to tell the inside story of the fire. Soon afterward, on May 7, Oberfohren was reported to have committed suicide.

The memorandum alleged that Dr. Paul Joseph Goebbels, minister for public enlightenment and propaganda, conceived the idea of setting the fire and that Captain Hermann Goering, acting Prussian minister of the interior, from whose office an underground passage led directly to the *Reichstag*, supervised the arson.

Scholars have since come to the conclusion that the Oberfohren Memorandum was a clever forgery. It was used in *The Brown Book of the Hitler Terror and the Burning of the Reichstag* (Victor Gollancz, Ltd., London, 1933) to show Nazi guilt in the arson. It is presented here as a summary of the communist case against the Nazis.

Manchester Guardian, April 27, 1933.

ALL WAS PREPARED. On Monday, 27 February, for some extraordinary reason, not one of the National-Socialist Propaganda General Staff was engaged in the election campaign. Herr Hitler, the indefatigable orator, Herr Goebbels, Herr Goering, all happened to be in Berlin. With them was the *Daily Express* correspondent, Sefton Delmer. So, in a cozy family party, these gentlemen waited for their fire.

Meanwhile the agents of Herr Goering, led by the Silesian SA leader, Reichstag deputy Heines, entered the Reichstag through the heating-pipe passage leading from the palace of the President of the Reichstag, Goering. Every SA and SS leader was carefully selected and had a special station assigned to him. As soon as the outposts in the Reichstag signalled that the Communist deputies Torgler and Koenen had left the building, the SA troop set to work. There was plenty of incendiary material, and in a few minutes it was prepared. All the men withdrew into the President's Palace, where they resumed their SA uniforms and whence they could disappear unhampered. The only one to be left behind was their creature, van der Lubbe, whom they had thoughtfully provided with a Communist leaflet on the United Front, a few odd photographs of himself, and even, it appears, a membership card of some Dutch Communist splinter group.

The incendiaries, Goebbels and Goering, had thought out everything very cleverly, but they had none the less made far too many mistakes, mistakes that are very difficult to understand considering the skill and ingenuity of the present Minister of Propaganda. Let us look at some of them. In the official announcement of 28 February (Prussian Press Service) we can read, *inter alia*: 'This fire is the most monstrous act of terror yet committed by Bolshevism in Germany. Among the many tons of subversive material that the police discovered in their raid on the Karl Liebknecht Haus were instructions for running a Communist terror campaign on the Bolshevik model. According to these documents, Government buildings, museums, palaces and essential buildings were to be set on fire. Further, instructions were given to place women and children, if possible those of police officials, at the head of terrorist groups in cases of conflict or disorder. The burning of the Reichstag was to have been the signal for bloody insurrection and civil war. Widespread looting was to have broken out in Berlin as early as 4 a.m. on Tuesday. It has been established that for today (28 February) acts of terror were planned against certain individuals, against private property, against the life and safety of the population.'

The astonished reader may well ask how it was that the police authorities and the Minister of the Interior waited until after the burning of the Reichstag on 27 February to take their anti-Bolshevik steps, when they had 'discovered' the plans for the insurrection as early as the 24th. Further, as early as Saturday, 25 February, an act of arson was discovered in the former Imperial Palace. But Herr Goering and Herr Levetzow did nothing at all to guard Government buildings, palaces or museums. That was one of the mistakes they made in their hurry.

But it was certainly not the only one. Who in his right senses can believe the fairy tale they have spread about the incendiary van der Lubbe? A hiker arrives from Holland. He spends the night of 17-18 February in Glindow near Potsdam. In the 'Green Tree Inn' he produces his Dutch passport and signs the visitors' book with his full name, birthplace, and place of usual residence. He is poorly dressed in a grey coat and soft hat, and in no way distinguishable from any of the other hikers that throng the roads. On 18 February, he leaves Glindow in the direction of Werder-Berlin. On the 19 February or so he reaches Berlin, and lo and behold, he immediately succeeds in joining the Action Committee of the plotters and is assigned a most important part in helping to fire the Reichstag barely ten days later. Whereupon this fine revolutionary sticks a Dutch passport, a United Front leaflet and so on in his pocket, stays behind in the Reichstag and is the only one to get himself arrested by the police. 'Look, everybody, here's the Communist who set fire to the Reichstag.' Herr Goebbels and Herr Goering have badly overestimated the credulity of world public opinion. It is an even happier chance that this van der Lubbe also volunteered the information that he was in touch with the SPD. In the Press Service report mentioned above we read: 'The Reichstag incendiary has admitted his contacts with the SPD. By this admission, the Communist-Social Democrat United Front has been implicated.' Goebbels and Goering went further still, although, on the whole, perhaps a little too far. For they also produced three scoundrels who had allegedly seen Deputies Torgler and Koenen in the Reichstag with van der Lubbe. The *Deutsche Allgemeine Zeitung* declared that Herr Torgler had spent several hours before the fire in the company of the incendiary who was later arrested, and also with a number of other individuals, some of whom were seen carrying torches. The only reason why these individuals were not caught was because they managed to escape through the subterranean heating passage leading to the palace of the Reichstag President.

The astonished reader may well wonder once again why Herr Torgler was allowed to run about the Reichstag with several persons, all equipped with torches, for several hours. And he may also marvel at the smartness of Herr Goering, or at least of his police, who discovered, even before the fire was extinguished, that the incendiaries must have got away through the subterranean heating passage.

It may, perhaps, be worth mentioning further that two reporters from the *Vorwärts* managed to slip through the cordon round the Reichstag, to get into a telephone booth in the Reichstag and to ring up the *Vorwärts* with the news that Herr Goering had set the Reichstag on fire. Naturally, they were both caught in the telephone booth, if only as 'proof' that it was the Social Democrats who had started the rumor that Goering had set fire to the Reichstag. Again Mr. Sefton Delmer of the *Daily Express*, who had waited with Goering, Hitler and Goebbels for the conflagration to break out, wired to his newspaper that shortly after the news of the fire became known, he met his friends in the Reichstag. When Hitler saw von Papen there, he said to Papen: 'If this fire, as I believe, turns out to be the handiwork of Communists, then nothing can now stop us crushing this murder pest with an iron fist.' A little later, Goering joined them as well and said to Herr Hitler: 'This is undoubtedly the work of Communists. A number of Communist deputies were in the Reichstag twenty minutes before the fire broke out. We have succeeded in arresting one of the incendiaries.' Alas, how obvious this dispatch of Mr. Sefton Delmer makes it why the Reichstag was burned!

25. The Enabling Act: The Law to Remove the Distress of People and State Legalizes the Nazi Revolution, March 24, 1933

"The national laws enacted by the National Cabinet are prepared by the Chancellor. . . ."

As soon as he was appointed chancellor on January 30, 1933, by President Paul von Hindenburg, Hitler decided to solidify his position by an act that would give legality to his revolution. He did this in the Enabling Act of March 24, 1933 – the Law to Remove the Distress of People and State. Even in his official decrees Hitler could not resist the use of propagandistic terms. Though he never repudiated the Weimar Constitution officially, Hitler in reality violated its spirit in acting in a manner which he regarded as legal use of the constitution.

THE REICHSTAG has resolved the following law, which is, with the approval of the National Council, herewith promulgated, after it has been established that the requirements have been satisfied for legislation altering the Constitution.

ARTICLE 1. National laws can be enacted by the National Cabinet as well as in accordance with the procedure established in the Constitution. This applies also to the laws referred to in article 85, paragraph 2, and in article 87 of the Constitution.

ARTICLE 2. The national laws enacted by the National Cabinet may deviate from the Constitution so far as they do not affect the position of

---

U.S., Department of State, *National Socialism: Basic Principles,* prepared by Raymond E. Murphy, F. B. Stevens, Howard Trivers, and Joseph M. Roland (Washington: Government Printing Office, 1943), pp. 217-18.

the *Reichstag* and National Council. The powers of the President remain undisturbed.

ARTICLE 3. The national laws enacted by the National Cabinet are prepared by the Chancellor and published in the *Reichsgesetzblatt.* They come into effect, unless otherwise specified, upon the day following their publication. Articles 68 to 77 of the Constitution do not apply to the laws enacted by the National Cabinet.

ARTICLE 4. Treaties of the Reich with foreign states which concern matters of national legislation do not require the consent of the bodies participating in legislation. The National Cabinet is empowered to issue the necessary provisions for the execution of these treaties.

ARTICLE 5. This law becomes effective on the day of publication. It becomes invalid on April 1, 1937; it further becomes invalid when the present National Cabinet is replaced by another.

Berlin, March 24, 1933

Reich President VON HINDENBURG

Reich Chancellor ADOLF HITLER

Reich Minister of the Interior FRICK

Reich Minister for Foreign Affairs
BARON VON NEURATH

Reich Minister of Finances
COUNT SCHWERIN VON KROSIGK

26. The Chancellor Explains to President von Hindenburg His Attitude Toward the Jews and Their Role in Germany, April 5, 1933

"Please be convinced that I shall try to take into account your noble sentiment. . . ."

Shortly after he came to political power, Hitler deemed it expedient to assure President Paul von Hindenburg about the nature of Nazi anti-Semitism. Apparently, the aged president had taken up the cause of Jews who had served with distinction in World War I. In a letter written in his own handwriting, Hitler assured von Hindenburg that he, Hitler, would try to take into consideration the president's "noble sentiment." The law to which Hitler referred in his last paragraph, the Law for the Restoration of the Civil Service, was promulgated on April 7, 1933. It became the model for additional legislation aimed at barring Jews from certain professions and also contained provisions in favor of Jewish war veterans. (See also the next document.)

APRIL 5, 1933

DEAR HERR PRESIDENT: The counteraction of the German people against the swamping of certain professions by the Jews is caused by two things:

First, the obvious injustice that exists on account of the outrageous slighting of the dominant German people [*Staatsvolk*]. For today there is a whole series of learned professions [*Intelligenzberufe*], e.g., the professions of the lawyers and doctors, in which in individual localities in the

Germany, Auswärtiges Amt, *Documents on German Foreign Policy*, Series C (Washington, D.C.: Government Printing Office), vol. 1, pp. 253-55.

Reich — in Berlin and in other cities — the Jews occupy up to 80 percent and more of all positions. At the same time hundreds of thousands of German intellectuals, including innumerable veterans of the war, are on the dole or have some sort of entirely subordinate position and become entirely demoralized.

Second, the serious shock to the authority of the State caused by the fact that here an alien body that was never entirely amalgamated with the German people, and whose ability is mainly in the business field, has pushed into governmental positions and furnishes here the mustard seed for a corruption about the extent of which today one still has no conception that would come close to being adequate. The cleanness of the old Prussian State depended in no small degree on the fact that the Jews had only a very limited access to the civil service. The officers' corps kept itself almost entirely clear of it. The German people to an overwhelming majority also recognize these defects emotionally and suffer together from their consequences. The counteraction in the present-day form was set off only by the entirely unjustified attack made by the Jews through their international atrocity and boycott agitation.

It is understandable that in such a muddled situation the counteraction involves serious consequences for the individual. But unemployment is no harder for a Jewish intellectual than the unemployment that has affected millions of our own people. And it has affected them as a result of general conditions for which they cannot be blamed, but for which on the whole one must make alien factors responsible which, even before November 1918 and particularly since then, have pursued a systematic destruction of the Reich.

Herr Field Marshal, in a generous and humane way you are taking up the cause of those members of the Jewish people who at one time were forced to perform war service as a result of general conscription. I have complete understanding for this noble humane sentiment, Herr Field Marshal. May I nevertheless respectfully point out that the members and supporters of my movement, who were Germans, were for years driven from all government positions without regard for wife and child and without regard for the war service they had performed. Even formerly the National Socialist party had the highest percentage of war veterans in its parliamentary group in the Reichstag. Everything was represented in it, beginning with generals and officers with the Pour le Mérite down to the simple private. And it's exactly the same with the members and supporters. Nevertheless the members of this largest movement of millions of the German people, whose primary aim in the struggle was the reestablishment of a German Wehrmacht, were not allowed to work in government enterprises even as workers or clerks. Those responsible for this cruelty were the same Jewish parties who are complaining today when their supporters with a thousand times more justification are barred from access to government positions in which they can be of little use but can do a limitless amount of damage. It was only through your intervention, Herr Field Marshal, that this outlawing of the members of my movement was done away with in individual cases, and then finally in general. Nevertheless, Herr Field Marshal, I respect the noble motives of your sentiment, and I have already discussed with Minister of Interior Frick the preparation of a law that will remove the solution of these questions from the arbitrariness of separate actions and regulate them in general by a law. And in this connection, I have also pointed out to the Minister of Interior the cases that you, Herr Field Marshal, wish to see excepted. The first deliberative discussions of this law were already held at the end of last week and it will provide for consideration for those Jews who either themselves performed war service or suffered injury through the war or who deserve well on any other grounds, or in a long term in office never gave cause for complaint. In general the first aim of this cleansing process is only intended to be the restoration of a certain health and natural relationship, and secondly, to remove from certain positions important to the state those elements which cannot be entrusted with the existence or nonexistence of the Reich. For in the coming years we will not be able to avoid taking precautions so that certain events that cannot be told to the rest of the world for higher reasons of state really remain secret. The only way to guarantee this is through the inner homogeneity of the administrative organs involved.

Herr Reich President, please be convinced that I shall try to take into account your noble sentiment to the greatest possible extent. I understand your inner motivations and, moreover, I myself often suffer from the harshness of a fate that forces one to make decisions which for humane reasons one would wish a thousand times to avoid.

The law under consideration will be drafted as quickly as possible, and I am convinced that this question, too, will then have found the best possible solution.

In sincere and deep respect, yours, etc.

ADOLF HITLER

27. Law for the Restoration of the Civil Service: The Opening Stage in the Persecution of the Jews, April 7, 1933

"Officials of non-Aryan descent are to be retired."

Five weeks after he assumed political power, on April 7, 1933, Hitler issued a decree making it plain that "public servants not of Aryan stock" – those who had one Jewish grandparent and were considered, therefore, to be one-quarter Jewish – were to be dismissed from civil service offices. On the protest of President Paul von Hindenburg, any non-Aryan civil servants who had held office since August 1, 1914, those who had fought at the front in World War I, and those whose fathers or sons had been killed in action, were excluded, but the exemption lasted only two and a half years. Under this act some two thousand non-Aryan office holders, including world-famous scientists and professors, were driven from office.

ARTICLE 1. (1) In order to restore a national civil service and also to simplify the civil service administration, certain officials may be dismissed from office in conformance with the following regulations, even when the details required by present laws are not present.

(2) Officials as defined by this law are both direct and indirect officials of the states, communities, and districts, officials of legal corporations, officials of establishments and businesses of equal status.

Officials as defined by this law include those who are temporarily retired.

(3) The *Reichsbank* and the German State Railway system are hereby given the power to make similar arrangements.

Reichsgesetzblatt, vol. 1, no. 34, April 7, 1933. Translated by the editor.

ARTICLE 2. (1) Officials who have entered the national civil service since November 9, 1918, who do not possess the essential training for their work, are to be dropped from the service. They will continue to be paid for three months.

(2) They have no claim to a pension, or for a pension for their heirs. Nor may they continue to use their title, uniform, or office badges.

(3) In cases involving distress, especially when the dismissed officials support destitute relatives, the individuals concerned may be given an annuity, subject to withdrawal at any time, consisting of up to one third of the existing base salary of the positions last held by them. They cannot, however, be reinsured under the provisions of the national insurance law.

ARTICLE 3. (1) Officials of non-Aryan descent are to be retired. Those who have honorary status are also to be dismissed.

(2) The preceding paragraph does not apply to officials who have been in service since August 1, 1914, or who fought in the World War at the front for the German Reich or its allies, or whose fathers or sons fell in the war. Further exceptions may be made by the Minister of the Interior in agreement with the competent minister in the case of officials who are resident in foreign countries.

ARTICLE 4. Those officials who have indicated by their previous political activity that they may not exert themselves for the national state without reservation may be dismissed. They will be paid for three months after their dismissal. From then on they will receive three-quarters of their pensions and corresponding maintenance for their heirs.

ARTICLE 5. (1) If the needs of the civil service demand it, every official must agree to a transfer to an office of the same rank or to one of lesser rank.

(2) An official designated for a lesser rank and income may, within a month, go on pension.

ARTICLE 6. In order to simplify administration, officials may be required to go on pension, even if they are still fit for service. When such officials are retired, their positions may not be filled.

ARTICLE 7. (1) All dismissals, transfers, and retirements are announced with finality by the highest national or state authorities. There is no legal redress.

(2) The procedures mentioned in Articles 2 and 6 must be taken at the latest by November 30, 1933. The time limit may be shortened by the Minister of the Interior if the highest competent authorities, national or state, declare that the provisions of this law have been implemented within their administrative area of authority.

ARTICLE 8. Officials retired or dismissed in conformance with Articles 3 and 4 will not receive pensions if they have not completed at least 10 years' service. This applies also in those cases in which, according to national or state laws, a pension is granted even after a shorter period of service.

28. The Burning of the Books — I: "Un-German Literature" Is Consigned to the Flames in a Nazi Ceremony, May 10, 1933

> *"Sigmund Freud — for falsifying our history and degrading its great figures."*

The entire world was given a front-page display of the Nazi attitude toward culture when thousands of books considered to be "un-German" were consigned to flames in some thirty university towns. On the evening of May 10, 1933, torchlight parades of thousands of students marched to a meeting place where books of authors opposed to the Nazi *Weltanschauung* were thrown ceremoniously into huge bonfires. The books included not only many by German-Jewish authors, such as Erich Maria Remarque, Lion Feuchtwanger, and Albert Einstein, but also the works of such non-German writers as André Gide, Jack London, and H. G. Wells. The display was organized by Dr. Paul Joseph Goebbels, minister for propaganda and public enlightenment, who proclaimed that the soul of the German people would once again express itself and that the flames of the burning books symbolized the beginning of a new era. (See also document 29.)

Editorial opinion throughout the world denounced the book-burning as an ignorant and barbaric display. Following is a factual report of the proceedings in Berlin sent by wireless to the *The New York Times* by its correspondent, Frederick T. Birchall.

BERLIN, May 10. — In most of the German university towns tonight the

---

The New York Times. May 11, 1933.

113

enthusiastic studenthoods are ceremoniously burning "the un-German spirit" as exemplified in literature, pamphlet, correspondence and record. It is all being done to the accompaniment of torchlight parades, martial music and much patriotic speechifying — the British Guy Fawkes Day intensified a thousandfold.

There are some thirty universities in Germany, at least one to each State. Each was to have had its bonfire, but the celebrations in Cologne, Heidelberg and other places were postponed until next week.

The celebrations held varied somewhat, but more in degree than in kind. Berlin naturally had the largest and what happened here was more or less typical of the celebrations elsewhere.

Probably 40,000 persons assembled in the great square between the opera house and the university and stood in a drizzle to watch the show. Perhaps as many more gathered along the five miles of streets through which the torchbearing parade of students escorted the borrowed trucks and private cars containing the books and pamphlets to be burned. But to the uninspired observer it savored strongly of the childish.

5,000 Students in Parade

Five thousand students, young men and young women together, marched in the parade. All the student corps were represented — red caps and green caps, purple and blue, with a chosen band of officers of the dueling corps in plush tam o' shanters, white breeches, blue tunics and high boots — with spurs. Bearing banners and singing Nazi songs and college melodies, they arrived.

It was toward midnight when they reached the great square. There on a granite block of pavement protected by a thick covering of sand had been built up a funeral pyre of crossed logs, some twelve feet square and five feet high. Until the parade appeared a Nazi band had striven to keep up enthusiasm.

Finally the head of the procession arrived. It passed the piled logs and formed within the great space reserved for it.

As they passed, the paraders tossed upon the logs the stumps of lighted torches that they had carried, until from end to end the mass was aflame.

Then came the books and pamphlets. The cars carrying them stopped at a distance and each group of students brought an armful and tossed it into the fire. A draft caught up the embers, bearing them far and wide. First the crowds cheered each new contribution, but they soon tired.

Then the students' president, Gutjahr, in a Nazi uniform, made a speech. He and his fellows had gathered, he said, to consign to the flames "un-German" books and documents that threatened to disintegrate the national movement. They took joy in it. Henceforth there must be purity in German literature.

Crowd Seems Disappointed

It was a boy's speech and it was received with boyish enthusiasm — by the students. The crowd seemed disappointed. To work up enthusiasm when fresh consignments reached the fire a student barker began to name the authors:

"Sigmund Freud — for falsifying our history and degrading its great figures!"

The crowd cheered.

"Emil Ludwig — burned for literary rascality and high treason against Germany!"

Loud cheers!

Then Erich Maria Remarque — "for degrading the German language and the highest patriotic ideal"; Alfred Kerr, late dramatic critic of the *Tageblatt*, denounced as "a dishonest literary adventurer"; Theodor Wolff, former editor of the *Tageblatt*, pilloried as "anti-German," and Georg Bernhard, former editor of the *Vossische Zeitung*. For these last there were available for burning only a few copies of their respective newspapers and a few magazine articles.

So it went until there appeared, amid Nazi salute and protected by uniformed satellites, the attraction of the evening, Dr. Paul Joseph Goebbels, the Minister of Propaganda, himself. Mounted on a tiny swastika-draped rostrum, he spoke.

"Jewish intellectualism is dead," he declared. "National socialism has hewn the way. The German folk soul can again express itself.

"These flames do not only illuminate the final end of the old era, they also light up the new. Never before have the young men had so good a right to clean up the debris of the past. If the old men do not understand what is going on, let them grasp that we young [Dr. Goebbels is under 40] men have gone and done it.

"The old goes up in flames, the new shall be fashioned from the flame in our hearts."

Much more, but all like that. Then the song "The Nation to Arms" and the Horst Wessel song. More literature on the fire. And more student singing. But the crowd disintegrating until it became a dreary duty to burn what literature was left.

It was not so large in quantity, because today a paper mill offered a small price for all it could get and the offer was accepted on condition that the student representatives should supervise the actual destruction. The proceeds will pay for the torches and the bands.

Original List Reduced

As to what went into the ceremonial bonfires tonight and will be included in the reconversion into raw material by the paper mills at the rate of one mark for 100 kilograms [currently about 27.5 cents for 220 pounds], the destruction is not quite so all-embracing as was at first threatened.

There is good reason to believe that the ripples of amusement that went through the outside world over the first rush of student enthusiasm had some effect on the older and wiser university heads. German propaganda authorities themselves, who recently had seen the effect of making Germany ridiculous as well as censurable, may even have been heard from. At any rate, not everything under attack went into the discard.

For several days whole truckloads of books, both seized and voluntarily offered for immolation, have been arriving at the students' house in the Oranienburgerstrasse, but these have undergone a weeding-out process. Students have been busy night and day going through the piles to insure that especially valuable books or others not on the German index expurgatorius should escape. Such of these as were found are to be returned to the libraries.

Nevertheless, plenty has been left that elsewhere in the world would be deemed innocuous if not positively beneficial, or at worst capable of carrying its own condemnation. In the pink-faced, healthy student-hood between the ages of 18 and 22 is found boundless enthusiasm, but not overmuch discretion. In this instance the enthusiasm had virtually free rein.

How Books Were Chosen

About such pictures and pamphlets as were gathered in from Dr. Magnus Hirschfeld's so-called Institute of Sexual Science the other day — which, with all the correspondence from outsiders who had taken the place seriously, went into the flames tonight — there could be little question. But there was so much more. Take this formula, laid down in one of the students' appeals for sacrificial material and note its comprehensiveness:

"Anything that works subversively on family life, married life or love or the ethics of our youth or our future or strikes at the roots of German thought, the German home and the driving forces in our people; any works of those who would subordinate the soul to the material, anything that serves the purpose of lies."

Almost anything could be understood by this student enthusiast to be covered by that. And so with "the seeping poison that hides under the mask of pacifism," to say nothing of the ban on all literature emanating from Jewish thinkers, all of which — although the works of Heine are strangely enough not among the sacrificed — are included in this comprehensive student anathema.

"The Jew, who is powerful in intellect, but weak in blood and without home and fireside, remains without understanding in the presence of German thought, fails to dignify it and, therefore, is bound to injure the German spirit."

Nobel Prize Winners Included

Inevitably the bonfire piles became large. World distinction and world praise had not counted in assembling them. Nobel Prize winners and all went into the *auto-da-fé*.

There was, for example, one of the first pacifist novels ever written. Bertha von Suttner got the Nobel Prize for "Lay Down Your Arms" in 1905, but it has now become "un-German" and was burned.

The works of Thomas Mann, a later Nobel Prize winner, went into the flames en bloc. What saved Sinclair Lewis may never be revealed, but many other 3,000,000-volume sellers became sacrifices, beginning with Erich Maria Remarque's "All Quiet on the Western Front."

The victims even included Count Coudenhove-Kalergi, the Japanese-Viennese author, who dreams of Pan-Europa. He falls under the ban because it is not a Prussian Pan-Europa and, moreover, might be suspected of having a Socialist tint.

For Berlin the first list alone — supplemented later — comprised four long typewritten pages containing the names of 160 authors, many of them almost unheard of before. It almost seemed as if any German student browsing in a second-hand bookstore, encountering a volume that he privately regarded as spicy, had been privileged to name a candidate.

The American Victims

Among the Americans, Helen Keller's "How I Became a Socialist" got into the fire. She had for company Upton Sinclair, Judge Ben Lindsey, Jack London and Morris Hillquit, among others. Judge Lindsey got there because he is regarded as assailing the marriage system. Robert Carr was burned in the shape of his "Wild-Blooming Youth," which might have been expected to be unknown to fame in Berlin but evidently isn't.

Socialist and Communist authors naturally figured largely. Karl Marx, Friedrich Engels, Lassalle, Bebel, Liebknecht, Kautsky, Bernstein and Wilferding among the Germans and Austrians. Lenin, Stalin, Zinovieff, Lunacharsky and Bukharin among the Russians, and Henry Lichtenberger, French philosopher who wrote on Franco-German relations, all went up in smoke as "un-German."

In the domain of belles lettres Heinrich Mann is included with Thomas Mann and then comes a long list including Emil Ludwig, who writes about Germany for THE NEW YORK TIMES; Lion Feuchtwanger, Arthur Schnitzler, Jakob Wassermann, Arnold and Stephan Zweig, Walther Rathenau, the German Foreign Minister who was assassinated by Nationalist gangsters; Hugo Preuss, who wrote the Weimar Constitution for the republic and spent the rest of his time expounding it, and countless others.

The bonfires are still burning as this is being written and there is going up in their smoke more than college boy prejudice and enthusiasm. A lot of the old German liberalism — if any was left — was burned tonight.

20,000 Books on Berlin Pyre
By The Associated Press

BERLIN, May 10. — More than 20,000 books were on the pile that students of the University of Berlin ignited in the Opera Square tonight.

Although the names of some German authors were read out as their books were consigned to the flames, the names of foreign authors on the list were not mentioned.

Dr. Paul Joseph Goebbels, the Propaganda Minister, told the assembled students:

"As you had the right to destroy the books, you had the duty to support the government. The fire signals to the entire world that the November revolutionaries have sunk to earth and a new spirit has arisen."

He pleaded for the students to recognize as comrades men in all walks of life as a sign to the world that Germany is completely united.

Lest the students "go too far," a commission of college professors had been named to "separate the wheat from the chaff" and preserve valuable books from the fires. This action followed upon a warning by Captain Hermann Wilhelm Goering, the Prussian Premier against forms of "racketeering."

100 Volumes Burned in Munich
Wireless to THE NEW YORK TIMES

MUNICH, May 10. — A hundred massively bound volumes— the works of "un-German" writers — were publicly burned in the Koenigsplatz tonight after a picturesque torchlight parade of students.

All the books destroyed came from the university library, but they were consigned to the flames lit by the students' inquisitorial tribunal because of their "disintegrating influence."

Funeral March Is Played
Wireless to THE NEW YORK TIMES

FRANKFORT-ON-MAIN, May 10. — Marxist literature and other "un-German" books went into the flames on the Römerberg tonight to the strains of Chopin's Funeral March as thousands of students of the University of Frankfort in full regalia stood at attention.

5,000 Pounds in Breslau
Wireless to THE NEW YORK TIMES

BRESLAU, May 10. — Five thousand pounds of "heretical" literature, among it books by Emil Ludwig, Erich Maria Remarque and Thomas Mann, went into the students' bonfire in the Schlossplatz tonight.

Professor Speller, the official speaker for the studenthood, proclaimed the purging fires as the symbol of the disappearance of everything smacking of "the un-German" and declared that they lit up a new task for the unbroken effectiveness of the German spirit. He said the flames also illuminated the newly welded blood community of the German people.

Kiel Fires Pacifist Works
Wireless to THE NEW YORK TIMES

KIEL, May 10. — The crusade against the "Un-German spirit," which has been in progress here for a week, culminated here tonight with the public burning of about 2,000 examples of pacifist literature and erotic publications gathered by the students of Kiel University.

Professor Kantorowicz's "Critical Study of England" and his memorial on Germany's war guilt went into the flames with the works of Marx, Kautsky and other Socialist writers.

One of the speakers charged that the Freudian theory undermined the ethics of German sex life and must therefore be stamped out.

29. The Burning of the Books — II: Dr. Goebbels, Minister for Public Enlightenment and Propaganda, Delivers His Speech of Justification, May 10, 1933

"The past lies in the flames."

Burning of despised symbols had long been a tradition among German students. On October 18, 1817, on the three hundredth anniversary of Luther's revolt (also the date of the Battle of Leipzig), 468 students of the *Burschenschaften* gathered at the Wartburg, near Eisenach, for a ceremonial bonfire to celebrate nationalistic ambitions for a united Germany. There the students, remembering Luther's public burning of the papal bull, collected the books of conservative and antinationalistic writers and burned them in a great public bonfire. Also consigned to the flames were a corporal's cane, a Prussian military manual, and stacks of conservative pamphlets.

To Dr. Paul Joseph Goebbels, minister for public enlightenment and propaganda, this tradition could be used to show the world the joy of the German people in their new revolution and their new sense of freedom. Accordingly, he encouraged the burning of "un-German books." Following is the speech he delivered to the students at the site of the book burning on the evening of May 10, 1933.

FELLOW STUDENTS! German men and women! The age of an exaggerating acute Jewish intellectualism is now at an end and the piercing of the German Revolution has again made the streets free for the German system. When, on the thirtieth of January of this year, the National Socialist

Der Angriff, May 11, 1933. Translated by the editor.

movement won its way to power, no one at that time could have known that Germany would be cleaned up so quickly and in so radical a fashion. The Revolution, which broke out at that time, was prepared — that we can only understand today — by us with extreme care and patient planning. . . .

This Revolution did not take place from above. It broke out from below. It was not dictated, but rather the people themselves wanted it. It is, therefore, in the best sense of the words, the implementation of the will of the people, and those men who organized, mobilized, and brought about this Revolution come from all strata, classes, and professions of the German people. An entire people have stood up and thrown away the chains of tyranny. That is the difference between this Revolution and the revolt of November 1918.

That revolt resulted in that sort of materialism which Marxism affirms. The powers of lower humanity (*Untermenschentum*) then conquered the political terrain, and then there followed in Germany fourteen years of unbelievable material and spiritual disgrace. This shame each one of us has been able to observe in his own life. Every worker, who lost his place at the machine, was aware of it; every apprentice laborer, who found his way to work blocked, was aware of it; every citizen, who saw his last penny taken from his pocket, was aware of it; every soldier, who had to grind his teeth and watch while national defense and national honor were ground underfoot, was aware of it. You students, too, are aware of it, for you have become the vanguard of a real revolutionary German spirit emerging out of the universities.

You young students are the bearers, front-rank troops, and champions of the young revolutionary ideas of this state, and just as in the past you were right in opposing the false state, the unsuitable state (*Unstaat*), to deny you respect and your regard for the unsuitable state, so now you have the duty to accept the new state, to support that state, and to give the authority of that new state new worth and new validity. A revolutionary must know everything. He must be able at once to destroy the unworthy and to build up the worthy. When you students take upon yourselves the task of casting this unworthy filth into the flames, then you must also take upon yourselves the duty of replacing it with a real German spirit of the streets. One learns about spirit through life and through the classroom, and the coming German man will not only be primarily a man of books but also a man of character. And that is the way we want to educate you. Youth must have the courage to look life in the eye pitilessly, to relinquish any fear of death, in order before death to assume a sense of honor — that is the task of the young generation.

Therefore, you have done well in the middle of this night to throw into the flames these unspiritual relics of the past. It is a strong, great, and symbolic performance, a performance which should document for all the world: here the spiritual foundations of the November Republic sink to the ground. But out of these ruins there will arise the phoenix of a new spirit, a spirit which we bear, which we demand, a spirit on which we have stamped its decisive character and its decisive features.

So I beg you, my fellow students, to stand up for the Reich and for its new authorities. So I beg you to dedicate yourselves to the work and duty and banners of responsibility. I also urge you to observe in these flames not only the symbol of the destruction of the old fortresses, but also the construction of a new fortress. You have already had to look life in the face, and few of you are so blessed with riches that you can enjoy this life in complete undisturbed freedom. You need not complain, even if you young people are poor in material resources, because you have won out in your souls. And I believe that never was a youth so proud of life, so proud of its tasks, and so proud of its duty, as you. And never have young people before had the right to cry out as Ulrich von Hutten called: "Oh Century, Oh Science, what a joy it is to live!"

You stand now before these tasks. In the past weeks and months you have stretched your hand to workers, comrades in the factories and in the civil service. The barriers, which have stood between all of us, are now broken down. The people have again found the people. And even if the oldsters have not seen it, we young people have accomplished it.

When, together with the workers, you wear the same brown uniform, and when you, without anyone knowing the difference, march in the same rows and with the same steps, you give the entire world the impression that the nation is again united. Under the storm of new ideas and the breathless tempo of this Revolution we have found one another again.

The past lies in the flames. The new will arise again from the flames of our hearts. We shall stay together and we shall go forward together, and we shall dedicate ourselves to the Reich. Just as in the past we had to fight the opposition, so now when we have the power and with it the responsibility, we join together in a solemn vow. Just as when we were fighting for power we took a vow, so today under this sky and with these flames we take a new oath: The Reich and the Nation and our Leader, Adolf Hitler — *Heil! Heil! Heil!*

30. Romain Rolland Denounces the Nazi Regime and Receives a Strained Rebuke, May 14, 1933

"The future will clarify for you — too late — your murderous mistake. . . ."

Reactions to the early excesses of the Nazi regime came from all over the world and not merely from such *émigrés* as Thomas Mann and Ernst Toller. Romain Rolland, French novelist and Nobel Prize winner, considered himself to be a devoted friend of Germany and of the Germans. On May 14, 1933, not quite four months after the accession of Hitler to political power, Rolland sent an outraged letter to the editor of the *Kölnische Zeitung,* a respected newspaper. Rolland made no secret of his disdain for the new barbarians who had trampled the good Germany underfoot and stained it with blood. The editors of the newspaper replied with a long and somewhat strained explanation, pleading for more understanding and regretting that Rolland had fallen victim to the false talk of German "barbarism" and "fascist terror." Rolland was not converted.

May 14, 1933

Dear Editor:

The article which the *Kölnische Zeitung* published about me in its issue of May 9, 1933, has been brought to my attention.

It is quite true that I love Germany, and have always defended her against the unfair attitude and lack of understanding by other nations. But the Germany which I love and which has nourished my spirit is that Germany composed of great world-citizens, of those "who regarded the

---

Kolnische Zeitung, May 21, 1933. Translated by the editor.

123

fortunes and misfortunes of other peoples as their own," of those who have worked for the union of nations and spirits.

This Germany is now being trampled underfoot, it is stained with blood, and it is being shamed by her "national" rulers, by the Germany of the swastika, which rejects the free spirit of men, Europeans, pacifists, Jews, socialists, and communists who strive to establish the internationalism of labor.

Do you not see that national-Fascist Germany is the worst possible enemy that the real Germany can have? Do you not see that it is rejecting this real Germany? This sort of thing is a crime not only against the human spirit but against your very own country. You drain her of a large part of her energy and you lose for her the great respect of her best friends in the world. Your leaders have only succeeded in bringing about the creation of a union of nationalists and internationalists of all countries against you. You do not seem to be aware of that. You prefer to speak of a "conspiracy" against Germany. But the fact of the matter is that you, yourselves, have been guilty of conspiring against yourselves.

In the past I have spoken out against the injustice done to Germany after the victory of 1918. I called for the revision of the Treaty of Versailles which was imposed upon you by force. I demanded the equality of Germany with all nations. But you just do not believe that I called for all this for the sake of a still greater injustice, of a Germany which herself violates the concept of the equality of human races and all those human rights which are sacred to us. Those hard-bitten opponents of treaty revision could not have done more to harm Germany than you yourselves have done. The future will clarify for you — too late — your murderous mistake, for which there is only one excuse — the fever of despair into which the blindness and harshness of the victors of Versailles plunged your people.

Despite what you have done I still retain my sympathy for Germany, for the real Germany which is dishonored by the terrorism and the insanity of Hitlerite fascism. I shall continue to do my writing, as I have done all my life, not for the egotism of any individual nation, but for all the nations together, for the international of the spirit of peoples.

P.S. You regard the accusations of the foreign press against Hitlerite fascism as lies. We have a great amount of proof concerning accused individuals and the most vicious horrors committed by Brown Shirts which were never punished or even denounced by official statements. But let us not talk of all that now! The official texts are quite enough for that. Can you deny the proclamations of your leaders, of Hitler, Goering, Goebbels, which have been published in the press and broadcast over the radio? Can you deny their incitement to violence, their statements on racialism which excoriate other people like the Jews? Can you deny this decaying odor which belongs to the Middle Ages, long since past in the West? Can you deny the vulgar intrusion of politics into the universities and schools? Do you really believe that the great anathema of art and science outweighs on the scales of world opinion the stupid excommunications of your inquisitors?

R.R.

Reply by the Editors of the *Kölnische Zeitung*

May 20, 1933

Dear Mr. Rolland,

We were not especially surprised to receive from you such a harsh reply to the lines about you which appeared in the *Kölnische Zeitung*. We realize that contemporary Germany has very little sympathy in the world, even among her old friends, and we know that serious efforts at understanding us have been very rare, indeed. This does not dishearten us. For you especially we shall be glad to repeat the effort to meet the serious charges which you make against Germany and her leaders.

We recall with gratitude the many works, both literary and practical, which you have written for the German cause. We recall your novel *Jean Christophe*, in which you gave such beautiful expression to your love for things German. We recall your profound work on Goethe and Beethoven, your help during the war and during the difficult postwar years, your attacks upon the brutality of the victors, and your demand for a really just peace. We shall not forget that, and it is the memory of that which now inspires what we have to say.

Germany has had a revolution, a revolution which is inspired not only by the fulfillment of the ancient German dream—the formation of a strong, unified state, but which goes beyond mere political innovations and shows a deep spiritual transformation. What this means in history is well known to you. You, yourself, sought to show it in your drama, *Danton*. When this drama was performed some years ago in Berlin, the scene which made the greatest impression was that before the revolutionary tribunal in which Danton is forced to retire. The stage depiction of stamping, shouting, and waving banners was filled with enthusiasm.

From that historic event in the history of your Fatherland, the German Revolution differs in that very thing which you so mistakenly misunderstand—in its disciplined and bloodless course. Of course, there were some excesses. These should be deplored and they were branded as such by the authorities. These were excesses committed by individual hot-heads and they were acts of violence which can be explained only by the fact that their perpetrators themselves had long been persecuted.

There were also exaggerated words uttered at the beginning of the revolution. But when you look at it in its entirety, you will see that the leaders held the reins of political developments firmly in their hands. You cannot use as a standard the welfare of a single individual during the storm of a revolution — you have shown this very well in your *Danton* — yet we were spared that cruel destiny which came to large sections of the French people in 1789, that sort of thing which today in Soviet Russia drives thousands into a meaningless death. When you compare Germany with the French past and with the conditions in Russia today, you must admit that Germany stands without shame before the bar of history. The German Revolution took place with considerably less bloodshed than any previous revolution.

The world is filled with the lies of propaganda atrocities. Even the most unprejudiced will not believe this and nothing convinces them except their own observations.

We graciously invite you, Mr. Rolland, to come here. We believe that we can assure you that you will suffer no embarrassment because of your attitude toward our government. We are too familiar with the sources of these lies and we know how to distinguish between slanderers and those who have been misled.

Even if we could convince you that Germany is not "stained with blood," there still remains the charge that she has violated the "sacred human rights" of liberty and equality. Our reply to this is that too close adherence to these rights is precisely what has brought Germany as well as all of Europe to the brink of ruination. Under cover of legally sanctioned liberty and equality, the Communists in Germany were able to undermine the bourgeois order, and as has been proven, were ready to convert it into bloody chaos. If this plan had been successful, it would have penetrated into other countries. Who knows if your peaceful home on Lake Geneva, which during the war was known as "the refuge of reason," would have continued to remain that way? The great service of Hitler and his ministers is precisely that they have averted the danger of new troubles for Europe. Maybe the world is not yet ready to recognize this, but some day it will render a more just verdict.

The Jews are not given liberty and equality, you say, by contemporary Germany. You utterly fail to understand that our situation differs from other countries in Europe. Many key posts in science, art, and economic life were held in Germany by Jews. They exploited this fact by not recognizing themselves the equality of races but rather furthered the interests of their own racial brothers. And added to the German Jews there came those elements from Eastern Europe, which streamed across the German borders after the war and took advantage of our weakness and poverty. They stimulated the opposition which was to be released in the National Revolution. The opposition received new strength when Jewish writers abroad started a veritable witches' Sabbath against Germany. Of course, the excitement generated here led to hardships and many tragic fates. But if you make it a point to examine German laws, you will find in them support for your idea of objective justice.

You speak, Mr. Rolland, of the "Germany of great world-citizens," which you love and which today has been dishonored by "racialism" and other "crimes." We intellectuals of Germany reject this charge. We want to retain the true vitality of a well-understood cosmopolitanism. We do not look on it in so abstract a fashion that it would seem possible to destroy one's own nationality. We know that it is only the strong attachment to homeland and Fatherland which makes people contribute something of value to the intellectual cooperation of nations. We are taught this by those German poets and thinkers whom you honor. They were not only universal-minded, but they also taught their people the idea of patriotism. Your own countrymen, Mr. Rolland, have denied this.

To give just one example, your countrymen preferred to see in Goethe only the world-citizen and not also the man whose great talents grew out of the German cultural soil. Therefore, they believed that they could have less respect for the people and the homeland of Goethe. In that way they gave support to that unholy chauvinism which is really un-German in concept and which is aroused in us only after the most unbearable pressure from without our country. This kind of chauvinism is really far removed from Germany, and there will be no change in the future. Witness the speech which Hitler addressed to the world on Wednesday, March 17, 1933. Germany places the peaceful cooperation of nations above all aspirations which can spring only from the blind anger of a nation for power. The German Government has given yet another indication of its cosmopolitan attitude. Look at the invitations sent out to all nations for participation in the Olympic games. All this clearly indicates that Germany has not rejected pacifism as such. She just refuses to recognize the rootless and aimless intellectualism which makes it more difficult for Germany to assert her right to life itself.

Indeed, foreign nations will just have to become accustomed to this fact, that German cosmopolitanism rooted in the national idea has its limits when the matter concerns the internal character of the German state. We can allow no intervention in this area, and it ill befits the representatives of democracy abroad to concern themselves with how Germany arranges its own house and to make this purely German matter a pretext for strong vilification.

You, also, Mr. Rolland, cling to democracy, and you believe that you must denounce the New Order in Germany. This New Order is being created by leaders who more than ever before in our history have won the confidence of the people. It is, therefore, democratic, though not in the

sense of a parliamentary regime. The latter form of government is undergoing crises, even in your own country and in other European states which
cling to such a system.

At the same time, you must not overlook the democratic nature of the
German Revolution. You must no longer say: "Germany provides us with
a horrible example of oppression," as you did in that anti-Fascist declaration which aroused our original comment. If you are right, there would no
longer be an independent *Kölnische Zeitung*, and we could not dare to
publish your violent attacks upon the German Government. Then we
could not carry on the free and candid conversation with you across our
borders.

But we do have this possibility. We shall use it further in order to
exhaust those miserable and secret sources which disseminate hatred and
calumny throughout Europe today. In these critical times such efforts are
doubly necessary. Such a dialogue can be fruitful and stimulating for both
parties only if certain preliminary problems are clarified.

Above all one must tone down this fallacious talk about "German barbarism" and "Fascist terror." That you, too, fell victim to this kind of talk,
despite your usual incorruptible judgment, is to be regretted. But it only
spurs us on all the more to earn an understanding on your part and to carry
on in the battle for truth.

Editors of the Kölnische Zeitung

31. Hitler's Decree for the *Gleichschaltung* (Coordination) of All Activities in the Third Reich, June 30, 1933

"General public enlightenment. . . ."

Hitler started his policy of *Gleichschaltung* (coordination) by ordering Hermann Goering to suppress all political opposition in Prussia. Within a few months after his accession to power, he extended the policy to coordinate every conceivable activity in the Third Reich. On June 30, 1933, he issued a decree defining the specific tasks of the Ministry for Public Enlightenment and Propaganda under the direction of Dr. Paul Joseph Goebbels. In this capacity and also as chief of the Reich Culture Chamber, Goebbels went ahead to coordinate all elements of German national life – press, radio, art, music, theater, and cinema. Each was regarded as a limb (*Gliederung*) of the body politic, and each was expected to project, foster, and nourish the Nazi image and the standards set by Hitler.

The New Germany was to reflect the personal ideology and wishes of its *Fuehrer*. Because Hitler was a passionate Wagnerite, special attention was to be given to promoting the compositions of Richard Wagner. Because the *Fuehrer* hated all forms of modern art, anything which came under that category was labeled "degenerate art" (*entartete Kunst*) and was banned. Most of all, German culture in all its forms was to be purged of even the slightest Jewish influence.

I [ADOLF HITLER], in full agreement with the Minister for Foreign Affairs, Minister of the Interior, Minister of Economics, Minister for Food and

---

Reichgesetzblatt, vol. 1, no. 37, April 11, 1933. Translated by the editor.

Agriculture, Minister of Post, Minister of Communications, and Minister for Public Enlightenment and Propaganda, decree the following:

The Minister for Public Enlightenment and Propaganda is to deal with everything concerning spiritual influence on the nation, publicity for the State, culture, and business, instruction of the public both inside and outside the nation in such matters, and administration concerning such purposes.

Therefore, all the following are transferred to the jurisdiction of the Minister for Public Enlightenment and Propaganda:

1. On the jurisdiction of the Foreign Office: intelligence reports and publicity in foreign countries, art, exhibitions of art, films, and sports in foreign countries.

2. On the jurisdiction of the Ministry of the Interior:

General public enlightenment on the domestic scene; The *Hochschule für Politik* (Academy of Politics);

Setting up and celebrating national holidays and state ceremonies, with the collaboration of the Minister of the Interior;

The press (together with the Institute of Journalism);

The radio;

The German Library in Leipzig;

Art;

Music (including philharmonic orchestras);

Theater;

Cinema;

Combatting of pornography and obscenity.

3. On the jurisdiction of the Ministry of Economics and the Ministry of Food and Agriculture:

Publicity for expositions, fairs, and other such matters.

4. On the jurisdiction of the Ministry of Posts and the Ministry of Communications:

Tourist publicity;

All radio matters which in the past were handled by the Ministry of Post are hereby transferred from its jurisdiction. . . . In matters of technical administration the Minister for Public Enlightenment and Propaganda is to participate insofar as it is necessary for the execution of his own duties, especially in the matter of loans to radio stations and the regulation of their dues. It is to be noted especially that representation of the Reich in the National Radio Corporation is transferred completely to the Minister for Public Enlightenment and Propaganda.

In all the areas designated above, including legislation, the Minister for Public Enlightenment and Propaganda is considered to be the head. The general regulations also apply for the participation of the remaining national matters.

32. Law Concerning the Formation of New Parties: The *Fuehrer* Abolishes All Opposition, July 14, 1933

". . . to be punished by confinement in a jail. . . ."

It was Hitler's will that his own NSDAP be the only political party allowed to exist in the Third Reich. The Law Concerning the Formation of New Parties, promulgated on July 14, 1933, abolished all other political parties.

ARTICLE 1. The National Socialist German Workers' Party is the only political party in Germany.

ARTICLE 2. Anyone who seeks to maintain the organization of another political party or to organize a new political party is to be punished by confinement in a jail from six months to three years unless his act is punishable by a still higher penalty under other laws.

Reichsgesetzblatt, vol. 1, no. 81, July 15, 1933, p. 479. Translated by the editor.

33. Law for the Protection of Heredity Health: The Attempt to Improve the German Aryan Breed, July 14, 1933

"The proceedings of the Health Inheritance Courts are secret."

For Hitler, the biological improvement of the German species was a matter of the utmost importance. In conformance with his racial doctrine, he encouraged early marriages and large families for "pure-blooded German Nordics." At the same time he wanted to discourage reproduction by Germans who had inheritable diseases or who were feeble-minded or alcoholic. The following law, enacted on July 14, 1933, and slated to become effective on January 1, 1934, recommended sterilization for certain elements of the population. Its main provisions follow.

ARTICLE 1. (1.) Anyone who suffers from an inheritable disease may be sterilized surgically if, in the judgment of medical science, it could be expected that his descendants will suffer from serious inherited mental or physical defects.

(2.) Anyone who suffers from one of the following is to be regarded as inheritably diseased within the meaning of this law:
1. congenital feeble-mindedness
2. schizophrenia
3. manic-depression
4. congenital epilepsy
5. inheritable St. Vitus dance (Huntington's Chorea)
6. hereditary blindness

Reichsgesetzblatt, vol. 1, no. 86, July 25, 1933, pp. 529-31. Translated by the editor.

7. hereditary deafness

8. serious inheritable malformations

(3.) In addition, anyone suffering from chronic alcoholism may also be sterilized.

ARTICLE 2. (1.) Anyone who requests sterilization is entitled to it. If he be incapacitated or under a guardian because of his low state of mental health or not yet 18 years of age, his legal guardian is empowered to make the request. In other cases of limited capacity the request must receive the approval of the legal representative. If a person be of age and has a nurse, the latter's consent is required.

(2.) The request must be accompanied by a certificate from a citizen who is accredited by the German Reich stating that the person to be sterilized has been informed about the nature and consequence of sterilization.

(3.) The request for sterilization can be recalled.

ARTICLE 3. Sterilization may also be recommended by (1.) the official physician, (2.) the official in charge of a hospital, sanitarium, or prison.

ARTICLE 4. The request for sterilization must be presented in writing to, or placed in writing by the office of the Health Inheritance Court. The statement concerning the request must be certified by a medical document or authenticated in some other way. The business office of the court must notify the official physician.

ARTICLE 7. The proceedings of the Health Inheritance Courts are secret.

ARTICLE 10. The Supreme Health Insurance Court retains final jurisdiction.

34. Propaganda Minister Goebbels Sums Up Six Months of Accomplishments of the Nazi Regime, July 17, 1933

"Hitler has the genuine will to work for peace in the world."

On July 17, 1933, Dr. Paul Joseph Goebbels, minister for public enlightenment and propaganda, delivered a speech in which he discussed the winding up of the National Socialist revolution and in glowing terms described the accomplishments of the Hitler government. Following are excerpts from this long speech, which was reported the next day in Goebbels's own newspaper, *Der Angriff* (Attack).

MY FELLOW COUNTRYMEN and countrywomen! Adolf Hitler has been in power for almost half a year. On last Friday the Reich Cabinet, led by him in an extended meeting lasting from eleven in the morning to midnight, discussed and adopted the final urgent legal proposals and thereby brought to a preliminary conclusion for the first part of our domestic reconstruction.

Of course, there still exist in our country some unteachable individuals who have the idea that since January thirtieth very little has been changed. A glance at the whole situation, at the accomplishments of this administration, at the sentiment in the country and along with it at the ever-increasing confidence of the people in Hitler and his co-workers will make it easy to punish these know-it-alls.

One does not have to exaggerate in stating that Hitler's cabinet in these past six months has implemented more in political deeds than all other past

---

Der Angriff, July 18, 1933. Translated by the editor.

administrations in fourteen years of German collapse and German shame. The tempo of the National Socialist Revolution has been breathtaking in its accomplishments. The futility of the November politicians was wiped out with an unmatched powerful punch and substituted for it the new values of National Socialist ideology. Things which a year ago seemed to be paradoxical today are shown to be almost trivial. What at one time was deemed to be impossible has long since been translated into reality, and the wrongs of the state and public life, which almost caused the destruction of the German people, have everywhere been overcome.

A government of political parties belongs conclusively to the past and will never again rise from the dead. The special interest groups of parliamentarianism have either been dissolved by the state or they have themselves put an end to their activities. No one sheds any tears over them — their only justification for existence was in taking advantage of class differences.

The National Socialist movement won its way to victory through its own power. It is the strong central authority, which is centered in the person of Hitler, and he and his colleagues will carry out the most difficult historical tasks ever placed before our times and our generation.

Today we recall almost with shudders the fact that a half-year ago a so-called State Minister-President [Heinrich Held, Bavarian Minister-President, 1924–1933], who had behind him no living people but a dying party [Bavarian *Volkspartei*], dared to threaten the Reich Government that he would personally see to the arrest of any Reich commissioner sent to Bavaria. This hero was no hero, and developments have passed him by without any opposition from him and his ilk. Through the new Reich Governor's law such things have been made impossible in the future. The Reich is ruled from one central spot, and any sabotage of its work for reconstruction just does not come into question.

All this was hypothetical for meeting the problems of our time head-on. It may well be that before we came on the scene one or another of the others understood those problems and knew how to use methods and ways of solving them. But the decisive fact is always whether or not one has the power to implement them and whether one has the possibility to bring together the opposing powers of public life and unite them into a common denominator.

That Hitler was able to overcome the multiple party state and unify the whole German people into one will and a readiness for common action is perhaps the greatest historical accomplishment of the past six months. It really brings to mind the fact that the Communist Party no longer rages, the Socialist Party of Germany no longer does its dirty business. . . . No one speaks of the bourgeois parties any more, and the National Socialist Party is recognized everywhere. . . .

A government without a solid, loyal and responsible bureaucracy will not last in the long run. Therefore, we need that new law [Reform of the Bureaucracy, April 7, 1933] to purify all those elements which in the last fourteen years because of their party platforms worked to the disadvantage of the state. . . . The purge of the bureaucracy, of men who proved themselves to be unworthy, has not yet ended, but also here we shall soon accomplish our task in the interests of general order, security, and stability, all of which are so urgent at this time.

Revolutions are not goals, but only means to an end. The goal is always the maintenance of the life of our people, and the maintenance of our national race. Revolutions which lead only to anarchy do not deserve the name. Real revolutions destroy only that which needs to be destroyed and solely to create room for the new and the necessary. This government maintains a watchful eye over those camouflaged Bolshevist elements who speak of a Second Revolution at that moment when the people and the nation are preparing to secure and build up the next centuries the results of our revolution.

Let no one believe that we lacked revolutionary zeal during the time when we were in opposition and when we took power, and you can bet that we won't be scared away by hyperrevolutionary talk which stirs up the chickens and frightens little children. A revolution is something great and holy. Only he can serve the revolution who has respect for the people and its future. Only he can substitute for the revolution if he has something better to offer, and he who does not understand what work means, but on the contrary, knows only how to twist phrases in order to make an impression on the conviction of others, he had better keep silent in the community.

Hitler began his revolution at precisely the right time. Now that we hold full political power in the state, we really do not need to consolidate our position with violence, for it is a legal one. . . .

Just before we came to power our opponents cried out: "Just a half year of governmental responsibility, and you will be lost!" The more cunning ones among them even believed that once we were tested we would be made innocuous for all time. We don't really know if they continue to hold such ideas today. The German people themselves have put us to the test, and it is our enemies who have been rendered innocuous.

The entire nation gives Hitler its confidence. At no time in German history has a government been able to represent its people as well as he has. When necessary it may proceed harshly against our opponents in order to demonstrate to them the principles we represent. It foregoes tenderness and magnanimity when it becomes absolutely necessary to bring back again to the great German people's community those who have been corrupted or those who still doubt.

This Government knows that it needs the people if it is to succeed in reaching its goal. It has begun on behalf of the people a great and important plan by which a war will be carried on against unemployment – the sickness of our times. It has shown courage and cleverness in its unparalleled powerful exertions in reducing the dwindling count of the jobless by two millions. Here lies the central problem of our work. Even if there is danger that one or another well-meant theory does not work, the administration and the people alike must concentrate all their energy at the present time and in the distant future on our great task.

If we are successful in solving that problem – and we shall and must be successful – then the thanks of the entire people will be certain, and no one will then make it a point to ask whether we took enough consideration of professorial and illusionary thoughts. The factories are resuscitated not by the multitude of theories, but only through serious work, the conscientiousness of preparation, and the effectiveness of great planning. The task of the Government is to move forward with initiative and strong hand, and it expects from the entire people their tireless and trusting support.

This Government has been successful in lightening the burden of taxation, in seeing to it that no new burdens are decreed, and at the same time it has not lessened its performance on behalf of the poor and the poorest. It realizes, indeed, that there is still great misery in Germany, but in that matter it is still of good conscience because it has left no stone unturned to correct that misery and to give people work again. It does not believe it wise to solve the problem of starvation by alms-giving, but rather in the creation of work so that everyone can earn his daily bread through his own work.

Also the entire world in the long run will come to understand the seriousness with which this Government has taken its work. Hitler has the genuine will to work for peace in the world. He has proclaimed that solemnly in his address to the *Reichstag* [May 17, 1933]. Our youthful Germany in no way has the intention of provoking and embarrassing others.

If the world just does not yet understand us, then it should at least recognize the sober reality with which we seek to solve our own difficult problems, without begging other states for assistance and without acting like Philistines to bring our troubles to the attention of the whole world. The justifiable pride with which we make certain to take care of our own troubles at home will – in the long run – remain not without deep impression among the fair-minded and honorable people of other nations. . . .

We have begun our work – from Chancellor and *Fuehrer* to the lowliest street-cleaner. Since May first this people has honored work not merely as an ethical thing, but they have done so with the deepest passion of which they are capable. Indeed, millions of hands are still idle, but soon they, too, will feel the fever of working for the reconstruction of People and Reich.

That is really what makes us so happy: to know that we bear the love and trust of the entire people, and that that people are ready to create with us and to go to work.

Imposing, indeed, is the picture of this nation, that so short a time ago was bleeding from a thousand wounds, has taken its destiny in its own hands and has gone to work to put an end to the misery of the times! For that the German people deserve the deeply felt thanks of the Reich Government, thanks which I, as the personal representative of the Chancellor and *Fuehrer*, bring to you here. The German people deserve it because they will work for their freedom and for their bread. With an unconquerable will to live they will become masters of their fate. They must only work together in common and use their own powers.

Courage and self-confidence — these are the keys if the nation is to continue what it has accomplished in the last six months, if the nation in trust and discipline continues to support and further the work of the *Fuehrer*, if it does not shrink before the magnitude of our pressing tasks; then shall we be successful in accomplishing this hard task. Then we shall be able better to thank the venerable and honorable Field Marshal and President for his noble-minded resoluteness and deep wisdom, with which he has blessedly held in his hand above us, and pay an even greater thanks than is possible through words: through deeds by all classes and professions of the united German people, who again enjoy the honor and respect of the whole world.

35. Concordat Between the Holy See and Nazi Germany: An Agreement to Regulate Tensions, July 30, 1933

"The German Reich guarantees the freedom of the profession and the public exercise of the Catholic Religion."

When he came to political power in 1933, Hitler at first decided to remain on good terms with the Roman Catholic church. He concluded a concordat between Germany and the Holy See on July 20, 1933, by which he guaranteed the integrity of the Catholic faith and provided for the safeguarding of the church's rights. Catholic schools, youth groups, and cultural societies were not to be disturbed if they kept out of politics.

Yet, underneath it all, there was strong hostility. One by one Hitler broke the terms of the concordat. Nazis began to speak of the enemies of Germany as "Judea and Rome." The ensuing struggle was marked by violence. Hitler arrested monks and nuns and accused them of smuggling gold out of Germany. He censored Catholic press, forbade Catholic religious processions, and banned pastoral letters. Following are extracts from the concordat.

His Holiness the Sovereign Pontiff Pius XI and the President of the German Reich, in their reciprocal desire to consolidate and develop the amicable relations existing between the Holy See and the German Reich, and wishing to regulate the relations between the Catholic Church and the

Text of the Concordat Between the Holy See and Germany (Washington, D.C.: National Catholic Welfare Conference News Service, 1933), pp. 1-6. Courtesy of National Catholic Welfare Conference.

State throughout the territory of the German Reich in a manner that is stable and satisfactory for the two parties, have resolved to conclude a solemn convention which completes the Concordat concluded with individual German States and assures to the others a uniform treatment for the solution of questions to which it pertains. . . .

ARTICLE 1. The German Reich guarantees the freedom of the profession and the public exercise of the Catholic Religion. It recognizes the right of the Catholic Church, within the limits of the general laws in force, to regulate and to administer freely her own affairs and to proclaim, in the field of her competence, laws and ordinances binding upon her members.

ARTICLE 2. The Concordats concluded with Bavaria (1924), Prussia (1929) and Baden (1932) remain in force and the rights and liberties of the Catholic Church which they recognize remain unchanged in the territory of these respective States. For the other States the dispositions contained in the present Concordat are binding integrally. They are obligatory also for the said three States with respect to matters not regulated in their respective Concordats, or which complete the dispositions already established. In the future the conclusion of Concordats with individual States shall be effected only in accord with the Government of the Reich. . . .

ARTICLE 4. The Holy See shall enjoy the full liberty of communicating and corresponding with the bishops, the clergy and with all those who belong to the Catholic Church in Germany. The same shall be valid for the bishops and other diocesan authorities in their communications with the faithful with respect to everything pertaining to their pastoral ministry.

ARTICLE 5. In the exercise of their sacerdotal activity, ecclesiastics shall enjoy the protection of the State in the same manner as the employees of the State. Offenses to their persons and to their quality as ecclesiastics, as well as interference in the exercise of their ministry, shall be punished under the terms of the general laws of the State, and protection on the part of the civil authorities when necessary is guaranteed. . . .

ARTICLE 9. Ecclesiastics shall not be required by magistrates or other authorities to give information on things or affairs which have been entrusted to them in the exercise of the care of souls and which for that reason fall under the secrecy of their spiritual office. . . .

ARTICLE 14. The Catholic Church, in principle, has the right to confer freely all the ecclesiastical offices and benefices, without the assistance of the State or the municipality, with the exception of the cases provided for in the accords established in the Concordats to which reference is made in Article 2. . . .

In addition, there shall be agreement on the following points:

1. Catholic priests who fill, in Germany, an ecclesiastical charge or who exercise an activity in the care of souls or in education must:

(a) Be German citizens;

(b) Have obtained a diploma which entitles them to attend a German higher institution of learning;

(c) Have at least finished three years of philosophical and theological studies either in a German university of the State or in a German ecclesiastical academy, or in a Pontifical university of Rome.

2. Before releasing Bulls of nomination of archbishops, bishops or coadjutors *cum jure successionis*, or any *praelatus nullius*, the name of the person chosen shall be made known to the Reichstatthalter of the respective State so as to assure that there are no objections to him of a general political character. . . .

ARTICLE 16. The bishops, before taking possession of their dioceses, shall place in the hands of the Reichstatthalter of the particular State, or else into the hands of the President of the Reich, an oath of allegiance according to the following formula: "Before God and on the Holy Gospels, I swear and promise, as is proper to a bishop, allegiance to the German Reich and to the State of. . . . I swear and promise to respect and cause to be respected by my clergy the Government established according to the constitutional laws of the State. Concerning myself, in dutiful solicitude for the welfare and interest of the German State, I will try, in the exercise of the holy ministry entrusted to me, to ward off all harm that might threaten it.". . .

ARTICLE 20. Except for other accords in force; the Church has the right to erect, for the training of the clergy, schools of philosophy and theology which depend exclusively on ecclesiastical authority, provided no State subsidy is claimed.

The erection, the direction and management of seminaries and ecclesiastical boarding schools shall be the concern of the ecclesiastical authorities alone, within the limits of the general laws in force.

ARTICLE 21. The teaching of the Catholic religion in the elementary, vocational, secondary and superior schools shall be a regular subject and shall be given in conformity with the principles of the Catholic Church. . . .

ARTICLE 23. The preservation and new erection of Catholic confessional schools shall remain guaranteed. In all the communities where parents, or those who hold the place of parents, propose it, elementary Catholic schools shall be conducted if it shall appear that, taking into account the number of pupils and the local conditions of school organization, it is possible to operate the school according to the terms of the regulations of the State. . . .

ARTICLE 27. To the German Army shall be conceded special services for Catholic officers, functionaries and soldiers belonging to the Army and their respective families.

The direction of the spiritual assistance to the Army belongs to the

Military Bishop. His ecclesiastical nomination shall be made by the Holy See, after the latter has been in communication with the Government of the Reich in order to name a suitable person. . . .

ARTICLE 31. Catholic organizations and associations which have exclusively religious, cultural and charitable aims, and which as such depend upon ecclesiastical authority, shall be protected in their institutions and in their activity. . . .

Wherever youth organizations—for sports or other purposes—exist and are supported by the Reich or the particular State, care shall be taken to make it possible for members to fulfill their religious duties on Sundays and Holy Days and to remove any obligation to do anything incompatible with their convictions and with their religious or moral duties.

ARTICLE 32. By reason of the present particular circumstances of Germany and in consideration of the guaranties created by the dispositions of the present Concordat, legislation which safeguards the rights and liberties of the Catholic Church in the Reich and in the States, the Holy See shall enact dispositions excluding ecclesiastics and religious from membership in political parties and from activity in this respect. . . .

ARTICLE 34. The present Concordat, the German and Italian texts of which shall have equal force, shall be ratified and the instruments of the ratifications shall be exchanged as soon as possible. It shall enter into effect the day of the exchange of the said instruments.

36. Hereditary Farm Law: The Nazi Government Seeks to Preserve the German Peasantry as the Blood Source of German Society, September 29, 1933

"A peasant must be a German citizen, of German or kindred blood. . . ."

On September 29, 1933, Hitler enacted a special law designed to create a farmer or yeoman aristocracy. The *Erdhofgesetz* was passed to establish more than 800,000 peasant families on plots of land called *Erbhofe* (hereditary estates), which could not be sold or mortgaged but had to be transmitted primarily through the male line. The *Fuehrer* hoped that by furthering good housing conditions he could raise the birth rate. In addition, he believed that Germany's future leaders would come from this hereditary small-landholding nobility of good Aryan descent. Following are the main provisions of the Hereditary Farm Law.

THE NATIONAL GOVERNMENT wishes to preserve the peasantry through the ancient German method of inheritance as the blood source of the German people.

The farms [covered by this law] shall be protected against excessive debts and breakdown through inheritance, in order that they remain permanently as heritages of the clan and in possession of free peasants.

Attempts will be made to assure a healthy partition of the large landed estates, because the existence of many prosperous small and medium-sized farms, distributed as equally as possible over the entire country, offers the best guarantee for a vigorous people and state.

Reichsgesetzblatt, vol. 1, no. 108, September 30, 1933, pp. 685-92. Translated by the editor.

The National Government has, therefore, decided on the following law. The fundamentals are:

ARTICLE 1. Land and forestry property of a minimum size of one soil subsistence and a maximum of 125 hectares [just under four acres] makes up a Hereditary Farm, if it is in possession of an individual belonging to the peasant class.

The owner of a Hereditary Farm is called a peasant.

A peasant must be a German citizen, of German or kindred blood, and is a man of honor.

The Hereditary Farm passes without being divided to the heir apparent.

All claims of joint heirs are limited to the remaining property of the peasant. Those descendants who are not classed as heirs apparent are to be given vocational training and a status consonant with the capabilities of the farm.

The Hereditary Farm is inalienable and unattachable.

ARTICLE 2. . . . (2.) The exact amount of land is to be regarded as a soil subsistence necessary to feed and clothe a family independently of market conditions and the general economy and to maintain the economic life of the farm. . . .

ARTICLE 15. The peasant must be an honorable man. He must be able to work his farm in orderly fashion. . . .

ARTICLE 20. The heirs to the farms are designated in this order:

1. The sons of the testator (the sons and grandsons take the place of a deceased son);

2. The father of the testator;

3. The brothers of the testator (the sons and grandsons take the place of a deceased brother);

4. The daughters of a testator (the sons and grandsons take the place of a deceased daughter);

5. The sisters of the testator (the sons and grandsons take the place of a deceased sister);

6. The female descendants of the testator and their descendants. . . . He who is closer to the male line of the testator excludes anyone who is more remote. In all other cases the male line has preference. . . .

ARTICLE 31. The surviving spouse of the testator may, when self-support is impossible, demand from the heir lifelong support on the farm in the customary circumstances.

37. Law to Promote National Labor: The German Worker Is Brought Under State Control, January 20, 1934

> *"It is the duty of the Council to promote mutual*
> *trust within the works community. . . ."*

The theory of national socialism, like that of Italian fascism, rejected the idea of an inevitable conflict between capital and labor. Slightly less than a year after Hitler came to political power, a special law was enacted to regulate labor. The act maintained the principle of leadership and stressed the national above individual welfare. Following is the official summary of the extensive act.

Leader of the Undertaking and Trust Council
The Act provides that within each undertaking the employer, as head or "Leader" (*Fuehrer*) of the undertaking, and his salaried and wage-earning employees as his "Followers" (*Gefolgschaft*) shall work together to promote the objects of the undertaking and the common welfare of people and State. The head of the undertaking is responsible toward his staff for all decisions affecting the business, and must seek to promote the welfare of his employees, who in turn must serve him with the loyalty on which the works community is founded.

The employer, or in the case of incorporated persons or groups of persons, his lawful representative, may delegate a person holding a responsible post in the management of the undertaking to act for him, and must do so when he does not himself conduct the business. For the purposes of the Act the term "undertaking" also includes the management.

International Labor Office, *Industrial and Labor Information* (Geneva: International Labor Office, 1934), pp. 245-50.

The Act does not, however, apply to the crews of craft engaged in maritime, inland and air navigation, or to wage-earning and salaried employees in the public services.

In undertakings normally employing not less than twenty persons, the head of the undertaking will be assisted by counsellors chosen from among the staff, who will act in an advisory capacity and form, with the head of the undertaking and under his leadership, the "Trust Council" of the undertaking. It is the duty of the Council to promote mutual trust within the works community and to discuss any measures for the improvement of work, the establishment and maintenance of general conditions of employment, and in particular of rules of employment, the maintenance and improvement of safety conditions in the undertaking, the promotion among all members of the undertaking of a spirit of solidarity both among themselves and with the undertaking, and the welfare of all members of the community. The Council must also try to settle all disputes arising within the undertaking and must be consulted prior to the infliction of any fines provided for in the rules of employment. The Council may delegate particular duties to its individual members.

In order to be eligible to serve on the Council an employee must be not less than twenty-five years of age and must have had at least one year's service in the business or undertaking concerned and at least two years' service in the same or an allied occupation or industry. He must be in full possession of his civil rights, must be a member of the German Labor Front, and must offer evidence of exemplary human qualities and every assurance that in all circumstances he will unreservedly support the interests of the national State. The head of the undertaking, in agreement with the Chief of the organization for establishing National Socialist "cells" in business undertakings, must draw up a list of the councillors and their substitutes in March of every year.

The staff of the undertaking is required to elect the Council from this list by secret ballot. If no Council is formed in this manner, the Labor Trustee has power to appoint the requisite number of councillors.

The Council must be convened as required by the head of the undertaking and must in any case be convened if a meeting is demanded by at least half the members. The duties of its members are honorary and may not be rewarded by payment, but the regular wage must be paid on account of any working time spent by members in performance of their duties. Any necessary expenditure must be borne by the management, which must also place at the disposal of the Council all facilities and institutions necessary for the conduct of its business and the orderly discharge of its duties. The Labor Trustee may cancel the appointment of any member of the Council on account of his practical or personal unsuitability.

The Council may by a majority decision appeal directly in writing to the Labor Trustee against any decision taken by the head of the undertaking in respect of general conditions of employment, and in particular of the rules of employment, which does not appear to be justified by the social or economic conditions of the undertaking. The enforcement of the decision contested is not stayed by the lodging of an appeal. The Labor Trustee has power to rescind the decision and himself issue the necessary regulations.

Labor Trustees

A Labor Trustee will be appointed for every large industrial area. It will be the duty of this officer to promote the maintenance of industrial peace, and in pursuance of this object:

(1) To supervise the constitution and procedure of the Trust Council and give a decision in any case of dispute:

(2) To appoint and dismiss members of the Council in cases specified in the Act;

(3) To investigate, on appeal by a majority of the Trust Council, decisions of the leader of the undertaking concerning the establishment of general conditions of employment, and in particular, of the rules of employment, and, if necessary, himself to take the necessary action;

(4) In the event of extensive dismissals, to undertake the duties hitherto devolving upon the Commissioner for dismissals under the Decree concerning the closing down of undertakings;

(5) To supervise the application of the provisions concerning rules of employment;

(6) To supervise the principles and provisions of collective rules and their application;

(7) To co-operate in enforcing the jurisdiction of the Social Honor Courts (see below);

(8) To keep the German Government regularly informed as to the development of social conditions in such manner as the Federal Minister of Labor and the Federal Minister of Economy may require.

The Federal Minister of Labor and the Federal Minister of Economy may allot to the Labor Trustee further duties under the Act.

The Decree concerning the closing down of undertakings is repealed. It is provided, however, that the Labor Trustee must be notified beforehand of any extensive dismissals contemplated, and that these may not take effect until a time-limit of four weeks has expired. This time-limit may be extended by the Labor Trustee to not more than two months. As under the provisions of the repealed Decree, the Labor Trustee may authorize the working of short time until the expiry of this period.

Deputy Labor Trustees may be appointed by the Federal Minister of Labor as required by the extent and special economic conditions of the industrial area concerned; to them the Federal Minister of Labor or the Labor Trustee may delegate all or part of the latter's functions in respect of a certain district or a certain branch of industry or of specified duties.

Any person who deliberately and persistently disregards general regulations issued in writing by the Labor Trustee in the execution of his duties is liable to a fine, which in especially serious cases may be replaced or supplemented by imprisonment. Proceedings in such cases may be opened only on the application of the Labor Trustee.

The Labor Trustee may appoint an expert board of advisers recruited from the various branches of industry within his jurisdiction, for consultation on general questions or matters of principle connected with his duties. In special cases, and more particularly prior to issuing collective rules, the Labor Trustee may also appoint a special committee of experts.

Rules of Employment and Collective Rules

Rules of employment for the staff must be drawn up in writing by the head of every undertaking normally employing at least twenty persons. These rules must cover the following conditions of employment:

(1) Beginning and end of normal daily hours of work and breaks;

(2) Date and manner of payment of wages and salaries;

(3) Principles for the calculation of piece or job work, where these systems are in force;   .

(4) Provisions concerning the nature, amount and collection of fines, where these are provided for;

(5) Reasons justifying summary dismissal without notice (apart from those laid down by law);

(6) Application of the sums due as compensation for unlawful breach of the relationship between employer and employee, in so far as this is payable under law, rules of employment, or contract of employment.

In addition to the above requirements of the Act, the rules of employment may also lay down provisions governing the rates of remuneration and other conditions of employment, and also further regulations respecting the conduct of the undertaking, the behavior of the employees in the undertaking and the prevention of accidents.

Where the rules of employment fix the remuneration due to wage-earning and salaried employees, minimum rates must be fixed, which nevertheless must leave scope for the remuneration of individual employees according to the quality of their services. In general also provision must be made for the possibility of appropriately rewarding special services. The provisions contained in the rules of employment are legally binding on the employer as minimum rates for his employees. The Labor Trustee, after consulting a committee of experts, may lay down guiding principles for the establishment of rules of employment and of individual contracts of employment. If it is urgently necessary for the protection of the employees of a given group of undertakings included within the district of the Labor Trustee that minimum standard conditions of employment should be established, the Labor Trustee, after consulting the committee of experts, may issue collective rules in writing, the terms of which are binding as minimum standards for the employments which they cover. Any provisions of rules of employment which conflict with these standards are void. The Labor Trustee may expressly withdraw any disputes arising out of the relations between employees and apprentices and their employers from the jurisdiction of the civil courts by stipulating that they shall be decided by an arbitration court.

The Labor Trustee may similarly issue collective rules to regulate the relations of home-workers with the employers whose orders they carry out. The Federal Minister of Labor or the Labor Trustee may deal in the same way with other home-workers, middlemen and independent workers of similar standing who are not economically independent.

Social Honor Court

Each member of a works community is responsible for the conscientious performance of the duties entailed by his position in that community. His conduct must be such as to deserve the consideration attaching to his position, and in particular he must be constantly mindful of his duty to devote his energies wholeheartedly to the services of the undertaking and to subordinate himself to the general good.

Any person who flagrantly disregards the social duties arising out of his membership of a works community will be charged before an Honor Court with offending against social honor. These duties will be deemed to have been disregarded by the following persons:

(1) Industrialists, heads of undertakings or other persons in supervisory positions who maliciously abuse their authority in the undertaking to exploit the labor of the employees or offend against their honor;

(2) Employees who endanger industrial peace in the undertaking by maliciously fostering discontent among their fellows, and in particular those who as members of the Trust Council deliberately exercise unjustifiable interference in the management or continually and maliciously try to undermine the corporate spirit of the undertaking;

(3) Members of the works community who repeatedly address frivolous and baseless complaints and appeals to the Labor Trustee or who persistently contravene his written instructions;

(4) Members of the Trust Council guilty of the unauthorized publication of confidential information concerning industrial or business secrets obtained in performance of their duties and of the confidential nature of which they were informed.

Public servants and soldiers are exempted from the jurisdiction of the Honor Courts.

The penalties which may be inflicted by the Honor Courts are: warning, reprimand, fine up to 10,000 marks, disqualification to act as leader of an undertaking or member of a Trust Council, removal to a different place of employment.

The procedure of the Honor Courts is mainly governed by the provisions of the code of penal procedure applicable to penal proceedings within the jurisdiction of the regional courts, but without the cooperation of the official legal services.

Cases relating to offences against social honor will be decided, on application by the Labor Trustee, by an Honor Court to be set up in each Labor Trustee's district. Each of these courts will consist of a chairman, who must be a public magistrate, and one leader of an undertaking and one member of a Trust Council as assessors. The leader of the undertaking and the member of the Trust Council are appointed by the chairman of the court from lists nominated by the German Labor Front.

Complaints concerning offences against social honor must be submitted to the Labor Trustee, who will investigate their substance.

If the chairman of the court, who may himself undertake further inquiries, considers that the Trustee's complaint is well founded, he may inflict a penalty in the form of a warning, reprimand, or fine of not more than 100 marks. Appeal against his decision may be lodged by the accused person or by the Labor Trustee. If the chairman does not decide the case himself, proceedings will be opened before the Honor Court, the Trustee being authorized to attend the principal proceedings and to submit proposals.

Appeal against decisions of the Honor Court may be made to the Federal Court of Honor, consisting of two higher officials of the magistrature, one leader of an undertaking, and one member of a Trust Council.

Protection against Dismissal

Any wage-earning or salaried employee dismissed after at least one year's service from an undertaking normally employing at least ten workers may appeal to the Labor Court against his dismissal if the latter is unduly harsh and is not justified by the conditions of the undertaking. No such appeal may be made, however, if the dismissal was in accordance with law or with collective rules. The appeal must be accompanied by a certificate from the Trust Council stating that the matter has already been discussed in the Council without effect.

If the Court decides that the dismissal should be cancelled it must also fix the compensation due from the employer in the event of his refusal to comply with the judgment, and the employer must then state whether he prefers to reinstate the worker or to pay the compensation.

The amount of the compensation is fixed proportionately to the length of service, but may not exceed four-twelfths of the last annual earnings of the person concerned.

Final and Transitional Provisions

Except for certain provisions, the Act will come into force on 1 May, 1934.

Leaders and employees of the legal advice centers set up by the German Labor Front, and the official lawyers authorized by the German Labor Front to represent a party in a particular case, will in future have full powers of representation in cases before the Labor Courts.

The Federal Minister of Labor has power to issue further regulations to administer and supplement the Act.

Lastly, it is provided that collective agreements in force at 1 December 1933 or which come into force after that date shall remain operative until 30 April 1934, failing their revision or suspension before that date by the Labor Trustee.

38. Law for the Reorganization of the Reich: Hitler Decrees Legality for His Dictatorship, January 30, 1934

"The popular assemblies . . . are hereby abolished."

On January 30, 1934, precisely one year after his assumption of political power as chancellor, Hitler issued a basic law for the reorganization of the German Reich. His purpose was to give legality to his dictatorship.

ARTICLE 1. The popular assemblies of the individual States are hereby abolished.

ARTICLE 2. (1.) The sovereign rights of individual States are hereby transferred to the Reich.

(2.) The governments of the individual States are to be subordinate to the Reich Government.

ARTICLE 3. The Federal Governors of the States are to be supervised by the Reich Minister of the Interior.

ARTICLE 4. The Reich Government may draw up new constitutional laws.

ARTICLE 5. The Reich Minister of the Interior is responsible for issuing the necessary legal decrees and administrative measures for implementing this law.

ARTICLE 6. This law becomes effective on the day of its promulgation.

Translated by the editor from the official text.

39. Propaganda Minister Goebbels Addresses the Film Industry at Kroll Opera House, February 9, 1934

"Then will the German film conquer its own people
as well as the entire world."

Dr. Paul Joseph Goebbels was assigned to use the full resources of the state for Hitler's policy of *Gleichschaltung* (coordination). For this work the propaganda minister utilized to the full a law passed on September 22, 1933, which formed the *Reichskulturkammer* (Reich Chamber of Culture). This chamber was divided originally into seven subordinate organizations for literature, music, theater, radio, fine arts, press, and films. Membership was compulsory for everyone in a specific profession. Anyone denied membership was in effect excluded from his profession.

Goebbels, a onetime unsuccessful playwright, was intensely interested in the film world. It was widely rumored throughout Germany that he had many liaisons with film actresses who could profit by association with him. On one occasion he was said to have been beaten badly by the husband of a film actress.

On February 9, 1934, Goebbels delivered an address at the Kroll Opera House to a gathering of all the important filmmakers in Germany. He took the opportunity to explain the role of films in the Third Reich. Following is a condensed version of this long speech.

IT IS NOW ALMOST a year since I spoke in my official capacity concerning the German film industry. At that time I could not very well talk about accomplishments, because we were faced with a negative situation, that is,

Völkischer Beobachter, February 11-12, 1934. Translated by the editor.

we had to give priority to the damages that had been done during the past fourteen years. Despite this I believed at that time that I could give all film producers good hopes for the future, because I was convinced, as has so often happened in history, that after such great political changes there would be great artistic and cultural innovations.

In my speech at the Kaiserhof I mentioned specifically that the uncertainty of the times could not be blamed on us because we were concerned with the matter of achieving political power. One thing was fundamentally changed: the latent crisis which lay over Germany was ended. One did not any longer need to fear that the ministers who were introducing reforms would fall from power. Since January thirtieth of the preceding year everybody knows that this regime is going to last forever. The situation has become stabilized, not only in political but also in industrial and artistic-cultural life.

The opponents of National Socialism have accused us of being cultural barbarians, that we are people who do not have the least interest in artistic things. But now creative Germany has learned the truth of the words of our *Fuehrer*, which he expressed three years before he became Chancellor. He said at that time that German artists, man for man, would rally behind our colors when they saw what we intended to do for them. Now we have had some twelve months to translate these words into deeds.

Since the time twelve months ago that I spoke for the first time about the German film industry, it has won its way past its most difficult economic and artistic crisis. No one can judge that better than those who do their daily work in German films.

We are convinced that films provide one of the most modern and economically feasible ways of influencing the masses. The government, therefore, must pay close attention to them.

We regard films, as we do every form of artistic and cultural activity, with a warm and passionate heart. We have looked upon films from above not only with the purpose of preventing them from causing bad trouble but also to give them official guidance. I believe that there does not exist in the whole world a government whose leader and minister of culture, in their first year after assuming political power, have seen almost every film produced in their country.

We have not been picayune nor bureaucratic in our attitude, but on the contrary we have been as generous as possible, because we realize that art demands generosity. An administration must hold strong reins on the inner discipline of its people, and must hold them even more tightly when they concern cultural and intuitive matters. Many film producers do not know with what warmth we have greeted their creative work and how thankful we are to them.

And now let us take a short glimpse into what we have accomplished in the year 1933 in the field of filmmaking. How did it look at the beginning of that year? Production was in chaos. There was a dark feeling of depression and a feeling that things had to be changed.

Meanwhile, the people were marching through lighted streets to a new future. German art has to thank us that we did not allow it to be separated from the people, but that we led the people back to German art.

That was something that had to be done if German films were not to lose their worldwide reputation.

The German public, after four years of war and twelve years of the Weimar Republic, finally came to recognize a movement motivated not by money but by idealism.

The desperate situation also had an effect on the finances of the film industry. Money was forthcoming only for junk films, because it was believed that only such films could pay their way. The tendency was to destroy films as an art form and use them only for simple amusement. It is in the nature of capital that it never thinks in terms of conviction or art or noble intentions, but always in terms of augmenting its value, doubling it or even increasing it threefold.

An attempt was made to overcome a dangerous situation through the production of monster films. The results were catastrophic, especially with those films which were meant to be artistic but which were not artistically made.

Then came experiments which were meant to be sure-fire and stable, such as military films and entertainment films and trashy operettas.

The idea was not to burden the filmgoer with deep ideas, because they were supposed to be the children of their day.

Indeed, the film world itself must bear to a great extent the blame for this state of affairs.

The result of all this was that honorable and struggling artists gradually began to desert the film world.

In courageous days art was without courage. In heroic times art was without heroism.

The decent German public has long since rejected this form of art. It fled to those who understood its needs. There it could find the realization of its longing. There it could find goals and ideals. There it could find exaltation, there a sense of character and heroism.

When we took over political power, the directors sat in their empty film ateliers. They had no more money. They did not even have a public. They did not know where to begin. Gradually the situation began to change for the better. Without a people there is no art, and without art there is no sense of fulfillment. The whole cultural world was in the process of capitulating to this breakdown. We took over this legacy.

We came to the decision to take up the struggle against this skepticism, and indeed we did so with every means at our disposal. The most important thing that had to be solved was the problem of organization, without giving the illusion that everything could be solved by that alone. But the organization had to be freed from its restrictions. For this reason we brought together in one over-all chamber all those who in any way had to do with the production of films [Reichsfilmkammer]. Our goal here was to serve only art and to do away with all restrictions that stood in the way.

The fact that we have not yet been completely successful is in large part due to you. It cannot be the task of the administration to create a genius. A genius appears spontaneously in life, and does not ask if he can appear on the scene. And the genius will find ways to achieve what he wants to achieve.

The ateliers are now filled once again with the stuff of life. Because we cannot expect the private capital market to spring forward all at once, we have arranged for state subventions, always with the secret hope that once the wheels are smoothed the private capital market will step in again.

I have begun an attempt to exert a favorable influence on the film critics. At the meeting of the Reichskulturkammer [on November 14, 1933], I declared that the German press seems to operate from either of two viewpoints: it criticizes everything that comes to its attention, or it criticizes nothing at all. In that way criticism loses its positive character.

A critic, who in the field of any artistic activity has contributed nothing himself, just does not have the right to look down at his nose at every artistic creation and condemn it. The critic must constantly be on his guard lest he by some nasty criticism destroy the life of an individual and, perhaps, in that way rob the nation of a great talent.

For some time now I have been working with the Reich Finance Minister and I believe that already today I can report to you that in a short time, in conjunction with important Reich tax reform, the entertainment tax on films will be lifted.

That will be an important step in the consolidation of the German film industry.

National Socialism is a philosophy of life, and it covers all of life. We can see in our very own existence how it has gradually changed all of us. Things which two years ago seemed altogether impossible have been achieved today. Everywhere in public life we see a return to a sense of nobility and solidity, a sense which encompasses everyone, and which makes all equal.

This is the kind of feeling I look for in art, and that feeling the German people, too, want to see. This sentiment, which today has moved millions of people to heroic sacrifice, will also permeate those who appear on the boards and before the camera. That does not mean that we act like puritanical parsons or preachers of morality who want to drive every witty conversation from the theater or the screen. We know well how much the German public today needs a little joy in its life.

We want to transfer this feeling not only to the area of art, but we want with it an open, free, and noble attitude toward life.

I do not want this evening to pass by without expressing to you my thanks for your active help for the administration. I also want to assure you that I have the intention of helping you and with that to help German films conquer the world.

You can, indeed, be proud of the fact that you are working in the field of German art. There is in life no greater happiness than to work for the welfare of a people. That is the greatest joy that a man can have, and the more he works in this way the greater will be his responsibility, but also his sense of accomplishment.

I am convinced that the German film will not conquer the world if it remains colorless and wishy-washy. The German film will conquer the world when it appears as a German film, when it reveals our essence, our character, our virtue, and if you wish, even our weaknesses. Then will the German film conquer its own people as well as the entire world and will win back artistic recognition among other peoples. Then will immortal Germany march over the silver screen.

40. The *Horst Wessel Lied*: The Nazis Find Their Poet of the Barricades

"Prepared for war and battle here we stand."

For some time Dr. Goebbels had been searching for a poet who could furnish him with a revolutionary song. He found his man in Horst Wessel, son of a Protestant chaplain, a student, a Nazi, and a Storm Trooper. A mixture of young idealist and street-brawling ruffian, Horst Wessel became a drop-out and went to live in the slums of Berlin with a former prostitute. A leader of the Nazis in his neighborhood, he took part in many street battles with the Communists. In February 1930, a gang composed of Communists or instigated by Communists invaded his room and killed him.

Horst Wessel left behind him a marching song of three stanzas that skillfully pieced together several Nazi slogans and which was set to the catchy music of several familiar tunes. This became the official song of the Nazi party and later the second official anthem of Germany after "Deutschland über Alles."

After Wessel's death, Dr. Goebbels used his propaganda apparatus to make Wessel a hero of national socialism, an idealistic youth who had given his life for the cause. Anti-Nazis labeled the minister's son a pimp, but this charge was undoubtedly exaggerated.

Translated by the editor.

1.

Die Fahne hoch, die Reihen dicht geschlossen!
S.A. marschiert mit ruhig festem Schritt.
Kam'raden, die Rotfront und Reaktion erschossen,
Marschieren im Geist in unsern Reihen mit.

2.

Die Strasse frei den braunen Bataillonen!
Die Strasse frei dem Sturmabteilungsmann!
Es schaun aufs Hakenkreuz voll Hoffnung schon Millionen,
Der Tag für Freiheit und für Brot bricht an.

3.

Zum letzten Mal wird nun Appell geblasen!
Zum Kämpfe stehn wir alle schon bereit.
Bald flattern Hitlerfahnen über allen Strassen,
Die Knechtschaft dauert nur noch kurze Zeit! . . .

1.

Hold high the banner! Close the hard ranks serried!
S.A. marches on with sturdy stride.
Comrades, by Red Front and Reaction killed, are buried,
But march with us in image at our side.

2.

Gangway! Gangway now for the Brown Battalions!
For the Storm Trooper clear roads o'er the land!
The Swastika gives hope to our entranced millions,
The day for freedom and for bread's at hand.

3.

The trumpet blows its shrill and final blast!
Prepared for war and battle here we stand.
Soon Hitler's banners will wave unchecked at last,
The end of German slav'ry in our land!

41. Nazi Ideology — I: Alfred Rosenberg, Official Nazi Philosopher, Discourses on the Myth of the Blood

"Nordic blood represents the mystery which has
replaced and overcome the old Sacraments."

Alfred Rosenberg (1893–1946), prophet-laureate of national social-ism, first published *The Myth of the Twentieth Century* in 1930. By 1938 the book had run into 142 editions and had sold 713,000 copies. For Rosenberg the key to the twentieth century was "the myth of Blood, which under the sign of the swastika unchained the racial world-revolution." "It is the awakening of the race-soul, which after long sleep victoriously ends the race-chaos." *The Myth* is a racial view of history, in contrast with the socio-economic interpretations usually made of the French and Russian world-revolutions. The following brief excerpts give an indication of the style of Rosenberg's writing and thinking.

A NEW EPOCH BEGINS TODAY in which world history will be written anew. The old conceptions of the human past have faded away. . . . A young but ancient feeling of life demands expression, a world view is born. . . .

A new and colorful picture of human and earthly history is beginning to be unveiled today, if we recognize honorably that we must investigate the division between blood and milieu, between blood and blood. But this recognition also includes the knowledge that the struggle of bloods and the mysticism of life are not two different things, but one and the same thing. Race is the symbolic expression of a soul. Racial virtue has a value in itself. . . .

Alfred Rosenberg, *Der Mythus des 20. Jahrhunderts* (Munich: n.p., 1934), pp. 21-23, 116-18 and passim. Translated by the editor.

Racial history is equivalent to natural history and the mystical soul. The history of the religion of the blood is the story of the rise and fall of peoples, of their heroes and thinkers, their inventors and artists. . . . A cultured nation will concede to no one the right to judge its creations, by censuring them as good or bad, right or wrong. . . . Each race has its soul, and each soul belongs to a race. . . . Each race produces in the long run only one supreme ideal. . . . This supreme value demands a definite grouping of the other life-values, which are conditioned by it. It thus determines the character of a race, of a people. . . .

If we tolerate, at the same time, and in the same place, two or more world outlooks, each one related to a different supreme value, which the *same* people are to share . . . we have sown the germs of a new catastrophe. . . .

History no longer means war of class against class nor of church dogma and dogma, but blood and blood, race and race. . . .

Soul means race, inwardly discerned. Conversely, race is the external aspect of a soul. . . .

Nordic blood represents that mystery which has replaced and overcome the old Sacraments. . . .

The race-bound national soul is the measure of all our thoughts, aspirations of will and deeds, the final criterion of our values. . . .

The foibles of our heroes ought not to be glossed over, but the eternal, the mythical, behind them ought to be intuited and formulated by the questing soul. In this very way there will arise a series of heroic spirits: Odin, Siegfried, Widukind, Frederick II (the Hohenstaufen), Eckehart, von der Vogelweide, Luther, Frederick the Great, Bach, Goethe, Beethoven, Schopenhauer, Bismarck. . . . To serve this new evolution is the mission of the school in the coming German Reich. It is its most important if not its only task in the decades to come to make the new evaluation self-evident to all Germans.

42. Nazi Ideology — II: Professor Hermann Gauch Compares Nordics with Non-Nordics

"It has not been proved that non-Nordics cannot mate with apes."

The teachings of Count Arthur de Gobineau, a Frenchman, and Houston Stewart Chamberlain, a Germanized Anglo-Saxon, became the basis for racial theory in the Third Reich. The idea of race purity (*Rassenreinheit*), called for by Hitler in *Mein Kampf*, was pursued with fanatical intensity by Nazi intellectuals. Its general tone may be ascertained from this statement by Professor Ernst Hauer: "Blood is sacred. It contains, from ancient times, the generating mystery of families, tribes and peoples. . . . The origin of the spirit is in the blood. There is a Divine power in the blood which forms human beings in conformity with their predestined patterns. . . . It thus comes about that we so ardently love blood and soil and fatherland and the history of our people with all its struggles, that we profoundly worship all this because God himself meets us here, materialized and immediate."

In the Third Reich, the disciplines of *Rassenkunde* (study of race) and *Rassenforschung* (racial research) were elevated to the plane of respectable "sciences." A standard work used in classrooms was Professor Hermann Gauch's *Neue Grundlagen der Rassenforschung* (New Foundations of Racial Research). In this book Gauch reclassified the animal world into Nordic men and lower animals (other races, including Jews).

Herman Gauch, *Neue Grundlagen der Rassenforschung* (Berlin, n.d.), pp. 165-66. Translated by the editor.

In NON-NORDICS, THE TEETH, corresponding to the snoutlike narrowness of the upper jaw, stand at a more oblique angle than in animals. The grinding motion of chewing in Nordics allows mastication to take place with the mouth closed, whereas men of other races are inclined to make the same smacking noise as animals. . . .

The Nordic mouth has further superiorities. Just as the color red has a stirring effect, the bright red mouth of Nordics attracts and provokes kisses and courtship. The Nordic mouth is kiss-capable. On the other hand, the non-Nordic's broad, thick-lipped mouth together with his wide-dilated nostrils display sensual eagerness, a false and malicious sneering expression and a dipping movement indicative of voluptuous self-indulgence.

Talking with the aid of hands and feet is characteristic of non-Nordics, whereas the Nordic man stands calmly, often enough with his hands in his pockets.

Generally speaking, the Nordic race alone can emit sounds of untroubled clearness, whereas among non-Nordics the pronunciation is impure, the individual sounds are more confused and like the noises made by animals, such as barking, sniffing, snoring, squeaking. . . . That birds can learn to talk better than other animals is explained by the fact that their mouths are Nordic in structure — that is to say, high, narrow, and short-tongued. The shape of the Nordic gum allows a superior movement of the tongue, which is the reason why Nordic talking and singing are fuller. . . .

If non-Nordics are more closely allied to monkeys and apes than to Nordics, why is it possible for them to mate with Nordics and not with apes? The answer is this: it has not been proved that non-Nordics cannot mate with apes.

43. Nazi Ideology — III: Ewald Banse, Professor of Military Science, Publishes a Book Approving German Militarism

"The sword will come into its own. . . ."

Immediately after Hitler took office, Ewald Banse was appointed professor of political science at Brunswick Technical College. His appointment was in all probability due to the fact that he had already published several books on military and geographical subjects which had attracted the attention of Hitler. Banse published *Raum und Volk im Weltkriege* (Space and People in World War), which was in effect a handbook on German militarism. He praised national sentiment as "self-respect and healthy egoism," and denounced international sentiment as "self-abandonment and a degeneration of the tissues."

The British quickly recognized a major propaganda weapon in Banse's ill-timed book. A British book agent signed a contract for an English translation in November 1933. The German government announced that the book was to be confiscated: "This book has unfortunately given anti-German propaganda abroad occasion to throw doubt on the peace policy of the government. . . . The German government is resolved not to allow its policy of peace to be the least disturbed by the propagandist exploitation of such private works." Despite threats of copyright violation, the British publisher went ahead and published the book under the title *Germany Prepares for War: A Nazi Theory of "National Defense."* Widely distributed, it later became an effective Allied propaganda instrument in World War II.

Ewald Banse, *Germany Prepares for War: A Nazi Theory of "National Defense"* (London and New York: n.p., 1934), pp. xix, 4-6, 56, 57, 347.

Significantly, though apparently disavowed by the Nazi regime, Banse retained his academic post and even wrote other books on the same subject. His *Wehrwissenschaft* (Military Science) again presented his view of war as a regeneration in which people may find true glory and his belief that in the waging of war not the means but the end must be considered.

Following are excerpts from Banse's *Raum und Volk im Weltkriege.*

THE SWORD WILL COME into its own again, and the pen, after fourteen years of exaggerated prestige, will be put in its place. The sword has lain rusting in the corner for fourteen years in the German countries, while the pen has had the stage to itself; and as a result we have gone to the dogs. Certainly, the pen is good, but the sword is good too and often far better, and we want both to be equally honored among the German people. A man can only protect himself against assault with the sword; if he tried to do it with the pen he would only make himself ridiculous and get the worst of it. . . .

War derives its nourishment from a country's spiritual and economic strength and translates it into military action through the agency of a leader; this in turn creates better opportunities for statesmanship than were previously forthcoming. . . .

Peace is the ideal state, but it carries with it the risk of stagnation and somnolence; war, on the contrary, is the grand stimulant and uplifter; quickening the whole pace of existence and opening up a completely different and, in most cases, novel world of ideas. . . .

Everything now depends on a highly exceptional order of activities, to do with discipline and the handling of arms, attacking and killing, heroism and contempt of death. While peace promises the industrious citizen a safe reward, war, by its very nature, does nothing of the kind to the hero. The citizen does the state the best service by keeping himself most carefully alive; the warrior does it his highest service when he falls. . . .

The actively warlike man is the man who does not fight to live, but lives to fight. War is his element. His eagle eye is ever on the alert for chances and opportunities of fighting; with his slight frame, which looks as if it were built for cutting through obstacles, he comes down like a wolf on the fold. This born warrior hurls himself without thinking into the mêlée; so far from trying to avoid or mitigate a quarrel, he looks for it and greets it with a cheer. For him battle is the everlasting yea, the fulfillment and justification of existence. He is hopelessly handicapped for the work of civil life; wherever swords are being sharpened in the world, there you will find his clear-cut profile. If he had his way, there would always be trouble somewhere. He will even put his sword at the disposal of a foreigner, if he provides him with a good fight. The essential Nordic original aristocracy of the West and beyond it has always been the largest contributor to this class, and has shed its blood on every battlefield in the world. Fighting for fighting's sake, not in defense of hearth and home, is the watchword of this kind. . . .

How utterly different . . . is the peace-loving man, the pacifist! Peace is the only state for which he is fitted and he will do anything to preserve it; he will endure any humiliation, including loss of liberty and even the most severe damage to his pocket, in order to avoid war. His dim, lusterless eye betokens servility (which does not rule out impertinence), his clumsy body is obviously built for toiling and stooping, his movements are slow and deliberate. This type is the born stay-at-home, small-minded, completely flummoxed by the smallest interruption of the normal course of events, looking at the whole world from the standpoint of his little ego and judging it accordingly. To this bourgeois or philistine, the warrior is the sworn foe, the deadly enemy who only exists to destroy his miserable rest. It remains a source of mixed wonder and horror to him that anybody can jeopardize his peace and security from mere pugnacity or on idealistic grounds. That is just the essential difference: the warrior . . . wagers his whole habitual existence, all he possesses, on the point of his sword, when it is a matter of maintaining his ego, his point of view, in a word, his honor, which is more to him than his individual life; the man of peace, be his muscles weak or strong, values honor and renown less than his own little life, which seems so great and important to him; he sets the individual destiny above the destiny of the nation. . . .

The lesson of World War I is that the German people, after inevitable convulsions, stand on the threshold of a national renaissance. Rejecting the poison of internationalism and pacifism, this renaissance dares once again to proclaim itself German on German territory. The German Renaissance has two principal missions: (1) to summon up the soul of Germany from the depths to perform its national, cultural and political task, so that on German soil all thought, all action and all speech shall be German; and (2) to combine German territory throughout its whole extent into a unified and therefore powerful state, whose boundaries will be far wider than those of 1914. . . .

Preparation for future wars must not stop at the creation, equipment and training of an efficient army, but must go on to train the minds of the whole people for the war and must employ all the resources of science to master the conditions governing the war itself and the possibility of endurance.

44. Twenty-Five Points of the German Religion: Professor Ernst Bergmann's Catechism for "Positive Christianity"

> *"The ethics of the German religion condemn . . .*
> *the Judeo-Christian idea of the fallen world and*
> *man."*

In the original Twenty-Five Points of the German Workers' party, Article 24 proclaimed liberty for all religious denominations "so far as they are not a danger to it and do not militate against the moral feelings of the German race." The party, it further stated, "stands for Positive Christianity." Despite guarantee of religious freedom, Nazi ideology became more and more critical of Christianity as an extension of unacceptable Judaism. Alfred Rosenberg, who eventually became the National Socialist party philosopher, denounced the "Oriental elements" of Christianity as unacceptable for German Aryan-Nordics. He insisted that there were fundamental differences between Christian mentality and the German mind.

In 1934, a year after Hitler became chancellor, Professor Ernst Bergmann wrote the following catechism which summarized the core of a new German religion, or what was called Positive Christianity. Eventually, there arose a German Faith movement (*Deutsche Glaubensbewegung*), which sought to subvert the old Protestant theology and replace it with a new religion more in consonance with Nazi ideology.

1. THE GERMAN HAS HIS OWN RELIGION, which flows like the living water of his own understanding, sentiment, and thought, and is engrained in his

---

Translated by the editor.

blood. We deem it to be the German religion, or the religion of the German people. We understand by it a German belief expressing the special character and the integrity of our race.

2. The German religion is a form of belief suited to our times, which we Germans would possess today if we had been able to come by our native German religion undisturbed.

3. The German today has need of a healthy and natural religion which makes him brave, pious, and strong in the struggle for people and Fatherland. This is the German religion.

4. The German religion has no dogmas because it is a religion.

5. The German religion is not to be regarded as a religion of revelation in the Christian form. It is based rather on a natural "revelation" of the divine will on earth and in the human mentality.

6. The German religion is a religion of the people. It has nothing in common with free thought, atheist propaganda, and the breakdown of current religions. We real followers of the German religion hold to a positive religion.

7. The German religion is not opposed to any Church. What it wants is a German Church representing a religious people.

8. The idea of God is a moral concept, which we believe is based on the eternal creative force of Nature, which works in the world and on man. Belief in a God of another world is of Semitic, not Indo-European, origin. This kind of belief in God is not consonant with true religion and piety.

9. The knowing Being or Mind grows inside the idea of a divine, living world. The mind is a natural outcome of the world of reality. It was not a completed thing at the beginning, but it became the goal of the apex of world development.

10. The will, understanding, and personality, all these belong to God's Being. They are, however, unique in that they are in the possession of man. Therefore, man takes the place of God on earth.

11. Man is not God. But he is the birthplace of God. God exists and appears in man. He never comes to earth. Therefore, the German religion is the religion of great faith in man.

12. The German religion recognizes no dualism or conflict between body and soul, any more than duality and conflict between God and the world and God and man. The body-soul, the Being, is a natural unity and complete in itself.

13. The living world is the womb of the high human mind. The All-Mother gives birth to Knowing, Being, and Mind. The concept of mother-child is, therefore, the correct expression of the God-world secret. We speak of a modern nature religion when we speak of the Mind-child God, who lives in the womb of the All-Mother.

14. The basic religious feelings are Union, Holiness, and Blessedness. On the other hand, the Christian sentiments of Sin, Guilt, and Repentance

are not really religious feelings. They are artificially engendered complexes in man.

15. The ethic of the German religion condemns the concept of inherited sin, and also the Judeo-Christian idea of a fallen world and man. This kind of teaching is not only non-Germanic but also immoral and non-religious. Anyone who practices this concept of sin is a menace to the morality of the people.

16. Anyone who is inclined to forgive sin, in reality sanctions sin. The act of forgiveness of sin really undermines religious ethics and tends to destroy the morale of the people.

17. At the heart of the German religious ethic stands a real understanding for the welfare of the people and the Fatherland, and not for the blessedness of the individual. Unlike the Christian ethic, the German ethic does not call for the salvation of the individual, but rather for the welfare of the people as a whole.

18. He who belongs to the German religion is not a slave of God, but actually lord of the divine power inside him. German ethics hence reject as non-German the concept of making man passive for receiving grace.

19. One cannot escape from life when he holds to the German religion, but he can be released into life. This statement holds true: Whoever loves man heals him before he is born, not before he dies. The real Saviour cares for man before he is born.

20. The ethic of the German religion is heroic. It is grounded on such German virtues as courage, chivalry, and faithfulness, all of which spring from the concept of honor.

21. We of the German religion demand the introduction of religious training in the schools. Christian instruction is no longer valid, because we do not believe Christianity to be a religion.

22. We of the German religion think of the Divine in images true to life, male-hero and woman-mother.

23. One of the two religious forms of the German religion is the Nordic Light-Hero, who embodies heroic manliness. This Nordic Light-Hero reflects the high human Mind and the heroic, helpful Leader. This image struggles triumphantly ahead as the Moral Ideal of the people.

24. The mother-child concept is the truest, most loving, sacred, and happiness-inducing of all the symbols of world and life. The mother figure is the original religious figure, from which the God-Father derives its splendor. In the German Church, alongside the manly-heroic figure is the faithful picture of the most blessed mother. This is necessary if the church is to be based on the laws of life.

25. The forms of the German religion and the German People's Church must be based on the living laws of thought behind them. The life of the family, the State, and the nation, must be reflected in a natural way, if the church is to be a modern people's church throbbing with life.

45. From London, Author and Refugee Lion Feuchtwanger Denounces the Nazi Regime

"The German Government is able to maintain itself in power solely and simply by constant and systematic lying. . . ."

Lion Feuchtwanger (1884-1958), author of best-selling novels on historical and political subjects, especially on Jews in positions of power, was born in Munich on July 7, 1884. During World War I his writings were suppressed because of their revolutionary content. After the war he won a global reputation for such novels as *The Ugly Duchess* (1923); *Jew Süss* (1926), translated into English as *Power*, and *Der Jüdische Krieg* (1932), translated as *Josephus*.

As soon as Hitler came to political power, Feuchtwanger, a Jew, was forced to flee his homeland. In March 1934 he issued from London a strong condemnation of the new Third Reich, one of the earliest and most severe attacks on the Hitler regime. His remarks served as an introduction to a list of some eight hundred cases of murder committed by the Nazis. His statement on "Murder in Hitler Germany" follows.

THE PRINCIPLES UPON WHICH NATIONAL-SOCIALISM is based are force and lies. Force and lies are not only means used for the achievement of its ends, but are in themselves constituent parts of the organism of National Socialism.

Convinced that the telling of lies in the interests of the National-Socialist Party is the highest social duty, the Government of the Third Reich has

---

*Quoted in Georgi Dimitrov, *The Reichstag Fire Trial: The Second Brown Book of the Hitler Terror* (London: John Lane, Bodley Head, 1934), pp. 317-19.

built up an apparatus for the propagation of falsehoods more comprehensive and more technically perfect than the world has ever known. This apparatus for the dissemination of falsehoods is the one constructive achievement of the National Socialists. Thanks to them the German Reich has been, as it were, hermetically sealed off from the rest of the world, so that it is defenseless against the falsehoods which are disseminated many millionfold daily by the special Ministry founded for the express purpose, through the loudspeaker and the printed page.

One can understand that the civilized world should express its indignation in the strongest terms at the monstrous audacity of this system for the dissemination of falsehoods. But indignation leads nowhere. The only way in which the National Socialist propaganda machine can be fought with the slightest possibility of success is by simple, restrained and constant reference to the proved facts.

In the following pages there are set forth some eight hundred cases of murders committed by National Socialists. It can with certainty be said that these constitute only a fraction of the deaths which have been brought about by the rulers of the Third Reich. Even according to the official statistics, under National Socialist rule the population of Germany has fallen by some four hundred thousand. The conjecture that murders committed by the National Socialists have contributed towards this fall in the population is justified.

The contents of the following pages are not, however, founded upon mere conjecture. They contain little more than an enumeration of the names of the murdered men, with the date and place of their death. It is an unemotional reckoning and makes dreary reading. Contrasted with the pretentious and glittering torrents of lies to which the enemy gives utterance our truths seem indeed crude and reticent. No high-sounding tumultuous words, but bare facts, figures and dates are to be found in the following pages. But the vital difference between them is that while the assertions of the National Socialists represent, at the very best interpretation, a Utopia, the data which are presented here are capable of actual proof.

Herr Hitler has, for example, stated that in no other country in the world is the individual as secure as in Germany. He has asserted that the whole National Socialist "Revolution" was attained at a cost of only fifty-one lives, and that the fifty-one who laid down their lives were only scoundrels. But in the pages which follow there will be found a list of nearly eight hundred men with the places and dates of their deaths. The German Government is invited to explain how it is that of these eight hundred murders only fifty-one were known to Herr Hitler, and upon what facts Herr Hitler relied in styling the fifty-one victims as scoundrels. The German Government is invited to examine the details of the list, to investigate the cases of murder which it recites and to submit each one by one to the examination of impartial, uncorrupted judges. The German Government will, of course, be very careful not to do any such thing. It is fully conscious of the fact that in a civilised country any single one of these murders would suffice to kindle the flame of revolution. It realizes that, were these murders known to them, the German people even from their deep present humiliation would rise and sweep away Herr Hitler and his associates with anger and abhorrence. The German Government is able to maintain itself in power solely and simply by constant and systematic lying: without the apparatus for the dissemination of these lies it would collapse in a night.

To National Socialism it must be conceded that their apparatus for lying is extraordinarily good, fashioned with an almost loving care it works flawlessly down to the smallest detail. Every means is used to sustain the illusion of peace and good order. No one who walks along the Kurfürstendamm in Berlin, the Jungfernstieg in Hamburg, or the Höhestrasse in Cologne, no one who goes to ski in the Garmisch-Partenkirschen sees anything but peace and good order. But this good order is maintained only through the deeds of violence perpetrated in the concentration camps, only by the commission of more murders like those which may be found listed in the following pages. The peace and good order of Germany are false appearances. The deeds and the omissions of the rulers of the Third Reich are both falsehoods. False are their spoken words and their silences. They rise with falsehood in the morning and lay themselves down with falsehood at night. False is their good order, false their justice and their judgments, false are their language, their science, their laws and their creeds, their Nationalism, their Socialism are false-hoods. Only these — their rapacity, their lust for revenge and their brutal-ity — are true.

Because this is so, because the very ground upon which these creatures, the rulers of Germany, stand is falsehood, it is doubly necessary to sap the foundations of their edifice and ceaselessly to oppose the glittering false-hoods of National Socialism with the sordid truth, the bloody and bestial reality.

Despite the power of their propaganda apparatus, the present rulers of Germany will not succeed forever in hiding the face of truth. The civilised world has already awakened to the reality which is veiled by the cloak of the Third Reich.

46. Vice-Chancellor Franz von Papen's Marburg Speech: A Call for More Freedom, June 17, 1934

*"It is a wholly reprehensible notion that a people
can be united through terrorism."*

On June 17, 1934, Vice-Chancellor Franz von Papen, disturbed by the direction the new National Socialist state was taking, delivered an address at the University of Marburg in which he criticized the government and called for a policy of greater freedom. He made it clear that, in his estimation, the matter of whether or not Germany would remain a Christian state was still open. He called for an end to the treatment of the German public as immature. There was severe economic distress throughout the country, he said, yet the situation was painted in glowing colors. Propaganda, he charged, was not enough to win the confidence of the people. Granted, one party now had absolute rule, but preparations should be made for the introduction of more freedom as a means of achieving a more democratic state.

Hitler was angered by von Papen's Marburg speech. He labeled his vice-chancellor "a ridiculous dwarf" and a "worm" and warned that such people would be "crushed by the fist of the entire German nation." During the Night of the Long Knives, the Blood Purge of June 30, 1934, which came two weeks after this speech, the vice-chancellor was fortunate to come away with his life.

Following are excerpts from von Papen's speech.

Rede des Vizekanzlers Franz von Papen vor dem Universitätsbund in Marburg am 17.6.1934 (Berlin, 1934), *passim.* Translated by the editor.

ON FEBRUARY 21, 1933, in the stormy days when National Socialism had just taken the reins of power in the Reich, I tried to explain the meaning of this change before an audience of Berlin students.

Speaking at a site dedicated to the search for truth and freedom of thought, I was careful to guard myself against being taken for one who supported the liberal conceptions of truth and freedom. The final truth, I said, lies only with God and the search for truth receives its ultimate meaning only when we start with that recognition.

Today I am once again privileged to speak on academic ground, in this medieval gem, the town of St. Elizabeth. I go back to that former exposition of mine. . . . This place is dedicated to science: therefore, it seems to me to be especially appropriate for testifying to the truth before the German people. . . . My inward obligation to Chancellor Hitler is so great . . . that both from a human and political standpoint, it would be a mortal sin not to say what in this decisive period of the German revolution should be said.

The events of the last year and a half have agitated the whole German people and stirred them deeply. It seems almost like a dream that, from the valley of melancholy, hopelessness, hatred, and division we should find our way back to the community of the German nation. . . .

An unknown soldier of the World War, who with contagious energy and unshakable faith has won the hearts of his countrymen, has set the German soul free. Together with his Field-Marshal he has placed himself at the head of a nation in order to turn a new page in the German book of destiny and restore mental unity. We have witnessed this reunion of minds in the intoxication of thousands of people, revealed in the flags and festivals of a nation which has rediscovered itself.

Now, however, as the enthusiasm has lessened and our labor is demanding its rights, it is clear that a catharsis of such historical dimensions produces of necessity a slag from which it must purify itself. This kind of defect occurs in all domains of life, material as well as intellectual.

The outside world regards us with disfavor and points its finger at these defects and finds in them a serious process of disintegration. Let us, however, not rejoice too soon. If we can succeed in freeing ourselves from these defects, we will give the finest proof of our strength internally and show how determined we are to prevent any adulteration of the German revolution.

Rumors must be dragged out of the dark into which they have receded. Open manly discussions would be of more service to the German people than, for example, the present state of the German press, of which Reich Minister for Public Enlightenment and Propaganda [Dr. Joseph Goebbels] has said: "It no longer has any physiognomy."

This defect exists beyond a doubt. The press would, indeed, do a good service when it informs the Government where faults have crept in, where corruption exists, where serious mistakes have been made, where unfit men hold office, where sins are committed against the spirit of the German revolution.

An anonymous secret news service, no matter how efficiently it is organized, can never act as a substitute for this task of the press. Editors are under a legal and conscientious responsibility, where anonymous purveyors of news are beyond control and are exposed to the dangers of Byzantinism. When proper organs of public opinion do not sufficiently clarify the mysterious obscurantism which currently seems to clothe German popular opinion, the statesman himself is obligated to intervene and call a spade a spade.

This kind of action should reveal that the Government is quite strong enough to withstand decent criticism. It is certainly aware of the old maxim: Only weaklings suffer no criticism.

If the outside world believes that liberty is dead in today's Germany, let it learn from the frankness of my exposition that the German Government can afford to allow the burning problems of the nation to be subjected to debate. However, this right can be claimed only by one who without reservation has placed himself at the service of National Socialism and has proved his loyalty to it. . . .

It is . . . inaccurate to twist a justified struggle against a certain kind of intellectualism into a struggle against the intellect itself. History tells us that it is necessary for a fundamental change and promoted by those who turned away from a change through a mass party movement. The claim for a revolutionary or a national monopoly by any one group seems to me to be exaggerated. . . .

The tasks of the reformer of life and those of the politician are quite different. This was recognized by the *Fuehrer* when he declared that the goal of his party was not a religious reformation but rather the political reorganization of our people.

It is quite impossible to organize all human life because then it would become mechanized. The State is a piece of organization; life means growth. . . .

I am convinced that Christian doctrine represents the religious form of all Occidental thought, and that with the rebirth of religious energies there will take place a renewal of the German people for a Christian treasure the value of which could scarcely be understood by men of the nineteenth century.

Before us is a struggle to decide whether or not the new Reich will be Christian or lose itself in sectarianism and pseudo-religious materialism. The decision will be a simple one, provided that the state authority makes certain to discontinue its efforts to bring about a forcible reformation. One must recognize that there is a political motivation in the opposition of Christian circles to governmental and party interference. People subjected to political interference in their religious life will naturally oppose it as strongly as possible.

Moreover, as a Catholic I understand that principle that religious conviction resting on freedom of conscience should refuse to allow itself to be controlled by politics. . . .

An enormous task is yet to be performed in Germany. Leadership will have to maintain a watch lest a new kind of class struggle emerge under new colors. Leadership wants a united nation. While recognizing national service, it must not divide people permanently into a privileged class and a class of lesser status. Such a division could not correspond with the nearly 100 percent profession of loyalty to the new state leadership revealed by the people of Germany on November 12, 1933.

It is understood that the supporters of the revolution will hold positions of power. But when the revolution is completed, then the Government can only represent the totality of the people. It must never be representative of special groups, because, if so, it could not possibly effect a popular union. . . .

Intellect bred in nature and blood has character, and it is incorruptible. It has a conscience. To this kind of mind respect for the nation is a matter of course. A nation is in danger when it denies the mind. Let us beware of the danger of excluding our intellectuals from our nation and let us remember that everything that is great comes from the mind — even in politics. Let no one say that intellectuals lack the vitality without which the nation cannot be led. Rightmindedness is so important that it will sacrifice itself for its convictions. We must not mistake vitality for brutality — adoration of force is dangerous for any people. . . .

The Reich Government is right when it frowns on the false glorification of individuals, the most un-Prussian thing conceivable. Great men are not created by propaganda but grow until their deeds are acknowledged by history. . . .

As an old soldier I know that the most rigid discipline must be accompanied by certain liberties. . . . The application of military discipline to the entire life of the nation must, therefore, be such that human nature is not offended. . . .

It is a wholly reprehensible notion that a people can be united through terrorism. The Government will counter any movement in this direction, because it knows that terrorism is a sign of bad conscience and that it is the worst course for any leader. . . .

It is important that we do not fall under the spell of polemics and catchphrases but, instead, that we take individual counsel. The Leader demands of his followers that "they must never forget that all human worth lies in individual values." . . .

One must never underestimate the wisdom of the people. One must return their confidence and not keep them permanently on a leash. The German people know full well the gravity of their situation, their economic distress, and they clearly see the defects of laws used in an emergency. They have a keen eye for coercion and injustice, and they mock any attempts to deceive them with whitewash.

No organization or kind of propaganda, no matter how excellent, can alone maintain confidence in the long run. I have all along had a different opinion concerning the propaganda movement. Not by incitement, especially of the young, not by threats against the helpless — only by confidential discussion can confidence and loyalty be maintained. . . .

If we disown our cultural heritage, if we pay no attention to and abuse our 1,700-year-old history and the 3,000-year-old history of Europe, then we shall miss the great chance offered to Europe and the nations of the twentieth century. . . .

The world is undergoing great changes. Only a people disciplined and conscious of its responsibility can take the lead. We Germans can win our true position if we are certain to match our intellect with our energy, wisdom with strength, and experience with readiness for action. History waits for us — if only we show ourselves worthy of it.

47. Blood Purge, June 30, 1934: The SA Advocates of a "Second Revolution" Are Eliminated

"The leader is against us, the Reichswehr opposes us. Comrades, to the streets!"

From the beginning of his movement, Hitler faced the dilemma implicit in the very name of his ideology, national socialism. *National* implied the rightist trend – capitalist, militarist, bourgeois; *socialism* indicated a leftist direction – radical, proletarian. Ernst Roehm, one of the *Fuehrer's* close friends, and others loudly called for a "Second Revolution" toward the left. Only the SA, Roehm's brown-shirted legions, could bring about this necessary revolution. But the *Fuehrer* gradually became convinced that his future lay with the monied barons of the Rhineland and with the power of the *Reichswehr,* the national army.

Hitler tried to reason with Roehm. "Forget the idea of a second revolution," he said. "Believe in me! Don't cause me any trouble." But Roehm and his followers would not listen. No one, he said, was going to break up his Brown Army, not even Hitler. It was a deadly decision. Goebbels and Himmler stayed with the Hitler bandwagon; Goering was already there.

The issue came to a head on June 30, 1934, when Hitler personally led a blood purge against dissenting elements of his party. What happened on that dark day was reported by wireless to *The New York Times* by its correspondent, Frederick T. Birchall.

BERLIN, JUNE 30. — On the eve of a self-proclaimed month of peace Germany has passed today through the throes of a violent purging that must

The New York Times, July 1, 1934.

profoundly affect her future. It is neither a revolution nor a coup d'état nor a counter-revolution but authoritative action intended to head off any of the three.

Chancellor Hitler in Munich, backed by General Hermann Wilhelm Goering, Premier of Prussia, in Berlin, has struck simultaneously at the rebel elements in his own Storm Troops and at certain reactionary elements temporarily allied with them or suspected of being so allied for their own ends in an attempt to upset the present regime in Germany.

When the day was over many Storm Troop leaders had been shot to death or had committed suicide.

In addition, General Kurt von Schleicher, Herr Hitler's predecessor as Chancellor, had been slain while resisting police who attempted to seize him as one of the plotters.

[Captain Ernst Roehm, chief of staff of the Storm Troops, committed suicide after having been ousted by Chancellor Hitler, according to The Associated Press, while Heinrich Klausener, chief of the Catholic Action, was shot to death by a Nazi special guard.]

The Official Version

The official version is that the attempt was a joint effort "to bring pressure" on the government with a threat of violent action behind it. There is mention of a "foreign power" as being involved. The discerning interpret this reference as being to Russia and the ultimate aim of the rebels as a new national bolshevism.

Whatever the cause, Chancellor Hitler has acted swiftly and decisively. Flying to Munich in the early hours of this morning from Bonn, where he had been ostensibly inspecting work camps, he assembled his trusted special guards in that city and proceeded to gather in the suspected leaders, who had already proceeded to preliminary action.

Captain Roehm, the leader of the conspiracy, was arrested in his bedroom in his country house outside Munich by Herr Hitler himself and then and there deposed from all his offices. His fellow-conspirators were gathered in by the dozen in Munich and around it.

The official story told to foreign correspondents by General Goering this afternoon says that some of them, both in Munich and in Berlin, committed suicide and others were shot while resisting.

Goering Acts Swiftly

Almost simultaneously in Berlin General Goering, by arrangement with Chancellor Hitler, was taking similar action. It came swiftly and unexpectedly just before noon. But here the members of the reactionary group believed to be acting with the rebel Storm Troop leaders were equally the objects of the assault.

Karl Ernst, group leader of the Berlin Storm Troops, was traced to a house near Bremen and surrounded there. He is dead and the official version is that he was shot while resisting arrest. The unofficial version is that he was brought by airplane to Berlin and executed on his arrival.

Police and special guards at the very outset sought to put General von Schleicher under arrest at his villa outside Potsdam. It is said that he attempted to draw a pistol. A volley of shots brought him down and his wife died with him.

Vice-Chancellor Franz von Papen, who seems to have been under suspicion of some connection with General Schleicher, although they were not friends, was temporarily arrested and questioned as to his relations with the reactionaries. He was, however, left at his home under guard, and after answering questions was no further molested.

Secretary Is Arrested

He was quite calm under examination and thoroughly convinced his questioners. However, his secretary and mouthpiece, Herr von Bose, was arrested and is said to be still in custody.

Police and special guards armed with rifles were placed around the homes of Cabinet Ministers. All public buildings were occupied and everywhere around important points were visible the rifle-bearing green-clad bodyguards of the Prussian Premier.

But apparently neither in Berlin nor Munich, except in isolated cases of individuals, was there the least resistance. Not only was the action so unexpected that it took the conspirators by complete surprise, but they appeared to have no really substantial following even among the storm troops themselves.

The dead are alleged tonight to include General von Schleicher and his wife and these six storm troop-leaders:

District Group Leader August Schneidhuber of Munich.
District Group Leader Edmund Heines of Silesia.
District Group Leader Karl Ernst of Berlin.
Group Leader Wilhelm Schmid of Munich.
Group Leader Hans Hayn of Saxony.
Group Leader Hans Peter von Heidelbreck of Pomerania.

Hard to Paint Full Picture

It is difficult within a few hours of events like these taking place over so wide an area as Germany, from news sources that have lost the habit of collecting news and aided only by newspapers restricted to official outgivings, to paint a complete picture of all that has happened today.

Fortunately, official utterances have been fairly liberal and ostensibly frank and themselves convey a fairly clear idea of developments in this great day of Germany's internal struggling.

The fullest account was supplied by General Goering to foreign correspondents summoned to his office early in the afternoon. This was supplemented in what purported to be an official text of what he said, given out this evening, by a further illuminating passage that no one present remembered having been spoken then. It was probably added as an afterthought. Here it is:

"The main go-between in the conspiracy was former Reich Chancellor General von Schleicher, who made conduction between Captain Roehm and a foreign power and those eternally dissatisfied figures of yesterday. I expanded my task by delivering a stroke against those dissatisfied ones also.

"It was self-understood that General von Schleicher had to be arrested. While being arrested, he attempted to make a lightning assault upon those men who were to arrest him. Thereby he lost his life."

Unofficial Versions

This is the sole authoritative version of General von Schleicher's death. Unofficial versions have it that the attempt to arrest him was made as he was leaving his villa near Potsdam with his wife to enter their motor to drive to Berlin and that she fell beside him under the rain of bullets that greeted his supposed attempt to draw a pistol.

But the most dramatic of all the scenes in this national drama were enacted near Munich and the outstanding figure in them was Chancellor Hitler himself. It seems that all along he had known of the conspiracy and his secret police were closely watching it. For several nights he had gone sleepless reading reports and giving instructions while awaiting the moment to strike.

After his interview with Franz Seldte, commander of the Stahlhelm, on Thursday, he went yesterday to the wedding of one of his followers near Essen merely to throw the conspirators off guard and assure them that all was well. After the wedding he inspected several labor camps, all the time keeping in touch with Premier Goering, who was the centre of information as to what was going on.

Early in the evening at Bonn the Chancellor ordered an airplane to be ready at the flying field at 2 o'clock in the morning, and at that time he started on his trip to Munich.

Arriving there at dawn, he learned that the storm troops in Munich and around had already been mobilized by the leaders who were in the conspiracy. They had circulated this slogan:

"The leader is against us, the Reichswehr opposes us. Comrades, to the streets!"

Adolf Wagner, the Bavarian Minister of the Interior, had been alarmed by the resulting influx the night before. He had sent some groups home and deposed some of the leaders. Chancellor Hitler sought out Herr Wagner.

In the meantime news of the Chancellor's arrival had spread like wildfire and the group leaders hurried to him, some voluntarily and some brought by an urgent summons. It was then barely 5 o'clock in the morning.

Chancellor Hitler called in his guards and ordered the arrest of the known rebels, himself tearing the insignia from their uniforms. Leaving them in custody, he motored on at top speed to Bad Wiessee, a resort outside Munich, where Captain Roehm was resting in his country house, and Herr Heines, Silesian leader and chief of police of Breslau, was spending the night. Captain Roehm was ill abed. It was only 5:30.

Strides In Unannounced

Unannounced, Herr Hitler with his guards strode into Captain Roehm's bedroom and himself declared that his Storm Troop chief of staff was under arrest. Captain Roehm made no protest and attempted no resistance. While he dressed for his transfer to prison, Herr Hitler walked across the hall to the chamber of Herr Heines, who was there with a youthful male companion.

"The scene that took place on Chancellor Hitler's arrival," says the official account, "is indescribable." Herr Hitler's own indignation was overwhelming. Herr Heines is listed tonight as among the dead, but as to how he came to his death the official records are silent.

Most of the possessions of both Captain Roehm and Herr Heines were taken into custody. The proceedings at the country house lasted almost two hours. At 8 o'clock the bodyguards of the two leaders arrived in motor trucks. But it was all over. They accepted the situation.

Herr Hitler motored back to Munich where, in the meantime, his special forces had been busy. Most of the storm troopers' leaders in Southern Germany were in the city. They had been ordered there for a conference. Suspects were hunted down and arrested at their lodgings, in their cars, on the streets and some even at railway stations as they sought to flee.

Hitler Issues Decree

Herr Hitler went to the Bavarian Ministry of the Interior, where he joined Herr Wagner and General von Epp, Governor of Bavaria. There the Chancellor issued a decree announcing the deposing of Captain Roehm and his expulsion from the party and the appointment of Chief Group Leader Viktor Lutze as Chief of Staff of the Storm Troops.

After dictating and signing the decree, Herr Hitler addressed a letter to his new Chief of Staff, who is Governor of Hanover. He has spent all his life there and had never before been brought to the attention of the German public at large. In the letter the Chancellor praised Herr Lutze as a "true and ideal Storm Troop leader" and declared he wanted the Storm

Troops developed into "a true and strong link in the National Socialist movement."

Informed over the telephone of his sudden elevation, Herr Lutze quickly accepted his task. The spirit in which the new chief of the Storm Troops has undertaken it may be gathered from the initial order of the day that he addressed to them on assuming office. It demanded from them unconditional faithfulness, the severest discipline and self-sacrificing devotion.

Goebbels With Hitler

Chancellor Hitler remained in Munich until evening. Then he flew back to Berlin. His plane landed at Tempelhof at 10 o'clock on a flying field illuminated literally like day in honor of his coming.

With him was a little group of trusted intimates including Dr. Paul Joseph Goebbels, the Minister of Propaganda, and it then came out that Dr. Goebbels had been with his leader throughout the whole exciting period in Munich. He had been summoned yesterday to meet Herr Hitler in the Rhineland, had flown there from Baden and had remained at his side.

Dr. Goebbels's hand can be seen in an official party communiqué describing the events of the morning which was issued in Munich in the afternoon. This official version stressed that Captain Roehm had taken part in an anti-Hitler plot and had caused other difficulties for the Chancellor. It also reported Herr Hitler's appeal for loyalty from the Storm Troops.

It is quite notable that the Reichswehr has not stirred. The purging has been accomplished only by the Nazi special guards with some aid from the police. Herr Hitler's foresight in creating this trusted special guard force, carefully selected and specially uniformed, is the subject of much commendation tonight.

Stahlhelm Stands Ready

Nevertheless, there is little doubt that should action by the Stahlhelm have been called for the veterans would have been ready. Their headquarters in Berlin have been open all day and their leaders have been receiving bulletins from branches all over the country. The bulletins were all of the same tenor — no disturbances anywhere and general quiet prevailing.

The Stahlhelm is quite content with the outcome. Everything has gone its way. The Stahlhelm men have no sympathy with General von Schleicher or with the conspiracy. Late this afternoon their leader, Herr Seldte, issued an order directing his men to refrain from wearing their uniforms until further notice and affirming loyalty to Chancellor Hitler and President von Hindenburg.

The Hitler Cabinet stands virtually intact. It is announced that there will be no changes except the substitution of Herr Lutze, the new chief of staff of the Storm Troops, for Captain Roehm as Minister Without Porfolio.

Colonel von Papen, whose speech defending the right of criticism, although a small thing, undoubtedly encouraged the malcontents to hasten their plans because of the encouragement it received, remains at his post. Dr. Goebbels, who fought him and had been rated as the intellectual leader of the radicals, goes through this at his leader's side.

Tomorrow and afterward may bring real revelations as to what has gone on behind the scenes before this battle was fought out in the open. It has lent new significance to the declaration of General Werner von Blomberg, the Defense Minister, Friday that the Reichswehr was the servant of the State with no share in party politics.

It has brought to sight a new future for a smaller and more carefully sifted Storm Troop aggregation. And it has put monarchist reaction on the one hand or a lapse to pseudo-bolshevism on the other far into the background. But what its other effects will be must be left to the future to determine.

48. Official Communiqué on the Crushing of the Radical Nazi Revolt, June 30, 1934

"He had to suppress at the root attempts in circles of an ambitious nature to propagate a new revolution."

Even while the Blood Purge was under way, Nazi propagandists, under the direction of Propaganda Minister Goebbels, furiously began to issue bulletins justifying the slaughter of both radicals and reactionaries. A series of decrees and proclamations appeared within a day in *The New York Times*.

MUNICH, JUNE 30. For many months individual elements have been trying to drive a wedge and produce conflicts between the Storm Troops and the party, as well as between the Storm Troops and the State. Suspicions of this became more and more confirmed, but it was also plain that these endeavors were to be charged to a limited clique of certain leanings.

Chief of Staff Roehm, in whom the leader placed an exceptional amount of confidence, not only did not oppose these endeavors but undoubtedly sponsored them. His well-known unfortunate characteristic gradually led to intolerable burdens which drove the leader of the movement and the Highest Leader of the Storm Troops [Hitler] into most serious conflicts of conscience.

Chief of Staff Roehm established contacts with General von Schleicher without the knowledge of Der Fuehrer [the Leader]. His go-betweens were another Storm Troop leader and an obscure person well known in Berlin, to whom Der Fuehrer had always strongly objected.

The New York Times, July 1, 1934.

Since these negotiations also led — of course without the knowledge of Der Fuehrer — finally to contacts with a foreign power, or rather to its representative, it was not possible to avoid intervention both from the standpoint of the party and the State.

Provocative incidents brought about according to the plan caused Der Fuehrer to fly from Bonn to Munich at 2 o'clock this morning, after visiting labor camps in Westphalia, in order to remove and arrest the most seriously compromised group or leaders. Der Fuehrer himself went with only a few companions to Wiessee in order to still any attempts at resistance.

The execution of the arrests revealed such immorality that any trace of pity was impossible. Some of these Storm Troop leaders had taken male prostitutes along with them. One of them was even disturbed in a most ugly situation and was arrested.

Der Fuehrer gave orders for this plague to be done away with ruthlessly. In the future he will not permit millions of decent people to be compromised by a few of such sick men. Der Fuehrer instructed Premier Goering of Prussia to take similar action in Berlin and especially to arrest the reactionary accomplices of this political plot.

At noon today Der Fuehrer spoke to assembled Hitler storm troop leaders and stressed his unshakable bond to the storm troops, at the same time declaring he intended from now on to remove and destroy without mercy all undisciplined and disobedient persons, as well as unsocial or sickly elements.

He pointed out that service in the storm troops was a service of honor, for which tens of thousands of brave storm troop men had made the greatest sacrifices. He expected, he said, from the leader of each unit proof that he was worthy of such sacrifice and that he would be an example to his troop.

Der Fuehrer pointed out furthermore that for years he had protected chief of staff Roehm against attacks, but that developments obliged him to place above all personal feelings the welfare of the movement and the State. He had to suppress at the root attempts in circles of an ambitious nature to propagate a new revolution.

49. Hitler Appoints Viktor Lutze New SA Chief of Staff and Issues an Order for Its Reform, June 30, 1934

"I demand . . . blind obedience and unquestioning discipline."

The Blood Purge of June 30, 1934, was designed to suppress Ernst Roehm's ambitions, reduce the SA drastically, and guarantee the military forces their preeminence in the Third Reich. While the slaughter was going on, the *Fuehrer* removed Roehm from his post as SA chief of staff and appointed Viktor Lutze in his place: "Munich, June 30. Under today's date I have removed Chief of Staff Roehm from his position and turned him out of the party and the Storm Troops. I appoint as Chief of Staff Chief Group Leader Lutze. Storm Troop leaders and special guard men who do not obey his orders or act against them will be removed from the Storm Troops by the party and will be arrested and dealt with. ADOLF HITLER, Highest Party and Storm Troop Leader."

In another decree Hitler informed Lutze that he was setting up a code of conduct for the Storm Troops. Asserting that he wanted "men, not apes," he forbade all SA men to spend money on banquets and banned moral "debauches." The decrees were published the next day in the *Völkischer Beobachter*.

Munich, June 30

To Chief Group Leader Lutze.

My dear Storm Troop Leader Lutze:

The most serious misdeeds of my Chief of Staff have forced me to

---

Völkischer Beobachter, July 1, 2, 1934. Translated by the editor.

remove him from office. You, my dear Chief Group Leader, have always been the same faithful and ideal Storm Troop leader through many years, in both good and bad days.

If under today's date I appoint you Chief of Staff, I do this because I am fully convinced by your true and faithful work you will be able to make the Storm Troops an instrument which the nation needs and which I have in mind. I expect you to accept the following series of duties, about which I hereby inform you.

1. I demand from every Storm Troop leader, just as from every Storm Trooper, blind obedience and unquestioning discipline.

2. I demand of every Storm Troop leader, just as every other political leader, that his conduct and reputation be a model for his organization and for our entire membership.

3. I demand that Storm Troop leaders, exactly as in the case of political leaders, who leave something to be desired in their public conduct, be removed without hesitation from the Party and from the SA.

4. I demand especially from the Storm Troop leader that he must be a model of simplicity and that he not live in great display. I do not want Storm Troop leaders to give costly dinners and take part in them. There was a time when we were not invited to them, and we have nothing to gain from them now. Millions of our countrymen today lack the merest necessities of life. They are not oblivious to those who have been blessed by good fortune, but it is unworthy of a National Socialist to widen the gap, which is already large enough, between misery and good fortune.

I explicitly forbid the use of Storm Troop or party funds for festivals or similar activities. It is irresponsible to use such funds, which in part come from the pennies of our poorest fellow citizens, for purposes of gluttony. The luxurious staff headquarters in Berlin, which it has now been discovered has spent up to 30,000 marks monthly for banquets, is hereby dissolved.

I prohibit all party groups to give banquets and dinners paid for with a variety of public funds. I forbid all party and Storm Troop leaders to take part in such banquets. The only exceptions allowed will be functions necessary for reasons of state, especially those for which the Reich President and the Reich Foreign Minister are responsible. I forbid all party leaders to give so-called diplomatic dinners. It is not necessary for Storm Troop leaders to engage in representation, but simply to do their duty.

5. I do not want Storm Troop leaders to go on business trips in expensive limousines or cabriolets, or to use public funds for such trips. Exactly the same applies to all leaders of the political organization.

6. Storm Troop leaders or political leaders who become intoxicated in public are unworthy to be leaders of our people.

The ban on grumbling criticism demands exemplary conduct. Mistakes can always be forgiven, but not bad behavior. Storm Troop leaders who behave in unseemly fashion in public, who take part in brawls or excessive conduct of any kind, are to be dismissed immediately without notice from the SA. I hold all those in posts of authority responsible for carrying out this order.

I expect that the State authorities will punish such misdemeanors more severely when they are committed by National Socialists than by non-National Socialists. A National Socialist leader, and especially a Storm Troop leader, should have an exceptional reputation among the people.

7. I expect all Storm Troop leaders to cooperate in preserving the reputation of the Storm Troop as a clean and upright institution. Every mother should be able to place her son in an SA unit, in the party, and in the Hitler Youth without fearing that he might be destroyed there ethically or morally. I, therefore, expect that every Storm Troop leader will take the utmost care to assure that there will be instant dismissal from the party and from the Storm Troops if an individual is guilty of a breach of Section 175 [homosexual crimes]. I want men in the party, not absurd apes.

8. I demand of every Storm Troop leader that he return my loyalty with his own. Especially, I demand from them that they reserve their strength for their own organization and that they do not mix in the affairs of others.*

9. Above all, I expect of a Storm Trooper that he will not demand more courage and sacrifice from those under his command than he is willing to ask from himself. I demand, therefore, that he show himself to be a real leader, friend, and comrade, in his dealings with his German fellow-citizens under his command, and I expect that he will value virtue in his men more than numbers.

10. And I expect of you as Chief of Staff that you do not forget your old faithful party comrades, the longtime fighters of the SA. I do not want to see the creation of thousands of unnecessary staff members, and I expect that promotions be made not on the basis of abstract knowledge but on the inborn capacity for leadership, many years of proven loyalty, and willingness to sacrifice. I have in my Storm Troops an unparalleled corps of the truest and bravest followers. These are the ones who have conquered Germany, not the latecomers of 1933 and after.

11. I want the SA man to be trained intellectually and physically to be a thorough National Socialist. The unique power of this organization is to be found in the anchor of the philosophy of our party.

12. I demand that obedience, loyalty, and comradeship be the basic principles of this organization. And so, just as every leader demands obedience from his men, so do I demand my Storm Troop leaders' respect for the law and obedience to my commands.

---

*Hitler here refers to the *Wehrmacht*, the army, which resented SA interference in its affairs.

50. Proclamation by Viktor Lutze, June 30, 1934

"Absolute loyalty! Severest discipline! Self-sacrificing devotion!"

The new chief of staff of the SA, Viktor Lutze, immediately issued a proclamation to the Brown Shirts, in which he called for unquestioning obedience to the *Fuehrer.*

SA COMRADES! Leaders and men!

The *Fuehrer* has called me to his side as chief of staff. I must and I will justify that trust placed in me through unbroken loyalty to the *Fuehrer,* and I pledge unending action for National Socialism and through it for our people.

It was just twelve years ago that I was named for the first time the leader of a small SA unit, and at that time I placed three virtues at the forefront of my activities and at the same time demanded them of the SA. These three virtues have made the SA great, and today, as I in these fateful hours can serve my *Fuehrer* in a post of high responsibility, present them as a code of conduct for the entire SA:

Absolute loyalty! Severest discipline! Self-sacrificing devotion!

In this way we shall march together — because we are National Socialists.

I am convinced that it can only be a march to freedom.

Long live the *Fuehrer!* Long live our people!

The Chief of Staff,
[signed]
Viktor Lutze

Völkischer Beobachter, July 1, 2, 1934. Translated by the editor.

51. The *Stahlhelm*, Organization of War Veterans, Is Ordered to Support Hitler, June 30, 1934

"In loyalty to Der Fuehrer, to the Reich President
and to the State we stand unchanged."

Simultaneously with Hitler's decrees, Franz Seldte, minister of labor in the Nazi government and head of the *Stahlhelm*, the organization of war veterans, issued an order calling on its members to remain loyal to Hitler and his regime.

BERLIN, June 30.

In view of the fateful hour which all Germans, and with them my old comrades, are experiencing, I take the occasion to point out that dignity, calm and self-discipline are especially to be expected from old soldiers. In loyalty to Der Fuehrer, to the Reich President and to the State we stand unchanged. The well-being of the State will always be for us the highest law.

At so earnest a moment no uniform belongs on the streets except the uniform of the State forces. Therefore I direct the National Socialist League of Front Fighters [the reorganized Stahlhelm] to refrain from wearing uniforms until further orders are received.

This order becomes effective immediately.

FRANZ SELDTE

The New York Times, July 1, 1934.

52. President von Hindenburg Sends Telegram of Congratulations to Hitler and Goering, July 2, 1934

". . . your determined action and gallant personal intervention. . . ."

Most of the slaughter in the Blood Purge was over by July 1, 1934. The next day the aged President Paul von Hindenburg aroused himself from his torpor and sent telegrams of congratulations to both Hitler and Goering for their success "in putting a halt to treason and rescuing the German people from great danger." The telegrams were published with great satisfaction by the Nazi party official newspaper, the *Völkischer Beobachter.*

From the Reich President von Hindenburg to the Fuehrer, *Telegram, July 2, 1934*

From reports submitted to me I see that you, through your determined action and gallant personal intervention have stopped treason in the bud. You have rescued the German people from a great danger. For that I express to you my heartfelt thanks and my sincere appreciation.

With best greetings,
[signed]   von Hindenburg

From the Reich President von Hindenburg to Minister-President Goering, Telegram, July 2, 1934

For your energetic and successful action in countering the attempt at high treason I send you my thanks and my appreciation.

With comradely greetings,
[signed]   von Hindenburg

Völkischer Beobachter, July 3, 4, 1934. Translated by the editor.

53. Hitler Issues a Decree Designed to Prevent Further Revolts Against His Authority, July 3, 1934

"Whoever takes it upon himself. . . ."

Within a few days after crushing the Roehm revolt, Hitler issued a decree designed to prevent any further challenges of his power as dictator. This decree was presented to the cabinet immediately after it congratulated him for his courageous action "in preventing a civil war."

MEASURES FOR THE SUPPRESSION of the Roehm revolt were taken during the evening of July 1, 1934. Whoever takes it upon himself—no matter for what purpose—to support any violent action will be turned over to normal justice for judgment.

[Signed]
Adolf Hitler

Reichsgesetzblatt, I, p. 529. Translated by the editor.

54. Death of von Hindenburg: Hitler Becomes President of the Third Reich, August 2, 1934

"He shall appoint his deputy."

The German cabinet met on the night of August 1, 1934, the evening preceding the death of President Paul von Hindenburg, and adopted a decree combining the offices of president and chancellor. It was to be effective immediately after the death of von Hindenburg. On August 2, 1934, Hitler became *Fuehrer* and chancellor of the Third Reich.

ARTICLE 1. The office of Reich President is united with that of Chancellor. Therefore, the authority until now exercised by the Reich President passes to the *Fuehrer* and Chancellor, Adolf Hitler. He shall appoint his deputy.

ARTICLE 2. This law becomes effective from the moment of the death of President von Hindenburg.

Reichsgesetzblatt, vol. 1, no. 89, August 2, 1934, p. 747. Translated by the editor.

55. Personal Oath of Loyalty to the *Fuehrer* Is Required of All Soldiers of the Armed Forces, August 2, 1934

". . . ready at all times to lay down my life for this oath."

A little over a month after the Blood Purge, Hitler ordered Reich Defense Minister Colonel-General Werner von Blomberg to present a formal oath for every member of the *Reichswehr*. Every member of the armed forces was required to pledge personal allegiance to the *Fuehrer* and to swear to lay down his life, if necessary, for that oath. On August 20, 1934, a similar oath was required for all officeholders in the Third Reich.

I SWEAR BEFORE GOD this holy oath: that I shall give absolute obedience to the *Fuehrer* of the German Reich and people, Adolf Hitler, the Supreme Commander of the Wehrmacht, and as a courageous soldier will be ready at all times to lay down my life for this oath.

Völkischer Beobachter, August 3, 1934. Translated by the editor.

56. Von Hindenburg's Political Testament Is Published, August 16, 1934

"My Chancellor, Adolf Hitler, and his movement, have in common led the German nation, above any distinctions of profession or class, to internal unity. . . ."

Paul Ludwig Hans von Beneckendorff und von Hindenburg (1847–1934) was a man with three lives. As adjutant to a battalion, he took part in the Franco-Prussian War of 1870–1871 and was among those who marched into Paris after the victory of Prussian arms. In 1914 he was recalled from retirement and was one of the moving forces behind the great victory of Tannenberg, August 26–31, 1914. The idol of his people, he was elected president of the Weimar Republic in 1925. Because of his advanced age and his devotion to duty and country, he became a legendary figure in the last days of the Weimar Republic. In 1933 he called Hitler to the chancellorship after having opposed him for some time.

Von Hindenburg died on August 2, 1934, three months before his eighty-eighth birthday. Two weeks later, on August 16, his political testament, dated May 11, 1934, was published with Hitler's approval. In it he spoke in retrospection of his life and maintained that it was necessary to restore the German Empire. Though he expressed high praise to "my Chancellor Adolf Hitler and his movement," his testament explicitly avoided naming the *Fuehrer* as his successor and gave the impression that he did not wish Hitler to be the future president of the Reich. It has been charged that Hinden-

Völkischer Beobachter, August 16, 1934. Translated by the editor.

burg may have been even more explicit and that certain passages in the original copy were suppressed before its publication.

The testament was brought by former Vice-Chancellor Franz von Papen at the request of Colonel Oskar von Hindenburg, the president's son, to Hitler at the Obersalzberg on August 15, 1934. With it was a note: "To the German nation and its chancellor, my testament. This letter is to be given to the Reich chancellor through my son."

Following is a translation of the complete text as published in the official national socialist newspaper, the *Völkischer Beobachter*, on August 16, 1934.

IN 1919 I WROTE IN MY MESSAGE to the German people:

"We are at the end! Just like Siegfried under the cunning spear of the angered Hagen, our exhausted front collapses. We seek in vain to drink new life from the dried-up spring of our inborn strength. Our task now is to preserve the remaining strength of our Army and to use it for the coming reconstruction of the Fatherland. The present is already lost. So there remains for us only one hope — for the future.

"Let us get to work!

"I understand well the thought of escape from the world, an idea which obsesses many officers because of the collapse of everything that was dear and true to them. The wish to know nothing more of a world where boiling passions hide the vital qualities of our people so that they can no longer be recognized, that is humanly understandable. Indeed, I must express it frankly, exactly the way I think: Comrades of the once grand and proud German Army, can you talk of losing heart? Direct your thoughts to those who more than a century ago created a new Fatherland for us. Their religion was their faith in themselves and in the sanctity of their cause. They created the new Fatherland, and grounded it not on doctrines foreign to us but on the foundation of the free development of the framework and on the principle of the common good. When she is able, Germany will embark on this course again.

"I am firmly convinced that now, as in those days, what has bound us to the past will be preserved, and where those links have been broken, they will be reassembled. Once again the old German Spirit will assert itself victoriously, but only after it has been purged in the flames of passion and suffering.

"Our opponents know full well the power of this spirit. They admired it and at the same time hated it in times of peace. They were in reality astonished by it and they feared it on the battlefields of the Great War. They tried to explain our strength to their own people by using the empty word 'Organization.' They were silent about the spirit which has lived and moved behind the veil of this word. But we shall use this spirit again and courageously reconstruct our nation.

"Germany, the focal point of so many of the endless values of human civilization and *Kultur*, will not be destroyed as long as it retains its faith in its great historical world-mission. I am confident that the depth and power of the best in our Fatherland will succeed in combining new ideas with the precious treasures of the past and blend them together in lasting fashion for the good of our Fatherland.

"This is the unshakable conviction I have as I leave the bloody fields of battle of international struggle. I have witnessed the heroism and agony of my Fatherland, and never, but never, shall I believe that this was its death agony.

"For the moment our whole former Constitution lies buried under the flood, a tide brought into existence by the storm of wild political passions and resounding words which seemed to destroy all our sacred traditions. But in time this flood will subside. Then, from the eternally boiling sea of human life there will again appear that rock to which the hopes of our fathers clung, that rock on which, nearly half a century ago, the future of our Fatherland was confidently founded — the German Empire!

"When the national idea, the national consciousness, has been restored again, then, out of the Great War, on which no nation can look back with such real pride and with such clear conscience as we, as well as out of the bitter misery of the current day, precious moral fruits will ripen for us. The blood of those who have fallen while believing in the greatness of the Fatherland will not then have flowed in vain.

"In this assurance I now lay down my pen and rely strongly on you — the Youth of Germany!"

I wrote those words in the darkest hours and in the belief that I was fast approaching the end of my life spent in the service of the Fatherland. Fate meant otherwise for me. A new chapter of my life was opened in the spring of 1925. Once again I was to cooperate in the destiny of my people.

It was only my firm confidence in the inexhaustible resources of Germany that gave me the courage to agree to my first and second elections to the Reich Presidency. This firm belief also gave me the inner strength to carry out unswervingly the demands of my difficult office.

The last part of my life has also been the most difficult for me. Many have failed to understand me in these confused times and have failed to grasp the fact that my only care has been to restore the disunited and discouraged German people to a self-conscious unity.

I began and carried out the duties of my offices in the realization that an introductory period of complete renunciation was required both in domestic and international politics. In my Easter message of the year 1925, I urged the nation to maintain its fear of God, its belief in social justice, and its devotion to peace and political sanity. I have not become tired of working for the domestic unity of our people nor have I become tired of cultivating the self-consciousness of their best qualities. At the same time, I was conscious that the political Constitution and the form of Government which were given to the nation in the time of its greatest distress and greatest weaknesses did not correspond with the needs and characteristics of our people. The time must come when this sentiment can enjoy widespread support. Therefore, it seemed to me to be my duty to rescue the country from the quicksands of oppression and degradation from outside, from internal distress and disruption, without endangering its existence before the hour struck.

The symbol and strong support for this superstructure must be the *Reichswehr*, the guardian of the State. On the firm foundation of the *Reichswehr* must rest the ancient Prussian virtues of self-understood duty, simplicity, and comradeship.

After the collapse the German *Reichswehr* maintained the continuation of the high traditions of the old Army. The *Reichswehr*, always and at all times, must reflect the pattern of State conduct, in order that, unmoved by any internal political developments, its high mission for the defense of the country may be maintained.

When I shall have returned to my comrades above, with whom I have fought on so many battlefields for the greatness and honor of our nation, then I shall call out to the younger generation:

"Prove yourselves worthy of your ancestors. Never forget that, if you would want to secure the peace and welfare of your homeland, it is necessary that you be prepared to sacrifice everything for its peace and honor. Never forget that your deeds, too, will become tradition at some future time."

The Field Marshal of the World War and its Commander-in-Chief gives his thanks to all the men who have built up the construction and organization of the *Reichswehr*.

In foreign policy the German people have had to travel the road to Calvary. A frightful treaty has weighed heavily upon us and has threatened, in its ever-increasing consequences, to bring our nation to the point of collapse. For a long time the surrounding world has failed utterly to understand that Germany must live, not only for her own sake, but also for Western Europe and as the standard-bearer of Western civilization.

The shackles that bind us were only loosened step by step without arousing an overwhelming resistance. If some of my comrades of the old days failed at the time to grasp the difficulties which existed in our path, then history will judge rightly how bitter but how necessary it was that I sign many a State document in order to maintain the existence of Germany.

In harmony with growing internal recovery and with the strengthening of the German nation, a progressive — and, God willing — a generous contribution toward the solution of all troublesome European problems could be striven for and eventually obtained on the basis of the nation's own national dignity and honor.

I thank Providence for allowing me, in the evening of my life, to be a witness to this hour of renewal. I thank all those who, with selfless patriotism, have collaborated with me in the reconstruction of Germany.

My Chancellor, Adolf Hitler, and his movement, have in common led the German nation, above any distinctions of profession or class, to internal unity — a decisive step of historical importance.

I know that much remains to be done, and I desire with all my heart that the act of reconciliation which embraces the entire German Fatherland will be the forerunner of the act of national exaltation and popular cooperation.

I say farewell to my German people in the full hope that what I longed for in 1919 and which by slow fruition led to January 30, 1933, may mature to the complete fulfillment and realization of the historic mission of our people.

In this firm belief in the future of the Fatherland, I am content to close my eyes in peace.

Berlin, May 11, 1934
[Signed]
von Hindenburg

57. Franco-German Agreement: The Saar Is Returned to Germany, February 18, 1935

"The French Government shall withdraw the personnel of French nationality."

From the beginning of his regime Hitler was determined to pursue an active foreign policy in an attempt to right what he regarded as the wrongs of the Treaty of Versailles. His first triumph in foreign policy came with the return of the Saar region to Germany. The Treaty of Versailles had given the League of Nations the responsibility for governing the Saar Basin. The mines of the region were placed under French control as compensation for the damages done to French coal fields by German troops during the World War.

On January 13, 1935, a plebiscite was held in the Saar territory under auspices of the League. The result was an overwhelming vote of 90 percent for the restoration of the Saar to Germany. The subsequent agreement for the cession of French property to Germany is condensed here.

The French Government and the German Government,

In view of the provisions of paragraphs 36 and 38 of the Annex to Articles 45 to 50 of the Treaty of Versailles:

In view of Parts III and V of the Franco-German Agreement of Rome, dated December 3, 1934;

In view of the resolution of the Council of the League of Nations dated January 17, 1935:

Have agreed on the following provisions as regards the conditions of

---

League of Nations, *Official Journal*, 1935, pp. 470-76.

France's cession to Germany of her rights of ownership over the mines, railways, and other immovable property situated in the Saar Territory.

Article 2

1. The property and rights transferred are enumerated in an inventory which has already been transmitted to the German Government and which will be regarded as annexed to the present agreement. The inventory is a list with a summary description enabling the installations to be identified; their nature, state or value may not be the subject of any dispute on questions of detail, nor may any aggregate estimate be made which would involve a settlement of accounts between the two parties. Any errors or omissions observed in the inventory or in the Land Register will form the subject of correction, to which the French State undertakes to lend its assistance as far as necessary, without thereby taking upon itself any pecuniary burden or any fresh obligation toward its successor or third parties. . . .

Article 3

1. The taking-over of the mines is fixed for midnight on the night of February 28/March 1, 1935, when the responsibility for operation and the management and profits or charges thereof will pass to the German Reich.

2. The French State remains a creditor for the value of the products dispatched with waybills or similar documents (records of meters, &c.) before March 1, 1935, rents and leases relating to the period previous to March 1, 1935, compensation due for damage caused before that date at the mines, and various deliveries made by the mines.

3. On the other hand, the French State is a debtor for wages and salaries earned at that date, taxes, charges, rents, &c., relating to the previous period, the cost of equipment arriving before March 1, 1935, at its storehouses, damage caused, and, in particular, any surface damages noted, as laid down in the Agreement of December 3, 1934.

4. Legal disputes and, in particular, surface damages shall be dealt with by the agents of the French liquidation service working on the spot in cooperation with the German Mine Services.

5. The French Government and the German Government are, however, prepared to consider a lump-sum settlement based on the following principles as soon as more accurate data regarding the matter are available:

(a) Damage caused to the railways, tramways, and roads to be estimated within the framework of the existing agreements by a commission consisting of four arbitrators, each party appointing two, and a Referee who shall be neither French nor German and who shall be appointed, in the absence of an agreement between the arbitrators, by the President of the Bank for International Settlements;

(b) The damage caused to property of other kinds (houses, &c.) and notifed before March 1, 1935, to be divided by the Arbitration Commission between the French Administration and the German Administration in such a manner as to insure the correct interpretation of the term "noted" appearing in the Agreement of December 3, 1934; payment for the damage thus charged to the French Administration to be estimated inclusively after a brief expert opinion has been given by the parties or by the Arbitration Commission;

(c) Outstanding lawsuits to be estimated under the same conditions.

The German Administration shall debit the French Administration with the lump sums thus fixed for these three categories of disputes and shall insure their liquidation in lieu of the French Administration, which shall be relieved of all obligations.

ARTICLE 4

1. The services of the French personnel shall terminate at midnight on the night of February 28/March 1, 1935. In order, however, to help the new owners to take over the services and to complete current transactions for which it assumes responsibility, such as the payment of wages on the due dates, &c., the Administration of the State mines shall retain the services of the necessary personnel and provide for their remuneration for a short period to be determined in each case.

2. The Administration of the State mines shall endeavor to release, within periods compatible with the service and with the position of its French personnel, the service dwellings occupied by the latter. In the present state of affairs, except for cases of *force majeure*, it proposes to release 250 dwellings for March 15, 1935, and 200 more for April 15, while, as regards the remainder, the French Administration will do all in its power to expedite their release and does not intend to retain any of the dwellings after April 30, 1935.

In order to insure the proper execution of this plan, the German Government will, for its part, take no steps to prevent French removal firms called into the Saar, after the local resources have been exhausted, from entering the territory and working there with their men.

3. The French personnel which have not yet left on April 1, 1935, shall be regarded, from the fiscal point of view, as already domiciled outside Germany. In general, the personnel remaining in the service dwellings after March 1, 1935, will continue to enjoy normal advantages in kind. The instruction given to the children of such personnel in the college and French school of Saarbruck will come to an end on April 1, 1935.

Article 5

1. The allocation of the archives will take place in the following manner:

The French Mines Administration will transmit to the German Administration:

Archives previous to 1930 which are still in existence;

Files of the personnel remaining in service;

Files of surface damages;

Files of purchases, sales or leases of buildings;

Files of lawsuits which have been concluded;

Copies of current commercial contracts taken over by the German Administration, together with the commission notes, transport contracts, execution cards, order notes, tariffs, lists of customers and supplies.

On the other hand, the French Administration will retain the commercial accountancy documents and cash vouchers necessary, in accordance with the rules of French public accountancy, to furnish evidence of its administration, the documents relating to the personnel leaving the service of the Mines, and the files of legal disputes which it undertakes to liquidate.

2. The two Administrations shall send each other copies of the documents in the files which they retain, in so far as this is necessary for dealing with current matters or matters in course of liquidation.

Article 6

1. On the conclusion of the operation referred to in Article 4, paragraph 1, a part of the French personnel not exceeding thirty persons shall remain on the spot as agents of the French liquidation service in order to deal with questions still remaining to be settled, and, in particular, the questions referred to in Article 3, paragraph 4. The German Administration shall place at the disposal of these agents, for their work, suitable offices and means of transport, and shall give them the necessary facilities for studying and settling disputes. . . .

3. The activity of these agents shall come to an end either by the inclusion of the lump-sum settlement provided for in Article 3, paragraph 5, or, on the expiry of their work, by agreement between the two Administrations.

Article 7

1. France transfers to Germany all her rights over the railways situated in the Saar.

2. All claims of the French State against the Reich in respect of the railways shall be deemed to be settled.

3. The transfer of rights shall take place at midnight on the night of February 28/March 1, 1935.

4. The provisions of the present article shall also apply to the settlement of the claims made by France in respect of the construction in the Saar of Customs stations on the old frontier between the Saar and the rest of Germany.

Article 13

The personnel of German nationality employed on the railway lines shall be taken over by the German Government. The French Government shall withdraw the personnel of French nationality. The payment of pensions to officials already in retirement, to disabled and injured workmen and to their surviving dependants, shall devolve on the State of which the beneficiary is a national on March 1, 1935. The French Government shall pay the German Government an amount equal to the payments made by German personnel to French pension funds and old age and invalidity insurance funds.

Article 36

The present Agreement, approved this day by the League of Nations in accordance with the procedure provided for by the Council resolution of January 17, 1935, shall be ratified. The exchange of the instruments of ratification shall take place in Rome as early as possible. The Agreement shall enter into force on the day on which the instruments of ratification are exchanged. If, however, by February 27, the ratifications have been secured although the instruments thereof have not yet arrived in Rome, the Embassies of the two countries shall draw up a formal record of this fact and the Agreement shall enter into force on February 28.

In faith whereof the undersigned plenipotentiaries, duly authorized, have signed the present Agreement.

Done in duplicate at Naples, February 18, 1935

58. Law Regarding Labor Service: The Coordination of Labor Is Completed, June 26, 1935

*". . . a free conception of labor, and above all, a
due respect for manual work."*

In conjunction with his aim of bringing every *Gliederung* (limb) of the body politic into line with national socialist philosophy, Hitler subjected German labor to *Gleichschaltung* (coordination). On June 26, 1935, at the *Fuehrer's* order, a compulsory labor service law was enacted which in effect denied an independent status for labor and outlawed the right to strike. Every German was to work for a specific time for the German nation. Through this labor service Hitler hoped to reduce unemployment and at the same time enhance his own political power.

THE REICH GOVERNMENT has decided upon this law which is hereby promulgated.

ARTICLE 1. (1) The Reich Labor Service [*Reichsarbeitsdienst*] is a service of honor to the German people.

(2) All young Germans of both sexes are obligated to serve their country in the Reich Labor Service.

(3) It is the purpose of the Reich Labor Service to educate German youth in the spirit of National Socialism so that they may obtain a true national community sentiment, a free conception of labor, and above all, a due respect for manual work.

Reichsgesetzblatt, vol. 1, no. 64, June 27, 1935, pp. 760-71. Translated by the editor.

(4) The Reich Labor Service is organized for the purpose of carrying out public welfare work.

Article 2. (1) The Reich Labor Service is under the jurisdiction of the Reich Minister of the Interior. His subordinate, the Reich Labor Leader, holds supreme authority over the Reich Labor Service.

(2) The Reich Labor Leader heads the Reich administration of the Labor Service. He determines the organization, arranges for distribution of work, and directs education and training.

Article 3. (1) The *Fuehrer* and Chancellor of the Reich decides on the number of people to be called annually for service and he determines the amount of service.

(2) Obligation for service commences at the earliest with the completion of the 18th year and ends at the latest with the completion of the 25th year.

(3) Individuals who are subject to compulsory service will be called ordinarily by the Reich Labor Service in the calendar year during which they complete their 19th year. It is possible to enroll in the Reich Labor Service at an earlier age.

(4) Those subject to compulsory labor and those serving voluntarily can be imprisoned for more than 30 days if they leave the service in any other way than that provided in Article 16.

Article 4. Those subject to compulsory service are recruited by the special office of the Reich Labor Service.

Article 5. (1) The following categories are excluded from Labor Service:

(a) those who have been punished with penal servitude;

(b) those who do not hold the rights of citizenship;

(c) those subject to the measures for protection and improvement as outlined in Article 42a of the Criminal Code;

(d) those who have been expelled from the National Socialist Party because of dishonorable activities;

(e) those who have been punished for treason.

(2) The Reich Minister of the Interior may make exceptions to (c) and (e) of Part 1 in this article.

(3) Those subject to compulsory service in the Labor Service who have lost their eligibility for public office may be called for service only after the end of their period of sentence.

Article 6. (1) No persons shall be recruited for the Labor Service who are unfitted for such service.

(2) Those subject to Labor Service who live abroad or who want to go abroad for a long period may be relieved of their obligation for labor service for a period of up to two years. In exceptional cases they may be permanently relieved. In any case they are to be relieved for the period of the stay abroad.

ARTICLE 7. (1) No one can serve in the Reich Labor Service who is of non-Aryan descent or who is married to a person of non-Aryan descent. Non-Aryan descent is determined according to the instructions laid down by the Reich Minister of the Interior, dated August 8, 1933, as stated in Article I-a, Section 3 of the Reich Law Concerning State Officials (*Reichsgesetzblatt* 1, p. 575).

(2) Non-Aryans who by Article 15, Section 2 of the Army Law have been declared worthy of military service may also be permitted to serve in the Reich Labor Service.

ARTICLE 8. Those subject to Labor Service who can show cause for urgent occupational activities may postpone their service from two to five years.

ARTICLE 9. Labor Service duties for young women are subject to special legal regulations.

ARTICLE 10. (1) Members of the Reich Labor Service include

(a) the permanent staff;

(b) recruits for the Labor Service;

(c) volunteers.

(2) Individuals may be engaged by labor contracts for special duties in the inside service.

ARTICLE 11. (1) The permanent staff consists of the regular leaders and officials and also the candidates for these posts. The regular leaders and officials are active as professionals in the Reich Labor Service.

(2) Any candidate for Leader is required, before he is appointed regular Troop Leader, to give written confirmation that he agrees to serve for a period of at least 10 years. He must supply proof of his Aryan descent. He must in addition have completed his active service in the Army.

(3) Regular leaders and officials are to be retired on reaching definite age limits.

(4) Those officials of other departments who are transferred to the Labor Service retain the salary and rights of their original office.

(5) The *Fuehrer* and Reich Chancellor appoints and dismisses all members of the Reich Labor Service from the rank of Work Leader up. All other members of the permanent staff are appointed and dismissed by the Reich Minister of the Interior on the recommendation of the Reich Labor Leader. The Reich Minister of the Interior may give this power to the Reich Labor Leader.

ARTICLE 12. (1) A regular leader or official may be dismissed from the service at any time in the following cases:

(a) in reasonable cases at his own request;

(b) if he no longer possesses the physical or mental powers necessary for the exercise of his duties and if, in line with the reports of the physician of the Labor Service, he cannot expect to regain the necessary powers within term of a year;

(c) if in the judgment of his superior he no longer possesses the ability to carry out his duties.

(2) Dismissal follows if such reasons barring membership as outlined in Articles 5 and 7 are discovered subsequently.

(3) Notice of dismissal and the reasons therefore in cases indicated in Section 1 preceding, letters (b) and (c), is to be given three months in advance for those members of the permanent staff who have served for a term of more than five years. For other permanent members notice will be given one month in advance. In all other cases there will be no definite time notice for dismissal.

ARTICLE 13. Membership in the Reich Labor Service begins from the day of entrance to the day of dismissal.

ARTICLE 14. Membership in the Reich Labor Service is not to be regarded as grounds for any status within the meaning of the labor law and Article 11 of the Decree for Welfare Administration.

ARTICLE 15. Members of the Reich Labor Service are subject to the disciplinary actions of the Reich Labor Service.

ARTICLE 16 (1) Those subject to compulsory Labor Service as well as volunteers may be dismissed from the Reich Labor Service ahead of time:

(a) on application, if after being called, a reason for postponement in accordance with Article 8 is concerned;

(b) if the necessary physical and mental powers for the performance of duty are no longer present.

(2) Advance dismissal of compulsory and voluntary members of the Labor Service is obligatory in the event of reasons against membership in the Reich Labor Service as described in Articles 5 and 7 are later established.

ARTICLE 17. (1) Members of the Reich Labor Service cannot take part in any active service of the National Socialist Party or in any of its affiliates. This is not to be interpreted as prejudicing their membership in the Party.

(2) Members of the Reich Labor Service must have permission for soliciting or exercising membership in organizations of any kind as well as for the formation of organizations inside or outside the Labor Service.

ARTICLE 18. Members of the Reich Labor Service must obtain permission to marry.

ARTICLE 19. Members of the Reich Labor Service must obtain permission to direct a business either for themselves or for the members of their family, and also for taking part in any other occupation which involves payments.

ARTICLE 20. (1) Members of the Reich Labor Service may refuse positions as guardians, trustees, advisors, or any other honorary activity in the Reich, State, or municipal service or in the Party service.

(2) Permission must be obtained for such positions. Such permission will be denied only in exceptional cases.

ARTICLE 21. In the event of sickness or accident, members of the Reich Labor Service are entitled to free medical attention and nursing according to special regulations set up for this purpose.

ARTICLE 22. Salaries of members of the Reich Labor Service are regulated by the payment decree of the Reich Labor Service.

ARTICLE 23. (1) All claims to property rights which come from membership in the Reich Labor Service are regulated by the special ordinances for Reich officials. The supreme agency for such ordinance is in the hands of the Reich Labor Leader.

(2) Decisions by agencies of the Reich Labor Service on enlistment (Articles 5,6,7), replacement (Article 8), and dismissal (Articles 12 and 16) are binding for all law courts. The same applies to decisions on temporary removals.

ARTICLE 24. Pensions for persons injured in service and for members of the permanent staff retiring after at least 10 years of service and their survivors are subject to the Law on Pensions for the Reich Labor Service.

ARTICLE 25. (a) The *Fuehrer* and Reich Chancellor or any agency he chooses may allow retiring members of the Reich Labor Service to wear the uniform of the Reich Labor Service, subject to recall.

(2) This grant may be granted only after honorable service of at least 10 years.

ARTICLE 26. The Reich Minister of the Interior will issue the legal and administrative decrees for the implementation and amplification of this law.

ARTICLE 27. This law is effective from July 1, 1935.

The Reich Minister of the Interior shall determine a later date for several provisions of this law to take effect.

Berlin, June 26, 1935

59. The Nuremberg Laws on Citizenship and Race: Legal Sanction Is Given to Nazi Anti-Semitism, September 15, 1935

"A citizen of the Reich may be only one who is of German or kindred blood. . . ."

On September 15, 1935, the so-called Nuremberg Laws on Citizenship and Race were decreed specifically against the Jews living in the Third Reich. Under these and subsequent laws the Jews were deprived of German citizenship. From this time on they were to be "subjects" of the Nazi Reich. They were not allowed to marry non-Jews, hold posts in the civil service or any branch of the government, practice law or medicine, or work as journalists, actors, teachers, or farmers. From now on they could work only in the most menial jobs. Within a year after promulgation of these laws, at least half the Jews in Germany were unemployed.

The Reich Citizenship Law of September 15, 1935

THE REICHSTAG HAS ADOPTED by unanimous vote the following law which is herewith promulgated.

ARTICLE 1. (1) A subject of the state is one who belongs to the protective union of the German Reich, and who, therefore, has specific obligations to the Reich.

(2) The status of subject is to be acquired in accordance with the provisions of the Reich and the state Citizenship Law.

ARTICLE 2. (1) A citizen of the Reich may be only one who is of German

Reichsgesetzblatt, vol. 1, no. 100, September 15, 1935, pp. 1142-47. Translated by the editor.

or kindred blood, and who, through his behavior, shows that he is both desirous and personally fit to serve loyally the German people and the Reich.

(2) The right to citizenship is obtained by the grant of Reich citizenship papers.

(3) Only the citizen of the Reich may enjoy full political rights in consonance with the provisions of the laws.

ARTICLE 3. The Reich Minister of the Interior, in conjunction with the Deputy to the *Fuehrer*, will issue the required legal and administrative decrees for the implementation and amplification of this law.

Promulgated: September 16, 1935. *In force:* September 30, 1935.

First Supplementary Decree of November 14, 1935

On the basis of Article III of the Reich Citizenship Law of September 15, 1935, the following is hereby decreed:

ARTICLE 1. (1) Until further provisions concerning citizenship papers, all subjects of German or kindred blood who possessed the right to vote in the *Reichstag* elections when the Citizenship Law came into effect, shall, for the present, possess the rights of Reich citizens. The same shall be true of those upon whom the Reich Minister of the Interior, in conjunction with the Deputy to the *Fuehrer* shall confer citizenship.

(2) The Reich Minister of the Interior, in conjunction with the Deputy to the *Fuehrer*, may revoke citizenship.

ARTICLE 2. (1) The provisions of Article I shall apply also to subjects who are of mixed Jewish blood.

(2) An individual of mixed Jewish blood is one who is descended from one or two grandparents who, racially, were full Jews, insofar that he is not a Jew according to Section 2 of Article 5. Full-blooded Jewish grandparents are those who belonged to the Jewish religious community.

ARTICLE 3. Only citizens of the Reich, as bearers of full political rights, can exercise the right of voting in political matters, and have the right to hold public office. The Reich Minister of the Interior, or any agency he empowers, can make exceptions during the transition period on the matter of holding public office. These measures do not apply to matters concerning religious organizations.

ARTICLE 4. (1) A Jew cannot be a citizen of the Reich. He cannot exercise the right to vote; he cannot occupy public office.

(2) Jewish officials will be retired as of December 31, 1935. In the event that such officials served at the front in the World War either for Germany or her allies, they shall receive as pension, until they reach the age limit, the full salary last received, on the basis of which their pension would have been computed. They shall not, however, be promoted according to their

seniority in rank. When they reach the age limit, their pension will be computed again, according to the salary last received on which their pension was to be calculated.

(3) These provisions do not concern the affairs of religious organizations.

(4) The conditions regarding service of teachers in public Jewish schools remain unchanged until the promulgation of new regulations on the Jewish school system.

ARTICLE 5. (1) A Jew is an individual who is descended from at least three grandparents who were, racially, full Jews. . . .

(2) A Jew is also an individual who is descended from two full-Jewish grandparents if:
  (a) he was a member of the Jewish religious community when this law was issued, or joined the community later;
  (b) when the law was issued, he was married to a person who was a Jew, or was subsequently married to a Jew;
  (c) he is the issue from a marriage with a Jew, in the sense of Section I, which was contracted after the coming into effect of the Law for the Protection of German Blood and Honor of September 15, 1935;
  (d) he is the issue of an extramarital relationship with a Jew, according to Section I, and born out of wedlock after July 31, 1936.

ARTICLE 6. (1) Insofar as there are, in the laws of the Reich or in the decrees of the National Socialist German Workers' party and its affiliates, certain requirements for the purity of German blood which extend beyond Article 5, the same remain untouched. . . .

ARTICLE 7. The *Fuehrer* and Chancellor of the Reich is empowered to release anyone from the provisions of these administrative decrees.

The Law for the Protection of German Blood and Honor, September 15, 1935

Imbued with the knowledge that the purity of German blood is the necessary prerequisite for the existence of the German nation, and inspired by an inflexible will to maintain the existence of the German nation for all future times, the *Reichstag* has unanimously adopted the following law, which is now enacted:

ARTICLE 1. (1) Any marriages between Jews and citizens of German or kindred blood are herewith forbidden. Marriages entered into despite this law are invalid, even if they are arranged abroad as a means of circumventing this law.

(2) Annulment proceedings for marriages may be initiated only by the Public Prosecutor.

ARTICLE 2. Extramarital relations between Jews and citizens of German or kindred blood are herewith forbidden.

ARTICLE 3. Jews are forbidden to employ as servants in their households female subjects of German or kindred blood who are under the age of forty-five years.

ARTICLE 4. (1) Jews are prohibited from displaying the Reich and national flag and from showing the national colors.

(2) However, they may display the Jewish colors. The exercise of this right is under state protection.

ARTICLE 5. (1) Anyone who acts contrary to the prohibition noted in Article 1 renders himself liable to penal servitude.

(2) The man who acts contrary to the prohibition of Article 2 will be punished by sentence to either a jail or penitentiary.

(3) Anyone who acts contrary to the provisions of Articles 3 and 4 will be punished with a jail sentence up to a year and with a fine, or with one of these penalties.

ARTICLE 6. The Reich Minister of Interior, in conjunction with the Deputy to the *Fuehrer* and the Reich Minister of Justice, will issue the required legal and administrative decrees for the implementation and amplification of this law.

ARTICLE 7. This law shall go into effect on the day following its promulgation, with the exception of Article 3, which shall go into effect on January 1, 1936.

60. Hitler's Decree to the Army on the Introduction of the Reich War Flag, November 7, 1935

"To follow the flag — that will be your pride."

As he went about the business of increasing the armed might of the Third Reich, Hitler was careful to seek and maintain the absolute loyalty of the *Wehrmacht,* the national army which he had designated to replace the *Reichswehr* of the Weimar Republic. In a decree dated November 7, 1935, the *Fuehrer* informed the soldiers of his army about the new war flag which was to be their banner in the future.

SOLDIERS OF THE *Wehrmacht!*

Today I give to the revived *Wehrmacht* the new Reich war flag as the banner of its service obligations.

Let the swastika [*Hakenkreuz*] be your symbol of the unity and cleanliness of the nation, the emblem of National Socialist philosophy, the pledge for the freedom and power of the Reich.

The Iron Cross is to remind you of the peerless tradition of the old *Wehrmacht,* on the virtues that animated it, on the model it gave to you.

To the Reich colors — black-white-red — you are to dedicate yourself in faithful service in life and to death.

To follow the flag — that will be your pride.

The former Reich war flag is honorably withdrawn.

I reserve the right to let it be used on special memorial days.

The *Fuehrer* and Supreme Commander of the *Wehrmacht,*

Adolf Hitler

Völkischer Beobachter, November 8, 1935. Translated by the editor.

61. Dissolution of the *Stahlhelm*: The Veterans Organization Is Subjected to Coordination, November 7, 1935

*"Under such circumstances I do not believe that it is
any longer necessary. . . ."*

The *Stahlhelm* (Steel Helmet), the nationalist ex-servicemen's organization, was organized in 1918 by Franz Seldte, a reserve officer in Magdeburg, and Theodor Duesterberg, a former officer on the general staff. Their aim was to oppose the German revolution and to work for the restoration of the Hohenzollern monarchy. The veterans group played an important role in the politics of the 1920s and early 1930s.

Hitler wanted no opposition of any kind. In a decree dated December 1, 1933, he incorporated all members of the *Stahlhelm* to the age of thirty-five into the SA, the *Sturmabteilung,* or Storm Troopers. He required all older members of the *Stahlhelm* to be formed into units of the SA Reserve. On February 17, 1934, the *Stahlhelm* was given the name of National Socialist League of Ex-Servicemen. On November 7, 1935, the *Fuehrer* dissolved the *Stahlhelm.* He announced his decision in a letter to co-founder Seldte, who was now serving in the cabinet as Reich minister of labor. The dissolution was another step in the gradual *Gleichschaltung* (coordination) of every organization or group in the Third Reich.

TODAY THE RECONSTRUCTION of the German *Wehrmacht* has been crowned through the attestation of the first year's recruits of the Third Reich. With

---

Völkischer Beobachter, November 9, 1935. Translated by the editor.

it the German *Wehrmacht* becomes for all time the bearer of German weapons and the guardian of German traditions. The Party is the expression of our formative will and of our political power.

Under such circumstances I do not believe that it is any longer necessary to maintain the continued existence of the *Stahlhelm*. The aim of the *Stahlhelm* was to guard the tradition of the old Army and to combine it with the struggle to reconstruct a strong Reich, which will find in its new *Wehrmacht* its certain security and the defender of its freedom.

Now, upon the achievement of this goal, I express to you as the leader of the *Stahlhelm* league and all its members my army's thanks for the work and the great sacrifice that you have made in service of these ideals.

In order to give the old constituents of the NSDFB (*Stahlhelm*), who already, even before the accession to power, fought for the freedom of the Reich, the possibility of taking part in additional arenas in the reconstruction of the National Socialist Third Reich, I am freeing these men from their former commitments. The takeover of the old members of the *Stahlhelm* cannot be handled in corporative fashion but must be treated on an individual basis. Outside of the general conditions for the takeover by the NSDAP and its limbs, the SA, SS, and the NSKK, I believe it is necessary that special procedures be instituted by the Chancellor of the Exchequer as well as by the leaders of each individual unit.

Final decisions on the transfer to the NSDAP will be the province of the Reich Chancellor of the Exchequer in common with the current leaders of the Party (*Gauleiter, Ortsgruppenleiter*).

The admission of former members of the *Stahlhelm* into the SA will be decided by the Chief of Staff of the SA.

The admission of former *Stahlhelm* members into the SS will be decided by the *Reichsfuehrer* of the SS [Heinrich Himmler].

The admission of the former *Stahlhelm* members in the NSKK [*Nationalsozialistische Kraftfahr Korps*—National Socialist Motor Corps] will be decided by the Corps-Leader of the NSKK.

This shall all be decided as necessity requires it.

Those members of the *Stahlhelm* who do not want to take part in political activities and who wish to continue to give attention to their soldierly reminiscences, are urged to join the Kyffhäuser Bund.

The liquidation of the *Stahlhelm* and its economic functions will be administered by the Reich Government. The Reich Chancellor of the Exchequer is ready to give his counsel in this process of liquidation. . . .

I thank you, Party member Seldte and your former fighting comrades, for your great idealistic work and for your many sacrifices in the reconstruction of the Reich, and I am at the same time convinced that history itself in the future will not forget this contribution to the German nation. The evaluation will be an even higher one if we achieve a unity as the result of all our struggles for the reconstruction of the Reich. What today may well seem to be a heavy sacrifice to the former members of the *Stahlhelm* is nothing more than a historical revalorization of former work and accomplishments. We can only speak of the future of our people if we are successful in overcoming the evil of the old German particularism and if we get away from regarding that situation as the foundation of our existence.

One People, One Reich, One Political Will, and a Sword!

I ask you and your comrade fighters to help us in this mighty work of German affirmation for life.

62. Heinrich Himmler Praises His *Schutzstaffel* as an Anti-Bolshevist Fighting Organization, November 12, 1935

> *". . . we march forward as a soldierly, National Socialist order of Nordic men. . . ."*

Two organizations played an important role in the history of the Third Reich – the SA and the SS. The SA, or *Sturmabteilung,* the Brown Shirts, led by Captain Ernst Roehm, was designed to win the battle of the streets against the Communists during the National Socialists' drive for political power. The SS, or *Schutzstaffel,* organized as a defense corps, started out as a small, highly disciplined personal bodyguard for Hitler. Later, under the leadership of Heinrich Himmler, it became the elite corps of the Nazi party, bound to Hitler by oath, pledged to fight for him to the death, and wearing black shirts for identification. More disciplined than the SA and dependent upon Hitler himself, the SS grew over the years into a formidable fighting force.

In 1929, leadership of the SS was entrusted by Hitler to Heinrich Himmler, a seemingly mild-mannered chicken farmer from Bavaria. By 1935 the organization was expanded to some two hundred thousand men. On November 12, 1935, Himmler appeared before a national convention of farmers held in Goslar and delivered an address on "The *Schutzstaffel* as an Anti-Bolshevist Fighting Organization." In a long, rambling speech, the SS leader gave his own version of Bolsheviks and Jews in history and then spoke at length on the "principles and virtues" of the SS. Following are condensed excerpts from the beginning and end of Himmler's speech.

Der 3. Reichsbauerntag in Goslar vom 10-17 (Berlin: Reichsnahrstand, 1935), vol. 3, pp. 45 ff. Translated by the editor.

MUCH IS SAID ABOUT Bolshevism today. Most people have the idea that this Bolshevism is a new thing that emerged in modern times. Many even believe that this Bolshevism, a battle of the lower elements of society organized and led by Jews, has for the first time become a new problem in world history.

We believe it is necessary to establish the fact that, as long as there are people on this earth, they must recognize the struggle between humanity and subhuman life, between human beings and Jews. One can come to the conclusion that this is a struggle between life and death, as natural a law as any other plague, such as the battle of the pest bacillus against the healthy body.

In order to understand the tactics of this Jewish-Bolshevist enemy, it is necessary to look at a few historical examples.

The Bible gives us one historical example of the destruction of an Aryan people by Bolshevist-Jewish methods. Read about it with open eyes — that part of Jewish history in which it is told how the Jews lived among the Persian people in all the cities and in all the villages and in the capital city Susa; how this Aryan Persian folk learned about the danger of the Jews in their midst; and how the minister Haman epitomized the will to solve the Jewish problem in Persia; further about the monarch, named Ahasveros in the Bible, but who was really Xerxes; how the court Jews separated him from his wife Casthi, and how the Jews through use of their girls and the prostitute Esther ensnared the king.

We then see how this blind and misled king, against the advice of his racially conscious minister Haman, saved the Jew Mordechai from the gallows — a shameful deed which was not the last of its kind in history — and how this Jew Mordechai was made vice-monarch, how he revealed his Bolshevism in a cold-blooded and vicious fashion by rounding up in all the cities and villages all the most noble of Persians and all other enemies of the Jews on a specially indicated day and under a decree of the monarch put them to death. The Bible tells us that some 75,000 Persians were then slaughtered. And another decree of the Aryan monarch ordered that the fourteenth and fifteenth days of the month Adar be made a legal holiday and celebrated year after year as a victory festival of the Jews, the Purim festival, which has been celebrated to the present day.

It is understandable that the old Persian people could not recover from this calamity. And the whole tragedy of this Jewish Bolshevism can be seen in the fact that the great religion of this people, Zoroastrianism, and also their language have been well-nigh forgotten. Now, after two thousand years, German scholars have subjected the words of Zoroaster to scientific investigation and have translated the old Persian language into German.

That is always the way of Bolshevism: it takes over control of a people, slices off their heads, or places them in administrative, industrial, scientific, cultural, spiritual, and bodily slavery.

How such tragedies take place we cannot explain completely. But we do know that in many cases our eternal enemy, the Jew, no matter what mantle he wears or what organization he operates, always has his bloody hand in the story. We see it when mothers and daughters were burned into ashes after witch trials. We see it in the Inquisition when the Spaniards were depopulated. And we see it in the terrible Thirty Years' War, when twenty-four millions of Germans were cut down to a hungry four millions.

Now I come to modern times — to the French Revolution, to the Reign of Terror, in which blonde and blue-eyed Frenchmen, the best of the French people, were slaughtered by the Jacobins, the Bolsheviks of their day. You get the truth here — the horror of the Reign of Terror was the work of the Free Masons, that excellent Jewish organization.

Now I come to the Russian Revolution. Here, too, I do not want to repeat the oft-told tale of dates and facts, but I want to cut down to the essential.

First, careful plans were made to use the Russian people and turn them by revolutionary propaganda to the desired direction. A number of Russian leaders, especially Stolypin, before they could introduce the reforms they envisioned, came under the influence of Jewish anarchists. They saw to it that Russia went to war against Germany. Here again you see how the Jewish-Free Mason combination led to World War.

The Free Masons changed the motto from "System of the Yellow Flag" to the "System of the Red Flag." In parliamentary language it was said that control was transferred from the democratic-bourgeois parties to the Socialist Party, called Social Democrats in our country, there called the Menshiviks. At its head was the Jew Kerensky, whose handling illustrates Aryan decency. His Jewish mother had been condemned to death because of anarchistic activities, but she was given her life by the mother of the last Czar because she was pregnant with this Kerensky.

That is it — through Aryan decency this Kerensky was spared, and he went on to overthrow the last Czar and prepare the way for Bolshevism.

Let me turn now to the *Schutzstaffel*, which is a part of that National Socialist German Workers' Party created by Adolf Hitler, and which has been given the special duty of maintaining the security of the Reich.

When the *Fuehrer* [on November 29, 1925] gave the command for the organization of the *Schutzstaffel*, and then in the year 1929 raised it to a great corps, it became clear to us that the *Schutzstaffel* could only fulfill its duty if it understood and carried out all the measures set up for it by the *Fuehrer*.

The first guiding principle for us is the knowledge of the true value of the blood and of the elite race. That principle projected in 1929 will hold as long as the *Schutzstaffel* exists.

It is necessary for us to concentrate on the choice of those physical specimens, those who come closest to the goal of Nordic-oriented humans. Physical characteristics, such as height and outward appearance, play an important role in this task.

It is really unnecessary for me to assure you that this principle has become sharper and sharper as the years have gone by. And I also make it plain to you that we will not remain inactive in promoting this principle.

The second principle and virtue that we support is that the *Schutzstaffel* must retain as its current and its permanent characteristics the will to freedom and the spirit to fight.

The third principle and virtue necessary for the very existence of the *Schutzstaffel* is the idea of loyalty and honor. Both are inseparable from one another. The idea was presented in two sentences, first in the sentence of the *Fuehrer*: "My honor is called loyalty" and second in the sentence of old German law: "All honor comes from loyalty."

Many things, so do we teach the SS man, can be forgiven on this earth, but never disloyalty. He who injures the concept of loyalty cuts himself off from our society. For loyalty is a matter of the heart, never of the brain. The heart must continue to beat, and when it stops, man dies, just as a people dies when it loses its sense of loyalty.

The fourth principle and virtue is obedience, obedience that is absolute and comes from the free will, obedience that is in the service of our world-view (*Weltanschauung*), obedience that never hesitates for an instant but blindly follows every order of the *Fuehrer*.

All these principles are understood by every SS man down to the finest detail. We believe it fair to assert that in the last six years the *Schutzstaffel* in general has followed these principles to the letter, and lives according to them. We know that from year to year more of these virtues are accepted and become the valued treasury of every SS man. They will be passed from generation to generation of SS men.

These principles and virtues have led to a set of laws which govern the life of our SS men and laid the groundwork for their future. The first SS law, decreed in the year 1931, set standards for marital engagements and marriage itself. In this respect we acted because of the value of the blood. We understood well that it was stupid to expect an ethnic elite unless we paid attention to the racial forbears of our SS men. We wanted to utilize good blood as a preparation for the future.

I should like to add a word about several other problems. First: in that little book: "Fifty Questions and Answers for the SS man," the first question is: "How does the oath read?"

The response is: "I swear before God this holy oath, that I shall give absolute obedience to the *Fuehrer* of the German Reich and people, Adolf Hitler, the Supreme Commander of the *Wehrmacht*, and as a courageous soldier will be ready at all times to lay down my life for this oath."

The second question reads: "Now do you believe in a God?"

The response reads: "Yes, I believe in an Almighty God."

The third question reads: "What do you feel about a person who does not believe in God?"

The response reads: "I hold him to be an arrogant, senseless, and stupid ass, and he doesn't belong to us."

You may well understand that we could not be the great organization we are, if we were not utterly convinced of the existence of a God, who reigns over us and our Fatherland, who created our people and this earth, and who sent us our *Fuehrer*.

We, the *Schutzstaffel*, came to life on command of the *Fuehrer* and we have grown and prospered. If I attempted to discuss with you today the organization, building, and tasks of the SS, no one would be able to understand me unless he from the depths of his heart and blood can grasp what we are trying to do. Everyone of us who wears the black tunic, no matter what his station in life — worker or sportsman or official or soldier — understands this. Everyone of us knows that he does not stand alone, but represents the will of 200,000 men. He knows that he represents this black corps and its sense of nobility and honor.

So, bolstered by our principles and laws, we march forward as a soldierly, National Socialist order of Nordic men, and as a sworn community of racial comrades who believe in their future. We want to be the forerunners of those who shall work for the eternal life of the German people.

63. Occupation of the Rhineland: Hitler Breaks Versailles Curb, Citing the Franco-Soviet Treaty as a Reason, March 7, 1936

"Thereby the Rhine pact of Locarno lost its inner meaning and practically ceased to exist."

In October 1933, Hitler made his first major breach of the Treaty of Versailles when he withdrew Germany from the sixty-two nation disarmament conference in Geneva and renounced its membership in the League of Nations. In March of 1935, following the return of the Saar in January, Hitler publicly denounced the disarmament clauses of the treaty.

Early in 1936, the Allies, preoccupied with the Ethiopian crisis, were disunited and unable to agree on a common course of action against Hitler. On March 7, 1936, the *Fuehrer* sent his troops into the Rhineland, thereby repudiating the Locarno Pacts of 1925, which regulated the Rhineland borders. According to the Versailles Treaty, the Rhineland was to remain demilitarized.

While German troops streamed into the Rhineland, Hitler spoke to the world on the strength of the German forces. At the same time, he offered to come to terms with the powers. He proposed a militarized zone on both sides of the Rhine, knowing well that the French would not accept the dismantling of their Maginot Line. He also offered Paris a twenty-five year nonaggression pact and suggested that Germany under such conditions might be willing to return to the League.

Following is the text of Hitler's memorandum to the ambassadors of the powers. It was distributed as German troops marched into the Rhineland.

Hitler memorandum distributed to ambassadors of foreign powers, March 7, 1936.

IMMEDIATELY AFTER IT BECAME KNOWN that on May 2, 1935, a pact had been signed between France and the U.S.S.R., the German Government called the attention of other signatory powers to the Rhine Pact of Locarno, and to the fact that the obligations which France assumed in the new pact are not compatible with her obligations under the Rhine pact.

The German government at that time gave its reasons in detail, both from a legal and a political standpoint.

As regards the legal position, this was elaborated in the German memorandum of May 25, 1935; as regards the political, in the numerous diplomatic conversations which followed in the wake of this memorandum.

The governments involved also know that neither the original to the German memorandum nor the arguments advanced by them through diplomatic channels or in public declarations could shake the standpoint of the German Government.

In fact, the entire discussions conducted since May, 1935, diplomatically and publicly, concerning these questions have in all points been able merely to confirm the interpretation of the German Government, to which it gave expression from the very beginning.

1. It is not denied that the Franco-Soviet pact is exclusively directed against Germany.

2. It is not denied that in that pact France assumed obligations in the event of a conflict between Germany and the Soviet Union which far exceed its mandate arising from the covenant of the League and which compel it to advance against Germany militarily, even then when it cannot, in so doing, fall back upon the recommendation, or in fact upon any known decision of the League Council.

3. It is not denied, therefore, that in such an event France arrogates to itself the right to decide, upon its own authority, as to who is the aggressor.

4. It is therefore established that France has assumed obligations toward the Soviet Union which practically mean that France must, under certain circumstances, act as though neither the League covenant nor the Rhine pact, which makes reference to this covenant, was operative.

This result of the Franco-Soviet treaty is not nullified by the fact that France has therein made a reservation of being not obligated to military procedure against Germany in the event of thereby laying itself open to sanctions by the guarantor powers, Italy and Britain.

As regards this reservation, the fact is decided that the Rhine pact does not rest alone upon guarantee obligations by Britain and Italy, but primarily upon obligations arising from relationship between France and Germany.

The only question at issue, therefore, is whether France, in undertaking the treaty obligations, kept within the bounds prescribed for it by the Rhine pact in relationship to Germany.

To this, however, Germany must reply in the negative.

The Rhine pact was to bring to realization the aim of securing peace in Western Europe by renunciation by Germany, on one side, and France and Belgium, on the other side, of application of military force for all time in their relations to one another.

It took no exception to the treaties with Poland and Czechoslovakia, laid upon the table at Locarno by the representative of France, but it was on the self-evident assumption that these treaties were adapted to the construction of the Rhine pact and contained no provision for handling Article XVI of the League covenant, such as that provided for the new Franco-Soviet arrangement.

The contents of those special arrangements, as it became known to the German Government, corresponded to this.

The exceptions permitted to the Rhine pact are, to be sure, not expressly focused upon Poland and Czechoslovakia but were formulated abstractly.

The meaning of all negotiations having to do with this point, however, was this: that a compromise was to be found between the Franco-German renunciation of war and the desire of France to retain obligations from pacts already operative.

If, on conclusion of the pact, certain exceptions to this renunciation of war beyond the right of self-defense were conceded, the political reason therefor, as was generally known, lay solely in the fact that France had previously assumed certain obligations of an ally toward Poland and Czechoslovakia which it was unwilling to sacrifice to the idea of absolute safeguarding of peace in the West.

Germany, at that time, agreed to these reservations upon renunciation of war because it has a clear conscience.

If, therefore, France now makes use of the abstract formulation of war possibilities, approved in the Rhine pact, in order now to conclude a new treaty against Germany with a militarily highly armed state; if, thereby, it further and in so decisive a manner narrows down the implications of war renunciation as agreed to with Germany, and if thereby, as pointed out, it does not even remain within the formal legal limits prescribed, it has thereby created a completely new situation and has destroyed the political system of the Rhine pact, both implied and actually.

The last debates and decisions of the French Parliament have proved that France is determined, despite the representations made by Germany, to give final effect to the pact with the Soviet Union; yet diplomatic conversations have developed the fact that France already considers itself bound by the signature to this pact, affixed May 2, 1935.

In the face of such a development in European policy, the German Reich Government cannot remain inactive if it does not want to reject or to renounce the interest the German people have duly entrusted to it.

In the course of negotiations in recent years the German Government has constantly emphasized that it is willing to stick to and to fulfill all obligations arising from the Rhine pact, as long as the other contracting parties likewise are willing, on their part, to stand by this pact.

This self-evident presupposition can now be regarded as no longer fulfilled on the part of France.

France has replied to the friendly offers tendered it again and again by Germany and to Germany's assurance of friendship by violating the Rhine pact, and by signing a military alliance directed exclusively against Germany.

Thereby the Rhine pact of Locarno lost its inner meaning and practically ceased to exist.

Germany, therefore, no longer considers herself bound to this now defunct pact.

The German Government is now compelled to meet the new situation which developed from this treaty — a situation aggravated by the fact that the Franco-Soviet treaty finds its complement in the treaty of alliance between Czechoslovakia and the Soviet Union, which is an exact parallel.

In the interest of the primitive right of a nation to secure her own borders and to safeguard her possibilities of defense, the German Government, therefore, beginning today, restituted full, unmitigated sovereignty of the Reich in the demilitarized zone of the Rhineland.

In order, however, to forestall any misconception of its intention, and in order to pledge the purely defensive character of these measures beyond doubt, and in order further to give expression to its eternally constant yearning for real pacification of Europe and States having equal rights and enjoying equal respect, the German Reich Government declares itself willing, on the basis of the following proposals, to enter upon new arrangements for erection of a system of new European peace safeguarding:

1. The German Reich government declares its willingness to enter at once upon negotiations with France and Belgium for creation of a bilateral demilitarized zone, and in advance, to agree to extend such a proposal to any desired depth of comprehensiveness, provided only there is complete parity.

2. The German Reich government proposes, for the sake of securing the inviolability and invulnerability of frontiers in the West, a non-aggression pact concluded between Germany, France and Belgium, whose duration it is ready to fix at twenty-five years.

3. The German Reich government desires to invite England and Italy to sign this pact as guarantor powers.

4. The German Reich government is agreeable, in case the Royal Netherlands government so desires and other contracting parties deem it expedient, to have the Netherlands included in this pact system.

5. The German government is ready, for the sake of further strengthening these security measures, to conclude between the Western powers an air pact, designed automatically and effectively to forestall the danger of a sudden air attack.

6. The Reich government repeats its offer to conclude non-aggression pacts with States bordering on the east of Germany, and a similar one with Poland.

Seeing that the Lithuanian government in the last few months has subjected its attitude toward the Memel territory to a certain revision, the Reich government takes back the exception which once applied to Lithuania, and declares its readiness to sign a nonaggression pact also with Lithuania, provided the guaranteed autonomy of the Memel territory is effectively carried out.

Now that Germany's equality at last is finally achieved and full sovereignty over the whole Reich territory is re-established, the Reich government regards the principal grounds for its withdrawal from the League of Nations removed.

It is ready to re-enter the League in expectation that in due course, by amicable negotiation, the question of colonial equality as well as the question of separation of the League of Nations Covenant from its Versailles basis shall be cleared up.

64. The *Fuehrer* Inaugurates a Four-Year Plan Designed to Improve the Economy of the Third Reich, August 1936

"The German economy must be fit for war within four years."

After three and a half years in office, Hitler came to be dissatisfied with the Reich Ministry of Economics and with the German business world in general. The German economy, he believed, had not progressed to the point where Germany could have a powerful say in world diplomacy. Accordingly, in the summer of 1936, the *Fuehrer* began a four-year economic mobilization plan under the direction of Hermann Goering. Following is a condensed version of Hitler's plan which he gave to Albert Speer, his chief architect. It will be noted that Hitler felt that there was a close nexus between economic strength and success in war.

Obersalzberg, August, 1936

THE POLITICAL SITUATION

Politics are the conduct and the course of the historical struggle for life of the peoples. The aim of these struggles is the assertion of existence.

No State will be able to withdraw or even remain at a distance from this historical conflict. *Since Marxism, through its victory in Russia, has established one of the greatest empires in the world as a forward base for its future operations, this question has become a menacing one. Against a democratic world ideologically rent within itself stands a unified aggressive will founded upon an authoritarian ideology.* The means of military

Germany, *Auswärtiges Amt, Documents on German Foreign Policy*, Series C (Washington, D.C.: Government Printing Office, 1949), vol. 5, pp. 853-62.

power available to this aggressive will are meantime increasing rapidly from year to year.

Germany will, as always, have to be regarded as the focal point of the Western world in face of the Bolshevist attacks. I do not regard this as an agreeable mission but rather as a handicap and encumbrance upon our national life regrettably resulting from our position in Europe. We cannot, however, escape this destiny. *A victory of Bolshevism over Germany would not lead to a Versailles Treaty but to the final destruction, indeed to the annihilation of the German people.*

The extent of such a catastrophe cannot be foreseen. How, indeed, would the whole of densely populated Western Europe (including Germany), after a collapse into Bolshevism, live through probably the most gruesome catastrophe for the peoples which has been visited upon mankind since the downfall of the States of antiquity? *In the face of the necessity of defense against this danger, all other considerations must recede into the background as being completely irrelevant.*

Germany's Defensive Capacity

Germany's defensive capacity is based upon several factors. I would give pride of place to the intrinsic value of the German people *per se.* A German people with an impeccable political leadership, a firm ideology and a thorough military organization certainly constitutes the most valuable factor of resistance which the world of today can possess. Political leadership is ensured by the National Socialist Party; ideological solidarity has, since the victory of National Socialism, been introduced to a degree that had never previously been attained. It must be constantly deepened and hardened on the basis of this concept. This is the aim of the National Socialist education of our people.

Military development is to be effected through the new Army. *The extent and pace of the military development of our resources cannot be made too large or too rapid!* It is a capital error to think that there can be any argument on these points or any comparison with other vital necessities. However much the general pattern of life of a people ought to be a balanced one, it is nonetheless imperative that at particular times certain disturbances of the balance, to the detriment of other, less vital, tasks, must be adopted. *If we do not succeed in developing the German* Wehrmacht *within the shortest possible time into the first Army in the world, in training, in the raising of units, in armaments, and, above all, in spiritual education as well, Germany will be lost!*

Germany's Economic Position

We are overpopulated and cannot feed ourselves from our own resources.

The final solution lies in extending the living space of our people and/or the sources of its raw materials and foodstuffs. It is the task of the political leadership one day to solve this problem.

The temporary easing can only be brought about within the framework of our present economy. In this connection, the following is to be noted:

It is not sufficient merely to draw up, from time to time, raw material or foreign exchange balances, or to talk about the preparation of a war economy in time of peace; on the contrary, it is essential to ensure peace-time food supplies and above all those means for the conduct of a war which it is possible to make sure of by human energy and activity. And I therefore draw up the following programme for a final solution of our vital needs:

1. Like the military and political rearmament and mobilization of our people, there must also be an economic one, and this must be effected in the same tempo, with the same determination, and, if need be, with the same ruthlessness.

2. For this purpose, in every sphere where it is possible to satisfy our needs through German production, foreign exchange must be saved in order that it can be applied to those requirements which can under no circumstances be supplied *except* by imports.

3. Accordingly, German fuel production must now be stepped up with the utmost speed and be brought to final completion within eighteen months. This task must be attacked and carried out with the same determination as the waging of war.

4. It is equally urgent that the mass production of synthetic rubber should be organized and secured.

5. The question of the cost of these raw materials is quite irrelevant, since it is in any case better for us to produce in Germany dearer tyres (sic) which we can use than for us to sell theoretically cheap tyres.

It is further necessary to increase the German production of iron to the utmost. The objection that we are not in a position to produce from the German iron ore, with a 26 percent content, as cheap a pig iron as from the 45 percent Swedish ores, etc., is irrelevant because we are not in fact faced with the question of what we would *rather* do but only of what we *can* do.

It is further necessary to prohibit forthwith the distillation of alcohol from potatoes. Fuel must be obtained from the ground and not from potatoes.

It is further necessary for us to make our supplies of *industrial* fats independent of imports as rapidly as possible and to produce them from our coal. This task has been solved chemically and is actually crying out to be done. The German economy will either grasp the new economic tasks or else it will prove itself quite incompetent to survive in this modern age when a Soviet State is setting up a gigantic plan. *But in that case it will not be Germany who will go under, but, at most, a few industrialists.*

It is further necessary to increase Germany's output of other ores, *re-*

gardless of cost, and in particular to increase the production of light metals to the utmost in order thereby to produce a substitute for certain other metals.

It is, finally, necessary for rearmament too to make use even now whenever possible of those materials which must and will replace high-grade metals in time of war. *It is better to consider and solve these problems in time of peace than to wait for the next war, and only then, in the midst of a multitude of tasks, to try to undertake these economic researches and methodical testings too.*

In short: I consider it necessary that now, with iron determination, 100 percent self-sufficiency should be attained in all those spheres where it is feasible, and not only should the national requirements in these most important raw materials be made independent of other countries but that we should also thus save the foreign exchange which in peacetime we require for our imports of foodstuffs. *Here I would emphasize that in these tasks I see the only true economic mobilization and not in the throttling of armament industries in peacetime in order to save and stockpile raw materials for war.*

But I further consider it necessary to make an immediate investigation into the outstanding debts in foreign exchange owed to German business abroad. There is no doubt that the outstanding claims of German business are today quite enormous. Nor is there any doubt that behind this in some cases there lies concealed the contemptible desire to possess, whatever happens, certain reserves abroad which are thus withheld from the grasp of the domestic economy. I regard this as deliberate sabotage of our national self-assertion and of the defense of the Reich, and for this reason I consider it necessary for the Reichstag to pass the following two laws: (1) a law providing the death penalty for economic sabotage, and (2) a law making the whole of Jewry liable for all damage inflicted by individual specimens of this community of criminals upon the German economy, and thus upon the German people.

Nearly four precious years have now gone by. There is no doubt that by now we could have been completely independent of foreign countries in the sphere of fuel supplies, rubber supplies, and partly also iron ore supplies. There has been time enough in four years to discover what we cannot do. It is now necessary to state what we can do.

I thus set the following tasks: (1) The German army must be operational within four years; and (2) the German economy must be fit for war within four years.

65. The German Evangelical Church Issues a Manifesto Defending Its Faith and Attacking Hitler's Conception of "Positive Christianity," August 23, 1936

"Come what may, we are bound to obey our heavenly Father."

From the beginning of his policy of *Gleichschaltung,* the coordination of every element in the Third Reich, Hitler found that his main opposition was in religious circles. Political parties and labor unions gave in to Nazi power almost immediately, but churchmen — having to face their consciences — were not as easily intimidated. This held true for both Protestant and Catholic faiths. (The Jews, relatively few in numbers, were not even considered to be important enough to be placed on a plane with other religions. They were to be purged from German life.)

Opposition from Protestants slowly gathered momentum. In March 1936 the Confessional Synod of the German Evangelical Church, meeting at Berlin-Dahlem, accused national socialism of "setting up the myth of race and people, or making idols out of blood, race, nation, honor and liberty, in place of God, and of demanding, as new religion, faith in eternal Germany, and of wishing to supplant the new faith in the eternal realm of our Lord and Saviour Jesus Christ." It was a serious and direct charge against the ideology of national socialism, and it was delivered at a time when it was dangerous to make accusations of this kind.

Hitler's battle against Christianity now assumed serious proportions. Opposition, nevertheless, continued. Karl Barth, the famous theologian, was dismissed from the University of Bonn for refusing to begin his lecture on God with the greeting *"Heil Hitler!"* In some

---

International Conciliation, no. 324 (November 1936).

schools the children had to memorize: "Which is our Bible? Our Bible is *Mein Kampf*."

In this atmosphere the German Evangelical church, opposed to Hitler's new faith of Positive Christianity, issued a ringing manifesto. The opening and concluding pages of this document follow.

To Evangelical Christians and the Authorities in Germany.

The German people are facing a decision of the greatest historical importance.

The question is whether the Christian faith is to retain its right to exist in Germany or not. Today the gospel of Jesus Christ is being attacked here systematically with unequaled violence. This is being done not only by those who reject any belief in God, but also by those who do not wish to deny God, but think they can reject the revelations of Jesus Christ. Powers of the State and of the party are being used against the gospel of Jesus Christ and against those who profess it.

It is hard for us to say this.

The Evangelical Church knows that it is bound to our people and its authorities by the word of God and has its duties toward them. On every Sunday divine aid is asked for the *Fuehrer* and the Fatherland in the Evangelical Church services. Three years ago millions of Evangelical Germans welcomed the new beginning in the life of our people with warm hearts. They did so with all the more joy because the government of the nation had said in its first proclamation of February 1, 1933, that it would "firmly protect Christianity as the basis of our whole moral system."

It is absolutely fantastic for Evangelical Christians to think that official organs in the German Fatherland turn against the gospel of Jesus Christ. But it is happening, nevertheless.

We have kept silence about this for a long time. We have allowed ourselves to be told that it was only the action of a few individuals who would be called to order. We have waited; we have made representations. And the *Fuehrer* has been told what was weighing down the hearts and consciences of Evangelical Christians.

Already on October 4, 1935, the then acting management of the German Evangelical Church, the National Council of Brothers, and the church governing bodies and councils of brothers affiliated with the acting management directed a communication to him in the name of the whole Confessional Church of Germany. It sounds like a cry of the deepest distress when this communication begins as follows:

It has gone so far among the German people that the honor of German citizens is being trampled in the dust because they are Christians. The

Christian population of Germany notes with great perturbation that it is being ridiculed and scorned in every way (in the press, theatres, lectures, and mass meetings) for its faith in the will of Jesus Christ, and its German sentiments and trustworthiness are being doubted.

Especial objects of such suspicions are those who are determined to cling loyally to the gospel. All attempts to improve this situation have remained vain, while at the same time we are being deprived in an ever-increasing degree of practically all possibility of public defense.

During this year the present acting management and the Council of the German Evangelical Church have sent to the *Fuehrer* a memorandum making apparent the whole misery and trouble of the Evangelical population. This memorandum is backed up point for point with detailed evidence. With the greatest conscientiousness, this memorandum and its contents were kept secret from the public, indeed even from the members of the Confessional Church, in order to give an opportunity to the *Fuehrer* of the Reich to give it a thorough examination and at the same time to avoid public misuse of this memorandum. Against our will and without the responsibility of the Confessional Church, this memorandum was published in the foreign press and thus became known also in Germany.

Now we are forced publicly to stand by our word. Now we must prove to the church what motivates us in connection with our people and our church. It is the duty of the Christian Church freely and publicly to oppose attacks upon the gospel, without fear of man. It is its duty especially to open the eyes of the rising generation to the danger menacing us all. It is in this sense of duty that we speak. What the result will be we leave in the hands of Him who has called us to His service. He has commanded it; He will take care of it.

The truth of the gospel is being attacked most openly, even by leading men of the State. We draw attention to the speech of National Director Dr. Ley [Dr. Robert Ley, head of the German Labor Front] on May 1, 1936, which was broadcast over the air and published in the whole German press.

The Evangelical Church is not permitted to repel such attacks before the general public. In the training camps the conception of the world contained in the Rosenberg Mythus, which exalts man and demeans God, frequently is taught. . . .

Protection for Christianity cannot mean that the gospel must be protected by human power. The gospel enjoys a higher protection! But it must mean that disparagements of the gospel be kept aloof from the public life of the German people and that the faith to which the church bears witness be not systematically destroyed in our young folk. This we demand, in the name of the living God, from all those holding office in Germany.

We must have the right publicly and freely to bear witness before the

German people of the faith of its fathers. The continual spying upon the work of the church must cease. The ban upon church meetings in public rooms must be lifted; the fetters placed upon the church press and the works of Christian charity must be removed. Above all must a halt be called upon State officials continually interfering in our internal affairs in the interest of those who, by their life and acts, are bringing about the destruction of the Evangelical Church.

A stop must be put to making it impossible for many evangelical Christians to attend divine service through parades, triumphal processions, demonstrations, and other affairs just on Sunday forenoon. It must be demanded that the German youth be not so in demand for political and sport service as to prejudice Christian family life and to leave no time for showing loyalty to the church.

This whole matter involves the right of the church of Jesus Christ to exist in this world. We ask all the authorities over the German people to bear in mind that they must give an accounting to the living God for all that they are doing. We entreat them to do nothing and to leave nothing undone that is against the will of God and against the freedom of conscience contained in the word of God.

We appeal to the entire Evangelical Christianity in Germany. We urge its members, true to the exhortations of the gospel: Do not allow yourselves to become embittered against the State and the people if you have to suffer for conscience's sake! Always and under all circumstances the Evangelical Christian owes loyalty to his State and to his people. And it also is loyalty when the Christian resists an order that conflicts with the word of God and thus recalls his authorities to obedience to God.

We entreat all evangelical Christians to pay attention to the rising generation and to maintain in it reverence for the gospel that gave strength and support to the German people through a thousand years of history. We call upon all evangelical Christians to confess firmly and openly their faith in the gospel of Jesus Christ. In this decisive hour Jesus Christ wants upright believers and resolute disciples. Now the following words hold good: "He who acknowledges me before men, him will I also acknowledge before my Heavenly Father."

We appeal to the servants of the church to bear witness to the gospel of Jesus Christ firmly and openly, without compromise and without fear of men. Many, for example, have lain in jail and in concentration camps and have had to endure banishment and other things. We do not know what still lies before us. But, come what may, we are bound to obey our Heavenly Father!

Let us do what we must and let us live in the joyous faith that men who fear only God and nothing else in the world are the best servants of their people.

We raise our hands to God the Father, the Son and the Holy Ghost! Be merciful to our people! Let Thy truth remain with us! Help it to victory! Amen.

The Council of Brothers of the Denominational Synod of the German Evangelical Church.

[Signed] D. KOCH

The Acting Management of the German Evangelical Church.

[Signed] MUELLER-DAHLEM

66. Decree on the Strength of the Reich Labor Service: Attention Is Given to Labor Service for Female Youth, September 6, 1935

". . . based temporarily on voluntary enlistments."

On September 6, 1936, Hitler decreed the term of service in and the strength of the Reich Labor Service (*Reichsarbeitsdienst*). To the decree he added a special section devoted to labor requirements for young girls (*Jungmädel*).

ARTICLE 1. The term of service in the Reich Labor Service for all those subject to military service is six months.

ARTICLE 2. The strength of the Reich Labor Service will be raised to 230,000 men, inclusive of the permanent staff, between October 1936 and the beginning of October 1937. The total will be 275,000 men, including permanent staff, in the period to the beginning of October 1939, and 300,000 men, including permanent staff, in the period to the beginning of October 1939.

ARTICLE 3. (1.) The Labor Service for female youth, based temporarily on voluntary enlistments, will be additionally developed in line with this plan.

(2.) The strength of the Labor Service for female youth is be raised to 25,000 Labor Maids in the period from April 1937 to March 1938.

Reichsgesetzblatt, vol. 1, no. 85, September 28, 1936, p. 757. Translated by the editor.

67. The Third Reich and the Japanese Government Sign an Agreement to Oppose the Spread of Communism, November 25, 1936

". . . to work in common against Communist disruptive influences. . ."

One of the factors drawing Nazi Germany and Imperial Japan together was a mutual hostility to communism. On November 25, 1936, the two countries signed an agreement at Berlin expressing opposition to the aims of the Communist Internationale.

THE GERMAN GOVERNMENT and the Japanese Government, recognizing that the aim of the Communist Internationale known as the Comintern is directed at disrupting and violating existing States with all means at its command and convinced that to tolerate the Communist Internationale's interference with the internal affairs of nations not only endangers their internal peace and social well-being but threatens world peace at large, animated by a desire to work in common against Communist disruptive influences, have arrived at the following agreement:

1. The high contracting parties agree to mutually inform each other concerning the activities of the Communist Internationale, to consult with each other concerning measures to combat this activity, and to execute these measures in close cooperation with each other.

2. The two high contracting States will jointly invite third parties whose domestic peace is endangered by the disruptive activities of the Communist Internationale to embark upon measures for warding these off in accordance with the spirit of this agreement or to join in it.

3. For this agreement, both the German and Japanese texts are regarded

---

The New York Times, November 26, 1936.

as original versions. It becomes effective the day of signing and is in force for a period of five years.

The high contracting State will, at the proper time before expiration of this period, arrive at an understanding with each other concerning the form this cooperation is to take.

Supplementary Protocol

A. The competent authorities of both high contracting parties will co-operate most clearly in connection with the exchange of information concerning the activities of the Communist Internationale, as well as in connection with publicity and defense measures against the Communist Internationale.

B. The competent authorities of both high contracting parties will within the framework of existing laws, take strict measures against those who, at home or abroad, directly or indirectly, are active in the service of the Communist Internationale or lend a helping hand to its disruptive work.

With a view to facilitating the cooperation of the competent authorities of both high contracting parties, specified in (A), a permanent commission will be created. In this commission the further defensive measures necessary for combating the disruptive work of the Communist Internationale will be considered and deliberated upon.

Berlin, November 25, 1936; that is, the November 25 of the eleventh year of the Showa Period.

RIBBENTROP
MUSHAKOJI

68. The Hitler Youth Is Formally Declared to Be a State Agency, December 1, 1936

"The future of Germany is dependent upon its youth."

One of Hitler's prime objectives was to win young Germans to national socialism. Accordingly, he founded the Hitler Youth as an important appendage to his system. On December 1, 1936, he decreed this law declaring the Hitler Youth an agency of the Nazi government.

THE FUTURE OF GERMANY is dependent upon its youth. Therefore, all German youth must be prepared for its future duties. The Reich Government has decided upon the following law which is hereby decreed:

ARTICLE 1. All German youth in the territory of the German Reich is brought together in the Hitler Youth.

ARTICLE 2. All German young people, outside of their homes and schools, are to be educated in the Hitler Youth, physically, spiritually, and morally, in the spirit of National Socialism for service to the nation and to the national community.

ARTICLE 3. The task of educating all German youth in the Hitler Youth is the responsibility of the Reich Youth Leader of the National Socialist German Workers' Party. The latter becomes the Youth Leader of the German Reich. He possesses the status of a chief Reich office with its seat in Berlin. He is responsible to the *Fuehrer* and the Reich Chancellor.

ARTICLE 4. The legal decrees and the general measures of administration needed to carry out this law will be issued by the *Fuehrer* and Reich Chancellor.

Translated by the editor from the official text.

69. The University of Bonn Cancels Thomas Mann's Honorary Degree, and the Famous Author Replies in a Scathing Denunciation, December 19, 1936

> *"God help our darkened and desecrated country! . . ."*

The novelist Thomas Mann (1875–1955), a great man in German letters, enjoyed a worldwide reputation. Together with James Joyce and Marcel Proust, he was considered to be among the preeminent novelists of the twentieth century. He was awarded the Nobel Prize for literature in 1929.

Mann's background was that of a German patriot. In 1914 he was swept away by the military spirit. At that time he regarded German militarism as the manifestation of German morality. "The militarism inherent in the German soul, its ethical conservatism, its soldier-like morality – an element of daemonism and heroism: this is what refuses to recognize the civilian spirit as the final ideal of mankind."* After this statement, Mann's conversion to Western democracy was slow but certain. He became a passionate defender of the Weimar Republic. When Hitler came to political power, Mann left Germany and remained abroad. In early 1936 he denounced the Nazi regime, as a result of which he lost his German citizenship.

Late in 1936 Mann was also deprived of his title of *Ehrendoktor* (Honorary Doctor), which he held at Bonn University. The ex-

---

Thomas Mann, *An Exchange of Letters*, translated by H. T. Lowe-Porter (New York: Knopf, 1937). Copyright 1937 and renewed 1965 by Alfred A. Knopf, Inc. Reprinted by permission of Alfred A. Knopf, Inc.

*Thomas Mann, "Thoughts on the War (1914)," quoted in Aurel Kolnai, *The War Against the West* (New York: n.p., 1938), pp. 514-15.

change of letters between the dean of the university and Mann's reply attracted global attention. Mann's reply was a devastating indictment of the Nazi *Weltanschauung.*

Philosophical Faculty
of the Friedrich-Wilhelm University
Bonn on Rhine

Bonn, December 19, 1936

To Herr Thomas Mann, Writer:
By the request of the Rector of the University of Bonn I must inform you that as a consequence of your loss of citizenship the Philosophical Faculty finds itself obliged to strike your name off its roll of honorary doctors. Your right to use this title is canceled in accordance with Article VIII of the regulations concerning the conferring of degrees.

[signature illegible]
— Dean

Thomas Mann's Communication to the University of Bonn, 1936

To the Dean of the Philosophical Faculty of the University of Bonn:
I have received the melancholy communication which you addressed to me on the nineteenth of December. Permit me to reply to it as follows:

The German universities share a heavy responsibility for all the present distresses which they called down upon their heads when they tragically misunderstood their historic hour and allowed their soil to nourish the ruthless forces which have devastated Germany morally, politically, and economically. This responsibility of theirs long ago destroyed my pleasure in my academic honor and prevented me from making any use of it whatever. Moreover, I hold today an honorary degree of Doctor of Letters conferred upon me more recently by Harvard University. I cannot refrain from explaining to you the grounds upon which it was conferred. My diploma contains a sentence which, translated from the Latin, runs as follows: ". . . we the President and Fellows with the approval of the honorable Board of Overseers of the University in solemn session have designated and appointed as honorary Doctor of Letters Thomas Mann, famous author, who has interpreted life to many of our fellow citizens and together with a very few contemporaries sustains the high dignity of German culture; and we have granted to him all the rights and privileges appertaining to this degree."

In such terms, so curiously contradictory to the current German view, do free and enlightened men across the ocean think of me and, I may add, not only there. It would never have occurred to me to boast of the words I have quoted; but here and today I may, nay, I must repeat them. If you,

Herr Dean (I am ignorant of the procedure involved), have posted a copy of your communication to me on the bulletin board of your university, it would gratify me to have this reply of mine receive the same honor. Perhaps some member of the university, some student or professor, may be visited by a sudden fear, a dismaying and swiftly suppressed presentiment, on reading a document which gives him in his disgracefully enforced isolation and ignorance a brief revealing glimpse of the free world of the intellect that still exists outside.

Here I might close. And yet at this moment certain further explanations seem to me desirable or at least permissible. I made no statement when my loss of civil rights was announced, though I was more than once asked to do so. But I regard the academic divestment as a suitable occasion for a brief personal declaration. I would beg you, Herr Dean (I have not even the honor of knowing your name), to regard yourself as merely the chance recipient of a communication not designed for you in a personal sense.

I have spent four years in an exile which it would be euphemistic to call voluntary, since if I had remained in Germany or gone back there I should probably not be alive today. In these four years the odd blunder committed by fortune when she put me in this situation has never once ceased to trouble me. I could never have dreamed, it could never have been prophesied of me at my cradle, that I should spend my later years as an émigré, expropriated, outlawed, and committed to inevitable political protest. From the beginning of my intellectual life I had felt myself in happiest accord with the temper of my nation and at home in its intellectual traditions. I am better suited to represent those traditions than to become a martyr for them: far more fitted to add a little to the gaiety of the world than to foster conflict and hatred in it. Something very wrong must have happened to make my life take so false and unnatural a turn. I tried to check it, this very wrong thing, so far as my weak powers were able – and in so doing called down on myself the fate which I must now learn to reconcile with a nature essentially foreign to it.

Certainly I challenged the wrath of these despots by remaining away and giving evidence of my irrepressible disgust. But it is not merely in the last four years that I have done so. I felt thus long before and was driven to it because I saw – earlier than my now desperate countrymen – who and what would emerge from all this. But when Germany had actually fallen into those hands I thought to keep silent. I believed that by the sacrifice I had made I had earned the right to silence; that it would enable me to preserve something dear to my heart, the contact with my public within Germany. My books, I said to myself, are written for Germans, for them above all; the outside world and its sympathy have always been for me only a happy accident. They are, these books of mine, the product of a mutually nourishing bond between nation and author and depend on conditions which I myself have helped to create in Germany. Such bonds as these are delicate and of high importance; they ought not to be rudely sundered by politics. Though there might be impatient ones at home who, muzzled themselves, would take ill the silence of a free man, I was still able to hope that a great majority of Germans would understand my reserve, perhaps even thank me for it.

These were my assumptions. They were not justified. I could not have lived or worked, I should have suffocated, had I not been able now and again to cleanse my heart, so to speak, to give from time to time free vent to my abysmal disgust at what was happening at home — the contemptible words and still more contemptible deeds. Justly or not, my name had once and for all been connected for the world with the conception of a Germany which it loved and honored. The disquieting challenge rang in my ears: that I and no other must in clear terms contradict the ugly falsification which this conception of Germany was now suffering. That challenge disturbed all the free-flowing creative fancies to which I would so gladly have yielded. It was a challenge hard to resist for one to whom it had always been given to express himself, to release himself through language, to whom experience had always been one with the purifying and preserving Word. . . .

To what a pass, in less than four years, have they brought Germany! Ruined, sucked dry body and soul by armaments with which they threaten the whole world, holding up the whole world and hindering it in its real task of peace, loved by nobody, regarded with fear and cold aversion by all, it stands on the brink of economic disaster, while its "enemies" stretch out their hands to snatch back from the abyss so important a member of the future family of nations, to help it, if only it will come to its senses and try to understand the real needs of the world at this hour, instead of dreaming dreams about mythical "sacred necessities." . . .

The meaning and purpose of the National Socialist State is this alone and can only be this: to put the German people in readiness for the "coming war" by ruthless repression, elimination, extirpation of every stirring of opposition; to make of them an instrument of war, infinitely compliant, without a single critical thought, driven by a blind and fanatical ignorance. Any other meaning and purpose, any other excuse this system cannot have; all the sacrifices of freedom, justice, human happiness, including the secret and open crimes for which it has blithely been responsible, can be justified only by the end — absolute fitness for war. If the idea of war as an aim in itself disappeared, the system would mean nothing but the exploitation of the people; it would be utterly senseless and superfluous. . . .

No, this war is impossible; Germany cannot wage it; and if its dictators are in their senses, then their assurances of readiness for peace are not tactical lies repeated with a wink at their partisans; they spring from a faint-hearted perception of just this impossibility. But if war cannot and shall not be — then why these robbers and murderers? Why isolation, world hostility, lawlessness, intellectual interdict, cultural darkness, and every other evil? Why not rather Germany's voluntary return to the European system, her reconciliation with Europe, with all the inward accompaniments of freedom, justice, well-being, and human decency, and a jubilant welcome from the rest of the world? Why not? Only because a regime which in word and deed denies the rights of man, which wants above all else to remain in power, would stultify itself and be abolished, if, since it cannot make war, it actually made peace!

I had forgotten, Herr Dean, that I was actually addressing you. Certainly I may console myself with the reflection that you long since have ceased to read this letter, aghast at language which in Germany has long been unspoken, terrified because somebody dares use the German tongue with the ancient freedom. I have not spoken out of arrogant presumption, but out of concern and a distress from which your usurpers did not release me when they decreed that I was no longer a German — a mental and spiritual distress from which for four years not an hour of my life has been free, and struggling with which I have had to accomplish my creative work day by day. The pressure was great. And as a man who out of diffidence in religious matters will seldom or never either by tongue or pen let the name of the Deity escape him, yet in moments of deep emotion cannot refrain, let me — since after all one cannot say everything — close this letter with a brief and fervent prayer: *God help our darkened and desecrated country and teach it to make its peace with the world and with itself!*

— Thomas Mann

70. Racial Purity: Hitler Reverts to the Dominant Theme of the National Socialist Program, January 30, 1937

"For the first time in our history, the German people have found the way to a higher unity."

In the pages of *Mein Kampf* and in nearly every speech on ideology he made, Hitler came back again and again to his lifelong theme of preserving the purity of German blood. He was convinced that there was a war to the death between the Aryans, the "culture-founding race," and the Jews, "the culture-destroying race." He called upon the German people to preserve the purity of their blood. In the following speech delivered in Berlin on January 30, 1937, at a time when the National Socialist party was increasing its strength, he summarized his concept of racial purity and what it meant to the German people. Following is a précis of this speech.

THE MOST IMPORTANT PLANK in the National Socialist program is to abolish the liberal idea of the individual and the Marxist idea of humanity and to substitute for them the folk community rooted in the soil and held together by the bond of common blood. This sounds simple, but it involves a principle which has great consequences.

For the first time and in the first country our people are being taught to understand that, of all the tasks we have to face, the most noble and the most sacred for all mankind is the concept that each racial species must preserve the purity of blood which God has given to it.

The greatest revolution won by National Socialism is that it has pierced the veil which hid from us the knowledge that all human errors may be

---

Völkischer Beobachter, January 31, 1937. Translated by the editor.

attributed to the conditions of the time and hence can be remedied, but there is one error that cannot be set right once it has been made by men — that is, the failure to understand the importance of keeping the blood and the race free from intermingling, and in this way to alter God's gift. It is not for human beings to discuss why Providence created different races. Rather it is important to understand the fact that it will punish those who pay no attention to its work of creation.

Unheard-of suffering and misery have been the lot of men because they have lost this instinct which is rooted in a deep sense of intuition. All this has been caused by mistaken education. Among us today there are millions and millions of people to whom this law has been clear and understandable. What individual prophets and the unspoiled nature of our forefathers saw clearly has now become a matter of scientific research in Germany.

I hereby prophesy that, just as knowledge that the earth moves around the sun led to a revolutionary change in the world picture, so will the blood-and-race doctrine of the National Socialist movement bring about a revolutionary change in our knowledge. Along with this goes a radical reconstruction of the picture which human history gives us of the past. It will also change the course of history in the future.

This will not lead to difficulties between nations. On the contrary, it will lead to a better understanding between them. But at the same time it will prevent the Jews, under the mask of world citizenship, from thrusting themselves among all nations as an element of domestic chaos.

This revolutionary vision of truth will bring about a radical change in German life. For the first time in our history, the German people have found the way to a higher unity.

The National Socialist movement limits its domestic activities to those individuals who belong to one people. It refuses to permit those of a foreign race to have any influence whatever on our political, intellectual, or cultural life. We refuse to give any members of a foreign race a dominant position in our national economic system.

In our folk community, which is based on ties of blood, in the results which National Socialism has obtained by training the public in the idea of this folk-community, lies the deepest reason for the great success of our Revolution.

71. *"Mit Brennender Sorge"*: Papal Encyclical Expresses Deep Anxiety for the Future, March 14, 1937

"We cease not to pray and beg for you, the children of the Church. . . ."

Both Protestants and Catholics resented the assault on Christianity by Nazi ideologues. Theologians were alienated by an ideology that they deemed hostile to their own beliefs. There were increasing protests in the 1930s.

It was a bitter reaction to Hitler's assault on Christian values. "Antiquity," said Hitler, "was better than modern times because it did not know Christianity and syphilis." He denounced Christianity, claiming that (1) it was a religion that sided with everything weak and low; (2) it was purely Jewish and Oriental in origin; (3) it began among sick, exhausted, and despairing men who had lost their belief in life; (4) Christian ideas of forgiveness of sin, resurrection, and salvation were just nonsense; (5) the Christian idea of mercy was altogether dangerous; (6) Christian love was silly because "love paralyzes"; and (7) the Christian idea of equality of all human beings meant that the inferior, the ill, the crippled, the criminal, and the weak are to be protected.

Christianity, said Hitler, just as much as Judaism, was opposed to the healthy Nordic pagan ideals he had for Germany. He would not destroy Christianity, but he would redefine it and use its more positive principles — such as "Render unto Caesar what is Caesar's" and "drive the money-changers out of the temple."

Encylical Letter of His Holiness, Pope Pius XI, Issued March 14, 1937, trans. Vatican Press, National Catholic Welfare Conference, Washington, D.C., 1937, pp. 1-35. Courtesy of the National Catholic Welfare Conference.

On March 14, 1937, Pope Pius XI, concerned by conditions inside Germany, issued an encyclical, "On the Condition of the Church in Germany," later to be called "*Mit brennender Sorge*" (With Deep Anxiety), after the opening three words of the text. Read from all Catholic pulpits in Germany, this was the first direct involvement of the papacy in the Nazi-Catholic controversy. The pope accused the Third Reich of violating the terms of the earlier Concordat with the Church and denounced the persecution of Catholics as "illegal as it is inhuman." "With personal emotion," he said, "we feel and suffer profoundly with those who have paid such a great price for their attachment to Christ and to the Church."

Following are excerpts from the papal encyclical.

TO THE VENERABLE
ARCHBISHOPS AND BISHOPS OF GERMANY
AND OTHER ORDINARIES IN PEACE
AND COMMUNION WITH THE APOSTOLIC SEE

ON THE CONDITION OF THE CHURCH IN GERMANY

POPE PIUS XI
VENERABLE BRETHREN
GREETING AND APOSTOLIC BENEDICTION

1. With deep anxiety and increasing dismay, We have for some time past beheld the sufferings of the Church, and the steadily growing oppression of those men and women who, loyally professing their faith in thought and deed, have remained true to her amidst the people of that land to which St. Boniface once brought the light and glad tidings of Christ and the Kingdom of God.

2. This anxiety of Ours has not been lessened by the accurate reports dutifully brought to Us by the representatives of the most reverend episcopate, who came to visit at Our sickbed. They related much that is consoling and edifying about the struggle for religion that is being waged by the faithful, and yet, despite their love for their people and their Fatherland, with every possible attempt to reach a dispassionate judgment, they could not pass over much that is bitter and sad. After receiving their accounts, We could say in great thankfulness to God: "I have no greater grace than this, to hear that my children walk in truth."[1] But the frankness befitting Our responsible apostolic office, and the desire to place before your eyes

---

[1] III John 1, 4.

and those of the entire Christian world the actual facts in all their gravity, require Us to add: A greater anxiety, a more bitter suffering in Our pastoral care, We have not, than to hear "many leave the way of truth."[2]

3. In the summer of 1933, Venerable Brethren, We accepted the offer made by the Government of the Reich to institute negotiations for a Concordat in connection with a proposal of the previous year, and to the satisfaction of you all brought them to a conclusion with a solemn agreement. In this We were guided by the solicitude incumbent on Us to safeguard the freedom of the Church in the exercise of her apostolic ministry in Germany and the salvation of the souls entrusted to her, and at the same time by the sincere wish of rendering an essential service to the progress and prosperity of the German people.

4. In spite of many serious misgivings at the time, We forced Ourselves to decide that We should not withhold Our consent. We wished to spare Our faithful sons and daughters in Germany, so far as was humanly possible, the anxiety and suffering which, in the given circumstances, We would certainly have otherwise had to expect. Through Our act We wished to prove to all, that seeking only Christ and the things of Christ, We do not refuse the hand of peace of Mother Church to anyone who does not himself reject it.

5. If the tree of peace which We planted with pure intention in German soil has not borne the fruit We desired in the interests of your people, no one in the wide world who has eyes to see and ears to hear can say today that the fault lies with the Church and her Head. The lessons of the past years make it clear where the responsibility lies. They disclose machinations that from the beginning had no other aim than a war of extermination. In the furrows where We labored to plant the seeds of sincere peace, others were sowing — like the enemy in Holy Scripture[3] — the tares of distrust, of discord, hatred, calumny, of secret and open enmity against Christ and His Church, an enmity in principle, fed from a thousand springs and working with every means at its disposal. With them and only with them, as well as with their open and silent supporters, lies the responsibility that now, instead of the rainbow of peace, the storm clouds of destructive religious conflicts are visible on the German horizon.

6. We have not tired, Venerable Brethren, of portraying to the responsible guides of the destinies of your country the consequences that necessarily follow if such trends are left unhindered and much more if they are viewed with favor. We have done everything to defend the sanctity of a word solemnly pledged, to protect the inviolability of obligations, freely undertaken, against theories and practices which, if officially approved,

---

[2]II Peter, 2, 3.
[3]Matthew, 13, 25.

must destroy all confidence and render valueless any word that might also be pledged in the future. . . .

8. The purpose of the present letter, however, Venerable Brethren, is a different one. As you kindly visited Us as We lay on Our bed of sickness, so today We turn to you and through you to the Catholic faithful of Germany, who, like all suffering and oppressed children, are particularly close to the heart of the Common Father. In this hour, when their faith is being tried like pure gold in the fire of tribulation and concealed and open persecution, when they are surrounded by a thousand forms of organized bondage in matters of religion, when the lack of true information and absence of the customary means of defense weigh heavy on them, they have a double right to words of truth and spiritual comfort from him, to whose first predecessor the significant words of the Saviour were spoken: "But I have prayed for thee, that thy faith fail not; and thou being once converted, confirm thy brethren."[4]

True Belief in God

9. Take care, Venerable Brethren, that first of all belief in God, the primary and irreplaceable foundation of all religion, be preserved true and unadulterated in German lands. He is not a believer in God who uses the word of God rhetorically but he who associates with the sacred word the true and worthy idea of God.

10. He who, in pantheistic vagueness, equates God with the universe, and identifies God with the world and the world with God does not belong to believers in God.

11. He who replaces a personal God with a weird impersonal Fate supposedly according to ancient pre-Christian German concepts denies the wisdom and providence of God, that "reacheth from end to end mightily and ordereth all things sweetly"[5] and directs everything for the best. Such a one cannot claim to be numbered among those who believe in God. . . . such can make the mad attempt of trying to confine within the boundaries of a single people, within the narrow blood stream of a single race, God the Creator of the world, the King and Lawgiver of all peoples before whose greatness all peoples are small as a drop of a bucket. . . .[6]

15. The Bishops of the Church of Christ set up "for the things that appertain to God"[7] must be watchful that such pernicious errors, which are usually followed by more pernicious practices, find no foothold among the faithful. It is the holy duty of your office, as far as in you lies, to

---

[4]Luke, 22, 32.
[5]Wisdom, 8, 1.
[6]Is., 40, 15.
[7]Heb., 5, 1.

do everything to bring it about that the commandments of God shall be regarded and obeyed as the obligatory basis of morally ordered private and public life, that the sovereign rights of God, the name and the word of God, be not blasphemed;[8] that the blasphemies — in word, writing and picture, at times countless as the sands by the sea — be made to cease; that over against the defying Promethean spirit of deniers, scorners and haters of God the propitiatory prayer of the faithful never falters but that, like incense, it may rise hour after hour to the Most High and stay His hand raised to punish.

16. We thank you, Venerable Brethren, your priests and all the faithful, who have done and continue to do their duty in defending the sovereign rights of God against the aggressive neo-paganism — that unfortunately in many instances is favored in influential quarters. Our thanks are doubly sincere and coupled with admiration and approval of those who in the exercise of their duty were found worthy of making earthly sacrifices for God's sake and of enduring earthly suffering.

True Belief in Christ

17. No belief in God will in the long run be preserved pure and genuine, if it is not supported by belief in Christ: "No one knoweth the Son, but the Father; neither does any one know the Father, but the Son and he to whom it shall please the Son to reveal him."[9] "This is eternal life: that they may know Thee, the only true God and Jesus Christ, whom Thou hast sent."[10] Hence no one may say: I am a believer in God; that is religion enough for me. The words of the Saviour allow no room for this kind of evasion. "Whosoever denieth the Son, the same hath not the Father. He that confesseth the Son hath also the Father."[11]

18. The fulness of divine revelation has appeared in Jesus Christ, the incarnate Son of God. "God, Who at sundry times and divers manners spoke in times past to the fathers through the prophets, in the fulness of time hath spoken to us by his Son."[12] The sacred books of the Old Testament are all God's Word, an organic part of His revelation. . . .

20. The climax of revelation reached in the Gospel of Jesus Christ is definite, is obligatory forever. This revelation knows no addition from the hand of man, above all, knows no substitution and no replacement by arbitrary "revelations" that certain speakers of the present day wish to derive from the myth of blood and race. Since Christ, the Anointed,

---

[8]Tit., 2, 5.
[9]Matthew, 11, 27.
[10]John, 17, 3.
[11]John, 2, 23.
[12]Hebrews, 1, 1.

accomplished the work of redemption, broke the dominion of sin, and merited for us the grace of becoming children of God — since then no other name has been given under heaven to men, through which they can be saved, but the name of Jesus.[13] No man, though all knowledge, all power, all outward might on earth should be embodied in him, can lay any other foundation than that which is already laid in Christ.[14] He who sacrilegiously disregarding the yawning abyss of essential distinction between God and creature, between the God-Man and the children of men, dares to place any mortal, were he the greatest of all times, beside Christ, or worse, above Him and against Him, must be told that he is a false prophet, in whom the words of Scripture find terrible application: "He that dwelleth in heaven, shall laugh at them."[15]

True Belief in the Church

21. Belief in Christ will not be preserved true and genuine, if not supported and protected by belief in the Church, "the pillar and ground of the truth."[16] Christ Himself, Godpraised forever in the ages, has erected this pillar of faith. His command, to hear the Church,[17] to hear His own words and commandments[18] in the words and commandments of the Church, is meant for the men of all times and places. . . .

22. The divine mission of the Church that works among men and must work through men may be lamentably obscured by human failings that again and again sprout up as tares amid the wheat of God's kingdom. He who has heard the Saviour's word about scandals and those who give scandal, knows how the Church and each individual has to judge on what was sin and is sin. . . .

Today We earnestly repeat: It is not enough to be counted a member of the Church of Christ. One must be also a living member of this Church — in spirit and in truth. And only they are such, who are in the grace of the Lord and ever walk in His presence — in innocence or in sincere and efficacious penance. If the Apostle of the Gentiles, the "Vessel of Election," kept his body under the rod of chastisement and mortification in order that he might not, after preaching to others, become himself a castaway,[19] can there be any other way but that of the closest union of apostolate and personal sanctification for the others to whose hands is committed the keeping and increase of the kingdom of God? . . . True, the spirit of God

---

[13]Acts, 4, 12.
[14]I Cor., 2, 11.
[15]Ps., 2, 4.
[16]I Timothy, 3, 15.
[17]Matthew, 18, 17.
[18]Luke, 10, 16.
[19]I Cor., 9, 27.

breatheth where He will.[20] He can raise up stones to prepare the way for His design.[21] He chooses the instruments of His will according to His Own plans, and not according to those of men. But He Who founded His Church and called it into being in the storm of Pentecost, does not blast the foundation of the establishment He Himself intended for salvation. Those who are moved by the spirit of God have of themselves the proper inward and outward attitude towards the Church, which is the precious fruit on the tree of the Cross, the Pentecostal gift of God's spirit to a world in need of guidance.

24. In your districts, Venerable Brethren, voices are raised in ever louder chorus urging men on to leave the Church. . . . When the tempter or oppressor comes to him with the Judas-like suggestion to leave the Church, then, even at the cost of heavy, earthly sacrifices he can only reply in the words of the Saviour: "Begone, Satan: for it is written: The Lord thy God thou shalt adore and Him only shalt thou serve."[22] But to the Church he will say: Thou my Mother from the days of my childhood, my comfort in life, my intercessor in death, may my tongue cleave to my palate, if I, yielding to earthly enticements or threats, should turn traitor to the promises of my baptism. But to those who think that they can continue outward leaving of the Church with inward loyalty to the Church, let the Saviour's words be earnest warning: "He that shall deny Me before men, I will also deny him before My Father Who is in heaven."[23]

The Belief in the Primacy

25. Belief in the Church will not be kept pure and genuine if it is not supported by belief in the primacy of the Bishop of Rome. At the very moment when Peter, foremost of all the Apostles and disciples, confessed faith in Christ, the Son of the living God, the answer of Christ rewarding his faith and his confession was the word that speaks of the building of His Church, the one Church, and on Peter the Rock.[24] . . .

No Changing the Sense of Holy Words and Ideas

26. You must be especially alert, Venerable Brethren, when fundamental religious conceptions are robbed of their intrinsic content and made to mean something else in a profane sense.

27. Revelation, in the Christian sense, is the word of God to man. To use the same word for the "whispered inspirations" of blood and race, for

---

[20]John, 3, 8.
[21]Matthew, 3, 9; Luke, 3, 8.
[22]Matthew, 4, 10; Luke, 4, 8.
[23]Matthew, 10, 33.
[24]Matthew, 16, 18.

the manifestations of the history of a people, is confusing in any case. Such false coinage does not deserve to be received into the vocabulary of a believing Christian.

28. Faith is the certain holding as true what God has revealed and through His Church proposes for belief, "the evidence of things that appear not."[25] The joyous and proud confidence in the future of one's people, dear to everyone, means something quite different from faith in the religious sense. To play one off against the other, to try to replace one by the other, and thereupon demand to be recognized as a "believer" by the convinced Christian, is an empty play on words or a wilful effacing of distinctions, or worse.

29. Immortality in the Christian sense is the continuance of the life of a man after temporal death, as a personal individual, to be rewarded or punished eternally. To designate with the word immortality the collective continued enjoyment of life in association with the continued existence of one's people on earth for an undetermined length of time in the future, is to pervert and falsify one of the principal truths of the Christian faith and strike at the foundations of every religious philosophy that demands a moral ordering of the world. If they do not want to be Christians, at least they should forego enriching the vocabulary of their unbelief from the Christian treasure of ideas.

30. Original sin is the inherited, though not personal, fault of the descendants of Adam, who sinned in him;[26] loss of grace, and therewith loss of eternal life, with the propensity to evil that each one must combat and overcome by grace, penance, struggle and moral endeavor. . . .

31. The Cross of Christ, though the mere name may have become to many a folly and a scandal,[27] is still for the Christian the hallowed sign of redemption, the standard of moral greatness and strength. In its shadow we live. In its kiss we die. On our graves it shall stand to proclaim our faith, to witness our hope turned towards the eternal light.

32. Humility in the spirit of the Gospel and prayer for the help of God's grace are compatible with self-respect, self-confidence and heroic purpose. The Church of Christ, that in all ages up to the present time counts more confessors and voluntary martyrs than any other body, does not need to receive instruction from such quarters about heroic purposefulness and heroic achievement. In its shallow twaddle about Christian humility being self-abasement and unheroic conduct, the disgusting pride of these reformers mocks itself.

33. Grace, in the loose sense of the term, can be said to be everything

---

[25]Hebrews, 11, 1.
[26]Romans, 5, 12.
[27]I Cor., 1, 23.

that the creature receives from the Creator. Grace in the proper and Christian sense of the word embraces, however, the supernatural manifestations of divine love, the loving kindness and working of God, whereby He raises men to that inward participation of life with Himself, that is called in the New Testatment sonship of God. "Behold what manner of charity the Father hath bestowed upon us, that we should be called and should be the sons of God."[28]

Moral Doctrine and Moral Order

34. The moral conduct of mankind is grounded on faith in God kept true and pure. Every attempt to dislodge moral teaching and moral conduct from the rock of faith, and to build them on the unstable sands of human norms, sooner or later leads the individual and the community to moral destruction. The fool who hath said in his heart there is no God, will walk the ways of corruption.[29] The number of such fools, who today attempt to separate morality and religion, has become legion. They do not or will not see that by expelling confessional, *i.e.* clear and definite, Christianity from instruction and education, from the formation of social and public life, they are treading the ways of spiritual impoverishment and decline. No coercive power of the State, no mere earthly ideals, though they be high and noble in themselves, will be able in the long run to replace the final and decisive motives that come from belief in God and Christ. . . .

Recognition of the Natural Law

35. It is part of the trend of the day to sever more and more not only morality but also the foundation of law and jurisprudence, from true belief in God and from His revealed commandments. Here We have in mind particularly the so-called natural law that is written by the finger of the Creator Himself in the tables of the hearts of men[30] and which can be read on these tables by sound reason not darkened by sin and passion. Every positive law, from whatever lawgiver it may come, can be examined as to its moral implications, and consequently as to its moral authority to bind in conscience, in the light of the commandments of the natural law. The laws of man that are in direct contradiction with the natural law bear an initial defect that no violent means, no outward display of power can remedy. By this standard must we judge the principle: "What helps the people is right." A right meaning may be given to this sentence if understood as expressing that what is morally illicit can never serve the true

[28]I John, 3, 1.
[29]Ps., 13, 1.
[30]Cf. Rom., 2, 15.

interests of the people. But even ancient paganism recognized that the sentence, to be perfectly accurate, should be inverted and read: "Never is anything useful, if it is not at the same time morally good. And not because it is useful, is it morally good, but because it is morally good, it is also useful."[31]

To Youth

39. As the vice regent of Him who said to the young man of the gospel: "If thou wilt enter into life, keep the commandments,"[32] do We especially address fatherly words to youth. By a thousand tongues today a gospel is preached in your ears that is not revealed by your Heavenly Father. A thousand pens write in the service of a sham Christianity that is not the Christianity of Christ. Day by day the press and the radio overwhelm you with productions hostile to your faith and Church and, with no consideration or reverence, attack what must be to you sacred and holy.

40. We know that many, very many, of you for the sake of loyalty to your religion and Church, for the sake of belonging to Church associations guaranteed by the Concordat, have borne and still endure bitter days of misunderstanding, of suspicion, of contempt, of denial of your patriotism, of manifold injury in your professional and social life. We are aware that many an unknown soldier of Christ stands in your ranks, who with heavy heart but head erect bears his lot and finds comfort solely in the thought of suffering reproach for the Name of Jesus.[33]

41. Today, when new perils and conflicts threaten, We say to this youth: "If anyone preach to you a gospel, besides that which you have received" at the knees of a pious mother, from the lips of a Catholic father, from the education of a teacher true to his God and his church, "let him be anathema."[34] . . .With confidence We expect from practicing Catholic youth that, in the difficult circumstances of obligatory State organization, they will insist unflinchingly on their right to keep Sunday in a Christian manner, that in the cult of physical fitness they will not forget the interests of their immortal souls; that they will not allow themselves to be overcome by evil, but will strive to overcome evil by good,[35] that their highest and holiest ambition will be so to run the race towards immortal life as to achieve the crown of victory."[36]

---

[31]Cicero, De officiis, 3, 30.
[32]Matthew, 19, 17.
[33]Acts, 5, 41.
[34]Gal., 1, 9.
[35]Rom., 12, 21.
[36]Cf. I Cor., 9, 24.

To Priests and Religious

43. We address a special word of recognition, encouragement and exhortation to the priests of Germany, on whom, in subordination to their Bishops, there rests the task of showing the flock of Christ in a trying time and under difficult circumstances, the right paths, by precept and example, by daily sacrifice and apostolic patience. Be not weary, beloved sons and sharers in the holy mysteries, in following the eternal High Priest, Jesus Christ, Who bestows love and care like the good Samaritan. . . .

47. We address a particularly heartfelt greeting to Catholic parents. . . .No one of those who today are oppressing you in the exercise of your rights in education and pretend to free you from your duty in this matter, will be able to answer for you to the Eternal Judge when He asks you the question: "Where are those I have given you?" May everyone of you be able to answer: "Of them thou hast given me, I have not lost anyone."[37]

48. Venerable Brethren, We are certain that the words which We address to you, and through you to the Catholics of the German Reich, in this decisive hour, will awaken in the hearts and actions of Our loyal children the echo that answers to the loving solicitude of the Common Father. If there is anything that We beseech of the Lord with particular fervor, it is this, that Our words may also reach the ears and hearts of those who have already begun to allow themselves to be inveigled by the enticements and threats of those who take their stand against Christ and His holy Gospel and cause them to reflect.

49. Every word of this letter has been weighed in the scales of truth and of charity. We did not desire to share any accountability, by reason of untimely silence, for a want of enlightenment, nor, by needless severity, for the hardening of heart of any one of those who are placed under Our pastoral responsibility and are no less included in Our pastoral charity because at the moment they are walking estranged in the ways of error. . . .

50. Just as other times of the Church, so will this be the harbinger of new advance and inward purification, if the readiness to suffer and confess the faith on the part of Christ's faithful is great enough to oppose to the physical violence of the persecutors of the Church the intransigeance of inward faith, the inexhaustibleness of hope that rests on eternity, the commanding power of active charity . . . .

Then—of this We are certain—will the enemies of the Church, who fancy that her hour has come, soon recognize that they rejoiced too soon and were too quick to dig her grave. Then will the day come when, instead

---

[37]John, 18, 9.

of the too hasty songs of victory raised by the enemies of Christ, the *Te Deum* of liberation can rise to heaven from the hearts and lips of Christ's faithful; a *Te Deum* of thanks to the Highest; a *Te Deum* of joy, that the German people, even in its erring sons of today, has trodden the way of religious home-coming, that they once more bend the knee in faith purified by suffering before the King of time and eternity, Jesus Christ, and that they prepare to fulfill that calling which the designs of the Eternal God point out to them, in the struggle against the deniers and destroyers of the Christian west, in harmony with all right-minded people of other nations.

51. He Who searches the heart and reins[38] is Our witness, that We have no more heartfelt wish than the restoration of a true peace between Church and State in Germany. But if, through no fault of Ours, there shall not be peace, the Church of God will defend her rights and liberties in the Name of the Almighty, Whose arm even today is not shortened. Trusting in Him "We cease not to pray and beg"[39] for you, the children of the Church, that the days of anguish may be shortened and that you may be found true in the day of searching; and We pray also for the persecutors and oppressors; may the Father of all light and all mercy grant them an hour of enlightenment, such as was vouchsafed to Paul on the road to Damascus, for themselves and all those who with them have erred and err.

52. With this prayer of supplication in Our heart and on Our lips, We impart as a pledge of divine assistance, as a help in your difficult and weighty decisions, as strength in the struggle, as consolation in suffering, to you, the episcopal Pastors of your loyal flock, to the priests and religious, to the lay apostles of Catholic Action, to all your diocesans, finally to the sick and imprisoned, in fatherly love, the Apostolic blessing.

Given at the Vatican, on Passion Sunday, March 14th, 1937.

PIUS PP. XI

---

[38]Ps., 7, 10.
[39]Coloss., 1, 9.

Part Four:

The
Road to War

72. The Hossbach Memorandum: Hitler Expresses His Intention of Obtaining *Lebensraum* for the German People, November 5, 1937

"The aim of German policy was to make secure and to preserve the racial community [Volksmasse] *and to enlarge it. It was therefore a question of space."*

Since his assumption of political power in 1933, Hitler had been careful in his public statements before the *Reichstag* and in interviews with journalists to project an image of a peaceful leader intent upon keeping his country out of war. His real thoughts were presented at a conference of top officials of the Third Reich held at the Reich Chancellery on November 5, 1937. At this conference meeting he outlined the steps he intended to take to obtain *Lebensraum,* or living space, for the German people.

Colonel Friedrich Hossbach, Hitler's adjutant, took careful notes. Five days later he wrote the highly secret document that came to be known as the *Hossbach Niederschrift* (Hossbach Memorandum). In this protocol Hitler's intentions were clear. After pledging his colleagues to secrecy, he informed them of his decisions and urged them to regard his words as a political testament in the event of his own death.

Most historians of World War II regard the Hossbach Memorandum as one of the most important documents of the immediate prewar period. Revisionist historians, however, reject it as of little significance. They insist that Hitler never wanted war, and there were no Nazi plans for conquest. Hitler himself, they say, was a blunderer who was pressed into aggression by outsiders under cir-

Germany, *Auswärtiges Amt, Documents on German Foreign Policy,* Series D vol. 1 (Washington, D. C.: Government Printing Office, 1949), pp. 29-39.

cumstances utterly beyond his control. He was, they add, no better or worse than other contemporary statesmen.

The reader is urged to read this Hossbach Memorandum carefully and judge for himself whether or not it reveals Hitler's plans for aggression.

BERLIN, November 10, 1937

MINUTES OF THE CONFERENCE IN THE REICH CHANCELLERY, BERLIN, NOVEMBER 5, 1937, FROM 4:15 TO 8:30 P.M.

Present: The *Fuehrer* and Chancellor,
Field Marshal von Blomberg, War Minister,
Colonel General Baron von Fritsch, Commander in Chief, Army,
Admiral Dr. h. c. Raeder, Commander in Chief, Navy,
Colonel General Goering, Commander in Chief, *Luftwaffe,*
Baron von Neurath, Foreign Minister,
Colonel Hossbach.

The *Fuehrer* began by stating that the subject of the present conference was of such importance that its discussion would, in other countries, certainly be a matter for a full Cabinet meeting, but he – the *Fuehrer* – had rejected the idea of making it a subject of discussion before the wider circle of the Reich Cabinet just because of the importance of the matter. His exposition to follow was the fruit of thorough deliberation and the experiences of his 4½ years of power. He wished to explain to the gentlemen present his basic ideas concerning the opportunities for the development of our position in the field of foreign affairs and its requirements, and he asked, in the interests of a long-term German policy, that his exposition be regarded, in the event of his death, as his last will and testament.

The *Fuehrer* then continued:

The aim of German policy was to make secure and to preserve the racial community [*Volksmasse*] and to enlarge it. It was therefore a question of space.

The German racial community comprised over 85 million people and, because of their number and the narrow limits of habitable space in Europe, constituted a tightly packed racial core such as was not to be met in any other country and such as implied the right to a greater living space than in the case of other peoples. If, territorially speaking, there existed no political result corresponding to this German racial core, that was a consequence of centuries of historical development, and in the continuance of these political conditions lay the greatest danger to the preservation of the German race at its present peak. To arrest the decline of Germanism

[*Deutschtum*] in Austria and Czechoslovakia was as little possible as to maintain the present level in Germany itself. Instead of increase, sterility was setting in, and in its train disorders of a social character must arise in course of time, since political and ideological ideas remain effective only so long as they furnish the basis for the realization of the essential vital demands of a people. Germany's future was therefore wholly conditional upon the solving of the need for space, and such a solution could be sought, of course, only for a foreseeable period of about one to three generations.

Before turning to the question of solving the need for space, it had to be considered whether a solution holding promise for the future was to be reached by means of autarky or by means of an increased participation in world economy.

Autarky:

Achievement only possible under strict National Socialist leadership of the State, which is assumed; accepting its achievement as possible, the following could be stated as results: —

A. In the field of raw materials only limited, not total, autarky.

1) In regard to coal, so far as it could be considered as a source of raw materials, autarky was possible.

2) But even as regards ores, the position was much more difficult. Iron requirements can be met from home resources and similarly with light metals, but with other raw materials — copper, tin — this was not the case.

3) Synthetic textile requirements can be met from home resources to the limit of timber supplies. A permanent solution impossible.

4) Edible fats — possible.

B. In the field of food the question of autarky was to be answered by a flat "No."

With the general rise in the standard of living compared with that of 30 to 40 years ago, there has gone hand in hand an increased demand and an increased home consumption even on the part of the producers, the farmers. The fruits of the increased agricultural production had all gone to meet the increased demand, and so did not represent an absolute production increase. A further increase in production by making greater demands on the soil, which already, in consequence of the use of artificial fertilizers, was showing signs of exhaustion, was hardly possible, and it was therefore certain that even with the maximum increase in production, participation in world trade was unavoidable. The not inconsiderable expenditure of foreign exchange to insure food supplies by imports, even when harvests were good, grew to catastrophic proportions with bad harvests. The possibility of a disaster grew in proportion to the increase in population, in which, too, the excess of births of 560,000 annually produced, as a consequence, an even further increase in bread consumption, since a child was a greater bread consumer than an adult.

It was not possible over the long run, in a continent enjoying a practically common standard of living, to meet the food supply difficulties by lowering that standard and by rationalization. Since, with the solving of the unemployment problem, the maximum consumption level had been reached, some minor modifications in our home agricultural production might still, no doubt, be possible, but no fundamental alteration was possible in our basic food position. Thus autarky was untenable in regard both to food and to the economy as a whole.

Participation in world economy:

To this there were limitations which we were unable to remove. The establishment of Germany's position on a secure and sound foundation was obstructed by market fluctuations, and commercial treaties afforded no guarantee for actual execution. In particular it had to be remembered that since the World War, those very countries which had formerly been food exporters had become industrialized. We were living in an age of economic empires in which the primitive urge to colonization was again manifesting itself; in the cases of Japan and Italy economic motives underlay the urge for expansion, and with Germany, too, economic need would supply the stimulus. For countries outside the great economic empires, opportunities for economic expansion were severely impeded.

The boom in world economy caused by the economic effects of rearmament could never form the basis of a sound economy over a long period, and the latter was obstructed above all also by the economic disturbances resulting from Bolshevism. There was a pronounced military weakness in those states which depended for their existence on foreign trade. As our foreign trade was carried on over the sea routes dominated by Britain, it was more a question of security of transport than one of foreign exchange, which revealed, in time of war, the full weakness of our food situation. The only remedy, and one which might appear to us as visionary, lay in the acquisition of greater living space — a quest which has at all times been the origin of the formation of states and of the migration of peoples. That this quest met with no interest at Geneva or among the satiated nations was understandable. If, then, we accept the security of our food situation as the principal question, the space necessary to insure it can only be sought in Europe, not, as in the liberal-capitalist view, in the exploitation of colonies. It is not a matter of acquiring population but of gaining space for agricultural use. Moreover, areas producing raw materials can be more usefully sought in Europe in immediate proximity to the Reich, than oveseas; the solution thus obtained must suffice for one or two generations. Whatever else might prove necessary later must be left to succeeding generations to deal with. The development of great world political constellations progressed but slowly after all, and the German people with its strong racial core would find the most favorable prerequisites for such achievement in the heart of the continent of Europe. The history of all ages – the Roman Empire and the British Empire – had proved that expansion could only be carried out by breaking down resistance and taking risks; setbacks were inevitable. There had never in former times been spaces without a master, and there were none today; the attacker always comes up against a possessor.

The question for Germany ran: where could she achieve the greatest gain at the lowest cost.

German policy had to reckon with two hate-inspired antagonists, Britain and France, to whom a German colossus in the center of Europe was a thorn in the flesh, and both countries were opposed to any further strengthening of Germany's position either in Europe or overseas; in support of this opposition they were able to count on the agreement of all their political parties. Both countries saw in the establishment of German military bases overseas a threat to their own communications, a safeguarding of German commerce, and, as a consequence, a strengthening of Germany's position in Europe.

Because of opposition of the Dominions, Britain could not cede any of her colonial possessions to us. After England's loss of prestige through the passing of Abyssinia into Italian possession, the return of East Africa was not to be expected. British concessions could at best be expressed in an offer to satisfy our colonial demands by the appropriation of colonies which were not British possessions – e.g., Angola. French concessions would probably take a similar line.

Serious discussion of the question of the return of colonies to us could only be considered at a moment when Britain was in difficulties and the German Reich armed and strong. The *Fuehrer* did not share the view that the Empire was unshakable. Opposition to the Empire was to be found less in the countries conquered than among her competitors. The British Empire and the Roman Empire could not be compared in respect of permanence; the latter was not confronted by any powerful political rival of a serious order after the Punic Wars. It was only the disintegrating effect of Christianity, and the symptoms of age which appear in every country, which caused ancient Rome to succumb to the onslaught of the Germans.

Beside the British Empire there existed today a number of states stronger than she. The British motherland was able to protect her colonial possessions not by her own power, but only in alliance with other states. How, for instance, could Britain alone defend Canada against attack by America, or her Far Eastern interests against attack by Japan!

The emphasis on the British Crown as the symbol of the unity of the

Empire was already an admission that, in the long run, the Empire could not maintain its position by power politics. Significant indications of this were:

(a) The struggle of Ireland for independence.

(b) The constitutional struggles in India, where Britain's half measures had given to the Indians the opportunity of using later on as a weapon against Britain, the nonfulfillment of her promises regarding a constitution.

(c) The weakening by Japan of Britain's position in the Far East.

(d) The rivalry in the Mediterranean with Italy who — under the spell of her history, driven by necessity and led by a genius — was expanding her power position, and thus was inevitably coming more and more into conflict with British interests. The outcome of the Abyssinian War was a loss of prestige for Britain which Italy was striving to increase by stirring up trouble in the Mohammedan world.

To sum up, it could be stated that, with 45 million Britons, in spite of its theoretical soundness, the position of the Empire could not in the long run be maintained by power politics. The ratio of the population of the Empire to that of the motherland of 9:1, was a warning to us not, in our territorial expansion, to allow the foundation constituted by the numerical strength of our own people to become too weak.

France's position was more favorable than that of Britain. The French Empire was better placed territorially; the inhabitants of her colonial possessions represented a supplement to her military strength. But France was going to be confronted with internal political difficulties. In a nation's life about 10 percent of its span is taken up by parliamentary forms of government and about 90 percent by authoritarian forms. Today, nonetheless, Britain, France, Russia, and the smaller states adjoining them, must be included as factors [*Machtfaktoren*] in our political calculations.

Germany's problem could only be solved by means of force and this was never without attendant risk. The campaigns of Frederick the Great for Silesia and Bismarck's wars against Austria and France had involved unheard-of risk, and the swiftness of the Prussian action in 1870 had kept Austria from entering the war. If one accepts as the basis of the following exposition the resort to force with its attendant risks, then there remain still to be answered the questions "when" and "how." In this matter there were three cases [*Fälle*] to be dealt with:

Case 1: Period 1943–1945.

After this date only a change for the worse, from our point of view, could be expected.

The equipment of the army, navy, and *Luftwaffe*, as well as the formation of the officer corps, was nearly completed. Equipment and armament were modern; in further delay there lay the danger of their obsolescence. In particular, the secrecy of "special weapons" could not be preserved forever. The recruiting of reserves was limited to current age groups; further drafts from older untrained age groups were no longer available.

Our relative strength would decrease in relation to the rearmament which would by then have been carried out by the rest of the world. If we did not act by 1943–45, any year could, in consequence of a lack of reserves, produce the food crisis, to cope with which the necessary foreign exchange was not available, and this must be regarded as a "waning point of the regime." Besides, the world was expecting our attack and was increasing its counter-measures from year to year. It was while the rest of the world was still preparing its defenses [*sich abriegeln*] that we were obliged to take the offensive.

Nobody knew today what the situation would be in the years 1943–45. One thing only was certain, that we could not wait longer.

On the one hand there was the great *Wehrmacht*, and the necessity of maintaining it at its present level, the aging of the movement and of its leaders; and on the other, the prospect of a lowering of the standard of living and of a limitation of the birth rate, which left no choice but to act. If the *Fuehrer* was still living, it was his unalterable resolve to solve Germany's problem of space at the latest by 1943–45. The necessity for action before 1943–45 would arise in cases 2 and 3.

Case 2.

If internal strife in France should develop into such a domestic crisis as to absorb the French Army completely and render it incapable of use for war against Germany, then the time for action against the Czechs had come.

Case 3.

If France is so embroiled by a war with another state that she cannot "proceed" against Germany.

For the improvement of our politico-military position our first objective, in the event of our being embroiled in war, must be to overthrow Czechoslovakia and Austria simultaneously in order to remove the threat to our flank in any possible operation against the West. In a conflict with France it was hardly to be regarded as likely that the Czechs would declare war on us on the very same day as France. The desire to join in the war would, however, increase among the Czechs in proportion to any weakening on our part and then her participation could clearly take the form of an attack toward Silesia, toward the north or toward the west.

If the Czechs were overthrown and a common German-Hungarian frontier achieved, a neutral attitude on the part of Poland could be the more certainly counted on in the event of a Franco-German conflict. Our agreements with Poland only retained their force as long as Germany's strength remained unshaken. In the event of German setbacks Polish action against East Prussia, and possibly against Pomerania and Silesia as well, had to be reckoned with.

On the assumption of a development of the situation leading to action on our part as planned, in the years 1943–45, the attitude of France, Britain, Italy, Poland, and Russia could probably be estimated as follows:

Actually, the *Fuehrer* believed that almost certainly Britain, and probably France as well, had already tacitly written off the Czechs and were reconciled to the fact that this question would be cleared up in due course by Germany. Difficulties connected with the Empire, and the prospect of being once more entangled in a protracted European war, were decisive considerations for Britain against participation in a war against Germany. Britain's attitude would certainly not be without influence on that of France. An attack by France without British support, and with the prospect of the offensive being brought to a standstill on our western fortifications, was hardly probable. Nor was a French march through Belgium and Holland without British support to be expected; this also was a course not to be contemplated by us in the event of a conflict with France, because it would certainly entail the hostility of Britain. It would of course be necessary to maintain a strong defense [*eine Abriegelung*] on our western frontier during the prosecution of our attack on the Czechs and Austria. And in this connection it had to be remembered that the defense measures of the Czechs were growing in strength from year to year, and that the actual worth of the Austrian Army also was increasing in the course of time. Even though the populations concerned, especially of Czechoslovakia, were not sparse, the annexation of Czechoslovakia and Austria would mean an acquisition of foodstuffs for 5 to 6 million people, on the assumption that the compulsory emigration of 2 million people from Czechoslovakia and 1 million people from Austria was practicable. The incorporation of these two States with Germany meant, from the politico-military point of view, a substantial advantage because it would mean shorter and better frontiers, the freeing of forces for other purposes, and the possibility of creating new units up to a level of about 12 divisions, that is, 1 new division per million inhabitants.

Italy was not expected to object to the elimination of the Czechs, but it was impossible at the moment to estimate what her attitude on the Austrian question would be; that depended essentially upon whether the *Duce* were still alive.

The degree of surprise and the swiftness of our action were decisive factors for Poland's attitude. Poland — with Russia at her rear — will have little inclination to engage in war against a victorious Germany.

Military intervention by Russia must be countered by the swiftness of our operations; however, whether such an intervention was a practical contingency at all was, in view of Japan's attitude, more than doubtful.

Should case 2 arise — the crippling of France by civil war — the situation thus created by the elimination of the most dangerous opponent must be seized upon *whenever it occurs* for the blow against the Czechs.

The *Fuehrer* saw case 3 coming definitely nearer; it might emerge from the present tensions in the Mediterranean, and he was resolved to take advantage of it whenever it happened, even as early as 1938.

In the light of past experience, the *Fuehrer* did not see any early end to the hostilities in Spain. If one considered the length of time which Franco's offensives had taken up till now, it was fully possible that the war would continue another 3 years. On the other hand, a 100 percent victory for Franco was not desirable either, from the German point of view; rather were we interested in a continuance of the war and in the keeping up of the tension in the Mediterranean. Franco in undisputed possession of the Spanish Peninsula precluded the possibility of any further intervention on the part of the Italians or of their continued occupation of the Balearic Islands. As our interest lay more in the prolongation of the war in Spain, it must be the immediate aim of our policy to strengthen Italy's rear with a view to her remaining in the Balearics. But the permanent establishment of the Italians on the Balearics would be intolerable both to France and Britain, and might lead to a war of France and England against Italy — a war in which Spain, should she be entirely in the hands of the Whites, might make her appearance on the side of Italy's enemies. The probability of Italy's defeat in such a war was slight, for the road from Germany was open for the supplementing of her raw materials. The *Fuehrer* pictured the military strategy for Italy thus: on her western frontier with France she would remain on the defensive, and carry on the war against France from Libya against the French North African colonial possessions.

As a landing by Franco-British troops on the coast of Italy could be discounted, and a French offensive over the Alps against northern Italy would be very difficult and would probably come to a halt before the strong Italian fortifications, the crucial point [*Schwerpunkt*] of the operations lay in North Africa. The threat to French lines of communication by the Italian Fleet would to a great extent cripple the transportation of forces from North Africa to France, so that France would have only home forces at her disposal on the frontiers with Italy and Germany.

If Germany made use of this war to settle the Czech and Austrian questions, it was to be assumed that Britain — herself at war with Italy — would decide not to act against Germany. Without British support, a warlike action by France against Germany was not to be expected.

The time for our attack on the Czechs and Austria must be made dependent on the course of the Anglo-French-Italian war and would not necessarily coincide with the commencement of military operations by these three States. Nor had the *Fuehrer* in mind military agreements with Italy, but wanted, while retaining his own independence of action, to exploit this favorable situation, which would not occur again, to begin and carry through the campaign against the Czechs. This descent upon the Czechs would have to be carried out with "lightning speed."

In appraising the situation Field Marshal von Blomberg and Colonel General von Fritsch repeatedly emphasized the necessity that Britain and France must not appear in the role of our enemies, and stated that the French Army would not be so committed by the war with Italy that France could not at the same time enter the field with forces superior to ours on our western frontier. General von Fritsch estimated the probable French forces available for use on the Alpine frontier at approximately twenty divisions, so that a strong French superiority would still remain on the western frontier, with the role, according to the German view, of invading the Rhineland. In this matter, moreover, the advanced state of French defense preparations [*Mobilmachung*] must be taken into particular account, and it must be remembered apart from the insignificant value of our present fortifications – on which Field Marshal von Blomberg laid special emphasis – that the four motorized divisions intended for the West were still more or less incapable of movement. In regard to our offensive toward the southeast, Field Marshal von Blomberg drew particular attention to the strength of the Czech fortifications, which had acquired by now a structure like a Maginot Line and which would gravely hamper our attack.

General von Fritsch mentioned that this was the very purpose of a study which he had ordered made this winter, namely, to examine the possibility of conducting operations against the Czechs with special reference to overcoming the Czech fortification system; the General further expressed his opinion that under existing circumstances he must give up his plan to go abroad on his leave, which was due to begin on November 10. The *Fuehrer* dismissed this idea on the ground that the possibility of a conflict need not yet be regarded as so imminent. To the Foreign Minister's objection that an Anglo-French-Italian conflict was not yet within such a measurable distance as the *Fuehrer* seemed to assume, the *Fuehrer* put the summer of 1938 as the date which seemed to him possible for this. In reply to considerations offered by Field Marshal von Blomberg and General von Fritsch regarding the attitude of Britain and France, the *Fuehrer* repeated his previous statements that he was convinced of Britain's nonparticipation, and therefore he did not believe in the probability of belligerent action by France against Germany. Should the Mediterranean conflict under discussion lead to a general mobilization in Europe, then we must immediately begin action against the Czechs. On the other hand, should the powers not engaged in the war declare themselves disinterested, then Germany would have to adopt a similar attitude to this for the time being.

Colonel General Goering thought that, in view of the *Fuehrer's* statement, we should consider liquidating our military undertakings in Spain. The *Fuehrer* agrees to this with the limitation that he thinks he should reserve a decision for a proper moment.

The second part of the conference was concerned with concrete questions of armament.

HOSSBACH

CERTIFIED CORRECT:
   Colonel (General Staff)

73. Hitler Dismisses His Two Top Generals and Appoints Himself Commander-in-Chief of All the Armed Forces, February 4, 1938

"From this moment on I take over command. . . ."

In the process of re-arming Germany after 1934, Hitler became disillusioned with two of his highest military officers, Field Marshal Werner von Blomberg, minister of defense and supreme commander of the *Wehrmacht,* and Colonel-General Werner Freiherr von Fritsch, commander-in-chief of the army. Both officers were in effect dismissed after being accused of scandalous conduct — von Blomberg of marrying a prostitute and von Fritsch of homosexual activities.

Werner von Blomberg (1878–1946), though not a convinced Nazi, had remained loyal to the *Fuehrer* and had won rapid promotion. Toward the end of 1937 von Blomberg, a widower, began to entertain seriously the thought of marrying his secretary, one Fräulein Eva Gruhn, despite her questionable past. The wedding finally took place on January 12, 1938, with Hitler himself and Hermann Goering as witnesses. When the *Fuehrer* learned of the scandal through Goering, he took advantage of the situation to get rid of his top officer.

On February 4, 1938, Hitler announced that he himself was taking over supreme command of the armed forces. That same day he sent a letter to von Blomberg praising him for his loyal service during the past five years in helping build the new *Wehrmacht.* Hitler's official order and his private letter to von Blomberg follow.

Reichsgesetzblatt, 1, p. 111. *Völkischer Beobachter,* February 5, 1938. Translated by the editor.

Order by the Fuehrer and Reich Chancellor on Command of the Wehrmacht, February 4, 1938

FROM THIS MOMENT ON I take over command of the entire *Wehrmacht*. The former office of the *Wehrmacht* in the Reich War Ministry shall become immediately under my command as my military staff.

At the top of the staff of the Supreme Command of the *Wehrmacht* shall be the former chief of the office of the *Wehrmacht* as "Chief of the Supreme Command of the *Wehrmacht*" [General Wilhelm Keitel]. He is to hold the rank of a Reich Minister.

The Supreme Command of the *Wehrmacht* at the same time takes over the affairs of the Reich War Ministry, and the Chief of the Supreme Command of the *Wehrmacht* shall exercise at my command the affairs of the former Reich War Minister.

The Supreme Command of the *Wehrmacht* shall be responsible during peacetime on my orders for the overall preparation for the defense of the Reich in all areas.

Letter of Thanks from the Fuehrer and Reich Chancellor to General Field Marshal von Blomberg, February 4, 1938

Since the completion in 1936 of the rebirth of full German sovereignty in military and territorial matters [occupation of the demilitarized zone in the Rhineland on March 7, 1936], you have often requested that I relieve you from those duties which have made severe demands on your health.

Now I have decided, after the completion of five years of reconstruction of our people and their *Wehrmacht*, to grant your oft-requested petition. May you, indeed, find in the time before you the opportunity for that recuperation which you deserve more than many others.

On January 30, 1933, you, General Field Marshal, were the first officer in the new Reich to take the oath of loyalty to the National Socialist state. You have held unflinchingly to that oath for five years. During this period of time there was completed the most unique military reorganization that the world has ever seen.

With this work your own name will be bound historically for all time.

I now express to you, for myself and for the German people, in this hour a renewed sentiment of heartfelt thanks.

[Signed] Adolf Hitler

74. Hitler Again Expresses His Contempt and Loathing for Communism and Bolshevism, February 20, 1938

> ". . . no matter where it may be, and where it men-
> aces us, we shall oppose it — with complete loath-
> ing."

From the beginning of his political career, Hitler made a speciality of attacking communism and bolshevism. His aim was clear: bolshevism had to be destroyed if Europe were to live. The Communists, he charged, were bloodthirsty apostles of ruin who wanted to overthrow Western civilization and allow it to fall to Asiatic barbarism. Communism, he charged, was the special creation of Jews, who were also responsible for the evils of capitalism. It was his duty and that of his movement, he insisted in virtually every speech he made, to prevent the appalling catastrophe of a communist triumph in Europe. National Socialists and Communists, he said, remained deadly enemies.

In a speech made in Berlin on February 20, 1938, Hitler again presented his views on communist machinations. Just a year and a half later, he was to make a solemn pact with bolshevik Russia to divide Poland between Germany and Soviet Russia.

THERE IS ONLY ONE COUNTRY with which we have not attempted to establish good relations. Nor do we desire to establish close relations with Soviet Russia. More than ever before we see bolshevism as the incarnation of the destructive element in human affairs.

We do not hold the Russian people responsible for this terrible ideology

---

Völkischer Beobachter, February 21, 1938. Translated by the editor.

of nihilism. We know well, indeed, that a small powerful group of Jewish intellectuals plunged that nation into a situation close to insanity. We would not be concerned by this very much had this ideology remained inside the borders of Russia, because Germany has had no intention of forcing her own way of life on the Russian people.

Unfortunately, however, this bolshevism led by international Jewry has sought from its breeding grounds in Soviet Russia to eat away at the very heart of the nations of the world, to overthrow the existing world order, and to substitute chaos for civilization.

We are not trying to make any contacts with bolshevism. To the contrary, bolshevism seeks persistently to corrupt the rest of mankind with its ideology and by it wants to plunge the entire world into a disaster of unparalleled magnitude. In this matter we remain ruthless enemies. We were successful in overcoming Communist machinations in our own country, and we do not have the least intention of permitting Germany to be destroyed from outside by the material forces of bolshevism.

We have been repeatedly assured by British statesmen of their wish to maintain the *status quo* in the world. If this be the case, let them apply that concept here. Whenever a European country falls prey to bolshevism, there is a shift in position. The areas thus bolshevized can no longer remain sovereign states with independent, national lives of their own, but they become mere parts of the Moscow revolutionary center.

I know well that Mr. Eden does not share this view. But Mr. Stalin does, and he is completely frank about it. Right now Mr. Stalin is much the better judge and interpreter of bolshevik ideology than a British cabinet minister. As a result, as far as any attempt to spread bolshevism is concerned, no matter where it may be, and where it menaces us, we shall oppose it — with complete loathing.

75. Report on the Accomplishments of the *Kraft Durch Freude* Organization, 1938

". . . 19,060 workers' courses and lectures. . . ."

Hitler was anxious to convince the German people and the world that his regime was accomplishing wonders. He was proud of the *Kraft durch Freude* (Strength Through Joy) organization, which had been set up in 1933 for the benefit of the workers. In 1938 an official report summarized the accomplishments of the KdF during the five years of its existence for the *Gau* (district) of Berlin. The report counted many millions of individuals as sharing in the events staged by the organization.

Sponsored Events	Participants
21,146 theater performances	11,507,432
989 concerts	705,263
20,527 cultural events of various forms	10,518,282
93 exhibitions	2,435,975
273 labor exhibits	525,621
61,503 tours through museums and workshops	2,567,596
19,060 workers' courses and lectures of the German Popular Education organization	1,009,922
388 sports events	1,432,569
1,196 vacation tours and sea journeys	702,591
3,499 short week-end journeys	1,007,242
5,869 tours	126,292
1,889 trips to other districts than the Reich capital	1,153,859

From Gerhard Starke, *Die Deutsche Arbeitsfront: Eine Darstellung über Zweck, Leistungen und Ziele* (Berlin; n.p., 1940).

76. *Anschluss*: Hitler Completes the Union Between Germany and Austria, March 12, 1938

> *"I am now determined to restore law and order in*
> *my homeland. . . ."*

From the beginning of his chancellorship, Hitler intended to bring his homeland, Austria, into the German sphere of influence and if need be to annex it. As early as 1934 there was an abortive attempt tied up with the assassination of Chancellor Engelbert Dollfuss. Thereafter, the *Fuehrer* saw to it that Austrian life was kept in a turmoil. In early 1938, with his position considerably stronger, he sent for Kurt von Schuschnigg, the Austrian chancellor, and threatened to blast his country to bits unless he agreed to a union with Germany. "I have a historic mission," Hitler told the stunned Austrian. "This mission I will fulfill because Providence has destined me to do so. Who is not with me is against me. . . . Don't think for one moment that anybody on earth is going to thwart my decision. Italy? I see eye to eye with Mussolini. . . . England? England will not lift one finger for Austria. . . . France? . . . Now it is too late for France."

On an earlier occasion Hitler had had to postpone his *Anschluss* with Austria because Mussolini, his Italian ally, was opposed to it and had sent troops to the Brenner Pass as a warning to the *Fuehrer*. Now Hitler had become too strong for the Italian dictator. In any case, on March 11, 1938, a day before his troops marched across

---

Bundesgesetzblatt für den Bundesstaat Österreich (Vienna: Österreichische Staatsdruckerei, 1938), no. 75. Translated by the editor. *Documents on Foreign Relations, 1918-1945*, Series D, 1937-1945 (Washington, D.C.: Government Printing Office, 1949), vol. 1, pp. 573-76.

the Austrian border, Hitler sent Mussolini a letter in which he explained his decision, "already irrevocable." Realizing that he now had no means of preventing the action of his impatient ally, Mussolini promptly gave his blessing. A delighted Hitler told his ambassador at Rome: "I shall never forget him for this. I thank him ever so much. Never, never shall I forget!"

Law for the Promulgation of Anschluss, March 12, 1938

ARTICLE 1. Austria is a state of the German Reich.

ARTICLE 2. On Sunday, April 10, 1938, there will be held a free, secret plebiscite of all German men and women residing in Austria who are 20 years of age or over, on the reunion with the German Reich.

ARTICLE 3. The plebiscite will be determined by majority vote.

Letter Sent by Hitler to Mussolini on March 11, 1938*

The Fuehrer *and Chancellor to Benito Mussolini*

MARCH 11, 1938

EXCELLENCY: In a fateful hour I am turning to Your Excellency to inform you of a decision which appears necessary under the circumstances and has already become irrevocable.

((In recent months I have seen, with increasing preoccupation, how a relationship was gradually developing between Austria and Czechoslovakia which, while difficult for us to endure in peacetime, was bound, in case of a war imposed upon Germany, to become a most serious threat to the security of the Reich.

In the course of these understandings [*accordi*], the Austrian State began gradually to arm all its frontiers with barriers and fortifications. Its purpose could be none other than:

1. to effect the restoration at a specified time;
2. to throw the weight of a mass of at least 20 million men against Germany if necessary.

It is precisely the close bonds between Germany and Italy which, as was to be expected, have exposed our Reich to inevitable attacks. Incumbent on me is the responsibiliity not to permit the rise of a situation in Central

---

*The passages in double parentheses were omitted by German insistence when the letter was published.

Europe which, perhaps, might one day lead to serious complications precisely because of our friendship with Italy. This new orientation of the policy of the Austrian State does not, however, reflect in any way the real desire and will of the Austrian people.))

For years the Germans in Austria have been oppressed and mistreated by a regime which lacks any legal basis. The sufferings of innumerable tormented people know no bounds.

Germany alone has so far received 40,000 refugees who had to leave their homeland, although the overwhelming majority of the people of Austria entirely share their ideology and their political views.

With a view to eliminating a tension which was becoming increasingly unbearable, I decided to make a last attempt to reach an agreement with Herr Schuschnigg and definitely establish full equality for all under the law.

During our conversation in Berchtesgaden, ((I called Herr Schuschnigg's attention in a most serious way to the fact that Germany is not disposed:

1. to permit a hostile military power to establish itself at its borders, the more so since such plans are clearly in contradiction to the true wishes of the Austrian people;

2.)) I called Herr Schuschnigg's attention to the fact that Germany could no longer tolerate mistreatment of the National-minded majority in Austria by a negligible minority. I myself am a son of this soil. Austria is my homeland, and from the circle of my own relatives I know what oppression and what sufferings the overwhelming majority of these people who embrace Nationalist ideas have to endure.

I called his attention to the fact that it was impossible — this case being in fact without a parallel in the world — for a great power to permit people of common blood, common origin, and common history to be persecuted, mistreated, and deprived of their rights for these very reasons.

Furthermore, I informed Herr Schuschnigg that if the equality of all Germans in Austria were not restored, we should some day be forced to assume the protection of these kinsmen, abandoned by everyone.

My demands were more than moderate.

In fact, according to all principles of reason, right, and justice, and even according to the precepts of a formalistic democracy, Herr Schuschnigg and his Cabinet should have resigned to make room for a government enjoying the confidence of the people. I did not demand this. I was satisfied with a number of assurances that henceforth, within the framework of the Austrian laws — which, although they had been enacted unjustly, were in force at the present time — all inhabitants of the country were to be treated in the same way, receive the same privileges or be subject to the same restrictions, and, lastly, some security was to be established in the military sphere ((in order that the Austrian State might not one day become a dependency of Czechoslovakia)).

Herr Schuschnigg made me a solemn promise and concluded an agreement to this effect.

From the beginning he failed to keep this agreement.

But now he has gone so far as to deal a new blow against the spirit of this agreement by scheduling a so-called plebiscite which actually is a mockery.

The results of this newly planned oppression of the majority of the people are such as were feared.

The Austrian people are now finally rising against the constant oppression, and this will inevitably result in new oppressive measures. Therefore, the representatives of this oppressed people in the Austrian Government as well as in the other bodies have withdrawn.

Since the day before yesterday the country has been approaching closer and closer to a state of anarchy.

In my responsibility as *Fuehrer* and Chancellor of the German Reich and likewise as a son of this soil, I can no longer remain passive in the face of these developments.

I am now determined to restore law and order in my homeland and enable the people to decide their own fate according to their judgment in an unmistakable, clear, and open manner.

May the Austrian people itself, therefore, forge its own destiny. Whatever the manner may be in which this plebiscite is to be carried out, I now wish solemnly to assure Your Excellency, as the *Duce* of Fascist Italy:

1. Consider this step only as one of national self-defense and therefore as an act that any man of character would do in the same way, were he in my position. You too, Excellency, could not act differently if the fate of Italians were at stake, and I as *Fuehrer* and National Socialist cannot act differently.

2. In a critical hour for Italy I proved to you the steadfastness of my sympathy. Do not doubt that in the future there will be no change in this respect.

3. Whatever the consequences of the coming events may be, I have drawn a definite boundary between Germany and France and now draw one just as definite between Italy and us. It is the Brenner.

This decision will never be questioned or changed. I did not make this decision in 1938, but immediately after the end of the World War, and I never made a secret of it.

I hope that Your Excellency will pardon especially the haste of this letter and the form of this communication. These events occurred unexpectedly for all of us. Nobody had any inkling of the latest step of Herr Schuschnigg, not even his colleagues in the Government, and until now I had always hoped that perhaps at the last moment a different solution might be possible.

I deeply regret not being able to talk to you personally at this time to tell you everything I feel.

Always in friendship,

Yours,

ADOLF HITLER

77. Decree on Jewish-Owned Property: The Campaign Against the Jews Is Intensified, April 26, 1938

"The duty to report holds likewise for the non-Jewish marital partner of a Jew."

After each success in foreign policy, Hitler invariably returned to his *bête noire*, the Jew. No one in the *Fuehrer's* immediate entourage dared to defend a Jew in his presence, for any such defense would bring on a raging tantrum. On April 26, 1938, the government issued another official decree aimed at the Jews in Germany. It required all Jews who owned property to the value of 5,000 marks or more to report their possessions to the authorities. Penalties were severe and included imprisonment. Following, in condensed form, were the main provisions of this new decree.

ARTICLE 1. Every Jew shall report and evaluate in accord with the following instructions his entire domestic and foreign property and estate on the day when this decree goes into force. Jews of foreign citizenship shall report and evaluate only their domestic property. The duty to report holds likewise for the non-Jewish marital partner of a Jew. Every reporting person's property must be given separately.

ARTICLE 2. Property does not include movable objects used by the individual or house furnishings as far as the latter are not classed as luxury objects.

ARTICLE 3. No report is necessary when the total worth of the property to be reported does not exceed 5,000 marks.

ARTICLE 4. The report is to be presented on an official form by June 30,

---

Condensed from *The New York Times*, April 29, 1938.

1938, to the administrative office responsible at the place of residence of the reporting individual.

ARTICLE 5. The reporting individual must report, after this decree goes into force, to the responsible officer every change of said individual's total property as far as it exceeds a proper standard of living or normal business transactions.

ARTICLE 8. Whoever with purpose or through carelessness does not fulfill the duty to report will be punished with imprisonment and a fine or one of the two said punishments. A delinquent is likewise punishable when the crime was committed abroad. An effort to commit such a crime is equally punishable. Besides the punishment provided above, confiscation of the property can also be imposed as far as said property was involved in a punishment action. When no definite individual can be prosecuted, confiscation alone can be imposed when the prerequisites for confiscation are demonstrated.

78. The People of Czechoslovakia Learn That Their Nation Has Been Wrecked, September 21, 1938

"Away with the cowardly government!"

One war correspondent termed the abandonment of Czechoslovakia a "cowardly, treacherous, and unnecessary sacrifice." British Prime Minister Neville Chamberlain had been strangely obsequious to Hitler. His peace pilgrimages to Berchtesgaden and Bad Godesberg were exercises in humiliation. But the story was finished. Czechoslovakia, the most democratic state to appear in the aftermath of World War I, had been sold down the river. An American foreign correspondent, George E. R. Geyde, was present in Prague on September 21, 1938, at a time when the Czechoslovak people finally began to realize what had happened to them. A year after writing this dispatch, Geyde was forced to flee the Czechoslovak Republic to avoid arrest under a Gestapo warrant.

PRAGUE, CZECHOSLOVAKIA, THURSDAY, SEPTEMBER 22 — Last night at 7:30, after twenty-four hours of agonizing pressure, the Czechoslovak people learned that their state had been wrecked — just twenty years after it had been created — by those who brought it into existence, Great Britain and France.

A communiqué issued by the government announced that it had agreed to cede Sudeten German territory to the Reich. It declared Britain and France had insisted that "only by territorial sacrifice on our part could security and peace be assured.

"They informed us that they could not extend aid in the event we were

---

The New York Times, September 22, 1938.

attacked by Germany and they were of the opinion such a conflict would have been inevitable had Czechoslovakia refused to cede the territories of the German population," the communiqué said, adding that the government had had no alternative but to accept.

Despite the censorship that was being applied — not, as had been expected, to protect the state from an external enemy during a war but to protect the government while it was agreeing to the final surrender — people had begun in the afternoon to suspect what was happening.

Even before the news got out in detail, demonstrations started that at first were quiet and full of pathos. By ten o'clock last night the capital bore the aspect of a city in the full swing not so much of a revolution as of a great national regeneration.

It was above all a furious demonstration against the government and one of trust in President Eduard Beneš and the army, although there were a number of Communist clenched fists raised and a few isolated Fascist threats against the President.

The demonstrations began spontaneously and the first ones were made with moving and touching dignity. They were carried out in front of cafes and hotels, and each demonstration ended with the singing of the national anthem while all heads were bared. The police, who were present in force, far from interfering, stood at salute as the national anthem was sung.

Many of the demonstrators, both men and women, wept unashamedly. More than one police officer standing near this correspondent was seen to pass his sleeves across his eyes.

On the sidewalks stood sad and red-eyed onlookers, watching the masses who marched, carrying the national colors, without any noticeable distinction of class or age. It was an unforgettable spectacle of a nation stricken down in peacetime, moved with great sorrow and vast anger.

On one street corner a news dealer told the writer:

"I have no London newspapers for sale tonight. The entire stock was bought up instantly after the news came out by a man who paid fifteen crowns each for them, tore them to shreds, ground them with his heel, spat on them, and turned away weeping."

In Prague it is estimated several hundred thousand persons took part in the demonstrations against the government and against capitulation.

Masses singing the national anthem and shouting for the commander-in-chief of the army, General Jan Syrovy, made their way down the Vaclavske Namesti to the Karel Bridge and swept across it, winding their way uphill toward the Hradschin Palace.

Halfway up they were confronted by strong detachments of mounted and foot police. The procession was headed by an automobile containing men displaying the national flag, and as they caught sight of it all the

police sprang to attention, saluted, and fraternized with the crowd, allowing it to sweep on and offering no obstacle.

Arriving at the Hradschin gates, the crowd halted. Moving speeches
were made by several impromptu speakers, the burden of which was trust
in President Beneš and such phrases as "We have been betrayed by our
allies and by cowards within our own camp." "Away with the cowardly
government!" "No capitulation!" and "We will defend our republic at the
side of our own army."

In many factories on the outskirts of the city workers downed their tools
before the end of the working day and marched into the city to take part in
the demonstrations.

There was one dramatic moment when the crowds on the Vaclavske
Namesti heard a voice from a loudspeaker — which had just been voicing
government warnings against joining demonstrations — declaiming furiously against the government and calling for a stouthearted defense of the
republic. After some minutes the voice stopped abruptly in the middle of a
sentence.

The explanation was that part of the crowd had forced its way into the
broadcasting center and one man had got before the microphone to voice
public sentiment before someone had thought of cutting off the current.

Similar spontaneous demonstrations in which all party distinctions
vanished occurred in Ostrau, Pilsca, Olmütz, and hundreds of other
towns and villages.

The crowds showed particular enthusiasm in demonstrating outside
barracks. In Prague officers and soldiers were carried on the crowds'
shoulders.

In Brno, an industrial area, German democratic elements joined with
the Czechs in demonstrations with the slogan: "No surrender! We will
defend ourselves to the last against the Nazi invaders. Away with the
government of capitulators!"

More than 100,000 copies of a leaflet calling on the citizens of the
republic to hold fast and defend their frontiers were circulated here last
night, signed by eighty-five influential parliamentarians of all parties,
secretaries of trade-unions, and leaders of cultural and economic bodies.

Together with these leaflets was issued an appeal to President Beneš
urging him to use his authority "against the enemies within our ranks." The
appeal asked the President to come forward, relying on the full support of
the whole nation, which trusted in him, and to take the direction of affairs
into his own hands.

"We know," the appeal said, "that you stand firm still — as firm as our
army by its guns on the fortifications. Draw your support from the whole
nation, which will never capitulate."

The leaflet, addressed to "our fellow citizens," began:

"The die is not yet cast. Czechoslovak democracy has not capitulated. A people does not capitulate. The government is not the nation.

"We have not yet lost one single rifle, one single gun, one airplane, or any of our fortifications. On the contrary, in the new unity of the whole people and its determination not to yield to the Nazis we have gained tremendous strength.

"Away with the enemies of the republic and the friends of the Nazis! The democrats of the world will stand by those who fight for their own, for truth and justice. Let us show the world our readiness to defend ourselves.

"Parliament alone has the right to decide the republic's fate. We demand the immediate assembling of Parliament, which will reject the capitulation.

"Long live the Czechoslovak Republic, its loyal army and its first commander-in-chief, President Beneš! Firm stands the President, firm stands the army, and firm stands the nation!"

The dramatic and tragic events leading up to last night's tremendous demonstrations began with the demand at midnight Tuesday by the British and French Ministers here that President Beneš give them an audience immediately.

Apparently someone had blundered in handling the Czech reply to the Anglo-French demands for the acceptance of the London plan. It was to have been sent to London and Paris in code for transmission to the respective governments yesterday morning. Someone, however, allowed the document — which in essence was a polite refusal of the plan — to be handed in clear language to the two Ministers, who immediately telephoned its contents to their respective capitals and received instructions to reject the note and renew the pressure.

At 2:15 A.M. President Beneš received the Ministers, who handed him a note couched in extremely harsh terms insisting that there must be full and immediate surrender to the London plan, which involved the republic's dismemberment and the loss of its frontiers that for more than a thousand years have marked the historic provinces in which Czechs and Germans have lived side by side. The British and French insistence that they should be torn apart in accordance with Chancellor Adolf Hitler's will was inexorable.

As the Cabinet's deliberations went on throughout the night there were calls from the two legations at intervals of something like an hour to know whether the business was not yet finished.

At four A.M. the committee of the Cabinet's political ministers met under Dr. Beneš's presidency in the Hradschin Palace. At six there was a full Cabinet meeting. President Beneš declined to exercise his privilege of attending it.

Premier Milan Hodza had to tell his ministers that the British and French diplomats had informed him that the country was now faced with a united front of Germany, Hungary, and Poland and that unless its surrender was immediate and complete, an invasion by all three armies would begin either yesterday or today.

Nobody, the Premier was told, would lift a finger to save Czechoslovakia, and she would disappear from the map entirely under complete partition.

The Cabinet ministers gloomily studied their maps, which showed them a country entirely surrounded by enemies save for a short strip bordering on Rumania. Hungary's entry was of no particular consequence, it was felt, but Poland's was fatal.

Soon after nine o'clock yesterday morning the Cabinet Council decided to surrender.

*   *   *

79. The Munich Agreement: The Western Allies Abandon Czechoslovakia in a Classic Case of Appeasement, September 29, 1938

". . . the Czechoslovak Government will be held responsible. . . ."

On September 12, 1938, Hitler announced that he wanted self-determination for all the Sudeten Germans in Czechoslovakia. He claimed that the Sudeten Germans were being persecuted mercilessly by the Czechs. On September 26, he delivered a speech at the Sportpalast in Berlin in which he informed Prime Minister Neville Chamberlain that, if the Sudeten problem were solved, Germany would have no more territorial problems in Europe. *The New York Times* reported, on September 27, 1938, Hitler's words: "We now come to the last problem which has to be solved and will be solved. It is the last territorial demand I have to make in Europe. In 1919, 2,500,000 Germans were torn away from their compatriots by a company of mad statesmen. The Czech state originated in a huge lie and the name of the liar is Beneš." *The Times* went on to say that "Herr Hitler's voice rose to a harsh scream as he pronounced the name of the Czech President. The heils from the audience reached a frantic pitch."

France and Russia were explicitly bound by treaty to defend the integrity of Czechoslovakia, while Britain was involved through commitments to France. The resulting crisis was the most dangerous since World War I. Chamberlain flew to Berchtesgaden and

Further Documents Respecting Czechoslovakia, including the Agreement Concluded at Munich on September 29, 1938. Presented by the Secretary of State for Foreign Affairs to Parliament by Command of His Majesty, Misc. no. 8 (1938), Cmd. 58948 (His Majesty's Stationery Office, London, 1938), pp. 2, 3-6.

Bad Godesberg to ask for peace. Britain and France, convinced
that Hitler was not bluffing, decided that they had to give in to the
Fuehrer. The climax of the crisis came at a meeting in Munich
called by Hitler for the purpose of fixing the means by which the
Sudetenland would be transferred to Germany. The resulting Munich Agreement maintained the peace by conceding to Hitler virtually everything for which he had asked. On returning to London,
Chamberlain announced that Munich meant "peace in our time."

GERMANY, THE UNITED KINGDOM, FRANCE AND ITALY, taking into consideration the agreement, which has been already reached in principle for the
cession to Germany of the Sudeten German territory, have agreed on the
following terms and conditions governing the said cession and the measures consequent thereon, and by this agreement they each hold themselves responsible for the steps necessary to secure its fulfilment:

1. The evacuation will begin on the 1st October.

2. The United Kingdom, France and Italy agree that the evacuation of
the territory shall be completed by the 10th October, without any existing
installations having been destroyed and that the Czechoslovak Government will be held responsible for carrying out the evacuation without
damage to the said installations.

3. The conditions governing the evacuation will be laid down in detail
by an international commission composed of representatives of Germany,
the United Kingdom, France, Italy and Czechoslovakia.

4. The occupation by stages of the predominantly German territory by
German troops will begin on the 1st October. The four territories marked
on the attached map will be occupied by German troops in the following
order: the territory marked No. I on the 1st and 2nd of October, the
territory marked No. II on the 2nd and 3rd of October, the territory
marked No. III on the 3rd, 4th, and 5th of October, the territory marked
No. IV on the 6th and 7th of October. The remaining territory of prepon-
derantly German character will be ascertained by the aforesaid international commission forthwith and be occupied by German troops by the
10th of October.

5. The international commission referred to in paragraph 3 will determine the territories in which a plebiscite is to be held. These territories will
be occupied by international bodies until the plebiscite has been completed. The same commission will fix the conditions in which the plebiscite
is to be held, taking as a basis the conditions of the Saar plebiscite. The
commission will also fix a date, not later than the end of November, on
which the plebiscite will be held.

6. The final determination of the frontiers will be carried out by the international commission. This commission will also be entitled to recommend to the four Powers, Germany, the United Kingdom, France and Italy, in certain exceptional cases minor modifications in the strictly ethnographical determination of the zones which are to be transferred without plebiscite.

7. There will be a right of option into and out of the transferred territories, the option to be exercised within six months from the date of this agreement. A German-Czechoslovak commission shall determine the details of the option, consider ways of facilitating the transfer of population and settle questions of principle arising out of the said transfer.

8. The Czechoslovak Government will within a period of four weeks from the date of this agreement release from their military and police forces any Sudeten Germans who may wish to be released, and the Czechoslovak Government will within the same period release Sudeten German prisoners who are serving terms of imprisonment for political offenses.

ADOLF HITLER
ED. DALADIER
MUSSOLINI
NEVILLE CHAMBERLAIN

Munich, September 29, 1938.

ANNEX TO THE AGREEMENT

His Majesty's Government in the United Kingdom and the French Government have entered into the above agreement on the basis that they stand by the offer, contained in paragraph 6 of the Anglo-French proposals of September 19th, relating to an international guarantee of the new boundaries of the Czechoslovak State against unprovoked aggression.

When the question of the Polish and Hungarian miniorities in Czechoslovakia has been settled, Germany and Italy for their part will give a guarantee to Czechoslovakia.

ADOLF HITLER
NEVILLE CHAMBERLAIN
MUSSOLINI
ED. DALADIER

MUNICH, September 29, 1938.

The four Heads of Government here present agree that the international commission, provided for in the agreement signed by them today, shall consist of the State Secretary in the German Foreign Office, the British,

French, and Italian Ambassadors accredited in Berlin, and a representative to be nominated by the Government of Czechoslovakia.

> ADOLF HITLER
> NEVILLE CHAMBERLAIN
> MUSSOLINI
> ED. DALADIER

MUNICH, September 29, 1938.

ADDITIONAL DECLARATION

The Heads of the Governments of the four Powers declare that the problems of the Polish and Hungarian minorities in Czechoslovakia, if not settled within 3 months by agreement between the respective Governments, shall form the subject of another meeting of the Heads of the Governments of the four Powers here present.

> ADOLF HITLER
> NEVILLE CHAMBERLAIN
> MUSSOLINI
> ED. DALADIER

MUNICH, September 29, 1938.

80. Night of Broken Glass: Nazis Smash, Loot, and Burn Jewish Shops and Synagogues, November 9-10, 1938

"Huge but mostly silent crowds looked on. . . ."

On November 7, 1938, a seventeen-year-old German-Jewish boy named Herschel Grynszpan, whose parents had been deported to Poland, shot and killed Ernst vom Rath, the third secretary of the German embassy in Paris. In fury, Dr. Paul Joseph Goebbels, minister for public enlightenment and propaganda, issued an order to the SS, the security police, and to the police to "allow a spontaneous demonstration" by the German people in revenge.

That order unleashed a horrible night for the Jews of Germany. On the evening of November 9, gangs of Storm Troopers and other Nazi party members attacked Jewish shops, homes, and synagogues throughout Germany. Bands of Nazis roved through the cities, leaving a trail of wreckage, while police stood idle. Thousands were arrested "for protection," perhaps as many as twenty thousand. Berlin became a center of looting and destruction. In Vienna, too, fires and bombs wrecked eighteen of twenty-one synagogues; Jews were beaten, and their furniture and goods flung from homes and shops.

Otto D. Tolischus, Berlin correspondent, sent the following report by wireless to *The New York Times.* Newspaper editorials throughout the world denounced the event as a shocking reversion to barbarism. The world press was virtually unanimous in condemning the Nazis for the outbreak of anti-Semitism. The *Petit Parisien,* in its issue of November 11, 1938, gave its reaction, which was similar to thousands of other editorials throughout the world:

The New York Times, November 11, 1938.

"The world is astonished that a civilized nation like Germany should permit such terrible reprisals against victims whose only relationship to the murderer is one of race. Even that could be explained if these acts had been committed by uncontrollable mobs. But Goebbels has been somewhat slow in issuing a call for order and it is apparent that for nearly twenty-four hours nothing has been done to prevent the disturbances. Unless this exhibition ends quickly it bids fair to tarnish the reputation for discipline and honor that the Nazi regime is always claiming as its own exclusive attribute."

The "exhibition" did not end quickly. Dr. Goebbels, who had issued orders to keep the fires away from German property, was astonished by the scope and energy of the attacks. He soon called a halt to the anti-Jewish activities, but it was a difficult task. The attacks went on for a week.

BERLIN, Nov. 10. — A wave of destruction, looting and incendiarism unparalleled in Germany since the Thirty Years War and in Europe generally since the Bolshevist revolution, swept over Great Germany today as National Socialist cohorts took vengeance on Jewish shops, offices and synagogues for the murder by a young Polish Jew of Ernst vom Rath, third secretary of the German Embassy in Paris.

Beginning systematically in the early morning hours in almost every town and city in the country, the wrecking, looting and burning continued all day. Huge but mostly silent crowds looked on and the police confined themselves to regulating traffic and making wholesale arrests of Jews "for their own protection."

All day the main shopping districts as well as the side streets of Berlin and innumerable other places resounded to the shattering of shop windows falling to the pavement, the dull thuds of furniture and fittings being pounded to pieces and the clamor of fire brigades rushing to burning shops and synagogues. Although shop fires were quickly extinguished, synagogue fires were merely kept from spreading to adjoining buildings.

Two Deaths Reported

As far as could be ascertained the violence was mainly confined to property. Although individuals were beaten, reports so far tell of the death of only two persons — a Jew in Polzin, Pomerania, and another in Bunzdorf.

In extent, intensity and total damage, however, the day's outbreaks exceeded even those of the 1918 revolution and by nightfall there was scarcely a Jewish shop, cafe, office or synagogue in the country that was not either wrecked, burned severely or damaged.

Thereupon Propaganda Minister Joseph Goebbels issued the following proclamation:

"The justified and understandable anger of the German people over the cowardly Jewish murder of a German diplomat in Paris found extensive expression during last night. In numerous cities and towns of the Reich retaliatory action has been undertaken against Jewish buildings and businesses.

"Now a strict request is issued to the entire population to cease immediately all further demonstrations and actions against Jewry, no matter what kind. A final answer to the Jewish assassination in Paris will be given to Jewry by way of legislation and ordinance."

What this legal action is going to be remains to be seen. It is known, however, that measures for the extensive expulsion of foreign Jews are already being prepared in the Interior Ministry, and some towns, like Munich, have ordered all Jews to leave within forty-eight hours. All Jewish organizational, cultural and publishing activity has been suspended. It is assumed that the Jews, who have now lost most of their possessions and livelihood, will either be thrown into the streets or put into ghettos and concentration camps, or impressed into labor brigades and put to work for the Third Reich, as the children of Israel were once before for the Pharaohs.

Thousands Are Arrested

In any case, all day in Berlin, as throughout the country, thousands of Jews, mostly men, were being taken from their homes and arrested – in particular prominent Jewish leaders, who in some cases, it is understood, were told they were being held as hostages for the good behavior of Jewry outside Germany.

In Breslau they were hunted out even in the homes of non-Jews where they might have been hiding. . . .

All pretense – maintained during previous comparatively minor anti-Jewish outbreaks – to the effect that the day's deeds had been the work of irresponsible, even Communist, elements was dropped this time and the official German News Bureau, as well as newspapers that hitherto had ignored such happenings, frankly reported on them. The bureau said specifically:

"Continued anti-Jewish demonstrations occurred in numerous places. In most cities the synagogue was fired by the population. The fire department in many cases was able merely to save adjoining buildings. In addition, in many cities the windows of Jewish shops were smashed.

"Occasionally fires occurred and because of the population's extraordinary excitement the contents of shops were partly destroyed. Jewish shop owners were taken into custody by the police for their own protection."

Excesses in Many Cities

Berlin papers also mention many cities and towns in which anti-Jewish excesses occurred, including Potsdam, Stettin, Frankfort on the Main, Leipzig, Luebeck, Cologne, Nuremberg, Essen, Duesseldorf, Konstanz, Landsberg, Kottbus and Eberswalde. In most of them, it is reported, synagogues were raided and burned and shops were demolished. But in general the press follows a system of reporting only local excesses so as to disguise the national extent of the outbreak, the full spread of which probably never will be known.

On the other hand, the German press already warns the world that if the day's events lead to another agitation campaign against Germany "the improvised and spontaneous outbreaks of today will be replaced with even more drastic authoritative action." No doubt is left that the contemplated "authoritative action" would have a retaliatory character. . . .

Possession of Weapons Barred

One of the first legal measures issued was an order by Heinrich Himmler, commander of all German police, forbidding Jews to possess any weapons whatever and imposing a penalty of twenty years' confinement in a concentration camp upon every Jew found in possession of a weapon hereafter.

The dropping of all pretense in the outbreak is also illustrated by the fact that although shops and synagogues were wrecked or burned by so-called Rollkommandos, or wrecking crews, dressed in what the Nazis themselves call "Rasüberzivil," or "bandit mufti," consisting of leather coats or raincoats over uniform boots or trousers, these squads often performed their work in the presence and under the protection of uniformed Nazis or police.

The wrecking work was thoroughly organized, sometimes proceeding under the direct orders of a controlling person in the street at whose command the wreckers ceased, lined up and proceeded to another place.

In the fashionable Tauenzienstrasse the writer saw a wrecking crew at work in one shop while the police stood outside telling a vast crowd watching the proceeding to keep moving.

"Move on," said the policemen, "there are young Volksgenossen [racial comrades] inside who have some work to do."

At other shops during the wrecking process uniformed Storm Troopers and Elite Guards were seen entering, and emerging while soldiers passed by outside.

Crowds Mostly Silent

Generally the crowds were silent and the majority seemed gravely disturbed by the proceedings. Only members of the wrecking squads shouted occasionally, "Perish Jewry!" and "Kill the Jews!" and in one case a person in the crowd shouted, "Why not hang the owner in the window?"

In one case on the Kurfuerstendamm actual violence was observed by an American girl who saw one Jew with his face bandaged dragged from a shop, beaten and chased by a crowd while a second Jew was dragged from the same shop by a single man who beat him as the crowd looked on.

One Jewish shopowner, arriving at his wrecked store, exclaimed, "Terrible," and was arrested on the spot.

In some cases on the other hand crowds were observed making passages for Jews to leave their stores unmolested.

Some persons in the crowds — peculiarly enough, mostly women — expressed the view that it was only right that the Jews should suffer what the Germans suffered in 1918. But there were also men and women who expressed protests. Most of them said something about Bolshevism. One man — obviously a worker — watching the burning of a synagogue in the Fasanenstrasse, exclaimed, "Arson remains arson." The protestors, however, were quickly silenced by the wrecking crews with threats of violence.

Warned Against Looting

To some extent — at least during the day — efforts were made to prevent looting. Crowds were warned they might destroy but not plunder, and in individual cases looters were either beaten up on the spot by uniformed Nazis or arrested. But for the most part, looting was general, particularly during the night and in the poorer quarters. And at least in one case the wreckers themselves tossed goods out to the crowd with the shout "Here are some cheap Christmas presents."

Children were observed with their mouths smeared with candy from wrecked candy shops or flaunting toys from wrecked toy shops until one elderly woman watching the spectacle exclaimed, "So that is how they teach our children to steal."

Foreign Jewish shops, it appears, were not at first marked for destruction and were passed over by the first wrecking crews. But in their destructive enthusiasm others took them on as well and even wrecked some "Aryan" shops by mistake.

Among the foreign wrecked establishments were three American-owned shops — the Loewenstein jewelry shop in Kanonierstrasse, near the office of THE NEW YORK TIMES, the owner of which shop is now in America; the Leipzig fur shop in Rosenthalerstrasse, owned by C. G. Schultz, who is also in America, and the Rose Bach rug shop in the Hauptstrasse. . . .

Damage in the Millions

BERLIN, Nov. 10 (AP). — In a great wave of anti-Jewish violence that swept Nazi Germany today millions of dollars' worth of Jewish property was destroyed. Jewish stores were looted. Synagogues were burned, dynamited or damaged in a dozen cities.

Bands of youths roved the streets of Berlin and other cities from early morning on, smashing windows of shops. In many places crowds that gathered after daybreak pushed into the establishments and came out with loot. Most of Berlin's 1,000 Jewish stores were plundered.

Sounds of breaking glass and shouts of looters died away only near midnight. Hundreds of Jews voluntarily spent the night in jails fearing worse violence as reports of burning and looting continued to come in from many cities.

Propaganda Minister Joseph Goebbels had appealed at 4 P.M. for an end to the demonstrations, but at first the appeal apparently had no effect in the West End of Berlin. Three hours later it was repeated by radio. Then policemen appeared in Koenigstrasse, where several Jewish shops are situated, arrested twenty-one looters and cleared the street.

Crowds Watch Gangs

In a tour of Berlin this afternoon this correspondent saw few Jewish stores or synagogues that had escaped damage. Many buildings were destroyed.

The rioting reached a high point at the center of Berlin, where, at noon, thousands gathered in the streets to watch gangs pound to bits dozens of stores.

Around another corner in the center of the city a tailor shop was looted. In the doorway, a tailor's dummy with a hat on its head hung with a rope around its neck.

Children "Fish" for Loot

While a large section of the German population seemed thoroughly ashamed at the exhibition of mob rule, those who participated in anti-Semitic actions had a gay time.

Before one Friedrichstrasse shop devoted to the sale of magic apparatus children lined up with brass poles that had hooks at the ends. With these they fished magicians' boxes of tricks for themselves out of the interior of the shop through a broken store window.

Older boys unconcernedly threw tables, chairs and other furniture out of smashed windows.

One group moved a piano from a shop into the street and played popular tunes for onlookers.

Before synagogues, demonstrators stood with Jewish prayer books from which they tore leaves as souvenirs for the crowds. This correspondent started out at daybreak with the milkman. On the tour the first damage seen was the destruction by fire of the wealthy synagogue in Fasanenstrasse, near the Zoo railway station. Clouds of smoke rose from three domes of the stone building. The interior was a furnace, with the tile roof about to collapse as the fire ate at rafters. Worship benches, books and other inflammable materials had been piled in the center.

During the morning this smoking synagogue could be seen by passengers on international trains arriving from the West. This temple, with the city's newest one in Prinzregentenstrasse, both huge structures, was virtually destroyed by fire.

Help Themselves to Shoes

Hundreds of stores gaped open when workmen passed them in the morning. Near Alexanderplatz some twenty workers from the city market were helping themselves at a shoe store. When this correspondent got there they were sitting on the curb, laughing and trying on pair after pair of shoes. . . . Traffic was halted along Friedrichstrasse, Charlottenstrasse and other streets crossing Kronenstrasse. An immense crowd filled the intersections.

The noise of breaking glass and cracking furniture accompanied loud anti-Jewish jeers. When the smashing crew had passed, it looked as if a tornado had swept the street. The pavement was covered with broken glass.

Typewriters, chairs, files and other office furniture, sample books and packing cases had been hurled into the street. Invoice sheets and price tags fluttered about.

Restaurants that previously had made no distinction between Jews and non-Jews posted signs: "No Jews Wanted."

The official German News Bureau expressed indignation that some Jewish proprietors had compelled "Aryan" employes to clean up the debris.

81. Goering Issues Three Decrees Holding the Jews Responsible for the Excesses of *Kristallnacht*, November 12, 1938

"Jews of German nationality will pay. . . ."

Within several days after the Night of Broken Glass, General Field Marshal Hermann Goering, as coordinator of the Four-Year Plan issued three decrees holding all German Jews responsible for the act of Herschel Grynszpan in Paris and for the subsequent events of revenge inside Germany. The Jews were fined one billion Reichsmarks, much of their property was confiscated, and Jewish shopkeepers were required to repair at their own expense all the damage done to their stores in the riots. In addition, further restrictions were placed on Jews, such as bans on walking on certain streets, using park benches, and driving automobiles. Public markets, playgrounds, and winter resorts were forbidden to them. So that some might not try to pass as Aryans, all Jews were ordered to wear the yellow Star of David as identification.

Expiation Decree for Jews of German Nationality, November 12, 1938

The hostile attitude of Judaism to the German people and to the Reich, an attitude which does not even hesitate at foul murder [a reference to the vom Rath assassination], calls for decisive defense and harsh atonement.

I order, on the basis of the decree for the implementation of the Four-Year Plan of October 18, 1936, the following:

Reichsgesetzblatt, 1938, 1, pp. 1579, 1580, 1581. Translated by the editor.

1

Jews of German nationality will pay a contribution of 1,000,000,000 Reichsmarks to the German Reich.

2

The measures for implementing this decree will be announced by the Reich Minister of Finance in consultation with the concerned Reich ministers.*

(1) 1. The contribution of a billion Reichsmarks will be made from the personal property of all Jews of German nationality and from stateless Jews [*Judensvermögensabgabe*].

2. Subject to this confiscation will be every Jew who, according to the required report of every Jew dated April 26, 1938, had to attest to all his property inside and outside Germany.

3. Jews of foreign nationality will not be subject to this confiscatory order.

(2) In mixed marriages only the Jewish partner is obligated to surrender his property.

(3) The confiscation will not apply to property valued at less than 5000 Reichsmarks.

(4) 1. The confiscation will apply to 20 percent of all property. . . .

(a) The obligation for payment ceases as soon as the total of one billion Reichsmarks is reached.

(b) The obligation for payment is extended in order to reach the total of one billion Reichsmarks.

Decree for the Expulsion of Jews from German Economic Life, November 12, 1938

1

(1) After January 1, 1939, Jews are forbidden to maintain a one-man business, any export business, or commission houses, as well as any individual handicraft trade.

(2) Further, from that day on, it is also decreed that Jews are forbidden to take part in exhibitions or fairs of and kind or to solicit business or exhibit goods at them.

(3) Jewish businessmen who violate these ordnances are to be arrested.

2

(1) From January 1, 1939, on, a Jew cannot remain a businessman any longer in the sense of the law of January 20, 1934.

(2) If a Jew has been a leading employee in a business enterprise, he will be dismissed after six months' notice. After this period of grace, he shall lose all contractual rights to his position, especially pensions and settlement claims.

---

*These decrees were issued on November 21, 1938.

3

(1) A Jew cannot be a member of a cooperative society.

(2) All Jewish members of cooperative societies will be dismissed as of December 31, 1938. Special notification is not necessary.

4

(1) The Reich Minister of Economics, in conjunction with the concerned Reich ministries, is empowered to issue implementation measures for this decree. He is empowered to make exceptions in cases where a transfer from Jewish to non-Jewish hands is called for, or the liquidation of a Jewish business, or in special cases.

Decree on Damage to Jewish Business, November 12, 1938

1

On the basis of the decree for the implementation of the Four-Year Plan of October 18, 1938, I order the following:

1

All damages, which through the indignation of the people due to the baiting of international Jewry against National Socialist Germany on the 8th, 9th, and 10th of November, 1938, were inflicted on Jewish businesses and dwellings are to be settled by the Jewish residents or businessmen.

2

(1) The costs of restoration shall be carried by the residents of the concerned Jewish businesses or dwellings.

(2) Insurance claims by Jews of German nationality will be brought to the attention of the Reich authorities.

(3) The Reich Economics Minister, in conjunction with the concerned Reich ministries, is empowered to issue implementation measures for this decree.

82. Reich Propaganda Minister Goebbels Comments on the Grynszpan Case in the *Völkischer Beobachter*, November 12, 1938

"The German people have become doubly vigilant."

Kristallnacht (Night of Broken Glass) caused shock and criticism throughout the entire world. Sensitive to world public opinion, Dr. Paul Joseph Goebbels, Reich minister for public enlightenment and propaganda, within several days wrote a special article for the *Völkischer Beobachter*. He explained how the German people had risen "spontaneously" in their wrath against the Jews, who in murdering two diplomats in foreign countries were working for the destruction of the Third Reich: on February 4, 1936, Wilhelm Gustloff, *Fuehrer* of the Swiss branch of the Nazi party, was shot while in his home at Davos by David Frankfurter, a Jew; and on November 7, 1938, Legation Secretary Ernst vom Rath was killed in Paris by Herschel Grynszpan, a Jew.

Goebbels's article was filled with resentment and contempt for Jews. He was careful, however, to point out that the government had ordered a cessation of demonstrations, undoubtedly a reaction to an inflamed world public opinion of *Kristallnacht*.

ON NOVEMBER 7 a seventeen-year-old Polish Jewish youth [Herschel Grynszpan] forced his way into the German Embassy in Paris and demanded to speak to someone in authority. When he was brought before Legation Secretary vom Rath, he took out his pistol and, without a word being said or any argument taking place, fired several shots at the German

Völkischer Beobachter, November 12, 1938. Translated by the editor.

diplomat. At his later interrogation he declared that he had never known the Legation Secretary personally. It was all the same to him who he shot. He wanted only to take revenge for his Jewish brothers in Germany. The investigation in Paris revealed that three months earlier Grynszpan had been ordered to leave France. He has consistently refused to tell where he lived during these three months. He had in his possession a false passport.

So the questions arise: Where was Grynszpan during the last three months? Who took care of his living expenses? Who gave him the false passport? Who trained him in pistol-shooting? There can be no doubt that he was given sanctuary by a Jewish organization, nor that he was systematically prepared for this cynical assassination.

Legation Secretary vom Rath died after excruciating pain several days later. The parallel with the Gustloff case is obvious. Just as in that murder, a young man was sought out by Jewish leaders in the background in order to hide their responsibility. The interrogation of both Jewish youths revealed an exact agreement on the nature of a defense and the tactics to be used by both assassins. Also it was revealed at the trial of Frankfurter that he wanted to strike not at an individual but at National Socialist Germany. In both cases one can see the well-prepared hand of the entire Jewish press.

Where can we find these men behind the scenes? For some weeks and months now a veritable war has been waged against Germany as a nation by the Jewish world press and murder provoked against individual prominent representatives of National Socialist Germany. At the head of this pack are the Jews Georg Bernhard and Emil Ludwig Cohn. Undoubtedly, the inspiration of the assassinations is to be found in these circles. In these same circles is a hitherto unmatched propaganda of assent for this murder. The reasons for the assassinations are obvious. World Jewry, after its feverish incitement to war during the summer months of this year, has undergone a terrible reversal. The Munich Agreement [September 29, 1938] reduced to a shambles its plan to destroy Germany. It had hoped through its infamous incitement to world war to bring Germany to her knees and to bring about the fall of the hated Nazi regime. After its plan was shattered at Munich, it wanted to take drastic and indecent action to halt the efforts for peace between the Great Powers of Europe in order to set the scene for a renewed hate campaign against Germany.

The murder of Legation Secretary vom Rath was to be a beacon for all Jewry in its battle against Germany. The murderer himself confessed that he wanted to give a warning signal by his act. However, this shot went astray. The world was not warned so much as the German people themselves.

It is certainly obvious that a nation of 80 million people will not in the long run remain silent and defenseless in the face of such provocation. The German people remained silent after the murder of Gustloff. After the murder of Legation Secretary vom Rath they have called spontaneously for reprisal against the Jews in Germany. The outbreak of fury by the people on the night of November 9–10 [Night of the Broken Glass] shows that the patience of the German people has now been exhausted.

But how does the anti-German, mostly Jewish-controlled foreign press react to the spontaneous reaction by Germans to those shots in Paris? In this part of the foreign press there is an attempt being made to convince the world that a kind of civil war reigns inside Germany. Countless atrocities are found by newsmongers and hawked about. It is charged that the spontaneous reaction of the German people was organized by official bodies. How little understanding do these scribblers have of Germany! How could such reactions have been expected if they were, indeed, organized?

One of the most striking things about what took place in the past several days against the Jews is the fact that, while it led to demolition, it never came to the stage of plunder. Naturally, the anti-German foreign press has claimed that this was all a purely criminal matter. Above all, the Jewish press of North America stirred up hatred in an inglorious way, mentioned the barbaric Middle Ages, and described Berlin as the theater of a civil war. It described the people who rose up against the Jews as "a Nazi mob" and "bands of gangsters." Unfortunately for them, these newspapers never really understood what was going on, and allowed themselves to fall into open contradictions. One reported that there were just one or two hundred people involved, another placed it at 20,000 to 30,000 demonstrating against the Jews. One of them reported that a huge mob surged through the streets, the other wrote that all there was was a small, unimportant group of young people. One announced that the vast majority of people just looked on without taking part in the demonstrations, while the other again reported that tremendous masses of people screamed out in joy. One declared that the mobs looked on passively, the other that the people showed their inner satisfaction. One insisted that the onlookers seemed to lose their minds, the other that they remained completely reserved.

To put it briefly, it is all a medley of lies, accusation, misrepresentations, and threats.

What shall we answer to all that? Basically, nothing. We hold the view that the reaction of the German people to that cowardly assassination in Paris must be explained by the ruthless vulgarity of the deed. It was neither organized nor prepared, but it broke out spontaneously from the nation.

The nation follows the healthy instinct which tells it that now for a second time a representative of Germany in a foreign country has been cut down by a Jewish youth, and that, if we take this deed silently and without reaction, then in the future German diplomatic representatives will be sitting ducks for assaults of this kind.

The German Government has seen to it that the reaction of the German people to this foul deed was limited to a short period. The German people, willingly and with discipline, have listened to the request of their Government. In a matter of hours the demonstrations and actions were brought to a halt.

This, however, should be known by the anti-German Jewish newspapers: by puffing up the incident, by threats and lies, they serve neither themselves nor those Jews who live in Germany. It could really be quite the opposite. The German people are an anti-Semitic people. They do not have the desire nor the willingness to have their rights diminished through the parasitical Jewish race nor will they allow the nation to be provoked.

It lies in the behavior of the Jews in Germany, and above all on the attitude of the Jews all over the world, as to what their future is in public life, in private life, and in business. The German Government is firmly determined to bring about law and order in our country, and law and order in this problem will be achieved better when attention is paid to the wishes and needs of the German people and to their solution of the problem. The shots fired by the Polish Jew Grynszpan in Paris were a warning signal. They worked out in a way that was not planned nor foreseen. The German people have become doubly vigilant. They know to the last man what the Jewish question means.

Anti-German foreigners would do well to allow Germans to find their own solution. If they feel the need to come to the defense of the German Jews, they can do as they like. It is not necessary to emphasize the fact that, because of governmental intervention made last Thursday, there has been a halt to the reaction of the public. No one has the right to act individually from now on. Laws and decrees to regulate this problem may be expected.

The German people can be assured: the Jew Grynszpan was a representative of Jewdom. The German vom Rath was a representative of the German people. In Paris Jewdom also shot at the German people. The German Government will reply to that legally but harshly.

83. Questionnaire for the Euthanasia Program, Spring 1939

"Incurable physical complaints — yes — no."

The extent and character of the euthanasia designed to purify the German race were indicated by this questionnaire used by medical directors or their deputies in determining whether individuals were eligible for being put to death. This document reveals the organizational background of the program. To accelerate processing, doctors were warned that the reports were to be filled out "on the typewriter," and returned to the Reich health leader *no later than* December 31, 1939.

Specimen   *Insert to Secret Journal no. 163/41*

Report Form I   To be filled out on the typewriter

Name of institution: _____ at _____

Patient's full name: _____

Date of Birth: _____ Place: _____ District: _____

Last residence: _____ District: _____

Married, single, widowed, divorced: _____ Religion: _____

Race* _____ Nationality: _____

Address of next of kin: _____

If regularly visited, by whom (address): _____

Alexander Mitscherlich, *Doctors of Infamy: The Story of Nazi Medical Crimes*, trans. Heinz Norden (New York: Schuman, 1949), pp. 96-97. Courtesy of Henry Schuman, Inc.

*Of German or kindred blood (of German blood, Jewish, first or second degree, Jewish half-breed, Negro [half-breed], gypsy [Half-breed], etc.)

Guardian or nurse (name, address): _____

Person bearing financial responsibility: _____ Since when in your
institution: _____

Record of other institutions, where and how long: _____

Sick since: _____ When admitted and from where: _____

Twin — yes — no. Blood relatives mentally ill: _____

Diagnosis: _____

Chief symptoms: _____

Predominantly bedridden — yes — no   Very restless — yes — no

Under restraint — yes — no   Incurable physical complaints — yes — no

War injury — yes — no

In schizophrenia: Fresh case _____ Final condition _____
Remissions: _____

In feeble-mindedness: Moron _____ Imbecile _____ Idiot _____

In epilepsy: Psych. changes: _____
Average frequency of seizures: _____

In senile disease: Marked confusion _____ Uncleanliness _____

Therapy (insulin, cardiazol, malaria, salvarsan, etc.): _____

Persistent effect — yes — no

Admitted on basis of Par. 51, Par. 42b, Criminal Code, etc.: _____

By: _____

Criminal record: See other side. See other side for character of employment. (Precise description of work and performance, for example: field
work, small output mechanic, good skilled worker. Do not give vague
data, such as housework, but state clearly: cleans rooms, etc. Always state
whether employed full-time, frequently, or only occasionally.)

Is discharge anticipated in immediate future: _____

Remarks: _____

Do not write in this space

_____   Place: _____ Date: _____

(Signature of medical director or his deputy)

84. In a Blistering Speech to the *Reichstag*, Hitler Responds to President Roosevelt's Peace Message, April 28, 1939

"I have conquered chaos in Germany...."

On April 15, 1939, President Franklin D. Roosevelt sent a message to Hitler and Mussolini urging them to observe a ten-year truce and asking them to pledge themselves not to attack thirty-one nations that he listed. On April 28 Hitler called a meeting of the *Reichstag* and delivered a long response to the American president. *The New York Times* reported the speech *in toto* and commented editorially that "Germany under national socialism is bent upon creating a new empire.... The new slogan is not racial unity but 'living room and power.'" In his polemics, Hitler sought to convince his fellow countrymen and at the same time to strengthen the anti-Roosevelt forces in the United States.

MEMBERS OF THE GERMAN *Reichstag!* The President of the United States of America has addressed a telegram to me with the curious contents of which you are already familiar. Before I, the addressee, actually received the document the rest of the world had already been informed of it by radio and newspaper reports; and numerous commentaries in organs of the democratic world press had already generously enlightened us as to the fact that this telegram was a very skillful, tactful document destined to impose upon the States in which people govern, the responsibility for warlike measures adopted by the plutocratic countries.

In view of these facts I decided to summon the German *Reichstag* so that you gentlemen might have the opportunity of hearing my answer first,

---

The New York Times, April 29, 1939, pp. 9-11.

and of either confirming that answer or rejecting it. In addition, I considered it desirable to keep to the method of procedure initiated by President Roosevelt and to inform the rest of the world on my part and by our means of my answer.

But I should like also to take this opportunity of giving expression to feelings with which the tremendous historical happiness of the month of March inspires me. . . .

The present Greater German Reich contains no territory which was not from the earliest times part of this Reich, not bound up with or subject to its sovereignty. Long before an American continent had been discovered — to say nothing of settled — by white people, this Reich existed, not merely in its present extent but with the addition of many regions and provinces which have since been lost.

Twenty-one years ago, when the bloodshed of war came to an end, millions of minds were filled with the ardent hope that a peace of reason and justice would reward and bless the nations which had been visited by the fearful scourge of the Great War. I say "reward" for all these men and women, whatever the conclusions arrived at by historians, bore no responsibility for these fearful happenings.

And if in some countries there still were politicians who even at that time could be charged with responsibility for this, the most atrocious massacre of all time, yet vast numbers of combatant soldiers of every country and nation were at most deserving of pity but were by no means guilty.

I myself, as you know, had never played a part in politics before the war, and only, like millions of others, performed such duties as I was called upon to fulfill as a decent citizen and soldier. It was therefore with an absolutely clear conscience that I was able to take up the cause of freedom and the future of my people, both during and after the war.

And I can therefore speak in the name of millions and millions of others equally blameless when I declare that all those who had only fought for their nation in loyal fulfillment of their duty were entitled to a peace of reason and justice, so that mankind might at last set to work to make good in joint effort the losses which all had suffered.

But the millions were cheated of this peace; for not only did the German people or other people fighting on our side suffer through the peace treaties, but these treaties had an annihilating effect on the victor countries.

For the first time appeared the misfortune that politics should be controlled by men who had not fought in the war. The feeling of hatred was unknown to soldiers, but not to those elderly politicians who had carefully preserved their own precious lives from the horror of war and who now descended upon humanity in the guise of insane spirits of revenge.

Hatred, malice and unreason were the intellectual forebears of the

Treaty of Versailles. Living space and States with history going back a thousand years were arbitrarily broken up and dissolved. Since time immemorial men who belong together have been torn asunder; the economic conditions of life have been ignored, while the peoples themselves have been converted into victors and vanquished, into masters possessing all rights and slaves possessing none. . . ."

However, when this new world order turned out to be a catastrophe, the democratic peace dictators of American and European origin were so cowardly that none of them ventured to take the responsibility for what occurred. Each put the blame on the others, thus endeavoring to save himself from the judgment of history. . . .

One of the most shameful acts of oppression ever committed is the dismemberment of the German nation and the political disintegration of her living space—which has, after all, been hers for thousands of years—was provided for in the dictate of Versailles.

I have never, gentlemen, left any doubt, that in point of fact it is scarcely possible anywhere in Europe to arrive at a harmony of State and national boundaries which will be satisfactory in every way. . . .

I

Mr. Roosevelt is of the opinion that I, too, must realize that throughout the world hundreds of millions of human beings are living in constant fear of a new war or even a series of wars.

This, he says, is of concern to the people of the United States for whom he speaks, as it must also be to the peoples of the other nations of the entire Western Hemisphere.

In reply to this it must be said in the first place that this fear of war has undoubtedly existed among mankind from time immemorial, and justifiably so.

For instance, after the peace treaty of Versailles fourteen wars were waged between 1919 and 1938 alone, in none of which Germany was concerned, but in which the States of the 'Western Hemisphere,' in whose name President Roosevelt also speaks, were indeed concerned.

In addition, there were in the same period twenty-six violent interventions and sanctions carried through by means of bloodshed and force.

Germany also played no part whatever in these. The United States alone has carried out military interventions in six cases since 1918. Since 1918 Soviet Russia has engaged in ten wars and military actions involving force and bloodshed.

Again Germany was concerned in none of these, nor was she the cause of any of these events. It would, therefore, be a mistake in my eyes to assume that the fear of war inspiring European and non-European nations can at this present time be directly traced back to actual wars at all.

II

The reason for this fear lies simply and solely in an unbridled agitation on the part of the press, an agitation as mendacious as it is base, in the circulation of vile pamphlets about the heads of foreign States, and in an artificial spreading of panic which in the end goes so far that interventions from another planet are believed possible and cause scenes of desperate alarm.

I believe that as soon as the responsible governments impose upon themselves and their journalistic organs the necessary restraint and truthfulness as regards the relations of the various countries to one another, and in particular as regards internal happenings in other countries, the fear of war will disappear at once, and the tranquility which we all desire so much will become possible.

In his telegram Mr. Roosevelt expresses the belief that every major war, even if it were to be confined to other continents, must have serious consequences while it lasts, and also for generations to come.

The answer: No one knows this better than the German people. For the peace treaty of Versailles imposed burdens on the German people which could not have been paid off even in a hundred years, although it has been proved precisely by American teachers of constitutional law, historians, and professors of history that Germany was no more to blame for the outbreak of the war than any other nation.

But I do not believe that every conflict must have disastrous consequences for the whole surrounding world, that is for the whole globe, provided the whole world is not systematically drawn into such conflicts by means of a network of nebulous pact obligations.

For, since in past centuries and — as I pointed out at the beginning of my answer — also in the course of the last decades, the world has experienced a continuous series of wars, if Mr. Roosevelt's assumption were correct humanity would already have a burden, in the sum total of the outcome of all these wars, which it would have to bear for millions of years to come.

III

Mr. Roosevelt declared that he had already appealed to me on a former occasion on behalf of a peaceful settlement of political, economic and social problems and without resort to arms.

The answer: I myself have always been an exponent of this view and, as history proves, have settled necessary political, economic, and social problems without force of arms, that is, without resort to arms.

Unfortunately, however, this peaceful settlement has been made more difficult by the agitation of politicians, statesmen, and newspaper representatives who were neither directly concerned nor even affected by the problems in question.

IV

Mr. Roosevelt believes that the 'tide of events' is once more bringing the threat of arms with it, and that if this threat continues a large part of the world is condemned to a common ruin.

The answer: As far as Germany is concerned, I know nothing of this kind of threat to other nations, although I every day read in the democratic newspapers lies about such a threat.

Every day I read of German mobilizations, of the landing of troops, of extortions — all this in regard to States with whom we are not only living in deepest peace but also with whom we are, in many cases, the closest friends.

V

Mr. Roosevelt believes further that in case of war victorious, vanquished, and neutral nations will all suffer.

The answer: As a politician I have been the exponent of this conviction for twenty years, at a time when unfortunately the responsible statesmen in America could not bring themselves to make the same admission as regards their participation in the Great War and its issue.

VI

Mr. Roosevelt believes lastly that it lies with the leaders of the great nations to preserve their peoples from the impending disaster.

The answer: If that is true, then it is a punishable neglect, to use no worse word, if the leaders of nations with corresponding powers are not capable of controlling their newspapers which are agitating for war, and so to save the world from the threatening calamity of an armed conflict.

I am not able to understand, further, why these responsible leaders, instead of cultivating diplomatic relations between nations, make them more difficult and indeed disturb them by recalling ambassadors, etc., without any reason.

VII

Mr. Roosevelt declared finally that three nations in Europe and one in Africa have seen their independent existence terminated.

The answer: I do not know which three nations in Europe are meant. Should it be a question of the provinces reincorporated in the German Reich I must draw the attention of Mr. Roosevelt to a historical error.

It is not now that these nations sacrificed their independent existence in Europe, but rather in 1918 when they, contrary to solemn promises, were separated from their communities and made into nations which they never wished to be and never were, and when they had forced upon them an independence which was no independence but at the most could only mean dependence upon an international foreign world which they hated.

As for the fact, however, that one nation in Africa is alleged to have lost its freedom – that too, is but an error; for it is not a question of one nation in Africa having lost its freedom – on the contrary practically all the previous inhabitants of this continent have been made subject to the sovereignty of other nations by bloody force, thereby losing their freedom.

Moroccans, Berbers, Arabs, Negroes, etcetera, have all fallen victim to foreign might, the swords of which, however, were inscribed not "Made in Germany," but "Made by Democracies."

VIII

Mr. Roosevelt then speaks of the reports which admittedly he does not believe to be correct but which state that further acts of aggression are contemplated against still other independent nations.

The answer: I consider every such unfounded insinuation as an offense against the tranquillity and consequently the peace of the world. I also see therein something which tends to frighten smaller nations or at least make them nervous.

If Mr. Roosevelt really has any specific instances in mind in this connection I would ask him to name the States which are threatened with aggression and to name the aggressor in question. It will then be possible to refute these monstrous general accusations by brief statements.

IX

Mr. Roosevelt states that the world is plainly moving toward the moment when this situation must end in catastrophe unless a rational way of guiding events is found.

He also declares that I have repeatedly asserted that I and the German people have no desire for war and that if this is true there need be no war.

The answer: I wish to point out first, that I have not conducted any war; second, that for years past I have expressed my abhorrence of war and, it is true, also my abhorrence of warmongers, and third, that I am not aware for what purpose I should wage a war at all. I should be thankful to Mr. Roosevelt if he would give me some explanation in this connection.

X

Mr. Roosevelt is finally of the opinion that the peoples of the earth could not be persuaded that any governing power has any right or need to inflict the consequences of war on its own or any other people save in the cause of self-evident home defense.

The answer: I should think that every reasonable human being is of this opinion; but it seems to me that in almost every war both sides claim a case of unquestionable home defense, and that there is no institution in this world, including the American President himself, which could clear up the problem unequivocally.

There is hardly any possibility of doubt, for example, that America's entry into the Great War was not a case of unquestionable home defense. A research committee set up by President Roosevelt himself has examined the cause of America's entry into the Great War, and reached the conclusion that the entry ensued chiefly for exclusively capitalistic reasons. Nevertheless, no practical conclusions have been drawn from this fact.

Let us hope, then, that at least the United States will in the future itself act according to this noble principle, and will not go to war against any country except in the case of unquestionable home defense.

XI

Mr. Roosevelt says further that he does not speak from selfishness, nor fear, nor weakness, but with the voice of strength and friendship for mankind.

The answer: If this voice of strength and friendship for mankind had been raised by America at the proper time, and if, above all, it had possessed some practical value, then at least there could have been prevented that treaty which has become the source of the direst derangement of humanity and history, namely, the dictate of Versailles.

XII

Mr. Roosevelt declares, further, that it is clear to him that all international problems can be solved at the council table.

The answer: Theoretically one ought to believe in this possibility, for common sense would correct demands on the one hand and show the compelling necessity of a compromise on the other.

For example, according to all common-sense logic and the general principles of a higher human justice, indeed, according to the laws of a divine will, all peoples ought to have an equal share of the goods of this world.

It ought not then to happen that one people needs so much living space that it cannot get along with fifteen inhabitants to the square kilometer, while others are forced to nourish 140, 150, or even 200 on the same area.

But in no case should these fortunate peoples curtail the existing living space of those who are, as it is, suffering, by robbing them of their colonies, for instance. I would therefore by very happy if these problems could really find their solution at the council table.

My skepticism, however, is based on the fact that it was America herself who gave sharpest expression to her mistrust in the effectiveness of conferences. For the greatest conference of all time was without any doubt the League of Nations.

That authoritative body, representing all the peoples of the world, created in accordance with the will of an American President, was supposed to solve the problems of humanity at the council table. . . .

XIII

Mr. Roosevelt continues that it is no answer to the plea for peaceful discussion for one side to plead that, unless they receive assurances beforehand that the verdict will be theirs, they will not lay aside their arms.

The answer: Do you believe, Mr. Roosevelt, that when the final fate of nations is in the balance a government or the leaders of a people will lay down their arms or surrender them before a conference, simply in the blind hope that in their wisdom or, if you like, their discernment, the other members of the conference will arrive at the right conclusion?

Mr. Roosevelt, there has been only one country and one government which has acted according to the recipe extolled in such glowing terms, and that country was Germany. The German nation once, trusting in the solemn assurances of President Wilson and in the confirmation of these assurances by the Allies, laid down its arms and thus went unarmed to the conference table.

It is true that as soon as the German nation had laid down its arms it was not even invited to the conference table, but, in violation of all assurances, was made to suffer the worst breaking of a word that had ever been known.

Then one day, instead of the greatest confusion known in history being resolved around the conference table, the cruelest dictated treaty in the world brought about a still more fearful confusion.

But the representatives of the German nation, who, trusting to the solemn assurance of an American President, had laid down their arms and therefore appeared unarmed, were not received, even when they came to accept the terms of the dictated treaty, as the representatives of a nation which, at all events, had held out with infinite heroism against a whole world for four years in the struggle for its liberty and independence; they were subjected to even greater degradations than can ever have been inflicted on the chieftains of Sioux tribes.

The German delegates were insulted by the mob, stones were thrown at them, and they were dragged like prisoners, not to the council table of the world but before the tribunal of the victors; and there, at the pistol's point, they were forced to undergo the most shameful subjection and plundering that the world had ever known.

I can assure you, Mr. Roosevelt, that I am steadfastly determined to see to it that not only now, but for all future time, no German shall ever enter a conference defenseless, but that at all time and forever every German negotiator should and shall have behind him the united strength of the German nation, so help me God.

XIV

The President of the United States believes that in conference rooms as in court it is necessary that both sides enter in good faith, assuming that substantial justice will accrue to both.

The answer: German representatives will never again enter a conference that is for them a tribunal. For who is to be the judge there? At a conference there is no accused and no prosecutor, but two contending parties. And if their own good sense does not bring about a settlement between the two parties, they will never surrender themselves to the verdict of disinterested foreign powers.

Incidentally, the United States itself declined to enter the League of Nations and to become the victim of a court which was able, by a majority vote, to give a verdict against individual interests. But I should be grateful to President Roosevelt if he would explain to the world what the new World Court is to be like.

Who are the judges here, according to what procedure are they selected, and on what responsibility do they act? And above all, to whom can they be made to account for their decision?

XV

Mr. Roosevelt believes that the cause of world peace would be greatly advanced if the nations of the world were to give a frank statement relating to the present and future policy of their governments.

The answer: I have already done this, Mr. Roosevelt, in innumerable public speeches. And in the course of this present meeting of the German *Reichstag*, I have again — as far as this is possible in the space of two hours — made a statement of this kind.

I must, however, decline to give such an explanation to any one else than to the people for whose existence and life I am responsible, and who, on the other hand, alone have the right to demand that I account to them. However, I give the aims of the German policy so openly that the entire world can hear it in any case.

But these explanations are without significance for the outside world as long as it is possible for the press to falsify and suspect every statement, to question it or to cover it with fresh lying replies.

XVI

Mr. Roosevelt believes that, because the United States as one of the nations of the Western Hemisphere is not involved in the immediate controversies which have arisen in Europe, I should therefore be willing to make such a statement of policy to him, as the head of a nation so far removed from Europe.

The answer: Mr. Roosevelt therefore seriously believes that the cause of international peace would really be furthered if I were to make to the nations of the world a public statement on the present policy of the German Government.

But how does Mr. Roosevelt come to expect of the head of the German State, above all, to make a statement without the other governments being invited to make such a statement of their policy as well?

I certainly believe that it is not feasible to make such a statement to the head of any foreign State, but rather that such statements should preferably be made to the whole world, in accordance with the demand made at the time by President Wilson, for the abolition of secret diplomacy.

Hitherto I was not only always prepared to do this but, as I have already said, I have done it only too often. Unfortunately, the most important statements concerning the aims and intentions of German policy have been in many so-called democratic States either withheld from the people or distorted by the press.

If, however, President Roosevelt thinks that he is qualified to address such a request to Germany or Italy, of all nations, because America is so far removed from Europe, we on our side might, with the same right, address to the President of the American Republic the question as to what aim American foreign policy has in view in its turn.

And on what intentions this policy is based—in the case of the Central and South American States, for instance. In this case Mr. Roosevelt would, rightly, I must admit, refer to the Monroe Doctrine and decline to comply with such a request as an interference in the internal affairs of the American continent. We Germans support a similar doctrine for Europe—and, above all, for the territory and the interests of the Greater German Reich.

/ Moreover, I would obviously never presume to address such a request to the President of the United States of America, because I assume that he would probably rightly consider such a presumption tactless.

XVII

The American President further declares that he would then communicate information received by him concerning the political aims of Germany to other nations now apprehensive as to the course of our policy.

The answer: How has Mr. Roosevelt learned which nations consider themselves threatened by German policy and which do not?

Or is Mr. Roosevelt in a position, in spite of the enormous amount of work which must rest upon him in his own country, to recognize of his own accord all these inner spiritual and mental impressions of other peoples and their governments?

XVIII

Finally, Mr. Roosevelt asks that assurance be given him that the German armed forces will not attack, and above all, not invade, the territory or possessions of the following independent nations he then names as those coming into question: Finland, Latvia, Estonia, Norway, Sweden, Denmark, the Netherlands, Belgium, Great Britain, Ireland, France, Portugal, Spain, Switzerland, Liechtenstein, Luxemburg, Poland, Hungary, Turkey, Iraq, the Arabias, Syria, Palestine, Egypt, and Iran.*

The answer: I have first taken the trouble to ascertain from the States mentioned, firstly, whether they feel themselves threatened, and secondly and above all, whether this inquiry by the American President was addressed to us at their suggestion, or at any rate, with their consent.

The reply was in all cases negative, in some instances strongly so. It is true that I could not cause inquiries to be made of certain of the States and nations mentioned because they themselves — as for example, Syria — are at present not in possession of their freedom, but are occupied and consequently deprived of their rights by the military agents of democratic States. . . .

The German Government is nevertheless prepared to give each of the States named an assurance of the kind desired by Mr. Roosevelt on the condition of absolute reciprocity, provided that the State wishes it and itself addresses to Germany a request for such an assurance together with appropriate proposals.

As concerns a number of the States included in Mr. Roosevelt's list, this question can probably be regarded as settled from the very start, since we are already either allied with them or at least united by close ties of friendship.

As for the duration of these agreements, Germany is willing to make terms with each individual State in accordance with the wishes of that State.

But I should not like to let this opportunity pass without giving above all to the President of the United States an assurance regarding those territories which would, after all, give him most cause for apprehension, namely the United States itself and the other States of the American continent.

And I here solemnly declare that all the assertions which have been circulated in any way concerning an intended German attack or invasion on or in American territory are rank frauds and gross untruths, quite apart from the fact that such assertions, as far as the military possibilities are concerned, could have their origin only in a stupid imagination.

---

*As Hitler recited the names of the countries, there were rising waves of laughter from the audience, especially at the mention of Palestine.

XIX

The American President then goes on to declare in this connection that he regards the discussion of the most effective and immediate manner in which the peoples of the world can obtain relief from the crushing burden of armaments as the most important factor of all.

Mr. Roosevelt perhaps does not know that this problem, insofar as it concerns Germany, has already been completely solved on one occasion. Between 1919 and 1923 Germany had already completely disarmed. . . .

At this point, as in all others where Germany believed that a promise would be kept, she was disgracefully deceived. All attempts to induce the other States to disarm, pursued in negotiations at the conference table over many years, came, as is well known, to nothing. This disarmament would have been but the execution of pledges already given and at the time just and prudent.

I myself, Mr. Roosevelt, have made any number of practical proposals for consultation and tried to bring about a discussion of them in order to make possible a general limitation of armaments to the lowest possible level.

I proposed a maximum strength for all armies of 200,000, similarly the abolition of all offensive weapons, of bombing planes, of poison gas, etc. It was not possible, however, to carry out these plans in the face of the rest of the world although Germany was herself at the time completely disarmed. I then proposed a maximum of 300,000 for armies.

This proposal met with the same negative reception. I then submitted a great number of detailed disarmament proposals — in each case before the forum of the German *Reichstag* and consequently before the whole world. It never occurred to anyone even to discuss the matter. The rest of the world began instead to increase still further their already enormous armaments.

And not until 1934, when the last of my comprehensive proposals — that concerning 300,000 as the maximum size of the army — was ultimately turned down did I give the order for German rearmament which was now to be very thorough.

Nevertheless, I did not want to be an obstacle in the way of disarmament discussion at which you, Mr. Roosevelt, intend to be present. I would ask you, however, not to appeal first to me and to Germany but rather to the others; I have a long line of practical experience behind me and shall remain skeptically inclined until reality has taught me to know better.

Mr. Roosevelt gives us his pledge, finally, that he is prepared to take part in discussions looking toward the most practical manner of opening up avenues of international trade to the end that every nation of the world may be enabled to buy and sell on equal terms in the world's market, as well as to possess assurances of obtaining the raw materials and products of peaceful economic life.

The answer: It is my belief, Mr. Roosevelt, that it is not so much a question of discussing these problems theoretically as of removing in practice the barriers which exist in international trade. The worst barriers, however, lie in the individual States themselves.

Experience so far shows at any rate that the greatest world economic conferences have come to nothing simply because various countries were not able to maintain order in their domestic economic systems; or else because they infected the international capital market with uncertainty by currency manipulation and above all by causing continual fluctuations in value of their currencies to one another.

It is likewise an unbearable burden for world economic relations that it should be possible in some countries for some ideological reason or other to let loose a wild boycott of agitation against other countries and their goods and so practically to eliminate them from the market.

It is my belief, Mr. Roosevelt, that it would be a great service if you, with your great influence, would remove these barriers genuinely to free world trade beginning with the United States. For it is my conviction that if the leaders of nations are not even capable of regulating production in their own countries or of removing boycotts pursued for ideological reasons which can damage trade relations between countries to so great an extent, there is much less prospect of achieving by means of international agreements any really fruitful step toward improvement of economic relations.

An equal right for all of buying and selling in world markets can only be guaranteed in this way. Further, the German people has made in this regard very concrete claims and I would appreciate it very much if you, Mr. Roosevelt, as one of the successors to the late President Wilson, were to devote yourself to seeing that promises be at last redeemed on the basis of which Germany once laid down her arms and gave herself up to the so-called victors.

I am thinking less of the innumerable millions extorted from Germany as so-called reparations than of territories stolen from Germany.

In and outside Europe, Germany lost approximately 3,000,000 square kilometers of territory, and that in spite of the fact that the whole German colonial empire, in contrast to colonies of other nations, was not acquired by way of war but solely through treaties of purchase.

President Wilson solemnly pledged his word that German colonial claims, like all others, would receive the same just examination. Instead of this, however, German possessions were given to nations that have always had the largest colonial empires, while our people were exposed to a

great anxiety which is now — as it will continue to be in future —
particularly pressing.

It would be a noble act if President Franklin Roosevelt were to redeem
the promises made by President Woodrow Wilson. This would, in the first
place, be a practical contribution to the moral consolidation of the world
and consequently to the improvement of its economic conditions.

Mr. Roosevelt also stated in conclusion that the heads of all the great
Governments are, in this hour, responsible for the fate of humanity.

They cannot fail to hear the prayers of the peoples to be protected from
the foreseeable chaos of war. And I, too, would be held accountable for
this.

Mr. Roosevelt! I fully understand that the vastness of your nation and
the immense wealth of your country allow you to feel responsible for the
history of the whole world and for the history of all nations. I, sir, am
placed in a much more modest and smaller sphere. You have 130,000,000
people on 9,500,000 square kilometers.

You possess a country with enormous riches in all mineral resources,
fertile enough to feed a half-billion people and to provide them with all
necessities.

I once took over a State which was faced by complete ruin, thanks to its
trust in the promises of the rest of the world and to the bad regime of
democratic governments. In this State there are roughly 140 people to each
square kilometer — not 15, as in America. The fertility of our country
cannot be compared with that of yours.

We lack numerous minerals which nature has placed at your disposal in
unlimited quantities.

Billions of German savings accumulated in gold and foreign exchange
during many years of peace were squeezed out of us and taken from us. We
lost our colonies. In 1933 I had in my country 7,000,000 unemployed, a
few million workers on half-time, millions of peasants sinking into poverty, destroyed trade, ruined commerce; in short, general chaos.

Since then, Mr. Roosevelt, I have only been able to fulfill one simple
task. I cannot feel myself responsible for the fate of the world, as this
world took no interest in the pitiful state of my own people.

I have regarded myself as called upon by Providence to serve my own
people alone and to deliver them from their frightful misery. Consequently, during the past six and one-half years, I have lived day and night
for the single task of awakening the powers of my people, in view of our
desertion by the whole of the rest of the world, of developing these powers
to the utmost and of utilizing them for the salvation of our community.

I have conquered chaos in Germany, re-established order and enor-
mously increased production in all branches of our national economy, by
strenuous efforts produced substitutes for numerous materials which we

lack, smoothed the way for new inventions, developed traffic, caused mighty roads to be built and canals to be dug, called into being gigantic new factories and at the same time endeavored to further the education and culture of our people.

I have succeeded in finding useful work once more for the whole of 7,000,000 unemployed, who so appeal to the hearts of us all, in keeping the German peasant on his soil in spite of all difficulties, and in saving the land itself for him, in once more bringing German trade to a peak and in assisting traffic to the utmost.

As precaution against the threats of another world war, not only have I united the German people politically, but I have also re-armed them; I have also endeavored to destroy sheet by sheet that Treaty which in its 448 articles contains the vilest oppression which peoples and human beings have ever been expected to put up with.

I have brought back to the Reich provinces stolen from us in 1919; I have led back to their native country millions of Germans who were torn away from us and were in misery; I have re-established the historic unity of German living space and, Mr. Roosevelt, I have endeavored to attain all this without spilling blood and without bringing to my people, and consequently to others, the misery of war.

I, who twenty-one years ago was an unknown worker and soldier of my people, have attained this, Mr. Roosevelt, by my own energy, and can, therefore, in the face of history, claim a place among those men who have done the utmost which can be fairly and justly demanded from a single individual.

You, Mr. Roosevelt, have a much easier task in comparison. You became President of the United States in 1933 when I became Chancellor of the Reich. In other words, from the very outset you stepped to the head of one of the largest and wealthiest States in the world.

You have the good fortune to have to feed scarcely fifteen people per square kilometer in your country. You have at your disposal the most unlimited mineral resources in the world. As a result of the large area covered by your country and the fertility of your fields, you are enabled to insure for each individual American ten times the amount of commodities possible in Germany. Nature has in any case enabled you to do this.

In spite of the fact that the population of your country is scarcely one-third greater than the number of inhabitants in Greater Germany, you possess more than fifteen times as much living space. Conditions prevailing in your country are on such a large scale that you can find time and leisure to give your attention to universal problems. Consequently, the world is undoubtedly so small for you that you perhaps believe that your intervention and action can be effective anywhere.

In this sense, therefore, your concerns and suggestions cover a much larger and wider area than mine, because my world, Mr. Roosevelt, in which Providence has placed me and for which I am therefore obliged to work, is unfortunately much smaller, although for me it is more precious than anything else, for it is limited to my people!

I believe, however, that this is the way in which I can be of the most service to that for which we are all concerned, namely, the justice, well-being, progress and peace of the whole human community.

85. To the Commanders-in-Chief of the *Wehrmacht* Hitler Reveals His Decision for War, August 21, 1939

"I am only afraid that at the last moment some swine or other will yet submit to me a plan for mediation."

Poland was the key to Hitler's plans for conquest. His diplomacy and propaganda centered on the Danzig Free State and those parts of Poland inhabited by people who spoke German. He made demands upon Poland for the recovery of Danzig and the cession of a strip of Polish territory giving Germany access to East Prussia – in other words, a *German corridor* across the Polish Corridor set up by the Treaty of Versailles. Polish authorities refused to place their country at Hitler's mercy. They pointed to an observation made by Frederick the Great: "He who rules Danzig and the mouth of the Vistula has more power than the king in Warsaw."

Hitler was infuriated by Polish unwillingness to give him what he wanted. He ordered a press and radio campaign to fill the air with lurid tales of systematic persecutions inflicted upon helpless German-speaking people living in Poland. The Poles would agree to his demands – or they would feel the lash of Nazi power.

Meanwhile, Hitler assured the world that he was a man of peace and was working only for a peaceful solution of international difficulties. In private, his attitude was far different. In a talk with his army commanders at the Berghof, his retreat on the Obersalzberg, he made it clear what he intended to do about Poland.

U.S., Department of State, *Documents on German Foreign Policy, 1918–1945*, Series D (Washington, D.C.: Government Printing Office, 1956), vol. 7, pp. 200-206.

This document is one of the most important to have come out of the Third Reich. Minutes of the talk were captured by American troops toward the close of the war and were submitted to the International Military Tribunal at Nuremberg. They refute those revisionist historians who seek to absolve Hitler of major blame for the immediate origins of the war. They reveal how Hitler was intent upon having his war as the only effective means of tearing up the Treaty of Versailles.

I HAVE CALLED YOU together to give you a picture of the political situation, in order that you may have some insight into the individual factors on which I have based my decision to act and in order to strengthen your confidence.

After this we shall discuss military details.

It was clear to me that a conflict with Poland had to come sooner or later. I had already made this decision in the spring, but I thought that I would first turn against the West in a few years, and only after that against the East. . . .

First of all two personal factors:

My own personality and that of Mussolini.

Essentially all depends on me, on my existence, because of my political talents. Furthermore, the fact that probably no one will ever again have the confidence of the whole German people as I have. There will probably never again in the future be a man with more authority than I have. My existence is therefore a factor of great value. But I can be eliminated at any time by a criminal or a lunatic.

The second personal factor is the *Duce*. His existence is also decisive. If anything happens to him, Italy's loyalty to the alliance will no longer be certain.

The other side presents a negative picture as far as authoritative persons are concerned. There is no outstanding personality in England and France.

It is easy for us to make decisions. We have nothing to lose; we have everything to gain. Because of our restrictions [*Einschränkungen*] our economic situation is such that we can only hold out for a few more years. Goering can confirm this. We have no other choice, we must act. . . .

All these favorable circumstances will no longer prevail in two or three years' time. No one knows how much longer I shall live. Therefore, better a conflict now. . . . The probability is still great that the West will not intervene. We must take the risk with ruthless determination. The politician must take a risk just as much as the general. We are faced with the harsh alternatives of striking or of certain annihilation sooner or later. . . .

We will hold our position in the West until we have conquered Poland. We must bear in mind our great production capacity. It is much greater than in 1914–1918. The enemy had another hope, that Russia would become our enemy after the conquest of Poland. The enemy did not reckon with my great strength of purpose. Our enemies are small fry. I saw them in Munich.

I was convinced that Stalin would never accept the English offer. Four days ago I took a special step, which led to Russia replying yesterday that she is prepared to sign. Personal contact with Stalin is established. The day after tomorrow von Ribbentrop will conclude the treaty. . . .

I am only afraid that at the last moment some swine or other will yet submit to me a plan for mediation. . . .

The destruction of Poland has priority. The aim is to eliminate active forces, not to reach a definite line. Even if war breaks out in the West, the destruction of Poland remains the priority. A quick decision in view of the season.

I shall give a propagandist reason for starting the war, no matter whether it is plausible or not. The victor will not be asked afterwards whether he told the truth or not. When starting and waging a war it is not right that matters, but victory.

Close your hearts to pity. Act brutally. Eighty million people must obtain what is their right. Their existence must be made secure. . . .

86. The Hitler-Stalin Pact: The Third Reich and the USSR Join in a Pact to Carve Up Poland, August 23, 1939

". . . questions which touch their common interests."

In the pact between Germany and the Soviet Union, signed on August 23, 1939, by Foreign Ministers Joachim von Ribbentrop and Vyacheslav Mikhailovich Molotov, it was agreed that Russia and Germany would not resort to war against each other for ten years. The announcement of this agreement created consternation in the West. But both partners, bitter opponents in the past, regarded the pact as advantageous. The text follows.

GUIDED BY THE DESIRE to strengthen the cause of peace between Germany and the Union of Socialist Soviet Republics, and basing themselves on the fundamental stipulations of the Neutrality Agreement concluded between Germany and the Union of Socialist Soviet Republics in April, 1926, the German Government and the Government of the Union of Socialist Soviet Republics have come to the following agreement:

ARTICLE 1. The two contracting parties undertake to refrain from any act of force, any aggressive act, and any attacks against each other undertaken either singly or in conjunction with any other Powers.

ARTICLE 2. If one of the contracting parties should become the object of war-like action on the part of a third Power, the other contracting party will in no way support the third Power.

ARTICLE 3. The Governments of the two contracting parties will in

German Library of Information, *Documents on the Events Preceding the Outbreak of the War*, compiled and published by the German Foreign Office (Berlin, 1939; New York, 1940), pp. 370-71.

future remain in consultation with one another in order to inform each other about questions which touch their common interests.

ARTICLE 4. Neither of the two contracting parties will join any group of Powers which is directed, mediately or immediately, against the other party.

ARTICLE 5. In case disputes or conflicts on questions of any kind should arise between the two contracting parties, the two partners will solve these disputes or conflicts exclusively by friendly exchange of views or if necessary by arbitration commissions.

ARTICLE 6. The present agreement is concluded for the duration of ten years with the stipulation that unless one of the contracting partners denounces it one year before its expiration, it will automatically be prolonged by five years.

ARTICLE 7. The present agreement shall be ratified in the shortest possible time. The instruments of ratification are to be exchanged in Berlin. The treaty comes into force immediately it has been signed.

Done in two original documents in the German and Russian languages, respectively.

Moscow, August 23, 1939.

For the German Government

RIBBENTROP

As plenipotentiary of the Government of the Union of Socialist Soviet Republics   MOLOTOV

87. The British Guarantee the Integrity of the Polish State, August 25, 1939

". . . . all the support and assistance in its power."

Immediately preceding the Munich crisis, Hitler stated that if the Sudeten problem were solved, he would have no more territorial claims in Europe. In the late days of August, however, the British government became convinced that the *Fuehrer* now had designs on Poland. On August 25, 1939, Britain gave a guarantee to Poland in a reciprocal treaty of mutual assistance.

ARTICLE 1. Should one of the Contracting Parties become engaged in hostilities with a European Power in consequence of aggression by the latter against that Contracting Party, the other Contracting Party will at once give the Contracting Party engaged in hostilities all the support and assistance in its power. . . .

British Command Paper, no. 6106, p. 37.

88. The *Fuehrer's* Reply to the British Government Is Handed to the British Ambassador, August 29, 1939

*"The demands of the German Government imply a
revision of the Treaty of Versailles. . . ."*

At 10:30 P.M. on the evening of August 28, 1939, Sir Nevile Henderson, the British ambassador to Berlin, handed to Hitler a memorandum from the British government, calling in diplomatic language
for a reasonable conclusion to the differences between Germany
and Poland: "A just settlement . . . may open the way to world
peace. Failure to reach it would ruin the hopes of better understanding between Germany and Great Britain, would bring the two
countries into conflict, and might well plunge the whole world into
war. Such an outcome would be a calamity without parallel in
history."

Hitler answered in equally diplomatic language. His reply, translated here, was handed to Henderson the next evening at 6:45 P.M.
He, too, the *Fuehrer* said, was anxious for sincere Anglo-German
understanding, but he would leave no doubt that such an understanding could not be purchased at the expense of "Germany's
renunciation of her vital interests."

THE BRITISH AMBASSADOR in Berlin has informed the British Government
of certain suggestions which I felt it incumbent upon me to put forward, in
order to (1) express once more the desire of the German Government for
sincere Anglo-German understanding, co-operation and friendship; (2)

German Library of Information, *Documents on the Events Preceding the Outbreak of War*, compiled and published by the German Foreign Office (Berlin,
1939; New York, 1940), pp. 480-82.

leave no room for doubt that such an understanding cannot be purchased at the expense of Germany's renunciation of her vital interests or even by the sacrifice of claims based just as much on general human rights as on the national dignity and honor of our nation.

It was with satisfaction that the German Government learned from the written reply of the British Government and the verbal declarations of the British Ambassador that the British Government for their part are also prepared to improve Anglo-German relations and to develop and to foster these in the spirit of the German suggestions.

The British Government are likewise convinced that the removal of the tension between Germany and Poland, which has become intolerable, is indispensable to the realization of this hope.

Since the autumn of 1938, and for the last time in March, 1939, verbal and written proposals have been submitted to the Polish Government, which, in consideration of the friendship then existing between Germany and Poland, might have led to a settlement of the questions under dispute which would have been acceptable to both parties. The British Government are aware that the Polish Government saw fit to reject these proposals finally in March of this year. At the same time the Polish Government made their rejection a pretext or an occasion for the adoption of military measures which have since then been continued on an ever-increasing scale. Poland had, in fact, mobilized as early as the middle of last month. In connection with the mobilization, numerous incidents took place in the Free City of Danzig at the instigation of the Polish authorities, and demands of a more or less threatening character amounting to an ultimatum were addressed to the Free City of Danzig. The closing of the frontier, which was at first in the nature of a customs measure, was afterwards carried out on military lines and was extended to affect traffic with the object of bringing about the political disintegration and the economic ruin of this German community.

Furthermore, the large group of Germans living in Poland was subjected to atrocious and barbarous ill-treatment and to other forms of persecution which resulted in some cases in the death by violence of many Germans domiciled there, or in their deportation under the most cruel circumstances. Such a situation is intolerable for a Great Power and has now forced Germany after months of inactive observation to undertake the necessary steps for the protection of her rightful interests. The German Government can only most seriously assure the British Government that a state of affairs has now been reached for which continued acquiescence or even inactive observation is no longer possible.

The demands of the German Government imply a revision of the Treaty of Versailles in this area, a fact which was recognized as necessary from the very outset; they constitute the return of Danzig and the Polish Corridor to Germany and the safeguarding of the German minorities domiciled in those territories remaining in Polish possession.

The German Government note with satisfaction that the British Government are also convinced on principle that some solution must be found for the state of affairs which has now developed. They further consider they may assume that the British Government entertain no doubt on the fact that this is a state of affairs which can no longer be remedied in a matter of days or even weeks but for which perhaps only a few hours yet remain. For in view of the disorganized state of Poland we must at any moment be prepared for the possibility of events occurring which Germany could not tolerate.

If the British Government still believe that these grave differences can be solved by direct negotiations, the German Government on their part regret at the outset that they are unable to share such an opinion. They have already tried to open up a way for peaceful negotiations of this nature, without meeting with the support of the Polish Government, and only seeing their efforts rejected by the abrupt initiation of measures of a military character in accordance with the general development indicated above.

There are two factors which the British Government consider important: (1) to remove most speedily the imminent danger of a conflagration by means of direct negotiations, and (2) to give the necessary economic and political safeguards by means of international guarantees for the future existence of the remaining Polish State.

To that, the German Government desire to make the following statement:

Despite their sceptical judgment of the prospects of such direct negotiations, the German Government are nevertheless prepared to accept the English proposal, and to enter into direct discussions. They do so solely because — as already emphasized — the written communication received from the British Government gives them the impression that the latter also desire a friendly agreement along the lines indicated to Ambassador Henderson. The German Government desire in this way to give to the British Government and to the British people a proof of the sincerity of the German intention of arriving at a state of permanent friendship with Great Britain.

The German Government nevertheless feel bound to point out to the British Government that in the case of a reorganization of the territorial conditions in Poland, the German Government are no longer in a position to take upon themselves any guarantees, or to participate in any guarantees, without the co-operation of the U.S.S.R.

Moreover, the German Government never had the intention, in their proposals, of attacking vital Polish interests or of questioning the existence of an independent Polish State. Under these conditions, the German Government therefore agree to accept the proposed intermediation of the British Government to send to Berlin a Polish representative invested with plenipotentiary powers. They expect his arrival on Wednesday, August 30, 1939.

The German Government will immediately draft the proposals for a solution acceptable to them, and, if possible, will make such proposals available for the British Government also before the Polish negotiator arrives.

89. German Ultimatum to Poland: Hitler Gives Poland Twenty-four Hours to Accept a Sixteen-Point Proposal, August 30–31, 1939

". . . the intolerable treatment of the minority in the territories cut off from the Reich."

On August 29, 1939, Hitler proposed to London that it arrange to send to Berlin on August 30 a Polish delegate with full power to negotiate. When the British objected to this procedure, Foreign Minister Joachim von Ribbentrop in a hurried voice read to the British ambassador at Berlin a sixteen-point proposal to settle the differences between the Third Reich and Poland. Not until the next day were the proposals given to the Poles. Von Ribbentrop then declared that the Poles, who had not even been able to send the draft to Warsaw, had rejected the peace offering.

The German ultimatum to Poland follows.

THE SITUATION BETWEEN THE GERMAN REICH and Poland is at the present time such that any further incident may lead to an outbreak of hostilities between the military forces of the two countries, which have already taken up their positions on their respective sides of the frontier. Any peaceful solution of the problem must be of such a nature that the events which originally brought about this state of affairs cannot be repeated on another occasion, thus causing a state of tension not only in Eastern Europe but also elsewhere.

The causes of this development are to be found in (1) the intolerable

---

German Library of Information, *Documents on the Events Preceding the Outbreak of War*, compiled and published by the German Foreign Office (Berlin, 1939; New York, 1940), pp. 485-88.

demarcation of the frontiers as dictated in the Treaty of Versailles, (2) the intolerable treatment of the minority in the territories cut off from the Reich.

In putting forward these proposals, the German Government are attempting to find a final solution, putting an end to the intolerable situation arising from the present demarcation of frontiers, securing to both parties their vital lines of communication, eliminating as far as possible the problem of the minorities and, in so far as this should prove impossible, rendering the fate of the minorities bearable by effectively guaranteeing their rights.

The German Government feel convinced that it is indispensable that economic and personal damage inflicted since 1918 should be investigated, and full compensation made therefor. Of course, the German Government regard this obligation as binding upon both parties.

The above considerations give rise to the following concrete proposals:

1. By reason of its purely German character and the unanimous will of its population, the Free City of Danzig shall be returned forthwith to the German Reich.

2. The territory known as the Polish Corridor, that is to say, the territory bounded by the Baltic Sea and a line running from Marienwerder to Graudenz, Kulm, Bromberg, (including these towns), and then in a westerly direction towards Schönlanke, shall itself decide whether it shall become part of the German Reich or remain with Poland.

3. For that purpose, a plebiscite shall be held in this territory. All Germans who were domiciled in this area on January 1, 1918, or who were born there on or before that day, and also all Poles, Cassubians, etc., who were domiciled in this area on that day or who were born there on or before the above-mentioned date, shall be entitled to vote. Germans who have been expelled from this territory shall return for the purpose of registering their votes.

In order to ensure an impartial plebiscite and to guarantee that the necessary and extensive preparations for the plebiscite shall be carried out correctly, an International Commission like the one formed in connection with the Saar plebiscite, and consisting of members appointed by the four Great Powers, Italy, the U.S.S.R., France and Great Britain, shall be formed immediately, and placed in charge of this territory. This commission shall exercise sovereign rights throughout the territory. To that end, the territory shall be evacuated by the Polish military forces, by the Polish police and by the Polish authorities within the shortest possible time to be agreed upon.

4. The Polish port of Gdynia to the extent of the Polish settlement is not included in this area, but, as a matter of principle, is recognized as Polish territory.

The details of the boundaries of this Polish port shall be decided on by Germany and Poland, and if necessary established by an International Court of Arbitration.

5. In order to allow for ample time for the necessary and extensive preparations for the carrying out of an impartial plebiscite, this plebiscite shall not take place before a period of twelve months has elapsed.

6. In order that during that period, Germany's lines of communication with East Prussia and Poland's access to the sea may be unrestrictedly ensured, certain roads and railway lines shall be determined, in order to facilitate unobstructed transit. In this connection only such taxes may be levied as are necessary for the upkeep of the lines of communication and for the carrying out of transport.

7. The allocation of this territory shall be decided on by the absolute majority of the votes cast.

8. In order to secure, after the plebiscite (irrespective of the result thereof), Germany's unrestricted communication with the province of Danzig-East Prussia, and Poland's access to the sea, Germany shall, in case the territory be returned to Poland as a result of the plebiscite, be given an extraterritorial traffic zone running from, say, Butow to Danzig or Dirschau, for the purpose of building a German motor highway (*Reichsautobahn*) and also a four-track railway line. The construction of the motor road and of the railway shall be carried out in such a manner that Polish lines of communication are not affected thereby, i.e., they are to be over-bridged or underbridged. This zone shall be one kilometer in width and shall be German territory.

Should the result of the plebiscite be in favor of Germany, Poland shall have the same rights as Germany would have had, to build an extraterritorial road and railway connection in order to secure her free and unrestricted access to her port of Gdynia.

9. In the event of the Polish Corridor being returned to the Reich, the latter declares herself prepared to arrange with Poland for an exchange of population, insofar as conditions in the Corridor lend themselves to such an exchange.

10. Any special rights claimed by Poland within the port of Danzig shall be negotiated on a parity basis in exchange for equal rights for Germany at the Port of Gdynia.

11. In order to avoid any sense of menace or danger on either side, Danzig and Gdynia shall henceforth have a purely commercial character; i.e., neither of these places shall be provided with means of military defense or fortifications.

12. The Peninsula of Hela, which according to the result of the plebiscite would be allocated either to Poland or to Germany, shall also be demilitarized in any case.

13. The German Government, having most serious complaints to make about the treatment of the minority by the Poles, and the Polish Government, considering themselves entitled to raise complaints against Germany, agree to investigate into all complaints about economic and personal damage, as well as other acts of terrorism.

Germany and Poland bind themselves to indemnify the minorities on either side for any economic damages and other wrongs inflicted upon them since 1918; and/or to revoke all expropriations or otherwise to completely indemnify the respective person or persons for these and other encroachments upon economic life.

14. In order to free the Germans remaining in Poland, as well as the Poles remaining in Germany, from the feeling of being deprived of the benefits of international law, and above all to afford them the certainty of their not being made to take part in actions and in furnishing services of a kind not compatible with their national convictions, Germany and Poland mutually agree to safeguard the rights of their respective minorities by most comprehensive and binding agreements for the purpose of warranting these minorities the preservation, free development and cultivation of their national customs, habits and traditions, to grant them in particular and for that purpose the form of organization considered necessary by them. Both parties undertake not to draft the members of the minority into military service.

15. In case of an agreement being reached on the basis of these proposals, Germany and Poland declare themselves prepared immediately to order and carry out the demobilization of their respective armed forces.

16. Any additional measures required to hasten the carrying through of the above agreement shall be mutually agreed upon between Germany and Poland.

90. Failure of a Mission: Sir Nevile Henderson Reports on His Unsuccessful Negotiations with Hitler to Prevent War, 1939

"It is the Fuehrer *alone who decides.* "

While the circumstances were still fresh in his mind, Sir Nevile Meyrick Henderson, the British ambassador in Berlin, recorded his firsthand impressions in his final report on the circumstances leading to the termination of his mission to Berlin. It was later published as a White Paper (Cmd 6115). The report concerns last-minute maneuvers and confirms the methods and techniques of Hitler during the final negotiations before the outbreak of war.

THE NATURE OF THE NAZI MOVEMENT

"Herr Hitler and National Socialism," the Report points out, "are the products of the defeat of a great nation in war and its reaction against the confusion and distress which followed that defeat. National Socialism itself is a revolution and a conception of national philosophy. Contrary to democracy which implies the subordination of the State to the service of its citizens, Nazism prescribes the subordination of its citizens to the service of the State, an all embracing Moloch, and to the individual who rules that State.

"So long as National Socialism remained an article for internal consumption, the outside world, according to its individual predilection, might criticise or sympathise or merely watch with anxiety. The government of Germany was the affair of the German people. It was not until the theory of German nationalism was extended beyond Germany's own fron-

---

Great Britain, Ministry of Information, *How Hitler Made the War* (London: His Majesty's Stationery Office, 1939), pp. 35-42.

tiers that the Nazi philosophy exceeded the limits compatible with peace.

"It would be idle to deny the great achievements of the man who restored to the German nation its self-respect and its disciplined orderliness. The tyrannical methods which were employed within Germany itself to obtain this result were detestable, but were Germany's own concern." As Sir Nevile Henderson points out, many of Herr Hitler's social reforms, such as the Labour Camps, were in spite of their complete disregard of personal liberty of thought, word or deed, on highly advanced lines. "Nor" he continues, "can the appeal of Nazism with its slogans so attractive to a not over-discerning youth be ignored. Much of its legislation in this respect will survive in a newer and better world, in which Germany's amazing power of organisation and the great contributions which she has made in the past to the sciences, music, literature and the higher aims of civilisation and humanity will again play a leading part."

HITLER AND THE PROBLEM OF GERMAN UNITY

"Nor was the unity of Great Germany in itself an ignoble ideal. It had long been the dream of some of the highest-minded of German thinkers, and it must be remembered that even in 1914 Germany was still immature as a political concept. In spite of the potential political danger for its weaker neighbours of a national philosophy which could so easily be distorted and extended beyond its due and legitimate frontiers, the unity of Great Germany was a reality which had to be faced, no less than that other reality, the paramount economic importance of Germany in Eastern, Central and South-Eastern Europe. It was not the incorporation of Austria and the Sudeten Germans in the Reich [in so far as it could be defended in accordance with the principle of self-determination] which so much shocked public opinion in the world as the unscrupulous and hateful methods which Herr Hitler employed" to precipitate that incorporation.

HITLER'S "SICKENING TECHNIQUE"

That principle constituted the whole basis of the Munich agreement of September, 1938, which Hitler violated six months later, and thus, as Sir Nevile states, "In 1939, as in 1914, the origin of war with Germany has been due to the deliberate tearing up by the latter of a scrap of paper. To the iniquities of a system which employed the barbarism of the middle ages in its persecution of the Jews, which subjected Roman Catholic priests and Protestant pastors alike to the inhumanities of the concentration camp for obedience to their religious faith, and which crushed out, in a fashion unparalleled in history, all individual liberty within the State itself, was added the violation not only of international agreements freely negotiated, but also of that principle of self-determination which Herr Hitler had invoked with such insistence so long as it suited his own purpose to do so. Up to last March the German ship of State had flown the German national flag, and in spite of the 'sickening technique' of Nazism it was difficult not to concede to Germany the right both to control her own destiny and to benefit from those principles which were accorded to others. On the 15th March, by the ruthless suppression of the freedom of the Czechs, its captain hoisted the skull and crossbones of the pirate, cynically discarded his own theory of racial purity and appeared under his true colours as an unprincipled menace to European peace and liberty.

"Two of the less attractive characteristics of the German are his inability either to see any side of a question except his own, or to understand the meaning of moderation. It would have been understandable to argue that a hostile Bohemia in the centre of Germany was an untenable proposition. But Herr Hitler could see no mean between rendering the Czechs innocuous as a potential enemy and destroying their liberty as an independent people. There is some surprising reason to believe that Herr Hitler himself was disagreeably and literally astonished at the reaction in Britain and the world generally, which was provoked by the occupation of Prague and his breach of faith with Mr. Chamberlain. But while he may have realised his tactical mistake, it did not deter him from prosecuting his further designs . . . Herr Hitler felt that it would not add much to the general execration of his aggression and ill-faith in March if he settled these two problems [i.e. Danzig and the Corridor, and Memel] simultaneously with Prague. The Democracies were, he thought, so averse to war that they would accept any *fait accompli*. They would be less disturbed if everything was done at once. Thereafter, the agitation would, he anticipated, gradually subside until, after consolidating his gains, he was once more in a position to strike again."

HITLER AND GREAT BRITAIN

Hitler's calculation in this matter is characteristic of his whole attitude towards the Western Powers, and towards Great Britain in particular. That attitude is described by Sir Nevile in a comment on his interview with Hitler of August 29 during which he says that Hitler delivered "a brief and in my opinion quite honest harangue . . . on the genuineness of his constant endeavour to win Britain's friendship, of his respect for the British Empire, and of his liking for Englishmen generally. I should like to state . . . emphatically," continues Sir Nevile, "that Herr Hitler's constant repetition of his desire for good relations with Great Britain was undoubtedly a sincere conviction," naturally on his own terms, namely a completely free hand in Central Europe, and even so it may be that he only desired them just so long as he was occupied in that part of the world; but, as Sir N. Henderson continues, "He will prove in the future a fascinating study for the historian and the biographer with psychological leanings. Widely different explanations will be propounded, and it would be out of place and time to comment at any length in this despatch on this aspect of Herr Hitler's mentality and character. But he combined, as I fancy many Germans do, admiration for the British race with envy of their achievements and hatred of their opposition to Germany's excessive aspirations. It is no exaggeration to say that he assiduously courted Great Britain, both as representing the aristocracy and most successful of the Nordic races, and as constituting the only seriously dangerous obstacle to his own far-reaching plan of German domination in Europe. This is evident in *Mein Kampf*, and, in spite of what he regarded as the constant rebuffs which he received from the British side, he persisted in his endeavours up to the last moment. Geniuses are strange creatures, and Herr Hitler, among other paradoxes, is a mixture of long-headed calculation and violent and arrogant impulse provoked by resentment. The former drove him to seek Britain's friendship and the latter finally into war with her. Moreover, he believes his resentment to be entirely justified. He failed to realise why his military-cum-police tyranny should be repugnant to British ideals of individual and national freedom and liberty, or why he should not be allowed a free hand in Central and Eastern Europe to subjugate smaller and, as he regards them, inferior peoples to superior German rule and culture. He believed he could buy British acquiescence in his own far-reaching schemes by offers of alliance with and guarantees for the British Empire. Such acquiescence was indispensable to the success of his ambitions and he worked unceasingly to secure it. His great mistake was his complete failure to understand the inherent British sense of morality, humanity and freedom.

"One of Herr Hitler's greatest drawbacks is that, except for two official visits to Italy, he has never travelled abroad. For his knowledge of British mentality he consequently relied on Herr von Ribbentrop as an ex-Ambassador to Britain, who spoke both French and English, and who had spent some years in Canada, and whom he regarded as a man of the world. If report be true Herr von Ribbentrop gave him consistently false counsels in regard to England, while his successes in other spheres induced Herr Hitler to regard him more and more as a second Bismarck, a conviction which Herr von Ribbentrop probably shared to the full."

THE TRAGEDY OF THE DICTATOR

"Even the most absolute Dictator is susceptible to the influence of his surroundings. Nevertheless Herr Hitler's decisions, his calculations, and his opportunisms were his own. As Field-Marshal Goering once said to me, 'when a decision has to be taken, none of us count more than the stones on which we are standing. It is the Fuhrer alone who decides'.

"I think there can be no doubt that Field-Marshal Goering himself would have preferred a peaceful solution, but in matters such as these it was Herr Hitler's decision which alone counted; and whatever Field-Marshal

Goering himself might feel, he was merely the loyal and submissive servant of his master. Moreover, he had come down definitely on the side of peace a year before and it may have been difficult for him to adopt this course a second time.

"In my report on the events of 1938 I drew your Lordship's special attention to the far reaching and unfortunate results of the Blomberg marriage. I am more than ever convinced of the major disaster which that – in itself – minor incident involved, owing to the consequent elimination from Herr Hitler's entourage of the more moderate and independent of his advisers, such as Field Marshal von Blomberg himself, Baron von Neurath, Generals Fritsch, Beck, &c. After February of last year Herr Hitler became more and more shut off from external influences and a law unto himself.

"People are apt, in my opinion, to exaggerate the malign influence of Herr von Ribbentrop, Dr. Goebbels, Herr Himmler and the rest. It was probably consistently sinister, not because of its suggestiveness (since Herr Hitler alone decided policy), nor because it merely applauded and encouraged, but because, if Herr Hitler appeared to hesitate, the extremists of the party at once proceeded to fabricate situations calculated to drive Herr Hitler into courses which even he at times shrank from risking. The simplest method of doing this was through the medium of a controlled Press. Thus what happened in September last year, was repeated in March this year, and again in August. Dr. Goebbels' propaganda machine was the ready tool of these extremists, who were afraid lest Herr Hitler should move too slowly in the prosecution of his own ultimate designs.

"The 1938 stories of Czech atrocities against its German minority, were rehashed up almost verbatim in regard to the Poles. Some foundation there must necessarily have been for a proportion of these allegations in view of the state of excitable tension which existed between the two peoples. Excess of zeal on the part of individuals and minor officials there undoubtedly was – but the tales of ill-treatment, expropriation and murder were multiplied a hundredfold. How far Herr Hitler himself believed in the truth of these tales must be a matter of conjecture. Germans are prone in any case to convince themselves very readily of anything which they wish to believe. Certainly he behaved as if he did believe, and, even if one may give him the benefit of the doubt, these reports served to inflame his resentment to the pitch which he or his extremists desired."

THE THREAT OF WAR

"There were, in fact, for Herr Hitler only two solutions: the use of force, or the achievement of his aims by the display of force. 'If you wish to obtain your objective by force, you must be strong; if you wish to obtain them by negotiation, you must be stronger still.' That was a remark which he made to a foreign Statesman who visited him this year, and it expresses in the concisest possible form the Hitler technique. It was exactly that which he displayed in September 1938. He was no more bluffing then than he was bluffing in August 1939. Up to the middle of August this year the fear of a war on two fronts, with Russia hostile or at least unfriendly, might possibly have deterred him and his military advisers from action against Poland. There was no Eastern front to give him cause for hesitation in 1938, and he could have counted then on Hungarian as well as Polish support in his nefarious plans for the dismemberment of Czecho-Slovakia. But for Munich he would without a shadow of doubt have invaded that country on the 29th September last year, just as surely as he invaded Poland on the 1st September this year, and the war would have come eleven months earlier. In both cases the methods employed were identical: the gradual mobilisation of the German army over a period of months and its secret concentration at the appointed positions, whence the advance could begin at almost any moment and within a very few hours.

"So it was again in 1939. If he could have secured his objectives by this display of force he might have been content for the moment, with all the additional prestige which another bloodless success would have procured for him with his own people. But it would only have been to start again once the world had recovered from the shock, and even his own people were beginning to be tired of these repeated crises. Millions of Germans had begun to long for a more peaceful existence. Guns instead of butter were becoming more and more unpopular except with the younger generation, and Hitler may well have wondered what might happen to his Nazi revolution if its momentum were allowed to stop. Moreover the financial and economic position of Germany was such that things could scarcely continue as they were without some form of explosion, internal or external. Of the two alternatives the most attractive from the point of view of his growing personal ambitions, and those of the clique which was nearest to him, was war.

"It is scarcely credible that he would have acted as he did if bloody war, rather than a bloodless victory, had not seemed the fairer prospect for him. He had always meant to teach the Poles a lesson for what he regarded as their base ingratitude in refusing the 'generous' demands which he had made to them in March. His only maneuvres since that date were with the object of creating circumstances favourable to his plans or of inducing Britain and France to abandon their Polish ally and to leave him a free hand in Central and Eastern Europe."

ADVICE OF THE SOLDIERS

"If anything did count, it was the opinion of his Military Advisers. I have always believed that it was they who, in the interests of Germany's strategical security, recommended the establishment of the Protectorate over Bohemia. And again this August, it was they, I fancy, who told Herr Hitler that further delay would be fatal lest the seasonal bad weather in Poland might upset their calculations for her swift overthrow. The army grudged him even the week between the 25th August and the 1st September which his last attempt to secure British neutrality or at least goodwill had cost it.

"Yet even so the advice of his soldiers was probably merely cover for the prosecution of Hitler's own plans. His impatience and precipitate action on that last day of August can scarcely have been other than premeditated. All through the summer he had been waiting on events to turn in his favour and had been making his preparations to seize the opportunity, when it was offered to him. The Russian pact appeared to give him the advantage which he was seeking and thereafter there was no time to lose, if mud was not to be added to Poland's allies."

THE NAZI-SOVIET PACT

"The secret [of the Russian pact] which on the German side had been known to not more than a few persons, had been well kept. It had been realised that German counter-negotiations had been proceeding throughout the summer, but it was hoped that they had been abandoned after the actual arrival at Moscow of the French and British military missions. . . [Giving his] first impression [of] Berlin on the morning of Monday, the 4th September, Sir Nevile concludes:

"A small crowd collected round the Embassy before our departure, but unlike 1914 it evinced no single sign of hostility. Mr. Kirk [the United States Chargé d'Affaires] rendered me one more last service by driving me to the station in his own car. The streets of Berlin were practically deserted and there was nothing to indicate the beginning of a war which is to decide whether force is to be the sole arbiter in international affairs; whether international instruments solemnly and freely entered into are to be modified, not by negotiation, but by mere unilateral repudiation; whether there is to be any faith in future in written contracts; whether the fate of a great nation and the peace of the world is to rest in the future in the hands of one man; whether small nations are to have any rights against the pretensions of States more powerful than themselves; in a word, whether government of the people by the people for the people is to continue in this world, or whether it is to be replaced by the arbitrary will and ambition of single individuals regardless of the peoples' will."

Part Five:

The
Third Reich
in
World War II

91. Nazi Germany Goes to War: The German Assault on Poland Is Reported by the London *Times*, September 1, 1939

*"The news of the German invasion amazed the offi-
cials of the Polish Foreign Office."*

At dawn on September 1, 1939, Hitler, without a declaration of war, sent his legions hurtling across the borders of Poland. The time was past for diplomatic activity, for threats and countercharges, for loud polemics, for appeals to reason and justice. The Nazi *Fuehrer* now had his war. Following is the first British dispatch of World War II reporting the thrust into Poland.

INVASION OF POLAND

GERMAN ATTACK ACROSS ALL FRONTIERS

WARSAW AND OTHER CITIES BOMBED

WAR WITHOUT A DECLARATION

WARSAW, Sept. 1—Hostilities began at 5:30 this morning on German-Polish frontiers with a heavy and apparently unannounced bombardment of Katowice from the air. The city was attacked with high explosive bombs. As far as is known there had been no declaration of war. Krakow, Tczew (near the Danzig border) and Tunel (between Krakow and Czenstochkowa) were attacked with incendiary bombs.

At 6:15 the air raid sirens sounded for the first time in Warsaw, but no bombs fell until 9 A.M., when the capital was attacked from the air with incendiary and explosive bombs. Many Polish fighters went up to inter-

---

Times (London), September 2, 1939.

cept raiders and there were thrilling aerial combats. The casualties resulting from this raid are unknown.

Subsequently during the day the capital was raided five or six times. On
one occasion, between 4:30 and 5:30, the bombers attacked the centre of
the city and flew down the Vistula bombing the bridges. Several of them
crashed. For the most part the bombers were chased away by the Polish
fighters and anti-aircraft fire, and the damage was almost entirely done
outside the city in the suburbs. Seven people were killed at a place 40 miles
from Warsaw. One flight of bombers in being chased unloaded their
bombs on the country resort of Otwock, 15 miles from the capital. Of
these 6 bombers, 4 escaped and 2 were brought down either by fighters or
the anti-aircraft guns. In the afternoon excited crowds watched the flight
of German bombers above Warsaw, swooping and twirling as light quick-
firing guns peppered the sky with puffs of smoke.

The outbreak of war was received most calmly by the inhabitants of
Warsaw. When the sirens sounded, the people ran into the streets and
looked up at the sky until A.R.P. squads drove them indoors.

Reports from Katowice state that the German aeroplanes have been
coming over in squadrons of 50 every half hour, and that there have been
many casualties. The anti-aircraft guns went into action only after the
second wave. Since mid-day telephonic communication has been cut off.
At that time a correspondent in Katowice reported that the population
was beginning to be shaken by the terrific bombing, but that there, as
elsewhere, they were behaving with extraordinary stoicism. . . .

The German invasion was launched from Slovakia, East Prussia, and
the main body of the Reich. Attack was made against Zrkopane from
Slovakia. . . .

The news of the German invasion amazed the officials of the Polish
Foreign Office, who had been up all night studying the latest dispatches.
Until late yesterday, when Herr Hitler's "minimum demands" were published by the official German news agency, it was thought that the exchange between London and Berlin was going on satisfactorily. . . .

The German excuse for invasion — namely, "the invasion by Polish di-
versionist bands near Gleiwitz" — is described as a tissue of lies.

92. Hitler Speaks to the *Reichstag* Justifying His Decision to Go to War and Asking for Support by the German People, September 1, 1939

"I ask of every German what I myself am prepared
to do at any moment: to be ready to lay down his
life for his people and for his country."

A few hours after German troops surged across the borders of Poland, Hitler appeared before the *Reichstag*, meeting at the Kroll Opera House, and delivered his war speech justifying Germany's attack on Poland. Most deputies were already dressed in military uniform. On the conclusion of the speech, the *Reichstag* passed a law incorporating Danzig into the Third Reich, declaring that all Danzig citizens were now German, voiding the constitution of the Free City, and extending to its territory the jurisdiction of German law.

Members of the German Reichstag:

For months we have been tormented by a problem once wished upon us by the dictated Treaty of Versailles and which has now assumed such a character as to become utterly intolerable. Danzig was and is a German city. The Corridor was and is German. All these districts owe their cultural development exclusively to the German people, without whom absolute barbarism would prevail in these eastern tracts of country. Danzig was separated from us. The Corridor was annexed by Poland. The German minorities living there were ill-treated in the most appalling manner.

German Library of Information, *Documents on the Events Preceding the Outbreak of War*, compiled and published by the German Foreign Office (Berlin: 1939; New York: 1940), pp. 498-504.

More than a million persons with German blood in their veins were compelled to leave their homes as early as 1919–1920. Here, as always, I have attempted to change this intolerable state of affairs by means of peaceful proposals for a revision. It is a lie when the world alleges that we always used pressure in attempting to carry out any revision. There was ample opportunity for fifteen years before National Socialism assumed power to carry through revisions by means of a peaceful understanding. This was not done. I myself then took the initiative in every single case, not only once, but many times, to bring forward proposals for the revision of absolutely intolerable conditions.

As you know, all these proposals were rejected. I need not enumerate them in detail: proposals for a limitation of armaments, if necessary even for the abolition of armaments, proposals for restrictions on methods of warfare, proposals for eliminating methods of modern warfare, which, in my opinion, are scarcely compatible with international law. You know the proposals which I made as to the necessity of restoring German sovereign rights in certain territories of the Reich, those countless attempts I made to bring about a peaceful solution of the Austrian problem and, later on, of the Sudetenland, Bohemia and Moravia. It was all in vain. One thing, however, is impossible: to demand that a peaceful revision should be made of an intolerable state of affairs — and then obstinately refuse such a peaceful revision. It is equally impossible to assert that in such a situation to act on one's own initiative in making a revision is to violate a law. For us Germans the dictated Treaty of Versailles is not a law. It will not do to blackmail a person at the point of a pistol, with the threat of starvation for millions of people, into signing a document and afterwards proclaim that this document with its forced signature was a solemn law.

In the case of Danzig and the Corridor I have again tried to solve the problems by proposing peaceful discussions. One thing was obvious: They had to be solved. That the date of the solution may perhaps be of little interest to the Western Powers is conceivable. But this date is not a matter of indifference to us. First and foremost, however, it was not and could not be a matter of indifference to the suffering victims. In conversations with Polish statesmen, I have discussed the ideas which you have heard me express here in my last speech to the *Reichstag*. No one can maintain that this was an unjust procedure or even unreasonable pressure.

I then had the German proposals clearly formulated, and I feel bound to repeat once more that nothing could be fairer or more modest than those proposals submitted by me. And I now wish to declare to the whole world that I, and I alone, was in a position to make such proposals. For I know quite definitely that I was thereby acting contrary to the opinion of millions of Germans.

Those proposals were rejected. But more than that, they were replied to by mobilization, by increased terrorism, by intensified pressure on the German minorities in those areas, and by a gradual economic and political strangulation of the Free City of Danzig, which during the past few weeks found its expression in military measures and traffic restrictions. Poland virtually began a war against the Free City of Danzig. Furthermore she was not prepared to settle the problem of the Corridor in a fair manner satisfying the interests of both parties. And lastly, Poland has never thought of fulfilling her obligations with regard to the minorities. In this connection I feel it necessary to state that Germany has fulfilled her obligations in this respect. Minorities domiciled in Germany are not subject to persecution. Let any Frenchman get up and declare that French citizens living in the Saar territory are oppressed, ill-treated or deprived of their rights. No one can make such an assertion.

For four months I have watched these developments without taking action but not without issuing repeated warnings. Recently I have made these warnings more and more emphatic. Over three weeks ago the Polish Ambassador was, at my request, informed that if Poland persisted in sending further notes in the nature of an ultimatum to Danzig and in further oppressing the German minorities, or if attempts were made to bring about the economic ruin of Danzig by means of customs restrictions, Germany would no longer stand aside and remain inactive. I have left no room for doubt that in this respect the Germany of today is not to be confused with postwar Germany. . . .

I am determined to eliminate from the German frontiers the element of insecurity, the atmosphere which permanently resembles that of civil war. I shall see to it that on the eastern frontier the same peaceful conditions prevail as on our other frontiers.

All actions in fulfillment of this aim will be carried out in such a way as not to contradict the proposals which I made known to you here, Members of the *Reichstag*, as my proposals to the rest of the world.

That is, I will not wage war against women and children! I have instructed my Air Force to limit their attacks to military objectives. But should the enemy think this gives him *carte blanche* to fight in the opposite way, then he will get an answer which will drive him out of his senses!

In the night Polish soldiers of the Regular Army fired the first shots in our own territory. Since 5:45 A.M. we have been returning their fire. And from now onwards every bomb will be answered by another bomb. Whoever fights with poison gas will be fought with poison gas. Whoever disregards the rules of human warfare can but expect us to do the same.

I will carry on this fight, no matter against whom, until such time as the safety of the Reich and its rights are secured!

For more than six years now I have been engaged in building up the German armed forces. During this period more than 90 billion *Reichs-*

marks have been expended in creating our armed forces. Today, they are the best equipped in the world and are far superior to those of 1914. My confidence in them can never be shaken.

In calling up these forces, and in expecting the German people to make sacrifices, if necessary unlimited sacrifices, I have done only what I have a right to do; for I myself am just as ready today as I was in the past to make every personal sacrifice. There is nothing I demand of any German which I myself was not prepared to do at any moment for more than four years. There shall not be any deprivations for Germans in which I myself shall not immediately share. From this moment my whole life shall belong more than ever to my people. I now want to be nothing but the first soldier of the German Reich.   Therefore, I have once again put on that uniform which was always so sacred and dear to me. I shall not lay it aside until after the victory — or I shall not live to see the end.

Should anything happen to me in this war, my first successor shall be Party Member Goering. Should anything happen to Party Member Goering, his successor shall be Party Member Hess. To these men as your leaders you would then owe the same absolute loyalty and obedience that you owe me. In the event that something fatal should happen to Party Member Hess, I am about to make legal provisions for the convocation of a Senate appointed by me, who shall then elect the worthiest, that is to say the most valiant among themselves.

As a National Socialist and a German soldier, I enter upon this fight with a stout heart! My whole life has been but one continuous struggle for my people, for the rebirth of Germany, and that whole struggle has been inspired by one single conviction: Faith in my people!

One word I have never known: Capitulation. If, however, there should be any one who thinks that we are on the verge of hard times, I would urge him to consider the fact that at one time a Prussian king ruling over a ridiculously small state confronted one of the greatest coalitions ever known and came forth victorious after three campaigns, simply because he was possessed of that undaunted spirit and firm faith which are required of us in these times.

As for the rest of the world, I can only assure them that November, 1918, shall never occur again in German history.

I ask of every German what I myself am prepared to do at any moment: to be ready to lay down his life for his people and for his country.

If any one thinks that he can evade this national duty directly or indirectly, he will perish. We will have nothing to do with traitors. We are acting only in accordance with our old principle. Our own life matters nothing, all that matters is that our people, that Germany shall live.

I expect of you, as deputies of the Reich, that you will do your duty in whatever position you are called upon to fill. You must bear the standard of resistance, cost what it may. Let no one report to me at any time that his province, his district, his group or his cell are losing heart. It is you who are responsible for public feeling. I am responsible for public feeling throughout Germany and you are responsible for public feeling in your provinces and districts. No one has the right to shelve this responsibility. The sacrifice that is demanded of us is not greater than the sacrifice which has been made by many generations in the past. All those men who before us have trod the hardest and most difficult path for Germany's sake did nothing less than we are called upon to do; the sacrifice they made was no less costly, no less painful, and therefore no easier than the sacrifice that may be demanded of us.

I also expect every German woman to take her place with unflinching discipline in this great fighting community.

German Youth, needless to say, will do, with heart and soul, what is expected and demanded of it by the nation and by the National Socialist State.

If we form this community, fused together, ready for anything, determined never to capitulate, our firm resolve will master every emergency.

I conclude with the words with which I once started my fight for power in the Reich. At that time I said: "If our will is so strong that no emergency can break it, then our will and our good German sword will master and subjugate even need and distress."

GERMANY — SIEG HEIL!

93. War Lord to the Front: The German Press Reports How the *Fuehrer* Goes to His Troops, September 4, 1939

> *"Fuehrer, command! We follow you, if necessary, to the death!"*

On September 1, as German troops swarmed into Poland, Hitler put on his military tunic and announced that he would wear no other clothes until the final victory. It was front-page news for the German public when the press reported that the *Fuehrer* was on his way to the front. The following dispatch appeared on the front page of the *Hamburger Anzeiger* three days after the beginning of hostilities. It was obviously designed as a morale builder for the German people.

BERLIN, September 4 — The *Fuehrer* last Saturday moved to join his soldiers on the Eastern Front.

All the streets and squares of Berlin, including the Wilhelmsplatz, are in deep darkness. The standard of the *Fuehrer* waves from the top of the Chancellery. The people are gathered in thick crowds. They press against the police lines.

Finally, the gates of the Reich Chancellery open. A second of expectant silence. An automobile with dimmed headlights proceeds slowly into the Wilhelmstrasse. Now the people cannot contain themselves any more. They break through the ranks of the security police and push forward. A single cry of joy fills the air. And then come the *"Heils!"* They reverberate along the whole length of the Wilhelmstrasse. It sounds like an oath: *"Fuehrer*, command, we follow in blind obedience, in unconditional readiness for sacrifice, in will of steel and belief in the victory of our just cause.

"Fuehrer, command! We follow you, if necessary, to the death."

Hamburger Anzeiger, September 4, 1939. Translated by the editor.

358

94. The German Foreign Office Publishes an Official Reply to the British War Blue Book and Claims that England Started the War, September 15, 1939

". . . a series of malicious intrigues and mendacity. . . ."

On September 15, 1939, soon after the outbreak of World War II, the German Foreign Office, on behalf of the German government, issued an official publication designed to refute the British War Book in its contention that Germany was exclusively to blame for the war. In more than five hundred pages of documents, a case was presented for German innocence and British guilt. London was accused of using all its diplomatic mechanisms for the purpose of giving Poland time to complete her mobilization "and to put off Germany with evasive subterfuges."

WE HEREWITH PRESENT for students of international affairs a summary of the reply of the German Government to the British War Blue Book on the origin of the war. The British War Blue Book was intended to present conclusive proof that Germany was solely to blame for the outbreak of war. To this end, England compiled a highly eclectic series of documents, which in themselves were designed to support this contention. In its reply to this publication, the German government has enumerated some of the omissions from the Blue Book, and pointed out the way in which they place some of the British documents in a different light. As a result the observer placing both sets of evidence side by side is inevitably led to a

---

German Library of Information, *Documents on the Events Preceding the Outbreak of War,* compiled and published by the German Foreign Office (Berlin, 1939; New York, 1940), pp. 517-25.

conclusion precisely opposite to that drawn by the British government. In the light of this supplementary evidence, the conduct of Lord Halifax assumes an appearance which is at best ambiguous. Furthermore it clearly appears that it was the conduct of the British Ambassador to Warsaw which, perhaps upon instructions, made the last attempt to settle the German-Polish problem by peaceful negotiation impossible. Bent upon war, British diplomacy, with subterfuges, delays, evasions, and outright falsehood, Germany charges, deliberately deceived not only Germany, but Britain's own allies, Poland and France.

England wanted war. Germany can bring proof after proof before the eyes of the world for that. Until now England has not been able to show anything to the contrary. For that reason she has resorted time and again to lies and distortions.

The British Blue Book which recently appeared and with which the German press has already concerned itself, even after the most exact examinations, shows itself to be no more than an unsuccessful attempt at exoneration. It is a new but weak attempt to pervert the truth. For those who know how to read, this English collection of documents is really a unique and positive proof of England's will to war.

The documents are arbitrarily gathered in the British Blue Book in order to create a one-sided impression. Other documents have been omitted, and in addition, the general contents can make no pretense to exactness and exhaustive presentation.

Malevolent and Dishonest

It would be too much to go into all these inexactitudes and contradictions. We wish however, from all these obscurations to single out one point which clearly proves that England did not act honorably as an intermediary between Poland and Germany as she alleged, but operated as just that force through whose well-considered intrigues the war became inevitable.

The Blue Book is proof in itself that British diplomacy did not attempt to effect direct Polish-German negotiations upon which, in the final phase of the last days of August, everything depended if war were to be prevented; on the contrary it malevolently prevented such negotiations.

British Contention

It is the contention of false English propaganda that Viscount Halifax endeavored until the end to bring Germany and Poland together around a conference table in order to reach a peaceful solution on the lines of the German thesis. Actually the goal of Halifax and his helper, the British Ambassador in Warsaw, Sir Howard Kennard, consisted of keeping the

Poles from entering into serious negotiations with the Germans. This is fully and completely confirmed by the British Blue Book. It appears scarcely believable but it is nevertheless true.

The Bare Facts

Documents in the Blue Book show:

1. That Halifax grossly duped the German Government when he declared that he had received an assurance from Warsaw that Poland was ready to negotiate.

2. Kennard consciously delayed the execution of a mission which he received from London, to recommend that Poland enter into negotiations with the Reich, until the deadline, which necessarily had to be set by the Reich, as a result of the Polish mobilization, had expired.

3. Polish willingness to negotiate on the moderate German proposals was not evident, only because the Poles believed themselves able to rely on British assistance.

4. The French Government, which manifestly was also interested in the dispatch of a Polish plenipotentiary or representative to Berlin in the last hour, was also deceived by England. In reality England did absolutely nothing toward bringing about these negotiations upon which war or peace were dependent.

5. Proof, which has already appeared in a German White Book,* that Poland, because of this English double-dealing, never sent a plenipotentiary or representative to Berlin and that the Polish Ambassador in Berlin was not authorized to enter any definite negotiations. Yes, that, so to speak, every form of discussion was forbidden him is fully demonstrated by the English Blue Book.

These are the naked facts which are revealed in documents published by the English. They not only prove England's responsibility for the war; they also reveal much more, namely that the British Government carried on their infamous double-dealing during the decisive days at the end of August. This fact was not clearly demonstrable until the release of the British documents.

In the following paragraphs we condense the documents which reveal the foul play of British diplomacy between August 28 and 31.

First Deception

On August 25 the Fuehrer gave Henderson the declaration in which the necessity for the solution of the problem of the Danzig Corridor as quickly as possible was pointed out and which again contained in the most gen-

---

*"Documents Concerning the Last Phase of the German-Polish Crisis," American edition, published by the German Library of Information.

erous form an offer of friendship to England. Three days later, on Aug. 28, Henderson appeared before the Fuehrer in order to give the latter, as an answer to the German proposals of August 25, a memorandum from the British Government.

In this memorandum the German Government was asked to enter into direct negotiations with the Polish Government.

The English memorandum says literally in this regard:

"His Majesty's Government has already received a definitive assurance from the Polish Government that it is prepared to agree to such procedure."

The British memorandum added that:

"If such conversations could lead to an understanding, a way would be open for a broader and more comprehensive understanding between Great Britain and Germany."

On the basis of these assertions and wishes, it appeared to the German Government that a peaceful solution of the problems confronting Europe was still possible, if — in spite of the provocative conduct of the Polish Government — Berlin agreed to direct negotiations with Poland. Furthermore, the German Government assumed, in view of the text of the English memorandum, that the Poles had already consented to such a procedure.

Reich Willing to Negotiate Despite Skepticism

On the afternoon of August 29 the German Government, therefore, declared, in spite of its skeptical judgment of the prospects of direct conversations, that it was ready to accept the English proposal and enter into these negotiations. A prerequisite was the dispatch of a fully empowered Polish emissary to Berlin, through the mediation of the British Government, on Wednesday, August 30. In the meantime, that is in the night between August 29 and 30, the German Government was to work out an acceptable solution and upon the arrival of the Polish negotiator to place it also at the disposal of the British Government. By consenting to this suggestion Germany took the most extreme step possible under the circumstances, to save peace. Because of his desire for peace Hitler accepted the English proposals in their full extent. The kernel of this Anglo-German exchange of notes on August 28 and 29 was the British declaration that there was already in London "a definitive assurance" from the Polish Government that it was ready for these conversations. It was only on the basis of this declaration that the German Government was in the position to grant a last respite before taking steps to end the intolerable tension on the German-Polish border.

From the Blue Book it follows that the British Government, meanwhile, was not at all interested in its own proposal that negotiations between Berlin and Warsaw should take place immediately. The proposal, manifestly, was made by the British only to gain time.

British Trick to Gain Time

In her memorandum of August 28th England declared that she had a definite acceptance from Poland; as a matter of fact there had been no negotiations with Poland about this matter at all. Halifax, it is true, had instructed the British Ambassador at Warsaw to persuade the Polish Government to agree to direct negotiations with Germany through British mediation. This dispatch was dated August 28th. But, Halifax added in the same breath, that the readiness of the Polish Government to enter into direct negotiations with Germany naturally did not signify in any way Polish acceptance of Germany's demands.

That was all the English did, as the Blue Book shows. Acceptance from Poland did not materialize, either on August 28 or on the two days following.

In view of the facts, we now know that the British declaration of August 28, to the effect that the British Government had in hand a definitive assurance of the readiness of the Polish Government to enter direct negotiations, was a lie.

Polish Acceptance Fictitious

At this time the British Government had nothing in hand. It had merely directed a proposal to Poland and Germany. The proposal to Poland was phrased in such a manner that the Polish Government could reject it; in fact, it could interpret it as a demand to reply in the negative. These facts, which will presently emerge even more clearly, conclusively prove that in the final phase of the crisis the most important British memorandum was constructed on falsehood.

When Halifax learned in the night between August 29 and August 30 of the German willingness to receive a Polish plenipotentiary he had to telegraph Sir Nevile Henderson,* since he really had no Polish acceptance in his hand (the telegram was dated August 30 at 2 o'clock in the morning):

"It is contrary to all reason to expect that a Polish agent can still come today to Berlin." Henderson replied that Hitler had called to his attention the previous night that one can fly from Warsaw to Berlin in ninety minutes. Since the entire diplomatic maneuvre of Halifax rested upon falsehood, this simple counter-argument naturally went unobserved in London. Halifax was really not at all interested that a Polish emissary should appear in Berlin.

Kennard refused to inform the Polish Government and invite it to nego-

---

*See the telegram from Sir H. Kennard to Viscount Halifax, (Document No. 72 in the "British War Blue Book," American Edition) which refers to a dispatch of a Polish plenipotentiary to discuss the conditions prepared by the German Government in the night of August 28, sometimes called the "Sixteen Points."

tiate. To the British Ambassador at Warsaw was assigned a delivery role in the decisive hours. At 10 o'clock in the morning of August 30, Halifax received a telegram from Kennard which reveals that the British Ambassador did not even transmit to Poland the demand of the British Government of August 28 to enter into direct conversation. It is possible that he was in possession of secret instructions, obviously not mentioned in the Blue Book. It is inconceivable that an Ambassador in such a situation would refuse to carry out the instructions of his government.

Kennard Message Reveals Double Game

The following must, therefore, be adduced from Kennard's published telegram of August 30:

Kennard declared he was convinced that it was impossible to persuade Beck or some other Polish emissary to depart for Berlin immediately to conclude an agreement on the basis proposed by Hitler. His telegram continues verbatim:

"If it is recalled that the Polish Government, in month of March, when it stood alone, was not prepared for war and rejected the German proposals, then it would definitely have been impossible for it to accept proposals which apparently exceeded those of March now that Poland had Britain as an ally and was assured of France's aid."

Kennard concluded his telegram:

"I shall naturally not volunteer any view to the Polish Government, neither shall I transmit Hitler's answer (this refers to the German answer of August 29, which expressed the German readiness to enter direct negotiations) until I have received instructions which I assume will be forthcoming at once."

This reply of the British Ambassador at Warsaw reveals with complete clarity the British interplay of lies and intrigues. Not only did the British Government possess no promise from Poland, as it claimed two days earlier, but its Ambassador in Warsaw did not even transmit the British proposal to the Polish Government solely on the ground that Poland would refuse to negotiate in any event because it felt itself strong enough, by virtue of its alliance with Britain, to reject the proposals of Hitler.

Collusion or Insubordination

Either Kennard's refusal to transmit his government's instructions to Poland was a flagrant insubordination or it was collusion. Perusal of the British Blue Book, therefore, proves that, while the Reich Government in Berlin was waiting in vain for a Polish negotiator, British diplomacy, which unequivocally pledged itself to do its best to this end, in reality not only failed to keep Poland informed of the drift of events and developments but also kept from the Polish Government Germany's readiness to negotiate.

The strange attitude of Kennard unquestionably suggests collusion with the Foreign Office. If Halifax actually had played the role of honest broker, one would assume that he would have instructed his Ambassador in Warsaw, after learning from the latter's telegram of August 28th that he had not as yet delivered the note to the Polish Government, to undertake forthwith everything in his power to compel Poland to enter negotiations. Throughout all of August 30th, no instructions to this effect went forward to Kennard. On the other hand, Halifax sent a message to Henderson in which he stated:

"We have taken cognizance of the German demand that a Polish emissary with complete credentials come to Berlin to receive the German proposals. We cannot counsel the Polish Government to consent to such a procedure, which is completely contrary to all reason."

Halifax must have known, in view of the existing state of affairs, that non-compliance with this condition could only mean war. And he knew it.

Facts Concealed

Now the exact situation had been reached which Britain desired to provoke and which was forecast in its mendacious telegram of August 28. The Blue Book conveniently conceals that on this self-same Aug. 30, Poland, instead of sending an emissary to Berlin, ordered general mobilization. All relevant disclosures in the Blue Book prove that mobilization was ordered without Poland being informed, by the dishonest broker Halifax or his aide Kennard, of developments. It was not until the morning of Aug. 31, when the time limit fixed by Germany had expired, that Halifax instructed the British Ambassador at Warsaw to apprise Beck of the German note of Aug. 29, and the British reply thereto. It was only then that the Poles were urged to get in touch with Berlin. The British Government, therefore, not only lied in its note of Aug. 28, but it waited until the morning of Aug. 31 before informing the Polish Government of the state of things in Berlin and of Germany's readiness to enter into negotiations.

British Intrigues and Subterfuges

The Blue Book admits Britain's sole responsiblity for Poland's refusal to negotiate. The German statement asserts:

"The telegram of Kennard of Aug. 30, cited above, confirms Germany's contention that Poland never indicated a willingness to reach an amicable agreement with us because it felt that the British guarantee sufficiently justified her to indulge in any sort of provocation."

Even the French were duped and kept uninformed through British duplicity. England evidently feared that France would desert the British chariot at the last minute, if it clearly realized the war-like intentions of British diplomacy.

"Paris, manifestly, was informed on Aug. 30 or 31, that the Reich Government had vainly awaited a Polish emissary." The German statement adds that just why he never appeared also was concealed from the Quai d'Orsay.

"On the evening of Aug. 31," to quote further, "Kennard reported to Halifax about his conversation with Beck. This telegram reveals that Beck merely instructed Lipski, Polish Ambassador to Berlin, to inform the German Foreign Office that Poland was giving the British proposals favorable consideration. Beck, however, according to Kennard's message, stated that 'Lipski will not be authorized to accept any document containing German proposals.' Beck also stated that under no circumstances would he go to Berlin. Thereby the German proposal to Poland to dispatch an emissary was definitely rejected — an objective successfully reached through British duplicity."

The German statement concludes:

"The British Blue Book proves conclusively that instead of promoting direct contacts between Berlin and Warsaw during the four decisive days of Aug. 28 to 31, Britain through a series of malicious intrigues and mendacity devoted its entire diplomatic mechanism to the purpose of giving Poland time to complete her mobilization and to put off Germany with evasive subterfuges. Such is the role Halifax and his diplomatic aides played in the days preceding the outbreak of war."

95. German-Soviet Treaty: Hitler and Stalin Complete the Partition of Poland, September 28, 1939

*". . . to assure the people living there a peaceful life
in keeping with their national character."*

On September 17, 1939, in conformance with its pact with the Third Reich, the Soviet Union invaded Poland. The USSR announced to the world that it was taking this action to protect Russian minorities in Eastern Poland. Eleven days later the Germans and Russians signed a treaty regulating the new boundaries set up as a result of the conquest of Poland. The text of the treaty follows.

THE GOVERNMENT OF THE GERMAN REICH and the Government of the U.S.S.R. consider it as exclusively their task, after the collapse of the former Polish state, to re-establish peace and order in these territories and to assure to the peoples living there a peaceful life in keeping with their national character. To this end, they have agreed upon the following:

ARTICLE I. The Government of the German Reich and the Government of the U.S.S.R. determine as the boundary of their respective national interests in the territory of the former Polish state the line marked on the attached map, which shall be described in more detail in a supplementary protocol.

ARTICLE II. Both parties recognize the boundary of the respective national interests established in Article I as definitive and shall reject any interference of third powers in this settlement.

U.S., Department of State, *Nazi-Soviet Relations, 1939–1941* (Washington, D.C.: Government Printing Office, 1948), pp. 105-8.

ARTICLE III. The necessary reorganization of public administration will be effected in the areas west of the line specified in Article I by the Government of the German Reich, in the areas east of this line by the Government of the U.S.S.R.

ARTICLE IV. The Government of the German Reich and the Government of the U.S.S.R. regard this settlement as a firm foundation for a progressive development of the friendly relations between their peoples.

ARTICLE V. This treaty shall be ratified and the ratifications shall be exchanged in Berlin as soon as possible. The treaty becomes effective upon signature.

Done in duplicate, in the German and Russian languages.
Moscow, September 28, 1939.

For the Government   *By authority of the*
of the German Reich: *Government of the U.S.S.R.:*
J. RIBBENTROP   W. MOLOTOW

CONFIDENTIAL PROTOCOL

The Government of the U.S.S.R. shall place no obstacles in the way of Reich nationals and other persons of German descent residing in the territories under its jurisdiction, if they desire to migrate to Germany or to the territories under German jurisdiction. It agrees that such removals shall be carried out by agents of the Government of the Reich in cooperation with the competent local authorities and that the property rights of the emigrants shall be protected.

A corresponding obligation is assumed by the Government of the German Reich in respect to the persons of Ukrainian or White Russian descent residing in the territories under its jurisdiction.

Moscow, September 28, 1939.

For the Government   *By authority of the*
of the German Reich: *Government of the U.S.S.R.:*
J. RIBBENTROP   W. MOLOTOW

SECRET SUPPLEMENTARY PROTOCOL

The undersigned Plenipotentiaries declare the agreement of the Government of the German Reich and the Government of the U.S.S.R. upon the following:

The Secret Supplementary Protocol signed on August 23, 1939, shall be amended in item 1 to the effect that the territory of the Lithuanian state falls to the sphere of influence of the U.S.S.R., while, on the other hand, the province of Lublin and parts of the province of Warsaw fall to the sphere of influence of Germany (cf. the map attached to the Boundary and

Friendship Treaty signed today). As soon as the Government of the U.S.S.R. shall take special measures on Lithuanian territory to protect its interests, the present German-Lithuanian border, for the purpose of a natural and simple boundary delineation, shall be rectified in such a way that the Lithuanian territory situated to the southwest of the line marked on the attached map shall fall to Germany.

Further it is declared that the economic agreements now in force between Germany and Lithuania shall not be affected by the measures of the Soviet Union referred to above.

Moscow, September 28, 1939.

For the Government	*By authority of the*
of the German Reich:	*Government of the U.S.S.R.:*
J. RIBBENTROP	W. MOLOTOW

SECRET SUPPLEMENTARY PROTOCOL

The undersigned Plenipotentiaries, on concluding the German-Russian Boundary and Friendship Treaty, have declared their agreement upon the following:

Both parties will tolerate in their territories no Polish agitation which affects the territories of the other party. They will suppress in their territories all beginnings of such agitation and inform each other concerning suitable measures for this purpose.

Moscow, September 28, 1939.

For the Government	*By authority of the*
of the German Reich:	*Government of the U.S.S.R.:*
J. RIBBENTROP	W. MOLOTOW

DECLARATION OF THE GOVERNMENT OF THE GERMAN REICH AND THE GOVERNMENT OF THE U.S.S.R. OF SEPTEMBER 28, 1939

After the Government of the German Reich and the Government of the U.S.S.R. have, by means of the treaty signed today, definitively settled the problems arising from the collapse of the Polish state and have thereby created a sure foundation for a lasting peace in Eastern Europe, they mutually express their conviction that it would serve the true interest of all peoples to put an end to the state of war existing at present between Germany on the one side and England and France on the other. Both Governments will therefore direct their common efforts, jointly with other friendly powers if occasion arises, toward attaining this goal as soon as possible.

Should, however, the efforts of the two Governments remain fruitless, this would demonstrate the fact that England and France are responsible for the continuation of the war, whereupon, in case of the continuation of the war, the Governments of Germany and of the U.S.S.R. shall engage in mutual consultations with regard to necessary measures.

Moscow, September 28, 1939.

For the Government	*By authority of the*
of the German Reich:	*Government of the U.S.S.R.:*
J. RIBBENTROP	W. MOLOTOW

96. Hitler as Military Leader: The *Fuehrer's* War Directives, 1939-1945

Although technically, General Wilhelm Keitel, *Chef OKW* (chief of the high command of the armed forces), was supposed to give direction to war operations, actually Hitler, as *Oberster Befehlshaber der Wehrmacht* (supreme commander of the armed forces), issued all major operations directives. The *Fuehrer* was convinced of his own genius as a military tactician and strategist. The professional military men who led the German forces were not altogether agreed, but few dared to contradict the war lord and risk his displeasure. Hitler regarded retreat of any kind as akin to treason, an attitude which appalled his military advisers.

Following is a summary of the directives issued by Hitler during the war.

No.	Date	Where Issued	Subject
1.	Aug. 31, 1939	Berlin	Plan of Attack on Poland
2.	Sept. 3, 1939	Berlin	Conduct of the War Against England and France
3.	Sept. 9, 1939	Berlin	Transfer of Defense Units from Poland to the West

The texts of the directives are given in *Hitlers Weisungen fur die Kriegfuehrung, 1939-45, Dokumente des Oberkommandos der Wehrmacht*, ed. Walther Hubatsch (Frankfurt am Main: Bernard and Graefe Verlag, 1962).

4.	Sept. 25, 1939	*Fuehrer* Headquarters	On the Quick Destruction of Continuing Polish Resistance
5.	Sept. 30, 1939	Berlin	Concerning the Partition of Poland
6.	Oct. 9, 1939	Berlin	Strategy on the Western Front
7.	Oct. 18, 1939	Berlin	Preparations for Attack in the West
8.	Nov. 20, 1939	Berlin	Additional Orders for Attack in the West
9.	Nov. 29, 1939	Berlin	Instructions for War on the British Economy
10.	Jan. 19, 1940 and Feb. 18, 1940	Berlin	*Fall Gelb* (Case Yellow): Offensive in the West
10a.	Mar. 1, 1940	Berlin	Operations Against Denmark and Norway
11.	May 14, 1940	*Fuehrer* Headquarters	Battles in the West
12.	May 18, 1940	Berlin	Operations on the Southern Flank of the Western Front
13.	May 24, 1940	*Fuehrer* Headquarters	Destruction of French, English, and Belgian Forces in the West
14.	June 8, 1940	*Fuehrer* Headquarters	Continuation of the Drive toward Paris
15.	June 14, 1940	*Fuehrer* Headquarters	Advance of the Right Flank of the Army along the Coast toward the Loire Estuary
16.	July 16, 1940	*Fuehrer* Headquarters	Preparation for *Operation Sea Lion* Landing in England
17.	Aug. 1, 1940	*Fuehrer* Headquarters	Conduct of Air and Sea Warfare Against England
18.	Nov. 12, 1940	*Fuehrer* Headquarters	Possible Winter Campaign in the Warm Mediterranean Area
19.	Dec. 10, 1940	*Fuehrer* Headquarters	*Operation Attila:* Occupation of Unoccupied France

20.	Dec. 13, 1940	*Fuehrer* Headquarters	*Operation Marita:* Attack on Greece
21.	Dec. 18, 1940	*Fuehrer* Headquarters	*Fall Barbarossa (Case Barbarossa):* Planned Attack on Soviet Russia
22.	Jan. 11, 1941	*Fuehrer* Headquarters	German Intervention in the Mediterranean Area
23.	Feb. 6, 1941	Berlin	Orders for Operations Against the English War Economy
24.	Mar. 5, 1941	*Fuehrer* Headquarters	On German-Japanese Cooperation
25.	Mar. 27, 1941	*Fuehrer* Headquarters	Operations Against Yugoslavia
26.	Apr. 3, 1941	*Fuehrer* Headquarters	Cooperation Between Germany and her Balkan Allies
27.	Apr. 4, 1941	*Fuehrer* Headquarters	Strategy and Tactics for the Attack on Greece
28.	Apr. 25, 1941	*Fuehrer* Headquarters	*Operation Mercury:* Seizure of Crete
29.	May 17, 1941	*Fuehrer* Headquarters	Proposed Defense of Conquered Greece
30.	May 23, 1940	*Fuehrer* Headquarters	Orders for the Support of Iraq
31.	June 9, 1941	*Fuehrer* Headquarters	Military Organization for the Balkans
32.	June 11, 1941	*Fuehrer* Headquarters	Preparation for Procedures after the Destruction of the Soviet Russian Armed Forces
32a.	June 14, 1941	*Fuehrer* Headquarters	On a Substantial Reduction in Personnel and Equipment following the Defeat of Soviet Russia
33.	July 19, 1941	*Fuehrer* Headquarters	Orders for Continued Operations on the Eastern Front
33a.	July 23, 1941	*Fuehrer* Headquarters	On Additional Attacks in the East
34.	July 30, 1941	*Fuehrer* Headquarters	Change of Strategy in Respect to the Moscow Front

34a.	Aug. 12, 1941	*Fuehrer* Headquarters	Supplementary Orders for the Various Fronts in Russia
35.	Sept. 6, 1941	*Fuehrer* Headquarters	Army Group Center to Go Over to the Offensive; Army Group North to Capture Leningrad
36.	Sept. 22, 1941	*Fuehrer* Headquarters	Objectives in the Arctic Theater of War
37.	Oct. 10, 1941	*Fuehrer* Headquarters	Reorganization of "D" Forces in the North
38.	Dec. 22, 1941	*Fuehrer* Headquarters	Transfer of an Entire Air Corps to the Central Mediterranean
39.	Dec. 8, 1941	*Fuehrer* Headquarters	Winter Defense on the Eastern Front
40.	Mar. 23, 1942	*Fuehrer* Headquarters	Response to a Possible Enemy Landing on Coastal Areas
41.	Apr. 5, 1942	*Fuehrer* Headquarters	Spring Campaign 1942 against Soviet Russia
42.	May 29, 1942	*Fuehrer* Headquarters	Special Instructions for Operations Against Unoccupied France and the Iberian Peninsula
43.	July 11, 1942	*Fuehrer* Headquarters	Preparation for New Operations in the Crimea
44.	July 21, 1942	*Fuehrer* Headquarters	Operations on the Finnish Plains
45.	July 23, 1942	*Fuehrer* Headquarters	Additional Orders on *Operations Brunswick*, Attack on the Caucasus
46.	Aug. 18, 1942	*Fuehrer* Headquarters	Instructions for Counteracting Partisans in Occupied Russia
47..	Dec. 28, 1942	*Fuehrer* Headquarters	German Counter Measures in the Southeast
48.	July 26, 1943	*Fuehrer* Headquarters	Instructions for Measures to Be Taken in the Mediterranean

49.	Sept. 28, 1943	*Fuehrer* Headquarters	*Operation Alaric:* Instructions for Procedures in Italy
50.	Sept. 28, 1943	*Fuehrer* Headquarters	Instructions for Operations in North Finland and North Norway
51.	Nov. 3, 1943	*Fuehrer* Headquarters	Possibility of a Two-Front War

[*From this point on the directives were unnumbered. By this time Hitler had lost the initiative for an offensive war and his armies were now on the defensive. The more important directives follow.*]

-	Jan. 28, 1944	— — —	Instructions for the Battle of Rome
-	Mar. 8, 1944	*Fuehrer* Headquarters	Commandants to Organize New Fortified Areas
-	Apr. 2, 1944	— — —	Holding a Defensive Line in the East
-	May 16, 1944	*Fuehrer* Headquarters	Use of Secret Weapons Against England
-	July 12, 1944	*Fuehrer* Headquarters	Problems on the Coordination of Shipping
-	July 13, 1944	— — —	Definition of Authority of Party and Army on Invasion of Europe
-	July 19, 1944	*Fuehrer* Headquarters	Preparation for Defense of the Third Reich
-	July 23, 1944	*Fuehrer* Headquarters	Reorganization of Command for Army Group North
-	July 26, 1944	Teleprint	Three Orders on the Defense of the Alpine Approaches in Northern Italy
-	Aug. 24, 1944	Teleprint	Defense of Belgium in the West
-	Aug. 29, 1944	— — —	Completion of Defenses in the German Bight
-	Sept. 1, 1944	Teleprint	Defense of the New West Wall

-	Sept. 3, 1944	Teleprint	Directions to Command-in-Chief West
-	Sept. 12, 1944	Teleprint	Defense of Austria
-	Sept. 22, 1944	— — —	Operations Inside the Third Reich
-	Nov. 28, 1944	*Fuehrer* Headquarters	Command for Units in Isolation
-	Jan. 21, 1945	Teleprint	Draconian Punishment for Inexact Reporting by Commanders
-	Jan. 28, 1945	Teleprint	Orders for the *Volksturm,* Emergency and Reserve Units
-	Feb. 5, 1945	Teleprint	Transport of Refugees from the East to Denmark
-	Mar. 20, 1945	Teleprint	Demolitions and Scorched Earth Policy
-	Apr. 7, 1945	Teleprint	Reorganized Command in the West
-	Apr. 15, 1945	— — —	Reorganization of Command in North and South Germany
-	Apr. 15, 1945	— — —	*Fuehrer* Order of the Day to Soldiers on the Eastern Front: "At this moment, when Fate has removed from the earth the greatest criminal of the day [President Franklin D. Roosevelt], the turning point of the war will be decided."

97. Order of Battle of the Thirty-Nine *Waffen-SS* Divisions in World War II, 1939-1945

Hitler regarded the *Waffen-SS;* or the Armed-SS, as the elite striking arm of the *Wehrmacht.* Many of its divisions took part in the major engagements of World War II. Division titles often had a patriotic connotation and sometimes were based on racial composition. The *SS-Division* was composed of German volunteers; the *SS-Freiwillingendivision* of racial Germans or Germanic volunteers; the *Division der Waffen-SS* of East Europeans. The main categories included the *Grenadierdivision* (infantry division); *Panzergrenadierdivision* (motorized infantry division); *Gebirgdivision* (mountain division); and *Kavallieriedivision* (cavalry division).

Title	Date of Origin	Composition	Final Disposition
1. SS-PANZERDIVISION-LEIBSTANDARTE ADOLF HITLER	1933	Germans	Surrendered, 1945
2. SS-PANZERDIVISION-DAS REICH	1939	Germans	Surrendered, 1945
3. SS-PANZERDIVISION-TOTENKOPF (DEATH'S HEAD)	1940	Germans	Surrendered, 1945
4. SS-POLIZEI-PANZERGRENADIERDIVISION-POLIZEI DIVISION	1940	Germans	Surrendered, 1945
5. SS-PANZERDIVISION-WIKING (VIKING)	1940	Germans	Surrendered, 1945
6. SS-GEBIRGSDIVISION-NORD (NORTH)	1940	Germans	Surrendered, 1945

7.	SS-FREIWILLIGEN-GEBIRGSDIVISION-PRINZ EUGEN	1942	Racial Germans	Surrendered, 1945
8.	SS-KAVALLERIEDIVISION-FLORIAN GEYER	1942	Germans/Racial Germans	Surrendered, 1945
9.	SS-PANZERDIVISION-HOHENSTAUFEN	1943	Germans	Surrendered, 1945
10.	SS-PANZERDIVISION-FRUNDSBERG	1943	Germans	Surrendered, 1945
11.	SS-FREIWILLIGEN-PANZERGRENADIERDIVISION-NORDLAND	1942	Germans/Scandinavians	Surrendered, 1945
12.	SS-PANZERDIVISION-HITLER JUGEND	1943	Germans	Surrendered, 1945
13.	WAFFEN-GEBIRGDIVISION DER SS-HANDSCHAR	1943	Yugoslavs	Dissolved, 1944
14.	WAFFEN-GRENADIERDIVISION DER SS-GALIZISCHE NO. 1 (GALICIAN NO. 1)	1943	Ukrainians	Surrendered, 1945
15.	WAFFEN-GRENADIERDIVISION DER SS-LETTISCHE NO. 1 (LATVIAN NO. 1)	1943	Latvians/Germans	Surrendered, 1945
16.	SS-PANZERGRENADIERDIVISION-REICHSFUEHRER-SS	1943	Germans/Racial Germans	Surrendered, 1945
17.	SS-PANZERGRENADIERDIVISION-GÖTZ VON BERLICHINGEN	1943	Germans/Racial Germans	Surrendered, 1945
18.	SS-FREIWILLIGEN-PANZERGRENADIERDIVISION-HORST WESSEL	1944	Germans/Racial Germans	Surrendered, 1945
19.	WAFFEN-GRENADIERDIVISION DER SS-LETTISCHE NO. 2 (LATVIAN NO. 2)	1944	Latvians	Surrendered, 1945
20.	WAFFEN-GRENADIERDIVISION DER SS-ESTNISCHE NO. 1 (ESTONIAN NO. 1)	1944	Estonians	Surrendered, 1945
21.	WAFFEN-GEBIRGSDIVISION DER SS-ALBANISCHE NO. 1 (ALBANIAN NO. 1) SKANDERBERG	1944	Albanians	Dissolved, 1944
22.	SS-FREIWILLIGEN-KAVALLERIEDIVISION-MARIA THERESA	1944	Racial Germans/Germans	Surrendered, 1945

23a. WAFFEN-GEBIRGSDIVISION DER SS- KAMA (CROATIAN NO. 2)	1944	Yugoslavs	Dissolved, 1944
23b. SS-FREIWILLIGEN- PANZERDIVISION- NEDERLAND (NETHERLANDS)	1945	Dutch	Surrendered, 1945
24. WAFFEN-GEBIRGSDIVISION DER SS- KARSTJÄGER	1944	Italians/ Racial Germans	Dissolved, 1945
25. WAFFEN-GRENADIERDIVISION DER SS-HUNYADI NO. 1 (HUNGARIAN NO. 1)	1944	Hungarians	Vanished
26. WAFFEN-GRENADIERDIVISION DER SS-HUNYADI NO. 2 (HUNGARIAN NO. 2)	1944	Hungarians	Vanished
27. SS-FREIWILLIGEN- GRENADIERDIVISION- LANGEMARCK (FLEMISH NO. 1)	1945	Flemings/ Belgians	Surrendered, 1945
28. SS-FREIWILLIGEN- GRENADIERDIVISION- WALLONIE (WALLOON)	1945	Walloons- Belgians	Surrendered, 1945
29a. WAFFEN GRENADIERDIVISION- DER SS- RUSSISCHE NO. 1 (RUSSIAN NO. 1)	1944	Russians	Made part of Vlasov Army, 1944
29b. WAFFEN-GRENADIERDIVISION DER SS- ITALISCHE NO. 1 (ITALIAN NO. 1)	1945	Italians	Vanished, 1945
30. WAFFEN-GRENADIERDIVISION DER SS- RUSSISCHE NO. 2 (RUSSIAN NO. 2)	1944	Russians	Made part of Vlasov Army, 1944
31. SS-FREIWILLIGEN- GRENADIERDIVISION	1945	Germans	Surrendered, 1945
32. SS-FREIWILLIGEN- PANZERDIVISION- BÖHMEN-MAHREN (BOHEMIA-MORAVIA)	1945	Germans/ Racial Germans	Surrendered, 1945
33. WAFFEN-GRENADIERDIVISION DER SS- JANUARY 30	1945	Germans	Surrendered, 1945
34. WAFFEN-GRENADIERDIVISION DER SS- CHARLEMAGNE	1945	French	Defeated at Berlin, 1945
35. SS-FRIEWILLIGEN- GRENADIERDIVISION- LANDSTORM NEDERLAND	1945	Dutch	Dissolved, 1945

36.	SS-POLIZEI-	1945	German	Dissolved, 1945
	GRENADIERDIVISION- DER SS		Policemen	
37.	WAFFEN-GRENADIERDIVISION-	1945	Germans	Surrendered, 1945
	DIRLEWANGER			
38.	SS-FREIWILLINGEN-	1945	Racial	Surrendered, 1945
	KAVALLIERIEDIVISION-		Germans	
	LÜTZOW			
39.	SS-PANZERGRENADIERDIVISION-	1945	SS cadets	Surrendered, 1945
	NIBELUNGEN			

98. Defeat at Sea: The *Graf Spee* Is Scuttled in Montevideo Harbor, December 17, 1939

"She's going down! She's going down by the stern!"

Panzerschiff Graf Spee, launched at Wilhelmshafen in 1934, was the pride of Nazi Germany and the symbol of her renascence as a naval power. The third and latest of Germany's pocket battleships, she had been designed by technicians to circumvent the Treaty of Versailles, which had limited German warships to no more than 10,000 tons displacement. In this ship, German designers had produced a fast, light, heavily armored battleship unmatched for its size in firing power and speed.

When World War II began, the *Graf Spee,* with Captain Hans Langdorff in command and with a crew of 1,107 aboard, sailed the southern seas to prey on Allied commerce. The British finally caught up with her on December 13, 1939. The German warship was badly mauled by a British heavy cruiser, the *Exeter,* and two light cruisers, the *Ajax* and the *Achilles.* Captain Langdorff sought refuge in the nearby neutral waters of Montevideo Harbor.

While the British ships lay outside to resume the battle, Uruguayan authorities ordered Langdorff to leave by December 17. The entire world waited in suspense. On Sunday afternoon, December 17, word came from Hitler to destroy the ship.

A radio report on what happened was sent to the American people by James Bowen, manager of the American Club in Montevideo, who had been pressed into service by the National Broadcasting Company. The club manager turned radio reporter sent in an extraordinary account by short-wave radio. It was good news for

Courtesy of the National Broadcasting Company.

the British. For the Germans, who had become inured to Nazi successes, it was a portent of worse news to come.

BOWEN. — There's been quite a little of excitement all day. It's been going back and forth — being pushed around. I had to cut off of one broadcast, due to almost falling in the water with the amplifier and microphone and all the equipment — it's being pushed by the crowd. There's been a crowd of 70 to 100,000 people or more pushing around the dock in and around the Maldonado all day long.

It looks now that the War of Nerves is absolutely over. We just gave you the Flash News Report since the *Graf Spee* had scuttled the ship — as we call it — had blown itself up. What method was used we can't tell you at the moment. The ship is 5 miles out, and all we can see at the present moment at the shore here is a lot of smoke and flame. The launches leaving the ship — we tried to get it with the glasses. The smoke seemed to overcast the action. She's still afloat; pieces of her have gone up; the hull is still afloat, and the *Tacoma* which left, as we wired you a short time ago, left shortly after the craft, is trying to stand by her. It's without doubt that the *Tacoma*, also being loaded with fuel oil, will very possibly take fire and also go up.

The launches trying to get away. Evidently, the report that we gave you of scuttling the ship was the truth, and the crew being transferred suddenly seemed to be in a terrible position being aboard the *Tacoma*.

The question of burning to death instead of being blown to death. It's been quite a time down here. A question of nerves — postponements of sailing hours, incoming ships, outgoing ships, everything being used as a method of postponing the inevitable.

The *Graf* left here a short time ago this afternoon before it began to get dusk and dropped anchor 5 miles off the coast. At that time there were two Argentine ships very close to the entrance of the La Plata River. The crew was standing off. The cruisers were known to be very close to the English banks just to the South.

The ship is moving — rolling from side to side. There goes another explosion! The bow is brought up. Evidently, the powder magazine has caught fire. She's going down! She's going down by the stern! The stern is completely under water! Flames are still shooting up in the air! Smoke! Evidently, this wasn't what we call exactly scuttling the ship, because the nautical term "scuttling a ship" is opening the sea valves and letting in the water. These boys evidently are making a good job of it and leaving nothing but the pieces. They aren't going to leave anything anyone can reclaim whatsoever.

Without a doubt there'll be no reclamation for any of the sailors. This afternoon in our broadcast we told you of the transfer of some of the sailors to the hospital, a transfer of 31 sailors to the hospital. It may be possible that those are the only sailors who'll remain of the pocket cruiser *Graf Spee*.

She's going down by the fore part. The bow is under! She seems to raise a little bit at the stern. That is possibly due to seeing it from here. Naturally, that would throw her bow a little bit in the air. Now she seems to be settling — going down a little bit. She's just about where we can see the afterstern gone completely. Part of the superstructure is gone. The stack is still there. She's down in the water due to the low depth of water. Her superstructure is out of the water. She is absolutely on the bottom. Only thing showing now is her superstructure, her stack, and part of her battle tower above water.

We have just received information which is not official and will probably need a long time to be confirmed. The confirmation or rumor is, or the advice which we'll have to accept as the rumor at the moment, the advice is that the explosion of the *Graf Spee* was done at the dictation of Mr. Hitler — absolutely. That of course will have to be proven in time like a number of things in the last war that we waited 20 years to find the truth. However, the first naval battle in this war fought in South American waters has probably come to its conclusion. And the heroism of all the sailors who took part in that battle is very well-known, especially the boys who are now in hospitals. They will have some memory, and the other boys will have none. We may possibly have another battle, if maritime reports are correct that the *Admiral Scheer* and the *Deutschland* are enroute to South American waters with a convoy of submarines and will be met by at least one-third of the British Fleet.

The flame — the *Graf Spee* is still a-flame so it's very hard to say whether or not anything will be saved due to the water action — possibly the action of the water will save something. It's a very strange sight having, as I have, seen the *Graf Spee* about 4 hours after her arrival in Montevideo, having made at least 10 trips around the *Graf Spee* in the last 3 days — noticing the changes and the checking up of the shell holes, repainting — and as we described last night, the work, the welding of plates. It brings about the logical suggestion that the decision to blow up the *Graf Spee* must have been made as a last-minute resort.

We are unable at the moment to determine what is happening to the crew even with glasses, due to the movement of launches and the movement of two or three tugs which left the harbor here after the *Graf Spee* had gone out. All the launches seem to be getting to the *Tacoma*. Whether the *Tacoma* is unloading the sailors that were transferred to her to the launches, it's impossible to define at the moment even with glasses. There's a lot of action, and the crowd around here are just about crowding us into the water. We are in a very bad way. However, we'll do the best we can. It's awfully hard to describe this. We know more or less what is going on, but we don't want to tell you what we think is going on. We want to tell you what we can see, and we can't see a great deal, due to the excessive action and movement. At least 300,000 people are here on the "rambler" as we call it—a wide highway wider even than the boardwalk at Atlantic City—and it's absolutely blocked—it's impossible to move.

You can't walk in one direction or another—you just have to follow the swing of the crowd. It's completely full of automobiles and people—accidents are happening. Now here come the tugboats from Montevideo. All the tugboats that have fought are borrowed to go to the assistance of the sailors. It's very hard for the tug to go on after the search. They're doing what they can. I think they're going to get very little myself, because I don't think they'll pick up much except pieces. It'll be sometime before there's anything done about the hull unless she's a menace to navigation. If she is, at that time they'll just give her a little more dynamite, and that will be all.

The *Graf* seems to be settling a little bit at the moment. It may be possible that the rest of her may go.

ANNOUNCER. — This is NBC in New York. You've been listening, ladies and gentlemen, to another in the series of the NBC On the Spot broadcasts. James Bowen, NBC's representative in Montevideo, Uruguay, has told us of the sinking of the *Graf Spee* and of the condition of the German supply ship *Tacoma*. The voice of Mr. Bowen was heard in the United States via RCA Communications.

Keep tuned to your favorite NBC station for the latest news. This is the National Broadcasting System.

99. The Nazi War Machine Crushes Norway: Correspondent Leland Stowe Tells the Story of a Paralyzing Conquest, April 9, 1940

"Norwegian people were stunned as the Belgian
people might have been stunned in 1914."

The so-called phony war during the winter of 1939–1940, in which neither Germany nor France and England moved, came to a sudden end on April 9th, 1940. On that day, Hitler sent his legions crashing into Denmark and Norway, and within a few days he was master of both countries.

Hitler regarded Scandinavia as vital to his cause. Sweden quickly announced her neutrality, which the *Fuehrer* grudgingly accepted as long as he could have access to Swedish ore. But control of Denmark and Norway was equally important, for they could provide the Third Reich with bases for air assaults on Britain, harbors for German naval units, and additional sources of food. At the same time, by holding both Denmark and Norway, Hitler could deny Britain the food products it needed desperately.

To confuse the Allies, Hitler sent a heavy concentration of troops to the Western front and the Swiss border. Then, early on the morning of April 9, 1940, he struck at both Scandinavian countries. Denmark fell within a few hours, Norway within twelve hours.

A week later, on April 16, American war correspondent Leland Stowe sent a historic dispatch to the *Chicago Daily News* describing the story behind the conquest.

STOCKHOLM, April 16 — For the first time the story behind Germany's paralyzing twelve-hour conquest of vital Norwegian ports on Tuesday, April

---

Baltimore Evening Sun, April 16, 1940. Courtesy of the *Chicago Daily News.*

9, can be told. Between midnight and noon on the bewildering day, Norway's capital, all her principal seaports and her most strategic coastal defenses fell into German hands like an overripe plum.

Norwegian people were stunned as the Belgian people must have been stunned in 1914, and most of them still have not the slightest conception of how this incomprehensible tragedy could have happened.

I spent these hours in Oslo, together with the only other American newspapermen who were on the spot — Warren Irvin, of National Broadcasting Company, and Edmund Stevens, of the *Christian Science Monitor* — and we ourselves could scarcely believe the evidence of our own eyes.

But I had to remain in Oslo through four days of German occupation to learn how this miracle of lightning naval and military occupation was made possible. Then I could scarcely believe my ears. After that, with the last train connections to Sweden severed, Irvin and myself decided to try somehow to get across the border. It was the only possible way to give a detailed account of the most astonishing thing that has happened since the second World War began.

Norway's capital and great seaports were not captured by armed force. They were seized with unparalleled speed by means of a gigantic conspiracy which must undoubtedly rank among the most audacious, most perfectly oiled political plots of the past century.

By bribery and extraordinary infiltration on the part of Nazi agents and by treason on the part of a few highly placed Norwegian civilian and defense officials, the German dictatorship built a Trojan horse inside of Norway. Then, when the hour struck, the German plotters spiked the guns of most of the Norwegian Navy and reduced its formidable fortresses to impotence.

Absolute control of only a handful of key men in administrative positions and the navy was necessary to turn the trick and everything had been faultlessly prepared. The conspiracy was about ninety per cent according to schedule. Only in two or three places was it marred by unexpected hitches, but Norway's sea gates were already wide open.

For the success of the German plan, the capture of three key cities was essential, these being Oslo, Bergen and Narvik. It is known that Narvik was betrayed to the Germans by its commanding officer. How Bergen's harbor defenses were taken remains a mystery, as far as I can learn. But most important of all to the Nazi plot was the immediate domination of Oslo fjord with its mighty fortresses and the forcing of its virtually impregnable narrows at Drobak, together with the seizure of the great Norwegian naval base at Horten.

Only in this manner could the Germans penetrate to Oslo and deliver an almost irreparable blow to Norway's parliamentary government. To seize all of Oslo fjord and force its narrows would have appeared impossible to any foreign government except the Nazi dictatorship, but by methods even more astonishingly efficient than those which it used against Austria and Czechoslovakia the inconceivable was accomplished. Until now, I believe, the outside world has had to guess how it was done.

To understand the conspiracy's scope one must go back somewhere near the climax of the plot. In Oslo I learned, on the most reliable authority, that Germany's sea forces and troop ships sailed from German ports for their Norwegian adventure during the night of Thursday, April 4 — three full days before the British mined the upper Norwegian coast between Bergen and Narvik.

I also was informed with impressive assurance that the German Army chiefs strongly opposed Fuehrer Adolf Hitler on the plan to invade Norway because they insisted that communication lines for an army of occupation in Norway would be most dangerously limited and exposed. Nazi radical leaders supported der Fuehrer and the decision was taken against the regular army chief's counsels.

On Friday night, April 5, while the German fleet and transports already were streaming toward Norway, an event of enormous historical importance occurred in Oslo and, until now, has probably never been reported. The German legation held a soiree to which it invited 200 persons representing Norway's influential personalities. All the members of the Government were invited, as well as many officers of the defensive forces, leading bankers, shipping executives and industrialists. The invitation emphasized the importance of the soiree by reading, "White ties, uniforms and decorations."

Despite the great formality imposed, it was no official dinner. Norway's elite had been invited to see an "unusually interesting film." It proved to be the motion picture, "Baptism of Fire," depicting in the most graphic details Germany's aerial destruction in Poland. For more than an hour the distinguished Norwegian audience sat in icy silence, gripped by the horror of many of the scenes. Afterward the German Minister explained that the film was not a war, but a peace, film, since it showed what nations which elected peace would save their people from suffering. The Norwegians left the German Legation that night filled with gloomy, ominous thoughts.

In Oslo I learned that Major Vidkun Quisling, leader of the pro-Nazi Norwegian party, called the Camling, and now Premier of the so-called National Government set up after the German occupation, was in Berlin at the time the film was shown in Oslo and while the expedition was being organized. He returned to Oslo on Saturday, April 6. On Sunday night the British sowed mine fields below Narvik. On Monday Berlin's press flamed against this provocation. In the first hours of Tuesday, April 9, Norway's naval defenses were betrayed to the German fleet and the first German troops landed at Fornebo, Oslo's airport, a few hours after daybreak.

This brings us to the methods by which Oslo fjord and Oslo itself were captured from the sea early in the morning hours of April 9. The Germans could not enter without controlling the vital Norse naval base at Horten. At 1:30 o'clock that morning — three and a half hours before Berlin's ultimatum was handed to Foreign Minister Dr. Halvdan Koht — the commander of three Norwegian warships at Horten received an urgent message. It was supposedly signed by Dr. Koht himself and accepted as coming direct from the Government via the Ministry of Foreign Affairs. It ordered Norwegian ships which were about to come up the fjord and to put all their men ashore immediately — without their arms.

Without questioning the origin of the order, the commander ordered all his men ashore except stokers and messmen.

From here on a slight hitch which was costly for the Germans occurred. The Norse minelayer *Olaf Trygvason* had unexpectedly put in for repairs the previous evening. Its presence apparently was unknown to the leaders of the conspiracy in Oslo. This was the only Norwegian war vessel which did not receive the order and so remained in condition to fight. Afterward the Norwegian sailor who verified these developments declared, "It was only through treason that the Germans got in."

Meanwhile, an even greater coup had been scored by the plotters. The narrows of Oslo fjord were mainland controlled from Drobak. About 11:30 o'clock in the morning of April 9 these mines were all rendered harmless by being electrically disconnected from the Drobak central. The mystery of who ordered this done remained unsolved when I left Oslo, but this move enabled the German cruiser to penetrate the narrows before dawn.

At 4:30, still half an hour before the German Minister handed the ultimatum to Dr. Koht, a German cruiser believed to have been the *Emden*, accompanied by two submarines, reached Horten. The three Norse war vessels were completely helpless but the little mine layer, *Olaf Trygvason*, blocked the entrance to the narrows. It immediately discharged torpedoes and sank the cruiser and a submarine. It was reported, though I was unable to confirm this, that the cruiser *Blücher* also was sunk by the narrows fort, called Oskarsborg.

In any case, all other crews were ashore without arms at Horten, and by daybreak the Germans landed marines and seized Horten. The way through the narrows was open and Oslo defenseless from the sea.

I talked to another Norwegian who was a member of the Horten naval base that night. He confirmed all the main details of the above events, including the fact that two German cruisers were sunk.

"Later the Germans got about one hundred men ashore," he related. "There was some fighting. We had four men killed; the Germans two. but there was nothing we could do. The officers on our ships ran up white flags. We didn't know why and I still don't know why. We thought they had orders from the Government."

In this fashion Norway's capital was betrayed from within and the German occupation of Oslo assured before its Government knew what had happened or Parliament had courageously refused to capitulate.

Before the Germans' capture of Horten the Oslo Government had already ordered mobilization as a precaution. Accordingly, before daybreak on April 9 scores of young Norwegians reported at the Horten railroad station. They were immediately surrounded by the German marines landing party and placed aboard other German ships which came up.

When German warships approached the formidable Oskarsborg fortress, at the narrows above Horten, so it was stated there afterward, they radioed the fortress commander not to shoot. According to report, the Nazis said, "We've got your own men aboard." The fortress guns remained silent and the German warships passed into Oslo's inner harbor. The occupation of Oslo was then inevitable.

Meanwhile, we had spent an eerie night in Oslo's Grand Hotel with a succession of air alarms, the first of which sounded at 12:35 o'clock in the morning, about the time mobilization was ordered. At first I could not believe my ears, as the sirens were so different from those in Helsinki. They sounded like motor cars honking in a traffic jam. Later Stevens and I decided that the Norwegians were only air-alarming as a precaution. So I refused to get up until 7 o'clock, when a Finnish diplomat informed me of the ultimatum and the Government's decision to leave.

At 7:45 o'clock, while we still had not the slightest idea what had happened in Oslo fjord and at Horten, five Nazi bombers suddenly came roaring over the rooftops, so low they almost touched them. We watched them some, expecting bombs momentarily. For two and a half hours German planes dived over the city, always only three or five in number. They were intended to terrorize the population into surrender and the authorities into inaction while the first troops landed by air at Fornebo outside the city.

Thousands of Osloans gazed curiously and fearfully, but no panic occurred. None of us dreamed that German warships were in the inner harbor and that Oslo was already doomed. We still thought that British ships and planes might come at any moment. It seemed utterly incredible that the narrows of Oslo fjord could have been forced by the Germans, and its powerful forts silenced.

The same madness of incomprehensible events continued all day long. First was mystification over the complete lack of defense of the city by its naval forces and coastal forts. Then it was the immunity of the low-flying Nazi planes to thousands of machine-gun bullets which pattered almost incessantly until about 10 o'clock. Then it was the further fact that only one anti-aircraft battery seemed to be firing against the German planes, and this became silent after firing only a few shells, all of which were inexplicably wide of the mark.

Finally, at 10:30 o'clock, came an equally fantastic lull in which German planes only circled occasionally and absolutely nothing seemed to happen. Tens of thousands of people clustered in the streets and on the sidewalks, looked and waited, utterly baffled. We all asked where were the British, but also where were the Germans.

Meanwhile, I had a great battle to get the telegraph office to accept a dispatch without a special Government press card.

At 9 o'clock in the morning Stevens and myself could find no responsible chief at his post in the telegraph building, only groups of perplexed employes standing in the corridors—those few who had reported for work. It was only through the personal intervention of Raymond Cox, first secretary, who remained in charge of the American Legation, that our first dispatches were finally accepted, and the only ones which were allowed to pass for more than twenty-four hours.

But Norway's capital in every quarter was the scene of dazed disorganization, completely without leadership. Apparently even the men who had been called to the colors did not know where to go or simply forgot about it. The streets were filled with men of fighting age, all standing watching the German planes, waiting and speculating, but doing nothing and going nowhere.

It was like this until 2:30 o'clock in the afternoon. Then, as I rushed up to the hotel desk, a porter asked me, "Aren't you going out to see the Germans come in?"

"What do you mean, the Germans?"

"Yes, they are marching up Carl Johan Boulevard any minute now."

I called Irvin and Stevens and we rushed outside into the strangest conceivable scene. Oslo's beautiful main boulevard was jammed with people all flocking to see the Germans come in. Strangest of all, Norwegian policemen were calmly forming lines along the sidewalks and clearing the streets for the Germans' triumphal entry. One of the policemen told me that the Germans would be there within ten minutes.

All this and what followed I told in a dispatch which was filed that afternoon—but the Germans had just taken over the telegraph building and I learned two days later that not a line of my dispatch was every sent. Meanwhile, we supposed that the world knew most of the story.

We waited half an hour on the hotel balcony with an excellent view all the way up the boulevard to its beginning, at the foot of the hill on which the royal palace stands. Shortly before 3 o'clock, two trucks filled with a dozen German soldiers rolled up the street. The soldiers lolled in them, with their guns dangling, as if they had been assured that they had not the slightest resistance to fear. From the rear of the second truck two machine guns poked their noses meaningfully straight down the boulevard. Their operators lay prone with intent, hard faces, ready to fire. This was the only show of force, and all that was needed.

At 3 o'clock there was a murmur through the crowd. We could see two mounted men swinging into the boulevard in front of the palace, then six more, then the head of a marching column in field gray. The mounted men were Norwegian policemen actually escorting the German troops which were occupying the capital. We looked uncomprehendingly. Later I was told that Norwegian policemen never carry any kinds of arms. This was also why they failed to fulfill the Government's order to arrest Major Quisling.

The German column marched steadily nearer through a lane of 20,000 or 30,000 Osloans, fully half of which were men of military age. A tall, broad-shouldered officer, Gen. Nikolaus von Falkenhorst, and two other officers marched directly behind the mounted police. Then came the German regulars in columns of threes, as if to make the line look as long as possible. One of nine carried light machine guns; all toted compact aluminum kits and bulky shoulder packs.

They were hard-muscled, stony-faced men. They marched with guns on their shoulders, with beautiful precision. Mostly, they stared straight ahead, but some could not restrain triumphant smiles toward the onlookers. Several times General von Falkenhorst and the other two officers returned Nazi salutes from persons in the crowd who must have been German advance agents who had been busy in Oslo for weeks before the crowning moment. From our hotel balcony two Nazis gave the salute. I noticed in particular the beaming face of a chic, slim, blond German woman whose husband had been very active in our hotel since we arrived on the previous Thursday.

It was a thin, unbelievably short column. It required only six or seven minutes to march past. It was composed of only two incomplete battalions — less than 1,500 men in all. Norway's capital of nearly 300,000 inhabitants was being occupied by a German force of approximately 1,500 men!

The last of the German troops went by without a single jeer or hiss, without a single tear noticeable on any Norwegian face. Like children, the people stared. Thousands of young men stood watching this occupation parade. Not one hand or voice was raised. We could discern no sign of resentment upon any face about us. This was the most incomprehensible thing among all the incomprehensible things of the fantastic twenty-four hours.

Somehow it seemed as if curiosity was the strongest sentiment in the throng of Osloans who watched the Germans come in. No other emotion was betrayed in the countless faces we scanned anxiously. The only indignant people we met or saw that day were foreigners. The Norwegians of Oslo seemed stunned beyond recovery. Every one acted curiously like children suddenly given a chance to see a parade of strange creatures out of prehistoric times — something which had no connection with real life. But within two hours real life was making itself felt in Oslo. The Germans had occupied the capital without dropping a bomb, without firing a shot within the city limits. They simply had paraded in and taken it over much as Frenchmen or Italians might parade into a colonial interior village somewhere in Africa. Now they went to work. It was the urgent task of the tiny force of 1,500 men to seize key places in the nation's capital. They did it swiftly, without any fear of interruption.

When I hurried into the telegraph building I had hopes. There were still no German troops guarding the door. But immediately I knew it was too late. The tip-off came when a women employee, who had always addressed me in perfect English, spoke to me in German and tried to refuse my message on the grounds that I had no special telegraph card. But her chief had already accepted my dispatch at 1 o'clock.

Finally, she accepted it reluctantly, together with $64 worth of Norwegian crowns, which had to be paid in advance. Then she told me in German that I must see Fraulein Hauge tomorrow morning or no more messages would be accepted. Of course, my own and all other dispatches for the next twenty-four hours were never sent. The Germans had closed all the wires, as well as telephone lines, to the outside world.

The next day, Wednesday, was as unbelievable as the events of April 9 had been. German troops now stood guard in the Parliament, the university, the city hall and other public buildings. My first shock came early in the morning as I passed the Storting (Parliament). Two score German soldiers filled the open windows on the third floor of the building, all singing lustily, while one pumped joyfully at his accordion. Osloans stood watching and listening on the sidewalks below. I looked closely, but as far as I could see they were simply curious and somewhat entertained.

As on the previous night after the occupation, the city's cafes were filled in almost normal fashion and a large number of young men were lolling in them as if there were no such thing as a regular Norwegian army, ready to offer resistance to an invader, only fifty miles north of the capital. Wherever we went we saw groups of young people clustered around German soldiers on guard. Some of them chatted pleasantly with the soldiers, some stared at their rifles and machine guns and asked questions about them. Many young girls gazed admiringly at the men in field-gray uniforms.

Outside the telegraph building I encountered an open car with half a dozen hardened German regulars who had a machine gun mounted for action. The crowd laughed and joked with the soldiers; one man, apparently half-intoxicated, shouted *"Deutschland über Alles!"* several times. The soldiers laughed. The chief of the machine gun crew looked down upon his admirers with an indescribable smile. He stood up proudly like a member of a conquering roman legion who realized that he had the right to do so.

Such scenes, far from infrequent, had not ended when I left Oslo on Friday. By that time, however, many young Norwegians had disappeared from the capital with packs on their backs. A great many more went when the Germans landed 20,000 troops on Oslo's quays on Thursday afternoon. This sight at last awakened many men from the daze which they had been in. Many others, however, still remained in the capital on Friday — seemingly a large part of the men.

On Wednesday evening we discovered that the Quisling government had been formed in room 430 of the Continental Hotel. I went there about a matter which was said to require the new Premier's personal decision. Three Germans in civilian clothes, and one Norwegian, were in room 430. After waiting, I saw Major Quisling very briefly, but he turned for advice to a sharp-faced German who introduced himself as Reichsamtsleiter Schoedt.

The Reichsamtsleiter decided the matter while another German assisted in giving further directions. From there, we were referred to the German Legation, where we were received courteously. It appeared that the German military censorship was not yet completely organized and nothing could be arranged about the transmission of dispatches until the next day.

Nevertheless, we made another call at the telegraph building. The public hall was deserted when we entered after passing German guards. Inside, two German privates were standing. While we wrote our cablegrams they began an exercise in mass psychology. They marched fifteen or twenty steps, slowly and calculatedly pounding the heels of their boots down on the cement floor at every step. Each step echoed loudly and menacingly against the ceiling. After a few second's pause, the two soldiers pounded their heels again.

They continued this exercise as long as we were in the hall. The echo of their hobnailed heels was amazingly eloquent.

This is how Norway's capital was captured without a bomb being dropped and without a shot being fired within several miles of the city.

I believe this to be the first story of any completeness to reach the outside world. I also believe it to be the most important newspaper dispatch I have ever had the occasion to write. It is my conviction, for the sake of history and also for the sake of the ultimate restoration of security and freedom in all three Scandinavian countries, that it is crying to be told now. I am closing it with the earnest hope that it will reach America and the outside world quickly.

100. Bombing of Rotterdam: Hitler Sets a Standard of Air Attack for Which German Cities Would Pay Heavily, May 14, 1940

"Modern warfare," said the German officer, "demands that whenever there is resistance it must be broken by all means possible."

The news was slow in coming out of the Netherlands. The German bombing of the center of Rotterdam took place on May 14, 1940. Not until six days later, on May 20, did word come to the world from the Netherlands Legation in Paris about the attack on an open city.

It was an almost incredible story. On Tuesday afternoon, May 14, two squadrons of German bombers flew over Rotterdam in close formation, and from a height of 4,500 feet dropped a cargo of delayed-action bombs on the heart of the great seaport. The city had already capitulated, but the raid, nevertheless, was carried on with savage fury. The communiqué from Paris reported: "Scenes reminiscent of Dante's 'Inferno' ensued, with fires and explosions everywhere. Buildings over an area of more than five square miles were destroyed. A moderate estimate is that in this monstrous work of destruction, horrifying as a nightmare and absolutely without precedent, at least 100,000 people must have perished."

The full story of Rotterdam was not revealed until May 23, 1940, when C. Brooks Peters, foreign correspondent for *The New York Times*, who was accompanying the German Army of Occupation in the Netherlands, wired the details to New York. The hand of German censorship shows clearly in this dispatch, especially in Peters' attention to distorted German figures on the Dutch dead and wounded and to the German explanation of the raid. Nevertheless,

The New York Times, May 23, 1940.

the report indicated that the bombing of an already capitulated city was unnecessary. German cities were destined to pay tenfold for this attack.

WITH THE GERMAN ARMY OF OCCUPATION, ROTTERDAM, May 23 — This beautiful Netherland city, principal shipping center for a far-flung Colonial empire, is today a sad skeleton of its former self. For on Tuesday, May 14, dive bombers of the German Air Force rained high explosives on approximately one square mile in the center of the city. The area bombed is a shambles with almost every single building so thoroughly razed that words cannot adequately describe the appearance of the wreckage.

Amazingly enough, the bombing occurred after the commanding Netherland general had capitulated. Negotiations had been in progress between the two commanders on surrender or evacuation of the city by Netherland troops. The defending general, it is said, after having broken off negotiations, reopened them but failed to inform the Germans in time, specifically the latters' commander.

Meantime, the Germans say, they instructed their air force to attack that part of the city allegedly occupied by troops immediately after expiration of the time limit. When they learned of the decision to surrender, the Germans declare, it was too late to recall "all the dive bombers that had set out to eject the enemy."

How many German planes were "recalled" and how many attacked is not definitely known. It is suggested by German military officials that the havoc had been worked by 27 planes in nine and one half minutes. The dive bombers did a thorough, accurate job. For they devastated and reduced to ashes the wide area they attacked without damage at all points in most places outside.

The entire central section of the city situated on the north bank of the Maas was affected. All the buildings flanking the river on the north bank were destroyed. Today they are still smoldering in some places.

It is not known how many civilians lost their lives in the holocaust — perhaps it will never be known. A German officer estimated the number at probably "several thousand" while Netherland sources placed the figure between 10,000 and 15,000. Later German figures given to us declared that 300 persons were killed and 365 wounded while 6,000 had been evacuated into the country before the attack began.

In modern warfare, a German officer explained, there are no longer "open" and "fortified" cities but merely "defended" and "undefended" cities. Rotterdam, he insisted, was "defended" and, he added, "modern warfare demands that whenever there is resistance it must be broken by all means possible."

By taking up posts within the city, Germans declare, the defenders exposed themselves and their city to this fate.

We drove through ruins patrolled by armed Netherland police. The faces of pedestrians were sober, pensive, somber. Coolsingle Street, whose tall buildings mostly had housed banks and business concerns, was reduced to street level. The telegraph building, although damaged, and a new modern 12-story apartment house unscathed except for broken windows, were almost the only upright buildings in the vicinity. The clock in the telegraph building had stopped at 4:30.

Small canals in this sector were filled with debris, broken bits of furniture and household furnishings. In the sectors adjoining the immediate center of attack, weary civilians were salvaging what remained of their belongings.

Germans who had taken up posts on the south bank of the Maas say Netherlanders destroyed whole blocks of buildings on the north side of the river to be able to cover the main bridge. Neutrals in Rotterdam believe the Germans were correct in this assertion. Netherland artillery, the Germans declare, stationed behind defensive positions fired at the Germans over the central part of the city and the river.

Tied to a wharf and camouflaged, the liner *Statendam* was still burning. Germans allege she was set afire by British and Netherland shells. Fighting within Rotterdam, Germans say, began at 8 A.M. on May 14. The Netherland commander procrastinated about evacuation or surrender, they declare, because he hoped reinforcements from the Utrecht sector would arrive in time to assist him.

We drove to Rotterdam in German Army cars from Dusseldorf, after a night almost three hours of which were spent in air-raid shelters, crossing the frontier near Gennep. Soon we came to the first line of defense, the Peel Line. All the way to Rotterdam, however, we saw few traces of heavy fighting, although almost every bridge had been blown up in a futile endeavor to hold up the German advance.

Barbed wire was everywhere, but heavy steel and concrete and wooden obstacles placed across the streets to impede the German advance had been pushed aside by German sappers. Bunkers that we saw along the road leading from Gennep via Hertogenbusch, Tilburg, Breda and Dordrecht to Rotterdam appeared to have been taken for the most part without a struggle. . . .

Germans say the very speed of their invasion rendered it merciful to the human pawns who sought to obstruct their passage. For, they say, only 100 Netherland soldiers were killed and 850 wounded in the entire campaign.

Neutral observers of the invasion allege that the Fifth Column played an important role in the occupation, diverting the attention of the troops in

The Hague and Rotterdam for some time. Ensconced in roof tops and windows, Netherland National Socialists fired on the Netherland defenders, who were obliged to divide their forces all over the interior towns in an effort to clean up this unlooked for enemy within. . . .

Through the entire campaign, it is said, only 700 British soldiers were on Netherland soil, and 80 of them were sappers who blew up the huge oil tanks at Rotterdam.

101. Fall of France: Hitler's Hour of Triumph at Compiègne, June 21, 1940

"The Frenchmen keep their eyes straight ahead."

In June 1940, Hitler's war machine turned on France, and within a few weeks that country was prostrate at the feet of the Nazi *Fuehrer*. On June 21, 1940, at exactly the same spot where on November 11, 1918, the Armistice that ended World War I had been signed by German plenipotentiaries in a little clearing in the forest of Compiègne, the German conquerer received three French envoys and handed them the German terms. The meeting took place in Marshal Foch's private railway car, the same car in which Foch had laid down the Armistice terms to Germany in 1918. Hitler furthermore insisted that exactly the same table in the shaky old *wagon-lit* be used.

The incident was witnessed and reported by a topflight war correspondent, William L. Shirer, who had been associated with the *Chicago Tribune* at one time and was now working for the Columbia Broadcasting System. Shirer's hastily improvised account was a model of great reporting. Reading from notes, with no time to polish his account, he delivered the story in conversational style.

ANNOUNCER — At this time, as the French government considers Germany's terms for an armistice, Columbia takes you to Berlin for a special broadcast by William Shirer in Germany. We take you now to Berlin. Go ahead, Berlin.

Broadcast by William L. Shirer, Columbia Broadcasting System, June 21, 1942. Courtesy of William L. Shirer.

SHIRER—Hello, America! CBS! William L. Shirer calling CBS in New York.

William L. Shirer calling CBS in New York, calling CBS from Compiègne, France. This is William L. Shirer of CBS. We've got a microphone at the edge of a little clearing in the forest of Compiègne, four miles to the north of the town of Compiègne and about forty-five miles north of Paris. Here, a few feet from where we're standing, in the very same old railroad coach where the Armistice was signed on that chilly morning of November 11, 1918, negotiations for another armistice—the one to end the present war between France and Germany—began at 3:30 P.M., German summer time, this afternoon. What a turning back of the clock, what a reversing of history we've been watching here in this beautiful Compiègne Forest this afternoon! What a contrast to that day twenty-two years ago! Yes, even the weather, for we have one of those lovely warm June days which you get in this part of France close to Paris about this time of year.

As we stood here, watching Adolf Hitler and Field Marshal Goering and the other German leaders laying down the terms of the armistice to the French plenipotentiaries here this afternoon, it was difficult to comprehend that in this rustic little clearing in the midst of the Forest of Compiègne, from where we're talking to you now, that an armistice was signed here on the cold, cold morning at five A.M. on November 11, 1918. The railroad coach—it was Marshal Foch's private car—stands a few feet away from us here, in exactly the same spot where it stood on that gray morning twenty-two years ago, only—and what an "only" it is, too— Adolf Hitler sat in the seat occupied that day by Marshal Foch. Hitler at that time was only an unknown corporal in the German army, and in that quaint old wartime car another armistice is being drawn up as I speak to you now, an armistice designed like the other that was signed on this spot to bring armed hostilities to halt between those ancient enemies— Germany and France. Only everything that we've been seeing here this afternoon in Compiègne Forest has been so reversed. The last time the representatives of France sat in that car dictating the terms of the armistice. This afternoon we peered through the windows of the car and saw Adolf Hitler laying down the terms. That's how history reversed itself, but seldom has it done so as today on the very same spot. The German leader in the preamble of the conditions which were read to the French delegates by Colonel General von Keitel, Chief of the German Supreme Command, told the French that he had not chosen this spot at Compiègne out of revenge but merely to right a wrong.

The armistice negotiations here on the same spot where the last armistice was signed in 1918, here in Compiègne Forest, began at 3:15 P.M. our time, a warm June sun beat down on the great elm and pine trees and cast purple shadows on the hooded avenues as Herr Hitler with the German plenipotentiaries at his side appeared. He alighted from his car in front of the French monument to Alsace-Lorraine which stands at the end of an avenue about two hundred yards from the clearing here in front of us where the armistice car stands. That famous Alsace-Lorraine statue was covered with German war flags, so that you cannot see its sculptured works or read its inscriptions. I had seen it many times in the postwar years, and doubtless many of you have seen it — the large sword representing the sword of the Allies, with its point sticking into a large, limp eagle, representing the old empire of the Kaiser, and the inscription underneath in front saying, "To the heroic soldiers of France, defenders of the country and of right, glorious liberators of Alsace-Lorraine."

Through our glasses, we saw the Fuehrer stop, glance at the statue, observe the Reich war flags with their big swastikas in the center. Then he strolled slowly toward us, toward the little clearing where the famous armistice car stood. I thought he looked very solemn; his face was grave. But there was a certain spring in his step, as he walked for the first time toward the spot where Germany's fate was sealed on that November day of 1918, a fate which, by reason of his own being, is now being radically changed here on this spot.

And now, if I may sort of go over my notes — I made from moment to moment this afternoon — now Hitler reaches a little opening in the Compiègne woods where the Armistice was signed and where another is about to be drawn up. He pauses and slowly looks around. The opening here is in the form of a circle about two hundred yards in diameter and laid out like a park. Cypress trees line it all around, and behind them the great elms and oaks of the forest. This has been one of France's national shrines for twenty-two years. Hitler pauses and gazes slowly around. In the group just behind him are the other German plenipotentiaries — Field Marshal Goering grasping his Field Marshal baton in one hand. He wears the blue uniform of the air force. All the Germans are in uniform. Hitler in a double-breasted gray uniform with the Iron Cross hanging from his left breast pocket. Next to Goering are the two German army chiefs, Colonel General von Keitel, Chief of the Supreme Command, and Colonel General von Brauchitsch, Commander-in-Chief of the German Army. Both are just approaching sixty, but look younger, especially General von Keitel, who has a dapper appearance, with his cap slightly cocked on one side. Then we see there Dr. Raeder, Grand Admiral of the German Fleet. He has on a blue naval uniform and the invariable upturned stiff collar which German naval officers usually wear. We see two nonmilitary men in Hitler's suite — his Foreign Minister, Joachim von Ribbentrop, in the field-gray uniform of the Foreign Office, and Rudolf Hess, Hitler's deputy, in a gray party uniform.

The time's now, I see by my notes, 3:18 P.M. in the Forest of Compiègne. Hitler's personal standard is run up on a small post in the center of the circular opening in the woods. Also, in the center, is a great granite block which stands some three feet above the ground. Hitler, followed by the others, walks slowly over to it, steps up, and reads the inscription engraved in great high letters on that block. Many of you will remember the words of that inscription. The Fuehrer slowly reads them, and the inscription says, "Here on the eleventh of November, 1918, succumbed the criminal pride of the German Empire, vanquished by the free peoples which it tried to enslave." Hitler reads it, and Goering reads it. They all read it, standing there in the June sun and the silence. We look for the expression on Hitler's face, but it does not change. Finally he leads his party over to another granite stone, a small one some fifty yards to one side. Here it was that the railroad car in which the German plenipotentiary stayed during the 1918 armistice negotiations stood from November 8 to 11. Hitler looks down and reads the inscription, which merely says: "The German plenipotentiary." The stone itself, I notice, is set between a pair of rusty old railroad tracks, the very ones that were there twenty-two years ago.

It is now 3:23 P.M., and the German leaders stride over to the armistice car. This car, of course, was not standing on this spot yesterday. It was standing seventy-five yards down the rusty track in the shelter of a tiny museum built to house it by an American citizen, Mr. Arthur Henry Fleming of Pasadena, California. Yesterday the car was removed from the museum by the German army engineers and rolled back those seventy-five yards to the spot where it stood on the morning of November 11, 1918. The Germans stand outside the car, chatting in the sunlight. This goes on for two minutes. Then Hitler steps up into the car, followed by Goering and the others. We watch them entering the drawing room of Marshal Foch's car. We can see nicely now through the car windows.

Hitler enters first and takes the place occupied by Marshal Foch the morning the first armistice was signed. At his sides are Goering and General Keitel. To his right and left at the ends of the table we see General von Brauchitsch and Herr Hess at the one end, at the other end Grand Admiral Raeder and Herr von Ribbentrop. The opposite side of the table is still empty, and we see there four vacant chairs. The French have not yet appeared, but we do not wait long. Exactly at 3:30 P.M. the French alight from a car. They have flown up from Bordeaux to a near-by landing field and then have driven here in an auto.

They glance at the Alsace-Lorraine memorial, now draped with swastikas, but it's a swift glance. Then they walk down the avenue flanked by three German army officers. We see them now as they come into the sunlight of the clearing—General Huntziger, wearing a brief khaki uniform; General Bergeret and Vice-Admiral Le Luc, both in their respective dark-blue uniforms; and then, almost buried in the uniforms, the one single civilian of the day, Mr. Noel, French Ambassador to Poland when the present war broke out there. The French plenipotentiaries passed the guard of honor drawn up at the entrance of the clearing. The guard snapped to attention for the French but did not present arms. The Frenchmen keep their eyes straight ahead. It's a grave hour in the life of France, and their faces today show what a burden they feel on their shoulders. Their faces are solemn, drawn, but bear the expression of tragic dignity. They walked quickly to the car and were met by two German officers, Lieutenant Colonel Tippelskirch, Quartermaster General, and Colonel Thomas, Chief of the Paris Headquarters. The Germans salute; the French salute: the atmosphere is what Europeans call "correct"; but you'll get the picture when I say that we see no handshakes — not on occasions like this. The historic moment is now approaching. It is 3:32 by my watch. The Frenchmen enter Marshal Foch's Pullman car, standing there a few feet from us in Compiègne Forest. Now we get our picture through the dusty windows of the historic old *wagon-lit* car. Hitler and the other German leaders rise from their seats as the French enter the drawing room. Hitler, we see, gives the Nazi salute, the arm raised. The German officers give a military salute; the French do the same. I cannot see Mr. Noel to see whether he salutes or how. Hitler, so far as we can see through the windows just in front of here, does not say anything. He nods to General Keitel at his side. We can see General Keitel adjusting his papers, and then he starts to read. He is reading the preamble of the German armistice terms. The French sit there with marblelike faces and listen intently. Hitler and Goering glance at the green table top. This part of the historic act lasts but a few moments. I note in my notebook here this — 3:42 P.M. — that is, twelve minutes after the French arrived — 3:42 — we see Hitler stand up, salute the three with hand upraised. Then he strides out of the room, followed by Goering, General von Brauchitsch, Grand Admiral Raeder is there, Herr Hess, and, at the end, von Ribbentrop. The French remain at the green-topped table in the old Pullman car, and we see General Keitel remains with them. He is going to read them the detailed conditions of the armistice. Hitler goes, and the others do not wait for this. They walk down the avenue back towards the Alsace-Lorraine monument. As they pass the guard of honor, a German band strikes up the two national anthems *Deutschland über Alles* and the *Horst Wessel Song.*

The whole thing has taken but a quarter of an hour — this great reversal of a historical armistice of only a few years ago.

CBS ANNOUNCER — You have just heard a special broadcast from the Compiègne Forest in France, where on the historic morning of November 11, 1918, representatives of the German army received from the Allies the terms of the armistice which ended the First World War, and where today,

June 21, 1940, representatives of the French government received from Fuehrer Adolf Hitler the terms under which a cessation of hostilities between Germany and France may be reached. As you know, the actual terms presented to the French plenipotentiaries have not yet been made public.

MUSIC — *Organ*

ANNOUNCER — This is the Columbia Broadcasting System.

102. A Triumphant Hitler Makes a Peace Offer to England, June 19, 1940

". . . I am not the vanquished seeking favors, but the victor speaking in the name of reason."

On July 19, 1940, a beaming Hitler appeared before the *Reichstag* and made an offer of peace to England. He would give the British a last chance to surrender before their complete annihilation. He would be willing to arrange a commonsense peace through negotiations. All he wanted in return was recognition of his conquests and acknowledgement of his role as the arbiter of Europe. The British maintained a contemptuous silence.

The significant parts of Hitler's address follow.

. . . Mr. Churchill should perhaps by way of exception believe me this time, if I now express these words as a prophet: a great empire is on the way to destruction — and I never had the idea of ruining or harming that empire. One thing I do know — the continuation of this war can only end in the complete destruction of one of the two belligerents. Mr. Churchill may believe that that will be Germany. I know that it will be England.

In this hour I believe I am conscience bound to make a renewed appeal to England. I believe I can do this because I am not the vanquished seeking favors, but the victor speaking in the name of reason.

Mr. Churchill may well turn aside my declaration with the cry that this appeal represents only my fear and my doubts about final victory. All I can say is that I have lightened my conscience in view of what is coming.

Verhandlung des Reichstages, Stenographische Berichte, 1939–1942, vol. 460, p. 78. Translated by the editor.

103. Berlin-Rome-Tokyo Axis: The Three Have-Not Powers Sign a Ten-year Tripartite Pact, September 27, 1940

". . . to assist one another with all political, economic and military means."

Hitler regarded close relations between the Axis Powers as a military necessity and one that would win the war for the Third Reich. On September 27, 1940, plenipotentiaries of Germany, Italy, and Japan signed in Berlin a ten-year military and economic treaty, by which they pooled their armaments and promised to assist one another in event of necessity, especially if one of them became involved in war with the United States. The former Rome-Berlin Axis was thereby extended into a three-way agreement, which all three regarded as an unbeatable combination.

THE GOVERNMENTS OF Germany, Italy, and Japan, considering it as a condition precedent of any lasting peace that all nations of the world be given each its proper place, have decided to stand by and cooperate with one another in regard to their efforts in Greater East Asia and regions of Europe respectively wherein it is their prime purpose to establish and maintain a new order of things calculated to promote the mutual prosperity and welfare of the peoples concerned.

Furthermore, it is the desire of the three governments to extend cooperation to such nations in other spheres of the world as may be included to put forth endeavors along lines similar to their own, in order that their ultimate aspirations for world peace may thus be realized.

The official English translation of the treaty as quoted in *World Almanac*, 1942, p. 273.

Accordingly, the governments of Germany, Italy and Japan have agreed as follows:

ARTICLE 1. Japan recognizes and respects the leadership of Germany and Italy in establishment of a new order in Europe.

ARTICLE 2. Germany and Italy recognize and respect the leadership of Japan in the establishment of a new order in Greater East Asia.

ARTICLE 3. Germany, Italy and Japan agree to cooperate in their efforts on aforesaid lines. They further undertake to assist one another with all political, economic and military means when one of the three contracting powers is attacked by a power at present not involved in the European war or in the Chinese-Japanese conflict.

ARTICLE 4. With the view of implementing the present pact, joint technical commissions, members of which are to be appointed by the respective governments of Germany, Italy and Japan, will meet without delay.

ARTICLE 5. Germany, Italy and Japan affirm that the aforesaid terms do not in any way affect the political status which exists at present as between each of the three contracting parties and Soviet Russia.

ARTICLE 6. The present pact shall come into effect immediately upon signature and shall remain in force ten years from the date of its coming into force. At the proper time before expiration of said term the high contracting parties shall at the request of any of them enter into negotiations for its renewal.

In faith whereof, the undersigned, duly authorized by their respective governments, have signed this pact and have affixed hereto their signatures.

Done in triplicate at Berlin, the 27th day of September, 1940, in the eighteenth year of the Fascist era, corresponding to the 27th day of the ninth month of the fifteenth year of Showa [the reign of Emperor Hirohito].

104. Coventry: Massive *Luftwaffe* Attack on British Midlands Manufacturing Center, November 15, 1940

"In Coventry tonight frenzied men tore at piles of brickwork and concrete covering the bodies of their women and children."

From the days of the opening *Blitzkrieg* against Poland, Hitler counted on his air force, the *Luftwaffe*, under the command of Hermann Goering, to lead the way to final victory. In the summer of 1940, when Britain stood alone, the *Fuehrer* unleashed the full strength of his air power on the island kingdom as a preliminary step to invasion. The badly outnumbered Royal Air Force made up for its deficiency in numbers by the quality of its pilots and aircraft. In the Battle of Britain, which took place between July 10 and the end of October 1940 and which centered on London, the Germans lost 1,733 raiders, the RAF 915 aircraft.

Frustrated, Hitler at first continued bombing the ports of Dover, Bournemouth, Portsmouth, and Southampton. Then, in November 1940, he shifted his attention to the industrial midlands. Just ninety-four miles northwest of London, Coventry stood on a small hill at the confluence of several tributaries of the Avon. The city of two hundred thousand, noted for its magnificent medieval cathedral, was also a manufacturing center for motor cars, munitions, and other war materials. It was a devastating attack: a good part of the city was wrecked, and its essential services paralyzed.

Alfred Wall, *Associated Press*, November 15, 1940. Courtesy of the Associated Press. *"Der Angriff an Coventry,"* in *Fahrten und Flüge gegen England: Berichte und Bilder, herausgegeben vom Oberkommando der Wehrmacht* (Berlin, 1941), pp. 138–39. Courtesy of Zeitgeschichte Verlag. Translated by the editor.

Following are two reports on the Coventry raid. The first, an AP dispatch, gives the bare details. The second describes the assault from the German side by an anonymous war correspondent who went along on a *Luftwaffe* plane.

Report by the Associated Press

COVENTRY, ENGLAND, NOVEMBER 15 — German bombers have blasted the heart out of this once peaceful city in the English midlands with a dusk-to-dawn raid which turned parts of the city into an inferno and left at least 1,000 dead and injured.

Coventry's beautiful and famous brownstone cathedral is a smoking wreck. Only its big main spire, 303 feet high, remains standing. All the rest of the medieval structure, started in 1373 and completed in 1450, lies in a tangle of broken stone and crumpled debris.

In a quick dash tonight into the still burning sector of the stricken town, a vital industrial center, I scrambled over great piles of brick and stone.

The town was like a scene out of Hades between dusk and dawn while German raiders dumped their bombs in ceaseless relays.

A full moon shone last night, but its brilliance was dimmed by a pall of smoke and the glare of fire from burning buildings.

Scarcely a street escaped the pounding of the raiders. It was the worst continuous attack experienced by any city — including London — since the siege of Britain began.

All night long, the narrow streets where Lady Godiva rode on her horse nearly 1,000 years ago trembled and crumbled with the thunder of diving planes, the screams of bombs and their explosions and the roar of anti-aircraft cannonade.

Searchlights stabbed vainly through the shroud of smoke in an attempt to spot the invaders. Rifles and machine guns crackled as the city's defenders tried to shoot scores of flares out of the sky.

At least two hospitals were hit. There were casualties in one; in another all glass was blown from the operating theatre.

Store after store was damaged, but authorities said that supplies were not affected materially and that there would be no food shortage.

The aeronautical expert of the press association also said the Germans "failed lamentably" to hit military targets.

Several other midlands towns were raided, and in one, 24 houses were demolished, 150 damaged extensively and a bomb dropped on a school shelter full of people.

In Coventry tonight frenzied men tore at piles of brickwork and concrete covering the bodies of their women and children.

Herbert Morrison, Minister of Home Security, came from London to direct the first relief efforts. With him came his wife.

The first thing they did was to halt a frightened caravan of refugees seeking safety in the country.

The awful experience of the night before was written in the pinched faces that peered at the Minister's limousine from trucks, wagons and automobiles.

Royal Air Force pilots took fire hoses from the hands of firemen reeling with fatigue, and played streams of water on the smoldering heaps of rubble which are all that remain of some of Britain's finest examples of Tudor architecture.

A German Account

On the night of November 15, 1940, in good weather and in clear moonlight, squadrons of German aircraft made a massive attack on the English armaments center of Coventry in the Midlands. In the late evening hours the devastating effects of countless bombs could be seen in the industrially important installations of the city. The roaring attacks continued without pause until early in the morning.

Coventry—how often has this city in the heart of England been the target of individual attacks by our flyers! In good and in bad weather. In the area of this city and its sister cities of Birmingham and Wolverhampton important factories of the English armaments industry have been hit. Here tools and motors were made for British aircraft.

The night was in full moon as we came to the ready room. We had an idea that our job this time was something special. The group commander began by giving us in the beginning in brief but precise words all necessary navigational and technical weather details. This attack, he says, must be an extraordinary success for our air force. Painfully accurate flying by our own pilots and careful bombing are of the greatest importance on this mission.

Our "Caesar," heavily loaded with bombs, is the first plane of its group to get away. It takes course for England. We all know that a long, difficult flight is before us. Fortunately, the storms that had bothered us in the last few nights had disappeared. Through clear skies, some clouds, and light haze we fly toward the English coast. In this favorable weather, cities, rivers, and canals are good signposts.

We are greeted by flak on the coast. Searchlights poke excitedly through the darkness. But we hold true to our course. Our first test through the enemy flak is soon behind us. From a fair distance we recognize the London area. Other planes must have already made their visits there. There are clouds of smoke over the city and we can see the flash of exploding bombs on the ground. From a great height we can see the curve of the

Thames. A cupola of lights rises up to meet us, and the first shells burst near us. But we hold our bombs — they are destined for another target that evening.

It has become very quiet in the plane. In the enclosed stall and in the canopy men study the maps by the dull lights of their little pocket flashlights. We are surrounded by deep black night. When the Midlands come into view, the game begins again with the searchlights and the antiaircraft guns.

A cry of surprise. Far to the north of us there is a tremendous fire. Is that Coventry already? That is out target — the great fire before us must be the work of our comrades who had flown in before us. Over the burning city many trace-bombers hang in their parachutes for minutes.

The picture is becoming clearer. German bombs must have caused tremendous damage in these hours before midnight. Conversation in the plane stops. We go to the attack. Calmly the commander gives the pilot his flight directions: "A little more to the right, just a bit more. So, now we are just right."

We come closer and closer. The terrible picture comes into focus. Thick smoke hovers over the city far out into the country. We can clearly see the flames crackling. An especially large burst of flame near countless others shows that a great industrial area must have been heavily hit.

We remain over the target. Flak is shot desperately at us. Around us the lightning of exploding shells.

We look directly into the destruction and see the great craters of fire and the greater part of the industrial city in flames. At this moment we release our bombs. A shudder goes through the plane. Down below there is a brilliant flash in a new explosion. We are not the first plane in our group of German fighter planes; others were there before us. Others will follow until the dawn of the new day, which will reveal the extent of the attack on Coventry.

105. *Dolchstoss*: In His Berlin Speech Hitler Supports the Stab-in-the-Back Theory, February 1, 1941

". . . the disaster of 1918 was nothing but the result
of a rare mixture. . . ."

Immediately after the end of World War I, German nationalists proposed the *Dolchstoss,* or stab-in-the-back theory, which held that German arms had been invincible in that conflict and that Germany never could have been conquered by her external enemies. Instead, the collapse was due, they charged, to treacherous actions on the home front by the radical Social Democrats and Jews in Berlin. This was the real explanation, it was said, for the *Zerrissenheit* (dismemberment) of the German public and the real cause for the loss of the war.

From the beginning of his political career, Hitler held to the *Dolchstoss* myth and placed it at the center of his political ideology. In speech after speech he insisted that the German army had never actually been conquered in World War I, but that disintegration at home was the cause. In the pages of *Mein Kampf* and in scores of speeches he came back again and again to the theme of "defeat through lies and deceit" and "collapse due to the poisons of Marxism and Judaism." Typical of this view was this excerpt from a speech delivered by Hitler in Berlin on January 30, 1941, in the midst of World War II.

THE GREAT WAR, which shook Europe from the years of 1914 to 1918, was primarily the work of British politicians. The whole world was eventually

Deutsche Allgemeine Zeitung, February 1, 1941. Translated by the editor.

mobilized against Germany, but she was not really conquered. We need not hesitate to say that today.

I did not want to speak about the past until that moment when I had made something of myself. Today, indeed, as one of those who have done well, I am in a position to judge and to criticize the past.

I can say this — the disaster of 1918 was nothing but the result of a rare mixture of personal incompetence on the part of the leaders of our people, an unheard of mixture such as has never taken place in the past and will, I can assure you, never be repeated in the future.

The German soldier withstood the onslaught of the entire world for more than four years. He would have held out even longer, had it not been for an additional factor — the belief of the German people in the honor of the so-called "democratic world" and its politicians. The German people in those days had faith in the promises of the world that was to cause them terrible suffering.

The British may well believe that it is enough today to play those old propaganda records of 1917-1918 in order to produce new effects, but I can only say that they have forgotten nothing. Indeed, unfortunately for them, they have also not learned anything. That is where they differ from the German people. Since those days the German people have learned and they have forgotten nothing.

There have been other breaches of faith in the pages of history. But what took place in 1918, 1919, 1920, and 1921 was not simply one breach of faith, but a whole series of such breaches. It was not just a matter of breaking one promise. Indeed, not a single promise was kept. Never in the past has a great nation such as Germany been so deceived as Germany was at that time.

What did they promise to us, this believing people? And what did they do to us? We were plundered and exploited. Foreign statesmen from America were utilized in order to convince the German people. Maybe that was the reason why the German people allowed themselves to be deceived in that manner.

Now, today, the German people are immune for all time against similar assaults on us.

106. In the Midst of War Hitler Denounces Churchill as the Victim of a Paralytic Disease or Drunken Delusions, May 4, 1941

". . . the most bloodthirsty amateur strategist in all history. . . ."

Hitler reserved his most biting contempt for two rival political leaders, Franklin D. Roosevelt and Winston Churchill. In his secret conversations he declared that both were psychotic. He was certain that Churchill was "off his head."*

Again and again he spoke of his rivals in angry terms. The Foreign Office might well tone down his speeches for the archives and for the judgment of history, but he, the *Fuehrer,* made no secret of his scorn for Churchill. In the following speech, delivered by Hitler in Berlin on May 4, 1941, he attacked Churchill in unrestrained language.

WHEN I WARNED against the night bombing of civilian populations, a strategy supported by Mr. Churchill, it was interpreted as a sign of German weakness. Churchill, the most bloodthirsty amateur strategist in all history, actually believed that the patience shown by the *Luftwaffe* for many months was proof of its inability to fly by night. For months this man ordered his paid propagandists to fool the British people into believing that the R.A.F. alone and no other air force could carry on this kind of war, and that through this policy the means had been found to force the Third Reich to its knees. That method was a ruthless attack by the British

---

Völkischer Beobachter, May 5, 1941. Translated by the editor.

*Adolf Hitler, *Hitler's Secret Conversations* (New York: Farrar, Straus & Young, 1953), pp. 147, 153.

Air Force on our civilian population, and added to it was the starvation blockade.

For three and a half months I issued warnings against this type of aerial warfare. That these warnings did not impress Mr. Churchill does not surprise me at all. What does this man care about the lives of others? What does culture or architecture mean to him? When hostilities commenced, he stated clearly that he wanted to have "his war," even at the expense of England's cities being reduced to ruins.

Now he has his war. He paid no attention to my own promise that every one of his bombs would be returned a hundred times, and he did not consider even for a moment the criminal nature of what he was doing. He says he is not the least depressed. He even tells us that after such bombing raids, the British people greeted him joyously and calmly, and that he always returned to London refreshed after his visits to the stricken areas. Maybe such sights strengthened Mr. Churchill in his decision to continue the war this way.

But we, too, are just as much determined to retaliate a hundredfold, if necessary, and to continue doing so until the British people at long last get rid of this criminal and his methods.

If Mr. Churchill considers it necessary from time to time to improve his waging of war by propaganda, I would like him to know that we, too, are quite ready to adopt similar methods. The call he made to the German nation to forsake me, a call made by this fool and his collaborators on May Day of all days, can be explained only as the symptoms of a paralytic disease or drunken delusions.

Churchill's abnormal state of mind led to his decision to make the Balkans a theater of war. For some five years this man has been running around Europe like a madman in search of arson possibilities. Unfortunately, he was able to find hirelings who would open the borders of their countries to this international arsonist. . . .

As a German and as a soldier, I believe it to be unworthy to ridicule a courageous foe. But it seems to me to be absolutely necessary to defend the truth from the wild exaggerations of a man who as a soldier is a bad politician and who as a politician is just as bad a soldier. Mr. Churchill started this war. Just as in the case of Norway and Dunkirk he always tries to make speeches portraying defeats as if they were victories. That is not honorable, but I understand it. If any other man had experienced as many defeats as a politician and as many catastrophes as a soldier, he would not have remained in office for even six months, unless he has the gift that Mr. Churchill has of lying with a pious expression on his face, and of distorting the truth until he can make terrible defeats into glorious victories.

Mr. Churchill may well be able to throw dust into the eyes of his own countrymen, but he cannot bypass the consequences of his defeats.

The British landed an army of 60,000 or 70,000 men in Greece. Before the defeat, this same man insisted that he had 240,000 men there. The aim of this army was to attack Germany from the south, inflict a defeat on her, and again, as in 1918, turn the tide of war. Yugoslavia, chosen by Churchill as an accomplice and driven into misfortune by him, was destroyed within two weeks after hostilities began. Within three weeks, the British troops in Greece were either killed, wounded, taken prisoner, drowned, or driven off.

I announced in my last speech that wherever Britons might set foot on the Continent, they would face us and be driven into the sea. Hence, I have prophesied more accurately than has Mr. Churchill. Now, with brazen effrontery, he says that this battle has cost us 75,000 lives, more than double the losses of the Western campaign. In fact, he goes beyond that. He tells his not-so-intelligent fellow countrymen through one of his paid propagandists that, after having killed enormous numbers of Germans, the British finally turned away because they were just sick of the slaughter, and, in the final analysis, withdrew for that reason alone.

Therefore, the Australians and New Zealanders would still be in Greece today if the English, with their rare combination of lion-like courage and puerile softheartedness, had not killed so many Germans that they finally withdrew, horrified by what they had done, boarded their ships, and sailed away.

That is in all probability the reason why we find virtually no one but Australians and New Zealanders among the killed or among those taken prisoners. That is the sort of nonsense a so-called democratic people will swallow.

107. The Hess Flight: The No. 3 Nazi Parachutes to Scotland After an Eight-Hundred-and-Fifty-Mile Flight to Warn the British, May 10, 1941

*"The most extraordinary flight of this or
any other war."*

Rudolf Hess, deputy *Fuehrer* of the Nazi party, member of the secret cabinet council, Reich minister without portfolio, and widely regarded as the number-three Nazi, had been a happy man in the shadow of his *Fuehrer*. After the beginning of World War II, however, he was gradually pushed into the background. He fretted and fumed about his bad luck. Realizing that Hitler intended to make war soon on the Russians, he decided that he would win back the good favor of the *Fuehrer* by a magnificent act of sacrifice. It was a tragedy, he thought, for Germans and British, blood brothers all, to fight one another. He would fly to England, make peace with his British cousins, and obtain their support against the common enemy – the Bolshevik Russians.

Hess's flight was an overnight sensation, but it was a fiasco. Prime Minister Winston Churchill refused to see him, but later stated: "Whatever be the moral guilt of a German who stood near to Hitler, Hess has, in my view, atoned for this by his devoted and frantic deed of lunatic benevolence. He came to us of his own free will, and, though without authority, has something of the quality of an envoy. He was a medical and not a criminal case and should be so regarded."

Following is the news report of Hess's flight by a correspondent of the Associated Press as it appeared in American newspapers.

Associated Press, May 13, 1941. Courtesy of the Associated Press.

LONDON. TUESDAY, MAY 13 — Rudolf Hess, No. 3 Nazi and high in German
war councils, has parachuted to safety in Scotland after a fantastic forbidden wartime flight from the Reich, where his disappearance has been
reported with the official comment that he suffered from hallucinations.

Circumstances surrounding the 850-mile flight by Adolf Hitler's close
confidant suggested that Hess had deliberately deserted the Nazi camp.

Unarmed and unresisting, he floated down Saturday to a Scottish farm
field where a farmer armed with a pitchfork awaited him. Suffering a
broken ankle but appearing in good humor, Hess was removed to a Glasgow hospital.

An official from the British Foreign Office sped to Glasgow from London to interview Hess, who, in coming to England, defied Hitler's long-
standing rule barring Hess from flying.

Hess was quoted as saying he had intended to land his Messerschmitt
plane but was unable to find a suitable spot and then stalled for a crash as
he bailed out.

Hours after Britain's official announcement of his parachute landing,
the German wireless ignored the London report, merely broadcasting the
original official German announcement that Hess was missing and had left
a confusing letter which suggested he was suffering mentally.

While the British statement did not specifically say that he had deserted,
it made three observations of seemingly inescapable significance.

That Hess had brought along photographs taken at varying years of his
life to establish his identity if it were questioned.

That he had arrived in a plane which could not possibly have had
enough gasoline for a return to Germany — and thus, inferentially, that his
trip was clearly not a one-man offensive but a one-way flight.

That the Messerschmitt's guns were empty.

This most extraordinary flight of this or any other war was disclosed in
London a few hours after the Germans in Berlin had announced that
Hess — Hitler's political heir but once removed — was missing, that he presumably had taken a forbidden plane flight and had cracked up, that he
appeared to have been suffering "hallucinations" and had "left behind a
confused letter."

The magnitude of his determination to escape was indicated in another
way, for he left behind his wife Ilse, whom he married in 1927, and their
three-year-old son. What their fate will be depends on Adolf Hitler.

The story of Hess's 850-mile strange and lonely flight to England as told
in the Government's announcement from Downing Street, showed that he
first crossed the Scottish coast last Saturday night.

He flew on in the direction of Glasgow, and later — just when was not
disclosed — he bailed out. His Messerschmitt crashed. Taken to the Glas-

gow hospital, he first identified himself as "Horn," but later by his correct name.

The announcement issued here said:

"Rudolf Hess, the deputy Fuehrer of Germany and party leader of the National Socialist party, has landed in Scotland in the following circumstances:

"On the night of Saturday, the tenth, a Messerschmitt 110 was reported by our patrol to have crossed the coast of Scotland and to be flying in the direction of Glasgow.

"Since the Messerschmitt 110 would not have enough fuel to return to Germany this report was at first disbelieved.

"Later on a Messerschmitt 110 crashed near Glasgow. Shortly afterward, a German officer, who had bailed out, was found with his parachute in the neighborhood, suffering from a broken ankle.

"He was taken to a hospital in Glasgow, where he at first gave the name of Horn but later on declared that he was Rudolf Hess.

"He brought with him various photographs of himself at different ages, apparently in order to establish his identity.

"These photographs were deemed to be photographs of Hess by several people who knew him personally. Accordingly, an officer of the Foreign Office who was closely acquainted with him before the war was sent up by airplane to see him in the hospital."

So fantastic was his solo flight out of the Reich that the British themselves, after thorough identification of their hostage, announced it only late tonight, two days after he landed in Scotland, and they were still openly at a loss what to make of it.

If Hess should talk he could lay bare to the British the entire framework of their Nazi enemy — information of inestimable value.

The announcement made the identification positive by referring to him as "Rudolf Hess, the deputy Fuehrer of Germany and party leader of Socialist party."

Subsequently, the Ministry of Information declared that he had been identified as Rudolf Hess beyond "all possible doubt."

108. Nazi Authorities Claim That Hess Was Mentally Deranged and a Victim of Hallucinations, May 12, 1941

"Under the circumstances, the National Socialist movement must regretfully assume. . . ."

Hitler, Propaganda Minister Paul Joseph Goebbels, and the Nazi hierarchy were shocked by news of Hess's flight to Scotland. The man who, on September 1, 1939, had been designated by Hitler as his second choice, next to Reich Marshal Hermann Goering, in the line of succession for leadership of the German state, was reported in Germany to have taken an airplane in Augsburg for an unknown destination "in violation of the *Fuehrer's* order prohibiting him from flying because of a physical ailment."

The news of the mysterious disappearance was withheld for forty-eight hours after Hess had been reported missing. Then, on May 12, 1941, came this official government communique, in which a letter Hess left behind was said to show a disordered mind.

RUDOLF HESS HAS MET with an accident.

Party Comrade Hess, who because of a disease that for a year has progressively worsened has been categorically forbidden by the Fuehrer to continue his flying activities, recently found means in violation of this command to come into possession of an airplane.

On Saturday, May 10, about 6 P.M., Party Comrade Hess took off from Augsburg for a flight from which until today he has not yet returned. A letter that he left behind unfortunately indicated, by its incoherence,

---

The New York Times, May 13, 1941.

symptoms of a mental derangement that permits the inference that Comrade Hess became the victim of hallucinations.

The Fuehrer immediately ordered the arrest of the adjutants of Party Comrade Hess, who alone knew of these flights and, knowing of their prohibition by the Fuehrer, did not prevent or immediately report them.

Under the circumstances, the National Socialist movement must regretfully assume that Comrade Hess has crashed or met with an accident somewhere on his flight.

109. The German Conquest of Crete: First Airborne Invasion in History, May 20, 1941

"It was a raging hell."

The war seemed to be going well for Hitler and the Third Reich. As soon as all Greece was under Nazi control, Hitler ordered the invasion of Crete. That island, like Malta, seemed safe for the Allies, protected as it was by the Royal Navy centered at Alexandria as well as by a strong garrison, under command of Major General Bernard C. Freyberg, a competent New Zealander.

On May 20, 1941, German paratroopers swarmed over the island in the first great airborne invasion in history. On the third and fourth days, the Royal Navy frustrated German seaborne landings, but the parachutists could not be contained. Among them was the former heavyweight boxing champion of the world, Max Schmeling. Soon the British position became hopeless. It was all over within ten days. The Royal Navy succeeded in evacuating seventeen thousand Empire troops.

In the following report the *Frankfurter Zeitung* later described the fighting during the first days of the invasion. The German public was delighted by the good news.

CNOSSUS ON CRETE — In the early hours of May 20 the motors of the Junkers transport planes are heard for the first time directly over the central and western portions of the island. The doors open. Many thousands of dead-tired troopers hurtle into the air, their chutes open and like inflated sails they glide with their living freight down toward the ground.

Frankfurter Zeitung, June 21, 1941. Translated by the editor.

The assault from the air on this island fortress was made at four separate places — at Erakleion (Candia), at Rethymno, at the main city of Canea, and to the west at Maleme airfield. Few Germans, few even among the paratroopers, have ever heard of these places. But those names were to burn themselves during the last two weeks into the hearts of the soldiers. They were the spots of heaviest combat. Those names will glow for centuries.

People talk about the "mathematical precision" of German victories. How foolish! But nowhere is it more silly than in connection with Crete. Missions can be planned with extreme care, but at the critical moment what counts most are the courage and ability of the combat troops and the fixity of purpose of the leadership. Many German paratroopers were caught while in the air in a hail of British defensive fire. Others, even after a gentle glide through the air or after a hard fall on foreign soil, and then after freeing themselves from the shrouds of their chutes, had to face the fire of the enemy.

It was a raging hell. Worst of all was the terror of the unknown into which the troops had jumped after the doors of their craft opened. But not a single one hesitated. Not one made the next man wait. Head over heels they tumbled into space down to the gray sand and into the glowing lightning of enemy fire.

Out of the sky into mortal danger they storm — the general as well as the junior officer and trooper, the staff physician as well as the mechanic. They cling to the good earth they have won and with their tommy guns they strike back at the enemy. They rush to the weapons that have come down by parachute and then defend themselves against the fire of the numerically superior enemy. Thus, it went on all that long Tuesday morning, the long afternoon, all through the night, and again the following morning.

Many things happened all at once. Reinforcements came out of the air, and to them the dead-tired comrades made their way. But they were outmanned and the pressure of the enemy became stronger and stronger. The sun shone pitilessly on the bare stones. There was little water. Many had no water at all. Their tongues stuck to the roofs of their mouths, their throats were parched. They lay on the open slopes or on the shore of Maleme. Enemy shells exploded among them. Their own artillery was far away in Greece.

The dead lay silent on the ground. Others who were wounded called for medical orderlies and for water.

Then came the night, the long, lonely night. Here and there groups of ten or twelve huddled together. The burning heat of the day gave way to a cutting cold. All knew that the next morning would be as hot as the preceding one. They would be thirsty again. Tired and exhausted, they would have to face a fresh and rested enemy. Yet — and all knew it — they could not give in. They would starve and thirst and fight until they won the victory.

The individual fighters knew little about the general situation. Each one had his own enemy in front of him — with whom he had to settle accounts — whether it was an Australian or a New Zealander, or whether it was the thirst and heat and cold and hunger. That German soldier knew only that he had to hold out and that he had to have a continuing faith in his leadership.

On the morning of the second day this was the situation: the paratroopers held the edges of the airfields at Candia and Rethymno. Both airfields, as well as both cities, were in British hands. Other paratroopers were in front of the main city of Canea. To the west, most of the airfield at Maleme was in German possession. The taking of the airfield was the happiest event of that first day. The outcome of the entire battle depended on this coup.

But thus far, it was all inconclusive. Even now no German plane could land in Maleme without danger, for the strip was covered with enemy fire. More — the big guns of the British in the south were plastering Maleme with their shells. German aircraft accomplished wonders, destroying many British emplacements and scattering marching columns. Without the *Luftwaffe* the troops who had landed could not possibly have halted their foes on the ground. The planes could not remain for long over Crete, and those British batteries were so strongly shielded that they could not be reached by bombs from the air.

As Wednesday morning dawned over Crete, it became clear that the crisis was at hand. Germans had landed at more spots. The enemy was no longer surprised, but he was at least put into disorder. The Germans had demonstrated their superiority in hand-to-hand fighting, and above all they had won a precious airfield. In this exciting moment, that airfield could not be used for the landing of transport planes. British fire still covered the area.

On the second day, more thousands of paratroopers jumped to reinforce the troops on the ground. They made the situation better by helping to counteract the pressure of the enemy, but the decision could not come from them. Everything depended on whether it would be possible to bring bigger army units to Crete. Anyone who that afternoon saw the shell-pocked and bomb-crippled airfield and the shores of Maleme could well doubt that it was possible to bring in such reinforcements.

On the morning of May 21, Junkers planes circled over Maleme, the airfield below them covered with holes and piles of sand and stones. Even if they managed to land in that mess, they would not be able to take off again. The pilots had no other choice than to fly back. With heavy hearts they turned their planes north and headed back to Greece. The Germans below, who had been fighting furiously, were now alone. With burning eyes they watched the planes disappear.

How long would it be before help came? They did not know. They knew only that they had to hold on.

Then came bad news about the fate of the sea squadrons. Mountain troops were to be brought in by motor boats. But the day went by and they did not appear. Only later was it learned that a British cruiser had come across the boats and had scattered them. Some 200 of these mountain troops and seamen lost their lives, but most of them were rescued.

Perhaps in few engagements has the steadfastness of the German soldier been demonstrated as well as in this one. Among those saved was a group of 64 men who had taken to rubber boats. All these men stayed together as a unit under the blistering sun during the third day of the attack. Their boats were so overcrowded that they had to throw their clothes overboard. By accident they came across a Greek cutter, which they hailed and boarded. They reached Maleme, anyhow. But they brought more than only themselves and their will power to the battle. They were "almost naked, but they had their weapons." They had never separated themselves from their guns and machine guns, even though shipwrecked. After a few hours they were ready and able to add their strength to that of their comrades.

In the history of war there are few examples as proud as this accurate account of the division's report . . . "almost naked, but with their weapons."

Meanwhile, the fate of Maleme and with it the outcome of the battle of Crete was being decided. On the afternoon of the second day the pilots of the transport planes were able to land a battalion of mountain troops on the airfield and the shores of Maleme. The big guns of the British still roared from the south, the field itself was still full of holes and rubble. But the pilots, threatened by instant death, nevertheless landed their precious cargo right in the middle of the airstrip with all its holes and stones. They had to make zigzag landings. Some, losing their momentum could not make it. That tiny spot was a veritable hell on earth.

But success came by that evening. At long last the first battalion of mountain troops was on Cretan soil.

110. The Third Reich Declares War on the USSR: The German Ambassador at Moscow Presents the Declaration, June 22, 1941

"Thereby the Soviet Government has broken its treaties with Germany and is about to attack Germany from the rear, in its struggle for life."

Just before the outbreak of World War II, Hitler had allied himself with Stalin for the task of carving up Poland between them. But the German *Fuehrer* was never comfortable in this alliance. It ran counter to his entire ideology expressed in *Mein Kampf*. Less than two years later he suddenly turned on his partner and unleashed his armies in a furious *Blitzkrieg* against the Bolshevik state beginning at dawn on Sunday, June 22, 1941.

An hour and a half later, the German ambassador at Moscow, on instructions from the German Foreign Office, presented the following German declaration of war to Vyacheslav Mikhailovich Molotov, the Soviet commisar for foreign affairs.

VERY URGENT   Berlin, June 21, 1941
STATE SECRET
By radio
For the Ambassador personally.

1) Upon receipt of this telegram, all of the cipher material still there is to be destroyed. The radio set is to be put out of commission.

2) Please inform Herr Molotov at once that you have an urgent com-

---

U.S., Department of State, *Nazi-Soviet Relations, 1939–1941* (Washington, D.C.: Government Printing Office, 1948), pp. 347–49.

munication to make to him and would therefore like to call on him immediately. Then please make the following declaration to him.

"The Soviet Ambassador in Berlin is receiving at this hour from the Reich Minister for Foreign Affairs a memorandum giving in detail the facts which are briefly summarized as follows:

"I. In 1939 the Government of the Reich, putting aside grave objections arising out of the contradiction between National Socialism and Bolshevism, undertook to arrive at an understanding with Soviet Russia. Under the treaties of August 23 and September 28, 1939, the Government of the Reich effected a general reorientation of its policy toward the U.S.S.R. and thenceforth adopted a cordial attitude toward the Soviet Union. This policy of goodwill brought the Soviet Union great advantages in the field of foreign policy.

"The Government of the Reich therefore felt entitled to assume that thenceforth both nations, while respecting each other's regime and not interfering in the internal affairs of the other partner, would arrive at good, lasting, neighborly relations. Unfortunately it soon became evident that the Government of the Reich had been entirely mistaken in this assumption.

"II. Soon after the conclusion of the German-Russian treaties, the Comintern resumed its subversive activity against Germany, with the official Soviet-Russian representatives giving assistance. Sabotage, terrorism, and espionage in preparation for war were demonstrably carried out on a large scale. In all the countries bordering on Germany and in the territories occupied by German troops, anti-German feeling was aroused and the German attempt to set up a stable order in Europe was combatted. Yugoslavia was gladly offered arms against Germany by the Soviet Russian Chief-of-Staff, as proved by documents found in Belgrade. The declarations made by the U.S.S.R. on conclusion of the treaties with Germany, regarding her intention to collaborate with Germany, thus stood revealed as deliberate misrepresentation and deceit and the conclusion of the treaties themselves as a tactical maneuver for obtaining arrangements favorable to Russia. The guiding principle remained the weakening of the non-Bolshevist countries in order the more easily to demoralize them and, at a given time, to crush them.

"III. In the diplomatic and military fields it became obvious that the U.S.S.R. — contrary to the declaration made at the conclusion of the treaties that she did not wish to Bolshevize and annex the countries falling within her sphere of influence — was intent on pushing her military might westward wherever it seemed possible and on carrying Bolshevism further into Europe. The action of the U.S.S.R. against the Baltic States, Finland, and Rumania, where Soviet claims even extended to Bucovina, showed this clearly. The occupation and Bolshevization by the Soviet Union of the sphere of influence granted to her clearly violated the Moscow agreements, even though the Government of the Reich for the time being accepted the facts.

"IV. When Germany, by the Vienna Award of August 30, 1940, settled the crisis in Southeastern Europe resulting from the action of the U.S.S.R. against Rumania, the Soviet Union protested and turned to making intensive military preparations in every field. Germany's renewed effort to achieve an understanding, as reflected in the exchange of letters between the Reich Foreign Minister and Herr Stalin and in the invitation to Herr Molotov to come to Berlin, brought demands from the Soviet Union which Germany could not accept, such as the guarantee of Bulgaria by the U.S.S.R., the establishment of a base for Soviet Russia land and naval forces at the Straits, and the complete abandonment of Finland. Subsequently, the policy of the U.S.S.R. directed against Germany became more and more obvious. The warning addressed to Germany regarding occupation of Bulgaria and the declaration made to Bulgaria after the entry of German troops, which was of a definitely hostile nature, were as significant in this connection as was the promise to protect the rear of Turkey in the event of a Turkish entry into the war in the Balkans, given in March 1941.

"V. With the conclusion of the Soviet-Yugoslav Treaty of Friendship of April 5 last, which was intended to stiffen the spines of the Yugoslav plotters, the U.S.S.R. joined the common Anglo-Yugoslav-Greek front against Germany. At the same time she tried *rapprochement* with Rumania, in order to induce that country to detach itself from Germany. It was only the rapid German victories that caused the failure of the Anglo-Russian plan for an attack against the German troops in Rumania and Bulgaria.

"VI. This policy was accompanied by a steadily growing concentration of all available Russian forces on a long front from the Baltic Sea to the Black Sea, against which countermeasures were taken by Germany only later. Since the beginning of the year this was been a steadily growing menace to the territory of the Reich. Reports received in the last few days eliminated the last remaining doubts as to the aggressive character of this Russian concentration and completed the picture of an extremely tense military situation. In addition to this, there are the reports from England regarding the negotiations of Ambassador Cripps for still closer political and military collaboration between England and the Soviet Union.

"To sum up, the Government of the Reich declares, therefore, that the Soviet Government, contrary to the obligations it assumed,

1) has not only continued, but even intensified its attempts to undermine Germany and Europe;

2) has adopted a more and more anti-German foreign policy;

3) has concentrated all its forces in readiness at the German border. Thereby the Soviet Government has broken its treaties with Germany and is about to attack Germany from the rear, in its struggle for life. The Fuehrer has therefore ordered the German Armed Forces to oppose this threat with all the means at their disposal."

End of declaration.

Please do not enter into any discussion of this communication. It is incumbent upon the Government of Soviet Russia to safeguard the security of the Embassy personnel.

RIBBENTROP.

111. In an Emotional Speech Hitler Justifies His Invasion of the Soviet Union, June 22, 1941

"I therefore decided today again to lay the fate and future of the German Reich and our people in the hands of our soldiers."

As his troops stormed across the borders of the Soviet Union, Hitler sent a letter to his partner Mussolini in which he explained: "The partnership with the Soviet Union, in spite of the complete sincerity of the efforts to bring a final conciliation, was, nevertheless, very irksome to me, for in some way or other it seemed to me to be a break with my whole origin, my concepts, and my former obligations. I am happy to be relieved now of these mental agonies." The way, he said, was actually forced on him by many factors beyond his control. He wanted everyone to know that he had never really changed his mind and that his prophecies in *Mein Kampf* were being fulfilled. Following is the proclamation Hitler delivered to the German people on the day of the invasion.

My GERMAN PEOPLE! National Socialists!

Burdened with heavy cares, forced to maintain a silence for many months, now I can at long last speak to you frankly.

When, on September 3, 1939, the English declared war on us, there was a renewed British attempt to interfere in European affairs. It was the old British strategy of opposing whomever on the Continent is strongest at a given time.

From the official version. Translated by the editor.

That is the way England acted in the past and brought about the destruction of Spain in the process. That is how she carried on war against Holland. That is how later she struck at France with the assistance of all Europe. That is also how at the turn of the century she began the encirclement (*Einkreisung*) of the German Reich at that time and in 1914 the World War. Germany was defeated in 1918 only because of her internal dissension. The results were deplorable.

There was a hypocritical announcement that the struggle at that time was only against the Kaiser and his Government. And the destruction of the German Reich began according to plan after the German Army had laid down its arms.

The French statesmen had made a declaration that there were 20 million Germans too many. In other words, that number would be decimated by hunger, disease, or emigration. Apparently that prophecy was being fulfilled to the letter. But at that time the National Socialist movement was beginning its work of unifying the German people and in that way starting the regeneration of the Reich. Our people began to emerge from distress, misery, and shameless disregard in a purely internal regeneration. There was no threat in all this to the existence of Britain.

Yet, a new policy of encirclement began against Germany, a policy born of hatred. Internally and externally, there existed that plot between Jews and democrats, a conspiracy familiar to all of us, between Bolsheviks and reactionaries, with the single aim of preventing the construction of a new German people's state, and of thrusting the Reich once again into weakness and misery. The hatred of this international conspiracy was directed not only against us but against those peoples who, like ourselves, were bypassed by good fortune and had to earn their daily bread in the struggle for existence.

The right of Italy and Japan to share in the wealth of the world was opposed just as much as that of Germany and in fact was completely denied.

The union of these states was, therefore, in reality only a means of self-protection against the egotistical world combination of wealth and power which threatened them.

As early as 1936 Prime Minister Churchill, as we know from statements made by the American General Wood before a committee of the American House of Representatives, stated that Germany once again was becoming too strong and, therefore must be destroyed. In the summer of 1939 the time seemed to be at hand for England to begin her contemplated process of destruction by once again attempting the encirclement of Germany.

A campaign of lies for this purpose was started. It consisted of declaring that other peoples were threatened, of fooling them with British guarantees of assistance, and of making them move against Germany precisely as they did in the days before the World War.

From May to August 1939, Britain was successful in broadcasting to the whole world that Lithuania, Latvia, Finland, and Bessarabia, in addition to the Ukraine, were all being threatened directly by Germany.

Several of these nations allowed themselves to be misled into accepting the promise of guarantees and thereby joined the new encirclement front against Germany.

In these circumstances I believed that I was entitled to assume responsibility before my own conscience and before the history of my German people not only of informing these countries or their governments of the falseness of British assertions, but also of assuring the strongest power in the East in solemn declaration of the limits of our interests.

National Socialists!

At that time you probably felt that this step was especially difficult and bitter for me. The German people never really were hostile to the Russian people. But for ten years Jewish Bolshevik rulers had been attempting from Moscow to set not only Germany but all Europe on fire.

At no time did Germany ever try to extend her National Socialist *Weltanschauung* into Russia. On the contrary, Jewish Bolshevik rulers in Moscow diligently attempted to force their domination on us as well as other European peoples through both ideological means and military force. The results were nothing but chaos, misery, and starvation in all nations.

On the other hand, I have been seeking for twenty years with as little intervention as possible and without ruining our production, to bring about a new social order in Germany which would not only conquer unemployment but would also allow every worker to win an even greater share of the fruits of his labor. The success of this policy of economic and social reconstruction of our nation, by carefully eliminating differences of class and rank, was a true people's community.

Therefore, it was with extreme difficulty that I brought myself in August 1939 to send my foreign minister to Moscow with the goal of frustrating this British policy aiming at the encirclement of Germany.

This I did not only from a sense of responsibility to the German people, but also in the hope that we would win permanent relief from tension and be able to reduce those sacrifices which might be demanded of us.

In Moscow we affirmed that the territories concerned, with the exception of Lithuania, were outside Germany's political interests. We also made a special agreement if Britain were to succeed into inciting Poland into war against Germany. Here, too, German claims were to be limited in nature — more so than justified by the power of German arms.

National Socialists!

The results of this treaty which I, myself, wanted, and which was arranged in the interests of the German people, were very severe, especially for Germany in the countries concerned. More than a half million Germans — small farmers, artisans, and workingmen — were required to leave their former homelands virtually overnight in order to escape from a new regime which threatened them with unlimited misery and sooner or later with complete extermination. And in the process thousands of Germans disappeared. We could not determine their fate or find out where they were living. Among them were no fewer than 160 German citizens.

I remained silent in the face of all that simply because I had to. After all, it was my final aim to bring about relief from tensions and, if at all possible, a permanent settlement with this state.

During our advance in Poland, Soviet rulers in Moscow suddenly claimed Lithuania — contrary to our solemn agreement. The German Reich really never had any intention of occupying Lithuania. It not only did not present any demands to the Lithuanian Government, but to the contrary declined as inconsistent with German policy the request of Lithuania at that time to send German troops to Lithuania. Despite this, I went along with that fresh Russian demand.

This was only the beginning of always renewed extortions by the Russians.

The victory in Poland won exclusively by German soldiers led me to make another peace offer to the Western Powers. It was refused because of the machinations of Jewish and international warmongers. Britain at that time still had hopes of being able to conclude a European coalition against Germany, an agreement which was to include the Balkans as well as Soviet Russia. London decided to send Mr. Cripps as Ambassador to Moscow with instructions to resume relations between England and Soviet Russia and to turn them into a pro-British direction. The British press reported on the progress of this mission to Moscow, concentrating on matters which did not require silence.

The first results came in the autumn of 1939 and the spring of 1940. Soviet Russia attempted to subjugate by armed power not only Finland but also the Baltic countries. She commenced this action with the ridiculous and false assertion that she must protect these countries from outside interests.

This could only apply to Germany, for no other country could penetrate into the Balkan theater or go to war there. Yet, I still had to remain silent. However, the men in power in the Kremlin at once went even farther.

Where Germany in the spring of 1940, in consonance with the so-called pact of friendship, withdrew her armies from the Far Eastern frontier, and for the most part cleared the area of German troops, the Russians already began something that could only be regarded as a deliberate threat to Germany.

Molotov personally made a statement at that time in which he said that there were twenty-two Russian divisions in the Baltic area alone in the spring of 1940. Because the Russian Government always claimed that it was called in by the local people, the purpose of the Russian presence there could only amount to a demonstration against us.

While, on May 5, 1940, our troops were smashing Franco-British power in the West, the Russians were continuing their military deployment to a more and more threatening extent. From August 1940 on, therefore, I decided it to be in the best interests of the Reich no longer to allow our eastern provinces, which had been devastated so often, to remain unprotected against this great concentration of Bolshevik divisions.

The result was British-Soviet Russian cooperation, which was intended primarily to tie up powerful forces in the East in such a manner that a radical conclusion to the war in the West, especially in the matter of airpower, could no longer be promised by the German High Command.

This was in line not only with the aims of the British but also of Russian Soviet policy. Both England and Soviet Russia intended to allow this war to go on as long as possible as a means of weakening all Europe and make it progressively more impotent.

In the final analysis Soviet Russia's threatened assault on Rumania was intended at the same time to obtain an important base, and to threaten not only Germany's economic life but also that of all Europe. The Reich, especially since the year 1918, has sought with continuing patience to win countries in Southeast Europe as trading partners. Therefore, we had the greatest interest in their internal constitutional organization and consolidation. But the advance of Soviet Russia into Rumania and the cooperation between Greece and England threatened to turn these regions also within a short time into a general theater of war.

In opposition to our principles and traditions, and at the urgent request of the Rumanian Government, which itself was responsible for this development, I advised agreement to the Soviet Russian demands for the sake of peace and for the cession of Bessarabia.

However, the Rumanian Government believes that it could answer to this development before its own people only if Germany and Italy, as a form of compensation, would at least guarantee the integrity of what was still left of Rumania.

I acquiesced in this matter with a heavy heart, mainly because when the German Government gives a guarantee, that means that it will be upheld. After all, we are neither Englishmen nor Jews.

I still believe at this late hour that I have served the cause of peace in that theater, although it has meant the assumption of important personal obligations. However, as a means of finally solving these problems and to bring about some clarification in the Russian attitude toward Germany, as well as to meet the pressure of continually augmented mobilization on our Eastern frontier, I invited Herr Molotov to come to Berlin. The Soviet Minister for Foreign Affairs then proceeded to demand that we clarify or agree to the following principles.

The first point was Molotov's question: Was the German guarantee for Rumania also directed against Soviet Russia in the event of a Russian attack on Rumania?

My response: The German guarantee is a general one and we regard it as unconditionally binding. Soviet Russia, however, never declared to us that she had other interests in Rumania beyond that of Bessarabia. The fact that Northern Bucovina was occupied was already a violation of our agreement. Therefore, I did not think that Russia could now suddenly make more extensive demands upon Rumania.

Molotov's second question had this background: Russia again felt menaced by Finland and she was determined not to tolerate this state of affairs. Was Germany prepared not to give any aid to Finland and above all would she immediately withdraw German relief troops marching through to Kirkenes?

I responded: Germany has absolutely no political interest in Finland. A new war, however, by Soviet Russia against the small Finnish state could not be regarded by the German Government as tolerable, all the more since we could never believe Russia to be menaced by Finland. Under no circumstances could we agree to the opening of another theater of war in the Baltic.

Molotov's third question: Was Germany ready to agree that Soviet Russia give a guarantee to Bulgaria and send Soviet Russian troops to Bulgaria for this purpose, at a time when Molotov was prepared to state that Soviet Russia had no intention of deposing the King?

My response: Bulgaria was a sovereign state. I did not know at all that Bulgaria had ever asked Soviet Russia for any kind of guarantee such as Rumania had asked of Germany. In addition, I would have to discuss the matter with my allies.

Molotov's fourth question: Under all conditions Soviet Russia needed free passage through the Dardanelles and for her protection also demanded occupation of several important bases on the Dardanelles and the Bosporus. Did Germany agree with this or not?

My response: Germany has been prepared at all times to agree to changing the Statute of Montreux in favor of the Black Sea states. But Germany was not prepared to agree to Russia taking possession of bases on the Straits.

National Socialists!

In this matter I took the only stand which I could conscientiously take, not only as the responsible leader of the German Reich but also as the representative of European culture and civilization.

The immediate result was that in Soviet Russia the activity against the Reich began to increase. Along with it went the immediate beginning of the attempt to undermine the new Rumanian state from inside and the attempt to overthrow the Bulgarian Government by propaganda.

With the assistance of the confused and immature leaders of the Rumanian Iron Guard, a *coup d'état* was staged in Rumania with the aim of overthrowing Chief of State Antonescu and to produce chaos in the country by removing all legal powers of the government and thus the preconditions for the implementation of the German guarantee.

Nevertheless, I still believed it best to remain silent.

Immediately after the failure of this undertaking, there was renewed reinforcement of Russian troops on Germany's eastern frontiers. The Russians sent in tank detachments and parachutists in constantly increasing numbers and in dangerous proximity to the German lines. Until a few weeks ago the German armed forces as well as the German public were not aware of a single tank or mechanized unit stationed on our eastern frontier.

If any proof for the coalition between England and Soviet Russia were needed, despite all the camouflage and diversions, that would be provided by the Yugoslavian conflict. At a time when I was making every possible attempt to pacify the Balkans, and in sympathetic cooperation with Mussolini, I invited Yugoslavia to join the Tripartite Pact. Meanwhile, England and Soviet Russia in a common plot organized the conspiracy which removed the government which had been ready to come to an agreement.

Today we can inform the German nation that the Serbian *Putsch* against Germany did not really take place only under the British but rather primarily under Soviet Russian auspices.

We also remained silent on that matter. Yet the Soviet leaders went one step farther. Not only did they organize the *Putsch* but a few days later concluded that well-known friendship pact with the Serbians in their desire to resist pacification in the Balkans and in their desire to incite them against the Germans.

This was no platonic intention. Moscow demanded the mobilization of the Serbian army.

Even now I still believed it better not to say anything. But the men in the Kremlin went even farther. The Government of the German Reich today possesses the documentary evidence to prove that Soviet Russia, as a means of bringing Serbia into this war, promised to supply her through Salonica with arms, aircraft, munitions, and other war materials to be used against Germany.

All this happened at the very moment when I myself advised Japanese Foreign Minister Matsuoka that my hope was always to ease tensions with Soviet Russia and through it to serve the cause of peace.

Only the rapid advance of our incomparable troops to Skoplje, as well as the capture of Salonica itself, frustrated the aims of this Soviet-Russian-Anglo-Saxon plot. Officers of the Serbian air force, however, fled to Russia, where they were quickly received as allies.

The triumph of the Axis Powers in the Balkans this summer frustrated the plan to involve Germany in long battles in Southeastern Europe. Meanwhile, the Soviet Russians were increasing their readiness for war in the hope that, in conjunction with England and aided by American supplies, they would crush Germany and Italy.

It was Moscow which broke and miserably betrayed the agreement of friendship. The rulers of the Kremlin did all this while, exactly as in the case of Finland and Rumania, they pretended peace up to the last moment and drew up seemingly innocent documents.

Even though I was forced to maintain silence again and again by these special circumstances, the moment has now come when to continue as a mere observer would not only be a sin of omission but in reality a crime against the German people, indeed, against the whole of Europe.

Today something like 160 Russian divisions stand at our frontiers. For weeks now there have been constant violations of this frontier, affecting not only us but from the far north down south to Rumania. Russian aviators believe it to be a sporting gesture to disregard these frontiers, apparently to prove to us that they already feel themselves to be masters of these territories. During the night of June 17 to June 18, Russian patrols again penetrated into the territory of the Reich and could be driven off only after prolonged firing.

This has brought us to the hour when it is necessary for us to take steps against the Jewish-Anglo-Saxon warmongers as well as against the Jewish rulers of the Bolshevik center in Moscow.

German people!

At this moment an advance is taking place which in extent compares with the greatest of its kind ever seen in this world. United with their Finnish comrades, the fighters of the Narvik victory stand at the Northern Arctic. German divisions commanded by the conqueror of Norway, in cooperation with the heroes of Finnish freedom, under their own marshal, are protecting Finnish soil.

The formations of the German Eastern Front, extending from East Prussia to the Carpathians, German and Rumanian soldiers, are all united under Chief of State Antonescu from the shores of the Pruth along the lower reaches of the Danube to the shores of the Black Sea.

The task of this front, therefore, is no longer the protection of single countries, but rather the safeguarding of Europe and with it the salvation of us all.

Therefore, I have decided today again to place the fate and future of the German Reich and our people in the hands of our soldiers.

May God help us in this struggle!

112. German Declaration of War on the United States, December 11, 1941

". . . under these circumstances brought about by President Roosevelt. . . ."

Article 3 of the 1940 Berlin-Rome-Tokyo Axis pact reads as follows: "Germany, Italy and Japan agree to cooperate in their efforts on aforesaid lines. They further undertake to assist one another with all political, economic and military means when one of the three contracting powers is attacked by a power at present not involved in the European war or in the Chinese-Japanese conflict."

In accordance with this agreement, Hitler declared war on the United States on December 11, 1941, just several days after the United States, in response to the attack on Pearl Harbor on December 7, 1941, declared war on Japan. Annoyed by American help to his enemies, Hitler deemed it best to wage war against the United States as well as the Soviet Union.

The German declaration of war, quoted here, was accompanied by a similar Italian declaration.

THE GOVERNMENT OF THE UNITED STATES having violated in the most flagrant manner and in ever-increasing measure all rules of neutrality in favor of the adversaries of Germany and having continually been guilty of the most severe provocations toward Germany ever since the outbreak of the European war, provoked by the British declaration of war against Germany on September 3, 1939, has finally resorted to open military acts of aggression.

U.S., Department of State *Bulletin* (Washington, D.C.: Government Printing Office, 1941), vol. 5, pp. 481–82.

On September 11, 1941, the President of the United States publicly declared that he had ordered the American Navy and Air Force to shoot on sight at any German war vessel. In his speech of October 27, 1941, he once more expressly affirmed that this order was in force. Acting under this order, vessels of the American Navy, since early September 1941, have systematically attacked German naval forces. Thus, American destroyers, as for instance the *Greer*, the *Kearny* and the *Reuben James*, have opened fire on German submarines according to plan. The Secretary of the American Navy, Mr. Knox, himself confirmed that American destroyers attacked German submarines.

Furthermore, the naval forces of the United States, under order of their Government and contrary to international law have treated and seized German merchant vessels on the high seas as enemy ships.

The German Government therefore establishes the following facts:

Although Germany on her part has strictly adhered to the rules of international law in her relations with the United States during every period of the present war, the Government of the United States from initial violations of neutrality has finally proceeded to open acts of war against Germany. The Government of the United States has thereby virtually created a state of war.

The German Government, consequently, discontinues diplomatic relations with the United States of America and declares that under these circumstances brought about by President Roosevelt, Germany too, as from today, considers herself as being in a state of war with the United States of America.

Accept, Mr. Chargé d'Affaires, the expression of my high consideration.

113. The Battle for Moscow: Soviet Reporter Konstantin Simonov Records the German Defeat on Soviet Soil, January 29, 1942

"Moscow was calm and stern in those days."

Hitler commenced his first general offensive against Moscow on October 2, 1941. Just two months later he ordered the editors of Berlin newspapers to reserve front-page space for an important announcement. "The Soviet Union is finished," he said.

But, unfortunately for the *Fuehrer*, the announcement of the fall of Moscow never came. The Germans reached the outskirts of the canal port of Khimki, five miles north of Moscow, but that was as far as they were able to move.

Hitler's armies had advanced some six hundred miles into the Soviet Union since the invasion of June. In the north, German armies were before Leningrad; in the south they were besieging Sevastopol; and in the center they were within sight of Moscow. It seemed to be a strong position. But the Germans were being subjected to one of the worst winters within memory. Most of the men were without winter clothing; so confident had Hitler been of defeating the Russians within a few weeks that he had neglected to outfit them with proper winter clothing. Added to the problem were the persistent attacks by Russian guerrillas, who snapped constantly at the German rear and broke their lines of communications. It was becoming more and more apparent that Hitler's armies were caught in a gigantic trap.

The story of Moscow was told by a popular Soviet reporter, Konstantin Simonov. Although this was tendentious reporting, it was greeted with joy by the Russian public.

Konstantin Simonov, *Moscow* (Moscow, 1943), pp. 19–23. Courtesy of the Foreign Languages Publishing House, Moscow.

ALL THROUGH OCTOBER, NOVEMBER, and the beginning of December, the Germans kept coming closer to Moscow every day. Their rout near Moscow began on December 5, when our troops launched their counteroffensive. The question of future victory had been decided when the country learned that the State Defense Committee, with Stalin at its head, was remaining in Moscow, and particularly on November 6 and 7, in accordance with the great Soviet traditions, the meeting of the Moscow Soviet was held and the parade passed through the Red Square, at both of which occasions Stalin spoke.

On these days, the Germans were at the very gates of Moscow. In places they were no more than sixty or seventy kilometers away. The danger was great and menacing. But just because the danger was so tremendous — in the parade, in the words of Stalin — there was such great force, such confidence in victory, such lofty, calm courage that every Soviet citizen, whether at the front or in the rear, no matter where he was on that day, felt with all his heart that Moscow would never be surrendered, and that in the end victory would be ours.

The Germans continued to advance on November 8, 9, 10, and 15, approaching ever closer to Moscow. And our troops continued to retreat with heavy fighting. But actually this could no longer be called a retreat. There was a feeling that near Moscow an enormous steel spring was slowly contracting, acquiring tremendous force in the process. It was contracting to strike in release.

Air raids on the city continued day and night. The Germans captured new villages daily. Their tanks would break through now in one place, now in another. Tens of thousands of Moscow women erected fortifications, dug trenches and anti-tank pits at the approaches to Moscow. They worked tirelessly, in mud and sleet and cold. They worked in the very same clothes they had on when they came, for there were no special work clothes for them. And Moscow itself was cold and uninviting, there was no fuel for heating purposes — every car that came from the East brought arms and arms alone. There were fewer people in Moscow. Some had gone to the front, others to build fortifications. But every one of those who remained did the work of three, and sometimes of four. The whole city seemed to have turned into a military camp. People spent their nights in the factories, sleeping two or three hours a day. The front was so close that newspaper correspondents managed to visit the forward positions and return to the city with fresh news for their papers twice a day.

All the principal war plants had been evacuated to the rear. But the Muscovites were faced with the task of continuing to forge arms for Moscow within the city itself. And all the small workshops, all the remaining plants began to produce arms for the troops fighting near Moscow. Places that used to put out primus stoves were now producing grenades; where household utensils used to be manufactured fuses and detonators were being turned out. A factory that used to manufacture adding machines began, for the first time in Moscow, to manufacture automatic rifles, turning out its first consignment of rifles for the twenty-fourth anniversary of the October Revolution. Thousands of skilled workers had been evacuated to the rear, comparatively few remaining in Moscow. But to their assistance came housewives, wives of men who had left for the front, juveniles and schoolchildren.

Moscow youngsters in the winter 1941–42! Some day a good children's author will write a wonderful book about them. They were everywhere. They replaced their fathers in the factories. They turned out automatic rifles, grenades, shells and mines. They replaced nurses in hospitals. They went on duty during air raids as the local A.R.P. posts. In their school workshops they made bags for presents and parcels for the front, made up mugs and knitted mittens and gloves. Like their grown-up brothers, sisters and fathers, they took part in the defense of Moscow. And if ever a monument to Moscow's defenders is erected on one of the Moscow squares, among the bronze figures, next to that of his father with an automatic rifle in his hands, there should be the fifteen-year-old son, who, in the autumn of 1941, forged this rifle for him.

Moscow was calm and stern in those days. The closer the Germans came, the closer it was to the beginning of December, the more alarmed, as it seemed, the Moscovites should have become at the decreasing distance between the Germans and Moscow, the calmer and more confident they became, the more furiously they fought at the front, the more intensely they worked in Moscow itself. The capital of a great people showed great examples of heroism.

The thinned divisions of the Moscow defenders fought with the fury of men whose backs are to the wall — thus far and no farther. And they went no farther. If the Germans succeeded in capturing a village or gained another bit of territory in those days, it meant that there was no longer a single defender left alive there.

And while the few remaining of Soviet defenders near Zvenigorod, Dedovsk, Chernays, Gryaz, Skhodnya, near Kashira and in the suburbs of Tula were harassing and bleeding with Hitler's divisions, which were already beginning to doubt their ultimate success and growing more savage as a result, echelons carrying tanks, cannon of various caliber, and regiments and battalions of eager young Red Army men, well clad in warm winter uniforms and equipped in full with the finest of armaments, were speeding regularly, a new echelon every ten or fifteen minutes, over the few trunk lines connecting the capital with the rear.

None knew where these echelons were unloaded, where this tremendous number of people, tanks, and guns disappeared. They had been moving through the whole of November and the beginning of December. But none of them appeared at the front. Only with their hearts and their soldier's intuition did the men at the front guess their presence. And this increased the force of their resistance tenfold.

Scores of divisions and tank brigades were swallowed up in the great forest around Moscow, somewhere quite near the front. These divisions and brigades were like a heavy executioner's sword, which Stalin had raised over the heads of the Germans, who were already appointing quartermasters for billeting troops in the warm houses of Moscow.

By December 4, the steel spring had contracted to its limit, and on December 5 all the reserves concentrated near Moscow, all that had been made ready for the blow with such painstaking care and iron self-restraint, all the troops and artillery, all the tanks, in a word all that had been concentrated around and beyond Moscow in accordance with Stalin's strategic plan to form a huge fist of crushing power, struck out at the Germans. The spring had contracted as far as it would go and now it was released with incredible force. The word which the whole country was waiting to hear with bated breath — "Offensive" — became a reality. Our army near Moscow had gone over to the offensive. The names of villages and towns near Moscow again began to appear in the war communiqués, but in reverse order now. Through snow and over ice, in the bitter frosts and blinding snowstorms, our army advanced steadily. That tremendous and great advance, which people later began to call the winter destruction of the Germans near Moscow had begun.

Moscow! Winter is again approaching. The first snowflakes glitter in the deflected white rays of automobile headlights. With a clattering of hoofs, a mounted patrol rides through a deserted square. The slender spires of the Kremlin towers pierce and vanish in the late November skies.

Moscow! Millions of Soviet fighters, from the snow-covered peaks of the Caucasus to the leaden waves of the Barents Sea, dream of you today. They see you before them — proud and invincible, having thrown back from your ancient walls the alien, iron-clad hordes.

Moscow — to the Russian people you have ever been a symbol of their Native Land, the symbol of life. And henceforward you have also become for them the symbol of victory, a victory which does not come of itself, but which must be won, as you won it under your ancient walls.

114. El Alamein: The Third Reich Sustains a Major Defeat in One of the Decisive Battles of World War II, October 23, 1942

". . . the whole horizon burst open into dragon tongues of flames. . . ."

North Africa turned out to be one of the critical theaters in World War II. Control of the Suez Canal and the Mediterranean Sea was the prize. The first of three Axis drives into Egypt was launched on September 12, 1940, from Libya, by Marshal Rodolfo Graziani's Italian forces. In five days the Italian drive reached Sidi Barani and then stalled. When the Italian army collapsed, Hitler was forced to reinforce his ally with the Afrika Korps, led by General (later Marshal) Erwin Rommel. Then began a seesaw battle between the able German general and his British opponents.

On July 1, 1942, Rommel paused at El Alamein, a stony, waterless desert spot seventy miles west of Alexandria. The next month British Prime Minister Winston Churchill placed General Bernard Montgomery in charge of the British Eighth Army. Throughout the summer reinforcements – tanks, jeeps, trucks, planes, ammunition – were rushed to Montgomery. Using deception on a vast scale, he convinced the Germans that he was going to strike from the south.

On October 21, 1942, Montgomery hurled the full strength of his armies at the Germans to the north. "Kill Germans, even the padres," Montgomery exhorted his troops, "one per weekday and two for Sundays!" What happened at El Alamein was a bitter defeat for Hitler. "It may almost be said," commented Churchill, "that before

Richard D. Macmillan, United Press International, October 26, 1942. Courtesy of United Press International.

Alamein we never had a victory. After Alamein we never had a defeat."

The battle was described by Richard D. Macmillan of the United Press in a remarkable dispatch.

INSIDE THE GERMAN LINES, on the Egyptian Front, Oct. 24 (Delayed) — The biggest battle of Egypt is under way.

The British have attacked violently and have penetrated the enemy positions at many points. Tanks are passing in strength through gaps in the minefields.

The heaviest fighting is inside the German lines, and I am with the Fifty-first Highland Division, which burst through the German outer defenses.

The British have already advanced well into the enemy sector at some points, although they were held up in others, and fighting of the heaviest kind, involving both infantry and tanks, is going on.

This offensive began with the speed of lightning.

A skirl of bagpipes resounded from the Highlanders' front positions last night and the sound of music in the chill, moonlit desert must have been clearly audible in the German front lines, a few hundred yards away.

Suddenly the music was drowned out by the greatest blast of guns ever heard in Egypt.

The Allied barrage had opened with a terrifying roar from hundreds of guns. The battle was on.

All that night I advanced with the Highlanders, under the full moon. The Highlanders, famous bayonet fighters, were having their first action against the Germans since their unit was re-formed after the battle of France.

The first burst of guns soon gave way to a deafening clamor from hundreds of tanks rumbling out of hiding places in dry water courses. The tanks churned up a sandstorm as they raced into battle on our right, left and center. They pushed up to the enemy lines under a monstrous flaring and blaring of artillery and rode roughshod over the startled German African Corps.

By dawn German and Italian prisoners were streaming back across the deep-rutted track of No Man's Land.

The British Eighth Army seemed to pack a knockout blow from the word go. In two years of campaigns in the Western Desert I have never seen the British go at it with such drive, such coordination of effort and such meticulous timing. It made one realize that this was an offensive inspired by a new spirit. The timing was so perfect that all divisions, brigades and battalions seemed like parts of one electric clock.

One instant all was silent in the desert, except for the bagpipies and the soft shuffle of marching feet, where dimly outlined troops moved in single file along the powdery, gleaming sand trails.

Then, as if some one had pushed a button, the whole horizon burst open into dragon tongues of flames, with a tempestuous noise.

The barrage from massed batteries of medium cannon continued incessantly for six hours — a new record for the North African campaign.

Only twenty minutes after the first big bang, troops with fixed bayonets were crossing the starting line, filing through corridors in our minefields and mopping up the enemy's forward posts.

They continued on through the enemy minefields. The sky across No Man's Land became a fairyland of multicolored lights as silver and red tracer bullets streaked the velvet darkness. There were angry splurges of red and ocher where shells exploded in countless profusion and munitions dumps went up in cascades of flame.

New lights began winking and flickering inside gasoline tins, to mark passageways for our troops advancing through the minefields. We went ahead in fairly quick time, stormed the first two minefields, and took our objectives at bayonet point.

As the Highlanders, led by kilted pipers, bayoneted and machine-gunned their way through the strong points, other British, Australian, New Zealand, and South African troops swung forward in general advance. Considerable headway was made before dawn.

Our tanks followed the infantry through the gaps and deployed to engage German tanks within the enemy's main lines. This marked a change in desert warfare, which previously had been based on preliminary attacks to clear the way for infantry.

Success of the Russians in destroying German tank spearheads in the battle of Stalingrad were believed to have influenced the change in tactics. Another consideration is that, by sending infantrymen ahead under artillery barrages to hack out a path for tanks, our tanks can deploy in mass formation, after they have crossed the minefields, and meet the full weight of the enemy's armor in force, instead of being strung out to be picked off by enemy guns as they approach in single file.

In the sector where I marched, we crossed a half-mile-wide No Man's Land that was dotted with patches of camel thorn. We threw ourselves on the earth and dug in from time to time as German artillery and machine guns replied to our barrage. The enemy guns were feeble in comparison with our massed fire.

A Highlander officer used a walking stick resembling a shepherd's crook to signal his men, mostly waving them forward. The Highlanders then pushed on to clean up a mixed force of Germans and Italians that was dug into holes at the fringe of the enemy's outer minefields.

The first wave of infantry was able to infiltrate the Axis minefields without much difficulty. It met a stronger defense line, which also broke under the Highlanders' bayonet charge. All was going according to plan along the line of advance, except that the right wing was held up by an exceptionally well-fortified strong point, where the Germans and Italians held on grimly.

By midnight our wave had swept through the first objective and had pushed on without a halt to the second, which was taken after stiff fighting.

The battlefield was shrouded in haze from dust and cordite flares, either sent up by our land forces or dropped from planes — mostly ours, which were constantly overhead, bombing and gunning the enemy emplacements, trenches and pillboxes.

We stumbled upon wounded. Stretcher bearers alternately crouched and ran through the barrages, picking up the wounded and moving them to ambulances — which tried to keep pace with the advance, but had considerable difficulty in weaving in and out among the slow columns of tanks, trucks, artillery and anti-tank guns, with their succeeding lines of support troops.

Our casualties at present do not seem high — not as high as had been expected. I saw many wounded during that first night, but never heard one of those gallant lads utter a murmur from pain.

The Scots had named the enemy strong points after their home towns. One Axis knoll was called Perth. Our fellows quickly headed for others, designated Stirling, Nairn and Killin. Stirling fell at 4 A.M.

When a slight breath of wind cleared up the foglike haze, we could see on every side British infantry extended in single file or clustered in small groups with bayonets gleaming in the moonlight. Then a curtain of dust and fumes obliterated the troops again.

The first of our tanks had poured through one gap by midnight. They were met by fierce fire from German 88s. That battle was still going on at dawn, and a bigger battle was looming.

In my advance with the Highlanders, I walked five and a half hours and covered nearly five miles, two of which were into the German lines. We went through two enemy minefields, but there were still more minefields and barbed wire protecting the main enemy positions ahead.

Throughout the night fresh Allied troops moved up, riding on tanks. Many of the men slept peacefully while the tanks lumbered into battle positions amid a welter of fury and carnage.

A major told me he was lucky to be able to fight in the desert, because he had been taken prisoner during his division's gallant stand at St. Valery on the Somme.

"I was held by the Germans in three prisons, then by the French," he said. "I was in and out of thirteen prisons, all told, but I managed to escape from each one and finally reached Oran, where I escaped from a stinking jail, where I was held with seventeen Arabs. I stole a small cutter and sailed to Gibraltar. The British Navy picked me up and I rejoined the regiment after a year's adventures in France, Algeria and Morocco."

He was moving up to the battle line when I saw him.

I met troops from all parts of the British Isles, many of them reinforcements that Prime Minister Winston Churchill had promised.

There was a Cockney who whistled "Tipperary" as he marched a group of German and Italian prisoners back along a gap.

"I'd be mighty glad to take these boys all the way home to Brixton prison," he said.

The Forty-fourth and Fiftieth British Divisions are among others now in the line.

115. Stalingrad: Nazi Germany Is Defeated in a Major Turning Point of the War, February 2, 1943

"God Almighty, put an end to all this torture!"

Stalingrad and the Caucasus were Hitler's prime objectives in the summer offensive of 1942. His aim was to cut Russia's main north-south line of communications by crossing the Volga in the Stalingrad area and at the same time seize the oil fields of the Caucasus. He made a critical mistake when he tried to take both Stalingrad and the Caucasus in one blow.

In the battle of Stalingrad, a German army of five hundred thousand, including Italians, Hungarians, and Rumanians, commanded by General Friedrich Paulus, opposed sixteen Soviet divisions led by General Vasily I. Chuikov. The attack commenced in September 1942. Stalin ordered the city to be defended at all costs. After two months of house-to-house fighting, the Germans took most of the city, but the Soviet garrison held out, thus giving General Georgi Zhukov time to prepare a counteroffensive.

Early in November, Hitler reaffirmed his intention of taking the city: "I wished to reach the Volga at a certain point, near a certain city. That city happens to bear the name of Stalin himself. . . . I wished to take that city: we do not make exaggerated claims, and I can now tell you that we have captured it. Only a very few small parts of it are not yet in our hands. Now people may ask: 'Why does the army not advance faster?' But I do not wish to see a second

---

True to Type, A Section of Letters and Diaries of German Soldiers and Civilians on the Soviet-German Front (London, n.d.), p. 77. Reprinted by permission of Hutchinson & Co., Ltd.

Verdun. I prefer to reach my objectives by limited assaults. Time is of no importance."

In December, a German relief force was routed. The Russians fought in the battered houses, the alleys, the streets, the court-yards, the shops. They erected barricades of rubble from which they fought the Germans to a standstill. "Stalingrad," said one observer, "was a monstrous graveyard of shattered buildings, shak-ing walls, and rotting flesh."

On February 2, 1943, Paulus surrendered the remnants of his army, after having been told by Hitler that he was to stand and die before Stalingrad. The casualties were staggering; the Germans lost some three hundred thousand men in the debacle.

What it was like for the Germans in Stalingrad was described in the diary of a German soldier.

. . . 5/12. (DECEMBER 5) Things are getting worse. Heavy snowfall. My toes are frost-bitten. Gnawing pain in my stomach.

Toward evening, after an exhausting march, we entered Stalingrad. We were welcomed by bursting shells but managed to reach a cellar. Thirty people are there already. We are indescribably filthy and unshaven. Can hardly move. There is very little food. Three or four fags to go round. A terrible, savage mob. I am very unhappy. All is lost. Constant bickering. Everybody's nerves are on edge. No mail gets here. Awful.

6/12. Same. We are lying here in the cellar with hardly a chance to go out as the Russians spot us at once. Now we get at least a quarter of a loaf a day, one tin for eight men and a pat of butter.

7/12. No change. Oh God, help me return home safe and sound! My poor wife, my dear father and mother! How hard it is for them now. God Almighty, put an end to all this torture! Give us peace again. If we could only go home soon, return to a human way of life!

9/12. At to-day's dinner the portions were a bit larger but each loaf and tin must be shared by twelve. Yesterday was my blonde wife's birthday. I have a hard cross to bear. Life has become absolutely useless. Here there is one row after another. All caused by hunger.

10/12. Have been fasting ever since yesterday. Only had some black coffee. I am in utter despair. Heavens, is this going to go on much longer? The wounded stay with us. We can't get them away. They've got us surrounded. Stalingrad is a hell on earth. We cook horse carcasses. There is no salt. Many are suffering from dysentery. It's a terrible life. What evil did I do to deserve such punishment? Here, in this cellar, thirty people live in awful congestion. At two in the afternoon it already gets dark. The nights are very long. Will it ever be day?

11/12. To-day we got one-seventh of a loaf, a bit of fat and a hot meal was promised us. But in the evening I just collapsed, I was so weak.

12/12. Still in Stalingrad. A new unit is issuing us our supplies. The food situation is still very bad. Yesterday I did get some horse meat but to-day there is nothing doing. Somehow I expect to pull through it all. Matters simply must improve. Lively doings last night: artillery fire and grenades. The earth fairly shook. Our corporal went into action. We shall follow soon. There are some dysentery cases among us. I am frightfully hungry. If things only eased up a bit. Only not get sick or be wounded. God in Heaven, protect me!

116. Opposition: Students of the *Weisse Rose* Distribute a Leaflet Denouncing Nazism and Pay for It with Their Lives, February 22, 1943

"Hitler cannot win the war, he can only prolong it!"

Although Hitler was able to count on a fanatically loyal following, there were individuals and small groups inside Germany who regarded him as the personification of evil and as a dictator who had forever stained the good name of Germany. Distaste for the *Fuehrer* and his Third Reich went through three closely related stages — opposition, resistance, and conspiracy.

Opposition to Nazism came at several universities. At the University of Munich twenty-three-year-old Sophie Scholl and her brother Hans belonged to an opposition group called the *Weisse Rose* (White Rose). Composed of students, faculty, artists, and scientists, this group called for rejection of Hitler and Nazism in order to "strive for the renewal of the mortally wounded German spirit." Arrested on February 18. 1943, Sophie Scholl, her brother, and Professor Kurt Huber were brought on February 22 before Roland Freisler, the presiding "hanging judge" of the dreaded *Volksgericht* (People's Court). The death sentence was carried out a few hours later.

Following is one of the leaflets of the White Rose society, the distribution of which was declared to be treason to the state.

Leaflet translated by the editor.

APPEAL TO ALL GERMANS!

The war goes on to its certain conclusion. As in the year 1918, the German Government tries to tell us that the U-boat campaign is succeeding, while in the East our armies are retreating without stopping and in the West an Allied invasion is expected momentarily. America has yet to reach the height of her arming for war, and today she is already armed beyond anything like it in the past. With mathematical certainty Hitler is leading the German people to destruction.

Hitler cannot win the war, he can only prolong it. His guilt and that of those who helped him have already gone beyond the point of no return. A just punishment comes nearer and nearer!

What must the German people do? It sees nothing and it hears nothing. Blinded, it staggers on to its destruction. "Victory at any cost!" are the words written on its banners. "I shall fight to the last man," says Hitler — even though the war has already been lost.

Germans! Do you want yourself and your children to suffer the same fate as the Jews? Do you want to be judged the same way your mis-leader will be judged? Shall we forever be the most hated and rejected people in all the world? Separate yourself, therefore, from the National Socialist subhumanity! Show by your deeds that you think otherwise!

This is the beginning of a new War of Liberation. The most decent of our people fight on our side! Tear up the cloak of indifference which you have placed around your hearts! *Decide yourself, before it is too late!*

Don't fall for that National Socialist propaganda that has put the fear of Bolshevism in your bones! Do you really think that the salvation of Germany is bound up for better or worse with National Socialism? A criminal conspiracy cannot possibly win a German victory. Abandon *immediately and in time* anything to do with National Socialism! There is going to be a terrible and just verdict for those who have shown themselves to be cowardly and irresolute.

This war was never a national one. What will be its lesson for us?

The imperialist concept of power, no matter from which side it comes, must have its teeth drawn for all time. One-sided Prussian militarism must never again be allowed to win power. Only in noble cooperation with other Europeans can the ground be prepared for a new political structure. Any centralized power, such as that the Prussian state sought to exercise inside Germany and in Europe, must be stifled in its germinal stage. The future Germany can be only a federal state. Only a sound federal state order can give Europe a new life. Workers must be freed by a rational socialism from their condition of abject slavery. The phantom of an autarchic economy must disappear in Europe. Every single person has the right to the good things of the world!

Freedom of speech, freedom of conscience, protection of the individual from despotism of the criminal power-state, these will be the foundation of the new Europe.

Support the Resistance! Distribute these leaflets!

117. On the Fall of Italy, Hitler Calls on Almighty God to Bestow the Laurel Wreath of Victory on Germany, September 10, 1943

". . . . the vanquished will be destroyed so that the victor can live."

By the fall of 1943, the war situation was bleak for the Third Reich. The Russians had won enormous victories, North Africa had been lost, and the people of Germany were being subjected to Allied bombing day and night. A heavy blow came with the unconditional surrender of Italy. Hitler had not spoken at length in public for nearly a year. Now he was forced by circumstances to explain the irreparable destruction of the Rome-Berlin Axis.

It was one of his weakest speeches. Angered, he spoke of the betrayal by the discredited Italians. Allied power was not the cause, he claimed. It was again a stab in the back by villainous traitors to the *Duce*. The old aggressive posturing was gone. The *Fuehrer* now spoke defensively of the ring of steel surrounding the homeland. He exhorted his fellow Germans not to desert the noble Nazi cause but to fight to the death and have faith in ultimate victory. Hitler's speech was convincing neither to the German public nor to himself. Defeat was in the air.

Following is a translation of the opening and closing remarks of Hitler's speech in Berlin on September 10, 1943.

FREED FROM THE HEAVY BURDEN of expectation which we have endured for a long time, I now believe it the right time to talk to the German people without lying either to them or to myself.

Hitler's speech in Berlin, September 10, 1943. Translated by the editor.

The collapse of Italy was something we could have expected for some time. This collapse was not really due to Italy's inability to defend herself adequately or to the fact that the necessary German help was not forthcoming. Rather it was due to those Italians who caused the capitulation by their systematic sabotage. What these men wanted for years has not been achieved. The Italian leaders have deserted their ally, the German Reich, and gone over to our common enemy.

In September 1939, England and France declared war on the Reich. Italy was bound by treaty immediately to declare her solidarity with Germany. This was expedient because the enemy had a special fate planned for both Germany and Italy. We know that Mussolini was firmly determined to order immediate mobilization in Italy in accordance with his treaty obligations. In August 1939 those same elements which today have brought about complete capitulation succeeded in preventing Italy from entering the war.

As *Fuehrer* of the German people, I understood the pressing internal difficulties of the *Duce*. Hence, I did not insist that Italy fulfill her treaty obligations. Quite to the contrary, I left it entirely to the Italian government either not to enter the conflict at all or, if it did enter, to do so at a time convenient to it. By June 1940 Mussolini had the internal requisites for Italy's entry into the war at the side of the Reich.

At that time the struggle in Poland had been decided, as well as that in Norway and France. I was grateful to Mussolini for his attitude, but I understood his difficulties, not with the Italian people, but with his internal enemies. Since that time the Reich and Italy have remained side by side in battle in many theaters of war and both our nations have shed their blood together. The *Duce* and I — not for a second — doubted that the outcome of this struggle was to decide the life or death of our nations. . . .

We all know that, in this merciless struggle, and in line with the contentions of the enemy, the vanquished will be destroyed so that the victor can live. Therefore, we intend with the greatest determination, to take large and small steps which will frustrate the intention of our enemies.

Many Italians who are motivated by a sense of honor are inextricably linked with us in this struggle. Italy's withdrawal means little in a military sense because in reality the struggle in that country has really been carried on for months mainly by German forces.

Now we can continue the struggle freed of all encumbrances. The attempt of international plutocrats to talk away German resistance in Italy is naive. In this case they are confusing the German nation with another nation. The hope that traitors can be found in our country rests on a complete ignorance of the nature of the National Socialist state. . . .

In any case, my own personal life has ceased to exist. I work from recognition and a sense of duty — that is my contribution to safeguarding the life of my country for future generations. I believe unconditionally in success, a belief grounded in my own life and in the destiny of our people.

In 1939 we were alone and isolated when we had to face the declarations of war. We acted in the belief that teaches us that heroic resistance is much better than any cowardly submission. I declared as early as September 1, 1939, in my speech to the *Reichstag* that the German people would be brought to their knees by neither time nor force of arms. Since then the enemy, mostly through our own power, has been driven back some 1,000 kilometers from the German borders. Only from the air is he able to terrorize our German homeland.

But in this matter we are using new technical and administrative conditions for breaking the hold of terror, and we shall be able to retaliate by more efficient means. Because of tactical necessity we might have to give up something on some front in the gigantic struggle, in order to avoid some special threat, but our enemy will never break the ring of steel constructed by the homeland and maintained through the heroism of our front-line soldiers in protecting the German Reich.

We expect in just these times that the nation will fulfill its duty defiantly and with dogged determination in all spheres. It has every reason to have confidence in itself. The home front can look with pride upon its soldiers, who, with heroic sacrifice of their blood, perform their duties under the most difficult circumstances. The men at the front, too, who have endured under superhuman burdens through many weeks and months, must also remember the homeland, which today has also become a fighting front. Here old men, boys, mothers, women, and girls do their duty.

Every soldier has the sacred duty of maintaining the greatest steadfastness even more than the people at home, and he must do whatever is called for in the struggle. Never in their entire history have the German people had a better right to be proud of themselves than in this greatest struggle of all time.

This determination will defeat any attempt to make slaves of the German people. May every German be consciously aware that his efforts and his readiness for sacrifice are responsible for the attitude of our people and for the destiny of future generations.

I cannot merely thank with words the German people – the men and women of the home front as well as soldiers on the battle line.

Our future generations will one day express their gratitude in the knowledge that here a free and socially secure life has been won through the greatest sacrifice. I take pride that I am the leader of this nation and I am grateful to God for every hour he grants me so that through my work I can win the greatest struggle of our times.

The measures we have taken for the protection of German interests in Italy are very hard indeed. Insofar as they affect Italy, they are being applied according to a preconceived plan and the results already have been good.

The example of Yugoslavia's betrayal has given us a salutary lesson and a valuable experience. The fate of Italy is a lesson to us never, in the hour of gravest crisis and deep distress, to forsake the commandment of national honor but to stand steadfastly by our allies, and to do what duty commands.

To a people which passes successfully through these trials ordained by Providence, the Almighty will in the end bestow the laurel wreath of victory.

No matter what happens, this people must and will be German.

118. The Schweinfurt Raid: Allied Air Power Helps Turn the Tide of War Against the Third Reich, October 14, 1943

"Then came a hell — great black balls of flak all around us."

The first two years of World War II saw one resounding Nazi success after another, but the direction of events slowly began to turn against Hitler and his war machine. After the *Luftwaffe* was defeated, the Allied counteroffensive in the air became a study in devastating revenge. The British and American air forces took part in round-the-clock operations, the former raiding by night and the latter by day. In 1943, some forty German cities and fifty other targets of lesser significance were thoroughly pummeled.

In the mounting air offensive the American Eighth Air Force was assigned the task of striking at Schweinfurt, center of the vital ball-bearing industry in southern Germany. The raid cost the Americans sixty Flying Fortresses and two P-47 fighters, some $20 million in equipment, and the lives of 593 men. Against these losses were measured ninety-nine Nazi planes, twenty-six probably shot down, and damage to seventeen others. Despite the heavy losses, the Allied High Command judged the raid as militarily justified.

The following dispatch to *Yank, The Army Weekly* described the devastating air battle.

A BOMBER BASE IN BRITAIN (By Cable) — It was still dark when they woke the crews. The fog lay thick and cold over the countryside that morning,

---

*Sergeant Walter Peters, in *Yank, The Army Weekly*, cable sent on October 14, 1943.

and inside the barracks all was pitch black and silent except for the deep, steady breathing of the sleeping Fortress gunners.

I had been awake for some time and I heard the door of the next hut slam shut, and then the sound of footsteps outside. Someone struck a match and announced that it was 6 o'clock. Then the door opened and the lights went on, cold and glaring when viewed from a warm bed.

The squadron operations officer, bundled up warmly against the morning's cold in a sheepskin jacket and flying boots, walked toward the center of the room. He started to read the list of names from a slip of paper, quietly so as not to wake up those who weren't flying that day.

"Baxter, Blansit, Cavanaugh, Hill, Sweeney," he said. The men whose names were called sat up sleepily, slid their feet a little wearily to the cold floor and stayed there on the bunks, most of them, for a few seconds before getting dressed. They shivered in the damp and cold.

"Briefing's at 0730," the officer said. Then he went on to another hut.

The men dressed quietly, trying not to disturb those who could sleep a little later and secretly envying them. Next to me bunked Sgt. Bill Sweeney, a former tire salesman and now a gunner. He lit a cigarette and came over to my bunk and said he thought this would be a fine day to christen his Fortress, which had made a dozen missions but until now was without a name. This was the first mission since the crew had decided a few days ago to name the ship *Yank*.

I drew back the blackout curtain carefully and looked out at the gray morning. "It looks pretty foggy to me," I said. "You never can tell about English weather," said Sweeney. "You're very goddam right you can't," said a sergeant gunner sitting on the next bunk. "You never can tell."

We headed for the combat mess. There, in the noise of conversation and the clatter of dishes, we had a big breakfast and polished it off with a cigarette before walking on to the briefing.

It was beginning to get light now. The briefing room, like the mess hall, was bright and noisy, until a mild-mannered Intelligence captain rose to speak. He had a long ruler in his hand and he kept toying with it as if it were a swagger stick.

Nobody knew where we were going, and there was a dead silence as he raised his ruler to the map. He pointed first to our base in Britain, then moved the ruler slowly over the North Sea into Belgium, as though he himself were exerting a tremendous effort to get us over the target.

The ruler moved through Belgium slowly and ate deeper and deeper into Germany until I thought for a moment we were being briefed for Austria. Way down in the southern reaches of Germany near Frankfort the ruler stopped. "This, gentlemen, is your target for today — Schweinfurt."

The men listened intently, leaning forward from the long rows of benches and chairs. The air was clouded now with cigarette smoke.

"Schweinfurt," the captain continued, "is the most important target in all of Germany. We cannot go ahead with other targets until it is seriously crippled."

The gunner ahead of us strained forward to get a better view of the map. "Half of Germany's ball bearings," the captain went on, "are produced at Schweinfurt, and ball bearings are important to Hitler. If we destroy these factories, we will have crippled the enemy's production of tanks and planes and submarines to a very great degree." Then the captain gave technical information about the target, the wind and the weather, and the briefing was over.

"I think this Schweinfurt is named after a very special kind of pig," said one of the radio operators as we headed toward the truck. We rode up the taxi strips to our head stand, where the crew stood around the ship. Station time was 30 minutes ahead, and the guns, ammunition, radio and bomb bays had been checked.

The skipper of *Yank* was a 21-year-old giant from Monterey, Calif., Capt. Ivan Klohe. While we waited for the take-off he wrestled with the two waist gunners, Sgts. Charlie Hill and Edward Cavanaugh. Though Cavanaugh was only a little over 5 feet tall, he succeeded in pinning the captain's shoulder to the ground, and Hill put a deadly lock on the captain's legs. The rest of the crew stood by and cheered for the gunners.

Then station time was announced. The men, suddenly serious, took their positions in the ship. I climbed into the nose with Lt. Howard J. Zorn, the navigator, and Lt. Richard J. Roth, the bombardier. "The right gun's yours," Roth said. *Yank* took its place on the runway.

Lt. Herbert Heuser, the co-pilot, announced over the interphone: "There goes *Piccadilly Queen.*" We watched as she sped down the black runway, at 50, 60, and then 90 miles an hour. It was a beautiful take-off. So was ours.

About 11,000 feet the pilot told us to check our oxygen masks. We put them on. Heuser imitated a fireside chat over the interphone. "My friends," he began, and the crew ate it up. Then he sang, and Cavanaugh and Zorn chimed in occasionally with a razzberry, a hard sound to produce over the interphone. There were more songs from Hill, from Sweeney and from Sgt. Roy (Tex) Blansit, the top-turret gunner. The war seemed beautiful at that point.

Our formation across the North Sea was perfect. We led the "Purple Heart" element, and in front of us the sky was literally clouded by B-17s. We counted as many as 190 and then quit counting. Zorn told us to look toward the long file of P-47 Thunderbolts on our right. They left a beautiful silver vapor trail behind them.

At 1302 the captain warned that we were approaching enemy territory.

We were above 20,000 feet and suddenly over the interphone somebody shouted: "Unidentified vessels down below." A couple of seconds later he said: "They're shooting." "Why the silly bastards," somebody else remarked.

By 1330 we were over Luxembourg. The sun was still with us, and the nose was so hot we didn't even bother using our electric suits. A pair of white silk gloves was enough to keep our hands warm. Enemy fighters were getting hot about that time, too.

Heuser did most of the calling, singing out the fighters' position in a cool and undisturbed voice. From his place he could see all of the planes, and he didn't miss a German. "Fighter at 5 o'clock high . . . fighter at 10 o'clock . . . Fighter at 8 o'clock low . . . fighter at 3 o'clock . . . fighter at 12 o'clock . . . ."

There were fighters everywhere, but mostly on our tail. "The whole goddam *Luftwaffe* is out today," somebody said over the interphone. There were even Dornier bombers. There were single-engined ME-109s and twin-engined 110s. There were JU-88s and a few 190s. There were ME-210s and heaven only knows what else.

"This is nothing," Zorn said, evidently trying to calm me down. "We've seen worse on other raids. In about 25 more minutes we'll come to the target."

The captain put the Fort into a little evasive action, banking to the left and then to the right. On our right we sighted a huge column of smoke, like a great black cloud. That was the target. Liberators and Fortresses had passed the ball-bearing works already, scoring hits on the plant.

The navigator told me to look out on the left side. A couple of planes were burning there, a Fort and an enemy fighter. Three white chutes and one brown were floating in the sky near by. The whites belonged to our boys. Under the brown chute was a German flyer.

"When the hell are we getting over the target?" Time had crawled by in the last 15 minutes. In 10 more we'd be there. Heuser was still calling the fighters off. They were coming in from all sides now, but not too close.

Looking back through the fuselage, we could see Tex's legs, his left one planted on a box of caliber-50s, the right one lazily dangling into space. From the interphone we knew that Tex was very busy in his top turret. His gun was tracking fighters all around the clock. Occasionally he concentrated his fire toward the tail, where his friend Sweeney was busy shooting at the enemy as they queued up from the rear.

A JU-88 and a 190 attacked Sweeney's position from 4 and 9 o'clock high. Tex's guns worked fast. Both planes peeled off. The 190 shied off but the 88 returned from about 500 yards to the rear, flying smack at Sweeney.

Tex called out directions to Sweeney. "You're shooting at him just a little high. Get him lower. A little lower." The 88 came closer and lobbed two of the rockets the Germans are using now — deadly looking affairs shooting out like huge red flames.

Tex kept on guiding Sweeney over the interphone. "A little lower, Bill." Bill fired a little lower. The 88 wavered, flipped over, and Sweeney and Tex saw the German catch fire and trail smoke. Then there was one JU-88 less, and one less JU-88 crew; they didn't get out.

Klohe headed the Fort northeast hitting a straight course for the tall column of smoke 6,000 feet high that marked the target. At our level and even higher flak blackened the sky. Roth was ready. It was only a matter of 20 seconds before he released the bombs.

Then came a hell — great black balls of flak all around us. It seemed impossible to escape the barrage. We weren't having fighter trouble now; our enemy was flak and there was nothing we could do about it except to take evasive action. Klohe did just that, and he did it beautifully. It seemed a miracle that we ever escaped.

Suddenly we heard a loud, jangling noise, even above the roar of the four engines. I looked toward the navigator. A fragment of flak had broken through the plate glass at his side. Zorn lifted his head quickly, took off his gloves and fur cap, and felt around the part of his face not covered by the oxygen mask. He winked when he found that he was okay.

The flak had stopped now but enemy fighters and fighter-bombers were back again. Heuser, too, was back on the job. "Fighter at 11 o'clock," Heuser announced. Zorn tracked the German with his 50s until the plane was out of sight. "Fighter at 12 o'clock," Heuser reported, and followed him. "Fighter at 5 o'clock," and Sweeney was back at his guns. "Fighter at 2 o'clock," and I grabbed my gun and tracked the German until Heuser bawled me out for using too much ammunition. I stopped fast.

Now Heuser's voice again: "Fighter at 3 o'clock." Tex saw the fighter, recognized it as a 190 and waited until it came closer before letting loose a barrage. Sweeney congratulated him. From where Sweeney was, he could see the 190 spiral down and the pilot bail out. That was Jerry No. 2 for the boys of *Yank*.

A third fighter was claimed by Cavanaugh, the left-waist gunner, who bagged an 88. The plane went spinning toward the ground in flames but the crew of two bailed out.

All this time Sgt. Ralph Baxter, the ball-turret gunner, and Hill in the right-waist position were engaging two 88s. Baxter had spotted the Germans diving after a lone B-17, forced out of formation with a feathered engine, and he called to Hill for a hand. Between them they saved the crippled Fort from destruction.

It was about 1650 now, as we were heading home, but the watch on the panel wasn't running any more. We cussed, and when some more fighters came at us, we cussed some more. A half hour later flak started bursting again, but it wasn't as heavy as the stuff at Schweinfurt. Zorn said he thought we were near Amiens, France.

Just then I heard another loud jangle of broken glass as flak hit the left front plate. Roth ducked, but Zorn went calmly about the business of navigating. I put on a helmet and then took it off a few seconds later; it interfered with my vision and I wanted to see. Roth picked up a piece of flak and handed it to me. "Maybe you'll want this for a souvenir," he said.

We tried guessing the time. I figured it was about 1730. We were well across the English channel and in a few minutes the English coast would be in sight. Klohe began losing altitude. At 17,000 feet Roth and Zorn took off their masks, and I did, too. Zorn smiled.

Tired but happy voices began coming over the interphone. They were kidding again. Heuser sang. Zorn told us how sharpshooter Sweeney hadn't been able to hit a single skeet out of 15 a year ago. Somebody else kidded Tex because he was once rejected by the Army for flat feet. Cavanaugh gave the captain a riding over the interphone, and Klohe dished it right back at him. Personally, I just sat back, relaxed with a cigarette. The mission was over.

119. D-Day: Beginning of the End for Nazi Germany, June 6, 1944

"If you'll excuse me, I'll just take a deep breath for a moment and stop speaking."

On June 6, 1944, a great armada of four thousand ships, guarded by seven hundred warships, set off from southern England for the Normandy coastline. After two years of planning, some two million Allied troops were ready for the greatest amphibious invasion in history. After false and misleading "wet runs," a great strike force was unleashed on Hitler's Fortress Europe. Operation Overlord was designed to set the stage for Hitler's defeat.

The way was cleared by a flotilla of mine sweepers. Then the big guns of the Allied battlewagons smashed the German coastal batteries, while destroyers raced in to rake the shores with shellfire. Overhead the skies were alive with eleven thousand Allied warplanes, unloading tons of bombs and many thousands of paratroopers. Gliders brought in more and more assault troops. Finally, a maze of landing craft pushed ashore to unload their troops. By the end of that first day, one hundred fifty thousand Allied troops, mostly American and British, were ashore at five beaches. It was a military achievement such as the world had never seen.

The following two reports describe the D-Day landings from the sea and the air. The first report by George Hicks for the Columbia Broadcasting System reported the scene from an American naval flagship in the English Channel. It aroused tremendous interest at

CBS broadcast by George Hicks, June 6, 1944. Courtesy of Columbia Broadcasting System; Leonard Mosley, in the London *Daily Telegraph*, June 6, 1941. Courtesy of the London *Daily Telegraph*.

the time. The second report by Leonard Mosley of the London *Daily Telegraph* described the invasion from the air.

George Hicks: From an American Naval Ship in the English Channel

This is George Hicks speaking. I am speaking now from a tower above the signal bridge of an American naval flagship and we're lying some few miles off the coast of France where the invasion of Europe has begun. It's now twenty minutes to six and the landing craft have been disembarked from their motor ships and are moving in in long irregular lines towards the horizon of France which is very plain to the naked eye.

Our own bombardment fleet lying out beyond us has begun to blast the shoreline and we can see the vivid yellow burst of flame quite clearly although the sound is too far away to be heard, and at the same time from the shore are answering yellow flames as the Nazi batteries are replying.

Overhead planes are high up in the thin cloud which is a gray screen over the sky but which is not thick nor heavy, and is not low enough to be an inconvenience to bombing.

The LCT's and LCI's have begun to pass along the side of us. Those are the amphibious beach-landing craft that carry the tanks, trucks, the bulldozers, and finally the men ashore. They have been churning along and are bouncing along in the choppy channel sea now, and all around us on either side are stretched the vast transports at anchor, which have disembarked the small craft. All over the surface of the sea here they can be seen cutting and zigzagging and then falling into those somewhat irregular lines that make a black pencil-point across the sea itself, heading towards the ribbon of land that's France and the coast of Normandy. . . .

It's now becoming quite near daylight as six A.M. approaches on June 6th, 1944. . . . We can hear the thud of shells or bombs landing on the French coastline, perhaps eight or ten miles before us, and the steel bridge on which we stand vibrates from the concussion of the heavy guns that are firing on the American and British battleships and heavy cruisers on the long line right behind us. I can count twenty-two of the squat square-nosed landing craft, carrying vehicles . . . as they turn and bounce in the chopping sea awaiting the exact timing to form their lines and start in toward the beach.

On our first (static) . . . it was the shore batteries of the Nazis that had spotted us here at sea (*static*) . . . and our naval bombardment squad has replied to them.

One battleship is in as close as three miles, and one of the famous American battleships, the *Texas* was . . . (*static*) . . . finally in her firing position. (*Static*) . . . battleships lying just a couple of miles off the French shore and firing broadsides into the land. The Germans are replying from the land with flashes and then the battleship lets go with its entire broadside again. The whole side of the battlewagon lights up in a yellow flare as a broadside goes off, and now we can see brown and gray smoke drifting up from her, from her gunbarrels . . . and now batteries are firing from the beach . . . the broadsides of the battleship are pouring it back at them. Overhead, high, planes are roaring . . . they just came in and dropped a salvo of bombs. . . .

The (*static*) . . . One of America's famous cruisers, is in off the shore near (*static*) . . . as well as the *Texas*, the *Nevada*, and the *Arkansas*; old battleships . . . They're just anchored off shore and blowing into the Nazi batteries on shore . . . The first Allied forces are reaching the beaches in France. . . .

That baby was plenty low!

I think I just made the statement that no German planes had been seen and I think there was the first one we've seen so far . . . just cleared our stack . . . let go a stream of tracers that did no harm . . .

(*Sound of ship's whistle*)

Our own ship has just given its warning whistle and now the flak is coming up in the sky. . . .

It's planes you hear overhead now . . . they are the motors of Nazis coming and going. . . . The reverberation of bombs. . . .

(*Sound of crash*)

That was a bomb hit, another one. That was a tracer line, shaped arching up into the darkness.

Very heavy firing now off our stern. . . . Fiery bursts and the flak and streamers going out (several words drowned out by voice in background and static) in the flak.

(*Sound of explosions*)

Now, it's died down. . . . We can't see the plane. . . . Here comes a plane. . . . More anti-aircraft fire . . . in more toward the shore . . . the Germans must be attacking low with their planes off our stern because the streamer fire of the tracers is almost parallel with the water. (*Noises in background*) . . . Flares are coming down now. You can hear the machinegunning. The whole seaside is covered with tracer fire . . . going up . . . bombs . . . machinegunning. The planes come over closer (*sound of plane*), firing low . . . smoke . . . brilliant fire down low toward the French coast a couple of miles. I don't know whether it's on the shore or is a ship on fire.

Here's very heavy ack-ack now — (*heavy ack-ack*) — right . . . the plane seems to be coming directly overhead . . . (*sound of plane and machinegun fire and ack-ack*)

Well, that's the first time we've shot our guns . . . directly right over our head . . . as we pick up the German bombers overhead.

VOICE: What was that — a bomb?

VOICE: Cruiser firing over there.

HICKS: Heavy fire from the naval warships . . . twenty mm. and forty mm. tracer . . . was the sound you just heard. . . .

Well, it's quiet for a moment now. . . .

If you'll excuse me, I'll just take a deep breath for a moment and stop speaking. . . .

Now the air attack has seemed to have died down. . . . See nothing in the night. . . .

Here we go again! (Noise) Another plane has come over . . . right over our port side . . . tracers are making an arc right over the bow now . . . disappearing into the clouds before they burst. . . .

Looks like we're going to have a night tonight. Give it to her, boys . . . another one coming over . . . a cruiser on . . . pouring it out . . . something burning is falling down through the sky and hurtling down . . . it may be a hit plane. (Terrific noises in background) . . . Here he goes . . . they got one! (Voices cheering) They got one (Voice: Did we?) Yeah. . . . Great splotches of fire came down and are smoldering now just off our port side in the sea . . . smoke and flames there. (Various sounds and voices in background) . . . The lights of that burning Nazi plane are just twinkling now in the sea and going out. . . .

To recapitulate, the first plane that was over . . . was a low-flying German JU-88 that was leading the flight and came on the convoy in surprise, we believe, because he drew up and only fired as he passed by, and perhaps he was as surprised as we were to see each other. . . . One bomb fell astern of this warship, a hundred and fifty yards away as the string of rockets were fired at a cruiser beside us on the port side. No damage was done and gun number forty-two on our port, just beside the microphone, shot down the plane that fell into the sea off to the port side. . . . Scheiner (?) of Houston, Texas, who is the gunnery control officer, and seaman Thomas Snyder (?) of Baltimore, Maryland, handled the direction finder. It was their first kill for this gun and the boys are all pretty excited about it. A twin-barrel forty mm. anti-aircraft piece.

They are already thinking of painting a big star on their chart and will be at that first thing tomorrow morning. . . . It's daylight. . . .

Leonard Mosley: With the Sky Troops

June 6 — At two minutes past one this morning I parachuted into Europe — six-and-a-half hours before our seaborne forces began the full-scale invasion. I was near the shore, hiding from Nazi patrols as I watched our first forces go ashore from the sea at 7:15 A.M. Those paratroops and glider-borne troops I consider the bravest, most tenacious men, I have ever known. They held the bridgehead against Hitler's armies for over sixteen hours, despite overwhelming odds. I believe that the things they have done are almost solely responsible for the great success of the invasion so far in this sector.

Our prime job as an airborne force was to silence a coastal battery, which might otherwise have blown our ships to bits as they came to the shore. We silenced it.

Our other job was to secure two important bridges over the canal and river north of Caen and to hold them against all comers until the main armies arrived. We are still holding them. They are still intact.

I emplaned in "C. for Charlie," a great black bomber, at 11:20 last night, and we took our place in the taxi-ing line of planes that stretched from one end to the other of one of the biggest airfields in Britain. There were Lancashire men, Yorkshiremen and Northumbrians.

Half an hour before us went the gliders and paratroopers who were going to try to take the vital bridges before they could be blown up. It was our job to bring them aid within thirty minutes of their surprise attack, and to prevent the Nazis from counter-attacking.

As our plane, the third in the formation, took the air and pointed for France, little Robson, next to me, was singing softly.

It was five minutes to one when the light snapped off and a door in the plane was opened. Under it we could see the coast of France. Flak from the coast defenses was spouting flame everywhere.

The red light flashed and swiftly changed to green, and we were all shuffling down the hole and jumping into space. We knew we were going down to enemy territory covered with poles and holes, and thick with Nazis waiting for us.

I looked, as I twisted down, for the church I had been told to use as a landmark, but the wind caught me and was whisking me east. I came down in an orchard outside a farmhouse.

As I stood up with my harness off and wiped the sweat of my brown-painted face I knew I was hopelessly lost. Dare I go to the farmhouse and ask for directions? Suddenly there was a rip and tear in my flapping jumping-smock, and I flung myself to the ground as machine-guns rattled. There were two smashing explosions — handgrenades. I could now see figures manoeuvring in the moonlight. I dived through a tangle of barbed wire into the next field, and began to run at the crouch.

Then, suddenly, at the farther edge there were two more figures, and they were coming towards me, carrying guns. There was a crash of Sten-gun fire, and both men crumpled up not 15 yards from me. Into the field stealthily came five men to challenge me — and I was with our own paratroopers again.

For two long weary hours we wandered the country. We hid from German patrols in French barns. We shot up a Nazi car speeding down a lane. A youth appeared with a German flask full of Normandy wine, and after we had drunk it he led us away from the enemy. Just after 3 A.M. we made our rendezvous.

I dropped my heavier equipment and made my way to the bridges where the battle had ceased. Over both the river and the canal, spans were in our hands and firmly held by paratroop machine-gunners. Only beyond, in the west country, could the noise of battle be heard as we beat back a German counter-attack. The situation was grim. We had taken the Nazis by surprise, but they knew what was happening now and we could expect their tanks at any moment.

At 3:20 A.M. every Allied paratrooper breathed a sigh of relief as he heard the roar of bombers towing gliders towards the dropping ground. We watched the gliders unhooking and then diving steeply for earth. One, hit by A.A., caught fire and flew around like a ball of flame. We heard the crunch of breaking matchwood as gliders bounced on rocks and careened into still-undestroyed poles. But out of every glider men were pouring, and jeeps and anti-tank guns and field guns — and we knew that even if Nazi tanks did come now we could hold them.

And now, as a faint glow began to appear in the sky, there was a roaring that rapidly grew to a thunderous roll. The climax of Phase One of the invasion was approaching. Bombers were swarming in like bees to give the coastal defenses their last softening-up before our seaborne forces landed.

We were about two miles away, but the shudder of explosions lifted us off the ground. Soon the sky was lit with a green and purple glow from the burning German dumps, and still more bombers came in and more bombs thudded to earth.

As dawn came I moved across country through Nazi patrols to get nearer to the coast. Everywhere there were traces of our airborne invasion — empty containers still burning their signal lights, wrecked gliders, and parachutes. It was hazardous going; one Nazi patrol was within a few yards of us, but we hid in a quarry and dodged them. Eventually we reached high ground overlooking the coast and waited until our watches showed 7:15.

A few minutes before it there was an earth-shaking holocaust of noise. Approaching the coast under cover of naval ships, the invasion barges were coming in, and firing as they came. It was a terrific barrage that must have paralysed the defenses.

Then ships began nudging towards the beaches, and we shook hands in the knowledge that the invasion had at last begun.

By 10 A.M. the area of ground where we had established headquarters was getting a roasting from shells and mortar bombs. Prisoners were coming in now. I went into the village to drink a glass of cider with the Mayor. "Thank God you've come now, monsieur," he said. "Next week all the men in the area were to be conscripted to drape barbed wire across the poles in the area where you dropped." He arranged to give us a regular supply of milk and eggs from the farm. "I've three sons in Nazi prison camps, and I hate Boches," he said. "We have waited a long time for the hour of liberation."

There were children playing in the streets unmindful of the war only a few yards away.

Just outside the town, along the road to Caen, one paratroop unit was fighting a grim battle against the Nazi panzers, including two Panther tanks. One of the posts had been over-run and their antitank guns destroyed, but everywhere men were fighting desperately yet confidently.

I made my way back to the bridges to contact one of our units holding the bridgehead on the other side. The road was impassable, and one walked at a crouch through a ditch. Every few hundred yards one "ran for it," with snipers' bullets smacking the mud around. Nazi counter-attacks were coming every few minutes. But these Lancashire lads were holding on, though their numbers were growing hourly smaller. The unit fought on until all opposition from the north-west ceased, and to their delight and relief a long line of green bereted men came into view. They were men of a noted commando unit.

More panzer grenadiers and self-propelled guns were massing on our southern flank. Around 6 P.M. a counter-attack was reaching full strength. We were all asking ourselves: Will relief come — relief from the sky?

They did not let us down. It was just on 9 P.M. when the sky was suddenly filled with twisting and turning fighter planes, and under them a great fleet of bombers and gliders. As the gliders unhooked they wheeled through clots of ack-ack fire and dived steeply for earth. They were bigger gliders this time. Smoothly, with only a low whine of wind, down they came. It was a glorious sight. It lasted half an hour and became a maelstrom of noise as the Nazis tried vainly to hold them back. But I saw only one glider and one tug-plane hit. Then they were all down on the dropping ground and more men and more guns were pouring out. A general said to me, "Well, it's very satisfactory. It is still all going according to plan." We are confident it will continue to go according to plan.

120. Dr. Theodor Morell, Hitler's Personal Physician and Injection Specialist, Prescribes an Extraordinary Variety of Drugs for His Patient, 1936-1945

". . . for spasms and colic."

Dr. Theodor Morell (ca. 1890–1948), Hitler's personal physician and injection specialist, began his career as a physician for the celebrities of Berlin. Many well-known actors, actresses, and film stars came to his office on the Kurfürstendamm. After he cured Heinrich Hoffmann, Hitler's court photographer, of a critical illness in 1935, Morell was called in as the *Fuehrer's* personal physician and served him in this capacity for nine years. Hitler, who was convinced of Morell's genius, forbade any criticism of his doctor and urged many of his colleagues to use his services.

As time went by and Hitler complained of more and more symptoms, his doctor poured more and more drugs into him. It is probable that high dosages of these drugs weakened the *Fuehrer* during his final days.

Following is a list of drugs prescribed for Hitler by Dr. Morell from 1936 on.

THE PREPARATIONS MARKED with an asterisk are those shown as still in current use in the *Rote Liste 1969: Verzeichnis pharmazeutischer Spezialpräparate* (Aulendorf 1969).

"List of Drugs Prescribed by Dr. Morell, 1936-1945," from *Hitler: Legend, Myth and Reality,* by Werner Maser (New York: Harper and Row, 1973), pp. 343-45. By permission of Harper and Row Publishers, Inc.

Brom-Nervacit (Potassium bromide, sodium barbitone, aminopyrine) every other month as a tranquillizer and hypnotic: 1-2 tablets.

Cardiazol (pentamethylenetetrazol) and *Coramine* (diethylnicotinamide) for the stimulation of the circulatory centre in the brain, the vascular nerves and the respiratory centres given at intervals in the form of a solution from 1941 onwards (when oedema of the legs developed): ten drops a week.

Chineurin (product containing quinine, influenza remedy) taken orally to treat colds.

Cortiron (deoxycortone acetate, product of adrenocortical hormone) intended to combat muscular weakness and to influence the absorption of fats and carbohydrate metabolism (alleged by Morell to have been administered once only): intramuscular injection.

Dr. Köster's Antigas Pills (extr. nuc. vom. extr. bellad. aa 0.5, extr. Gent.) to combat flatulence; from 1936-43 (with occasional interruptions), before each meal.

Eubasin (sulphonamide) injected to combat infection and colibacilli: 5 ccm intragluteally.

Euflat (active bile extract: radix angelica, papaverine, aloe, coffea tosta, pancreatin and fel tauri) to promote digestion and also to inhibit flatulence; in the form of pills from 1939-44.

Eukodal (chlorohydrate of dihydroxycodeine, produced from thebaine) narcotic, analgesic and anti-spasmodic.

Eupaverin (isoquinoline derivative) for spasms and colic.

Glucose (5-10 per cent in solution added to other injections) to supplement calories and to enhance the action of strophantine, injected from 1937-40 (except for short interruptions): 10 ccm every two or three days.

Glyconorm (metabolic enzymes, containing cozymase I and II, vitamins and amino-acids) to promote the digestion of vegetable foods and reduce flatulence: administered occasionally (rarely, according to Morell), from 1938-40: 2 ccm intramuscular injections.

Homatropin POS eyedrops (homatropine-hydrobromide. 0.1 g; sod. chlor. 0.08 g; aqua dest. ad 10 ml) for treatment of the right eye.

Intelan (vitamins A, D_3, and B_{12}) to stimulate the appetite, help convalescence, protect against infection, promote physical resistance and combat tiredness, given therapeutically from 1942-44 (like *Vitamultin*): in tablet form, twice daily before meals.

Camomile for enemas: at patient's request.

Luizym (enzyme preparation; digestive enzyme; cellulose, hemicelluloses amylase and proteases) against digestive weakness (disturbance of protein digestion) and flatulence: one tablet after meals.

Mutaflor (emulsion of a strain of Escherichia coli) for causal therapy of symptoms connected with abnormal intestinal flora (e.g. meteorism, eczema and migraine, depressive states), given by Morell from 1936–40 for the regulation of intestinal flora in enteric capsules (colibacilli: normally about 25 thousand million organisms per capsule): on the first day, one yellow capsule, on the second, third and fourth, one red capsule, and from the fifth day onwards, two red capsules. (In 1943 *Trocken-Coli-Hamma was given for this purpose.*)

Omnadin (combination of proteins, lipoids from the bile and animal fat) to inhibit colds in the early stages of infection (sometimes in combination with *Vitamultin-Calcium*): intramuscular injection, 2 ccm.

Optalidon (patent analgesic of barbiturates and amidopyrines: allyl isobutylbarbituric acid = 0.05 g, dimethylaminophenazon, pyramidon = 0.125 g, caffeine = 0.025 g) for headaches: 1–2 tablets taken orally.

Orchikrin (extract of the seminal vesicles and prostate of young bulls, reinforced male sex hormone) to promote potency and combat exhaustion and depression (administered once only, according to Morell): 2.2 cm intramuscular injection.

Penicillin-Hamma: After the assassination attempt of 20 July 1944, over a period of eight to ten days in powder form, for treatment of the right hand.

Progynon B-oleosum (benzoic ester of follicular hormone) to improve the circulation of the gastric mucosa, and to prevent spasms of the stomach walls and vesicles, by intramuscular injection 1937–38.

Prostacrinum (extract of seminal vesicles and prostate) for the prevention of depression, given over a short period in 1943 at two day intervals: 2 ampoules, by intramuscular injection.

Prostrophanta (composite injection: 0.3 mg strophanthin in combination with glucose and Vitamin-B; nicotinic acid) given like strophanthin.

Septoid, for respiratory infections (Morell believed that by administering this drug he could also slow down the progress of arteriosclerosis); maximum dose, 20 ccm, injected.

Strophanthin (glycoside from Strophanthus gratus) for the treatment of coronary sclerosis: from 1941–44, in two to three week cycles, intravenous injections 0.2 mg daily.

Sympatol (p-hydroxyphenyl methylamino ethanol tartrate) to increase the minute volume of the heart, to promote cardiac activity and to help overcome cardiac and vascular insufficiency: from 1942 onwards (with occasional interruptions), 10 drops daily.

Tonophosphan (sodium salt of dimethylaminomethylphenylphosphinic acid) non-toxic preparation of phosphorus used both to supplement phosphorus and to stimulate the smooth muscles. From 1942–44, injected subcutaneously from time to time.

Trocken-Coli-Hamma: see under *Mutaflor.*

Ultraseptyl (sulphonamide) to combat inflammation of the upper respiratory tract: 1–2 tablets orally. To prevent concretions (e.g. kidney stones), taken with fruit juice or water after meals.

Veritol 1 (4-hydroxyphenyl)–2-methylamino-propane. In 1 g (20 drops): 0.01 g, in 1 ml ampoule solution: 0.02 g Veritol-sulphate. For the treatment of the left eye, from March 1944.

Vitamultin-Calcium (A, B complex, C, D, E, K, P) injected in combination with other drugs from 1938 to 1944: every other day 4.4 ccm.

The above list is complete save for Morell's product, the 'golden' *Vitamultin* tablets containing *Pervitin* and caffeine.

121. Conspiracy: Hitler Survives Bomb Attempt on His Life at His Secret War Headquarters, July 20, 1944

"The specter of 1918 hovered ominously over Germany in yesterday's developments."

By the summer of 1944, the opposition to Hitler had gone beyond resistance to conspiracy. There had been several occasions when assassins and plotters had sought to take his life: On November 8, 1939, a bomb planted in the Bürgerbräukeller, from which Hitler had set out to make his abortive *Putsch* exploded shortly after Hitler had left. On March 21, 1943, Colonel Freiherr von Gersdorff, chief of intelligence of army group center, volunteered on a suicide mission to place two British bombs in the *Fuehrer's* overcoat pocket. The plan failed when Hitler changed his schedule at the last moment. In February 1944 the conspirators in the army received an unexpected reinforcement when Field Marshal Erwin Rommel, the popular Desert Fox, joined the group led by General Ludwig Beck to assassinate Hitler.

The major attempt came on July 20, 1944, when Lieutenant-Colonel Klaus Philipp Schenck, Count von Stauffenberg, arrived at Hitler's secret war headquarters, the "wolf's lair" at Rastenburg in East Prussia. What happened there was reported in *The New York Times*.

The New York Times, July 21, 1944.

HITLER ESCAPES BOMB

FUEHRER 'BRUISED'

Bomb Wounds 13 Staff Officers, One Fatally — Assassin Is Dead

---

'USURPERS' BLAMED

Hitler Names New Chief of Staff — Himmler to Rule Home Front

By JOSEPH SHAPLEN

Adolf Hitler had a narrow escape from death by assassination at his secret headquarters, the Berlin radio reported yesterday, and a few hours later in a radio broadcast to the German people he blamed an "officers' clique" for the attempt to kill him. His address disclosed a movement in the armed forces to overthrow him and his regime. He announced that a purge of the conspirators was under way.

Thirteen members of his military staff were injured, one fatally and two seriously, by a bomb set off at an undisclosed place while many of his highest advisers were assembled around him. The man who played the role of assassin, Hitler said, was Colonel Count von Stauffenberg, one of his collaborators, who stood only six feet away from him as he hurled the bomb. Von Stauffenberg is dead, Hitler announced.

Waiting to see Hitler before the assassination attempt was Benito Mussolini. Reich Marshal Hermann Goering, who rushed to Hitler's side, was in the immediate vicinity. Hitler escaped with singes and bruises.

Army Clique Blamed

While Dr. Joseph Goebbels and Nazi radio propagandists at first tried to put the blame for the attempt to kill the Fuehrer upon the Allies, Hitler himself exploded the bombshell by announcing that the culprits were a group of German Army officers. He thus confirmed reports of a serious rift between the Nazi High Command and German military elements. . . .

Count von Stauffenberg is the son of Freiherr Schenck von Stauffenberg of Wilfingen, Wuertemberg. Hitler did not give the presumably executed count's Christian name, but there are three sons in the family, Werner, 39; Friedrich, 30, and Hans, 32 years old. . . .

Himmler's appointment as commander in chief of the home forces was foreshadowed in a Stockholm dispatch published in THE NEW YORK TIMES yesterday indicating that events of great import were brewing in Germany.

New Chief of Staff Named

The special powers with which Himmler was vested were those of Commander in Chief of the German home army, with instructions "to create order once and for all," a description considered pregnant with emphasis of a growing conflict between the Nazi hierarchs and insurgent military elements.

At the same time Hitler indicated a shake-up in the German High Command with the announcement that Col. Gen. Heinz Guderian, tank force commander, had been named Chief of Staff. He will replace Field Marshal Gen. Wilhelm Keitel, who has "retired for reasons of health."

How serious was the clash between the Nazi ruling circle and the "usurpers" of whom Hitler spoke was evident also from his statement that accounts would be settled "in a National Socialist manner" with his enemies in the armed forces.

He announced that Col. Gen. Hans Stumpf had been appointed commander in chief of all units of the Luftwaffe in the Reich and warned that "only his and my orders" are to be obeyed. He commanded also that Himmler was to be supported by all branches of the Luftwaffe.

Goering's part in the present confused political situation in Germany appeared mysterious in the light of yesterday's developments. He was in the immediate vicinity of the attempted assassination, but was absent at the critical moment, a circumstance recalling his conduct in the Munich beer hall bombing of Nov. 8, 1939, in which Hitler barely escaped, as he was during the historic Reichstag fire of 1933. Just as on those occasions, The Associated Press pointed out, Goering hurried to the scene of the latest attempt on Hitler's life immediately afterward.

Army-Navy Split Indicated

It appeared from United Press dispatches last night, however, that for the time being Goering remained at Hitler's side. He issued orders yesterday commanding members of the air force to confirm orders by telephone when in doubt as to their authenticity, an amazing development, indicating that Hitler no longer can put implicit faith in the officers and men of the Luftwaffe.

A further indication of the cleavage between Hitler and his immediate entourage on the one side and the professional naval and military elements on the other was seen in a speech by Admiral Karl Doenitz, supreme German naval commander, transmitted by the German Home Service and

monitored by the Federal Communications Commission. Admiral
Doenitz declared that a "mad clique of generals that had nothing in common with the army itself had staged a plot."

"In their stupidity," he added, "they hoped to eliminate Germany from
the war by getting rid of Hitler."

The Doenitz statement declared that the navy "stands firm" and would
accept orders only from him and the navy's own leaders.

Hitler Uses Old Technique

Hitler's own characterization of the situation compared it to 1918, when
Germany was making her last vain effort to hold back the deluge. He
spoke of the "stab in the back," a slogan he used so successfully in stirring
up the German masses against the Weimar Republic, whose leaders he had
accused of bringing about the German defeat in World War I by under-
mining morale and letting down the armed forces in the field. The specter
of 1918 hovered ominously over Germany in yesterday's developments.

A telephone dispatch from THE NEW YORK TIMES bureau in Berne,
Switzerland, last night noted that telephone communications between the
Reich and the outside world had been cut since midnight Tuesday. All
attempts to reach the Reich by telephone through neutral quarters last
night received the answer "gespert" — closed.

After Hitler, Doenitz and Goering had spoken on the radio a mysterious
broadcast was picked up in London on the Frankfort wavelength by a
"Wehrmacht officer" who appealed to like-minded men to help "save our
cause."

The British radio, in a broadcast recorded by the Office of War Information, announced that telephone and telegraph communications between
Berlin and Stockholm had been resumed at 3:30 A.M. yesterday (Berlin
time) after an interruption of fourteen hours.

There was a suggestion that, contrary to the German announcement,
the attempt to kill Hitler and his staff had taken place on Wednesday and
not yesterday, and had perhaps occurred at Berchtesgaden, Hitler's private retreat, where he was holding a conference with his immediate military and naval advisers. Mussolini was reported to have been received by
Hitler at Berchtesgaden on Tuesday.

The first formal announcement of the attempted assassination came
from the official German DNB agency. It was quoted by The Associated
Press as follows:

"Special announcement: Today an attempt was made on the life of the
Fuehrer with explosives.

"The following members of his entourage were severely injured: Lieutenant General Schmundt, Colonel Brandt and Adviser Berger.

"The following suffered lighter injuries: Colonel General Jodl, Generals

Korten, Euhle, Bodenschatz, Heusinger and Scherff, Admirals Voss and von Puttkamer, Captain Assmann and Lieutenant Colonel Borgmann.

"The Fuehrer himself suffered no injuries except light burns and bruises. He has immediately resumed his work and, as scheduled, received the Duce for a lengthy conversation. A short time after the attempt, the Reichsmarshal (Hermann Goering) arrived to see the Fuehrer."

Late last night The Associated Press quoted the German radio as saying "the officers' conspiracy has completely collapsed."

The German radio declared that "ringleaders have either been shot or have committed suicide." Count von Stauffenberg was again mentioned among those executed.

"No incidents have been reported from anywhere," the radio continued, "and other guilty persons are being called to account," indicating that the bloody purge announced by Hitler was in full swing. Members of the armed forces, according to The United Press, were again warned against accepting "false" orders from the "usurpers," and it was intimated that Marshal Keitel, demoted chief of the German General Staff, might be among them.

122. Escape from Assassination: Texts of Talks by Hitler, Goering, and Doenitz, July 20, 1944

"This I consider to be confirmation of the task given to me by Providence to continue in pursuit of the aim of my life, as I have done hitherto."

Hitler miraculously survived the attempt on his life at Rastenburg. The bomb, which had burst only a few feet from the *Fuehrer*, had merely stunned him, punctured his eardrums, and bruised his right arm. After von Stauffenberg left the conference table, another officer moved the briefcase a few feet behind one of the table's heavy oak supports. This action saved the *Fuehrer's* life.

Immediately after the blast, Hitler, speaking as commander-in-chief, Hermann Goering, representing the *Luftwaffe*, and Admiral Karl Doenitz, speaking for the German navy, gave talks on the radio to assure the public that the *Fuehrer* had been saved by a miracle. These talks are reproduced here.

Meanwhile, von Stauffenberg, certain that Hitler had been killed, went on to Berlin to meet his fellow conspirators at the War Ministry. He and the other plotters were quickly arrested. Hitler's vengeance was terrible. Several hundred conspirators were slaughtered, some of them with strangling wire. Hitler had scenes of the executions filmed, and he spent hours watching the death throes of those who had attempted to take his life.

Texts reported by the Federal Communications Commission, Washington, D.C., July 20, 1944.

Hitler's Speech

German men and women: I do not know how many times an attempt on my life has been planned and carried out. If I address you today I am doing so for two reasons: first, so that you shall hear my voice and know that I personally am unhurt and well and, second, so that you shall hear the details about a crime that has no equal in German history.

An extremely small clique of ambitious, unscrupulous and at the same time foolish, criminally stupid, officers hatched a plot to remove me and, together with me, virtually to exterminate the staff of the German High Command. The bomb that was placed by Col. Graf von Stauffenberg exploded two meters [slightly more than two yards] away from me on my right side. It wounded very seriously a number of my dear collaborators. One of them has died. I personally am entirely unhurt apart from negligible grazes, bruises or burns.

This I consider to be confirmation of the task given to me by Providence to continue in pursuit of the aim of my life, as I have done hitherto. For I may solemnly admit before the whole nation that since the day I moved into the Wilhelmstrasse I have been imbued with one thought only: to do my duty to the best of my knowledge and ability. Also since it became clear to me that war was inevitable and could no longer be postponed I lived practically only in work and worry throughout countless days and sleepless nights.

At an hour in which the German army is waging a very hard struggle there has appeared in Germany a very small group, similar to that in Italy, that believed that it could thrust a dagger into our back as it did in 1918. But this time they have made a very great mistake. The assertion of these usurpers that I was no longer alive is disproved at this moment, as I am talking to you, my dear German fellow-countrymen. The circle that comprises these usurpers is extremely small. It has nothing to do with the German armed forces, and particularly nothing with the German army.

Himmler Made Home Commander

It is a very small clique of criminal elements, which will now be exterminated quite mercilessly.

I order, therefore, at this moment that no civilian authority has to accept any order from an authority that these usurpers arrogantly assume. Secondly; that no military authority and no leader of troops and no soldier should obey any order by these usurpers; that on the contrary everyone is in duty bound either to arrest a person bearing or issuing such an order or to kill him immediately if he offers resistance.

To create order at last, I have appointed Reich Minister Himmler to be commander of the army at home. Into the General Staff I have called Colonel General Guderian to replace the chief of the General Staff, who had to retire for health reasons, and I have summoned another proved leader of the eastern front to be his assistant. In all other Reich authorities there is no change.

Charges Attempts at Sabotage

I am convinced that by stamping out this very small clique of traitors and conspirators we will now at last create that atmosphere in the rear, at home, that the fighting front needs, for it is impossible that in the front line hundreds of thousands and millions of honest men offer their utmost, while at home a very small clique of miserable, ambitious types constantly attempts to sabotage this.

This time we will settle accounts in such a manner as we National Socialists are wont.

I am convinced that every decent officer and every brave soldier will understand at this hour what fate would have overtaken Germany if the attempt today had succeeded. Only very few, perhaps, are capable of visualizing the consequences. I myself thank providence and the Lord, not because I have been spared — my life is only care and work for my people — I thank them that I shall be allowed in the future also to carry this burden and to carry on with my work to the best of my abilities, as I have to answer for it with my conscience and before my conscience.

Therefore every German, whoever he may be, has a duty, (shouting) to counter these elements at once and with ruthless determination and either to arrest them at once or — should they offer resistance anywhere — to wipe them out at once. Appropriate orders have been issued to all troops. They are being strictly carried out with the obedience typical of the German Army.

Once more I may greet with joy especially you, my old fighting comrades, now that I have been again spared a fate that did not contain horrors for me personally, but that would have brought horror over the German people. But we also see here a clear sign of providence that I must carry on with my work and that I shall carry on with it.

Goering's Speech

Comrades of the Luftwaffe:

An incredible, mean attempt at murder was today committed against our Fuehrer by a colonel, Count Stauffenberg, acting on orders of a miserable clique of former generals who had to be chased from their posts for a leadership that was cowardly as it was incompetent.

The Fuehrer was saved miraculously by the working of an almighty Providence. These criminals are now trying to spread confusion among the troops by issuing false orders, be it as a new Government of the Reich or as usurpers.

Orders Aid to Himmler

I, therefore, have given the following order:

Colonel General Stumpf assumes on my order the leadership of all formations of the Luftwaffe inside Reich territory as commander in chief of the Luftwaffe of the Reich.

Only my and his orders are to be obeyed. When in doubt, confirm by telephone. Reich leader of the S.S. Himmler is, if requested, to be given every assistance by all commands of the Luftwaffe. Dispatch flights can be carried out only with my or his permission.

Officers and soldiers, whatever your rank, and also civilians: wherever these criminals appear or approach you and try to draw you into their contemptible plans, they are to be arrested at once and to be shot.

Where you yourselves are being employed for the extermination of these traitors you are to proceed ruthlessly. These are the self-same curs who tried to betray and sabotage the front. All officers who have abetted in these crimes have put themselves outside the pale of the nation, outside the army and outside all military honor, and outside their oath and loyalty.

Their extermination will give us new strength. Against this treason the Luftwaffe pits the loyalty that it has sworn and its ardent love to the Fuehrer and unreserved application of all its strength to victory.

Long live our Fuehrer, whom Almighty God has today blessed so manifestly!

Doenitz's Speech

Men of the German Navy:

Sacred anger and unbounded fury is in us in face of the criminal attempt that was designed to take the life of our beloved Fuehrer. Providence has determined differently; she has guarded and protected our Fuehrer and thereby not abandoned our German fatherland in its fateful struggle.

A mad small clique of generals that has nothing in common with our brave Army has in cowardly disloyalty instigated this murder to commit a most base betrayal of the Fuehrer and the German people. If these rascals and henchmen of our enemies, whom they served with unprincipled, dastardly and false cleverness — in reality their stupidity is unlimited — believe that by removal of the Fuehrer they can free us from our hard but inexorable and fateful struggle, they do not see in their fearful and blind limitation that their criminal act would have thrown us into terrible chaos and would deliver us unarmed into the hands of our enemies. Extermination and enslavement of our men and hunger and unbelievable misery would be the consequences.

Unspeakable unhappiness would be the lot of the people — infinitely more cruel and more difficult than even the hardest days that the present war . . . entail.

We will get even with these traitors. The German Navy stands fast in allegiance to its oath and in well-tried loyalty to the Fuehrer. Our devotion to duty and readiness for battle are unconditional.

You will accept orders only from me as Commander in Chief of the German Navy and from your own military commanders so as to prevent any misleading by forged instructions. You will ruthlessly annihilate any person who should turn out to be a traitor.

Long live our Fuehrer, Adolf Hitler!

123. The Allies Prepare a Protocol on the Occupation and Administration of the Greater Berlin Area, September 12, 1944

"The Protocol will come into force on the signature of Germany of the Instrument of Unconditional Surrender."

As early as September 12, 1944, the United States, the United Kingdom, and Soviet Russia agreed on the zones of occupation to be assigned each power after the expected surrender of Nazi Germany. The amendment of November 14, 1944, allocated the northwestern parts of Germany and Greater Berlin to the United Kingdom, established the Bremen enclave for the United States, and assigned the southwestern part of Germany and the southern part of Berlin to the United States. Later, French occupation zones were provided for both in Germany and Greater Berlin.

Protocol on Zones of Occupation and Administration of the "Greater Berlin" Area, September 12, 1944

The Governments of the United States of America, the United Kingdom of Great Britain and Northern Ireland, and the Union of Soviet Socialist Republics have reached the following agreement with regard to the execution of Article 11 of the Instrument of Unconditional Surrender of Germany: —

1. Germany, within her frontiers as they were on the 31st December,

U.S., Senate, Committee on Foreign Relations, *Documents of German History, 1944–1961* (Washington, D.C.: Government Printing Office, 1962), pp. 1–5.

1937, will, for the purposes of occupation, be divided into three zones, one of which will be allotted to each of the three Powers, and a special Berlin area, which will be under joint occupation by the three Powers.

2. The boundaries of the three zones and of the Berlin area, and the allocation of the three zones as between the U.S.A., the U.K. and the U.S.S.R. will be as follows: —

Eastern Zone (as shown on the annexed map "A")

The territory of Germany (including the province of East Prussia) situated to the East of a line drawn from the point on Lübeck Bay where the frontiers of Schleswig-Holstein and Mecklenburg meet, along the western frontier of Mecklenburg to the frontier of the province of Hanover, thence, along the eastern frontier of Hanover, to the frontier of Brunswick; thence along the western frontier of the Prussian province of Saxony to the western frontier of Anhalt, thence along the western frontier of Anhalt; thence along the western frontier of the Prussian province of Saxony and the western frontier of Thuringia to where the latter meets the Bavarian frontier; then eastwards along the northern frontier of Bavaria to the 1937 Czechoslovakian frontier, will be occupied by armed forces of the U.S.S.R., with the exception of the Berlin area, for which a special system of occupation is provided below.

North-Western Zone (as shown on the annexed map "A")

The territory of Germany situated to the west of the line defined above, and bounded on the south by a line drawn from the point where the western frontier of Thuringia meets the frontier of Bavaria; thence westwards along the southern frontiers of the Prussian provinces of Hessen-Nassau and Rheinprovinz to where the latter meets the frontier of France will be occupied by armed forces of***

South-Western Zone (as shown on the annexed map "A")

All the remaining territory of Western Germany situated to the south of the line defined in the description of the North-Western Zone will be occupied by armed forces of***

The frontiers of States (Länder) and Provinces within Germany, referred to in the foregoing descriptions of the zones, are those which existed after the coming into effect of the decree of 25th June, 1941 (published in the Reichsgesetzblatt, Part I, No. 72, 3rd July, 1941).

Berlin Area (as shown on the annexed 4 sheets of map "B")

The Berlin area (by which expression is understood the territory of "Greater Berlin" as defined by the Law of the 27th April, 1920) will be jointly occupied by armed forces of the U.S.A., U.K., and U.S.S.R., assigned by the respective Commanders in Chief. For this purpose the territory of "Greater Berlin" will be divided into the following three parts: —

North-Eastern part of "Greater Berlin" (districts of Pankow, Prenzlauerberg, Mitte, Weissensee, Friedrichshain, Lichtenberg, Treptow, Köpenick) will be occupied by the forces of the U.S.S.R.:

North-Western part of "Greater Berlin" (districts of Reinickendorf, Wedding, Tiergarten, Charlottenburg, Spandau, Wilmersdorf) will be occupied by the forces of***

Southern part of "Greater Berlin" (districts of Zehlendorf, Steglitz, Schöneberg, Kreuzberg, Tempelhof, Neukölln) will be occupied by the forces of***

The boundaries of districts within "Greater Berlin," referred to in the foregoing descriptions, are those which existed after the coming into effect of the decree published on 27th March, 1938 (Amtsblatt der Reichshauptstadt Berlin No. 13 of 27th March, 1938, page 215).

3. The occupying forces in each of the three zones into which Germany is divided will be under a Commander-in-Chief designated by the Government of the country whose forces occupy that zone.

4. Each of the three Powers may, at its discretion, include among the forces assigned to occupation duties under the command of its Commander-in-Chief, auxiliary contingents from the forces of any other Allied Power which has participated in military operations against Germany.

5. An Inter-Allied Governing Authority (Komendatura) consisting of three Commandants, appointed by their respective Commanders-in-Chief, will be established to direct jointly the administration of the "Greater Berlin" Area.

6. This Protocol has been drawn up in triplicate in the English and Russian languages. Both texts are authentic. The Protocol will come into force on the signature by Germany of the Instrument of Unconditional Surrender.

The above text of the Protocol between the Governments of the United States of America, the United Kingdom and the Union of Soviet Socialist Republics, on the zones of occupation in Germany and the administration of "Greater Berlin" has been prepared and unanimously adopted by the European Advisory Commission at a meeting held on 12th September, 1944, with the exception of the allocation of the North-Western and South-Western zones of occupation in Germany and the North-Western and Southern parts of "Greater Berlin," which requires further consider-

ation and joint agreement by the Governments of the U.S.A., U.K. and
U.S.S.R.

Representative of the Government of the U.S.A. on the European Advisory Commission:	Representative of the Government of the U.K. on the European Advisory Commission:	Representative of the Government of the U.S.S.R. on the European Advisory Commission:
J. G. Winant	W. Strang	F. T. Gousev
JOHN G. WINANT	WILLIAM STRANG	F. T. GOUSEV

LANCASTER HOUSE,
LONDON, S.W.1.

12th September, 1944.

124. In a Last Gamble to Change the Tide of War Hitler Unleashes His Vengeance Weapons Against Britain, November 10, 1944

"The first one I saw reminded me of the moon exploding."

In late October 1944 a desperate Hitler unveiled his second *Vergeltungswaffe* (vengeance weapon), a supersonic rocket. Containing approximately the same quantity of high explosives as the V-1 flying bomb, the V-2 rockets were designed to penetrate deeply into the ground before exploding. They flew through the atmosphere going up to sixty or seventy miles and outstripped the sound of their own propelling blast. By a phenomenon of physics, people in the vicinity could hear the rockets strike and explode before they could hear the noise heralding the approach. No warning, therefore, was possible against this weapon. The sort of defensive measures used against the V-1 were useless now.

Hitler was making a last attempt to destroy the morale of the British people. Joseph Goebbels, his propaganda minister, was sure that this was the ultimate weapon. The V-2s were, indeed, dangerous, but they could not win the war for Germany. As Allied armies overran the launching sites, they brought about a diminution of the barrage. But the Germans continued using V-2s to the end of the war.

How London reacted to the V-2s was described by Henry B. Jameson, an AP newsman, in the following story.

LONDON, Nov. 10 (A.P.) — The new V-2 rockets fall like shooting stars and although they are nothing compared to the buzz bombs as a terror weapon, they make a whale of a bang that can be heard for ten miles.

One man who lived through such an explosion less than 50 yards away

Associated Press, November 11, 1944. Courtesy of the Associated Press.

said, "I didn't hear any noise whatever before the explosion—then I thought it was the end of the world."

Another man, describing the same incident, said a "terrific explosion" was preceded by a noise like thunder. Others say the rockets looked like great balls of fire, and a few even claim to have been close enough to call them "great black arrows."

The first one I saw at night in the country reminded me of the moon exploding. There was a brilliant flash, followed by a jolting bang.

Many persons have reported hearing double explosions, one at the time of the flash in the sky and a second presumably when the rocket landed.

While censorship regulations still prevent publication of detailed damage reports, the "flying telegraph poles" so far have been too inaccurate to be of much military value.

Many narrow escapes have been disclosed, however, since the secret of "*Vergeltungswaffe*" No. 2 was launched.

In one incident a Mrs. French, an employe of a bakery which was demolished, was having tea with the proprietor and his wife after the shop had closed. "Something seemed to fall on top of us," said the proprietor. "Mrs. French was killed instantly, but my wife and I, sitting on the other side of the table, were only badly cut."

An elderly woman walking along a sidewalk when a rocket fell near by saw "a vivid flash"—and the next moment found herself sitting in the middle of the street—hardly scratched.

Houses, schools, hospitals, churches, public houses and other buildings have been among those destroyed or damaged in rocket attacks.

Eyewitnesses who have seen them fall estimate their length from 30 to 50 feet and from two to four feet in diameter, with a warhead about the same size as the flying bomb.

"I saw a black cloud of smoke and then what appeared to be a very bright star traveling fast," said George Matthews, who saw his neighbor's house demolished. "Then later there was an orange-and-red explosion which appeared to have two distinct reports."

Frank Turner said it was almost a minute from the time he saw "something in the sky that looked like a red football" until he was rocked on his heels by an explosion.

Many pieces of exploded rockets have been recovered in scattered sections of the country.

Some parts of mechanism, from which experts may be able to piece together a composite picture of the rocket, also have been found.

Twisted-off-looking pieces of machinery littered the ground near the scene of several explosions. Tough white metal, some in rolls and some in flat sheets a yard square, have been picked up. There were also numerous lengths of metal chain like those on the wheels of oversized bicycles; curiously shaped blocks of wood and bright red iron piping apparently from the tail section resembling gutters with many slotted holes.

125. The Allies Agree on Control Machinery for Germany, November 14, 1944

". . . when Germany is carrying out the basic requirements of unconditional surrender."

Two months after the zones of occupation of a defeated Germany were decided upon by the United States, the United Kingdom, and Soviet Russia, the three governments reached an agreement on the organization of Allied control machinery during that period when Germany would be carrying out the terms of unconditional surrender. An attempt was made to include precise arrangements which would prevent friction among the victorious powers.

Agreement on Control Machinery in Germany, November 14, 1944

The Governments of the United States of America, the United Kingdom of Great Britain and Northern Ireland and the Union of Soviet Socialist Republics have reached the following Agreement with regard to the organization of the Allied control machinery in Germany in the period during which Germany will be carrying out the basic requirements of unconditional surrender: —

ARTICLE 1.

Supreme authority in Germany will be exercised, on instructions from their respective Governments, by the Commanders-in-Chief of the armed

U.S., Senate, Committee on Foreign Relations, *Documents of German History, 1944–1961* (Washington, D.C.: Government Printing Office, 1962), pp. 5–8.

forces of the United States of America, the United Kingdom and the Union of Soviet Socialist Republics, each in his own zone of occupation, and also jointly, in matters affecting Germany as a whole, in their capacity as members of the supreme organ of control constituted under the present Agreement.

ARTICLE 2.

Each Commander-in-Chief in his zone of occupation will have attached to him military, naval and air representatives of the other two Commanders-in-Chief for liaison duties.

ARTICLE 3.

(a) The three Commanders-in-Chief, acting together as a body, will constitute a supreme organ of control called the Control Council.

(b) The functions of the Control Council will be: —

(i) to ensure appropriate uniformity of action by the Commanders-in-Chief in their respective zones of occupation:

(ii) to initiate plans and reach agreed decisions on the chief military, political, economic and other questions affecting Germany as a whole, on the basis of instructions received by each Commander-in-Chief from his Government;

(iii) to control the German central administration, which will operate under the direction of the Control Council and will be responsible to it for ensuring compliance with its demands;

(iv) to direct the administration of "Greater Berlin" through appropriate organs.

(c) The Control Council will meet at least once in ten days; and it will meet at any time upon request of any one of its members. Decisions of the Control Council shall be unanimous. The chairmanship of the Control Council will be held in rotation by each of its three members.

(d) Each member of the Control Council will be assisted by a political adviser, who will, when necessary, attend meetings of the Control Council. Each member of the Control Council may also, when necessary, be assisted at meetings of the Council by naval or air advisers.

ARTICLE 4.

A permanent Co-ordinating Committee will be established under the Control Council, composed of one representative of each of the three Commanders-in-Chief, not below the rank of General Officer or the equivalent rank in the naval or air forces. Members of the Co-ordinating Committee will, when necessary, attend meetings of the Control Council.

ARTICLE 5.

The duties of the Co-ordinating Committee, acting on behalf of the Control Council and through the Control Staff, will include: —
(a) the carrying out of the decisions of the Control Council;
(b) the day-to-day supervision and control of the activities of the German central administration and institutions;
(c) the co-ordination of current problems which call for uniform measures in all three zones;
(d) the preliminary examination and preparation for the Control Council of all questions submitted by individual Commanders-in-Chief.

ARTICLE 6.

(a) The members of the Control Staff appointed by their respective national authorities, will be organized in the following Divisions: —
Military; Naval; Air; Transport, Political; Economic; Finance; Reparation, Deliveries and Restitution; Internal Affairs and Communications; Legal; Prisoners of War and Displaced Persons; Man-power.
Adjustments in the number and functions of the Divisions may be made in the light of experience.
(b) At the head of each Division there will be three high-ranking officials, one from each Power. The duties of the three heads of each Division, acting jointly, will include: —
(i) exercising control over the corresponding German Ministries and German central institutions;
(ii) acting as advisers to the Control Council and, when necessary, attending meetings thereof;
(iii) transmitting to the German central administration the decisions of the Control Council, communicated through the Co-ordinating Committee.
(c) The three heads of a Division will take part in meetings of the Co-ordinating Committee at which matters affecting the work of their Division are on the agenda.
(d) The staffs of the Divisions may include civilian as well as military personnel. They may also, in special cases, include nationals of other United Nations, appointed in their personal capacity.

ARTICLE 7.

(a) An Inter-Allied Governing Authority *(Komendatura)* consisting of three Commandants, one from each Power, appointed by their respective Commanders-in-chief, will be established to direct jointly the administration of the "Greater Berlin" area. Each of the Commandants will serve in rotation, in the position of Chief Commandant, as head of the Inter-Allied Governing Authority.

(b) A Technical Staff, consisting of personnel of each of the three Powers, will be established under the Inter-Allied Governing Authority, and will be organized to serve the purpose of supervising and controlling the activities of the local organs of "Greater Berlin" which are responsible for its municipal services.

(c) The Inter-Allied Governing Authority will operate under the general direction of the Control Council and will receive orders through the Co-ordinating Committee.

ARTICLE 8.

The necessary liaison with the Governments of other United Nations chiefly interested will be ensured by the appointment of such Governments of military missions (which may include civilian members) to the Control Council, having access, through the appropriate channels, to the organs of control.

ARTICLE 9.

United Nations' organizations which may be admitted by the Control Council to operate in Germany will, in respect of their activities in Germany, be subordinate to the Allied control machinery and answerable to it.

ARTICLE 10.

The Allied organs for the control and administration of Germany outlined above will operate during the initial period of the occupation of Germany immediately following surrender, that is, the period when Germany is carrying out the basic requirements of unconditional surrender.

ARTICLE 11.

The question of the Allied organs required for carrying out the functions of control and administration in Germany in a later period will be the subject of a separate Agreement between the Governments of the United States of America, the United Kingdom and the Union of Soviet Socialist Republics.

The above text of the Agreement on Control Machinery in Germany between the Governments of the United States of America, the United Kingdom and the Union of Soviet Socialist Republics has been prepared and unanimously adopted by the Representatives of the United States of

America, the United Kingdom and the Union of Soviet Socialist Republics on the European Advisory Commission at a meeting held on 14th November, 1944, and is now submitted to their respective Governments for approval.

For the Representative of the Government of the United States of America on the European Advisory Commission:	Representative of the Government of the United Kingdom on The European Advisory Commission:	Representative of the Government of the Union of Soviet Socialist Republics on the European Advisory Commission:
PHILIP E. MOSELY	WILLIAM STRANG	F. T. GOUSEV

LANCASTER HOUSE,
LONDON, S.W. 1

14th November, 1944.

Part Six:

Götterdämmerung and Residue

126. Nero Decree: Hitler Orders the Destruction of All Industrial Installations, March 30, 1945

> *"The order . . . is aimed exclusively at preventing the enemy from using these installations and facilities to add to his fighting strength."*

On March 19, 1945, Hitler issued through Martin Bormann a decree calling for the radical destruction of the nation's life in a scorched earth policy. Areas which the German army could not hold were to be evacuated. "The *Fuehrer* expects that the districts of the interior will display the needful understanding for the inescapable demands of the hour." On March 30, 1945, Hitler issued more detailed instructions.

Fuehrer's Headquarters
March 30, 1945

In order to assure uniform implementation of my decree of March 19, 1945, I hereby make the following order:

1. The order already given for destruction of industrial installations is aimed exclusively at preventing the enemy from using these installations and facilities to add to his fighting strength.

2. No measures should be taken which would decrease our own fighting strength. Production must be carried on to the last possible moment, even at the risk of a factory falling into the hands of the enemy before it could be destroyed.

All kinds of industrial installations, including plants for producing food, should not be destroyed unless they are threatened immediately by the enemy.

Translated by the editor.

3. Bridges and other installations for transport must be destroyed in order to deny the enemy their use for a long time, but the same effect can be won with industrial installations by smashing them permanently.

The total destruction of especially important plants, such as munitions and chemical plants, will be within the province of the Minister of Armaments and War Production.

4. The signal for destroying industrial installations and other plants will be given by the concerned *Gauleiter* and Defense Commissioner, who will supervise the work. Implementation of this order will be made solely by the Ministry of Armaments and War Production. All other agencies of the Party, the State, and the Armed Forces will assist in the process.

5. The Minister of Armaments and War Production will issue instructions for the implementation of this decree, with my agreement. He can pass on detailed instructions to the Reich Defense Commissioners.

6. These basic instructions concern plants and installations in the immediate war zone.

(Signed) ADOLF HITLER

127. Buchenwald: Weimar Germans Are Forced to View the Horrors of a Nazi Death Factory, April 16, 1945

"The German people saw all this today, and they wept."

Buchenwald, located on a wooded hill several miles from Weimar, shrine of German culture, was one of three major concentration camps established in 1933 (Sachsenhausen in the north; Dachau in the south; and Buchenwald in Central Germany). An extermination factory, Buchenwald was the scene of starvation, beatings, torture, and illness. Inmates were required to work in an adjacent armaments factory for the manufacture of machine guns, small arms, and ammunition.

Buchenwald was liberated on April 10, 1945, by the U.S. Eightieth Division. Several days later, on April 16, correspondent Gene Currivan sent a dispatch to *The New York Times* describing how Germans from neighboring Weimar were required to view the terrible death factory. Currivan's story took on the macabre quality of Dante's *Inferno*.

BUCHENWALD, APRIL 16, 1945 — German civilians — 1200 of them — were brought from the neighboring city of Weimar today to see for themselves the horror, brutality, and human indecency perpetrated against their "neighbors" at the infamous Buchenwald concentration camp. They saw sights that brought tears to their eyes, and scores of them, including German nurses, just fainted away.

They saw more than 20,000 nondescript prisoners, many of them barely

The New York Times, April 18, 1945.

living, who were all that remained of the normal complement of 80,000. The Germans were able to evacuate the others before we overran the place on April 10.

There were 32,705 that the "visiting" Germans didn't see, although they saw some of their bodies. It was this number that had been murdered since the camp was established in July, 1937. There was a time when the population reached more than 110,000, but the average was always below that. It included doctors, professors, scientists, statesmen, army officers, diplomats, and an assortment of peasants and merchants from all over Europe and Asia.

There was a group of British officers among those left behind and one of seven French generals, but this was obviously an oversight in the great confusion that followed the news of our approach.

Five generals died and one escaped. This government-controlled camp was considered second only to that at Dachau, near Munich, as the world's worst atrocity center.

It had its gallows, torture rooms, dissection rooms, modern crematoria, laboratories where fiendish experiments were made on living human beings, and its sections where people were systematically starved to death.

This correspondent made a tour of the camp today and saw everything herein described. The statistics and an account of the events that happened before our troops liberated the camp were obtained from a special committee of prisoners, some of whom had been in the camp since its inception and others who had been German prisoners for twelve years. Their information was documented and in most cases confirmed by the records.

This story has already been told in part, but not until today has the full import of the atrocities been completely felt.

One of the first things that the German civilian visitors saw as they passed through the gates and into the interior of the camp was a display of "parchment." This consisted of large pieces of human flesh on which were elaborate tatooed markings. These strips had been collected by a German doctor who was writing a treatise on tattoos, and also by the twenty-eight-year-old wife of the *Standartenfuehrer*, or commanding officer. This woman, according to prisoners, was an energetic sportswoman who, back in Brandenburg, used to ride to hounds. She had a mania for unusual tattoos, and whenever a prisoner arrived who had a rare marking on his body, she would indicate that that trophy would make a valuable addition to her collection.

In addition to the "parchments" were two large table lamps, with parchment shades also made of human flesh.

The German people saw all this today, and they wept. Those who didn't weep were ashamed. They said they didn't know about it, and maybe they didn't, because the camp was restricted to Army personnel, but there it was right at their back doors for eight years.

The visitors stood in lines, one group at a time passing by the table on which the exhibits were displayed. A German-speaking American sergeant explained from an adjacent jeep what they were witnessing, while all around them were thousands of liberated "slaves" just looking on. Even the barracks roof was crowded with them. They watched silently. Some of them looked as if they were about to die, but this assemblage of "slaves" constituted the more healthy elements of the camp.

In barracks farther down the line were three thousand sick who could not move and 4800 aged who were unable to leave their squalid quarters. In addition, there were untold hundreds just roaming around, not knowing where they were or what was going on.

There were human skeletons who had lost all likeness to anything human. Most of them had become idiots, but they still had the power of locomotion. Those in the sick bay were beyond all help. They were packed into three-tier bunks, which ran to the roof of the barnlike barracks. They were dying there, and no one could do anything about it.

The German visitors were to see them, too – and much more – but at the moment they were merely seeing "Exhibit A" and fainting.

Some Germans were skeptical at first, as if this show had been staged for their benefit, but they were soon convinced. Even as they had milled along from one place to another, their own countrymen, who had been prisoners there, told them the story. Men went white and women turned away. It was too much for them.

These persons, who had been fed on Nazi propaganda since 1933, were beginning to see the light. They were seeing with their own eyes what no quantity of American propaganda could convince them of. Here was what their own government had perpetrated.

But they hadn't seen anything yet. In a barracks building in front of them was a scientific laboratory where captured scientists worked with material supplied by their overlords. There were shelves of bottles filled with various organs of the human body. In one was half a human head. It had been cut longitudinally to show all its component parts. This head once belonged to a prisoner, as did all the other human parts so displayed. In another room were a dozen death masks, skulls, and shrunken human heads. A Czechoslovak scientist and surgeon who worked in the laboratory told us the history of each part, each head, each mask – because he had known the human beings to which they belonged. Some had been his own countrymen.

The German visitors saw this, too.

And then they were taken to another laboratory, where victims had been injected with typhus so that Germany could have typhus serum. There were still a score of "patients" who were still alive, although the Polish doctor left behind, who had been forced to give these injections even to his own people, said the death rate had been ninety-eight per cent.

This sight was too much for many German housewives, especially a little farther on, where only the children were kept. One nine-year-old boy, who had had only the first few injections, seemed quite chipper. He was Andor Gutman, a Hungarian Jew of Budapest. He had been in the camp three years. When asked where his parents were, he replied, without any emotion: "My father was killed and my mother was burned to death."

As one watched the Germans filing out of this building there was hardly a dry eye, although some tried to maintain their composure. There was real horror ahead, but some of them just couldn't go on.

From there they were taken to the living quarters. The stench, filth, and misery here defied description. Those human wrecks standing in the corridor were beyond the stage where any amount of hospitalization could restore them to normal, while others peering helplessly from their bunks would be fortunate when they died. . . .

128. Berlin Bunker: The Last Days of Hitler in His "Cloud-Cuckoo Land," April 20–30, 1945

"I don't care what happens. I shall stay here and die."

Hitler decided to remain in Berlin and commit suicide in its ruins. Above his bunker dug below the Chancellery, Berlin was a dying city. Great clouds of smoke hovered in the sky as Russian artillery shells exploded incessantly and gunfire thundered through the rubble. Surrounded by his closest friends, the *Fuehrer* gave way to despair. *"Meine Herren,"* he said, *"*I see that all is lost. I shall remain in Berlin. I shall fall here in the Reich Chancellery – I can serve the German people best in that way. There is no sense in continuing any longer."

On his last day on earth, Hitler married his mistress, Eva Braun, in an underground ceremony. After dictating his last will and political testament, he took his own life. His body was drenched in gasoline and burned in the courtyard.

The British historian, Hugh R. Trevor-Roper, described the atmosphere in the bunker as "a cloud-cuckoo land." What it was like was reported by Gerhardt Herrgesell, Hitler's principal secretary for the last two years of the war, in this interview with Pierre J. Huss, correspondent for International News Service.

HERRGESELL IS THIRTY-FIVE. He was a member of the SS and he served briefly on the Russian front. He was a champion short-hand writer who had studied law, and in September 1944, he was assigned to be one of two

International News Service, May 15, 1945. Courtesy of United Press International.

stenographers always at Hitler's elbow even in most secret and limited conferences.

He and the other stenographer were flown out of Berlin from the Gatow Airfield late on the evening of April 22, 1945, under orders from Hitler to proceed to Berchtesgaden and transcribe their notes for posterity. Herrgesell said the Condor plane in which he left Berlin was the last transport to leave the capital. It carried the wives and children of some Nazi officials. Herrgesell heard that Hitler's adjutant, Julius Schaub, got out some time later aboard a fighter plane. [Hence it would have been possible for Hitler to leave also.]

Just before he left, Herrgesell said, Eva Braun gave him a tiny package, apparently containing a ring, and wrote a long farewell letter to be handed over to a Herr Mueller, at Obersalzberg, for an unidentified person.

Hitler's headquarters had been at the Berlin Chancellery since January 16, Herrgesell said. By April 1, all meetings had been shifted down below into the bunkers, where some ten to fifteen high officers took part in conferences with Hitler at a map table.

The living quarters of Hitler and Eva Braun were a couple of small adjoining rooms. The electrically-lighted bunker, just behind the old part of the Chancellery, was two stories deep, sixteen feet square with an upholstered bench along the wall. It had all the comforts that could be provided and was well stocked with food and luxuries from all over plundered Europe.

Early in the afternoon of April 21, a heavy-calibre Russian shell rocked the bunker in the middle of a conference.

But until the next afternoon, April 22, Hitler's order forbidding all talk of a lost war remained in effect. Herrgesell quoted Hitler as having said in March or early April:

"We shall fight until the last scrap of German ground is gone."

This motto stood while the entire reduced Chancellery quarters staff awaited a decision as to when to leave for the so-called national redoubt in South Germany. Until the last everything continued to pivot around Hitler, everyone hoped he would give the word to go south although it was clearly and silently understood that as soon as Hitler abandoned the capital the war would degenerate into a last stand in Bavaria. Nevertheless, most of them wanted this chance to save their skins.

Absent from Berlin was Heinrich Himmler, who commanded the army of the Upper Rhine and later the Vistula group.

At noon on April 20, Chief of Staff Krebs, who had succeeded Gen. Heinz Guderian, characterized the situation in Berlin as being critical. Whereupon Hitler ordered the bulk of Fuehrer headquarters transferred to Berchtesgaden, retaining only a skeleton staff representing the army, navy and air force.

There were no Wehrmacht troops left in the capital except for stray units of volksgrenadiers, volksturmers, non-combat soldiers and herds of picked-up and mobilized clerks, dishwashers and waiters, Herrgesell said. The only regular troops at Berlin's disposal were those of the Twelfth Army facing the American Ninth Army along the Elbe to defend Berlin.

It was fairly quiet the 20th but the next day about 10:20 A.M. Russian shells started falling in the government area. During the day they came in every few seconds in a shifting radius interspersed with strafing raids.

"It seemed that every few minutes somebody ran into the bunker excitedly to warn the Fuehrer that the Russians were closing in," said Herrgesell. "One of the busiest back and forth was Goebbels, who was defense boss of Berlin. We two stenographers had a hard time keeping tab on the goings and comings. Nobody even seemed to notice we were there. Jodl, Keitel, Bormann, Hitler's SS Adjutant Fuensche and Himmler's liaison SS officer Fegelein with a handful of Wehrmacht representatives, hung within beck and call. Goering had left. I never saw Doenitz and von Ribbentrop in those days but heard Hitler talking to them on the phone occasionally."

In the forenoon of Sunday, April 22, five hundred Chancellery clerks, guards, cooks and minor officials were mobilized into Hitler's special escort body and sent to the Alexanderplatz to try and block any Russian breakthrough in that direction. For the first time during the afternoon Herrgesell heard Hitler make a vague remark suggesting the war was lost.

" 'It doesn't make any sense to continue any longer,' he said. 'I shall remain here.' "

"Since he didn't elaborate, the entourage let it pass as a tired man's offhand remark.

"By 5 P.M. shells were pretty audible through the open bunker door. It was obviously our last chance to get away unless Hitler had some secret escape prepared. Then at 5:30 P.M., Hitler told Jodl, Keitel and Bormann he wished to see them alone and in his usual gruff way told Fegelein and a handful of others to get out.

"He told Bormann to shut and lock the steel door. We two stenographers sat in dead silence, scarcely daring to breathe and we knew that the fatal moment was at hand."

Hitler wore dark trousers, a field-gray tunic, a white collar with a black tie. An Iron Cross was his only decoration. His grey-flecked moustache was unchanged but his famous forelock was less conspicuous. His face, formerly tanned by the sun, was puffy and florid. His eyes were sleepy-weary. He talked in front of a small map table while the others stood informally around.

The shorthand notes of that dramatic fifteen to twenty minutes were only ten pages. Most was ranting by all present, with Hitler blaming everyone except himself for Germany's downfall and finally yelling: "Get out, get out! Go to South Germany. I'll stay here. I'll stay here. It's all over anyhow."

Keitel's bull-voice cut in: "We won't leave you. I'd be ashamed to face my wife and children if I deserted you."

Hitler waved that aside and again demanded that they go south. Bormann said: "This would be the first time I ever disobeyed you. I won't go."

Jodl, who had been quietly standing aside and was known to be a rare man who would occasionally tell Hitler the straight truth, spoke up calmly as the others momentarily stopped arguing. "I shall not stay in this mousehole. Here one cannot establish headquarters and direct a battle or do anything. We are soldiers, *mein Fuehrer*. Give us an army group and orders to fight wherever possible. But I won't stay in this mouse-hole."

In other days Hitler undoubtedly would have exploded and ordered Jodl shot. But this time he snorted and shrugged saying: "Do what you wish — it doesn't mean anything to me any more. I don't care what happens. I shall stay here and die."

Keitel broke in boldly, stating that what sufficient armies remained would continue to fight and could "turn the tide."

"No, it's all over," Hitler said. He told Bormann to start packing.

Then Jodl said: "*Mein Fuehrer*, do you yield herewith complete leadership for continuation of the war?"

Hitler, intentionally or otherwise, evaded a direct answer and turned wearily to Keitel and Bormann: "Go to South Germany," he said, and then he added somewhat incoherently: "Goering will build a government. Goering is my successor anyhow — *ja*, Goering will negotiate everything."

The last obviously was sarcastic, for Hitler now regarded Goering as a traitor to the Nazi cause.

Jodl then repeated his previous question but again was sidetracked when Hitler just said "You must all go south right away." He rose to indicate the conference had ended and declined to listen further.

"Outside I heard Keitel telling the others they must take Hitler by force to Berchtesgaden," Herrgesell said, "but apparently no one knew just what to do except to rush about and telephone. As it turned out they got several like Doenitz to phone Hitler in an effort to persuade him to leave."

Krebs, Guensche and Fegelein all tried to argue Hitler out of his decision. He didn't even shout back, merely motioning everyone aside with repetition of the words: "It's all over. I stay here."

Von Ribbentrop telephoned and strove to convince Hitler he at last had authentic information indicating tension among the Allies and said something about direct word from the British cabinet that a split between the Western Allies and Russia was assured. Hitler formerly had staked much hope on this. But now he showed no interest and said: "Ach, that's what you say. Thanks. *Heil*," and hung up the phone.

129. Belsen: A British Reporter Gives an Eyewitness Account of a Nazi Concentration Camp, April 24, 1945

"None of this is propaganda. This is the plain and simple truth."

Bergen-Belsen was a concentration camp about ten miles northwest of Celle (Hanover) near the village of Bergen on the road to Hamburg. There were no gas chambers in Belsen, but many inmates died of disease and starvation. Its commandant in 1944 was the notorious Josef Kramer, called the "Beast of Belsen."

It was almost certain that after the war claims would be made by Nazi leaders that stories of concentration camps were exaggerated propaganda. This in fact happened at the Nuremberg war trials. Gene Currivan's report on Buchenwald was substantiated by the following broadcast about conditions at Belsen, sent on April 24, 1945, to the United States by Oxford historian Patrick Gordon Walker, BBC commentator and chief editor of Radio Luxembourg.

I WENT TO BELSEN. It was a vast area surrounded by barbed wire. The whole thing was being guarded by Hungarian guards. They had been in the German Army and are now immediately and without hesitation serving us. They are saving us a large number of men for the time being. Outside the camp, which is amidst bushes, pines, and heather, all fairly recently planted, were great notices in red letters: DANGER — TYPHUS.

We drove into what turned out to be a great training camp, a sort of Aberdeen, where we found the officers and Oxfordshire Yeomanry. They began to tell us about the concentration camp.

Courtesy of U.S. War Department, Washington, D.C.

It lies south of the training area and is behind its own barbed wire. The Wehrmacht is not allowed near it. It was entirely guarded by SS men and women. This is what I discovered about the release of the camp that happened about the fifteenth. I got this story from Derek Sington, political officer, and from officers and men of Oxfordshire Yeomanry.

Typhus broke out in the camp, and a truce was arranged so that we could take the camp over. The Germans originally had proposed that we should by-pass the camp. In the meanwhile, thousands and thousands of people would have died and been shot. We refused these terms, and demanded the withdrawal of the Germans and the disarmament of the SS guards. Some dozen SS men and women were left behind under the command of Higher Sturmfuehrer Kramer, who had been at Auschwitz. Apparently they had been told all sorts of fairy tales about the troops, that they could go on guarding, and that we would let them free and so forth.

We only had a handful of men so far, and the SS stayed there that night. The first night of liberty, many hundreds of people died of joy.

Next day some men of the Yeomanry arrived. The people crowded around them, kissing their hands and feet — and dying from weakness. Corpses in every state of decay were lying around, piled up on top of each other in heaps. There were corpses in the compound in flocks. People were falling dead all around, people who were walking skeletons. One woman came up to a soldier who was guarding the milk store and doling the milk out to children, and begged for milk for her baby. The man took the baby and saw that it had been dead for days, black in the face and shriveled up. The woman went on begging for milk. So he poured some on the dead lips. The mother then started to croon with joy and carried the baby off in triumph. She stumbled and fell dead in a few yards. I have this story and some others on records spoken by the men who saw them.

On the sixteenth, Kramer and the SS were arrested. Kramer was taken off and kept in the icebox with some stinking fish of the officers' home. He is now going back to the rear. The rest, men and women, were kept under guard to save them from the inmates. The men were set to work shoveling up the corpses into lorries.

About thirty-five thousand corpses were reckoned, more actually than the living. Of the living, there were about thirty thousand.

The SS men were driven and pushed along and made to ride on top of the loaded corpses and then shovel them into their great mass open graves. They were so tired that they fell exhausted amongst the corpses. Jeering crowds collected around them, and they had to be kept under strong guard.

Two men committed suicide in their cells. Two jumped off the lorry and tried to run away and get lost in the crowd. They were shot down. One jumped into a concrete pool of water and was riddled with bullets. The other was brought to the ground, with a shot in the belly. The SS women were made to cook and carry heavy loads. One of them tried to commit suicide. The inmates said that they were more cruel and brutal than the men. They are all young, in their twenties. One SS woman tried to hide, disguised as a prisoner. She was denounced and arrested.

The camp was so full because people had been brought here from East and West. Some people were brought from Nordhausen, a five-day journey, without food. Many had marched for two or three days. There was no food at all in the camp, a few piles of roots amidst the piles of dead bodies. Some of the dead bodies were of people so hungry that though the roots were guarded by SS men they had tried to storm them and had been shot down then and there. There was no water, nothing but these roots and some boiled stinking carrots, enough for a few hundred people.

Men and women had fought for these raw, uncooked roots. Dead bodies, black and blue and bloated, and skeletons had been used as pillows by sick people. The day after we took over, seven block leaders, mostly Poles, were murdered by the inmates. Some were still beating the people. We arrested one women who had beaten another women with a board. She quite frankly admitted the offense. We are arresting these people.

An enormous buried dump of personal jewelry and belongings was discovered in suitcases. When I went to the camp five days after its liberation, there were still bodies all around. I saw about a thousand.

In one place, hundreds had been shoveled into a mass grave by bulldozers; in another, Hungarian soldiers were putting corpses into a grave that was sixty feet by sixty feet and thirty feet deep. It was almost half full.

Other and similar pits were being dug. Five thousand people had died since we got into the camp. People died before my eyes, scarcely human, moaning skeletons, many of them gone mad. Bodies were just piled up. Many had gashed wounds and bullet marks and terrible sores. One Englishman, who had lived in Ostend, was picked up half dead. It was found that he had a great bullet wound in the back. He could just speak. He had no idea when he had been shot. He must have been lying half unconscious when some SS man shot him as he was crawling about. This was quite common. I walked about the camp. Everywhere was the smell and odor of death. After a few hours you get used to it and don't notice it any more. People have typhus and dysentery.

In one compound I went, I saw women standing up quite naked, washing among themselves. Nearby were piles of corpses. Other women suffering from dysentery were defecating in the open and then staggering back, half dead, to their blocks. Some were lying groaning on the ground. One had reverted to the absolute primitive.

A great job had been done in getting water into the camp. It has been pumped in from the outside and carried by hoses all over the camp with frequent outlet points. There are taps of fresh clean water everywhere. Carts with water move around.

The Royal Army Service Corps has also done a good job in getting food in.

I went into the typhus ward, packed thick with people lying in dirty rags of blankets on the floor, groaning and moaning. By the door sat an English Tommy talking to the people and cheering them up. They couldn't understand what he said, and he was continually ladling milk out of a caldron. I collected together some women who could speak English and German and began to make records. An amazing thing is the number who managed to keep themselves clean and neat. All of them said that in a day or two more, they would have gone under from hunger and weakness.

There are three main classes in the camp: the healthy, who have managed to keep themselves decent, but nearly all of these had typhus; then there were the sick, who were more or less cared for by their friends; then there was the vast underworld that had lost all self-respect, crawling around in rags, living in abominable squalor, defecating in the compound, often mad or half mad. By the other prisoners they are called Mussulmen. It is these who are still dying like flies. They can hardly walk on their legs. Thousands still of these cannot be saved, and if they were, they would be in lunatic asylums for the short remainder of their pitiful lives.

There were a very large number of girls in the camp, mostly Jewesses from Auschwitz. They have to be healthy to survive. Over and over again I was told the same story. The parades at which people were picked out arbitrarily for the gas chambers and the crematorium, where many were burned alive. Only a person in perfect health survived. Life and death was a question of pure chance.

Rich Jews arrives with their belongings and were able to keep some. There were soap and perfume and fountain pens and watches. All amidst the chance of sudden, arbitrary death, amidst work commandos from which the people returned to this tomb so dead beat that they were sure to be picked for the gas chamber at the next parade, amidst the most horrible death, filth, and squalor that could be imagined.

People at Auschwitz were saved by being moved away to work in towns like Hamburg and were then moved back to Belsen as we advanced. At Auschwitz every women had her hair shaven absolutely bald.

I met pretty young girls whose hair was one inch long. They all had their numbers tattooed on their left arm, a mark of honor they will wear all their lives.

One of the most extraordinary things was the women and men — there were only few — who had kept themselves decent and clean.

On the first day many had on powder and lipstick. It seems the SS stores had been located and looted and boots and clothes had been found. Hundreds of people came up to me with letters, which I have taken and am sending back to London to be posted all over the world. Many have lost all their relatives. "My father and mother were burned. My sister was burned." This is what you hear all the time. The British Army is doing what it can. Units are voluntarily giving up blankets. Fifty thousand arrived while I was there and they are being laundered. Sweets and chocolate and rations have been voluntarily given.

Then we went to the children's hut. The floors had been piled with corpses there had been no time to move. We collected a chorus of Russian girls from twelve to fourteen and Dutch boys and girls from nine to fifteen. They sang songs. The Russian children were very impressive. Clean and quite big children, they had been looked after magnificently amidst starvation. They sang the songs they remembered from before captivity. They looked happy now. The Dutch children had been in camp a long time and were very skinny and pale. We stood with our backs to the corpses, out in the open amidst the pines and the birch trees near the wire fence running around the camp.

Men were hung for hours at a time, suspended by their arms, hands tied behind their back, in Belsen. Beatings in workshops were continuous, and there were many deaths there. Just before I left the camp a crematorium was discovered. A story of Auschwitz was told to me by Helen — and her last name, she didn't remember. She was a Czechoslovak.

When the women were given the chance to go and work elsewhere in the work zones like Hamburg, mothers with children were, in fact, given the choice between their lives and their children's. Children could not be taken along. Many preferred to stay with their children and face certain death. Some decided to leave their children. But it got around amongst the six-year-old children that if they were left there they would at once be gassed. There were terrible scenes between children and their mothers. One child was so angry that though the mother changed her mind and stayed and died, the child would not talk to her.

That night when I got back at about eleven o'clock very exhausted, I saw the Jewish padre again and talked to him as he was going to bed. Suddenly, he broke down completely and sobbed.

The next morning I left this hellhole, this camp. As I left, I had myself deloused and my recording truck as well. To you at home, this is one camp. There are many more. This is what you are fighting. None of this is propaganda. This is the plain and simple truth.

130. Hitler's Last Will: The Trapped *Fuehrer* Dictates His Final Bequests, April 29, 1945

"I myself and my wife — in order to escape the disgrace of . . . capitulation — choose death."

On the morning of April 29, 1945, all Berlin was engulfed in a sea of flames. Hitler, the lifelong bachelor, went through a marriage ceremony with Eva Braun. While the wedding was being celebrated, the *Fuehrer* sent for his secretary, Frau Gertrud Junge, and dictated two documents: his Last Will and his Political Testament (q.v.). In his private will, Hitler explained his marriage, disposed of his property, and announced his impending death. The next afternoon at 3:30 P.M., Hitler and Eva Braun committed suicide. The bodies were burned and buried in the Chancellery garden or taken away by the Russians.

As I DID NOT consider that I could take responsibility, during the years of struggle, of contracting a marriage, I have now decided, before the closing of my earthly career, to take as my wife that girl who, after many years of faithful friendship, entered, of her own free will, the practically besieged town in order to share her destiny with me. At her own desire she goes as my wife with me into death. It will compensate us for what we both lost through my work in the service of my people.

What I possess belongs — in so far as it has any value — to the Party.

Translated in the Office of United States Chief of Counsel for the Prosecution of Axis Criminality, *Nazi Conspiracy and Aggression* (Washington, D.C.: Government Printing Office, 1946–1948), vol. 6, pp. 259–60.

Should this no longer exist, to the State; should the State also be destroyed, no further decision of mine is necessary.

My pictures, in the collections which I have bought in the course of years, have never been collected for private purposes, but only for the extension of a gallery in my home town of Linz on Donau.

It is my most sincere wish that this bequest may be duly executed.

I nominate as my Executor my most faithful Party comrade, Martin Bormann.

He is given full legal authority to make all decisions. He is permitted to take out everything that has a sentimental value or is necessary for the maintenance of a modest simple life, for my brothers and sisters, also above all for the mother of my wife and my faithful co-workers who are well-known to him, principally my old Secretaries Frau Winter etc. who have for many years aided me by their work.

I myself and my wife — in order to escape the disgrace of deposition or capitulation — choose death. It is our wish to be burnt immediately on the spot where I have carried out the greatest part of my daily work in the course of a twelve years' service to my people.

Given in Berlin, 29th April 1945, 4:00 A.M.

[*Signed*] A. HITLER

[*Witnesses*]
DR. JOSEPH GOEBBELS
MARTIN BORMANN
COLONEL NICHOLAS VON BELOW

131. Hitler's Political Testament: Apologia and Last Warning Against "International Jewry," April 29, 1945

"I die with a happy heart. . . ."

After writing his last will, Hitler then left a "political testament" for the German people. In the first part he insisted that he had not wanted to go to war in 1939 and placed the blame for the conflict on "International Jewry." In the second part he expelled those he decided were traitors to his cause, including Hermann Goering and Heinrich Himmler, appointed his successors, and outlined the form of government they should adopt.

The authenticity of Hitler's political testament was challenged by a writer to the *London Daily Telegraph,* who noted the "un-German" characteristics of the typescript. H. R. Trevor-Roper, the British historian, regards the validity of the testament as established beyond the possibility of a doubt by a mass of internal and circumstantial evidence, including expert scrutiny of the signatures and the testimony of Frau Gertrud Junge, who typed the documents. Trevor-Roper points to this last advertisement of the Nazi movement, designed as a valedictory to the world and a message to later generations, as "nothing but the old claptrap, the negative appeal, the purposeless militarism, of the Revolution of Destruction."

Translated in the Office of the United State Chief of Counsel for the Prosecution of Axis Criminality, *Nazi Conspiracy and Aggression* (Washington, D.C.: Government Printing Office, 1946–1948), vol. 6, pp. 260–63.

First Part of the Political Testament

More than thirty years have now passed since I in 1914 made my modest contribution as a volunteer in the first world war that was forced upon the Reich.

In these three decades I have been actuated solely by love and loyalty to my people in all my thoughts, acts, and life. They gave me the strength to make the most difficult decisions which have ever confronted mortal man. I have spent my time, my working strength, and my health in these three decades.

It is untrue that I or anyone else in Germany wanted the war in 1939. It was desired and instigated exclusively by those international statesmen who were either of Jewish descent or worked for Jewish interests. I have made too many offers for the control and limitation of armaments, which posterity will not for all time be able to disregard for the responsibility for the outbreak of this war to be laid on me. I have further never wished that after the first fatal world war a second against England, or even against America, should break out. Centuries will pass away, but out of the ruins of our towns and monuments the hatred against those finally responsible whom we have to thank for everything, International Jewry and its helpers, will grow.

Three days before the outbreak of the German-Polish war I again proposed to the British ambassador in Berlin a solution to the German-Polish problem — similar to that in the case of the Saar district, under international control. This offer also cannot be denied. It was only rejected because the leading circles in English politics wanted the war, partly on account of the business hoped for and partly under influence of propaganda organized by International Jewry.

I have also made it quite plain that, if the nations of Europe are again to be regarded as mere shares to be bought and sold by these international conspirators in money and finance, then that race, Jewry, which is the real criminal of this murderous struggle, will be saddled with the responsibility. I further left no one in doubt that this time not only would millions of children of Europe's Aryan people die of hunger, not only would millions of grown men suffer death, and not only hundreds of thousands of women and children be burnt and bombed to death in the towns, without the real criminal having to atone for this guilt, even if by more humane means.

After six years of war, which in spite of all setbacks, will go down one day in history as the most glorious and valiant demonstration of a nation's life purpose, I cannot forsake the city which is the capital of this Reich. As the forces are too small to make any further stand against the enemy attack at this place and our resistance is gradually being weakened by men who are as deluded as they are lacking in initiative, I should like, by remaining in this town, to share my fate with those, the millions of others, who have also taken upon themselves to do so. Moreover I do not wish to fall into the hands of an enemy who requires a new spectacle organized by the Jews for the amusement of their hysterical masses.

I have decided therefore to remain in Berlin and there of my own free will to choose death at the moment when I believe the position of the *Fuehrer* and Chancellor itself can no longer be held.

I die with a happy heart, aware of the immeasurable deeds and achievements of our soldiers at the front, our women at home, the achievements of our farmers and workers and the work, unique in history, of our youth who bear my name.

That from the bottom of my heart I express my thanks to you all, is just as self-evident as my wish that you should, because of that, on no account give up the struggle, but rather continue it against the enemies of the Fatherland, no matter where, true to the creed of a great Clausewitz. From the sacrifice of our soldiers and from my own unity with them unto death, will in any case spring up in the history of Germany, the seed of a radiant renaissance of the National Socialist movement and thus of the realization of a true community of nations.

Many of the most courageous men and women have decided to unite their lives with mine until the very last. I have begged and finally ordered them not to do this, but to take part in the further battle of the Nation. I beg the heads of the Armies, the Navy and the Air Force to strengthen by all possible means the spirit of resistance of our soldiers in the National Socialist sense, with special reference to the fact that also I myself, as founder and creator of this movement, have preferred death to cowardly abdication or even capitulation.

May it, at some future time, become part of the code of honor of the German officer — as is already the case in our Navy — that the surrender of a district or of a town is impossible, and that above all the leaders here must march ahead as shining examples, faithfully fulfilling their duty unto death.

Second Part of the Political Testament

Before my death, I expel the former *Reichsmarschall* Hermann Goering from the party and deprive him of all rights which he may enjoy by virtue of the decree of June 29th, 1941; and also by virtue of my statement in the *Reichstag* on September 1st, 1939. I appoint in his place *Grossadmiral* Doenitz, President of the Reich and Supreme Commander of the Armed Forces.

Before my death I expel the former *Reichsfuehrer-SS* and Minister of the Interior Heinrich Himmler, from the party and from all offices of State. In his stead I appoint *Gauleiter* Karl Hanke as *Reichsfuehrer-SS* and Chief of the German Police, and *Gauleiter* Paul Giesler as Reich Minister of the Interior.

Goering and Himmler, quite apart from their disloyalty to my person, have done immeasurable harm to the country and the whole nation by secret negotiations with the enemy, which they have conducted without my knowledge and against my wishes, and by illegally attempting to seize power in the State for themselves. . . .

Although a number of men, such as Martin Bormann, Dr. Goebbels, etc., together with their wives, have joined me of their own free will and did not wish to leave the capital of the Reich under any circumstances, but were willing to perish with me here, I must nevertheless ask them to obey my request, and in this case set the interests of the nation above their own feelings. By their work and loyalty as comrades they will be just as close to me after death, as I hope that my spirit will linger among them and always go with them. Let them be hard but never unjust, but above all let them never allow fear to influence their actions, and set the honor of the nation above everything in the world. Finally, let them be conscious of the fact that our task, that of continuing the building of a National Socialist State, represents the work of the coming centuries, which places every single person under an obligation always to serve the common interest and to subordinate his own advantage to this end. I demand of all Germans, all National Socialists, men, women and all the men of the Armed Forces, that they be faithful and obedient unto death to the new government and its President.

Above all I charge the leaders of the nation and those under them to scrupulous observance of the laws of race and to merciless opposition to the universal poisoner of all peoples, International Jewry.

Given in Berlin, this 29th day of April 1945. 4:00 a.m.

ADOLF HITLER

[*Witnesses*]
DR. JOSEPH GOEBBELS   WILHELM BURGDORF*
MARTIN BORMANN   HANS KREBS†

---

*General Wilhelm Burgdorf, *Wehrmacht* adjutant at the *Fuehrer's* headquarters.
†General Hans Krebs, Chief of Staff.

132. JCS/1067: The U.S. Military Government Issues a Directive for the Occupation of the American Military Zone in Defeated Germany, April 1945

> *"Germany will not be occupied for the purpose of liberation but as a defeated enemy nation."*

Nazi Germany officially surrendered unconditionally on May 7, 1945. The critical task now became the method by which Germany was to be governed by the occupying powers — England, Russia, the United States, and France. Fully a month before the surrender, the United States Joint Chiefs of Staff sent General Dwight D. Eisenhower a directive known as JCS/1067 to be used as a guide in the occupation of the American zone in the defeated country. Most policies outlined in this directive were adopted in substance later (July 12–August 2, 1945) at the Potsdam Conference. Critics claimed that JCS/1067 was violated again and again in practice by the American military authorities. The result was, it was charged, that American occupation policies were not as effective as they might have been.

Following are extracts from the directive to Eisenhower in April 1945.

1. *The Purpose and Scope of this Directive:*
This directive is issued to you as Commanding General of the United States forces of occupation in Germany. As such, you will serve as United States member of the Control Council and will also be responsible for the

---

U.S., Department of State, *The Axis in Defeat: A Collection of Documents on American Policy Toward Germany and Japan,* pub. 2423 (Washington, D.C.: Government Printing Office; 1945), pp. 40–59, passim.

administration of military government in the zone or zones assigned to the United States for purposes of occupation and administration. It outlines the basic policies which will guide you in those two capacities after the termination of the combined command of the Supreme Commander, Allied Expeditionary Force.

This directive sets forth policies relating to Germany in the initial post-defeat period. As such it is not intended to be an ultimate statement of policies of this Government concerning the treatment of Germany in the post-war world. It is therefore essential that, during the period covered by this directive, you assure that surveys are constantly maintained of economic, industrial, financial, social and political conditions within your zone and that the results of such surveys and such other surveys as may be made in other zones are made available to your Government, through the Joint Chiefs of Staff. These surveys should be developed in such manner as to serve as a basis for determining changes in the measures of control set forth herein as well as for the progressive formulation and development of policies to promote the basic objectives of the United States. Supplemental directives will be issued to you by the Joint Chiefs of Staff as may be required.

As a member of the Control Council you will urge the adoption by the other occupying powers of the principles and policies set forth in this directive and, pending Control Council agreement, you will follow them in your zone. It is anticipated that substantially similar directives will be issued to the Commanders-in-Chief of the U. K., U.S.S.R. and French forces of occupation.

Part I. General and Political

2. *The Basis of Military Government:*

   a. The rights, power and status of the military government in Germany are based upon the unconditional surrender or total defeat of Germany.

   b. Subject to the provisions of paragraph 3 below, you are, by virtue of your position, clothed with supreme legislative, executive, and judicial authority in the areas occupied by forces under your command. This authority will be broadly construed and includes authority to take all measures deemed by you necessary, appropriate or desirable in relation to military exigencies and the objectives of a firm military government.

   c. You will issue a proclamation continuing in force such proclamations, orders and instructions as may have heretofore been issued by Allied Commanders in your zone, subject to such changes as you may determine. Authorizations of action by the Supreme Commander, Allied Expeditionary Force, may be considered as applicable to you unless inconsistent with this or later directives.

3. *The Control Council and Zones of Occupation:*

a. The four Commanders-in-Chief, acting jointly, will constitute the Control Council in Germany which will be the supreme organ of control over Germany in accordance with the agreement on Control Machinery in Germany. For purposes of administration of military government, Germany has been divided into four zones of occupation.

b. The authority of the Control Council to formulate policies and procedures and administrative relationships with respect to matters affecting Germany as a whole will be paramount throughout Germany. You will carry out and support in your zone the policies agreed upon in the Control Council. In the absence of such agreed policies you will act in accordance with this and other directives of the Joint Chiefs of Staff. . . .

4. *Basic Objectives of Military Government in Germany:*

a. It should be brought home to the Germans that Germany's ruthless warfare and fanatical Nazi resistance have destroyed the German economy and made chaos and suffering inevitable and that the Germans cannot escape responsibility for what they have brought upon themselves.

b. Germany will not be occupied for the purpose of liberation but as a defeated enemy nation. Your aim is not oppression but to occupy Germany for the purpose of realizing certain important Allied objectives. In the conduct of your occupation and administration you should be just but firm and aloof. You will strongly discourage fraternization with the German officials and population.

c. The principal Allied objective is to prevent Germany from ever again becoming a threat to the peace of the world. Essential steps in the accomplishment of this objective are the elimination of Nazism and militarism in all their forms, the immediate apprehension of war criminals for punishment, the industrial disarmament and demilitarization of Germany, with continuing control over Germany's capacity to make war, and the preparation for an eventual reconstruction of German political life on a democratic basis.

d. Other Allied objectives are to enforce the program of reparations and restitution, to provide relief for the benefit of countries devastated by Nazi aggression, and to ensure that prisoners of war and displaced persons of the United Nations are cared for and repatriated.

5. *Economic Controls:*

a. As a member of the Control Council and as zone commander, you will be guided by the principle that controls upon the German economy may be imposed to the extent that such controls may be necessary to achieve the objectives enumerated in paragraph 4 above and also as they may be essential to protect the safety and meet the needs of the occupying forces and assure the production and maintenance of goods and services required to prevent starvation or such disease and unrest as would endanger these forces. No action will be taken in execution of the reparations program or otherwise which would tend to support basic living conditions in Germany or in your zone on a higher level than that existing in any one of the neighboring United Nations.

b. In the imposition and maintenance of such controls as may be prescribed by you or the Control Council, German authorities will to the fullest extent practicable be ordered to proclaim and assume administration of such controls. Thus it should be brought home to the German people that the responsibility for the administration of such controls and for any breakdowns in those controls will rest with themselves and German authorities.

6. *Denazification:*

a. A Proclamation dissolving the Nazi Party, its formations, affiliated associations and supervised organizations, and all Nazi public institutions which were set up as instruments of Party domination, and prohibiting their revival in any form, should be promulgated by the Control Council. You will assure the prompt effectuation of that policy in your zone and will make every effort to prevent the reconstitution of any such organization in underground, disguised or secret form. Responsibility for continuing desirable non-political social services of dissolved Party organizations may be transferred by the Control Councils to appropriate central agencies and by you to appropriate local agencies.

b. The laws purporting to establish the political structure of National Socialism and the basis of the Hitler regime and all laws, decrees and regulations which establish discriminations on grounds of race, nationality, creed or political opinions should be abrogated by the Control Council. You will render them inoperative in your zone.

c. All members of the Nazi Party who have been more than nominal participants in its activities, all active supporters of Nazism or militarism and all other persons hostile to Allied purposes will be removed and excluded from public office and from positions of importance in quasi-public and private enterprises such as (1) civic, economic and labor organizations, (2) corporations and other organizations in which the German government or subdivisions have a major finanical interest, (3) industry, commerce, agriculture, and finance, (4) education, and (5) the press, publishing houses and other agencies disseminating news and propaganda. Persons are to be treated as more than nominal participants in Party activities and as active supporters of Nazism or militarism when they have (1) held office or otherwise been active at any level from local to national in the Party and its subordinate organizations, or in organizations which further militaristic doctrines, (2) authorized or participated affirmatively in any Nazi crimes, racial persecutions or discriminations, (3) been

HITLER'S THIRD REICH

avowed believers in Nazism or racial and militaristic creeds, or (4) voluntarily given substantial moral or material support or political assistance of any kind to the Nazi Party or Nazi officials and leaders. No such persons shall be retained in any of the categories of employment listed above because of administrative necessity, convenience or expediency.

  d. Property, real and personal, owned or controlled by the Nazi Party, its formations, affiliated associations and supervised organizations, and by all persons subject to arrest under the provisions of paragraph 8, and found within your zone, will be taken under your control pending a decision by the Control Council or higher authority as to its eventual disposition.

  e. All archives, monuments and museums of Nazi inception, or which are devoted to the perpetuation of German militarism, will be taken under your control and their properties held pending decision as to their disposition by the Control Council.

  f. You will make special efforts to preserve from destruction and take under your control records, plans, books, documents, papers, files, and scientific, industrial and other information and data belonging to or controlled by the following:

  (1) The Central German Government and its subdivisions, German military organizations, organizations engaged in military research, and such other governmental agencies as may be deemed advisable;

  (2) The Nazi Party, its formations, affiliated associations and supervised organizations;

  (3) All police organizations, including security and political police;

  (4) Important economic organizations and industrial establishments including those controlled by the Nazi Party or its personnel;

  (5) Institutes and special bureaus devoting themselves to racial, political, militaristic or similar research or propaganda. . . .

PART II. ECONOMIC

General Objectives and Methods of Control:

  16. You will assure that the German economy is administered and controlled in such a way as to accomplish the basic objectives set forth in paragraphs 4 and 5 of this directive. Economic controls will be imposed only to the extent necessary to accomplish these objectives, provided that you will impose controls to the full extent necessary to achieve the industrial disarmament of Germany. Except as may be necessary to carry out these objectives, you will take no steps (a) looking toward the economic rehabilitation of Germany, or (b) designed to maintain or strengthen the German economy.

  17. To the maximum extent possible without jeopardizing the successful execution of measures required to implement the objectives outlined in paragraphs 4 and 5 of this directive you will use German authorities and

agencies and subject them to such supervision and punishment for non-compliance as is necessary to ensure that they carry out their tasks. . . .

Labor, Health, and Social Insurance:

23. You will permit the self-organization of employees along democratic lines, subject to such safeguards as may be necessary to prevent the perpetuation of Nazi or militarist influence under any guise or the continuation of any group hostile to the objectives and operations of the occupying forces.

24. You will permit free collective bargaining between employees and employers regarding wage, hour and working conditions and the establishment of machinery for the settlement of industrial disputes. Collective bargaining shall be subject to such wage, hour and other controls, if any, as may be instituted or revived by your direction. . . .

Agriculture, Industry and Internal Commerce:

27. You will require the Germans to use all means at their disposal to maximize agricultural output and to establish as rapidly as possible effective machinery for the collection and distribution of agricultural output.

28. You will direct the German authorities to utilize large-landed estates and public lands in a manner which will facilitate the accommodation and settlement of Germans and others or increase agricultural output.

29. You will protect from destruction by the Germans, and maintain for such disposition as is determined by this and other directives or by the Control Council, all plants, equipment, patents and other property, and all books and records of large German industrial companies and trade and research associations that have been essential to the German war effort or the German economy. You will pay particular attention to research and experimental establishments of such concerns. . . .

133. Admiral Karl Doenitz, Hitler's Successor, Broadcasts a Proclamation to the German People, May 1, 1945

"Our Fuehrer, Adolf Hitler, has fallen."

In his political testament dictated just before his suicide, Hitler appointed Grand Admiral Karl Doenitz, who had demonstrated his personal loyalty, to be his successor as president of the Reich and supreme commander of the armed forces. On May 1, 1945, from a studio in Hamburg, Doenitz broadcast to the German people his opening proclamation on assuming authority.

ANNOUNCER: It is reported from the *Fuehrer's* headquarters that our *Fuehrer,* Adolf Hitler, fighting to the last against bolshevism, fell for Germany this afternoon in his operational headquarters in the Reich Chancellery.

On April 30, the *Fuehrer* appointed Grand Admiral Doenitz his successor. The Grand Admiral and successor of the *Fuehrer* now speaks to the German people.

DOENITZ: "German men and women, soldiers of the armed forces: Our *Fuehrer,* Adolf Hitler, has fallen. In the deepest sorrow and respect the German people now.* . . . The *Fuehrer* has appointed me to be his successor. Fully conscious of the responsibility, I take over the leadership of the German people at this fateful hour. . . ."

The New York Times, May 2, 1945.
*The radio broadcast was not clear at this point.

134. Admiral Doenitz Issues His First Order of the Day to the German Armed Forces and Calls for Further Resistance, May 1, 1945

*"German soldiers! Do your duty! The existence of
our people is at stake."*

As soon as he had informed the German people in a proclamation that he had become the successor to Hitler, Grand Admiral Karl Doenitz issued an order of the day to the armed forces in which he urged them to continue their battle against the Russians. He also called for further resistance against the British and Americans as long "as they impede me in the struggle against bolshevism." There was little point to the order. The Germans had already been defeated on the battlefields. The next day, Doenitz sent an envoy to General Bernard L. Montgomery with a proposal to capitulate in the West but to continue the struggle in the East. Montgomery rejected the proposal brusquely and called for unconditional surrender. On May 4, 1945, the Germans in Holland, northwest Germany, and Denmark capitulated. Three days later came the final unconditional surrender at Reims.

German armed forces, my comrades:
The Fuehrer has fallen. Faithful to his great ideal to save the nations of Europe from Bolshevism, he has given his life and has met a hero's death. In him one of the greatest heroes of German history has appeared. With proud respect and grief we lower our standards.

The New York Times, May 2, 1945.

The *Fuehrer* has designated me to be at the head of the State† and Supreme Commander. . . . I am resolved to continue the struggle against the Bolsheviks. . . . Against the British and Americans I am bound to continue to fight as far and as long as they impede me in the struggle against Bolshevism. . . . For every single one of you the oath of loyalty to the *Fuehrer* is transferred straight to my person as the *Fuehrer*'s appointed successor.

German soldiers! Do you duty! The existence of our people is at stake.

---

†In his political testament, Hitler appointed Doenitz to the posts of president of the Reich and supreme commander of the armed forces. Doenitz here used the term "head of the State."

135. Final Capitulation at Reims: Collapse of the Third Reich, May 7, 1945

"The mad dog of Europe was put out of the way; the strange, insane monstrosity that was Nazi Germany has been beaten into submission."

The Third Reich was in chaos. Tens of thousands of prisoners had been taken by the Allies. Many others were desperately seeking to surrender to the Americans or to the British rather than to the dreaded Russians. The German government ordered all U-boats to return to home ports.

On May 5, 1945, Admiral Hans Georg von Friedeburg, representing Admiral Karl Doenitz, the new head of state, arrived at General Dwight D. Eisenhower's headquarters. Friedeburg indicated that he wanted to "negotiate," but he was told immediately that there was no point in negotiating anything. There would be total, unconditional surrender of all German armed forces everywhere. Eisenhower made it plain, through his deputy, General Walter Bedell Smith, that unless the Germans ceased all pretense and delay, he would close the entire Allied front in the west to fleeing German refugees.

The end came on May 7, 1945, when representatives of the Third Reich signed the instrument of surrender in a small red schoolhouse at Reims, France. Charles Collingwood of the Columbia Broadcasting System broadcast this eyewitness account later from SHAEF, Supreme Headquarters Allied Expeditionary Force.

CBS broadcast by Charles Collingwood, May 8, 1945. Courtesy of Charles Collingwood.

GERMANY SURRENDERED at 2:45 on the morning of May 7, 1945. At that moment, General Jodl, Chief of Staff of the German Army, signed the last document. He sat there very straight, with his head bent over the papers and when he had signed the last one, he put the cap back on the pen and looked up at the men sitting across the plain wooden table. Opposite him sat General Bedell Smith, Eisenhower's Chief of Staff. General Smith looked tired. He'd been negotiating for thirty-three hours, but his mouth was hard and so were his eyes. . . .

With sixteen other correspondents I witnessed this scene, which formalized the most complete and resounding defeat in the history of the world, which meant relief and hope to millions of sorely tried people. It was the end of the war, the climax of a series of piecemeal surrenders. The final surrender took place at a quarter to three on Monday morning. . . .

The only people in the room now besides us correspondents are a milling mass of photographers in constant movement climbing up and down ladders, aiming cameras, and around the walls there is a battery of recording apparatus set up to catch every word by our friends the radio engineers of SHAEF, the people who get our broadcasts through.

The whole place is brilliantly lit. It looks like a movie set. About two-thirty in the morning General Carl Spaatz walks in. He is followed in quick succession by the Russians. Then Air Marshal Robb comes in; Admiral Burrough. Pretty soon Bedell Smith himself enters, the man who bore the brunt of the long hours of negotiations. He looks tired, but there's a look of grim satisfaction about his tight mouth. The other generals come in. The last is the little French general, Sevez. He looks out of breath as though he'd run up the stairs. Everyone stands about by their chairs, waiting for the Germans. Spaatz makes a soldierly pleasantry to the Russians and they grin broadly. Everyone tries to appear completely at ease, but the air is tense, tense, tense.

Then the Germans come in. Jodl's face is like a death mask; drawn, unnatural-looking, and with every muscle in it clenched. Admiral Friedeburg is more relaxed, but he, too, is not enjoying himself. Jodl's aide bobs about like a head waiter in a restaurant. Their uniforms are immaculate and rather spectacular in the German fashion. Both Jodl and his aide have the double red stripe of the German General Staff on the sides of their cavalry breeches. They reach the table, bow in unison, and wait. General Smith motions them to sit down. Everyone sits down.

Then the cameramen start bounding about after the fashion of cameramen, like so many monkeys in the zoo. They run at top speed all around the room, up and down ladders, flash-bulbs going all the time. It's an incredible scene. The generals are clearly annoyed, but still the photographers untiringly dash about, getting in the way of General Strong,

Eisenhower's G-2, who is by this time handing around the documents to be signed.

Jodl signs the surrender, at 2:41, and then General Smith who hands it to the Russian General Suslaparov — and finally the French General Sevez signs it. This happens four times . . . a copy for each nation. Meanwhile, Admiral Burrough and General Smith sign a paper relating to the conditions for disarming the German Navy. And Smith and Spaatz sign one for the ground and air forces.

By 2:45 the last signature has been affixed. The photographers are still in full cry, leaping over one another to get their pictures. It has become completely ridiculous, but still they go on. They're fascinated by the face of General Suslaparov's interpreter. He's a Russian with a head completely bald, not a hair, and a glittering eye which he fixed on the Germans like the very eye of doom. To get a good shot at him, a photographer leans over the Germans, elbowing Jodl out of the way, and flashes his bulb at the Russian.

The Germans sit there, through it all, stiff, unblinking, tasting to the bitter dregs their cup of humiliation.

Then came the most dramatic moment of all. Everything had been signed. There was no longer any possibility of quibbling or evasion. The German Third Reich, which had once made the world tremble, had collapsed in blood-stained fragments. Colonel General Jodl, Chief of Staff of the German Army, asked General Bedell Smith's permission to speak. He stood up stiffly, like a man holding himself in against some unbearable pain.

In a strangled voice, like a sob, he said: "With this signature the German people and the German armed forces are, for better or worse, delivered into the victor's hands. In this hour, I can only express the hope that the victor will treat them with generosity."

I will let you hear now how it sounded. Here is a recording made at the table of his actual words as General Jodl spoke in that moment filled with such tremendous meaning.

(Collingwood plays the recording.)

When General Jodl sat down after that, it was all over. At a sign from General Smith, the Germans stood up, bowed again, and quickly left the room.

Up to this time they had not yet seen General Eisenhower or Air Chief Marshal Tedder, his deputy. All the negotiations were undertaken by General Smith and General Strong, but after the surrender, Jodl and Friedeburg were taken to the Supreme Commander. Eisenhower and his deputy, Air Chief Marshal Tedder, stood side-by-side behind Eisenhower's desk, unsmiling.

The Germans bowed and stood there. Eisenhower asked them curtly whether they had understood the terms of surrender and whether they agreed to carry them out. The Germans said "Yes," and then they were taken away.

It was all over — the Germans had surrendered — and later General Eisenhower said a few words. This is what he said:

"In January, 1943, the late President Roosevelt and Premier Churchill met in Casablanca. There were pronounced the formula of unconditional surrender for the Axis powers. In Europe, that formula has now been fulfilled. The Allied force, which invaded Europe on June 6, 1944, has, with its great Russian ally, and forces advancing in the south, utterly defeated the Germans by land, sea and air. Thus, unconditional surrender has been achieved by teamwork, teamwork not only among all the Allies participating but amongst all the services — land, sea and air. To every subordinate that has been in this command, of almost five million Allies, I owe a debt of gratitude that can never be repaid. The only repayment that can be made to them is the deep appreciation and lasting gratitude of all free citizens of all the United Nations."

With these words General Eisenhower finished the evening's ceremonies. It was all over. Eisenhower relaxed, everyone relaxed. One almost forgave the photographers. The most terrible war in human history had finally come to an end. The mad dog of Europe was put out of the way, the strange, insane monstrosity that was Nazi Germany had been beaten into submission. To millions of people this was the end of suffering. It was perhaps the best news the world had ever had — the surrender of Reims had been signed.

136. The Formal Act of German Military Surrender, Berlin, May 8, 1945

"... *hereby surrender unconditionally.* ..."

The act of military surrender was signed at Reims on May 7, 1945, at 2:41 A.M. to take effect at 11:01 the next day. This document was signed by General Alfred Jodl on behalf of the German High Command, General W. B. Smith on behalf of the Supreme Commander, Allied Expeditionary Force, and General Ivan Suslaparov on behalf of the Soviet High Command. The document was then sent to Berlin for the formal act to be signed.

One half hour before midnight, May 8, 1945, the Instrument of Unconditional Surrender was officially ratified in Berlin. For the first time in modern history, the entire armed forces of a nation, officers and enlisted men alike, became prisoners of war. Following is the text of the German act of surrender.

1. WE THE UNDERSIGNED, acting by authority of the German High Command, hereby surrender unconditionally to the Supreme Commander, Allied Expeditionary Force and simultaneously to the Supreme High Command of the Red Army all forces on land, at sea, and in the air who are at this date under German control.

2. The German High Command will at once issue orders to all German military, naval and air authorities and to all forces under German control to cease active operations at 2301 hours Central European time on 8th May 1945, to remain in the positions occupied at that time and to disarm completely, handing over their weapons and equipment to the local allied

---

U.S., Senate, Committee on Foreign Relations, *Documents on Germany, 1944–1961* (Washington, D.C.: Government Printing Office; 1962), pp. 11–12.

commanders or officers designated by Representatives of the Allied Supreme Commands. No ship, vessel, or aircraft is to be scuttled, or any damage done to their hull, machinery or equipment, and also to machines of all kinds, armament, apparatus, and all the technical means of prosecution of war in general.

3. The German High Command will at once issue to the appropriate commanders, and ensure the carrying out of any further orders issued by the Supreme Commander, Allied Expeditionary Force and by the Supreme High Command of the Red Army.

4. This act of military surrender is without prejudice to, and will be superseded by any general instrument of surrender imposed by, or on behalf of the United Nations and applicable to Germany and the German armed forces as a whole.

5. In the event of the German High Command or any of the forces under their control failing to act in accordance with this Act of Surrender, the Supreme Commander, Allied Expeditionary Force and the Supreme High Command of the Red Army will take such punitive or other action as they deem appropriate.

6. This Act is drawn up in the English, Russian and German languages. The English and Russian are the only authentic texts.

Signed at Berlin on the 8 day of May, 1945.

FRIEDEBURG   KEITEL   STUMPF
On behalf of the German High Command

In the presence of:

On behalf of the   On behalf of the
Supreme Commander   Supreme High Command
Allied Expeditionary Force   of the Red Army
A W TEDDER   G ZHUKOV

At the signing also were present as witnesses:

F. DE LATTRE-TASSIGNY   CARL SPAATZ
General Commanding in Chief   General, Commanding United
First French Army   States Strategic Air Forces

137. Devastated Berlin: Newsman Describes the Capital of the Third Reich as a Modern Carthage, May 9, 1945

"The Blitz of London was a bank holiday compared with this . . ."

On May 2, 1945, the German defenders of Berlin, after two weeks of desperate fighting, surrendered. The capital of the Third Reich presented an incredible spectacle. American and British bombardment from the air and Russian artillery had smashed the great metropolis beyond recognition. Scarred skeletons of buildings teetered precariously on their foundations. The streets were filled with rubble, the air with dust. Bodies lay where they had fallen. There was no water, no electricity, no telephone service. Shops were bare. The people, shattered by panic and fear, moved in the subways or burrowed into the ruins to share quarters with the rats.

In the following dispatch, Harold King, writing for the Combined Allied Press, described the ruined city as a modern Carthage.

BERLIN, MAY 9 (AP) — This town is a city of the dead. As a metropolis it has simply ceased to exist. Every house within miles of the center seems to have had its own bomb.

I toured the Nazi capital from the east to the center and back to the south this morning in company with Air Chief Marshal Sir Arthur Tedder and the Russian military commander of Berlin, General Berzarin.

The scene beggars description. I have seen Stalingrad; I have lived through the entire London *Blitz*; I have seen a dozen badly damaged Russian towns, but the scene of utter destruction, desolation and death

Associated Press, May 9, 1945.

which meets the eye in Berlin as far as the eye can rove in all directions is
something that almost baffles description.

"The *Blitz* of London was a bank holiday compared with this," one of
my colleagues remarked.

Dozens of well-known thoroughfares, including the entire Unter den
Linden from one end to the other, are wrecked beyond repair. The town is
literally unrecognizable.

The Alexander Platz, in the east end, where the Gestapo headquarters
was, is a weird desert of rubble and gaping, smoke-blackened walls. From
the Brandenburg Gate, everything within a radius of from 2 to 5 miles is
destroyed. There does not appear to be one house in a hundred which is
even useful as shelter.

Among hundreds of well-known landmarks which have disappeared or
been irreparably damaged are the former Kaiser's palace, the opera house,
the French, British, American and Japanese embassies, Goering's Air Ministry, Goebbels' Propaganda Ministry, the Bristol and Adlon Hotels.

Hitler's Chancellery in the Wilhelmstrasse is like some vast abandoned
ancient tomb of the dead. It has had several direct hits, and it is impossible
yet to tell who lies buried beneath the rubble, perhaps Hitler himself.

The only people who look like human beings in the streets of what was
Berlin are the Russian soldiers. There are 2,000,000 inhabitants in the
town, the Russian authorities told me, but they are mostly in the remoter
suburbs. In the central part of the town you only see a few ghostlike figures
of women and children — few men — queueing up to pump water.

If Stalingrad, London, Guernica, Rotterdam, Coventry wanted aveng-
ing, they have had it, and no mistake about it.

The Red flag, or rather several Red flags, fly on top of the Reichstag
which is burned hollow. The Tiergarten opposite the Reichstag looks like a
forest after a big fire. There was heavy street fighting here.

I motored from the Tempelhof airport in a fast car and during 30 minutes unhampered driving, I spotted only six houses which you were not
able to see straight through and in which there were signs of habitation.

The population and Red Army soldiers are attempting to clear some of
the main streets.

The Russian command has already erected at all main squares and
crossings huge sketch maps, without which it would be impossible to find
one's way about.

Except for an occasional Russian army car or horses drawing Russian
army carts, there is complete silence over the city, and the air is filled with
rubble dust.

One sign of life, however, are the interminable columns of displaced
persons of all European nationalities who seem to be marching through
Berlin in various directions, carried forward by a homing instinct more

than by any clear idea of where they are going. These columns of freed slaves are sometimes a mile long.

They trudge along slowly, one or two abreast, drawing tiny carts, or six or eight of them at a time dragging with ropes wagons which need a lusty horse. In these columns there are many little groups, carrying the flag of their nationality — Italians, French, Belgians, mostly. Many are in soldier's uniform and appear to be escaped or freed prisoners of war.

The Russian military command of this modern Carthage is already feeding hundreds of thousands of Berliners. The Red Army has seized what food stocks the town had, and has added from its own supplies.

Berliners get 500 grams of bread a day (more than many got in Moscow in the winter of 1942), a little meat, sugar, coffee, potatoes. Attempts are being made to get the water supply working. The Russians are obviously not wreaking any vengeance on the population.

I asked one well-known Russian writer, who was attending the surrender ceremonial, why the Russians bothered about the population.

"We must look after the people," he said with a note of surprise at the question. "We cannot let 2,000,000 people die."

Many wounded German soldiers lying in underground hospitals have been sent to Russian-organized hospitals, and are looked after by German doctors and German nurses.

138. Allied Declaration on the Defeat of Germany and the Assumption of Supreme Authority by the Victor Powers, June 5, 1945

". . . Germany, which bears responsibility for the war. . . ."

On June 5, 1945, the victorious Allied Powers drew up a special declaration to make provisions for the cessation of hostilities by the German armed forces, to maintain order inside defeated Germany, to set up administration for the defeated country, and to state those immediate requirements to which Germany should comply. It was the requiem of defeat for the shattered Third Reich.

THE GERMAN ARMED FORCES on land, at sea and in the air have been completely defeated and have surrendered unconditionally and Germany, which bears responsibility for the war, is no longer capable of resisting the will of the victorious Powers. The unconditional surrender of Germany has thereby been effected, and Germany has become subject to such requirements as may now or hereafter be imposed upon her.

There is no central Government or authority in Germany capable of accepting responsibility for the maintenance of order, the administration of the country and compliance with the requirements of the victorious Powers.

It is in these circumstances necessary, without prejudice to any subsequent decisions that may be taken respecting Germany, to make provision for the cessation of any further hostilities on the part of the German armed forces, for the maintenance of order in Germany and for the administra-

U.S. Senate, Committee on Foreign Relations, *Documents of German History, 1944–1961* (Washington, D.C.: Government Printing Office, 1962), pp. 8–17.

tion of the country, and to announce the immediate requirements with which Germany must comply.

The Representatives of the Supreme Commands of the United States of America, the Union of Soviet Socialist Republics, the United Kingdom and the French Republic, hereinafter called the "Allied Representatives," acting by authority of their respective Governments and the interests of the United Nations, accordingly make the following Declaration: —

The Governments of the United States of America, the Union of Soviet Socialist Republics and the United Kingdom, and the Provisional Government of the French Republic, hereby assume supreme authority with respect to Germany, including all the powers possessed by the German Government, the High Command and any state, municipal, or local government or authority. The assumption, for the purposes stated above, of the said authority and powers does not effect the annexation of Germany.

The Governments of the United States of America, the Union of Soviet Socialist Republics and the United Kingdom, and the Provisional Government of the French Republic, will hereafter determine the boundaries of Germany or any part thereof and the status of Germany or of any area at present being part of German territory.

In virtue of the supreme authority and powers thus assumed by the four Governments, the Allied Representatives announce the following requirements arising from the complete defeat and unconditional surrender of Germany with which Germans must comply: —

Article 1.

Germany, and all German military, naval and air authorities and all forces under German control shall immediately cease hostilities in all theatres of war against the forces of the United Nations on land, at sea and in the air.

Article 2.

(a) All armed forces of Germany or under German control, wherever they may be situated, including land, air, anti-aircraft and naval forces, the S.S., S.A. and Gestapo, and all other forces of auxiliary organizations equipped with weapons, shall be completely disarmed, handing over their weapons and equipment to local Allied Commanders or to officers designated by the Allied Representatives.

(b) The personnel of the formations and units of all the forces referred to in paragraph (a) above shall, at the discretion of the Commander-in-Chief of the Armed Forces of the Allied State concerned, be declared to be prisoners of war, pending further decisions, and shall be subject to such conditions and directions as may be prescribed by the respective Allied Representatives.

(c) All forces referred to in paragraph (a) above, wherever they may be, will remain in their present positions pending instructions from the Allied Representatives.

(d) Evacuation by the said forces of all territories outside the frontiers of Germany as they existed on the 31st December, 1937, will proceed according to instructions to be given by the Allied Representatives.

(e) Detachments of civil police to be armed with small arms only, for the maintenance of order and for guard duties, will be designated by the Allied Representatives.

ARTICLE 3.

(a) All aircraft of any kind or nationality in Germany or German-occupied or controlled territories or waters, military, naval or civil, other than aircraft in the service of the Allies, will remain on the ground, on the water or aboard ships pending further instructions.

(b) All German or German-controlled aircraft in or over territories or waters not occupied or controlled by Germany will proceed to Germany or to such other place or places as may be specified by the Allied Representatives.

ARTICLE 4.

(a) All German or German-controlled naval vessels, surface and submarine, auxiliary naval craft, and merchant and other shipping, wherever such vessels may be at the time of this Declaration, and all other merchant ships of whatever nationality in German ports, will remain in or proceed immediately to ports and bases as specified by the Allied Representatives. The crews of such vessels will remain on board pending further instructions.

(b) All ships and vessels of the United Nations, whether or not title has been transferred as the result of prize court or other proceedings, which are at the disposal of Germany or under German control at the time of this Declaration, will proceed at the dates and to the ports and bases specified by the Allied Representatives. . . .

ARTICLE 8.

There shall be no destruction, removal, concealment, transfer or scuttling of, or damage to, any military, naval, air, shipping, port, industrial and other like property and facilities and all records and archives, wherever they may be situated, except as may be directed by the Allied Representatives.

ARTICLE 9.

Pending the institution of control by the Allied Representatives over all means of communication, all radio and telecommunication installations and other forms of wire or wireless communications, whether ashore or afloat, under German control, will cease transmission except as directed by the Allied Representatives.

ARTICLE 10.

The forces, ships, aircraft, military equipment, and other property in Germany or in German control or service or at German disposal of any other country at war with any of the Allies, will be subject to the provisions of this Declaration and of any proclamations, orders, ordinances or instructions issued thereunder.

ARTICLE 11.

(a) The principal Nazi leaders as specified by the Allied Representatives, and all persons from time to time named or designated by rank, office or employment by the Allied Representatives as being suspected of having committed, ordered or abetted war crimes of analogous offenses, will be apprehended and surrendered to the Allied Representatives.

(b) The same will apply in the case of any national of any of the United Nations who is alleged to have committed an offense against his national law, and who may at any time be named or designated by rank, office or employment by the Allied Representatives.

(c) The Germany authorities and people will comply with any instructions given by the Allied Representatives for the apprehension and surrender of such persons.

ARTICLE 12.

The Allied Representatives will station forces and civil agencies in any or all parts of Germany as they may determine.

ARTICLE 13.

(a) In the exercise of the supreme authority with respect to Germany assumed by the Governments of the United States of America, the Union of Soviet Socialist Republics and the United Kingdom, and the Provisional Government of the French Republic, the four Allied Governments will take such steps, including the complete disarmament and demilitarization of Germany, as they deem requisite for future peace and security.

(b) The Allied Representatives will impose on Germany additional political, administrative, economic, financial, military and other requirements arising from the complete defeat of Germany. The Allied Representatives, or persons or agencies duly designated to act on their authority, will issue proclamations, orders, ordinances and instructions for the purpose of laying down such additional requirements, and of giving effect to the other provisions of this Declaration. All German authorities and the German people shall carry out unconditionally the requirements of the Allied Representatives, and shall fully comply with all such proclamations, orders, ordinances and instructions.

ARTICLE 14.

This Declaration enters into force and effect at the date and hour set forth below. In the event of failure on the part of the German authorities or people promptly and completely to fulfil their obligations hereby or hereafter imposed, the Allied Representatives will take whatever action may be deemed by them to be appropriate under the circumstances.

ARTICLE 15.

This Declaration is drawn up in the English, Russian, French, and German languages. The English, Russian and French are the only authentic texts.

BERLIN, GERMANY,
  June 5, 1945

139. The Potsdam Conference: The Allies Decide the Future of Germany, July 17–August 2, 1945

> *"War criminals . . . shall be arrested and brought to judgment."*

The Potsdam Conference, officially called the Berlin Conference, met from July 17 to August 2, 1945, for the purpose of deciding the future of Germany after the fall of the Third Reich. The United States was represented by President Harry S Truman and Secretary of State James F. Byrnes; the Soviet Union by Joseph Stalin and Foreign Minister Vyacheslav Mihailovich Molotov; and Great Britain by Prime Minister Winston Churchill and Foreign Secretary Anthony Eden. The parley was interrupted briefly on July 26, 1945, to allow Churchill to go to England for the final returns of the general election of July 5. After the Socialists won in a landslide, the new prime minister, Clement R. Attlee, was sent to Potsdam to replace Churchill.

On August 2, 1945, the conference reached its climax with the issue of a six-thousand-word communiqué dealing with the denazification, demilitarization, and decentralization of Germany. The following extracts give the political and economic principles agreed upon to govern the treatment of Germany in the initial control period and to prepare for her reconstruction.

The Potsdam Agreement, Joint Report on Results of the Anglo-Soviet-American Conference (Berlin, 1945), released August 2, 1945. From *The New York Times*, August 3, 1945.

III. Germany

THE ALLIED ARMIES are in occupation of the whole of Germany, and the German people have begun to atone for the terrible crimes committed under the leadership of those whom, in the hour of their success, they openly approved and blindly obeyed.

Agreement has been reached at this conference on the political and economic principles of a coordinated Allied policy toward defeated Germany during the period of Allied control.

The purpose of this agreement is to carry out the Crimea Declaration on Germany. German militarism and Nazism will be extirpated, and the Allies will take in agreement together, now and in the future, the other measures necessary to assure that Germany never again will threaten her neighbors or the peace of the world.

It is not the intention of the Allies to destroy or enslave the German people. It is the intention of the Allies that the German people be given the opportunity to prepare for the eventual reconstruction of their life on a democratic and peaceful basis. If their own efforts are steadily directed to this end, it will be possible for them in due course to take their place among the free and peaceful peoples of the world.

The text of the agreement is as follows:

The Political and Economic Principles To Govern the Treatment of Germany in the Initial Control Period

A. Political Principles

1. In accordance with the agreement on control machinery in Germany, supreme authority in Germany is exercised, on instructions from their respective governments, by the Commanders-in-Chief of the armed forces of the United States of America, the United Kingdom, the Union of Soviet Socialist Republics, and the French Republic, each in his own zone of occupation, and also jointly in matters affecting Germany as a whole, in their capacity as members of the Control Council.

2. So far as is practicable, there shall be uniformity of treatment of the German population throughout Germany.

3. The purposes of the occupation of Germany by which the Control Council shall be guided are:

(*i*) The complete disarmament and demilitarization of Germany and the elimination or control of all German industry that could be used for military production. To these ends:

(*a*) All German land, naval and air forces, the S.S., S.A., S.D., and *Gestapo,* their organizations, staffs and institutions, including the General Staff, the Officers' Corps, Reserve Corps, military schools, war veterans' organizations and all other military and quasimilitary organizations, together with all clubs and associations which serve to keep alive the military tradition in Germany, shall be completely and finally abolished in such manner as permanently to prevent the revival or reorganization of German militarism and Nazism.

(*b*) All arms, ammunition and implements of war and all specialized facilities for their production shall be held at the disposal of the Allies or destroyed. The maintenance and production of all aircraft and all arms, ammunition and implements of war shall be prevented.

(*ii*) To convince the German people that they have suffered a total military defeat and that they cannot escape responsibility for what they have brought upon themselves, since their own ruthless warfare and the fanatical Nazi resistance have destroyed the German economy and made chaos and suffering inevitable.

(*iii*) To destroy the National Socialist Party and its affiliated and supervised organizations, to dissolve all Nazi institutions, to ensure that they are not revived in any form, and to prevent all Nazi and militarist activity or propaganda.

(*iv*) To prepare for the eventual reconstruction of German political life on a democratic basis and for eventual peaceful cooperation in international life by Germany.

4. All Nazi laws which provided the basis of the Hitler regime or established discrimination on grounds of race, creed or political opinion shall be abolished. No such discriminations, whether legal, administrative or otherwise shall be tolerated.

5. War criminals and those who have participated in planning or carrying out Nazi enterprises involving or resulting in atrocities or war crimes shall be arrested and brought to judgment. Nazi leaders, influential Nazi supporters and high officials of Nazi organizations and institutions and any other persons dangerous to the occupation or its objectives shall be arrested and interned.

6. All members of the Nazi Party who have been more than nominal participants in its activities and all other persons hostile to Allied purposes shall be removed from public and semi-public office, and from positions of responsibility in important private undertakings. Such persons shall be replaced by persons who, by their political and moral qualities, are deemed capable of assisting in developing genuine democratic institutions in Germany.

7. German education shall be so controlled as completely to eliminate Nazi and militarist doctrines and to make possible the successful development of democratic ideas.

8. The judicial system will be reorganized in accordance with the principles of democracy, of justice under law and of equal rights for all citizens without distinction of race, nationality or religion.

9. The administration of affairs in Germany should be directed toward the decentralization of the political structure and the development of local responsibility. To this end:

(*i*) Local self-government shall be restored throughout Germany on democratic principles and in particular through elective councils as rapidly as is consistent with military security and the purposes of military occupation;

(*ii*) All democratic political parties with rights of assembly and of public discussion shall be allowed and encouraged throughout Germany;

(*iii*) Representative and elective principles shall be introduced into regional, provincial and state (land) administration as rapidly as may be justified by the successful application of these principles in local self-government;

(*iv*) For the time being no central German government shall be established. Notwithstanding this, however, certain essential central German administrative departments, headed by state secretaries, shall be established, particularly in the fields of finance, transport, communications, foreign trade and industry. Such departments will act under the direction of the Control Council.

10. Subject to the necessity for maintaining military security; freedom of speech, press and religion shall be permitted, and religious institutions shall be respected. Subject likewise to the maintenance of military security, the formation of free trade unions shall be permitted.

B. Economic Principles

11. In order to eliminate Germany's war potential, the production of arms, ammunition and implements of war as well as all types of aircraft and seagoing ships shall be prohibited and prevented. Production of metals, chemicals, machinery and other items that are directly necessary to a war economy shall be rigidly controlled and restricted to Germany's approved war peacetime needs to meet the objectives stated in paragraph 15. Productive capacity not needed for permitted production shall be removed in accordance with the reparations plan recommended by the Allied Commission on reparations and approved by the governments concerned or if not removed shall be destroyed.

12. At the earliest practicable date, the German economy shall be decentralized for the purpose of eliminating the present excessive concentration of economic power as exemplified in particular by cartels, syndicates, trusts and other monopolistic arrangements.

13. In organizing the German economy, primary emphasis shall be given to the development of agriculture and peaceful domestic industries. . . .

IV. Reparations from Germany

In accordance with the Crimea decision that Germany be compelled to compensate to the greatest possible extent for the loss and suffering that she has caused to the United Nations and for which the German people cannot escape responsibility, the following agreement on reparations was reached.

1. Reparation claims of the U.S.S.R. shall be met by removals from the zone of Germany occupied by the U.S.S.R. and from appropriate German external assets.

2. The U.S.S.R. undertakes to settle the reparation claims of Poland from its own share of reparations.

3. The reparation claims of the United States, the United Kingdom and other countries entitled to reparations shall be met from the western zones and from appropriate German external assets.

4. In addition to the reparations to be taken by the U.S.S.R. from its own zone of occupation, the U.S.S.R. shall receive additionally from the western zones:

(A) 15 per cent of such usable and complete industrial capital equipment, in the first place from the metallurgical, chemical and machine manufacturing industries, as is unnecessary for the German peace economy and should be removed from the western zones of Germany, in exchange for an equivalent value of food, coal, potash, zinc, timber, clay products, petroleum products, and such other commodities as may be agreed upon.

(B) 10 per cent of such industrial capital equipment as is necessary for the German peace economy and should be removed from the western zones, to be transferred to the Soviet Government on reparations account without payment or exchange of any kind in return.

Removals of equipment as provided in (A) and (B) above shall be made simultaneously.

5. The amount of equipment to be removed from the western zones on account of reparations must be determined within six months from now at the latest.

6. Removals of industrial capital equipment shall begin as soon as possible and shall be completed within two years from the determination specified in paragraph 5. The delivery of goods covered by 4 (A) above shall begin as soon as possible and shall be made by the U.S.S.R. in agreed installments within five years of the date hereof. The determination of the amount and character of the industrial capital equipment unnecessary for the German peace economy and therefore available for reparations shall be made by the Control Council under policies fixed by the Allied Commission on Reparations, with the participation of France, subject to the final approval of the zone commander in the zone from which the equipment is to be removed.

7. Prior to the fixing of the total amount of equipment subject to re-

moval, advance deliveries shall be made in respect of such equipment as will be determined to be eligible for delivery in accordance with the procedure set forth in the last sentence of paragraph 6.

8. The Soviet Government renounces all claims in respect of reparations to shares of German enterprises which are located in the western zones of occupation in Germany as well as to German foreign assets in all countries except those specified in paragraph 9 below.

9. The Governments of the United Kingdom and the United States of America renounce their claims in respect of reparations to shares of German enterprises which are located in the eastern zone of Germany, as well as to German foreign assets in Bulgaria, Finland, Rumania and Eastern Austria.

10. The Soviet Government makes no claims to gold captured by the Allied troops in Germany.

V. Disposal of the German Navy and Merchant Marine

The Conference agreed in principle upon arrangements for the use and disposal of the surrendered German Fleet and merchant ships. It was decided that the three Governments would appoint experts to work out together detailed plans to give effect to the agreed principles. A further joint statement will be published simultaneously by the three Governments in due course. . . .

140. Nuremberg Trial: Hermann Goering Takes the Stand and Begins His Defense, March 13, 1946

"We did not want power and governmental authority for power's sake, but we needed power and governmental authority in order to make Germany free and great."

Hermann Goering took the stand at Nuremberg in the afternoon session of March 13, 1946. He gave testimony in his own defense for three days. Led by his lawyer, Dr. Otto Stahmer, he began with a factual description of his background, his meeting with Hitler, and his motives in helping build the Nazi party. He then traced his activities as a Nazi leader to the early days of 1934. Following are excerpts from Goering's testimony on his first day on the stand.

DR. STAHMER: If the High Tribunal agree, I wish to call the former Reich Marshal, Defendant Hermann Goering, to the witness stand.

[*The Defendant Goering took the stand.*]

THE PRESIDENT: Will you give your name please?

HERMANN WILHELM GOERING (Defendant): Hermann Goering.

THE PRESIDENT: Will you repeat this oath after me: I swear by God—the Almighty and Omniscient—that I will speak the pure truth—and will withhold and add nothing.

[*The witness repeated the oath in German.*]

THE PRESIDENT: You may sit down if you wish.

DR. STAHMER: When were you born and where?

International Military Tribunal, Nuremberg, *Trial of the Major War Criminals* (Nuremberg: Allied Control Authority for Germany, 1947), vol. 9, pp. 235–61.

GOERING: I was born on 12 January 1893 in Rosenheim, Bavaria.

DR. STAHMER: Give the Tribunal a short account of your life up to the outbreak of the first World War, but briefly, please.

GOERING: Normal education, first a tutor at home; then cadet corps, then an active officer. A few points which are significant with relation to my later development: The position of my father as first Governor of Southwest Africa; his connections at that time, especially with two British statesmen, Cecil Rhodes and the elder Chamberlain. Then the strong attachment of my father to Bismarck; the experiences of my youth, half of which was spent in Austria to which I already felt a close attachment, as to a kindred people. At the beginning of the first World War I was a lieutenant in an infantry regiment.

DR. STAHMER: With what rank did you participate in the first World War?

GOERING: As I just mentioned, at first as a lieutenant in an infantry regiment in the so-called border battles. From October 1914 on I was an aircraft observer. In June 1915 I became a pilot, at first with a reconnaissance plane, then for a short time with a bomber and in the autumn of 1915 I became a fighter pilot. I was seriously wounded in aerial combat. After recovery I became the leader of a fighter squadron, and after Richthofen was killed I became the commander of the then well-known "Richthofen Squadron."

DR. STAHMER: What war decorations did you receive?

GOERING: First the Iron Cross (Second Class), then Iron Cross (First Class), then the Zahring Lion with Swords, the Karl Friedrich Order, the Hohenzollern with Swords (Third Class), and finally the Order *Pour le Mérite*, which was the highest decoration possible.

DR. STAHMER: Tell the Tribunal when and under what circumstances you came to know Hitler.

GOERING: I should like to mention one basic fact in advance. After the collapse in the first World War I had to demobilize my squadron. I rejected the invitation to enter the *Reichswehr* because from the very beginning I was opposed in every way to the republic which had come to power through the revolution; I could not bring it into harmony with my convictions. Shortly afterwards I went abroad to find a position there. But after a few years I longed to get back to my own country. First, I spent quite some time at a hunting lodge in the mountains and studied there. In some way I wanted to participate in the fate of my country. Since I could not and would not do that as an officer for the reasons mentioned above, I had first of all to build up the necessary foundation, and I attended the University of Munich in order to study history and political science. I settled down in the neighborhood of Munich and bought a house there for my wife. Then one day, on a Sunday in November or October of 1922, the demand having been made again by the *Entente* for the extradition of our military leaders, at a protest demonstration in Munich—I went to this protest demonstration as a spectator, without having any connection with it. Various speakers from parties and organizations spoke there. At the end Hitler, too, was called for. I had heard his name once before briefly and wanted to hear what he had to say. He declined to speak and it was pure coincidence that I stood nearby and heard the reasons for his refusal. He did not want to disturb the unanimity of the demonstration; he could not see himself speaking, as he put it, to these tame, bourgeois pirates. He considered it senseless to launch protests with no weight behind them. This made a deep impression on me; I was of the same opinion.

I inquired and found that on the following Monday evening I could hear Hitler speak, as he held a meeting every Monday evening. I went there, and there Hitler spoke in connection with that demonstration, about Versailles, the treaty of Versailles, and the repudiation of Versailles.

He said that such empty protests as that of Sunday had no sense at all — one would just pass on from it to the agenda — that a protest is successful only if backed by power to give it weight. Until Germany had become strong, this kind of thing was of no purpose.

This conviction was spoken word for word as if from my own soul. On one of the following days I went to the office of the NSDAP. At that time I knew nothing of the program of the NSDAP, and nothing further than that it was a small party. I had also investigated other parties. When the National Assembly was elected, with a then completely unpolitical attitude I had even voted democratic. Then, when I saw whom I had elected, I avoided politics for some time. Now, finally I saw a man here who had a clear and definite aim. I just wanted to speak to him at first to see if I could assist him in any way. He received me at once and after I had introduced myself he said it was an extraordinary turn of fate that we should meet. We spoke at once about the things which were close to our hearts — the defeat of the fatherland, and that one could not let it rest with that.

The chief theme of this conversation was again Versailles. I told him that I myself to the fullest extent, and all I was, and all I possessed, were completely at his disposal for this, in my opinion, most essential and decisive matter: the fight against the Treaty of Versailles.

The second point which impressed me very strongly at the time and which I felt very deeply and really considered to be a basic condition, was the fact that he explained to me at length that it was not possible under the conditions then prevailing to bring about, in co-operation with only that element which at that time considered itself national — whether it be the political so-called nationalist parties or those which still called themselves national, or the then existing clubs, fighter organizations, the Free Corps, *et cetera*—with these people alone it was not possible to bring about a reconstruction with the aim of creating a strong national will among the

German people, as long as the masses of German labor opposed this idea. One could only rebuild Germany again if one could enlist the masses of German labor. This could be achieved only if the will to become free from the unbearable shackles of the Treaty of Versailles were really felt by the broad masses of the people, and that would be possible only by combining the national conception with a social goal.

He gave me on that occasion for the first time a very wonderful and profound explanation of the concept of National Socialism; the unity of the two concepts of nationalism on the one hand and socialism on the other, which should prove themselves the absolute supporters of nationalism as well as of socialism — the nationalism, if I may say so, of the bourgeois world and the socialism of the Marxist world. We must clarify these concepts again and through this union of the two ideas create a new vehicle for these new thoughts.

Then we proceeded to the practical side, in regard to which he asked me above all to support him in one point. Within the Party, as small as it was, he had made a special selection of these people who were convinced followers, and who were ready at any moment to devote themselves completely and unreservedly to the dissemination of our idea.

He said that I knew myself how strong Marxism and communism were everywhere at the time, and that actually he had been able to make himself heard at meetings only after he had opposed one physical force disturbing the meeting with another physical force protecting the meeting; for this purpose he had created the SA. The leaders at that time were too young, and he had long been on the lookout for a leader who had distinguished himself in some way in the last war, which was only a few years ago, so that there would be the necessary authority. He had always tried to find a "Pour le Mérite" aviator or a "Pour le Mérite" submarine man for this purpose, and now it seemed to him especially fortunate that I in particular, the last commander of the "Richthofen Squadron," should place myself at his disposal.

I told him that in itself it would not be very pleasant for me to have a leading part from the very beginning, since it might appear that I had come merely because of this position. We finally reached an agreement that for 1 to 2 months I was to remain officially in the background and take over leadership only after that, but actually I was to make my influence felt immediately. I agreed to this, and in that way I came together with Adolf Hitler. . . .

On the Sunday, before the 9th of November, there was a large parade in Munich. The whole Bavarian Government was there. the *Reichswehr*, the police and the Fatherland associations, and we too, marched past. Suddenly, on that occasion, we saw that the figure in the foreground was no longer Herr Von Kahr but the Bavarian Crown Prince Rupprecht. We were very much taken aback by that. The suspicion arose among us that Bavaria wished to follow a course which would possibly lead to a considerable disintegration, and Bavaria might secede from the body of the Reich. But nothing was farther from our intentions than to permit that. We wanted a strong Reich, a unified Reich; and we wanted to have it cleansed of certain parties and authorities which were now ruling it.

We had become distrustful of the so-called "March on Berlin." When this became a certainty and Herr von Kahr had called the well-known meeting in the *Bürgerbräukeller*, it was high time to frustrate such plans and to guide the whole undertaking in the direction of the "Greater Germany" idea. Thus the events of 9 November 1923 materialized in very short time. But as far as I personally am concerned, I was — and I never made a secret of this — ready from the beginning to take part in every revolution against the so-called November Republic, no matter where and with whom it originated, unless it originated with the Left, and for these tasks I had always offered my services.

Then I was severely wounded at the *Feldherrnhalle* — the events are well known — and with this incident I close this first chapter. . . .

DR. STAHMER: Had the Party come to power in a legal way, in your opinion?

GOERING: Of course the Party had come to power in an entirely legal way, because the Party had been called upon by the Reich President according to the Constitution, and according to the principles in force the Party should have been called upon much earlier than that. The Party gained strength and came to power only by way of normal elections and the franchise law then valid.

DR. STAHMER: What measures were now taken to strengthen this power after Hitler's appointment?

GOERING: It was a matter of course for us that once we had come into power we were determined to keep that power under all circumstances. We did not want power and governmental authority for power's sake, but we needed power and governmental authority in order to make Germany free and great. We did not want to leave this any longer to chance, to elections, and parliamentary majorities, but we wanted to carry out the task to which we considered ourselves called.

In order to consolidate this power now, it was necessary to reorganize the political relationship of power. That was carried out in such a manner that, shortly after the seizure of governmental authority in the Reich and in Prussia, the other states followed automatically and more or less strong National Socialist governments were formed everywhere.

Secondly, the so-called political officials who according to the Reich

Constitution could be recalled at any time, or could be dismissed, would naturally have to be replaced now, according to custom, by people from the strongest party. . . .

DR. STAHMER: What offices did you hold after the seizure of power?

GOERING: First I was President of the *Reichstag*, as before, and I remained that until the end. In the Reich Cabinet I was given at first the post of Reich Minister and Reich Commissioner for Aviation, not the Air Force. In parentheses I should like to say that from the very beginning it was clear to me that we had to establish an air force.

In Prussia I was given the position of the Prussian Minister of the Interior, then on 20 April 1933, in addition, the post of Prime Minister of Prussia.

The Reich Commissariat for Aviation had become before this, I believe already in March 1933, a Reich Ministry for Aviation.

Then there were still several not very important offices, President of the State Council, and so on. . . .

DR. STAHMER: Did you in your capacity as Prussian Minister of the Interior create the *Gestapo* and the concentration camps which have so often been mentioned here? When and for what purpose were they established?

GOERING: I mentioned before that for the consolidation of power the first prerequisite was to create along new lines that instrument which at all times and in all nations is always the inner political instrument of power, namely, the police. There was no Reich police, only provincial police. The most important was the Prussian police. . . .

Before our time there was also a political police in Prussia. That was Police Department Ia, and its task was first of all the supervision of and the fight against the National Socialists, and also, in part, against the Communists.

Now, I could have simply put new people into this political police and let it continue along the old lines. But the situation had changed because of our seizure of power, for at this time, as I have mentioned before, the Communist Party was extraordinarily strong. It had over 6 million voters, and in its Red Front Organization it had a thoroughly revolutionary instrument of power. It was quite obvious to the Communist Party that if we were to stay in power for any length of time, it would ultimately lose its power.

Looking back, the danger positively existed at that time of political tension, and with atmosphere of conflict, that revolutionary acts might have taken place on the part of the Communists, particularly as, even after we came to power political murders and political shootings of National Socialists and policemen by that party did not stop, but at times even increased. Also the information which I received was such that I was made extremely fearful of a sudden swing in that direction. Therefore with this department as it was, I could not ward off that danger. I needed reliable political police not only in the main office, but also in the branch offices. I therefore had to enlarge this instrument.

In order to make clear from the outset that the task of this police was to make the State secure I called it the Secret State Police, and at the same time I established branch offices of this police. I took in a great number of political officials who were experienced, and at the beginning took fewer people from the Party circles because for the time being I had to attach importance to professional ability. . . .

I know — as was afterwards proved — that the headquarters of the Communists in Berlin, the Liebknecht House, was strongly fortified and contained very many arms; we had also at that time brought to light very strong connections between the Russian Trade Delegation and the German Communist Party. Even if I arrested, as I did, thousands of communist functionaries at one blow, so that an immediate danger was averted at the outset, the danger as such was by no means eliminated. . . . Thus the Secret State Police was created by me for these tasks, first of all in Prussia, because I had nothing to do with the other states at that time. The organization of the rest of the police is not of such importance here.

DR. STAHMER: The concentration camps?

GOERING: When the need became evident for creating order first of all, and removing the most dangerous element of disorder directed against us, I decided to have the communist functionaries and leaders arrested all at once. I therefore had a list made for that purpose, and it was clear to me that even if I arrested only the most important and most dangerous of these functionaries it still would involve several thousands, for it was necessary to arrest not only the party functionaries but also those from the Red Front Organization, as the Communists also had affiliated organizations. These arrests were in accordance with reasons of State security and State necessity. It was a question of removing a danger. Only one possibility was available here, that of protective custody — that is, whether or not one could prove that these people were involved in a traitorous act or an act hostile to the State, whether or not one could expect such an act from them, such an act must be prevented and the possibility eliminated by means of protective custody. That was nothing new and it was not a National Socialist invention. Already before this such protective custody measures had been carried out, partly against the Communists, and chiefly against us, the National Socialists. The prisons were not available for this purpose, and also I want to stress from the very beginning that this was a political act for the defense of the State. Therefore, I said that these men should first of all be gathered into camps — one to two camps were

proposed at that time — because I could not tell them how long the intern-
ment of these people would be necessary nor how the number would be
increased by the further exposure of the entire communist movement. . . .

DR. STAHMER: Did you supervise the treatment of the prisoners?

GOERING: I naturally gave instructions that such things should not happen.
That they did happen and happened everywhere to a smaller or greater
extent I have just stated. I always pointed out that these things ought not to
happen, because it was important to me to win over some of these people
for our side and to re-educate them.

DR. STAHMER: Did you do anything about abuses of which you heard?

GOERING: I took a personal interest in the concentration camps up to the
spring of 1934. At that time there were two or three camps in Prussia.

Witness Korner has already mentioned the case of Thaelmann. I would
like to speak about it briefly, because it was the most striking case, as
Thaelmann was the leader of the Communist Party. I could not say today
who it was who hinted to me that Thaelmann had been beaten.

I had him called to me in my room directly, without informing the
higher authorities and questioned him very closely. He told me that he had
been beaten during, and especially at the beginning, of the interrogations.
Thereupon, as the witness who was present has said already, I told
Thaelmann that I regretted that. At the same time I told him, "Dear
Thaelmann, if you had come to power, I probably would not have been
beaten, but you would have chopped my head off immediately." And he
agreed. Then I told him that in the future he must feel free to let me know if
anything of this sort should happen to him or to others. I could not always
be there, but it was not my wish that any act of brutality should be
committed against them. . . .

DR. STAHMER: How long were you in charge of the *Gestapo* and the concentration camps and until what date?

GOERING: Actually I was in charge until the beginning of 1934, that is, at
the beginning of 1934 Diels was the head and he gave me frequent reports
about the *Gestapo* and about the concentration camps. Meanwhile, outside Prussia a re-grouping of police had taken place with the result that
Himmler was in charge of the police in all the provinces of Germany with
the exception of Prussia only. Probably following the example of my
measures, he had installed the Secret State Police there, because the police
at that time was still a matter of the states. There were the police of
Bavaria, Württemberg, Baden, Hesse, Saxony, *et cetera.* . . .

These efforts, I believe, started as early as in the late summer of 1933.
Shortly after I had transferred the Prussian Ministry of the Interior to the
Reich Ministry of the Interior, in the spring of 1934, and so was no longer a
departmental minister, Himmler, I assume, probably urged the *Fuehrer*
more strongly to put him in charge of the Prussian police as well. At that

time I did not expressly oppose it. It was not agreeable to me; I wanted to handle my police myself. When, however, the *Fuehrer* asked me to do this and said that it would be the correct thing and the expedient thing, and that it was proved necessary for the enemy of the State to be fought throughout the Reich in a uniform way, I actually handed the police over to Himmler, who put Heydrich in charge. But legally I still retained it, because there was still no Reich police in existence. . . .

In 1936 the Reich Police Law was issued, and thereby the office of the Chief of the German Police was created. By virtue of this law the police was then legally and formally turned over to the *Reichsfuehrer* SS, or, as he was called, the Chief of the German Police.

DR. STAHMER: You mentioned before the Roehm *Putsch*. Who was Roehm, and with what event was this *Putsch* connected?

GOERING: Roehm had become leader of the SA, Chief of Staff of the SA.

THE PRESIDENT: I think we had better adjourn. It is 5 o'clock now.

[*The Tribunal adjourned until 14 March 1946 at 1000 hours.*]

141. Justice Robert H. Jackson, Chief American Prosecutor, Makes His Summation at the Conclusion of the Nuremberg Trial, July 20, 1946

"Can anyone be surprised that they continue the habits of a lifetime in this dock?"

The Nuremberg Tribunal sat continuously from November 20, 1945, to October 1, 1946. The transcript of the proceedings and the documents introduced fill some forty-two large volumes. Although special courts had been set up in the past to judge political crimes by extraordinary authority, no such court had ever attained universal recognition. Day after day, a huge mass of evidence was introduced to bring to the attention of the world a sordid story of crimes against peace, against humanity, and against defenseless minorities.

There were differences of opinion concerning the validity of the trial and its judicial competence. Many jurists were disturbed by the ex *post facto* implications of the proceedings. Those who defended the trial insisted that the testimony itself proved the need for mass proceedings against leaders of the Third Reich. Those who attacked it pointed out that the hands of Allied leaders were not clean and that the trial amounted to a demonstration of the victors' vengeance.

On July 20, 1946, Justice Robert H. Jackson, the chief American prosecutor, began his final summation. The following condensation of his remarks gives the case for the prosecution as well as a formal opinion of Hitler's Third Reich.

Office of the United States Chief of Counsel for the Prosecution of Axis Criminality, *Nazi Conspiracy and Aggression* (Washington, D.C.: Government Printing Office, 1947), Supplement A, pp. 7–59.

MR. PRESIDENT AND MEMBERS OF THE TRIBUNAL:

An advocate can be confronted with few more formidable tasks than to select his closing arguments where there is great disparity between his appropriate time and his available material. In eight months – a short time as state trials go – we have introduced evidence which embraces as vast and varied a panorama of events as has ever been compressed within the framework of a litigation. It is impossible in summation to do more than outline with bold strokes the vitals of this trial's mad and melancholy record, which will live as the historical text of the Twentieth Century's shame and depravity.

It is common to think of our own time as standing at the apex of civilization, from which the deficiencies of preceding ages may patronizingly be viewed in the light of what is assumed to be "progress." The reality is that in the long perspective of history the present century will not hold an admirable position, unless its second half is to redeem its first. These two-score years in this Twentieth Century will be recorded in the book of years as one of the most bloody in all annals. Two World Wars have left a legacy of dead which number more than all the armies engaged in any war that made ancient or medieval history. No half-century ever witnessed slaughter on such a scale, such cruelties and inhumanities, such wholesale deportations of peoples into slavery, such annihilations of minorities. The Terror of Torquemada pales before the Nazi Inquisition. These deeds are the overshadowing historical facts by which generations to come will remember this decade. If we cannot eliminate the causes and prevent the repetition of these barbaric events, it is not an irresponsible prophecy to say that this Twentieth Century may yet succeed in bringing the doom of civilization. . . .

The Crimes of the Nazi Regime

The strength of the case against these defendants under the conspiracy count, which it is the duty of the United States to argue, is in its simplicity. It involves but three ultimate inquiries: First, have the acts defined by the Charter as crimes been committed; second, were they committed pursuant to a common plan or conspiracy; third, are these defendants among those who are criminally responsible?

The charge requires examination of a criminal policy, not of a multitude of isolated, unplanned, or disputed crimes. The substantive crimes upon which we rely, either as goals of a common plan or as means for its accomplishment, are admitted. The pillars which uphold the conspiracy charge may be found in five groups of overt acts, whose character and magnitude are important considerations in appraising the proof of conspiracy.

1. THE SEIZURE OF POWER AND SUBJUGATION OF
GERMANY TO A POLICE STATE

The Nazi Party seized control of the German state in 1933. "Seizure of power" is a characterization used by defendants and defense witnesses, and so apt that it has passed into both history and every-day speech. . . .

New political crimes were created. . . . It was made a treason, punishable with death, to organize or support a political party other than the Nazi party. Circulating a false or exaggerated statement, or one which would harm the state or even the Party, was made a crime. Laws were enacted of such ambiguity that they could be used to punish almost any innocent act. It was, for example, made a crime to provoke "any act contrary to the public welfare."

The doctrine of punishment by analogy was introduced to enable conviction for acts which no statute forbade. Minister of Justice Guertner explained that National Socialism considered every violation of the goals of life which the community set up for itself to be a wrong *per se*, and that the act could be punished even though it was not contrary to existing "formal" law.

The *Gestapo* and the SD were instrumentalities of an espionage system which penetrated public and private life. Goering controlled a personal wire-tapping unit. All privacy of communication was abolished. Party *blockleiters*, appointed over every 50 households, continuously spied on all within their ken. Upon the strength of this spying individuals were dragged off to "protective custody" and to concentration camps, without legal proceedings of any kind, and without statement of any reason therefor. The partisan political police were exempted from effective legal responsibility for their acts.

With all administrative offices in Nazi control and with the *Reichstag* reduced to impotence; the judiciary remained the last obstacle to this reign of terror. But its independence was soon overcome and it was reorganized to dispense a venal justice. Judges were ousted for political or racial reasons and were spied upon and put under pressure to join the Nazi Party. After the Supreme Court had acquitted three of the four men whom the Nazis accused of setting the *Reichstag* fire, its jurisdiction over treason cases was transferred to a newly established "People's Court" consisting of two judges and five party officials. The German film of this "People's Court" in operation, which we showed in this chamber, revealed its presiding judge pouring partisan abuse upon speechless defendants. Special courts were created to try political crimes, only party members were appointed judges, and "Judges' letters" instructed the puppet judges as to the "general lines" they must follow.

The result was the removal of all peaceable means either to resist or to change the government. Having sneaked through the portals of power, the Nazis slammed the gate in the face of all others who might also aspire to enter. Since the law was what the Nazis said it was, every form of opposition was rooted out, and every dissenting voice throttled. Germany was in the clutch of a police state, which used the fear of the concentration camp as a means to enforce non-resistance. The Party was the State, the State was the Party, and terror by day and death by night were the policy of both.

2. THE PREPARATION AND WAGING OF WARS OF AGGRESSION

From the moment the Nazis seized power, they set about feverish but stealthy efforts, in defiance of the Versailles Treaty, to arm for war. In 1933 they found no air force. By 1939 they had 21 squadrons, consisting of 240 echelons or about 2,400 first-line planes, together with trainers and transports. In 1933 they found an army of 3 infantry and 3 cavalry divisions. By 1939 they had raised and equipped an army of 51 divisions, four of which were fully motorized and four of which were *Panzer* divisions. In 1933 they found a navy of one cruiser and 6 light cruisers. By 1939 they had built a navy of 4 battleships, 1 aircraft carrier, 6 cruisers, 22 destroyers, and 54 submarines. They had also built up in that period an armament industry as efficient as that of any country in the world.

We need not trouble ourselves about the many abstract difficulties that can be conjured up about what constitutes aggression in doubtful cases. I shall show you, in discussing the conspiracy, that by any test ever put forward by any responsible authority, by all the canons of plain sense, these were unlawful wars of aggression in breach of treaties and in violation of assurances.

3. WARFARE IN DISREGARD OF INTERNATIONAL LAW

It is unnecessary to labor this point on the facts. Goering asserts that the Rules of Land Warfare were obsolete, that no nation could fight a total war within their limits. He testified that the Nazis would have denounced the Conventions to which Germany was a party, but that General Jodl wanted captured German soldiers to continue to benefit from their observance by the Allies.

It was, however, against the Soviet people and Soviet prisoners that Teutonic fury knew no bounds, in spite of a warning by Admiral Canaris that the treatment was in violation of International Law.

We need not, therefore, for purposes of the Conspiracy count, recite the revolting details of starving, beating, murdering, freezing, and mass extermination admittedly used against the eastern soldiery. Also, we may take as established or admitted that lawless conduct such as shooting British and American airmen, mistreatment of Western prisoners of war, forcing French prisoners of war into German war work, and other deliberate violations of the Hague and Geneva Conventions, did occur, and in obedience to highest levels of authority.

4. ENSLAVEMENT AND PLUNDER OF POPULATIONS IN OCCUPIED COUNTRIES

The defendant Sauckel, Plenipotentiary General for the Utilization of Labor, is authority for the statement that "out of five million foreign workers who arrived in Germany, not even 200,000 came voluntarily." It was officially reported to defendant Rosenberg that in his territory "recruiting methods were used which probably have their origin in the blackest period of the slave trade." Sauckel himself reported that male and female agents went hunting for men, got them drunk, and "shanghaied" them to Germany. These captives were shipped in trains without heat, food, or sanitary facilities. The dead were thrown out at stations, and the newborn were thrown out the windows of moving trains. . . .

Populations of occupied countries were otherwise exploited and oppressed unmercifully. Terrorism was the order of the day. Civilians were arrested without charges, committed without counsel, executed without hearing. Villages were destroyed, the male inhabitants shot or sent to concentration camps, the women sent to forced labor, and the children scattered abroad. The extent of the slaughter in Poland alone was indicated by Frank, who reported: "If I wanted to have a poster put up for every seven Poles who were shot, the forests of Poland would not suffice for producing the paper for such posters."

Those who will enslave men cannot be expected to refrain from plundering them. Boastful reports show how thoroughly and scientifically the resources of occupied lands were sucked into the German war economy, inflicting shortage, hunger, and inflation upon the inhabitants. Besides this grand plan to aid the German war effort there were the sordid activities of the Rosenberg *Einsatzstab*, which pillaged art treasures for Goering and his fellow-bandits. It is hard to say whether the spectacle of Germany's No. 2 leader urging his people to give up every comfort and strain every sinew on essential war work while he rushed around confiscating art by the trainload should be cast as tragedy or comedy. In either case it was a crime.

International Law at all times before and during this war spoke with precision and authority respecting the protection due civilians of an occupied country, and the slave trade and plunder of occupied countries was at all times flagrantly unlawful.

5. PERSECUTION AND EXTERMINATION OF JEWS AND CHRISTIANS

The Nazi movement will be of evil memory in history because of its persecution of the Jews, the most far-flung and terrible racial persecution of all time. Although the Nazi party neither invented nor monopolized anti-Semitism, its leaders from the very beginning embraced it, incited it, and exploited it. They used it as "the psychological spark that ignites the mob." After the seizure of power, it became an official state policy. The persecution began in a series of discriminatory laws eliminating the Jews from the civil service, the professions, and economic life. As it became more intense it included segregation of Jews in ghettos, and exile. Riots were organized by party leaders to loot Jewish business places and to burn synagogues. Jewish property was confiscated and a collective fine of a billion marks was imposed upon German Jewry. The program progressed in fury and irresponsibility to the "final solution." This consisted of sending all Jews who were fit to work to concentration camps as slave laborers, and all who were not fit, which included children under 12 and people over 50, as well as any others judged unfit by an SS doctor, to concentration camps for extermination. . . .

The *Gestapo*-appointed "Church specialists" were instructed that the ultimate aim was "destruction of the confessional Churches." The record is full of specific instances of the persecution of clergymen, the confiscation of Church property, interference with religious publications, disruption of religious education, and suppression of religious organizations.

The chief instrumentality for persecution and extermination was the concentration camp, sired by defendant Goering and nurtured under the overall authority of defendants Frick and Kaltenbrunner.

The horrors of these iniquitous places have been vividly disclosed by documents and testified to by witnesses. The Tribunal must be satiated with ghastly verbal and pictorial portrayals. From your records it is clear that the concentration camps were the first and worst weapons of oppression used by the National Socialist State, and that they were the primary means utilized for the persecution of the Christian Church and the extermination of the Jewish race. This has been admitted to you by some of the defendants from the witness stand. In the words of defendant Frank: "A thousand years will pass and this guilt of Germany will still not be erased." . . .

THE COMMON PLAN OR CONSPIRACY

The prosecution submits that these five categories of premeditated crimes were not separate and independent phenomena but that all were committed pursuant to a common plan or conspiracy. The defense admits that these classes of crimes were committed but denies that they are connected one with another as parts of a single program. . . .

A glance over the dock will show that, despite quarrels among themselves, each defendant played a part which fitted in with every other, and that all advanced the common plan. It contradicts experience that men of such diverse backgrounds and talents should so forward each other's aims by coincidence.

The large and varied role of Goering was half militarist and half gangster. He stuck a pudgy finger in every pie. He used his SA muscle-men to help bring the gang into power. In order to entrench that power he contrived to have the *Reichstag* burned, established the *Gestapo*, and created the concentration camps. He was equally adept at massacring opponents and at framing scandals to get rid of stubborn generals. He built up the *Luftwaffe* and hurled it at his defenseless neighbors. He was among the foremost in harrying the Jews out of the land. By mobilizing the total economic resources of Germany he made possible the waging of the war which he had taken a large part in planning. He was, next to Hitler, the man who tied the activities of all the defendants together in a common effort.

The parts played by the other defendants, although less comprehensive and less spectacular than that of the *Reichsmarshall* were nevertheless integral and necessary contributions to the joint undertaking, without any one of which the success of the common enterprise would have been in jeopardy. There are many specific deeds of which these men have been proven guilty. No purpose would be served — nor indeed is time available — to review all the crimes which the evidence has charged up to their names. Nevertheless, in viewing the conspiracy as a whole and as an operating mechanism it may be well to recall briefly the outstanding services which each of the men in the dock rendered to the common cause.

The zealot HESS, before succumbing to wanderlust, was the engineer tending the Party machinery, passing orders and propaganda down to the Leadership Corps, supervising every aspect of Party activities, and maintaining the organization as a loyal and ready instrument of power. When apprehensions abroad threatened the success of the Nazi scheme for conquest, it was the duplicitous RIBBENTROP, the salesman of deception, who was detailed to pour wine on the troubled waters of suspicion by preaching the gospel of limited and peaceful intentions. KEITEL, weak and willing tool, delivered the armed forces, the instrument of aggression, over to the Party and directed them in executing its felonious designs.

KALTENBRUNNER, the grand inquisitor, took up the bloody mantle of Heydrich to stifle opposition and terrorize compliance, and buttressed the power of National Socialism on a foundation of guiltless corpses. It was ROSENBERG, the intellectual high priest of the "master race," who provided the doctrine of hatred which gave the impetus for the annihilation of Jewry, and put his infidel theories into practice against the eastern occupied territories. His wooly philosophy also added boredom to the long list of Nazi atrocities. The fanatical FRANK, who solidified Nazi control by establishing the new order of authority without law, so that the will of the Party was the only test of legality, proceeded to export his lawlessness to Poland, which he governed with the lash of Caesar and whose population he reduced to sorrowing remnants. FRICK, the ruthless organizer, helped the Party to seize power, supervised the police agencies to insure that it stayed in power and chained the economy of Bohemia and Moravia to the German war machine.

STREICHER, the venomous vulgarian, manufactured and distributed obscene racial libels which incited the populace to accept and assist the progressively savage operations of "race purification." As Minister of Economics FUNK accelerated the pace of rearmament, and as *Reichsbank* president banked for the SS the gold teeth fillings of concentration camp victims — probably the most ghoulish collateral in banking history. It was SCHACHT, the facade of starched respectability, who in the early days provided the window dressing, the bait for the hesitant, and whose wizardry later made it possible for Hitler to finance the colossal rearmament program, and to do it secretly.

DOENITZ, Hitler's legatee of defeat, promoted the success of the Nazi aggressions by instructing his pack of submarine killers to conduct warfare at sea with the illegal ferocity of the jungle. RAEDER, the political admiral, stealthily built up the German navy in defiance of the Versailles Treaty, and then put it to use in a series of aggressions which he had taken a large part in planning. VON SCHIRACH, poisoner of a generation, initiated the German youth in Nazi doctrine, trained them in legions for service in the SS and *Wehrmacht*, and delivered them up to the Party as fanatic, unquestioning executors of its will.

SAUCKEL, the greatest and cruelest slaver since the Pharaohs of Egypt, produced desperately needed manpower by driving foreign peoples into the land of bondage on a scale unknown even in the ancient days of tyranny in the kingdom of the Nile. JODL, betrayer of the traditions of his profession, led the *Wehrmacht* in violating its own code of military honor in order to carry out the barbarous aims of Nazi policy. VON PAPEN, pious agent of an infidel regime, held the stirrup while Hitler vaulted into the saddle, lubricated the Austrian annexation, and devoted his diplomatic cunning to the service of Nazi objectives abroad.

SEYSS-INQUART, spearhead of the Austrian fifth-column, took over the government of his own country to make a present of it to Hitler, and then, moving north, brought terror and oppression to the Netherlands and pillaged its economy for the benefit of the German juggernaut. VON

NEURATH, the old-school diplomat, who cast the pearls of his experience before the Nazis, guided Nazi diplomacy in the early years, soothed the fears of prospective victims, and as Reich Protector of Bohemia and Moravia, strengthened the German position for the coming attack on Poland. SPEER, as Minister of Armaments and War Production, joined in planning and executing the program to dragoon prisoners of war and foreign workers into German war industries which waxed in output while the laborers waned in starvation. FRITZSCHE, radio propaganda chief, by manipulation of the truth goaded German public opinion into frenzied support of the regime and anesthetized the independent judgment of the population so that they did without question their masters' bidding. And BORMANN, who has not accepted our invitation to this reunion, sat at the throttle of the vast and powerful engine of the Party, guiding it in the ruthless execution of Nazi policies, from the scourging of the Christian Church to the lynching of captive Allied airmen.

The activities of all these defendants, despite their varied backgrounds and talents, were joined with the efforts of other conspirators not now in the dock, who played still other essential roles. They blend together into one consistent and militant pattern animated by a common objective to reshape the map of Europe by force of arms. . . .

The defendants have been unanimous, when pressed, in shifting the blame on other men, sometimes on one and sometimes on another. But the names they have repeatedly picked are Hitler, Himmler, Heydrich, Goebbels, and Bormann. All of these are dead or missing. No matter how hard we have pressed the defendants on the stand, they have never pointed the finger at a living man as guilty. It is a temptation to ponder the wondrous workings of a fate which has left only the guilty dead and only the innocent alive. It is almost too remarkable.

The chief villain on whom blame is placed, —some of the defendants vie with each other in producing appropriate epithets—is Hitler. He is the man at whom nearly every defendant has pointed an accusing finger.

I shall not dissent from this consensus, nor do I deny that all these dead or missing men shared the guilt. In crimes so reprehensible that degrees of guilt have lost their significance they may have played the most evil parts. But their guilt cannot exculpate the defendants. Hitler did not carry all responsibility to the grave with him. All the guilt is not wrapped in Himmler's shroud. It was these dead whom these living chose to be their partners in this great conspiratorial brotherhood, and the crimes that they did together they must pay for one by one.

It may well be said that Hitler's final crime was against the land that he had ruled. He was a mad messiah who started the war without cause and prolonged it without reason. If he could not rule he cared not what happened to Germany. . . .

Hitler ordered every one else to fight to the last and then retreated into death by his own hand. But he left life as he lived it, a deceiver; he left the official report that he had died in battle. This was the man whom these defendants exalted to a *Fuehrer*. It was they who conspired to get him absolute authority over all Germany. And in the end he and the system they created for him brought the ruin of them all. . . .

We have presented this Tribunal an affirmative case based on incriminating documents which are sufficient, if unexplained, to require a finding of guilt on Count One against each defendant. In the final analysis, the only question is whether the defendants' own testimony is to be credited as against the documents and other evidence of their guilt. What, then, is their testimony worth?

The fact is that the Nazi habit of economizing in the use of truth pulls the foundations out from under their own defenses. Lying has always been a highly approved Nazi technique. Hitler, in *Mein Kampf*, advocated mendacity as a policy. Von Ribbentrop admits the use of the "diplomatic lie." Keitel advised that the facts of rearmament be kept secret so that they could be denied at Geneva. Raeder deceived about rebuilding the German navy in violation of Versailles. Goering urged Ribbentrop to tell a "legal lie" to the British Foreign Office about the *Anschluss*, and in so doing only marshaled him the way he was going. Goering gave his word of honor to the Czechs and proceeded to break it. Even Speer proposed to deceive the French into revealing the specially trained among their prisoners.

Nor is the lie direct the only means of falsehood. They all speak with a Nazi doubletalk with which to deceive the unwary. In the Nazi dictionary of sardonic euphemisms "Final solution" of the Jewish problem was a phrase which meant extermination; "Special treatment" of prisoners of war meant killing; "Protective custody" meant concentration camp; "Duty labor" meant slave labor; and an order to "take a firm attitude" or "take positive measures" meant to act with unrestrained savagery. Before we accept their word at what seems to be its face, we must always look for hidden meanings. Goering assured us, on his oath, that the Reich Defense Council never met "as such." When we produced the stenographic minutes of a meeting at which he presided and did most of the talking, he reminded us of the "as such" and explained this was not a meeting of the Council "as such" because other persons were present. Goering denies "threatening" Czechoslovakia — he only told President Hacha that he would "hate to bomb the beautiful city of Prague."

Besides outright false statements and doubletalk, there are also other circumventions of truth in the nature of fantastic explanations and absurd professions. Streicher has solemnly maintained that his only thought with respect to the Jews was to resettle them on the Island of Madagascar. His reason for destroying synagogues, he blandly said, was only because they were architecturally offensive. Rosenberg was stated by his counsel to have always had in mind a "chivalrous solution" to the Jewish problem. When it was necessary to remove Schuschnigg after the *Anschluss*, Ribbentrop would have had us believe that the Austrian Chancellor was resting at a "villa." It was left to cross-examination to reveal that the "villa" was Buchenwald Concentration Camp. The record is full of other examples of dissimulations and evasions. Even Schacht showed that he, too, had adopted the Nazi attitude that truth is any story which succeeds. Confronted on cross-examination with a long record of broken vows and false words, he declared in justification — "I think you can score many more successes when you want to lead someone if you don't tell them the truth than if you tell them the truth."

This was the philosophy of the National Socialists. When for years they have deceived the world, and masked falsehood with plausibilities, can anyone be surprised that they continue the habits of a lifetime in this dock? Credibility is one of the main issues of this trial. Only those who have failed to learn the bitter lessons of the last decade can doubt that men who have always played on the unsuspecting credulity of generous opponents would not hesitate to do the same now.

It is against such a background that these defendants now ask this Tribunal to say that they are not guilty of planning, executing, or conspiring to commit this long list of crimes and wrongs. They stand before the record of this trial as blood-stained Gloucester stood by the body of his slain King. He begged of the widow, as they beg of you: "Say I slew them not." And the Queen replied, "Then say they were not slain. But dead they are, . . ." If you were to say of these men that they are not guilty, it would be as true to say there has been no war, there are no slain, there has been no crime.

142. Judgment at Nuremberg: The International Military Tribunal Brings in Verdicts on Twenty-Two Individuals and Seven Organizations, October 1, 1946

"There is nothing to be said in mitigation."

After a trial lasting from November 20, 1945, to October 1, 1946, a trial which captured the interest of the entire world, the International Military Tribunal brought in its verdicts on the historically important case. There were four different kinds of indictments: conspiracy to prepare aggressive war; crimes against the peace ("waging a war of aggression"); war crimes (killing of hostages, use of slave labor, murder); and crimes against humanity (extermination camps). Of the seven organizations indicted, four were found guilty – Leadership Corps of the NSDAP, the SS, the SA, and the *Gestapo* – and three were declared innocent – the Reich cabinet, the General Staff, and the High Command of the army.

Of the twenty-two individuals tried, three were acquitted, von Papen, Schacht, and Fritsche. Of those who were found guilty, twelve were sentenced to death by hanging. Hess, Funk, and Raeder were sentenced to life imprisonment. The remaining four received sentences of from ten to twenty years' imprisonment.

Following is a condensation of the judgments with reasons for the individuals' guilt or innocence.

Goering

Goering is indicted on all four Counts. The evidence shows that after Hitler he was the most prominent man in the Nazi regime. He was Commander-in-Chief of the *Luftwaffe*, Plenipotentiary for the Four Year Plan,

International Military Tribunal, *Nuremberg Trial of the Major War Criminals* (Nuremberg: Allied Control Commission, 1948), vol. 22, pp. 524–89.

and had tremendous influence with Hitler, at least until 1943, when their relationship deteriorated, ending in his arrest in 1945. He testified that Hitler kept him informed of all important military and political problems.

Crimes against Peace

From the moment he joined the Party in 1922 and took command of the street-fighting organization, the SA, Goering was the adviser, the active agent of Hitler, and one of the prime leaders of the Nazi movement. As Hitler's political deputy he was largely instrumental in bringing the National Socialists to power in 1933 and was charged with consolidating this power and expanding German armed might. He developed the *Gestapo* and created the first concentration camps, relinquishing them to Himmler in 1934, conducted the Roehm purge in that year, and engineered the sordid proceedings which resulted in the removal of Von Blomberg and Von Fritsch from the Army. In 1936 he became Plenipotentiary for the Four Year Plan and in theory and in practice was the economic dictator of the Reich. Shortly after the Pact of Munich, he announced that he would embark on a five-fold expansion of the *Luftwaffe* and speed up rearmament with emphasis on offensive weapons.

Goering was one of the five important leaders present at the Hossbach conference of 5 November 1937, and he attended the other important conferences already discussed in this Judgment. In the Austrian *Anschluss* he was indeed the central figure, the ringleader. He said in court: "I must take 100 percent responsibility. . . . I even overruled objections by the *Fuehrer* and brought everything to its final development." . . .

After his own admissions to this Tribunal, from the positions which he held, the conferences he attended, and the public words he uttered, there can remain no doubt that Goering was the moving force for aggressive war second only to Hitler. He was the planner and prime mover in the military and diplomatic preparation for war which Germany pursued.

War Crimes and Crimes against Humanity

The record is filled with Goering's admissions of his complicity in the use of slave labor. "We did use this labor for security reasons so that they would not be active in their own country and would not work against us. On the other hand, they served to help in the economic war." And again: "Workers were forced to come to the Reich. That is something I have not denied." The man who spoke these words was Plenipotentiary for the Four Year Plan charged with the recruitment and allocation of manpower. As *Luftwaffe* Commander-in-Chief he demanded from Himmler more slave laborers for his underground aircraft factories: "That I requested inmates of concentration camps for the armament of the *Luftwaffe* is correct and it is to be taken as a matter of course." . . .

Goering persecuted the Jews, particularly after the November 1938 riots, and not only in Germany, where he raised the billionmark fine as stated elsewhere, but in the conquered territories as well. His own utterances then and his testimony now shows this interest was primarily economic — how to get their property and how to force them out of the economic life of Europe. As these countries fell before the German Army, he extended the Reich anti-Jewish laws to them; the *Reichsgesetzblatt* for 1939, 1940, and 1941 contains several anti-Jewish decrees signed by Goering. Although their extermination was in Himmler's hands, Goering was far from disinterested or inactive, despite his protestations in the witness box. By decree of 31 July 1941 he directed Himmler and Heydrich to "bring about a complete solution of the Jewish question in the German sphere of influence in Europe."

There is nothing to be said in mitigation. For Goering was often, indeed almost always, the moving force, second only to his leader. He was the leading war aggressor, both as political and as military leader; he was the director of the slave labor program and the creator of the oppressive program against the Jews and other races, at home and abroad. All of these crimes he has frankly admitted. On some specific cases there may be conflict of testimony, but in terms of the broad outline his own admissions are more than sufficiently wide to be conclusive of his guilt. His guilt is unique in its enormity. The record discloses no excuses for this man.

Conclusion

The Tribunal finds the Defendant Goering guilty on all four Counts of the Indictment.

Hess

Hess is indicted under all four Counts. He joined the Nazi Party in 1920 and participated in the Munich *Putsch* on 9 November 1923. He was imprisoned with Hitler in the Landsberg fortress in 1924 and became Hitler's closest personal confidant, a relationship which lasted until Hess's flight to the British Isles. On 21 April 1933, he was appointed Deputy to the *Fuehrer*, and on 1 December 1933 was made Reich Minister without Portfolio. He was appointed member of the Secret Cabinet Council on 4 February 1938, and a member of the Ministerial Council for the Defense of the Reich on 31 August 1939. In September 1939, Hess was officially announced by Hitler as successor designate to the *Fuehrer* after Goering. On 10 May 1941, he flew from Germany to Scotland.

Crimes against Peace

As Deputy to the *Fuehrer*, Hess was the top man in the Nazi Party with responsibility for handling all Party matters and authority to make decisions in Hitler's name on all questions of Party leadership. As Reich Minister without Portfolio he had the authority to approve all legislation suggested by the different Reich Ministers before it could be enacted as law. In these positions, Hess was an active supporter of preparations for war. His signature appears on the law of 16 March 1935, establishing compulsory military service. Throughout the years he supported Hitler's policy of vigorous rearmament in many speeches. He told the people that they must sacrifice for armaments, repeating the phrase, "Guns instead of butter." It is true that between 1933 and 1937 Hess made speeches in which he expressed a desire for peace and advocated international economic cooperation. But nothing which they contained can alter the fact that of all the defendants none knew better than Hess how determined Hitler was to realize his ambitions, how fanatical and violent a man he was, and how little likely he was to refrain from resort to force, if this was the only way in which he could achieve his aims. . . .

With him on his flight to England, Hess carried certain peace proposals which he alleged Hitler was prepared to accept. It is significant to note that this flight took place only 10 days after the date on which Hitler fixed 22 June 1941 as the time for attacking the Soviet Union. In conversations carried on after his arrival in England, Hess wholeheartedly supported all Germany's aggressive actions up to that time and attempted to justify Germany's action in connection with Austria, Czechoslovakia, Poland, Norway, Denmark, Belgium, and the Netherlands. He blamed England and France for the war.

War Crimes and Crimes against Humanity

There is evidence showing the participation of the Party Chancellery, under Hess, in the distribution of orders connected with the commission of War Crimes; that Hess may have had knowledge of, even if he did not participate in, the crimes that were being committed in the East, and proposed laws discriminating against Jews and Poles; and that he signed decrees forcing certain groups of Poles to accept German citizenship. The Tribunal, however, does not find that the evidence sufficiently connects Hess with these crimes to sustain a finding of guilt. . . .

That Hess acts in an abnormal manner, suffers from loss of memory, and has mentally deteriorated during this Trial, may be true. But there is nothing to show that he does not realize the nature of the charges against him, or is incapable of defending himself. He was ably represented at the Trial by counsel, appointed for that purpose by the Tribunal. There is no suggestion that Hess was not completely sane when the acts charged against him were committed.

Conclusion

The Tribunal finds the Defendant Hess guilty on Counts One and Two; and not guilty on Counts Three and Four.

Von Ribbentrop

Ribbentrop is indicted under all four Counts. He joined the Nazi Party in 1932. By 1933 he had been made foreign policy adviser to Hitler, and in the same year the representative of the Nazi Party on foreign policy. In 1934 he was appointed Delegate for Disarmament Questions and in 1935 Minister Plenipotentiary at Large, a capacity in which he negotiated the Anglo-German Naval Agreement in 1935 and the Anti-Comintern Pact in 1936. On 11 August 1936 he was appointed Ambassador to England. On 4 February 1938, he succeeded Von Neurath as Reich Minister for Foreign Affairs as part of the general reshuffle which accompanied the dismissal of Von Fritsch and Von Blomberg.

Crimes against Peace

Ribbentrop was not present at the Hossbach conference held on 5 November 1937, but on 2 January 1938, while still Ambassador to England, he sent a memorandum to Hitler indicating his opinion that a change in the *status quo* in the East in the German sense could only be carried out by force and suggesting methods to prevent England and France from intervening in a European war fought to bring about such a change. When Ribbentrop became Foreign Minister, Hitler told him that Germany still had four problems to solve: Austria, Sudetenland, Memel, and Danzig, and mentioned the possibility of "some sort of a showdown" or "military settlement" for their solution. . . .

War Crimes and Crimes against Humanity

Ribbentrop participated in a meeting of 6 June 1944, at which it was agreed to start a program under which Allied aviators carrying out machine gun attacks should be lynched. In December 1944 Ribbentrop was informed of the plans to murder one of the French generals held as a prisoner of war and directed his subordinates to see that the details were worked out in such a way as to prevent its detection by the protecting powers. Ribbentrop is also responsible for War Crimes and Crimes against Humanity because of his activities with respect to occupied countries and Axis satellites. . . .

He played an important part in Hitler's "final solution" of the Jewish question. . . . At the same conference Hitler had likened the Jews to "tuberculosis bacilli" and said if they did not work they were to be shot.

Ribbentrop's defense to the charges made against him is that Hitler made all the important decisions, and that he was such a great admirer and faithful follower of Hitler that he never questioned Hitler's repeated assertions that he wanted peace or the truth of the reasons that Hitler gave in explaining aggressive action. The Tribunal does not consider this explanation to be true. Ribbentrop participated in all of the Nazi aggressions from the occupation of Austria to the invasion of the Soviet Union. Although he was personally concerned with the diplomatic rather than the military aspect of these actions, his diplomatic efforts were so closely connected with war that he could not have remained unaware of the aggressive nature of Hitler's actions. In the administration of territories over which Germany acquired control by illegal invasion, Ribbentrop also assisted in carrying out criminal policies, particularly those involving the extermination of the Jews. There is abundant evidence, moreover, that Ribbentrop was in complete sympathy with all the main tenets of the National Socialist creed, and that his collaboration with Hitler and with other defendants in the commission of Crimes against Peace, War Crimes and Crimes against Humanity was wholehearted. It was because Hitler's policy and plans coincided with his own ideas that Ribbentrop served him so willingly to the end.

Conclusion

The Tribunal finds that Ribbentrop is guilty on all four Counts.

Keitel

Keitel is indicted on all four Counts. He was Chief of Staff to the then Minister of War von Blomberg from 1935 to 4 February 1938; on that day Hitler took command of the Armed Forces, making Keitel Chief of the High Command of the Armed Forces. Keitel did not have command authority over the three *Wehrmacht* branches which enjoyed direct access to the Supreme Commander. OKW was in effect Hitler's military staff.

Crimes against Peace

Keitel attended the Schuschnigg conference in February 1938 with two other generals. Their presence, he admitted, was a "military demonstration," but since he had been appointed OKW chief just one week before, he had not known why he had been summoned. Hitler and Keitel then continued to put pressure on Austria with false rumors, broadcasts, and troop maneuvers. . . .

Keitel testified that he opposed the invasion of the Soviet Union for military reasons, and also because it would constitute a violation of the Non-Aggression Pact. Nevertheless he initialed "Case Barbarossa," signed by Hitler on 18 December 1940, and attended the OKW discussion with Hitler on 3 February 1941. On 16 June he directed all Army units to carry out the economic directives issued by Goering in the so-called "Green Folder" for the exploitation of Russian territory, food, and raw materials.

War Crimes and Crimes against Humanity

On 4 August 1942 Keitel issued a directive that paratroopers were to be turned over to the SD. On 18 October Hitler issued the Commando Order, which was carried out in several instances. After the landing in Normandy, Keitel reaffirmed the order, and later extended it to Allied missions fighting with partisans. He admits he did not believe the order was legal, but claims he could not stop Hitler.

On 16 September 1941, Keitel ordered that attacks on soldiers in the East should be met by putting to death 50 to 100 Communists for one German soldier, with the comment that human life was less than nothing in the East. On 1 October he ordered military commanders always to have hostages to execute when German soldiers were attacked. . . .

On 12 May 1941, five weeks before the invasion of the Soviet Union, the OKW urged upon Hitler a directive of the OKH that political commissars be liquidated by the Army. Keitel admitted the directive was passed on to field commanders. And on 13 May Keitel signed an order that civilians suspected of offenses against troops should be shot without trial, and that prosecution of German soldiers for offenses against civilians was unnecessary. . . .

On 7 December 1941, as already discussed in this opinion, the so-called *Nacht und Nebel* decree, over Keitel's signature, provided that in occupied territories civilians who had been accused of crimes of resistance against the army of occupation would be tried only if a death sentence was likely; otherwise they would be handed over to the *Gestapo* for transportation to Germany.

Keitel directed that Russian prisoners of war be used in German war industry. On 8 September 1942 he ordered French, Dutch, and Belgian citizens to work on the Atlantic Wall. He was present on 4 January 1944 when Hitler directed Sauckel to obtain 4 million new workers from occupied territories.

In the face of these documents Keitel does not deny his connection with these acts. Rather, his defense relies on the fact that he is a soldier and on the doctrine of "superior orders," prohibited by Article 8 of the Charter as a defense.

There is nothing in mitigation. Superior orders, even to a soldier, cannot be considered in mitigation where crimes so shocking and extensive have been committed consciously, ruthlessly, and without military excuse or justification.

Conclusion

The Tribunal finds Keitel guilty on all four Counts.

Kaltenbrunner

Kaltenbrunner is indicted under Counts One, Three, and Four. He joined the Austrian Nazi Party and the SS in 1932. In 1935 he became leader of the SS in Austria. After the *Anschluss* he was appointed Austrian State Secretary for Security and, when this position was abolished in 1941, he was made Higher SS and Police Leader. On 30 January 1943, he was appointed Chief of the Security Police and SD and head of the Reich Security Head Office (RSHA), a position which had been held by Heydrich until his assassination in June 1942. He held the rank of *Obergruppenfuehrer* in the SS.

Crimes against Peace

As leader of the SS in Austria Kaltenbrunner was active in the Nazi intrigue against the Schuschnigg Government. On the night of 11 March 1938, after Goering had ordered Austrian National Socialists to seize control of the Austrian Government, 500 Austrian SS men under Kaltenbrunner's command surrounded the Federal Chancellery and a special detachment under the command of his adjutant entered the Federal Chancellery while Seyss-Inquart was negotiating with President Miklas. But there is no evidence connecting Kaltenbrunner with plans to wage aggressive war on any other front. The *Anschluss*, although it was an aggressive act, is not charged as an aggressive war, and the evidence against Kaltenbrunner under Count One does not, in the opinion of the Tribunal, show his direct participation in any plan to wage such a war.

War Crimes and Crimes against Humanity

When he became Chief of the Security Police and SD and head of the RSHA on 30 January 1943, Kaltenbrunner took charge of an organization which included the main offices of the *Gestapo*, the SD, and the Criminal Police. As Chief of the RSHA, Kaltenbrunner had authority to order protective custody to and release from concentration camps. Orders to this effect were normally sent over his signature. Kaltenbrunner was aware of conditions in concentration camps. He had undoubtedly visited Mauthausen, and witnesses testified that he had seen prisoners killed by the various methods of execution, hanging, shooting in the back of the neck, and gassing, as part of a demonstration. . . .

The murder of approximately 4 million Jews in concentration camps . . . was also under the supervision of the RSHA when Kaltenbrunner was head of that organization, and special missions of the RSHA scoured the occupied territories and the various Axis satellites arranging for the deportation of Jews to these extermination institutions. Kaltenbrunner was informed of these activities. . . .

Kaltenbrunner has claimed that when he took office as Chief of the Security Police and SD and as head of the RSHA he did so pursuant to an understanding with Himmler under which he was to confine his activities to matters involving foreign intelligence and not to assume overall control over the activities of the RSHA. He claims that the criminal program had been started before his assumption of office; that he seldom knew what was going on; and that when he was informed he did what he could to stop them. It is true that he showed a special interest in matters involving foreign intelligence. But he exercised control over the activities of the RSHA, was aware of the crimes it was committing, and was an active participant in many of them.

Conclusion

The Tribunal finds that Kaltenbrunner is not guilty on Count One. He is guilty under Counts Three and Four.

Rosenberg

Rosenberg is indicted on all four Counts. He joined the Nazi Party in 1919, participated in the Munich *Putsch* of 9 November 1923, and tried to keep the illegal Nazi Party together while Hitler was in jail. Recognized as the Party's ideologist, he developed and spread Nazi doctrines in the newspapers *Völkischer Beobachter* and *NS Monatshefte,* which he edited, and in the numerous books he wrote. His book *Myth of the Twentieth Century* had a circulation of over a million copies. . . .

Crimes against Peace

Rosenberg bears a major responsibility for the formulation and execution of occupation policies in the Occupied Eastern Territories. He was informed by Hitler, on 2 April 1941, of the coming attack against the Soviet Union, and he agreed to help in the capacity of a "Political Adviser." On 20 April 1941 he was appointed Commissioner for the Central Control of Questions Connected with the East European Region. In preparing the plans for the occupation, he had numerous conferences with Keitel, Raeder, Goering, Funk, Ribbentrop, and other high Reich authorities. In April and May 1941 he prepared several drafts of instructions concerning the setting up of the administration in the Occupied Eastern Territories. On 20 June 1941, two days before the attack on the U.S.S.R., he made a speech to his assistants about the problems and policies of occupation. Rosenberg attended Hitler's conference of 16 July 1941, in which policies of administration and occupation were discussed. On 17 July 1941, Hitler appointed Rosenberg Reich Minister for the Occupied Eastern Territories and publicly charged him with responsibility for civil administration.

War Crimes and Crimes against Humanity

Rosenberg is responsible for a system of organized plunder of both public and private property throughout the invaded countries of Europe. Acting under Hitler's orders of January 1940 to set up the *"Hohe Schule,"* he organized and directed the *"Einsatzstab Rosenberg,"* which plundered museums and libraries, confiscated art treasures and collections, and pillaged private houses. His own reports show the extent of the confiscations. In *"Aktion-M"* (*Möbel*), instituted in December 1941 at Rosenberg's suggestion, 69, 619 Jewish homes were plundered in the West, 38,000 of them in Paris alone, and it took 26,984 railroad cars to transport the confiscated furnishings to Germany. As of 14 July 1944, more than 21,903 art objects, including famous paintings and museum pieces, had been seized by the *Einsatzstab* in the West. . . .

Rosenberg had knowledge of the brutal treatment and terror to which the Eastern people were subjected. He directed that the Hague Rules of Land Warfare were not applicable in the Occupied Eastern Territories. He had knowledge of and took an active part in stripping the Eastern territories of raw materials and foodstuffs, which were sent to Germany. He stated that feeding the German people was first on the list of claims on the East, and that the Soviet people would suffer thereby. His directives provided for the segregation of Jews, ultimately in ghettos. His subordinates engaged in mass killings of Jews, and his civil administrators in the East considered that cleansing the Eastern Occupied Territories of Jews was necessary. . . . His signature of approval appears on the order of 14 June 1944, for the *"Heu Aktion,"* the apprehension of 40,000 to 50,000 youths, aged 10–14, for shipment to the Reich.

Upon occasion Rosenberg objected to the excesses and atrocities committed by his subordinates, notably in the case of Koch, but these excesses continued and he stayed in office until the end.

Conclusion

The Tribunal finds that Rosenberg is guilty on all four Counts.

MR. BIDDLE*:

Frank

Frank is indicted under Counts One, Three, and Four. Frank joined the Nazi Party in 1927. He became a member of the *Reichstag* in 1930, the Bavarian State Minister of Justice in March 1933, and when this position was incorporated into the Reich Government in 1934, Reich Minister

---

*Because of the length of the verdicts, members of the Tribunal and President Lord Justice Geoffrey Lawrence took turns reading it aloud. This refers to Mr. Francis Biddle, the United States member.

without Portfolio. He was made a *Reichsleiter* of the Nazi Party in charge of legal affairs in 1933, and in the same year President of the Academy of German Law. Frank was also given the honorary rank of *Obergruppen-fuehrer* in the SA. In 1942 Frank became involved in a temporary dispute with Himmler as to the type of legal system which should be in effect in Germany. During the same year he was dismissed as *Reichsleiter* of the Nazi Party and as President of the Academy of German Law.

Crimes against Peace

The evidence has not satisfied the Tribunal that Frank was sufficiently connected with the common plan to wage aggressive war to allow the Tribunal to convict him on Count One.

War Crimes and Crimes against Humanity

Frank was appointed Chief Civil Administration Officer for occupied Polish territory and, on 12 October 1939, was made Governor General of the occupied Polish territory. On 3 October 1939, he described the policy which he intended to put into effect by stating: "Poland shall be treated like a colony; the Poles will become the slaves of the Greater German World Empire." The evidence establishes that this occupation policy was based on the complete destruction of Poland as a national entity, and a ruthless exploitation of its human and economic resources for the German war effort. All opposition was crushed with the utmost harshness. A reign of terror was instituted, backed by summary policy courts which ordered such actions as the public shootings of groups of 20 to 200 Poles and the widespread shooting of hostages. The concentration camp system was introduced in the Government General by the establishment of the noto-rious Treblinka and Maidanek camps. . . .

Frank introduced the deportation of slave laborers to Germany in the very early stages of his administration. On 25 January 1940, he indicated his intention of deporting a million laborers to Germany, suggesting on 10 May 1940 the use of police raids to meet this quota. On 18 August 1942, Frank reported that he had already supplied 800,000 workers for the Reich and expected to be able to supply 140,000 more before the end of the year.

The persecution of the Jews was immediately begun in the Government General. The area originally contained from 2,500,000 to 3,500,000 Jews. They were forced into ghettos, subjected to discriminatory laws, deprived of the food necessary to avoid starvation, and finally systematically and brutally exterminated. On 16 December 1941, Frank told the Cabinet of the Government General: "We must annihilate the Jews wherever we find them and wherever it is possible in order to maintain there the structure of the Reich as a whole." By 25 January 1944, Frank estimated that there were only 100,000 Jews left.

At the beginning of his testimony, Frank stated that he had a feeling of "terrible guilt" for the atrocities committed in the occupied territories. But his defense was largely devoted to an attempt to prove that he was not in fact responsible; that he ordered only the necessary pacification measures; that the excesses were due to the activities of the Police which were not under his control; and that he never even knew of the activities of the concentration camps. It has also been argued that the starvation was due to the aftermath of the war and policies carried out under the Four Year Plan; that the forced labor program was under the direction of Sauckel; and that the extermination of the Jews was by the Police and SS under direct orders from Himmler.

It is undoubtedly true that most of the criminal program charged against Frank was put into effect through the Police, that Frank had jurisdictional difficulties with Himmler over the control of the Police, and that Hitler resolved many of these disputes in favor of Himmler. It therefore may well be true that some of the crimes committed in the Government General were committed without the knowledge of Frank, and even occasionally despite his opposition. It may also be true that some of the criminal policies put into effect in the Government General did not originate with Frank but were carried out pursuant to orders from Germany. But it is also true that Frank was a willing and knowing participant in the use of terrorism in Poland; in the economic exploitation of Poland in a way which led to the death by starvation of a large number of people; in the deportation to Germany as slave laborers of over a million Poles; and in a program involving the murder of at least 3 million Jews.

Conclusion

The Tribunal finds that Frank is not guilty on Count One but is guilty under Counts Three and Four.

M. DE. VABRES*:

Frick

Frick is indicted on all four Counts. Recognized as the chief Nazi administrative specialist and bureaucrat, he was appointed Reich Minister of the Interior in Hitler's first cabinet. He retained this important position until August 1943, when he was appointed Reich Protector of Bohemia and Moravia. In connection with his duties at the center of all internal and domestic administration, he became the Prussian Minister of the Interior, Reich Director of Elections, General Plenipotentiary for the Administra-

---

*Professor Donnedieu de Vabres, the French member of the Tribunal.

tion of the Reich, and a member of the Reich Defense Council, the Ministerial Council for Defense of the Reich, and the "Three Man College." As the several countries incorporated into the Reich were overrun, he was placed at the head of the central offices for their incorporation.

Though Frick did not officially join the Nazi Party until 1925, he had previously allied himself with Hitler and the National Socialist cause during the Munich *Putsch,* while he was an official in the Munich Police Department. Elected to the *Reichstag* in 1924, he became a *Reichsleiter* as leader of the National Socialist faction in that body.

Crimes against Peace

An avid Nazi, Frick was largely responsible for bringing the German nation under the complete control of the NSDAP. After Hitler became Reich Chancellor, the new Minister of the Interior immediately began to incorporate local governments under the sovereignty of the Reich. The numerous laws he drafted, signed, and administered, abolished all opposition parties and prepared the way for the *Gestapo* and their concentration camps to extinguish all individual opposition. He was largely responsible for the legislation which suppressed the trade unions, the Church, the Jews. He performed the task with ruthless efficiency. . . .

War Crimes and Crimes against Humanity

Always rabidly anti-Semitic, Frick drafted, signed, and administered many laws designed to eliminate Jews from German life and economy. His work formed the basis of the Nuremberg Decrees, and he was active in enforcing them. Responsible for prohibiting Jews from following various professions and for confiscating their property, he signed a final decree in 1943, after the mass destruction of Jews in the East, which placed them "outside the law" and handed them over to the *Gestapo.* These laws paved the way for the "final solution," and were extended by Frick to the incorporated territories and to certain of the occupied territories. While he was Reich Protector of Bohemia and Moravia, thousands of Jews were transferred from the Terezin ghetto in Czechoslovakia to Auschwitz, where they were killed. He issued a decree providing for special penal laws against Jews and Poles in the Government General. . . .

During the war nursing homes, hospitals, and asylums in which euthanasia was practiced as described elsewhere in this Judgment, came under Frick's jurisdiction. He had knowledge that insane, sick, and aged people, "useless eaters," were being systematically put to death. Complaints of these murders reached him, but he did nothing to stop them. A report of the Czechoslovak War Crimes Commission estimated that 275,000 mentally deficient and aged people, for whose welfare he was responsible, fell victim to it.

Conclusion

The Tribunal finds that Frick is not guilty on Count One. He is guilty on Counts Two, Three and Four.

THE PRESIDENT*:

Streicher

Streicher is indicted on Counts One and Four. One of the earliest members of the Nazi Party, joining in 1921, he took part in the Munich *Putsch*. From 1925 to 1940 he was *Gauleiter* of Franconia. Elected to the *Reichstag* in 1933, he was an honorary general in the SA. His persecution of the Jews was notorious. He was the publisher of *Der Stürmer*, an anti-Semitic weekly newspaper, from 1923 to 1945 and was its editor until 1933.

Crimes against Peace

Streicher was a staunch Nazi and supporter of Hitler's main policies. There is no evidence to show that he was ever within Hitler's inner circle of advisers; nor during his career was he closely connected with the formulation of the policies which led to war. He was never present, for example, at any of the important conferences when Hitler explained his decisions to his leaders. Although he was a *Gauleiter* there is no evidence to prove that he had knowledge of these policies. In the opinion of the Tribunal, the evidence fails to establish his connection with the conspiracy or common plan to wage aggressive war as that conspiracy has been elsewhere defined in this Judgment.

Crimes against Humanity

For his 25 years of speaking, writing, and preaching hatred of the Jews, Streicher was widely known as "Jew-Baiter Number One." In his speeches and articles, week after week, month after month, he infected the German mind with the virus of anti-Semitism and incited the German people to active persecution. Each issue of *Der Stürmer*, which reached a circulation of 600,000 in 1935, was filled with such articles, often lewd and disgusting.

Streicher had charge of the Jewish boycott of 1 April 1933. He advocated the Nuremberg Decrees of 1935. He was responsible for the demolition on 10 August 1938 of the synagogue in Nuremberg. And on 10 November 1938, he spoke publicly in support of the Jewish program which was taking place at that time. . . .

With knowledge of the extermination of the Jews in the Occupied Eastern Territories, this defendant continued to write and publish his propa-

---

*Lord Justice Geoffrey Lawrence, the British president of the Tribunal.

ganda of death. Testifying in this Trial, he vehemently denied any knowledge of mass executions of Jews. But the evidence makes it clear that he continually received current information on the progress of the "final solution." . . .

In the face of the evidence before the Tribunal it is idle for Streicher to suggest that the solution of the Jewish problem which he favored was strictly limited to the classification of Jews as aliens, and the passing of discriminatory legislation such as the Nuremberg Laws, supplemented if possible by international agreement on the creation of a Jewish state somewhere in the world, to which all Jews should emigrate.

Streicher's incitement to murder and extermination at the time when Jews in the East were being killed under the most horrible conditions clearly constitutes persecution on political and racial grounds in connection with War Crimes, as defined by the Charter, and constitutes a Crime against Humanity.

Conclusion

The Tribunal finds that Streicher is not guilty on Count One, but that he is guilty on Count Four.

GEN. NIKITCHENKO*:

Funk

Funk is indicted under all four Counts. Funk, who had previously been a financial journalist, joined the Nazi Party in 1931, and shortly thereafter became one of Hitler's personal economic advisers. On 30 January 1933, he was made Press Chief in the Reich Government, and on 11 March 1933 became Under Secretary in the Ministry of Propaganda and shortly thereafter a leading figure in the various Nazi organizations which were used to control the press, films, music, and publishing houses. Funk took office as Minister of Economics and Plenipotentiary General for War Economy in early 1938, and as President of the *Reichsbank* in January 1939. He succeeded Schacht in all three of these positions. . . .

Crimes against Peace

Funk became active in the economic field after the Nazi plans to wage aggressive war had been clearly defined. One of his representatives attended a conference on 14 October 1938, at which Goering announced a gigantic increase in armaments and instructed the Ministry of Economics to increase exports to obtain the necessary exchange. On 28 January 1939, one of Funk's subordinates sent a memorandum to the OKW on the use of

---

*Major-General I. T. Nikitchenko, the Russian member of the Tribunal.

prisoners of war to make up labor deficiencies which would arise in case of mobilization. On 30 May 1939, the Under Secretary of the Ministry of Economics attended a meeting at which detailed plans were made for the financing of the war. . . .

War Crimes and Crimes against Humanity

In his capacity as Under Secretary in the Ministry of Propaganda and Vice-Chairman of the Reich Chamber of Culture, Funk had participated in the early Nazi program of economic discrimination against the Jews. On 12 November 1938, after the pogroms of November, he attended a meeting held under the chairmanship of Goering to discuss the solution of the Jewish problem and proposed a decree providing for the banning of Jews from all business activities, which Goering issued the same day under the authority of the Four Year Plan. . . .

In 1942 Funk entered into an agreement with Himmler under which the *Reichsbank* was to receive certain gold and jewels and currency from the SS and instructed his subordinates, who were to work out the details, not to ask too many questions. As a result of this agreement the SS sent to the *Reichsbank* the personal belongings taken from the victims who had been exterminated in the concentration camps. The *Reichsbank* kept the coins and bank notes and sent the jewels, watches, and personal belongings to Berlin municipal pawn shops. The gold from the eyeglasses and gold teeth and fillings were stored in the *Reichsbank* vaults. Funk has protested that he did not know that the *Reichsbank* was receiving articles of this kind. The Tribunal is of the opinion that he either knew what was being received or was deliberately closing his eyes to what was being done.

As Minister of Economics and President of the *Reichsbank*, Funk participated in the economic exploitation of occupied territories. He was President of the Continental Oil Company which was charged with the exploitation of the oil resources of occupied territories in the East. . . .

In the fall of 1943, Funk was a member of the Central Planning Board which determined the total number of laborers needed for German industry and required Sauckel to produce them, usually by deportation from occupied territories. Funk did not appear to be particularly interested in this aspect of the forced labor program and usually sent a deputy to attend the meetings, often SS General Ohlendorf, the former chief of the SD inside of Germany and the former commander of *Einsatzgruppe D*. But Funk was aware that the board of which he was a member was demanding the importation of slave laborers and allocating them to the various industries under its control.

As President of the *Reichsbank*, Funk was also indirectly involved in the utilization of concentration camp labor. Under his direction the *Reichsbank* set up a revolving fund of 12,000,000 *Reichsmarks* to the credit of the SS for the construction of factories to use concentration camp laborers.

In spite of the fact that he occupied important official positions, Funk was never a dominant figure in the various programs in which he partici-pated. This is a mitigating fact of which the Tribunal takes notice.

Conclusion

The Tribunal finds that Funk is not guilty on Count One but is guilty under Counts Two, Three, and Four.

THE PRESIDENT: The Court will adjourn for 10 minutes.

[*A recess was taken.*]

MR. BIDDLE:

Schacht

Schacht is indicted under Counts One and Two of the Indictment. Schacht served as Commissioner of Currency and President of the *Reichsbank* from 1923 to 1930; was reappointed President of the bank on 17 March 1933; Minister of Economics in August 1934; and Plenipotentiary General for War Economy in May 1935. He resigned from these two positions in November 1937 and was appointed Minister without Portfolio. He was reappointed as President of the *Reichsbank* for a one-year term on 16 March 1937, and for a four-year term on 9 March 1933, but was dismissed on 20 January 1939. He was dismissed as Minister without Portfolio on 22 January 1943.

Schacht was an active supporter of the Nazi Party before its accession to power on 30 January 1933 and supported the appointment of Hitler to the post of Chancellor. After that date he played an important role in the vigorous rearmament program which was adopted, using the facilities of the *Reichsbank* to the fullest extent in the German rearmament effort. The *Reichsbank*, in its traditional capacity as financial agent for the German Government, floated long-term Government loans, the proceeds of which were used for rearmament. He devised a system under which five-year notes, known as "mefo" bills, guaranteed by the *Reichsbank* and backed, in effect, by nothing more than its position as a bank of issue, were used to obtain large sums for rearmament from the short-term money market. As Minister of Economics and as Plenipotentiary General for the War Economy he was active in organizing the German economy for war. He made detailed plans for industrial mobilization and the co-ordination of the Army with industry in the event of war. . . .

Schacht, by April 1936, began to lose his influence as the central figure in the German rearmament effort when Goering was appointed co-ordinator for raw materials and foreign exchange. . . .

It is clear that Schacht was a central figure in Germany's rearmament program, and the steps which he took, particularly in the early days of the Nazi regime, were responsible for Nazi Germany's rapid rise as a military power. But rearmament of itself is not criminal under the Charter. To be a Crime against Peace under Article 6 of the Charter it must be shown that Schacht carried out this rearmament as part of the Nazi plans to wage aggressive wars. . . .

Schacht was not involved in the planning of any of the specific wars of aggression charged in Count Two. His participation in the occupation of Austria and the Sudetenland (neither of which is charged as aggressive war) was on such a limited basis that it does not amount to participation in the common plan charged in Count One. He was clearly not one of the inner circle around Hitler which was most closely involved with this common plan. He was regarded by this group with undisguised hostility. The testimony of Speer shows that Schacht's arrest on 23 July 1944, was based as much on Hitler's enmity toward Schacht growing out of his attitude before the war as it was on suspicion of his complicity in the bomb plot. The case against Schacht therefore depends on the inference that Schacht did in fact know of the Nazi aggressive plans.

On this all-important question evidence has been given for the Prosecution and a considerable volume of evidence for the Defense. The Tribunal has considered the whole of this evidence with great care, and comes to the conclusion that this necessary inference has not been established beyond a reasonable doubt.

Conclusion

The Tribunal finds that Schacht is not guilty on this Indictment, and directs that he shall be discharged by the Marshal, when the Tribunal presently adjourns.

M. DE VABRES:

Doenitz

Doenitz is indicted on Counts One, Two, and Three. In 1935 he took command of the first U-Boat flotilla commissioned since 1918, became in 1936 commander of the submarine arm, was made Vice-Admiral in 1940, Admiral in 1942, and on 30 January 1943 Commander-in-Chief of the German Navy. On 1 May 1945 he became the Head of State, succeeding Hitler.

Crimes against Peace

Although Doenitz built and trained the German U-Boat arm, the evidence does not show he was privy to the conspiracy to wage aggressive wars or that he prepared and initiated such wars. He was a line officer performing strictly tactical duties. He was not present at the important conferences when plans for aggressive wars were announced, and there is no evidence he was informed about the decisions reached there. Doenitz did, however, wage aggressive war within the meaning of that word as used by the Charter. Submarine warfare which began immediately upon the outbreak of war, was fully co-ordinated with the other branches of the *Wehrmacht*. It is clear that his U-boats, few in number at the time, were fully prepared to wage war. . . .

War Crimes

Doenitz is charged with waging unrestricted submarine warfare contrary to the Naval Protocol of 1936, to which Germany acceded, and which reaffirmed the rules of submarine warfare laid down in the London Naval Agreement of 1930.

The Prosecution has submitted that on 3 September 1939 the German U-Boat arm began to wage unrestricted submarine warfare upon all merchant ships, whether enemy or neutral, cynically disregarding the Protocol, and that a calculated effort was made throughout the war to disguise this practice by making hypocritical references to international law and supposed violations by the Allies.

Doenitz insists that at all times the Navy remained within the confines of international law and of the Protocol. He testified that when the war began, the guide to submarine warfare was the German Prize Ordinance, taken almost literally from the Protocol; that pursuant to the German view, he ordered submarines to attack all merchant ships in convoy and all that refused to stop or used their radio upon sighting a submarine. When his reports indicated that British merchant ships were being used to give information by wireless, were being armed and were attacking submarines on sight, he ordered his submarines on 17 October 1939 to attack all enemy merchant ships without warning on the ground that resistance was to be expected. Orders already had been issued on 21 September 1939 to attack all ships, including neutrals, sailing at night without lights in the English Channel. . . .

Conclusion

The Tribunal finds that Doentiz is not guilty on Count One of the Indictment, and is guilty on Counts Two and Three.

THE PRESIDENT:

Raeder

Raeder is indicted on Counts One, Two, and Three. In 1928 he became Chief of Naval Command and in 1935 *Oberbefehlshaber der Kriegsmarine* (OKM); in 1939 Hitler made him *Grossadmiral*. He was a member of the Reich Defense Council. On 30 January 1943, Doenitz replaced him at his own request, and he became Admiral Inspector of the Navy, a nominal title.

Crimes against Peace

In the 15 years he commanded it, Raeder built and directed the German Navy; he accepts full responsibility until retirement in 1943. He admits the Navy violated the Versailles Treaty, insisting it was "a matter of honor for every man" to do so, and alleges that the violations were for the most part minor, and Germany built less than her allowable strength. . . .

Raeder endeavored to dissuade Hitler from embarking upon the invasion of the U.S.S.R. In September 1940 he urged on Hitler an aggressive Mediterranean policy as an alternative to an attack on Russia. On 14 November 1940 he urged the war against England "as our main enemy" and that submarine and naval air force construction be continued. He voiced "serious objections against the Russian campaign before the defeat of England," according to notes of the German Naval War Staff. He claims his objections were based on the violation of the non-aggression pact as well as strategy. But once the decision had been made, he gave permission 6 days before the invasion of the Soviet Union to attack Russian submarines in the Baltic Sea within a specified warning area and defends this action because these submarines were "snooping" on German activities.

It is clear from this evidence that Raeder participated in the planning and waging of aggressive war.

War Crimes

Raeder is charged with war crimes on the high seas. The *Athenia*, an unarmed British passenger liner, was sunk on 3 September 1939, while outward bound to America. The Germans 2 months later charged that Mr. Churchill deliberately sank the *Athenia* to encourage American hostility to Germany. In fact, it was sunk by the German U-Boat *U-30*. Raeder claims that an inexperienced U-boat commander sank it in mistake for an armed merchant cruiser, that this was not known until the *U-30* returned several weeks after the German denial and that Hitler then directed the Navy and Foreign Office to continue denying it. Raeder denied knowledge of the propaganda campaign attacking Mr. Churchill.

The most serious charge against Raeder is that he carried out unrestricted submarine warfare, including sinking of unarmed merchant ships, of neutrals, non-rescue and machine-gunning of survivors, contrary to the London Protocol of 1936. . . .

The Commando Order of 18 October 1942 which expressly did not apply to naval warfare was transmitted by the Naval War Staff to the lower naval commanders with the direction it should be distributed orally by flotilla leaders and section commanders to their subordinates. Two Commandos were put to death by the Navy, and not by the SD, at Bordeaux on 10 December 1942. The comment of the Naval War Staff was that this was "in accordance with the *Fuehrer's* special order, but is nevertheless something new in international law, since the soldiers were in uniform." Raeder admits he passed the order down through the chain of command and he did not object to Hitler.

Conclusion

The Tribunal finds that Raeder is guilty on Counts One, Two and Three.

GEN. NIKITCHENKO:

Von Schirach

Von Schirach is indicted under Counts One and Four. He joined the Nazi Party and the SA in 1925. In 1929 he became the Leader of the National Socialist Students' Union. In 1931 he was made Reich Youth Leader of the Nazi Party with control over all Nazi youth organizations including the *Hitler Jugend*. In 1933, after the Nazis had obtained control of the Government, von Schirach was made Leader of Youth in the German Reich, originally a position within the Ministry of the Interior, but, after 1 December 1936, an office in the Reich Cabinet. In 1940, von Schirach resigned as head of the *Hitler Jugend* and Leader of Youth in the German Reich, but retained his position as *Reichsleiter* with control over Youth Education. In 1940 he was appointed *Gauleiter* of Vienna, Reich Governor of Vienna, and Reich Defense Commissioner for that territory.

Crimes against Peace

After the Nazis had come to power von Schirach, utilizing both physical violence and official pressure, either drove out of existence or took over all youth groups which competed with the *Hitler Jugend*. A Hitler decree of 1 December 1936 incorporated all German youth within the *Hitler Jugend*. By the time formal conscription was introduced in 1940, 97 percent of those eligible were already members.

Von Schirach used the *Hitler Jugend* to educate German youth "in the spirit of National Socialism" and subjected them to an intensive program of Nazi propaganda. He established the *Hitler Jugend* as a source of replacements for the Nazi Party formations. In October 1938 he entered into an arrangement with Himmler under which members of the *Hitler Jugend* who met SS standards would be considered as the primary source of replacements for the SS. . . .

Crimes against Humanity

In July 1940, von Schirach was appointed *Gauleiter* of Vienna. At the same time he was appointed Reich Governor for Vienna and Reich Defense Commissioner, originally for Military District 17, including the *Gaue* of Vienna, Upper Danube, and Lower Danube and, after 17 November 1942, for the *Gau* of Vienna alone. As Reich Defense Commissioner, he had control of the civilian war economy. As Reich Governor he was head of the municipal administration of the City of Vienna and, under the supervision of the Minister of the Interior, was in charge of the governmental administration of the Reich in Vienna. . . .

The Tribunal finds that von Schirach, while he did not originate the policy of deporting Jews from Vienna, participated in this deportation after he had become *Gauleiter* of Vienna. He knew that the best the Jews could hope for was a miserable existence in the ghettos of the East. Bulletins describing the Jewish extermination were in his office.

While *Gauleiter* of Vienna, von Schirach continued to function as *Reichsleiter* for Youth Education and in this capacity he was informed of the *Hitler Jugend's* participation in the plan put into effect in the fall of 1944 under which 50,000 young people between the ages of 10 and 20 were evacuated into Germany from areas recaptured by the Soviet forces and used as apprentices in German industry and as auxiliaries in units of the German Armed Forces. In the summer of 1942, von Schirach telegraphed Bormann urging that a bombing attack on an English cultural town be carried out in retaliation for the assassination of Heydrich which, he claimed, had been planned by the British.

Conclusion

The Tribunal finds that von Schirach is not guilty on Count One. He is guilty under Count Four.

MR. BIDDLE:

Sauckel

Sauckel is indicted under all four Counts. Sauckel joined the Nazi Party in 1923, and became *Gauleiter* of Thuringia in 1927. He was a member of the Thuringian legislature from 1927 to 1933, was appointed *Reichsstatthalter* for Thuringia in 1932, and Thuringian Minister of the Interior and head of the Thuringian State Ministry in May 1933. He became a member of the *Reichstag* in 1933. He held the formal rank of *Obergrupperfuehrer* in both the SA and the SS.

Crimes against Peace

The evidence has not satisfied the Tribunal that Sauckel was sufficiently connected with the common plan to wage aggressive war or sufficiently involved in the planning or waging of the aggressive wars to allow the Tribunal to convict him on Counts One or Two.

War Crimes and Crimes against Humanity

On 21 March 1942, Hitler appointed Sauckel Plenipotentiary General for the Utilization of Labor, with authority to put under uniform control "the utilization of all available manpower, including that of workers recruited abroad and of prisoners of war." Sauckel was instructed to operate within the fabric of the Four Year Plan, and on 27 March 1942, Goering issued a decree as Delegate for the Four Year Plan transferring his manpower sections to Sauckel. On 30 September 1942, Hitler gave Sauckel authority to appoint commissioners in the various occupied territories and "to take all necessary measures for the enforcement" of the decree of 21 March 1942.

Under the authority which he obtained by these decrees, Sauckel set up a program for the mobilization of the labor resources available to the Reich. One of the important parts of this mobilization was the systematic exploitation, by force, of the labor resources of the occupied territories. Shortly after Sauckel had taken office, he had the governing authorities in the various occupied territories issue decrees establishing compulsory labor service in Germany. Under the authority of these decrees Sauckel's commissioners, backed up by the police authorities of the occupied territories, obtained and sent to Germany the laborers which were necessary to fill the quotas given them by Sauckel. . . .

There is no doubt, however, that Sauckel had over-all responsibility for the slave labor program. At the time of the events in question he did not fail to assert control over the fields which he now claims were the sole responsibility of others. His regulations provided that his commissioners should have authority for obtaining labor, and he was constantly in the field supervising the steps which were being taken. He was aware of ruthless methods being taken to obtain laborers and vigorously supported them on the ground that they were necessary to fill the quotas.

Sauckel's regulations also provided that he had responsibility for transporting the laborers to Germany, allocating them to employers and taking care of them, and that the other agencies involved in these processes were subordinate to him. He was informed of the bad conditions which existed. It does not appear that he advocated brutality for its own sake, or was an advocate of any program such as Himmler's plan for extermination through work. His attitude was thus expressed in a regulation: "All the men must be fed, sheltered, and treated in such a way as to exploit them to the highest possible extent at the lowest conceivable degree of expenditure." The evidence shows that Sauckel was in charge of a program which involved deportation for slave labor of more than 5,000,000 human beings, many of them under terrible conditions of cruelty and suffering.

Conclusion

The Tribunal finds that Sauckel is not guilty on Counts One and Two. He is guilty under Counts Three and Four.

M. DE VABRES:

Jodl

Jodl is indicted on all four Counts. From 1935 to 1938 he was Chief of the National Defense Section in the High Command. After a year in command of troops, in August 1939 he returned to become Chief of the Operations Staff of the High Command of the Armed Forces. Although his immediate superior was Defendant Keitel, he reported directly to Hitler on operational matters. In the strict military sense, Jodl was the actual planner of the war and responsible in large measure for the strategy and conduct of operations.

Jodl defends himself on the ground he was a soldier sworn to obedience, and not a politician; and that his staff and planning work left him no time for other matters. He said that when he signed or initialed orders, memoranda, and letters, he did so for Hitler and often in the absence of Keitel. Though he claims that as a soldier he had to obey Hitler, he says that he often tried to obstruct certain measures by delay, which occasionally proved successful as when he resisted Hitler's demand that a directive be issued to lynch Allied "terror fliers."

Crimes against Peace

. . . Jodl testified that Hitler feared an attack by Russia and so attacked first. This preparation began almost a year before the invasion. Jodl told Warlimont as early as 29 July 1940 to prepare the plans since Hitler had decided to attack; and Hitler later told Warlimont he had planned to attack in August 1940 but postponed it for military reasons. He initialed Hitler's directive of 12 November 1940 that preparations verbally ordered should be continued and also initialed "Case Barbarossa" on 18 December. On 3 February 1941, Hitler, Jodl, and Keitel discussed the invasion, and he was present on 14 June when final reports on "Case Barbarossa" were made.

War Crimes and Crimes against Humanity

On 18 October 1942 Hitler issued the Commando Order, and a day later a supplementary explanation to commanding officers only. The covering memorandum was signed by Jodl. Early drafts of the order were made by Jodl's staff, with his knowledge. Jodl testified he was strongly opposed on moral and legal grounds but could not refuse to pass it on. He insists he tried to mitigate its harshness in practice by not informing Hitler when it was not carried out. He initialed the OKW memorandum of 25 June 1944 reaffirming the order after the Normandy landings.

A plan to eliminate Soviet commissars was in the directive for "Case Barbarossa." The decision whether they should be killed without trial was to be made by an officer. A draft contains Jodl's handwriting suggesting this should be handled as retaliation, and he testified this was his attempt to get around it. . . .

There is little evidence that Jodl was actively connected with the slave labor program, and he must have concentrated on his strategic planning function. But in his speech of 7 November 1943 to the *Gauleiter* he said it was necessary to act "with remorseless vigor and resolution" in Denmark, France, and the Low Countries to compel work on the Atlantic Wall.

By teletype of 28 October 1944, Jodl ordered the evacuation of all persons in northern Norway and the burning of their houses so they could not help the Russians. Jodl says he was against this, but Hitler ordered it and it was not fully carried out. A document of the Norwegian Government says such an evacuation did take place in northern Norway and 30,000 houses were damaged. On 7 October 1941, Jodl signed an order that Hitler would not accept an offer of surrender of Leningrad or Moscow, but on the contrary he insisted that they be completely destroyed. He says this was done because the Germans were afraid those cities would be mined by the Russians as was Kiev. No surrender was ever offered.

His defense, in brief, is the doctrine of "superior orders," prohibited by Article 3 of the Charter as a defense. There is nothing in mitigation. Participation in such crimes as these has never been required of any soldier and he cannot now shield himself behind a mythical requirement of soldierly obedience at all costs as his excuse for commission of these crimes.

Conclusion

The Tribunal finds that Jodl is guilty on all four Counts.

THE PRESIDENT:

Von Papen

Von Papen is indicted under Counts One and Two. He was appointed Chancellor of the Reich on 1 June 1932, and was succeeded by von Schleicher on 2 December 1932. He was made Vice Chancellor in the Hitler Cabinet on 30 January 1933, and on 13 November 1933, Plenipotentiary for the Saar. On 26 July 1934, he was appointed Minister to Vienna, and was recalled on 4 February 1938. On 29 April 1939, he was appointed Ambassador to Turkey. He returned to Germany when Turkey broke off diplomatic relations with Germany in August 1944.

Crimes against Peace

Von Papen was active in 1932 and 1933 in helping Hitler to form the Coalition Cabinet and aided in his appointment as Chancellor on 30 January 1933. As Vice Chancellor in that Cabinet he participated in the Nazi consolidation of control in 1933. On 17 June 1934, however, von Papen made a speech at Marburg which contained a denunciation of the Nazi attempts to suppress the free press and the Church, of the existence of a reign of terror, and of "150 percent Nazis" who were mistaking "brutality for vitality." On 30 June 1934, in the wave of violence which accompanied the so-called Roehm Purge, von Papen was taken into custody by the SS, his office force was arrested, and two of his associates, including the man who had helped him work on the Marburg speech, were murdered. Von Papen was released on 3 July 1934.

Notwithstanding the murder of his associates, von Papen accepted the position of Minister to Austria on 26 July 1934, the day after Dollfuss had been assassinated. His appointment was announced in a letter from Hitler which instructed him to direct relations between the two countries "into normal and friendly channels" and assured him of Hitler's "complete and unlimited confidence." As Minister to Austria, von Papen was active in trying to strengthen the position of the Nazi Party in Austria for the purpose of bringing about the *Anschluss*. . . .

After the annexation of Austria von Papen retired into private life and there is no evidence that he took any part in politics. He accepted the position of Ambassador to Turkey in April 1939 but no evidence has been offered concerning his activities in that position implicating him in crimes.

The evidence leaves no doubt that von Papen's primary purpose as Minister to Austria was to undermine the Schuschnigg regime and strengthen the Austrian Nazis for the purpose of bringing about the *Anschluss*. To carry through this plan he engaged in both intrigue and bullying. But the Charter does not make criminal such offenses against political morality, however bad these may be. Under the Charter von Papen can be held guilty only if he was a party to the planning of aggressive war. There is no evidence that he was a party to the plans under which the occupation of Austria was a step in the direction of further aggressive action, or even that he participated in plans to occupy Austria by aggressive war if necessary. But it is not established beyond a reasonable doubt that this was the purpose of his activity, and therefore the Tribunal cannot hold that he was a party to the common plan charged in Count One or participated in the planning of the aggressive wars charged under Count Two.

Conclusion

The Tribunal finds that von Papen is not guilty under this Indictment, and directs that he shall be discharged by the Marshal, when the Tribunal presently adjourns.

GEN. NIKITCHENKO:
Seyss-Inquart

Seyss-Inquart is indicted under all four Counts. Seyss-Inquart, an Austrian attorney, was appointed State Councillor in Austria in May 1937 as a result of German pressure. He had been associated with the Austrian Nazi Party since 1931, but had often had difficulties with that party and did not actually join the Nazi Party until 13 March 1938. He was appointed Austrian Minister of Security and Interior with control over the police pursuant to one of the conditions which Hitler had imposed on Schuschnigg in the Berchtesgaden conference of 12 February 1938.

Activities in Austria

Seyss-Inquart participated in the last stages of the Nazi intrigue which preceded the German occupation of Austria and was made Chancellor of Austria as a result of German threats of invasion. . . .

As Reich Governor of Austria, Seyss-Inquart instituted a program of confiscating Jewish property. Under his regime, Jews were forced to emigrate, were sent to concentration camps, and were subjected to pogroms. At the end of his regime he co-operated with the Security Police and SD in the deportation of Jews from Austria to the East. While he was Governor of Austria, political opponents of the Nazis were sent to concentration camps by the *Gestapo*, mistreated, and often killed. . . .

Criminal Activities in Poland and the Netherlands

In September 1939, Seyss-Inquart was appointed Chief of Civil Administration of South Poland. On 12 October 1939, Seyss-Inquart was made Deputy Governor General of the Government General of Poland under Frank. On 18 May 1940, Seyss-Inquart was appointed Reich Commissioner for Occupied Netherlands. In these positions he assumed responsibility for governing territory which had been occupied by aggressive wars and the administration of which was of vital importance in the aggressive war being waged by Germany.

As Deputy Governor General of the Government General of Poland, Seyss-Inquart was a supporter of the harsh occupation policies which were put in effect. In November 1939, while on an inspection tour through the Government General, Seyss-Inquart stated that Poland was to be so administered as to exploit its economic resources for the benefit of Germany. Seyss-Inquart also advocated the persecution of Jews and was informed of the beginning of the AB Action which involved the murder of many Polish intellectuals.

As Reich Commissioner for Occupied Netherlands, Seyss-Inquart was ruthless in applying terrorism to suppress all opposition to the German occupation, a program which he described as "annihilating" his opponents. In collaboration with the local Higher SS and Police Leaders he was involved in the shooting of hostages for offenses against the occupation authorities and sending to concentration camps all suspected opponents of occupation policies, including priests and educators. . . .

Seyss-Inquart contends that he was not responsible for many of the crimes committed in the occupation of the Netherlands because they were either ordered from the Reich, committed by the Army, over which he had no control, or by the German Higher SS and Police Leader who, he claims, reported directly to Himmler. It is true that some of the excesses were the responsibility of the Army, and that the Higher SS and Police Leader, although he was at the disposal of Seyss-Inquart, could always report directly to Himmler. It is also true that in certain cases Seyss-Inquart opposed the extreme measures used by these other agencies, as when he was largely successful in preventing the Army from carrying out a scorched earth policy, and urged the Higher SS and Police Leaders to reduce the number of hostages to be shot. But the fact remains that Seyss-Inquart was a knowing and voluntary participant in War Crimes and Crimes against Humanity which were committed in the occupation of the Netherlands.

Conclusion

The Tribunal finds that Seyss-Inquart is guilty under Counts Two, Three, and Four; Seyss-Inquart is not guilty on Count One.

MR. BIDDLE:

Speer

Speer is indicted under all four Counts. Speer joined the Nazi Party in 1932. In 1934 he was made Hitler's architect and became a close personal confidant. Shortly thereafter he was made a department head in the German Labor Front and the official in charge of capital construction on the staff of the Deputy to the *Fuehrer*, positions which he held through 1941. On 15 February 1942, after the death of Fritz Todt, Speer was appointed Chief of the Organization Todt and Reich Minister for Armaments and Munitions (after 2 September 1943, for Armaments and War Production). The positions were supplemented by his appointments in March and April 1942 as Plenipotentiary General for Armaments and as a member of the Central Planning Board, both within the Four Year Plan. Speer was a member of the *Reichstag* from 1941 until the end of the war.

Crimes against Peace

The Tribunal is of opinion that Speer's activities do not amount to initiating, planning, or preparing wars of aggression, or of conspiring to that end. He became the head of the armament industry well after all of the wars had been commenced and were under way. His activities in charge of German armament production were in aid of the war effort in the same way that other productive enterprises aid in the waging of war; but the Tribunal is not prepared to find that such activities involve engaging in the common plan to wage aggressive war as charged under Count One, or waging aggressive war as charged under Count Two.

War Crimes and Crimes against Humanity

The evidence introduced against Speer under Counts Three and Four relates entirely to his participation in the slave labor program. Speer himself had no direct administrative responsibility for this program. Although he had advocated the appointment of a Plenipotentiary General for the Utilization of Labor because he wanted one central authority with whom he could deal on labor matters, he did not obtain administrative control over Sauckel. Sauckel was appointed directly by Hitler, under the decree of 21 March 1942, which provided that he should be directly responsible to Goering, as Plenipotentiary of the Four Year Plan.

As Reich Minister for Armaments and Munitions and Plenipotentiary General for Armaments under the Four Year Plan, Speer had extensive authority over production. His original authority was over construction and production of arms for the OKH. This was progressively expanded to include naval armaments, civilian production, and finally, on 1 August 1944, air armament. . . .

Speer was also directly involved in the utilization of forced labor as chief of the Organization Todt. The Organization Todt functioned principally in the occupied areas on such projects as the Atlantic Wall and the construction of military highways, and Speer has admitted that he relied on compulsory service to keep it adequately staffed. . . .

Speer was also involved in the use of prisoners of war in armament industries, but contends that he only utilized Soviet prisoners of war in industries covered by the Geneva Convention.

Speer's position was such that he was not directly concerned with the cruelty in the administration of the slave labor program, although he was aware of its existence. For example, at meetings of the Central Planning Board he was informed that his demands for labor were so large as to necessitate violent methods in recruiting. . . .

In mitigation it must be recognized that Speer's establishment of blocked industries did keep many laborers in their homes and that in the closing stages of the war he was one of the few men who had the courage to tell Hitler that the war was lost and to take steps to prevent the senseless destruction of production facilities, both in occupied territories and in Germany. He carried out his opposition to Hitler's scorched earth program in some of the Western countries and in Germany by deliberately sabotaging it at considerable personal risk.

Conclusion

The Tribunal finds that Speer is not guilty on Counts One and Two, but is guilty under Counts Three and Four.

Von Neurath

Von Neurath is indicted under all four Counts. He is a professional diplomat who served as German Ambassador to Great Britain from 1930 to 1932. On 2 June 1932 he was appointed Minister of Foreign Affairs in the Von Papen Cabinet, a position which he held under the Cabinets of von Schleicher and Hitler. Von Neurath resigned as Minister of Foreign Affairs on 4 February 1938, and was made Reich Minister without Portfolio, President of the Secret Cabinet Council, and a member of the Reich Defense Council. On 18 March 1939, he was appointed Reich Protector for Bohemia and Moravia and served in this capacity until 27 September 1941. He held the formal rank of *Obergruppenfuehrer* in the SS.

Crimes against Peace

As Minister of Foreign Affairs, von Neurath advised Hitler in connection with the withdrawal from the Disarmament Conference and the League of Nations on 14 October 1933; the institution of rearmament; the passage, on 16 March 1935, of the law for universal military service; and the passage, on 21 May 1935, of the secret Reich Defense Law. He was a key figure in the negotiation of the Naval Accord entered into between Germany and England on 18 June 1935. Von Neurath played an important part in Hitler's decision to reoccupy the Rhineland on 7 March 1936, and predicted that the occupation could be carried through without any reprisals from the French. On 18 May 1936, he told the American Ambassador to France that it was the policy of the German Government to do nothing in foreign affairs until "the Rhineland had been digested," and that as soon as the fortifications in the Rhineland had been constructed and the countries of central Europe realized that France could not enter Germany at will, "all those countries will begin to feel very differently about their foreign policies and a new constellation will develop."

Von Neurath took part in the Hossbach conference of 5 November 1937. He has testified that he was so shocked by Hitler's statements that he had a heart attack. Shortly thereafter, he offered to resign, and his resignation was accepted on 4 February 1938, at the same time that von Fritsch and von Blomberg were dismissed. Yet with knowledge of Hitler's aggressive plans he retained a formal relationship with the Nazi regime as Reich Minister without Portfolio, President of the Secret Cabinet Council, and a member of the Reich Defense Council. . . .

Criminal Activities in Czechoslovakia

Von Neurath was appointed Reich Protector for Bohemia and Moravia on 18 March 1939. Bohemia and Moravia were occupied by military force. . . .

As Reich Protector, von Neurath instituted an administration in Bohemia and Moravia similar to that in effect in Germany. The free press, political parties, and trade unions were abolished. All groups which might serve as opposition were outlawed. Czechoslovakian industry was worked into the structure of German war production, and exploited for the German war effort. Nazi anti-Semitic policies and laws were also introduced. Jews were barred from leading positions in government and business. . . .

In mitigation it must be remembered that he did intervene with the Security Police and SD for the release of many of the Czechoslovaks who were arrested on 1 September 1939, and for the release of students arrested later in the fall. On 23 September 1941 he was summoned before Hitler and told that he was not being harsh enough and that Heydrich was being sent to the Protectorate to combat the Czechoslovakian resistance groups. Von Neurath attempted to dissuade Hitler from sending Heydrich, and when he was not successful offered to resign. When his resignation was not accepted he went on leave, on 27 September 1941, and refused to act as Protector after that date. His resignation was formally accepted in August 1943.

Conclusion

The Tribunal finds that von Neurath is guilty under all four Counts.

THE PRESIDENT:

Fritzsche

Fritzsche is indicted on Counts One, Three, and Four. He was best known as a radio commentator, discussing once a week the events of the day on his own program, "Hans Fritzsche Speaks." He began broadcasting in September 1932; in the same year he was made the head of the Wireless News Service, a Reich Government agency. When on 1 May 1933, this agency was incorporated by the National Socialists into their Reich Ministry of Popular Enlightenment and Propaganda, Fritzsche became a member of the Nazi Party and went to that Ministry. In December 1938 he became head of the Home Press Division of the Ministry; in October 1942 he was promoted to the rank of Ministerial Director. After serving briefly on the Eastern Front in a propaganda company, he was, in November 1942, made head of the Radio Division of the Propaganda Ministry and

Plenipotentiary for the Political Organization of the Greater German Radio.

Crimes against Peace

As head of the Home Press Division, Fritzsche supervised the German press of 2,300 daily newspapers. In pursuance of this function he held daily press conferences to deliver the directives of the Propaganda Ministry to these papers. He was, however, subordinate to Dietrich, the Reich Press Chief, who was in turn a subordinate of Goebbels. It was Dietrich who received the directives to the press of Goebbels and other Reich Ministers, and prepared them as instructions which he then handed to Fritzsche for the press. . . .

War Crimes and Crimes against Humanity

The Prosecution has asserted that Fritzsche incited and encouraged the commission of war crimes, by deliberately falsifying news to arouse in the German people those passions which led them to the commission of atrocities under Counts Three and Four. His position and official duties were not sufficiently important, however, to infer that he took part in originating or formulating propaganda campaigns.

Excerpts in evidence from his speeches show definite anti-Semitism on his part. He broadcast, for example, that the war had been caused by Jews and said their fate had turned out "as unpleasant as the *Fuehrer* predicted." But these speeches did not urge persecution or extermination of Jews. There is no evidence that he was aware of their extermination in the East. The evidence moreover shows that he twice attempted to have publication of the anti-Semitic *Der Stürmer* suppressed, though unsuccessfully.

In these broadcasts Fritzsche sometimes spread false news, but it was not proved he knew it to be false. For example, he reported that no German U-Boat was in the vicinity of the *Athenia* when it was sunk. This information was untrue; but Fritzsche, having received it from the German Navy, had no reason to believe it was untrue.

It appears that Fritzsche sometimes made strong statements of a propagandistic nature in his broadcasts. But the Tribunal is not prepared to hold that they were intended to incite the German people to commit atrocities on conquered peoples, and he cannot be held to have been a participant in the crimes charged. His aim was rather to arouse popular sentiment in support of Hitler and the German war effort.

Conclusion

The Tribunal finds that Fritzsche is not guilty under this Indictment, and directs that he shall be discharged by the Marshal when the Tribunal presently adjourns.

GEN. NIKITCHENKO:

Bormann

Bormann is indicted on Counts One, Three, and Four. He joined the National Socialist Party in 1925, was a member of the Staff of the Supreme Command of the SA from 1928 to 1930, was in charge of the Aid Fund of the Party, and was *Reichsleiter* from 1933 to 1945. From 1933 to 1941 he was Chief of Staff in the office of the *Fuehrer's* Deputy and, after the flight of Hess to England, became head of the Party Chancellery on 12 May 1941. On 12 April 1943 he became Secretary to the *Fuehrer*. He was political and organizational head of the *Volksstürm* and a general in the SS.

Crimes against Peace

Bormann, in the beginning a minor Nazi, steadily rose to a position of power and, particularly in the closing days, of great influence over Hitler. He was active in the Party's rise to power and even more so in the consolidation of that power. He devoted much of his time to the persecution of the Churches and of the Jews within Germany.

The evidence does not show that Bormann knew of Hitler's plans to prepare, initiate, or wage aggressive wars. He attended none of the important conferences when Hitler revealed piece by piece these plans for aggression. Nor can knowledge be conclusively inferred from the positions he held. It was only when he became head of the Party Chancellery in 1941, and later in 1943 Secretary to the *Fuehrer*, when he attended many of Hitler's conferences, that his positions gave him the necessary access. Under the view stated elsewhere which the Tribunal has taken of the conspiracy to wage aggressive war, there is not sufficient evidence to bring Bormann within the scope of Count One.

War Crimes and Crimes against Humanity

By decree of 29 May 1941 Bormann took over the offices and powers held by Hess; by decree of 24 January 1942 these powers were extended to give him control over all laws and directives issued by Hitler. He was thus responsible for laws and orders issued thereafter. On 1 December 1942, all *Gaue* became Reich defense districts, and the Party *Gauleiter* responsible to Bormann were appointed Reich Defense Commissioners. In effect, this made them the administrators of the entire civilian war effort. This was so not only in Germany, but also in those territories which were incorporated into the Reich from the absorbed and conquered territories.

Through this mechanism Bormann controlled the ruthless exploitation of the subjected populace. His order of 12 August 1942 placed all Party agencies at the disposal of Himmler's program for forced resettlement and denationalization of persons in the occupied countries. Three weeks after the invasion of Russia, he attended the conference of 16 July 1941 at Hitler's field quarters with Goering, Rosenberg, and Keitel; Bormann's report shows that there were discussed and developed detailed plans of enslavement and annihilation of the population of these territories. . . .

Bormann was extremely active in the persecution of the Jews not only in Germany but also in the absorbed or conquered countries. He took part in the discussions which led to the removal of 60,000 Jews from Vienna to Poland in co-operation with the SS and the *Gestapo*. He signed the decree of 31 May 1941 extending the Nuremberg Laws to the annexed Eastern territories. In an order of 9 October 1942 he declared that the permanent elimination of Jews in Greater German territory could no longer be solved by emigration, but only by applying "ruthless force" in the special camps in the East. On 1 July 1943 he signed an ordinance withdrawing Jews from the protection of the law courts and placing them under the exclusive jurisdiction of Himmler's *Gestapo*.

Bormann was prominent in the slave labor program. The Party leaders supervised slave labor matters in the respective *Gaue*, including employment, conditions of work, feeding, and housing. . . .

Conclusion

The Tribunal finds that Bormann is not guilty on Count One, but is guilty on Counts Three and Four.

THE PRESIDENT: Before pronouncing sentence on any of the defendants, and while all the defendants are present, the Tribunal takes the occasion to advise them that any application to the clemency of the Control Council must be lodged with the General Secretary of this Tribunal within 4 days from today.

The Tribunal will now adjourn and will sit again at 10 minutes to three.
[*A recess was taken until 1450 hours.*]

Afternoon Session

THE PRESIDENT: In accordance with Article 27 of the Charter, the International Military Tribunal will now pronounce the sentences on the defendants convicted on this Indictment:

"Defendant Hermann Wilhelm Goering, on the Counts of the Indictment on which you have been convicted, the International Military Tribunal sentences you to death by hanging.

"Defendant Rudolf Hess, on the Counts of the Indictment on which you have been convicted, the Tribunal sentences you to imprisonment for life.

"Defendant Joachim von Ribbentrop, on the Counts of the Indictment on which you have been convicted, the Tribunal sentences you to death by hanging.

"Defendant Wilhelm Keitel, on the Counts of the Indictment on which you have been convicted, the Tribunal sentences you to death by hanging.

"Defendant Ernst Kaltenbrunner, on the Counts of the Indictment on which you have been convicted, the Tribunal sentences you to death by hanging.

"Defendant Alfred Rosenberg, on the Counts of the Indictment on which you have been convicted, the Tribunal sentences you to death by hanging.

"Defendant Hans Frank, on the Counts of the Indictment on which you have been convicted, the Tribunal sentences you to death by hanging.

"Defendant Wilhelm Frick, on the Counts of the Indictment on which you have been convicted, the Tribunal sentences you to death by hanging.

"Defendant Julius Streicher, on the Counts of the Indictment on which you have been convicted, the Tribunal sentences you to death by hanging.

"Defendant Walter Funk, on the Counts of the Indictment on which you have been convicted, the Tribunal sentences you to imprisonment for life.

"Defendant Karl Doenitz, on the Counts of the Indictment on which you have been convicted, the Tribunal sentences you to ten years' imprisonment.

"Defendant Erich Raeder, on the Counts of the Indictment on which you have been convicted, the Tribunal sentences you to imprisonment for life.

"Defendant Baldur von Schirach, on the Count of the Indictment on which you have been convicted, the Tribunal sentences you to twenty years' imprisonment.

"Defendant Fritz Sauckel, on the Counts of the Indictment on which you have been convicted, the Tribunal sentences you to death by hanging.

"Defendant Alfred Jodl, on the Counts of the Indictment on which you have been convicted, the Tribunal sentences you to death by hanging.

"Defendant Arthur Seyss-Inquart, on the Counts of the Indictment on which you have been convicted, the Tribunal sentences you to death by hanging.

"Defendant Albert Speer, on the Counts of the Indictment on which you have been convicted, the Tribunal sentences you to twenty years' imprisonment.

"Defendant Konstantin von Neurath, on the Counts of the Indictment on which you have been convicted, the Tribunal sentences you to fifteen years' imprisonment."

The Tribunal sentences the Defendant Martin Bormann, on the Counts of the Indictment on which he has been convicted, to death by hanging.

I have an announcement to make. The Soviet member of the International Military Tribunal desires to record his dissent from the decisions in the cases of the Defendants Schacht, von Papen, and Fritzsche. He is of the opinion that they should have been convicted and not acquitted.

He also dissents from the decisions in respect to the Reich Cabinet and the General Staff and High Command, being of the opinion that they should have been declared to be criminal organizations.

He also dissents from the decision in the case of the sentence on the Defendant Hess and is of the opinion that the sentence should have been death, and not life imprisonment.

This dissenting opinion will be put into writing and annexed to the Judgment, and will be published as soon as possible.

[*The Tribunal adjourned.*]

143. Finale: Kingsbury Smith of International News Service Witnesses the Executions at Nuremberg, October 16, 1946

Sauckel: "I am dying innocent!"

After the judgments were passed on twenty-two of Hitler's lieutenants at Nuremberg, those condemned to death, with the exception of Ernst Kaltenbrunner, applied to the Allied Control Council at Berlin for mercy. Their appeals were rejected. Hermann Goering, Alfred Jodl, and Wilhelm Keitel then asked to be executed by firing squad, but their requests were denied. Two hours before he was scheduled to hang, Goering swallowed a vial of poison that had been smuggled into his cell. The executions began at eleven minutes past 1:00 A.M. on October 16, 1946. Master Sergeant John G. Woods, United States Army, was assigned the task of hanging the convicted men. Eight newspaper correspondents – two each from the United States, Britain, France, and Russia – were selected to report the executions. Following is the report by Kingsbury Smith, European general manager of International News Service.

Nuremberg, October 16 – Ex-*Reichsmarschall* Hermann Wilhelm Goering succeeded in cheating the gallows of Allied justice by committing suicide in his prison cell a short time before the ten other condemned remnants of the Nazi hierarchy were hanged today.

Despite the fact that an American security guard was supposed to be watching his every movement, the crown prince of Nazidom managed to

---

New York Journal-American, October 16, 1946. Courtesy of United Press International.

hide in his mouth, chew, and swallow a vial containing cyanide of potassium.

Goering swallowed the poison while Colonel Burton C. Andrus, American security commandant, was walking across the prison yard to the death row block to read to him and the ten other condemned Nazi leaders the International Military Tribunal's sentence of death.

Within little more than an hour after the reading of this sentence to the condemned men in their cells, Goering was scheduled to be led out to a near-by small gymnasium building in the jailyard to lead the parade of death of the Nazi political and military chieftains to the scaffold.

Goering had not previously been told that he was going to die this morning, nor had any of the other condemned men.

How he guessed this was to be his day of doom and how he managed to conceal the poison on his person is a mystery that had confounded the security forces.

With former Foreign Minister Joachim von Ribbentrop taking the place of Goering as the first to mount the scaffold, the ten other condemned princes of Nazidom were hanged one by one in the bright, electrically lighted barnlike interior of the small gymnasium inside one of the prison yards of the Nuremberg city jail.

The execution of von Ribbentrop and the others took approximately one hour and a half. The once-arrogant diplomatic doublecrosser of Nazidom entered the execution hall at 1:11 this morning. The trap was sprung at 1:16 and he was pronounced dead at 1:30.

The last to walk up the thirteen forbidding wooden steps to one of the two gallows used for the execution was Artur Seyss-Inquart, Austrian traitor and Nazi *Gauleiter* for Holland. He dropped to his death at 2:45 A.M. and was pronounced dead at 2:57.

All ten of the Nazis attempted to show bravery as they went to their deaths. Most of them were bitterly defiant, some grimly resigned, and others asked the Almighty for mercy.

All but Alfred Rosenberg, the pagan party theorist, made brief, last-minute statements on the scaffold, nearly all of which were nationalistic expressions for the future welfare and greatness of Germany.

The only one, however, to make any reference to Nazi ideology was Julius Streicher, that arch Jew-baiter. Displaying the most bitter and enraged defiance of any of the condemned, he screamed "Heil Hitler" at the top of his voice as he was about to mount the steps leading to the gallows.

Streicher appeared in the execution hall, which had been used only last Saturday night for a basketball game by American security guards, at twelve and a half minutes after two o'clock.

As in the case of all the condemned, a warning knock by a guard outside preceded Streicher's entry through a door in the middle of the hall.

An American lieutenant colonel sent to fetch the condemned from the death row of the cell block to the near-by prison wing entered first. He was followed by Streicher, who was stopped immediately inside the door by two American sergeants. They closed in on each side of him and held his arms while another sergeant removed the manacles from his hands and replaced them with a leather cord.

The first person whom Streicher and the others saw upon entering the gruesome hall was an American lieutenant colonel who stood directly in front of him while his hands were being tied behind his back as they had been manacled upon his entrance.

This ugly, dwarfish little man, wearing a threadbare suit and a well-worn bluish shirt buttoned to the neck but without a tie, glanced at the three wooden scaffolds rising up menacingly in front of him.

Two of these were used alternately to execute the condemned men while the third was kept in reserve.

After a quick glance at the gallows, Streicher glared around the room, his eyes resting momentarily upon the small group of American, British, French, and Russian officers on hand to witness the executions.

By this time Streicher's hands were tied securely behind his back. Two guards, one to each arm, directed him to No. 1 gallows on the left entrance. He walked steadily the six feet to the first wooden step, but his face was twitching nervously. As the guards stopped him at the bottom of the steps for official identification requests, he uttered his piercing scream:

"Heil Hitler!"

His shriek sent a shiver down the back of this International News Service correspondent, who is witnessing the executions as sole representative of the American press.

As its echo died away, another American colonel standing by the steps said sharply:

"Ask the man his name."

In response to the interpreter's query Streicher shouted:

"You know my name well."

The interpreter repeated his request, and the condemned man yelled:

"Julius Streicher."

As he mounted the platform Streicher cried out:

"Now it goes to God!"

After getting up the thirteen steps to the eight-foot-high and eight-foot-square black-painted wooden platform, Streicher was pushed two steps to the mortal spot beneath the hangman's rope.

This was suspended from an iron ring attached to a crossbeam which rested on two posts. The rope was being held back against a wooden rail by the American Army sergeant hangman.

Streicher was swung around to face toward the front.

He glanced again at the Allied officers and the eight Allied correspondents representing the world's press who were lined up against a wall behind small tables directly facing the gallows.

With burning hatred in his eyes, Streicher looked down upon the witness and then screamed:

"Purim Fest 1946!"*

The American officer standing at the scaffold said:

"Ask the man if he has any last words."

When the interpreter had translated, Streicher shouted:

"The Bolsheviks will hang you one day."

As the black hood was being adjusted about his head, Streicher was heard saying:

"Adele, my dear wife."

At that moment the trap was sprung with a loud bang. With the rope snapped taut and the body swinging wildly, a groan could be heard distinctly within the dark interior of the scaffold.

It was originally intended to permit the condemned to walk the seventy-odd yards from the cells to the execution chamber with their hands free, but they were all manacled in the cells immediately following the discovery of Goering's suicide.

The weasel-faced Ribbentrop in his last appearance before mankind uttered his final words while waiting for the black hood to be placed over his head. Loudly, in firm tones, he said:

"God save Germany!"

He then asked:

"May I say something else?"

The interpreter nodded. The former diplomat wizard of Nazidom who negotiated the secret German non-aggression pact with Soviet Russia on the eve of Germany's invasion of Poland, and who approved orders to execute Allied airmen, then added:

"My last wish is that Germany realize its entity and that an understanding be reached between East and West. I wish peace to the world."

The ex-diplomat looked straight ahead as the hood was adjusted before the trap was sprung. His lips were set tight.

Next in line to follow Ribbentrop to the gallows was Field Marshal Wilhelm Keitel, symbol of Prussian militarism and aristocracy.

Here came the first military leader to be executed under the new concept of Allied international law — the principle that professional soldiers cannot escape justice for waging aggressive wars against humanity by claiming that they were merely carrying out orders of their superiors.

---

*Purim is a Jewish holiday celebrated in the spring and commemorating the hanging of Haman, Biblical oppressor of the Jews.

Keitel entered the death arena at 1:18, only two minutes before the trap was dropped beneath Ribbentrop and while the latter was still hanging at the end of his rope.

The Field Marshal could not, of course, see the ex-Foreign Minister, whose body was concealed within the first scaffold and whose rope still hung taut.

Keitel did not appear as tense as Ribbentrop. He held his head high while his hands were being tied, and walked erect with military bearing to the foot of the second scaffold, although a guard on each side held his arms.

When asked his name he answered in a loud sharp tone, "Wilhelm Keitel!" He mounted the gallows steps as he might have climbed to a reviewing stand to take the salute of the German Army. He certainly did not appear in need of the guards' help.

When turned around at the top of the platform, Keitel looked over the crowd with the traditional iron-jawed haughtiness of the proud Prussian officer. When asked if he had anything to say he looked straight ahead and speaking in a loud voice said:

"I call on Almighty God to have mercy on the German people. More than two million German soldiers went to their deaths for the Fatherland. I follow now my sons."

Then, while raising his voice to shout, "All for Germany," Keitel's black-booted, uniformed body plunged down with a bang. Observers agreed he had shown more courage on the scaffold than he had in the courtroom, where he tried to hide his guilt behind Hitler's ghost.

Then he claimed that it was all the *Fuehrer's* fault, that he merely carried out orders and had no responsibility.

This despite the fact that documentary evidence presented during the trial showed he "approved and backed" measures for branding Russian prisoners, directed "Draconian measures" to terrorize the Russian people into submission, and issued secret orders for invasion of Poland three months before the attack took place.

With both Ribbentrop and Keitel hanging at the end of their ropes, there was a pause in the grim proceedings.

The American colonel directing the executions asked the American general representing the Allied Control Commission if those present could smoke. An affirmative answer brought cigarettes into the hands of almost every one of the thirty-odd persons present.

These included two official representatives of the German government in the American zone — Dr. Wilhelm Hoegner, Minister-President of Bavaria, and Dr. Jacob Leisner, Chief Prosecutor of Nuremberg.

Officers and GI's walked around nervously or spoke a few words to one another in hushed voices while Allied correspondents scribbled furiously their notes of the historic, though ghastly event.

In a few minutes an American Army doctor accompanied by a Russian Army doctor and both carrying stethoscopes walked to the first scaffold, lifted the curtain, and disappeared within.

They emerged at 1:30 A.M. and spoke to a short, heavy-set American colonel wearing combat boots. The colonel swung around and facing official witnesses, snapped to attention to say:

"The man is dead."

Two GI's quickly appeared with a stretcher, which was carried up and lifted into the interior of the scaffold. The hangman, a sergeant, mounted the gallows steps, took a large commando-type knife out of a sheath strapped to his side, and cut the rope.

Ribbentrop's limp body with the black hood still over his head was speedily removed from the far end of the room and placed behind a black canvas curtain. This all had taken less than ten minutes.

The directing colonel turned to the witnesses and said: "Lights out, please, gentlemen," and then, addressing another colonel he called "Norman," said, "O.K." The latter went out the door and over to the condemned block to fetch the next man.

This creature was Ernst Kaltenbrunner, *Gestapo* chief and director of the greatest mass murder Europe has seen since the Dark Ages.

Kaltenbrunner, master killer of Nazidom, entered the execution chamber at 1:36 A.M. wearing a sweater beneath his double-breasted coat. With his lean, haggard face furrowed by old dueling scars, the terrible successor of Reinhard Heydrich had a frightening look as he glanced around the room.

He was nervous and he wet his lips as he turned to mount the gallows, but he walked steadily. He answered his name in a calm, low voice. When he turned around on the gallows platform he first faced a U.S. Catholic Army chaplain attired in a Franciscan habit.

Kaltenbrunner was asked for his last words and answered quietly:

"I would like to say a word.

"I have loved my German people and my Fatherland with a warm heart.

"I have done my duty by the laws of my people and I am sorry my people were led this time by men who were not soldiers and that crimes were committed of which I have no knowledge."

This sounded like strange talk from a man, one of whose agents — a man named Rudolf Hoess — confessed at a previous trial that under Kaltenbrunner's orders he gassed three million human beings at the Auschwitz concentration camp.

As the black hood was about to be placed over his head Kaltenbrunner, still speaking in a low, calm voice, used a German phrase which translated means:

"Germany, good luck!"

His trap was sprung at 1:30 A.M.

Field Marshal Keitel had been pronounced dead at 1:44 A.M., and three minutes later guards had removed his body. The scaffold was made ready for Alfred Rosenberg, master mind behind the Nazi race theories, who sought to establish Nazism as a pagan religion.

Rosenberg was dull and sunken-cheeked as he looked around the court. His complexion was pasty brown. But he did not appear nervous and walked with a steady step to and up the gallows.

Apart from giving his name and replying "No" to a question as to whether he had anything to say, this atheist did not utter a word. Despite his disbelief in God he was accompanied by a Protestant chaplain, who followed him to the gallows and stood beside him praying.

Rosenberg looked at the chaplain once, but said nothing. Ninety seconds after he entered the execution hall he was swinging from the end of a hangman's rope. His was the swiftest execution of any of those condemned.

Then there was a brief lull in the morbid proceedings until Kaltenbrunner was pronounced dead at 1:52 A.M. Hans Frank, the *Gauleiter* of Poland and former SS general, was next in the parade of death. He was the only one of the condemned to enter the chamber with a smile on his lips.

Although nervous and swallowing frequently, this man, who was converted to Catholicism after his arrest, gave the appearance of being relieved at the prospect of atoning for his evil deeds.

He answered to his name quietly and when asked on the platform if he had any last statement replied in a low voice that was almost a whisper:

"I am thankful for the kind treatment during my captivity and I ask God to accept me with mercy."

Frank then closed his eyes and swallowed again as the black hood went over his head.

The sixth man to leave his prison cell and walk with handcuffed wrists across the corner of the small yard separating the condemned block from the death house was sixty-nine-year-old Wilhelm Frick, former Nazi Minister of the Interior.

He entered the execution chamber at five and a half minutes after two, six and a half minutes after Rosenberg had been pronounced dead. He seemed to be the least steady of any so far and stumbled on the thirteenth step of the gallows. His only words were "Long live eternal Germany" before he was hooded and dropped through the trap.

Following Streicher's melodramatic exit and removal of Frick's corpse after he was pronounced dead at 2:20 A.M., Fritz Sauckel, the slave-labor director and one of the worst of the blood-stained men of Nazidom, was brought to face his doom.

Wearing a sweater with no coat and looking wild-eyed, Sauckel proved to be the most defiant of any except Streicher.

Here was the man who drove millions into a land of bondage on a scale unknown since the pre-Christian era. Gazing around the room from the gallow's platform, he suddenly screamed:

"I am dying innocent. The sentence is wrong. God protect Germany and make Germany great again. God protect my family."

The trap was sprung at 2:26 A.M., and, like Streicher, this hatred-filled man groaned loudly as the fatal noose snapped tightly under the weight of his body.

Ninth to come was Colonel General Alfred Jodl, Hitler's strategic adviser and close friend. With the black coat collar of his *Wehrmacht* uniform turned up at the back as though hurriedly put on, Jodl entered the death house with obvious signs of nervousness.

He wet his lips constantly and his features were drawn and haggard as he walked forward, not nearly so steady as Keitel in mounting the gallows steps. Yet his voice was calm when he uttered his last six words on earth:

"My greetings to you, my Germany."

At 2:34 Jodl plunged into the black hole of the scaffold's death. Both he and Sauckel hung together in that execution chamber until the latter was pronounced dead six minutes later and removed.

The Czechoslovakian-born Seyss-Inquart was the last actor to make his appearance in the ghastly scene of Allied justice. He entered the death chamber at 2:38½ A.M., wearing the glasses which made his face a familiar and despised figure in all the years he ruled Holland with an iron hand and sent thousands of Dutchmen to Germany for forced labor.

Seyss-Inquart looked around with noticeable signs of unsteadiness and limped on his left clubfoot as he walked to the gallows. He mounted the steps slowly, with guards helping him on his way.

When Seyss-Inquart spoke his last words his voice was very low but intense. He said:

"I hope that this execution is the last act of the tragedy of the Second World War and that the lesson taken from this World War will be that peace and understanding should be between peoples.

"I believe in Germany."

Index

Afrika Korps, 445
Allied control machinery, 1944, 493–97
Allied declaration on German default, 540–44
Allied protocol on Berlin, 487–90
Alsace-Lorraine, 401, 403
Andrus, Col. Burton C., 608
Anschluss, 280–81
Anti-Semitism, 26–30, 108–10
Article 48, 20–21
Article 231, 16, 18

Banse, Ewald, 164–66
Bebel, Ferdinand August, 117
Beer-Hall *Putsch*, 33–36
Below, Nicholas, 517
Belsen concentration camp, 511–17
Beneš, Eduard, 287–89, 291
Bergen-Belsen, 511–17
Bergmann, Ernst, 167
Berlin Conference. *See* Potsdam Conference
Berlin, devastation of, 577–79
Berlin-Rome-Tokyo Axis, 406–7, 439
Bernhard, Georg, 115
Birchall, Frederick T., 113–19
Bismarck, Otto von, 67
Blomberg, Field Marshal Werner von, 81, 195, 264, 272, 274–75
Blood Purge of 1934, 178–84
Bolshevism, 119–23, 276–77
Bonn, University of, 242–46
Bomb attempt on Hitler's life, July 20, 1944, 477–81
Books, burning of, 113–19, 120–21
Bormann, Martin, 501–2, 509, 510, 517, 521, 568, 603–4, 606
Bowen, James, 302

Brauchitsch, Field Marshal Walther von, 412–13
Braun, Eva, 508
British War Blue Book, 359–66
Bruening, Heinrich, 71, 72
Buchenwald concentration camp, 503–6, 570
Bukharin, Nikolai Ivanovich, 117
Burgdorf, Wilhelm, 521
Bürgerbräukeller, 33
Byrnes, James F., 545

Catholic Church, 247–60
Caucasus, 450
Chamberlain, Houston Stewart, 162
Chamberlain, Neville, 291–94
Christianity, 247–60
Churchill, Winston, 405, 414, 417, 431, 449, 534, 545
Clemenceau, Georges, 16
Collingwood, Charles, 531–34
Communism, 276–77
Compiègne, 399–404
Concordat between Holy See and Nazi Germany, 139–42
Coordination, 83–260
Coudenhove-Kalergi, Count, 117
Cousey, F. T., 490, 497
Coventry, bombing of, 408–11
Crete, German attack on, 422–25
Currivan, Gene, 503–6
Czechoslovakia, 206–9, 291–94

D-Day, 466–72
Daladier, Edouard, 293–94
Danzig, 327, 353, 354, 355
Delmer, Seton, 105
"Deutschland über Alles," 158

Doenitz, Admiral Karl, 328, 329,
    330, 405, 479, 480, 567, 588–89,
    605
Dolchstoss, 412–13
Drexler, Anton, 23
Düsseldorf speech, von Papen's,
    60–69
Düsterberg, Theodor, 70–74, 216

Eden, Anthony, 277, 545
Eighth Air Force, 400
Einstein, Albert, 113
Eisenhower, Dwight D., 522, 532–34
El Alamein, 445–49
Elections of April 10, 1932, 70–74
Eltz-Rubenbach, Baron von, 82
Enabling Act, 1933, 106–7
Engels, Friedrich, 117
Euthanasia questionnaire, 307–10
Evangelical Church, 233–37

Feder, Gottfried, 23
Fegelein, Gen. Hermann, 510
Feuchtwanger, Lion, 113, 117,
    170–72
Flying Fortress, 460
Foch, Ferdinand, 400, 402, 403
France, fall of, 399–404, 580–81
Fourteen Points, 16
Franco-German agreement on Saar,
    1935, 201–5
Freud, Sigmund, 113, 115
Freyberg, Gen. Bernard C., 422
Frick, Wilhelm, 81, 107, 502–3, 605,
    613
Friedeburg, Adm. Georg von, 531–36
Fritsch, Gen. Frh. Werner von, 264,
    272, 274–75
Fritsche, Hans, 568, 601–2, 605, 606
Funk, Walther, 585–86, 605

Gauch, Hermann, 162
German declaration of war on the
    United States, 437–40
German-Japanese Pact, 239–40
German-Soviet Treaty, 367–70
German Workers' Party, 22–25
Germany Prepares for War, 164
Gersdorff, Col. Friedrich von, 477
Gestapo, 565, 571
Geyde, George E. R., 286–89

Gide, André, 113
Gleichschaltung (coordination),
    83–261
Gobineau, Count Joseph Arthur, 102
Godesberg, Bad, 292
Goebbels, Dr. Paul Joseph, 53–55,
    102, 103, 113–19, 120–22, 129–30,
    134–38, 153–57, 174, 179, 185–86,
    295, 300, 305–8, 420–21, 478, 517,
    521
Goering, Hermann, 37, 38, 82, 93,
    94, 102, 103, 104, 105, 179, 181,
    264, 273, 274, 302–4, 402–3, 408,
    420, 479, 480, 481, 482–86, 518,
    551–59, 566, 568, 571–72, 585, 607,
    608
Graf Spee, 382–85
Gruhn, Eva, 274
Grynszpan, Herschel, 295, 305–8
Guderian, Col. Gen. Heinz, 479
Gustloff, Wilhelm, 305

Hacha, Dr. Emil, 569
Halifax, Viscount (later first earl of),
    360
Hauer, Prof. Ernst, 162
Henderson, Nevile, 333–36, 341–47
Hereditary Farm Law, 143–44
Hergesell, Gerhardt, 507–10
Hess, Rudolf, 53, 401–3, 417–19,
    420–22, 574, 604, 606
Heydrich, Reinhard, 568
Hicks, George, 466–69
Hillquit, Morris, 117
Himmler, Heinrich, 219–23, 288, 483,
    485, 518, 568, 572
Hindenburg, Oskar Von, 197
Hindenburg, Paul von Beneckendorf
    und von, 70–74, 75–76, 77–79, 80,
    81–82, 108–10, 111, 192–94,
    196–99, 200
Hirschfeld, Magnus, 116
Hitler, Adolf: and *Anschluss*,
    279–83; anti-Semitism, 26–30; in
    beer-hall *Putsch*, 33–36; in Berlin
    bunker, 507–10; and bolshevism,
    58–59; bomb attempt on life of,
    472–81, 482, 486; and book
    burning, 126; and British
    government, 333–36; chancellor,
    appointment as, 81–82; Churchill,

denunciation of, 414–16; and civil service, 111–12; and communism, 50–52, 276–77; and Czechoslovakia, 286–89; dismissal of generals, 274; *Dolchstoss* speech, 412–13; drugs, use of, 473–76; *Düsseldorf* speech, 60–69; and elections of April 10, 1932, 71–74; and Enabling Act, 106–7; and England, 333–36, 405; final days, 507–10; and Four-Year Plan, 229–32; and France, fall of, 399–404; and *Gleichschaltung* (coordination), 129–30; and Hossbach Memorandum, 263–73; and Italy, fall of, 456–59; and Jews, 58–59, 108–10; laws of, 106–7, 111–12, 131; and *Mein Kampf*, 42–49; as military leader, 371–76; Nero decree, 501–2; and Nuremberg Trials, 568, 569, 571; and Poland, 337–40; political testament, 518–19; proclamations and decrees, 90–91, 215, 501–2; on racial purity, 247–48; *Reichstag*, speeches to, 311–26, 353–57; and Rhineland occupation, 224–27; and Rotterdam bombing, 395–98; and Saar, return of, 201–5; speeches, 58–59, 60–69, 90–91, 92, 353–57, 412–13; and the SS, 219–23; and Stalin pact, 330–31; treason, trial for, 42–43; and U.S.S.R., 430–38; vengeance weapons after attempt on life, 491–92; and Versailles, Treaty of, 56–57; and von Hindenburg, 77–79, 192–93; 194; and the *Wehrmacht*, 327–29; and the *Weisse Rose*, 453–55; will, 516–17
Hitler-Stalin Pack, 1939, 330–31
Hitler-Stalin, on Poland, 367–70
Hitler Youth, as state agency, 241
Hodza, Milan, 289–90
Hoegner, Wilhelm, 611
Hoess, Adolf, 612
Horst Wessel Song, 115, 158–59, 407
Hossbach, Col. Friedrich, 263–73
Hossbach Memorandum, 265–73
Hugenberg, Alfred, 81
Hutten, Ulrich von, 122

International Military Tribunal, at Nuremberg, 551–614

Jackson, Robert H., 560–70
JCS 1067, 522–27
Jewish property, Decree on, 284–85
Jews, 26–30, 53–55, 108–10, 211–14, 284–85, 295–301, 302–4, 519–21, 565
Jodl, Gen. Alfred, 480, 509–10, 539, 584–95, 605–6, 614
Joyce, James, 242
Junge, Gertrud, 518
Jungmädel, 238

Kahr, Gustav von, 34 ff.
Kaltenbrunner, Ernst, 565, 566, 578–79, 603, 605, 607, 612, 613
Kantoworicz, E., 119
Kautsky, Karl, 117, 119
Keitel, Field Marshal Wilhelm, 400, 403, 479, 481, 509–10, 536, 569, 576–77, 605, 610, 613
Keller, Helen, 117
Kennard, Sir Howard, 360, 366
King, Harold, 537–39
Koch, D., 237
Kölnische Zeitung, and Thomas Mann, 123–28
Kraft durch Freude (Strength through Joy), 278
Krebs, Hans, 521
Kristallnacht (Night of Broken Glass), 295–301, 302–4
Kroll Opera House, 153, 353
Krosigk, Schwerin von, 81, 187

Labor Service, 238
Labor Service Law, 206–7
Langsdorff, Capt. Hans, 382–85
Lassalle, Ferdinand, 117
Lattre-Tassigny, F. de, 536
Law for the Protection of Heredity Health, 132–33
Law for the Reorganization of the Civil Service, 111–12
Law for the Reorganization of the Reich, 152
Law on Formation of New Parties, 131
League of Nations, 201–5, 224

Lebensraum (living space), 263
Leisner, Jacob, 611
Ley, Robert, 235
Lichtenberger, Henri, 117
London, Jack, 113, 117
Lossow, Gen. Otto von, 34
Lubbe, Marinus van der, 103, 105
Ludendorff, Gen. Erich, 33, 34,
    37–39
Ludwig, Emil, 119
Luftwaffe, 460, 479, 571
Luther, Martin, 120
Lutze, Viktor, 187–90

Macmillan, Richard D., 445–49
Mann, Thomas, 117, 119, 127,
    242–46
Marburg speech, Franz von Papen's,
    173–77
Marx, Karl, 117, 119
Marxism, Hitler on, 50–52
Mein Kampf, 42–49, 247, 426, 569
Meissner, Otto von, 77
"Mit Brennender Sorge," 249–60
Molotov, Vyacheslav M., 331, 368,
    369, 370, 430, 434, 435, 545
Montevideo, 382–85
Montgomery, Gen. Bernard L.,
    445–49, 529
Morrell, Dr. Theodor, 473–76
Moscow, 441–44
Mosley, Leonard, 467, 469–72
Mueller-Dahlem, 237
Munich Agreement, 291–94
Mushakoji, 240
Mussolini, Benito, 273–74, 279–82,
    328, 430, 456–57
Myth of the Twentieth Century, 160

Nazi ideology, 160–66
Nero Decree, 501–2
Neurath, Baron Konstantin von, 107,
    264, 600–601
Night of Broken Glass, 295–301,
    302–4
Norway, invasion of, 386–94
NSDAP, 571
Nuremberg, 328
Nuremberg, judgment at, 571–606
Nuremberg Laws, 211–14
Nuremberg Trials, 551–59, 560–68

Oberfohren Memorandum, 96, 102–5

P–47, 46
Papal encyclical, 1937, 249–60
Papen, Franz von, 78, 81, 105,
    173–77, 180, 186–98, 606
Paulus, Gen. Friedrich, 450–51
Peters, C. Brooks, 395–98
Peters, Sgt. Walter, 460–65
Pius XI, 139, 249–60
Poland, German ultimatum to,
    336–40
Poland, guarantee to, 1939, 332
Polish Corridor, 327, 353
Positive Christianity, 167–69, 273–77
Potsdam Conference, 545–50
Preuss, Dr. Hugo, 20, 117
Protocols of the Elders of Zion, 26
Proust, Marcel, 242

Questionnaire, euthanasia, 307–10

Raeder, Grand Admiral Erich, 264,
    401–4, 509–10, 569, 603, 605
Rastenburg, 477–81
Rath, Ernst vom, 295, 302–4
Rathenau, Walther, 117, 118
Reich Labor Law, 206–10
Reichstag fire, 95–101, 102–5
Reims, surrender at, 531–34, 535
Remarque, Erich Maria, 113, 115,
    117
Rhineland industrialists, 60–69
Rhineland, occupation of, 224–27
Ribbentrop, Joachim von, 240, 331,
    337, 368, 369, 370, 401–3, 429,
    510, 575–76, 610, 612
Roehm, Ernst, 33, 174–84, 192–93
Roehm revolt, 192–93
Rommel, Field Marshal Erwin,
    445–49
Rolland, Romain, 123–28
Roosevelt, Franklin D., 211, 414, 534
Rosenberg, Alfred, 160–61, 570,
    579–80, 605, 608, 613
Rotterdam, bombing of, 395–98
Royal Air Force, 408

SA, 174–84
Saar, 201–5, 224

Sauckel, Fritz, 564, 567, 592–93, 605, 613
Schacht, Hjalmar Horace Greeley, 507–8, 570, 605
Schirach, Baldur von, 591–92, 605
Schleicher, Gen. Kurt von, 21, 80, 180
Schmeling, Max, 422
Schnitzler, Arthur, 117
Schuschnigg, Kurt von, 279, 281
Schweinfurt raid, 460–65
Seldte, Franz, 81, 171, 216
Sevez, Gen. François, 533
Seyss-Inquart, Arthur, 597–98, 605, 614
SHAEF, 532
Shaplen, Joseph, 478–81
Shirer, William L., 399–404
Simonov, Konstantin, 441–44
Sinclair, Upton, 117
Smith, Gen. Walter Bedell, 533, 535
Smith, Kingsbury, 607–14
Spaatz, Gen. Carl Andrew, 532–36
Speer, Albert, 229, 590–99
Spengler, Otto, 59
Sportpalast, Berlin, 291
SS, 219–23, 571
Stahlhelm, 94, 191, 216–18
Stahmer, Otto, 551–59
Stalingrad, Battle of, 450–52
Stauffenberg, Count Klaus Philipp von, 477–81
Streicher, Julius, 53, 567, 584–85, 605, 608–9, 610, 614
Stowe, Leland, 286–94
Strength Through Joy, 278
Stumpf, Col. Gen. Hans, 479, 536
Suez Canal, 445
Surrender, German military, 535–36
Susloparov, Gen. Ivan, 533, 535
Suttner, Bertha von, 117
Syrovy, Gen. Jan, 287

Tedder, Air Marshal Arthur William, 533, 536
Thaelmann, Ernst, 70–74
"Tipperary," 449
Tolischus, Otto D., 295–301

Trevor-Roper, Hugh R., 517, 518
Tripartite Pact, 406–7
Truman, Harry S, 545
Twenty-five Points of the German Workers' Party, 22–25
Twenty-five Points of the German Religion, 167–69
Toller, Ernst, 123
Torgler, Ernst, 104

USSR, 330–31, 426–29, 430–38, 441–44, 450–52

V-1, 491–92
V-2, 491–92
Vengeance weapons, 491–92
Versailles, Treaty of, 15–19, 56–57, 58, 61, 67, 201–5, 230, 327, 553
Völkischer Beobachter, 23, 26, 50–52, 75–76, 85–89, 90–91, 153–57, 187–90, 193–99, 247–48, 276–77, 414–16, 705–8

Waffen-SS, divisions in World War II, 377–80
Wagner, Richard, 129
Walker, Patrick Gordon, 511–17
Wall, Alfred, 408–9
War Directives, Hitler's, 371–76
Wasserman, Jakob, 127
Wehrmacht, 215, 274–75, 327–29, 377, 509
Weimar, 503
Weimar Republic, 15, 88, 215
Weisse Rose, 453–55
Wells, H. G., 113
White Paper, Cmd. 6115, 341–47
White Rose Society, 451–53
Wilson, Woodrow, 16, 57
Winant, J. G., 490, 497
Wolff, Theodor, 115

Ybarra, T. B., 37–39

Zhukov, Gen. Georgi, 536
Zinovieff, Gregori, 117
Zweig, Stephan, 117